BIOGRAPHICAL INDEX OF ARTISTS IN CANADA

This index has been compiled as a quick reference guide to biographies of almost 8,800 professional and amateur artists active in Canada from the seventeenth century to the present. The artists represent 42 professional categories, from animation to topography. In addition to Canadian artists, the index has entries on more than 800 British, American, and European artists, all of whom spent part of their careers in Canada.

Each entry provides the artist's name, date and place of birth and death (or years the artist flourished, if birth and death dates are unavailable), nationality (if not Canadian), type of artist (major medium/media used), and sources in which biographical information may be found. Several hundred cross-references link the various names used by some artists during the course of their careers.

† EVELYN DE R. MCMANN retired in 1978, having been responsible for indexing Canadian art for the Fine Arts and Music Division of the Vancouver Public Library for fourteen years. Her previous books include *Royal Canadian Academy of Art: Exhibitions and Members, 1880–1979* and *Canadian Who's Who Index, 1898–1984.*

EVELYN DE R. McMANN

BIOGRAPHICAL INDEX OF ARTISTS IN CANADA

UNIVERSITY OF TORONTO PRESS
Toronto Buffalo London

Toronto Buffalo London

Reprinted 2017

ISBN 978-0-8020-2790-0 (cloth)
ISBN 978-1-4875-8688-1 (paper)

Printed on acid-free paper

National Library of Canada Cataloguing in Publication Data

McMann, Evelyn de R. (Evelyn de Rostaing), 1913–1998
Biographical index of artists in Canada

ISBN 978-0-8020-2790-0 (bound). – ISBN 978-1-4875-8688-1 (Pbk.)

1. Artists – Canada – Biography – Indexes. I. Title

N6548.M29 2003 709′.2′271 C2001-904049-0

University of Toronto Press acknowledges the financial assistance to its publishing program of the Canada Council for the Arts and the Ontario Arts Council.

University of Toronto Press acknowledges the financial support for its publishing activities of the Government of Canada through the Book Publishing Industry Development Program (BPIDP).

CONTENTS

INTRODUCTION

The history of art in Canada has three distinct periods, beginning with the years of Nouvelle France prior to 1759, when the first classes in painting and the decorative arts were offered in the Quebec Seminary. This period was followed by the British regime, which culminated in Confederation in 1867, and which saw the arrival of many fine artists in the army, navy, and government services who recorded the pioneer life of the people. The third and present era of Canadian art was heralded by the establishment of the Royal Canadian Academy of Arts in 1880. To obtain a membership diploma artists gave one of their best works to the academy. These were presented to the government, and became the nucleus of the National Gallery of Canada collection.

This index has been compiled as a quick reference guide to biographies of almost 8,800 artists active in Canada from the seventeenth century to the present. These artists have worked in forty-two professional categories, from painting and sculpture to animation. In addition to Canadian artists, the index has entries on more than 800 British, American, and European artists. Many standard references ignore the Canadian activity of these foreign artists. Several hundred cross-references link the various names used by some artists during the course of their careers.

The biographies have been gathered from more than 150 sources: art dictionaries, national biographies, who's who series, catalogues of permanent collections in art galleries, and Canadian art histories. The selection was confined to those sources that may be found in many university, public, and art gallery libraries.

The majority of the biographies were found in J. Russell Harper's *Early Painters and Engravers in Canada*, catalogues of the National Gallery of Canada, the *Dictionary of Canadian Biography*, Colin S. MacDonald's *Dictionary of Canadian Art*, and major exhibition catalogues. Biographies of non-Canadians have been augmented by dictionaries published in Great Britain, the United States, and Europe.

No distinction has been made between professional, amateur, and naive artists. There are some persons who have had little or no instruction in carving, painting, or sculpture, but whose works are considered worthy of acceptance by exhibition judges, and are purchased by art galleries.

Inevitably, compiling the index has required making a number of decisions. The same name may appear with different spellings in various sources; places and dates of birth and death are not always available or precise; names of the countries of birth or death change; activity in 'the

Arctic' had to be examined to determine whether it occurred in what is now Canada, or in Alaska or Greenland. Where there has been doubt, I have based the entry on the most apparently reliable source, or sources.

It has been my good fortune to receive the assistance of many kind friends and acquaintances who have improved the quality of the index. Their replies to my questions have been most gratefully received and valued: Ian Montagnes, editor of the index; David Karel, Assistant Dean Faculté des Lettres, l'Université Laval; Charles C. Hill, Curator of Canadian Art, Pierre Landry, Acting Associate Curator of Canadian Art, Peter Trepanier, Head Special Collections, and Murray Waddington, Head Librarian, National Gallery of Canada; Jim Burant, Chief Art Acquisition and Research, National Archives of Canada; Kathryn Bridges, Pictorial Records, British Columbia Archives; Cheryl Siegle, Librarian, Art Gallery of Vancouver; Diana Cooper, Fine Arts Reference Librarian, University of British Columbia; and the Vancouver Public Library's Subject Divisions, in particular the staff of Fine Arts and Music.

Evelyn de Rostaing McMann
Vancouver
July 1995

GUIDE TO ENTRIES

Entries provide the following information:

- name
- date and place of birth and death (when available)
- years an artist flourished (when birth and death dates are unavailable)
- nationality (if not Canadian)
- type of artist (major medium/media used)
- sources in which biographical information may be found

Abbreviations for types of artists, place names and nationalities, and sources are given on pages xiii–xxvi.

Names

Most names appear in the index as they appear in the sources. However, an artist may be identified in more than one way, depending on the source. To assist users of the index in locating entries in the sources, several devices have been used:

COLVILLE, David Alexander (some sources list him as Colville, Alex)
HARRINGTON/HARRISON (sources differ in the spelling of the surname: used when the variant spellings are close together alphabetically)

Some authors are listed in different sources under different surnames or by a signature other than their surname. In such cases superscript numbers have been inserted. Thus:

SMITH[1], Ann Harris[2] DBA[1,2] (she is listed under both Smith and Harris in the source)
LAMBE, Sarah M.[2] (Zaidee M.[3]) H[2,3] MM RCA (she is listed under both names in the source)
MILLER, Grace Wilson[2] ACA[2] (she is listed under Wilson in the source)
ROSS, Mary (m John Beck[2]) MA[2] (she is listed as Mary Beck in the source)
MOORE, Helen (m Henry Stuart[2]) WHC[2] (she is included in her husband's biography in the source)

HALL, Bertha Adams[2] (s Berto[3]) F[2] Des[3] (she is listed under Adams in the first source, and under her signature Berto in the second)

In addition, *see* references have been used.

Entries for Inuit artists include census numbers assigned to the artist by the Canadian government. For the 1941 decennial census, each Inuit person was allotted a number on a disc, e.g., E 174. In 1945 a number was added to indicate the geographical district in which the person lived: E1 to E9 for the nine districts in the Eastern Arctic, and W1 to W3 for districts in the Western Arctic. Depending on the district, the disc number E 174, for example, became E1-174. In 1971 disc numbers were discontinued and 'Project Surnames' were introduced. Kiawak E1-174 became Kiawak Ashoona. Because the disc numbers were used as a signature for many years by many artists, they are retained in the index. Entries are further complicated by variations in transliteration of the Inuit names, so that the same artist may appear in different sources as, for example, Amitook, Amatuk, and Ometuoq.

Dates and places of birth and death

Birth and death dates are provided when available, based on the most consistently reliable sources. Even with so many sources, it has been impossible to determine some dates of birth or death, or to decide between conflicting dates. Places of birth and death are given when available. Dates and places are treated as follows:

b London 1819, d England 1905 (born in London in 1819; died in England, location unknown, in 1905)
b Montreal 1896 – d 1961 (born and died in the same city)
b Ottawa 1865, d 1901 (place of death unknown)
b Toronto 1863 (place and date of death unknown)
b Halifax 1936– (still living)
b 1857/61, d 1914 (birth dates vary in different sources)

Sources

The sources indexed in this work are identified by abbreviations. Directories published regularly over a number of years are identified by the last, or latest, year in which a biography appears. Editions and volumes are identified as part of the abbreviation:

CWW10	*Canadian Who's Who*, 1910 edition
DCB9	*Dictionary of Canadian Biography*, vol. 9

Mo98,12	Morgan 1898 edition, and 1912 edition
WWA43d56	*Who's Who in American Art,* the last biography was in the 1943 edition, the death was reported in the 1956 edition

Page numbers are given when the source does not list the artist's name in correct alphabetical order. In *Burke's Peerage and Baronetage* the entries are in order of the name of the peerage and baronetage, and references include page numbers; the 10th edition of 1970 and the 1978 reprint have the same pagination.

Full bibliographic references are given with their abbreviations in the list which begins on page xvii.

One valuable source does not appear because it does not include biographies. *Artists in Canada,* published by the National Gallery of Canada, lists by name approximately 40,000 artists and where their files are held in university, public, and art gallery libraries. It was particularly useful in providing dates not available in the sources.

ABBREVIATIONS

Professional Categories

anim	animator	illus	illustrator
cal	calligrapher	litho	lithographer
car	caricaturist	med	medallist
cart	cartoonist	met	metal worker
carv	carver	min	miniaturist
cer	ceramist	mmed	mixed media artist
coll	collage artist	mos	mosaic artist
con	conceptualist	mtech	mixed techniques artist
crto	cartographer	mur	muralist
des	designer	paint	painter
dior	dioramist	panor	panoramist
drgt	draughtsman	pas	pastelist
drw	drawer	prt	print maker
enam	enamellist	sculp	sculptor
engr	engraver	sil	silhouettist
etch	etcher	ske	sketcher
fab	fabric artist	stgl	stained-glass maker
fre	frescoist	tap	tapestry maker
glpt	glass painter	tex	textile artist
gra	graphic artist	topog	topographer
illum	illuminator	wlhg	wall-hanging artist

General

Adm	Admiral	Comdt	Commandant
aka	also known as	d	died
b	born	fl	flourished
Brig	Brigadier	FM	Field Marshal
Bro	Brother	Ft	Fort
bu	buried	Gen	General
c	circa (about)	GovGen	Governor General
Capt	Captain	Isld	Island, Islands
Cdr	Commander	Lt	Lieutenant
cen	century	m	married
Co	County, Company	Maj	Major
Col	Colonel	Msgr	Monsignor

nr	near	re	renamed
p	page	Res	Reserve
pp	pages	ret	retired
Prov	Province	RN	Royal Navy
q.v.	*quod vide* (which see)	s	signature
RA	Royal Academy	Tp	Township
R Adm	Rear Admiral	V Adm	Vice Admiral
RCA	Royal Canadian Academy	x	error

Place names and nationalities

Major foreign cities are not identified by country, e.g., London, New York, Paris. In Canada major cities are not identified by province, e.g., Calgary, Edmonton, Montreal, Toronto, Vancouver, Winnipeg. City names are spelled in full, e.g., New York is the city, NY is the state. Quebec is the city, Que is the province. Upper Canada and Canada West are identified as Ontario, Lower Canada and Canada East are identified as Quebec. Place names of old villages and towns that have vanished from maps and gazetteers are listed as near (nr) a present place, e.g., Gugen nr Shediac, NB. The change of a place name is noted, e.g., Port Arthur renamed (re) Thunder Bay, Ont. Without a town or city in the biographies the full name of the country is noted, e.g., b Hungary 1962. The name of the country as it was when an artist was born is kept, e.g., b Russia 1906.

Canada

Alta	Alberta	NWT	Northwest Territories
BC	British Columbia	Ont	Ontario
Man	Manitoba	PEI	Prince Edward Island
NB	New Brunswick	Que	Quebec
Nfld	Newfoundland	Sask	Saskatchewan
NS	Nova Scotia	YT	Yukon Territory

Great Britain

Aber	Aberdeenshire, Scotland	CI	Channel Islands, England
Argyl	Argyllshire, Scotland		
Ayrs	Ayrshire, Scotland	Corn	Cornwall, England
Banf	Banffshire, Scotland	Cumb	Cumberland, England
Beds	Bedfordshire, England	Derb	Derbyshire, England
Berks	Berkshire, England	Dev	Devon, England
Bucks	Buckinghamshire, England	Dor	Dorset, England
Cambs	Cambridgeshire, England	Dur	Durham, England
Ches	Cheshire, England	Exe	Exeter, England

Glam	Glamorganshire, Wales	Ork	Orkney, Scotland
Glos	Gloucestershire, England	Oxon	Oxfordshire, England
Hants	Hampshire, England	Pemb	Pembrokeshire, Wales
Herts	Hertfordshire, England	Per	Perthshire, Scotland
I of M	Isle of Man, England	Selk	Selkirkshire, Scotland
I of W	Isle of Wight, England	Shrops	Shropshire, England
Kinc	Kincardineshire, Scotland	Som	Somerset, England
Kirc	Kircudbrightshire, Scotland	Staf	Staffordshire, England
Lancs	Lancashire, England	Suf	Suffolk, England
Leics	Leicestershire, England	Sur	Surrey, England
Lincs	Lincolnshire, England	Sus	Sussex, England
Mon	Monmouthshire, Wales	War	Warwickshire, England
Monts	Montgomeryshire, Wales	Westm	Westmorland, England
N Ire	Northern Ireland	Wilts	Wiltshire, England
N'land	Northumberland	W Loth	West Lothian, Scotland
Norf	Norfolk, England	Wor	Worcestershire, England
Notts	Nottinghamshire, England	Yorks	Yorkshire, England

United States of America

Ala	Alabama	NC	North Carolina
Calif	California	ND	North Dakota
Colo	Colorado	Nebr	Nebraska
Conn	Connecticut	NH	New Hampshire
DC	District of Columbia	NJ	New Jersey
Fla	Florida	NM	New Mexico
Ga	Georgia	NY	New York
Ill	Illinois	Okla	Oklahoma
Ind	Indiana	Oreg	Oregon
Kans	Kansas	Pa	Pennsylvania
Ky	Kentucky	RI	Rhode Island
La	Louisiana	SC	South Carolina
Mass	Massachusetts	SDak	South Dakota
Md	Maryland	Tenn	Tennessee
Me	Maine	Tex	Texas
Mich	Michigan	Va	Virginia
Minn	Minnesota	Vt	Vermont
Miss	Mississippi	Wash	Washington
Mo	Missouri	Wis	Wisconsin
Mont	Montana	Wyo	Wyoming

Countries, regions, nationalities

Alb	Albania	Alg	Algeria

Amer	America, American
Au	Austria
Aus	Australia
Bah	Bahamas
Ban	Bangladesh
Bel	Belgium, Belgian
Ber	Bermuda
Bul	Bulgaria
Bur	Burma
BWI	British West Indies
Chi	China
Cz	Czechoslovakia
Dn	Denmark, Danish
Egy	Egypt
Eng	England, English
Est	Estonia
Fin	Finland
Fr	France, French
Ge	Germany, German
Gr	Greece
Hu	Hungary
Indo	Indonesia
Ire	Ireland
Is	Israel
It	Italy, Italian
Jam	Jamaica
Kor	Korea
Lat	Latvia
Leb	Lebanon
Lith	Lithuania
Malay	Malaysia
Maur	Mauritius
Mor	Morocco
Neth	Netherlands, Netherlander
N Ire	Northern Ireland
Nor	Norway
NZ	New Zealand
Pak	Pakistan
Phil	Philippines
Pol	Poland
Port	Portugal
Pru	Prussia
Rom	Romania
Rus	Russia, Russian
SA	Union of South Africa
Scot	Scotland, Scottish
S Dom	Santo Domingo
Sib	Siberia
Sp	Spain, Spanish
Swe	Sweden
Swi	Switzerland, Swiss
Tan	Tanganyika
Tri	Trinidad
Tur	Turkey
Ug	Uganda
Ukr	Ukraine
USSR	Union of Soviet Socialist Republics
Ven	Venezuela
Yu	Yugoslavia

ABBREVIATIONS OF WORKS CITED

AA — Baker, Suzanne Devonshire. *Artists of Alberta.* Edmonton: University of Alberta Press, 1980.

AAA year — *American Art Annual.* Washington, DC, and New York: American Federation of Arts, 1898–1933.

AAW 1–3 — Dawdy, Doris Ostrander. *Artists of the American West: A Biographical Dictionary.* 3 vols. Chicago: Swallow Press, Sage Books, 1974; Athens, Ohio: Swallow Press, Ohio University Press, 1981–5.

ABC — Morys-Edge, Derek. *Artists of British Columbia.* Vancouver: Chartwell Publishing, 1986.

ABH — Kinneir, Joan, ed. *The Artist By Himself.* New York: St Martin's Press, 1988.

AC — Hughes, Edan Milton. *Artists in California, 1786–1940.* San Francisco: Hughes Publishing, 1986.

ACA — Hubbard, Robert H., ed. *An Anthology of Canadian Art.* Toronto: Oxford University Press, 1960.

AE — Agnes Etherington Art Centre. *Permanent Collection.* Kingston, Ont.: Agnes Etherington Art Centre, Queen's University, 1968.

AGO — Art Gallery of Ontario. *Canadian Collection.* Toronto: McGraw-Hill of Canada, 1970.

AH — Hogarth, Paul. *Artists on Horseback: The Old West in Illustrated Journalism, 1857–1900.* Toronto: General Publishing in co-operation with Riveredge Foundation, Calgary; New York: Watson-Guptill, 1972.

AKL — *Allgemeines Künstlerlexikon: Die bildenden Künstler aller Zeiten und Völker.* 8 vols. Munich-Leipzig: G.K. Saur, 1992– .

AM — Wehle, Harry Brandeis. *American Miniatures, 1750–1850, and a Biographical Dictionary of the Artists by Theodore Bolton.* Garden City, NY: Doubleday for the Metropolitan Museum of Art, 1927.

ANC — Waters, Clara Erskine Clement, and Laurence Hutton. *Artists of the Nineteenth Century and Their Works.* 1879. 7th rev. ed. Reprint (2 vols in 1). St Louis, Mo.: North Point Inc.; New York: Arno Press, 1969.

ANZ — Germaine, Max. *Artists and Galleries of Australia and New Zealand.* Sydney, New York: Lansdowne Editions, 1979.

AO — *Artists of the Okanagan.* Kelowna, BC: Mainline Senior Writers and Publishers Association, 1988.

APH	Burant, Jim, et al. *A Place in History: Twenty Years of Acquiring Paintings, Drawings and Prints at the National Archives of Canada.* Ottawa: National Archives of Canada, 1991.
App	*Appleton's Cyclopedia of American Biography.* James Grant Wilson and John Fiske, eds. 6 vols. New York: D. Appleton and Company, 1887–9.
AW	Curry, Larry. *The American West: Painters from Catlin to Russell.* New York: Viking Press in association with Los Angeles County Museum of Art; Toronto: Macmillan, 1972.
B	Benezit, Emmanuel. *Dictionnaire critique et documentaire des peintres, sculpteurs, dessinateurs et graveurs.* 10 vols. Paris: Librarie Grund, 1976.
BB	Brender à Brandis, G., and Danuta M.A.K. Kamocki. *The White Line: Wood Engravings in Canada Since 1945.* Erin, Ont.: Porcupine's Quill, 1990.
BCA	British Columbia Archives, Victoria, BC.
BCS	*BC Sculptors.* [Vancouver]: Sculptors' Society of Canada, Western Chapter, [1972].
BDSA	Newman, Marketa, and Eva Jana Newman. *Biographical Dictionary of Saskatchewan Artists.* Vol. 1, *Women Artists.* Saskatoon: Fifth House Publishers, 1990.
BE	*Britannica Encyclopaedia of American Art.* Chicago: Encyclopaedia Britannica Educational Corp., 1973.
BI	Peppin, Brigid, and Lucy Micklethwait. *Book Illustrators of the Twentieth Century.* New York: Arco Press, 1984.
BM	Long, Basil S. *British Miniatures,* 3rd ed. London: Holland Press, 1966.
BP	*Burke's Peerage and Baronetage,* 105th ed. London: Burke's Peerage and Baronetage, 1970. Reprinted 1978.
Bry	Bryan, Michael. *Bryan's Dictionary of Painters and Engravers: Biographical and Critical.* Revised and enlarged by George C. Williamson. New York: Macmillan, 1925.
BSA	McKechnie, Sue. *British Silhouette Artists and Their Works, 1760–1860.* London: P. Wilson for Sotheby Parke Bernet, 1978.
C	*The CANSCAIP Companion: A Biographical Record of Canadian Children's Authors, Illustrators and Performers.* Barbara Greenwood, general ed. Markham, Ont.: Pembroke Publishers, 1991.
CA 1–3	Naylor, Colin, ed. *Contemporary Artists,* 3 eds. London and Chicago: St James Press; New York: St Martin's Press, 1977–89.
CAE 1,2	*Canadian Artists in Exhibition/Artistes Canadiens en expositions,* 2 eds. Toronto: Roundstone Council for the Arts and Canadian Art Publications, 1973–4.
CBC	Stott, Jon C., and Raymond E. Jones. *Canadian Books for Children: A Guide to Authors and Illustrators.* Toronto: Harcourt Brace Jovanovich Canada, 1980.

CC 1,2 — *Creative Canada: A Biographical Dictionary of Twentieth-Century Creative and Performing Arts*. Compiled by the Reference Division, McPherson Library, University of Victoria. 2 vols. Toronto: University of Toronto Press, 1971–2.

CE 1,2 — *Canadian Encyclopedia*. 1st ed., 3 vols; 2nd ed., 4 vols. Edmonton: Hurtig Publishers, 1985–8.

CGA 1–3 — Horn, Maurice. *Contemporary Graphic Artists: Biographical and Critical Guide to Current Illustrators, Animators, Cartoonists, Designers and Other Graphic Artists*. 3 vols. Detroit: Gale Research, 1986–8.

CLA — Canadian Library Association. *Canadian Biographies: Artists and Authors*. Ottawa: Canadian Library Association, 1947–51.

CNS year — *Canadian Newspaper Service Reference Book: Biographical Reference Data and General Information*. Montreal: Canadian Newspaper Service Ltd., 1927–72.

Co — Colombo, John Robert. *Colombo's Canadian References*. Toronto: Oxford University Press, 1976.

CWW year — *Canadian Who's Who*. Kieran Simpson, ed. Toronto: University of Toronto Press, 1910– .

DAA — Baignell, Mathew. *Dictionary of American Art*. New York: Harper and Row, 1979.

DAB — *Dictionary of American Biography*. 27 vols. New York: Charles Scribner's Sons, 1928– .

DAS — Opitz, Glenn B. *Dictionary of American Sculptors: 18th Century to the Present*. Poughkeepsie, NY: Apollo Books, 1984.

DBA — Johnson, Jane, and A. Greutzner, compilers. *Dictionary of British Artists, 1880–1940*. Woodbridge, Suffolk: Antique Collectors' Club, 1976.

DBBI — Houfe, Simon. *Dictionary of British Book Illustrators and Caricaturists, 1800–1914*. 2nd rev. ed. Woodbridge, Suffolk: Antique Collectors' Club, 1981.

DBE — Grant, Maurice Harold. *Dictionary of British Etchers*. London: Maurice Harold Grant, 1952.

DBF — Burbridge, R. Brinsley. *Dictionary of British Flower, Fruit and Still Life Painters*, vol. 2: *1850–1950*. Leigh-on-Sea: F. Lewis Publishers, 1974.

DBHP — Lewis, Frank. *Dictionary of British Historical Painters*. Leigh-on-Sea: F. Lewis Publishers, 1979.

DBLP — Grant, Maurice Harold. *Dictionary of British Landscape Painters: From the 16th Century to the Early 20th Century*. Leigh-on-Sea: F. Lewis Publishers, 1952.

DBMaP — Wilson, Arnold. *Dictionary of British Marine Painters*. Leigh-on-Sea: F. Lewis Publishers, 1967.

DBMP — Wilson, Arnold. *Dictionary of British Military Painters*. Leigh-on-Sea: F. Lewis Publishers, 1973.

DBWA Mallalieu, H.L. *Dictionary of Watercolour Artists up to 1920.* 2nd ed., vol. 2. Woodbridge, Suffolk: Antique Collectors' Club, 1986.

DCA Smith, V. Babbington, ed. *Dictionary of Contemporary Artists.* Oxford, Eng.; Santa Barbara, Calif.: Clio Press, 1981.

DCAA 1–3 Cummings, Paul. *Dictionary of Contemporary American Artists.* 3 eds. New York: St Martin's Press; London: St James Press, 1971–88.

DCB 1–13 *Dictionary of Canadian Biography, 1000–1910,* 13 vols. Toronto: University of Toronto Press, 1966– .

DEA Gray, Philip Howard. *Directory of Eskimo Artists in Sculpture and Prints.* Bozeman, Mont.: Philip Howard Gray, 1974.

Des Desbarats, Peter, and Terry Mosher. *The Hecklers: A History of Canadian Political Cartooning and a Cartoonists' History of Canada.* Toronto: McClelland and Stewart and National Film Board of Canada, 1979.

DeV 1–9 DeVolpi, Charles Patrick. Pictorial Record Series. Montreal: DeV-Sco Publications, 1962–6; Toronto: Longmans, 1971–4.

1. *British Columbia, 1778–1891.* 1973.
2. *Eastern Townships, 1830s–1860s.* 1962.
3. *Montreal, 1535–1885.* 2 vols. 1963.
4. *Newfoundland, 1497–1887.* 1972.
5. *Niagara Peninsula, 1697–1880.* 1966.
6. *Ottawa, 1807–1882.* 1964.
7. *Quebec, 1608–1875.* 1971.
8. *Toronto, 1813–1882.* 1965.
9. *Nova Scotia, 1605–1878.* 1974.

DFA McKendry, Blake. *Dictionary of Folk Artists in Canada: From the 17th Century to the Present.* Elginburg, Ont.: Blake McKendry, 1988.

DFP 2,3 Paviere, Sydney H. *Dictionary of Flower, Fruit and Still Life Painters,* vol. 2, *1786–1840*; vol. 3, *1841–1885.* Leigh-on-Sea: F. Lewis Publishers, 1964.

DIA Strickland, Walter George. *Dictionary of Irish Artists.* New York: Hacker Art Books, 1968.

DMA Brewington, Dorothy E.R. *Dictionary of Marine Artists.* Salem, Mass.: Peabody Museum of Salem; Mystic, Conn.: Mystic Seaport Museum, 1982.

DMS Maillard, Robert, general ed. *New Dictionary of Modern Sculpture.* New York: Tudor Publishing, 1976.

DNB *Dictionary of National Biography.* 21 vols. 9 supplements. London: Smith, Elder 1885–1900.

DP *Debrett's Peerage and Baronetage.* London: Debrett Peerage Ltd.; London: Macmillan; New York: St Martin's Press, 1990.

DScP	Halsby, Julian, and Paul Harris. *Dictionary of Scottish Painters, 1600–1960*. Edinburgh: Canongate Publishing; Oxford: Phaidon Press in association with Bourne Fine Art, 1990.
DSP	Archibald, Edward H.H. *Dictionary of Sea Painters*, 2nd ed. Woodbridge, Suffolk: Antique Collectors' Club, 1989.
DVLP	Paviere, Sydney H. *Dictionary of Victorian Landscape Painters*. Leigh-on-Sea: F. Lewis Publishers, 1968.
DVP	Wood, Christopher. *Dictionary of Victorian Painters, 1820–1914*, rev. 2nd ed. Woodbridge, Suffolk: Antique Collectors' Club, 1978.
DWA	Petteys, Chris, et al. *Dictionary of Women Artists: An International Dictionary of Women Artists Born before 1900*. Boston: G.K. Hall, 1985.
DWP	Fisher, Stanley W. *Dictionary of Watercolour Painters, 1750–1900*. London and New York: Foulsham S. Co., 1972.
EC	*Encyclopedia Canadiana*. 10 vols. Ottawa: Canadiana Company of Canada; Grolier Society of Canada, 1957.
EMA	Henry, John Frazier. *Early Maritime Artists of the Pacific Northwest Coast, 1741–1841*. Seattle: University of Washington Press; Vancouver: Douglas & McIntyre, 1984.
F	Fielding, Mantle. *Dictionary of American Painters, Sculptors, and Engravers*. Revised and updated by Glenn B. Opitz. 2nd ed. Poughkeepsie, NY: Apollo Books, 1986.
FCA	Miller, Muriel, and Gail H. Corbett, eds. *Famous Canadian Artists*. Peterborough, Ont.: Woodland Publishing, 1983.
Fo	Foskett, Daphne. *Miniatures: Dictionary and Guide*. Woodbridge, Suffolk: Antique Collectors' Club, 1987.
G	Graves, Algernon. *The Royal Academy of Arts: A Complete Dictionary of Contributors and Their Works from Its Foundation in 1769 to 1904*. 8 vols. London: Henry Graves & Co., and George Bell & Sons, 1905.
GM	Ainslie, Patricia. *Images of the Land: Canadian Block Prints, 1919–1945*. Calgary: Glenbow Museum, 1985.
GW	Groce, George G., and David H. Wallace. *New York Historical Society's Dictionary of Artists in America, 1564–1860*. New Haven: Yale University Press, 1957.
H	Harper, J. Russell. *Early Painters and Engravers in Canada*. Toronto: University of Toronto Press, 1970.
H74	Harper, J. Russell. *A People's Art: Primitive, Naïve, Provincial and Folk Painting in Canada*. Toronto: University of Toronto Press, 1974.
H77	Harper, J. Russell. *Painting in Canada: A History*. 2 eds. Toronto: University of Toronto Press, 1966–77.
Hu	Hughes, Margaret E. *A Guide to Canadian Painters*. Toronto: King's Printer [Ontario], 1940.

IA1	Reed, Walt. *The Illustrator in America, 1900–60*. New York: Reinhold Publishing, 1967.
IA2	Reed, Walt, and Roger Reed. *The Illustrator in America, 1880–1980: A Century of Illustration*. New York: Madison Square Press for the Society of Illustrators, 1984.
IBYP	Ward, Martha Eades. *Illustrators of Books for Young People*. 2nd ed. Metuchoen, NJ: Scarecrow Press, 1975.
ICB 1–4	*Illustrators of Childrens Books*. (1) *1744–1945*. (2) *1946–56*. (3) *1957–66*. (4) *1967–76*. Boston: Horn Book Inc., 1947–78.
IO	Wolff, Hennie. *Index of Ontario Artists*. Toronto: Visual Arts of Ontario and Ontario Association of Art Galleries, 1978.
J	Jackson, E. Neville. *Silhouettes: A History and Dictionary of Artists*. 1938. Reprint. New York: Dover Publications, 1981.
JAI 4–6	Holtze, Sally Holmes. *Junior Authors and Illustrators*, vols. 4–6. New York: H.W. Wilson, 1978–89.
K	Karel, David. *Dictionnaire des artistes de langue français en Amérique du Nord: Peintres, sculpteurs, dessinateurs, graveurs, photographes et orfèvres*. Quebéc: Musée du Quebéc, Les Presses de l'Université Laval, 1992.
KB	Kobayashi, Terry, and Michael Bird. *A Compendium of Canadian Folk Artists*. Erin, Ont.: Boston Mills Press, 1985.
Ke	Kerr, Joan, ed. *Dictionary of Australian Artists, Painters, Sketchers, and Engravers to 1870*. Oxford: Oxford University Press, 1992.
L	*Larousse Dictionary of Painters*. New York: Larousse & Co., 1981.
LeJ	Le Jeune, Louis-Marie. *Dictionnaire général de biographie, histoire, literature ... du Canada*. 2 vols. Ottawa: Université d'Ottawa, 1931.
M	MacDonald, Colin S. *Dictionary of Canadian Artists*. vols 1–7. Ottawa: Canadian Paperbacks, 1967– .
MA	Hashey, Mary H., comp. *Maritime Artists*. N.p.: Maritime Art Association, 1967.
McC	McCracken, Harold. *Great Painters and Illustrators of the Old West*. Reprint. New York: Dover Publications, 1988.
MF	Dey-Bergmoser, Olga, and Khaletum Majumber. *Many Faces, Many Spaces: Artists in Ontario*. Edited by Elizabeth J. Coulter. Oakville, Ont.: Mosaic Press, 1987.
MFMS	Dey-Bergmoser, Olga, and Betty Coulter, eds. *More Faces, More Spaces: Artists in Canada*. Oakville, Ont.: Mosaic Press, 1991.
MM	McMann, Evelyn de R. *Montreal Museum of Fine Arts, formerly Art Association of Montreal: Spring Exhibitions, 1880–1970*. Toronto: University of Toronto Press, 1988.
Mo 98,12	Morgan, Henry James. *Canadian Men and Women of the Time*. 2 eds. Toronto: Briggs, 1898, 1912.
MP	Gaunt, William. *Marine Painting: An Historical Survey*. London: Secker & Warburg, 1975.

MPE Cordingly, David. *Marine Painting in England, 1700–1900.* London: Studio Vista, 1974.

MQ Musée du Quebéc. *500 ouvres choisies.* Quebéc: Musée du Quebéc, 1983.

NAC National Archives of Canada. Ottawa.

NCAB *National Cyclopedia of American Biography: Being the History of the United States.* 76 vols. Clifton, NJ: James T. White, 1890– .

NGC1 Hubbard, R.H. *National Gallery of Canada: Catalogue of Paintings and Sculpture, Canadian School,* vol. 3. Toronto: University of Toronto Press for the Trustees, 1960.

NGC2 *National Gallery of Canada Catalogue of Canadian Art.* 2 vols. Ottawa: National Gallery of Canada, 1988– .

NGC67 Hubbard, R.H., and J.R. Ostiguy. *Three Hundred Years of Canadian Art: An Exhibition Arranged in Celebration of the Century of Confederation.* Ottawa: National Gallery of Canada, 1967.

NGC68 Woodehouse, R.F. *Check-list of the War Collections of World War I, 1914–1918, and World War II, 1939–1945.* Ottawa: National Gallery of Canada, 1968.

O date Ontario Library Review. *Who's Who in Canadian Art: From O.L.R. November 1947 – August 1962.* Toronto: Government Printer, 1947–1962.

OC Osborne, Harold, ed. *Oxford Companion to Art.* Oxford: Clarendon Press, 1970.

OCD Chilvers, Ian, ed. *Concise Oxford Dictionary of Art and Artists.* Oxford and New York: Oxford University Press, 1990.

OELP Grant, Maurice Harold. *A Chronological History of Old English Landscape Painters in Oil: From the XVIth Century to the XIXth.* 8 vols. Leigh-on-Sea: F. Lewis Publishers, 1957–61.

P *Phaidon Dictionary of Twentieth Century Art.* London: Phaidon Press, 1973.

PHA Kasas, Ernest Gyimesy, and Leslie L. Konnyu, eds. *Professional Hungarian Artists Outside of Hungary.* St Louis, Mo.: American Hungarian Review, 1977.

PMC Hamilton, Ross, ed. *Prominent Men of Canada, 1931–1932.* Montreal: National Publishing of Canada, 1932.

PNL Bell, Michael, comp. *Painters in a New Land: From Annapolis Royal to the Klondike.* Toronto: McClelland and Stewart, 1973.

Po year Badeux, Guy, ed., text by Charles Gordon. *Portfolio* [year] *in Canadian Caricature.* Montreal: Croc Publishing. Ludcom Inc., 1986–7; Montreal: Eden Press, 1988; Toronto: Macmillan, 1989– .

PP Finch, Roger. *Pierhead Painters: Naïve Ship Portrait Painters, 1750–1950.* London: Barrie & Jenkins, 1983.

PS Cordingly, David. *Painters of the Sea: A Survey of Dutch and English Marine Paintings from British Collections.* London: Lund

Humphries in association with the Royal Pavilion Art Gallery and Museum, 1979.

R 1,2 — Roberts, Charles G.D., and Arthur L. Tunnell, eds. *A Standard Dictionary of Canadian Biography: The Canadian Who Was Who, 1875–1933.* 2 eds. Toronto: Trans Canada Press, 1934–8.

RA — Royal Academy of Arts. *Exhibitions 1905–1970: A Dictionary of Artists and Their Work in the Summer Exhibitions of the Royal Academy of Arts.* 6 vols. East Ardsley, Yorkshire: EP Publishing, 1973–82.

RCA — McMann, Evelyn de R. *Royal Canadian Academy of Arts/Académie royale des arts du Canada: Exhibitions and Members, 1880–1979.* Toronto: University of Toronto Press, 1981.

Red — Redgrave, Samuel. *A Dictionary of Artists of the English School: Painters, Sculptors, Architects and Ornamentalists with Notes of Their Lives and Work,* 2nd ed. 1878. Bath, Somerset: Kingsmead Reprints, 1970.

ROM — Allodi, Mary. *Canadian Watercolours and Drawings in the Royal Ontario Museum.* 2 vols. Toronto: Royal Ontario Museum, 1971.

S — Sarnia Public Library and Art Gallery. *The Collection.* Sarnia, Ont.: Sarnia Public Library and Art Gallery, 1981.

SAA 1–72 — *Something about the Author: Facts and Pictures about Authors and Illustrators of Books for Young People.* Vols 1–72. Detroit: Gale Research, 1971– .

Sam — Samuels, Peggy, and Harold Samuels. *Illustrated Biographical Encyclopedia of Artists of the American West.* Garden City, NY: Doubleday, 1976.

SC — *Shell Canada Collection: A Selection of Canadian Art Assembled by the Employees of Shell Canada Limited.* Calgary: Shell Canada, 1977.

SP — Finch, Roger. *The Ship Painters.* Lavenham, Suffolk: Terence Dalton Ltd., 1975.

St — Stacey, Robert H. *Lives and Works of the Canadian Artists.* Toronto: Dundurn Press, 1977–8.

SW — Halsby, Julian. *Scottish Watercolours, 1740–1940.* London: B.T. Batsford, 1986.

T — *Canadian Childhoods: A Tundra Anthology in Words and Art.* Montreal: Tundra Books, 1989.

TB 1–3 — Thieme, Ulrich, and Felix Becker. *Allgemeines Lexikon der bildenden Künstler von der Antike bis zur Gegenwart.* 37 vols. Leipzig: E.A. Seamans, 1907–62.

TCBA — Driskell, David C., catalogue notes by Leonard Simon. *Two Centuries of Black American Art.* New York: Alfred A. Knopf, 1976.

TN — Tooby, Michael, ed. *The True North: Canadian Landscape Painting,*

	1896–1939. London: Lund Humphries in association with Barbican Art Gallery, 1991.
UG	Nasby, Judith M. *University of Guelph Art Collection: A Catalogue of Paintings, Drawings, Prints and Sculpture.* Guelph, Ont.: University of Guelph, 1980.
US	Findlay, Isobel, ed. *University of Saskatchewan Permanent Art Collection.* Saskatoon: University of Saskatchewan, 1980.
W 1–3	Wallace, W. Stewart, ed. *Dictionary of Canadian Biography,* 1945 ed. *Macmillan Dictionary of Canadian Biography,* 1963, 1978 eds. Toronto: Macmillan, 1945–78.
WA	Marks, Claude. *World Artists, 1950–1980: An H.W. Wilson Biographical Dictionary.* New York: H.W. Wilson Company, 1984.
WBA 1,2	Waters, Grant M. *Dictionary of British Artists Working 1900–1950.* 2 vols. Eastbourne: Eastbourne Fine Art Publications, 1975.
WECa	Horn, Maurice, ed., assisted by Richard E. Marshall. *The World Encyclopedia of Cartoons.* New York: Chelsea House, 1980.
WECo	Horn, Maurice, ed. *World Enclyclopedia of Comics.* 2 vols. New York: Chelsea House, 1976.
WENA	Bihalji-Merin, Oto. *World Encyclopedia of Naïve Art: A Hundred Years of Naïve Art.* London: F. Muller, 1984.
WHC	Cooke, W. Martha E. *W.H. Coverdale Collection of Canadiana: Paintings, Watercolours, and Drawings, Manoir Richeliue Collection.* Ottawa: Public Archives Canada, 1983.
WI	Hodgson, Pat. *War Illustrations.* London: Osprey Publishing, 1977.
WWA year	*Who's Who in American Art.* Washington, DC: American Federation of Arts, 1935–47; New York: R.R. Bowker, 1953– .
WWB year	*Who's Who in Art: Being a Series of Alphabetically Arranged Biographies of Leading Men and Women in the World of Art Today.* London: Art Trade Press, 1927– .
WWC year	*Who's Who in Canada,* 1898– . Agincourt, Ont.: Global Press; Toronto: Canadian Publishing Corp., 1922– .
WWGA 1,2	Amstutz, Walter, ed. *Who's Who in Graphic Art.* 2 eds. Zurich: Amstutz & Herdeg Graphics Press, 1962; Dudendorf, Switzerland: De Clivo Press, 1982.
WWNA	Appleton, Marion Brymner, ed. *Who's Who in Northwest Art: A Directory of Persons in the Pacific Northwest Working in the Media of Painting, Sculpture, Graphic Arts, and Handicrafts.* Seattle, Wash.: Frank McCaffrey, 1941.
WWW	*Who Was Who: A Companion Volume to 'Who's Who,' Containing the Biographies of Those Who Have Died ... 1897–1990.* 8 vols. London: Adam and Charles Black, 1920– .
WWWA	*Who Was Who in America: With World Notables; Biographies of*

the Non-living with Dates of Death Appended. 11 vols. New Providence, NJ: Marquis Who's Who; Reed Reference Publishing, 1943– .

Y — Young, William, ed. and comp. *Dictionary of American Artists, Sculptors, and Engravers from the Beginnings through the Turn of the Twentieth Century.* Cambridge, Mass.: William Young & Co., 1968.

BIOGRAPHICAL INDEX OF ARTISTS IN CANADA

AADLAND, Mavis, b Kevan, Mont 1915– , paint CAE1

AALTO, Harri Anselm, b Tampere, Fin 1946– , drw paint sculp AKL IO

AALUK, Christine, E3-360 (m Octave Sivanerktok), b Repulse Bay, NWT 1938– , sculp DEA

AARONS, Andrew Lewis, b London 1939– , paint AKL IO

AARONS, Anita O. (m Albert Dare; m Merton Chambers), b Sydney, Aus 1912– , sculp paint AKL ANZ WWA89

ABBEY, Carol, b Kimberly, BC 1937– , paint ABC

ABBOT, Hazel Newham/Newnham, b Montreal 1894, paint AAW2 AKL DWA WWA76

ABBOT, John Bethune, b Montreal 1852 – d 1929, paint AKL H Hu MM Mo12 RCA

ABEL, Gabrielle, b Prague 1943– , paint AKL CAE1

ABERDEEN, Ishbel Maria Majoribanks, Lady (m John Campbell Hamilton Gordon[2], 1st Marquis of Aberdeen and Termair), b London 1857, d Aberdeen 1939, Scot, paint AKL BPp9 CE1,2 DNB[2] DP DWA EC H LeJ Mo98,12 W1–3 WWW

ABRAHAM, Nicolas, b France, fl 1653, paint sculp AKL H K

ACHARD, Charles, fl 1704, sculp K

ACHIM/ACHAIM, André, b Longueuil, Que c 1792 – d 1843, sculp K

ACKERMANN, George, b England, fl 1866–77, Eng, drw DFA H H77 KB ROM WHC

ACKERMANN, Robert, b Canada c 1812/17, fl 1870, engr AKL DFA H KB WHC

ACLAND, Henry Wentworth, Sir, b Kellerton, Exe 1815, d Oxford, Eng 1900, Eng, paint APH DNB WWW

ACLAND, Laurence, b Salt Lake City, Utah 1949– , gra paint AKL IO

ACRES, John Edward, fl 1800–26, paint AKL B BM Fo G GW H TB1

ACRES, William Henry, b London, Ont 1942– , paint AKL IO

ACS, Joseph Ferenc, b Hungary 1936– , paint SC

ACULIAK, E9-1593, b Port Harrison, NWT 1910 – d 1968, sculp S

ADAMS, Francis, fl 1853–77, engr litho AKL B H TB1

ADAMS, Frederick, b London, Ont 1880, paint sculp AAW3 AKL WWNA

ADAMS, Glenn Nelson, b Montreal 1928– , paint AKL M WWA78

ADAMS, Henry, fl 1859, paint AKL H

ADAMS, Irvine Clinton, b Swan Lake, Man 1902– , paint WWA70

ADAMS/ADAMES, J.E., fl 1815–16, min AKL H

ADAMS, James Lowell, b Philadelphia 1943– , paint AKL CAE1

ADAMS, Jean F.M. *See* JEFFERYS, Jean F.M. Adams

ADAMS, John, fl 1819–37, paint AKL H

ADAMS, Lily Osman, b Toronto 1865/70 – d 1945, paint AGO AKL DWA H Hu RCA

ADAMS, Ruth, b Calgary 1920– , gra paint AKL CAE1,2

ADAMSON, Amy L., b Edmonton 1909– , paint AKL WWNA

ADAMSON, Ann Mabel Cawthra[2] (1899 m Agar Allan Masterson

Adamson[3]), fl 1893–1904, paint H[2] Mo12[3] RCA

ADAMSON, Daniel, fl 1858, paint AKL H

ADAMSON, James M.F., fl 1891–3, paint AKL H RCA

ADAMSSON, Peter Magnus. *See* ALMINI, Peter Magnus

ADASKIN, Gordon, b Toronto 1931– , gra paint AKL CWW93 M RCA US

ADENEY, Christopher, b Toronto 1929– , etch paint AKL IO M

ADNEY, Edwin Tappan, b Athens, Ohio 1868, d Woodstock, NB 1950, paint illus AAA19 AKL B F M MM RCA TB1,3 WWWA Y

ADRIAN, Robert (b Adrian Robert Smith), b Toronto 1935– , paint AKL M

AFFLECK, Joan, b Windsor, Ont 1947– , drw paint AKL IO

AGGIAK, E7-815, b Cape Dorset, NWT 1922– , sculp DEA

AGLIALORO, Fortunato, b Ventimiglia, It 1949– , paint AKL IO S

AGNAKNAK/AGNARKNAK, Luke, E2-365 (m Myra Kookeeyout, E2-210, q.v.), b Baker Lake, NWT 1931– , sculp DEAp5

AGNEW, George Harvey, b Toronto 1895, d 1971, paint CWW67

AGNEW, John, b Ireland c 1835, engr AKL H

AHEARN, Margaret Howit Fleck (1892 m Thomas Ahearn), b Montreal, paint CWW10 Mo12

AHEARN, Morris/Maurice, fl 1878–89, paint AKL H

AHIER, Charles, fl 1900–17, paint AKL DFA H MM

AHN, Harry, b Korea 1939– , paint AKL IO

AHN, Seung Wan, b Seoul, Kor 1948– , paint MF

AHRENS/AHERNS[2], Carl Henry von, b Winfield, Ont 1863, d Toronto 1936, paint AAW1,3 AKL B CC1 H[2] H77 M MM Mo12 NGC1,2 PMC RCA ROM TB3 UG W1–3

AIDE-CREQUY, Jean-Antoine, Abbé, b Quebec 1749 – d 1780, paint AKL B CE1,2 DCB4 H H77 K KB TB1

AIKINS, Louise A., fl 1889, paint AKL H MM

AIKINSON, John, fl 1838–52, paint AKL H

AINSLIE/AINSLEY, Henry Francis, Col, b c 1803, d 1879, Eng, topog AKL DBMP DFA H KB

AIRD, Helen. *See* BAILLIE, Helen Phoebe Aird

AIREY, Richard, Gen Sir, b England 1803, d Leatherhead, Eng 1881, Eng, paint AKL DFA DNB H KB

AIROLA, Paavo Olavia, b Karelia, Fin 1915, d 1983, paint AKL CWW83 M MM RCA TB3 WWA82d84

AISLIN. *See* MOSHER, Terry

AITKEN, James Alfred, b Edinburgh 1846, d Glasgow 1897, Scot, paint AKL B DBA DBWA DVP DWP G H MM RCA TB1

AITKEN, Melita (m R.J. Aitken), b Drumbo, Ont 1866, d Vancouver 1945, paint AKL B DBA DFA DWA H Hu MM RA RCA WWNA

AITKEN, Peter, b Dundas, Ont 1858, fl 1912+, engr etch AKL B CWW10 F H Mo12 TB1 WWWA Y

AITKEN, Ross (s A. Jenkins), b Edinburgh 1943– , paint S

AJMO, Jean Pierre, b Quebec 1938– , drw sculp AKL M

AKED, Aleen, b England, fl 1930s, sculp DAS RCA WWA59

AKEEAKTASHUK/AKEEAKTASHOOK, b nr Irukjuak River, Que 1898, d Craig Harbour, NWT 1954, sculp AKL CE2 Co DEA

AKERMAN, William, fl 1873–82, paint AKL H

AKERS, Charles Style, b England, fl 1846–70, paint Ke

AKINS, Thomas Beamish, b Liverpool,

NS 1809, d Halifax 1892, paint AKL DFA H KB

AKPALIAPIK, Manasie, b Arctic Bay, NWT 1955– , sculp CWW93

AKROYD, Jack, b Halifax, Yorks 1921– , paint mos AKL M

ALAN, Rose Beatrice (Bea[2]), b Montreal 1910– , paint AKL[2] M

ALARY/ALARIE, Siméon, b c 1849, fl 1917, paint AKL H K

ALARY/ALARIE, Zénon, b St-Jean-Port-Joli, Que 1894, fl 1941, d 1974, carv DFA K

ALASHUA, E7-1149, b Cape Dorset, NWT 1914– , prt DEA

ALBERGA, Pino, b Italy 1940– , paint AKL

ALBERT, Antoine, b Que Prov 1820 – d 1864, paint AKL H K

ALBERT, Theresia, b W Germany 1954– , paint ABC

ALBINSON, Ernest Dewey, b Minneapolis 1898, Amer, paint AAA33 AKL MM TB2 WWA38

ALCAN/ALKAN, Felix, b c 1851, fl 1877–83, paint AKL DFA H K

ALDEN, James Madison, b Roxbury, Mass 1834, d Orlando, Fla 1922, Amer, paint AAW1 AC AKL AW DFA GW H Sam Y

ALDRICH, Pelham, fl 1875–6, Eng, topog DFA H

ALDWINCKLE, Eric, b Oxford, Eng 1909, d Toronto 1980, des paint AKL CWW80 M NGC68 O.N47 RCA TB1 WWA78

ALEXANDER, Arthur, fl 1882, paint AKL H

ALEXANDER, Charles (b Charles Alexander Smith[2]), b Galt/Hamburg/London, Ont 1864, d London 1915, paint AKL B DBA G H Hu[2] MM Mo12[2] RCA TB1,2

ALEXANDER, David, b Vancouver 1947– , paint CWW93

ALEXANDER, Earla M., b Picton, Ont 1916– , paint sculp AKL IO

ALEXANDER, Lady Eveline Marie Michell (1837 m Sir James Edward Alexander, q.v.), fl 1837–1906, Eng, paint AKL DFA DWA H WHC

ALEXANDER, Harold Rupert Leofric George, 1st Earl of Tunis, GovGen of Canada 1946–52, b London 1891, d Windsor Forest, Berks 1969, Eng, paint AKL BP CE1,2 CWW49 DNB DP EC MM RCA WWW

ALEXANDER, Hugh, b 1913– , paint DFA KB

ALEXANDER, Irene. *See* PORTER, Irene Cattelle

ALEXANDER, James Edward, Gen, Sir (m Eveline Alexander, q.v.), b Sterling, Scot 1803, d Ryde, I of W 1885, Scot, paint AKL DFA DMA DNB H LeJ ROM WHC

ALEXANDER, Martha. *See* LOGAN, Martha Alexander

ALEXANDER, Robert Samuel (m Irene Cattelle Porter, q.v.), b Vancouver 1916, d N Vancouver 1974, paint AKL CLA M RCA WWNA

ALEXANDER, William Walker, b Toronto 1869 – d 1948, illus prt AKL AGO M MM NGC2 RCA

ALEXIE/ALEXCEE[2], Frederick (Weeksem), b 1853, d Port Simpson, BC 1933, carv paint AGO AKL DFA[2] H

ALFORD, Edward John Gregory, b Bowden, Ches 1890, d New York 1960, Amer, paint AKL CWW58 WWA62 WWB66

ALFRED, Paul (b Alfred Ernest Meister), b Hanley, Staff 1892, d Ottawa 1959, paint AKL Hu M MM NGC1,2 RCA WWA62

ALFSEN, John Martin, b Alpena, Mich 1902, d Toronto 1971, paint AKL AGO CC2 CWW67 H77 Hu M NGC2 TB3 WWA70d73

ALIKATUKTUK, Thomasie, b Pangnitung, NWT 1953– , prt AKL

ALISAUSKAS, Ona Marie, b Toronto 1951– , drw AKL IO

ALLAIN, Marie-Hélène, b Sainte Marie de Kent, NB 1939– , sculp AKL

ALLAMAND, Jeanne Charlotte. *See* BERCZY, Jeanne Charlotte Allamand
ALLAN, Wayne, b 1941– , sculp AKL IO
ALLAN, William, b England 1847 – d 1909, Eng, topog AKL DFA H
ALLAN, William George, b Ottawa 1929– , sculp AKL IO RCA
ALLAN, William Mill, b Scotland 1864, d Victoria, BC 1951, paint AKL DFA H
ALLANSON, John, b Newcastle, Eng c 1813, d Toronto 1853, engr AKL B DCB8 GW H TB1 Y
ALLARD, Alfred, b Quebec 1842, sculp K
ALLARD, René, b Chateauneuf-sur-Sarthe, Fr 1878, paint AKL B K
ALLARD, Roger, fl 1922+, carv K
ALLARD, Thomas (?), fl 1809–36, carv K
ALLEN, Gladys W., b Reading, Berks, fl 1924+, des CNS40
ALLEN, Lillian Beatrice, b Winnipeg, fl 1970s, paint CLA
ALLEN, Margaret Prosser Allison[2], b Vancouver 1913– , Amer, paint sculp AKL WWA78 WWNA[2]
ALLEN, Ralph, b Raunds, Eng 1926– , paint AE AGO AKL B CC1 M MM NGC2 RCA TB3 US WWA93
ALLEN, Thomas, fl 1756–72, Eng, paint AKL B Bry DBMaP DMA DSP Red TB1
ALLER, Robert C., b Dauphin, Man 1922– , paint AKL MM
ALLEYN, George Edmund, b Quebec 1931– , paint sculp AE AGO AKL CC2 CE2 M MM NGC1,2 NGC67 RCA S TB3
ALLIES, Louis (aka Henri), b France, fl 1764, paint AKL H K
ALLISON, Frank Drummond, b Saint John, NB 1883 – d 1951, paint AKL CLA MA MM RCA
ALLISON, Louise Muir (m William Gordon Stockwell), b Rothesay, NB, fl 1935+, paint CNS40 MM
ALLISON, Margaret Prosser. *See* ALLEN, Margaret Prosser Allison
ALLISON, Rosemary, b Jamaica 1953– , illus CBC
ALLISON, Tony, b Flin Flon, Man 1946– , drw sculp AKL CAE1,2 SC
ALLISTER, William, b Benito, Man 1919– , paint AKL CC2
ALLOM, Thomas, b London 1804, d Barnes, Sur 1872, paint AKL H
ALLOWAY, Mary Wilson (m Clement John Alloway), b Montreal, fl 1877, paint Mo12
ALLOWAY, William Forbes, b Ireland 1852, d Winnipeg 1930, paint CWW10
ALLSOPP, Judith A., b Bartlesville, Okla 1943– , paint prt CAE1 IO SC
ALLWARD, Hugh Lachlan Cruickshank, b Toronto 1899 – d 1971, paint AKL NGC1,2 RCA
ALLWARD, Walter Seymour, b Toronto 1876 – d 1955, sculp AKL CC1 Co CWW52 EC M Mo12 NGC1,2 O.N48 RCA W2–3 WWA53
ALMEIDA, Henry Rosalio, b Caracas, Ven 1913– , gra paint AGO NGC2 S
ALMERAS, Louis, b France c 1834, fl 1892, carv K
ALMINI, Peter Magnus (b Adamsson), b Rossmark, Swe 1825, paint AKL H
ALPEN-WHITESIDE, Dale, b St Boniface, Man 1947– , gra paint WWA93
ALPERT, Patricia Joy, b Toronto 1931– , drw paint AKL IO
ALSTYNE, Thelma S.S. van. *See* VAN ALSTYNE, Thelma Selina Scribbans
ALT, Marino, b Tartu, Est 1918– , gra paint AKL
ALTWERGER, Libby Deborah, b Toronto 1915– , paint AKL IO RCA WWA93
ALTWERGER, Sandra Rochelle, b Toronto 1942– , paint prt AKL IO
AMA. *See* MOHR, Jurgen Klaus
AMAROOK/AMAROUK[2], Michael, E2-275, b Baker Lake, NWT 1941– , sculp AKL DEA[2]

AMBLER, Christopher Gifford, b Bedford, Yorks 1886, Eng, illus paint IBYP SAA29
AMBROSE, G. William, fl 1860–74, paint AKL DFA H
AMEDEE, Marie (Soeur), b Quebec, fl 1966, paint sculp AKL M
AMES, Anne (m Edgar Ames), b Victoria, BC, fl 1941, paint AKL WWNA
AMESS, Frederick Arthur, b London 1909, d N Vancouver 1970, paint AKL CC2 WWNA
AMESS, James Henry Osborne, b Sunderland, Dur 1875, paint AKL WWNA
AMHERST, Elizabeth Frances. *See* HALE, Elizabeth Frances Amherst
AMIOT, Patrick, b Montreal 1959– , carv sculp CWW93
AMITTUO. *See* DAVIDIALUK, Alasua Amittuq
ANAITOK, Augustin, b Pelly Bay, NWT 1935– , sculp AKL
ANCEL, Julien, b Gueblange, Fr 1846, d Fort Chipewyan, Alta 1899, des K
ANCERL, Susan/Suzan Ann, b Trutnov, Cz 1955– , mur sculp AKL IO
ANDERSON, Aksel H., b Copenhagen 1925– , sculp SC
ANDERSON, Alexander Caulfield, b Calcutta 1814, d Victoria, BC 1844, paint DFA H
ANDERSON, Donald Kenneth, b Toronto 1920– , paint AKL M NGC68
ANDERSON, Eiliv Howard, b Robsart, Sask 1934– , drw CWW93
ANDERSON, Frederick N., b Hunter, Wash 1917– , fl 1978, Amer, paint AKL
ANDERSON, G.S.L., b Sweden 1920– , paint CWW84
ANDERSON, Helen Violet, b Brockville, Ont 1882, paint AKL B Hu MM Mo12 RCA
ANDERSON, J.B., fl 1877, illus AKL H
ANDERSON, James, Lt, b England 1760 – d 1835, Eng, paint DMA
ANDERSON, James W., fl 1874, paint AKL H
ANDERSON, John B., Lt, b England, fl 1841–9, Eng, paint AKL DFA DMA H
ANDERSON, John Newton Pomeroy, b Calcutta 1940– , paint AKL CAE2 IO
ANDERSON, Linda M., b Victoria, BC 1943– , paint ABC
ANDERSON, Mark, b Fort Dauphin, Man 1940– , sculp AKL
ANDERSON, Michael, fl 1838–53, paint AKL DFA H
ANDERSON, Millicent Gore. *See* GORE, Millicent
ANDERSON, Reginald S., b Oakland, Calif 1890, paint CWW61
ANDERSON, Robert J., b Sherbrooke, Que 1934– , paint AKL IO
ANDERSON, Ronald Trent, b Madison, Wis 1938– , paint AKL MM WWA73
ANDERSON, Tobey C., b Washington, DC 1946– , drw paint sculp DCA IO
ANDERSON, Wally, b Toronto 1937– , gra AKL RCA
ANDERSON, Wm. O., Capt, fl 1875–86, paint AKL H
ANDRE, Françoise Marise Sylviane (m Charles Stegeman, q.v.), b Les Sables d'Olonée, Fr 1926– , paint AE AKL M MM RCA WWA73
ANDRE, John (Jean), Maj, b Geneva 1750, d Tappan-on-Hudson, NY 1780, Eng, paint min AKL B BM BSA DBE DNB Fo GW J NCAB Red TB1 WWA
ANDRE, Paul, b Montreal 1933 – d 1983, paint AKL CAE2 M
ANDREAE, Janice Lee, b Guelph, Ont 1949– , drw paint IO
ANDREW, David Neville, b Redruth, Eng 1934– , paint AKL DCA IO WWA93
ANDREW, George W., fl 1883, engr AKL H
ANDREW, Helen Kate Woods (m John

A. Andrew), b England c 1854, d 1939, paint AKL DWA H

ANDREWS, A.S. (Miss), fl 1892, paint AKL H MM

ANDREWS/ANDRUS, Ambrose, b W. Stockbridge, Mass 1801, d 1860, Amer, paint AKL B F G GW H

ANDREWS, George Henry, b Lambeth, London 1816, d Hammersmith, London 1898, Eng, illus paint AKL B Bry DBA DBLP DBMaP DBWA DeV3,5–8 DMA DSP DVP DWP G H RCA ROM Sam TB1

ANDREWS, Kim, b 1939– , paint WWA93

ANDREWS, Stephen James, b Saskatoon 1922– , paint AKL CWW93 M NGC1,2 RCA

ANDREWS, Sybil (m Walter M. Morgan), b Bury St Edmonds, Eng 1898, d Victoria, BC 1993, etch paint AKL CE2 DBA M WBA2 WWA91 WWB34

ANDREWS, William W., fl 1815–23, drw H

ANDRICH, Tom, b Winnipeg 1945– , sculp AKL CAE1

ANDRUS, Ambrose. *See* ANDREWS/ANDRUS, Ambrose

ANGATAGUAK, Joseph, E1-486, b Rankin Inlet, NWT 1935– , sculp CAE1 DEA

ANGER/ANGERS[2], Marie-Elmina (Soeur Marie de Jésus[3]), b Pointe-aux-Trembles, nr Montreal 1844, d Quebec 1901, paint DCB13[2] H[3] K

ANGERS, Felicité, b Neuville, Que 1854 – d 1921, paint K

ANGERS, Henri, b Neuville, Que 1870, d Quebec 1963, sculp DFA K MQ NGC2

ANGHICK/ANGHIK[2], Abraham Apakark, b Pavlatuk, nr Yellowknife, NWT 1951– , paint sculp AKL[2] DCA CWW93[2]

ANGLISS, George (m Kay Angliss, q.v.), b Penticton, BC 1921– , paint AA AKL

ANGLISS, Kay (m George Angliss, q.v.), b Haney, BC 1923– , gra paint AA AKL SC

ANGLOSAGLO, Luke. *See* ANGUHADLUQ/ANGLOSAGLO, Luke

ANGOTIGULU, E7-978 (m Jamasie, E7-977), b Cape Dorset, NWT 1910– , prt DEA

ANGUHADLUQ/ANGLOSAGLO[2], Luke, E2-294, b Chantry Inlet, NWT 1895, d Baker Lake, NWT 1982, prt AKL CAE1[2] CE1,2 Co DEAp19[2] UG

ANGUS, Myron, b St Mary's, Ont 1926– , paint AKL M

ANINGNERK, Philipa, E2-155, b Baker Lake, NWT 1944– , prt US

ANIRIK, b Cape Dorset, NWT c 1909– , gra AKL

ANISMAN, Roslyn. *See* POLLOCK, Florrie

ANNA, E7-916, b Cape Dorset, NWT 1910 – d 1971, prt AKL DEA

ANNA. *See* MIOLEE, Anna Louise

ANNAND, Robert William, b Truro, NS 1923– , paint AKL CC1 M NGC1,2 RCA TB3 WWA70

ANNAQTUUSI TULURIALIK, Ruth, b Baker Lake, NWT 1934– , tap AKL

ANNASKOF. *See* SKOF, Anna Maria

ANNAU, Ernest, b Szeged, Hu 1931– , des ske CWW93 RCA

ANNESLEY, David, b London 1936, d 1977, paint sculp AKL

ANTIGNA, Marc (André-Marc[2]), b Paris 1869, d 1941, min paint AKL[2] B DBA H K MM RCA

ANTOINE, Père. *See* MARTIN DE LINO, Antoine

ANTROBUS, E. (Mrs), fl 1881–4, paint AKL H

APRAHAMIAN, Mirella, b Beirut, Leb 1939– , gra AKL

AQIGAAQ, Mathew, b Kazan River Falls, NWT, sculp CWW93

AQJANGAJUK/AXANGAYUK[2], Shaa[3], E7-289, b Shartoweetuk, nr Cape Dorset, NWT 1937– , prt sculp CE1,2 CWW93[3] DEAp36[2]

ARBUCKLE, Frances Anne Johnston. *See* JOHNSTON, Frances Anne

ARBUCKLE, George Franklin (m Frances Anne Johnston, q.v.), b Toronto 1909– , paint AGO AKL CC2 CWW80 Hu IO M MM NGC1,2 RCA TB2,3 WWA82

ARCAND, Arthur, fl 1880–4, illus paint AKL H K

ARCHAMBAULT, Edmond, fl 1868–80, paint AKL H K

ARCHAMBAULT, Janvier, fl 1828–47, carv K

ARCHAMBAULT, Joseph E., fl 1861–70, paint H K

ARCHAMBAULT, Louis de Gonzaque Pascal, b Montreal 1915– , mur sculp ACA AGO AKL CAE1,2 CC1 CE1,2 Co CWW93 DCA M MM MQ NGC1,2 NGC67 P RCA TB3 WWA93 WWB90

ARCHAMBAULT, Pierre, b Montreal 1943– , paint sculp AKL CAE1

ARCHAMBAULT, Violet (m J.G. Archambault), b Kentville, NS, fl 1966, paint M

ARCHER, George Barnes, b Campbellford, Ont 1880, paint CWW36

ARCHIBALD, Mary, fl 1881, paint AKL H RCA

ARCHIE. *See* DALE, Archibald

ARDIEL, June Victoria M., b London, Ont 1921– , paint CWW93

ARDOUIN, Charles J.R., Quebec c 1804, fl 1819–71, engr AKL H K

AREM. *See* BIERMAN, Robert Maximillian

AREZINA, Dushka (s Dushka), b Belgrade, Yu 1942– , paint IO

ARGYLL, John Douglas Sutherland Campbell[3], Marquis of Lorne[2], 9th Duke of Argyll (m HRH Princess Louise, q.v.), GovGen of Canada 1878–83, b London 1845, d I of W 1914, Scot, paint BPp103 CE1,2[2] DNB[3] DP EC[2] H[2] Mo12[2] W1–3[2]

ARIE, Dubi, b Warsaw 1910– , paint sculp AKL IO

ARISS, Herbert Joshua (m Margot Joan Phillips Ariss, q.v.), b Guelph, Ont 1916/17– , paint AGO AKL CWW93 IO M MM NGC2 O.My50 RCA TB3 WWA93

ARISS, Margot Joan Phillips (m Herbert Joshua Ariss, q.v.), b Belleville, Ont 1929– , etch sculp AKL WWA93

ARLU/ARLUK[2]/ARLOOK[3], George, E3-1049, b Rankin Inlet, NWT 1949– , sculp AKL CE1,2[2] CWW93[2] DEAp29 SC[3]

ARLUTNAR, Therese, b Eskimo Point, NWT 1926– , sculp AKL

ARMINGTON, Caroline Helena Wilkinson (m Frank Milton Armington, q.v.), b Brampton, Ont 1875, d New York 1939, paint prt AAA31 AGO AKL B CWW36 DBA DWA F Hu MM NGC2 NGC68 TB2 WWA38d40

ARMINGTON, Frank Milton (m Caroline H.W. Armington, q.v.), b Fordwick, Ont 1876, d New York 1941, etch paint AAA33 AGO AKL B CWW48 DBA F Hu MM Mo12 NGC2 NGC68 RCA TB2 WBA1 WWA40d47

ARMITAGE, George, Sr, b England c 1809, fl 1867, sculp H

ARMITAGE, George, Jr, b 1831, sculp H

ARMOUR, Phyllis (Mrs Hertzberg), b Toronto c 1885, d 1975, sculp Hu MM RCA

ARMSTRONG, Arnold Edwin, b Cornwall, Ont 1896, d 1958, paint Hu

ARMSTRONG, David Geoffrey, b Toronto 1928– , paint prt AKL IO SC WWA93

ARMSTRONG, Elizabeth Adela. *See* FORBES, Elizabeth Adela Armstrong

ARMSTRONG, Henry Fry, b Sunderland, Eng 1868, drw Mo98,12

ARMSTRONG, James G., fl 1879 90, engr AKL H

ARMSTRONG, William, b Dublin 1822, d Toronto 1914, paint AAW1

AGO AKL CE1,2 DeV7 DFA H H77 NGC1,2 NGC67 PNL RCA ROM Sam WHC

ARMSTRONG, William Walton, b Toronto 1916– , drw paint AKL CWW93 M MM NGC1,2 WWA70

ARNOLD, Gregory Harland, b Meota, Sask 1916, d Calgary, Alta 1968, gra paint sculp AKL M SC TB3

ARNOLDIN, Carmelo M., b Italy 1943– , paint IO

ARNOTT, Frank E.P., b Toronto 1908– , paint AKL IO

ARONSON, Marion, b Montreal 1913– , paint CLA

ARSENAULT, Réal, b Quebec 1931– , gra paint sculp AKL NGC2

ARSENAULT, Sylvain, b Rogerville, NB 1931– , cart Des

ARTHUR, Katherine. *See* BEHENNA, Katherine Arthur

ARTHUR, Paul Rodney, b Liverpool, Eng 1924– , des gra Co CWW93 RCA

ARTHURS, Anna J. Austin (m George Allan Arthur[2]), b Toronto 1845, paint AKL CWW36[2] DWA H Hu RCA

ARTHURS, Stephen J., b Saint John, NB 1951– , paint IO

ASCOTT, Roy, b Bath, Eng 1934– , paint CWW70

ASH, Stuart Bradley, b Hamilton, Ont 1942– , des gra AKL CWW93 RCA WWGA2

ASHEVAK/ACHEALAK, E7-975 (m Mary Ashevak, E7-861, q.v.), b Cape Dorset, NWT 1932– , prt sculp DEA US

ASHEVAK, Karoo[2], b Spence Bay, NWT 1940 – d 1974, sculp AKL CAE1[2] CE1,2[2] DEAp34

ASHEVAK, Mary[2], E7-861 (m Ashevak, E7-975, q.v.), b Cape Dorset, NWT 1932– , prt DEAp146[2]

ASHEVAK, Tommy, b Netchuk, nr Spence Bay, NWT 1931– , paint sculp AKL

ASHEVAK. *See* JOHNNIEBO, E7-1034; KENOJUAK, E7-1035

ASHKEWIE/ASHKEWE[2], Delmer, b Cape Croker Res, NWT 1945/7– , illus paint AKL[2] IO

ASHMORE, Cyril Frank, b Sheffield, Eng 1894, d 1977, illus paint AKL M

ASHOONA. *See* KIAWAK/KIUGAK, Ashoona, E7-1103; KOOMWARTOK/KUMWARTOK, Ashoona, E7-1102; OTTOCHIE, Ashoona, E7-1105; PITSEOLAK, E7-1100; QAQAQ/HAKA/KAKA/QAKA, Ashoona, E7-1101

ASHRAF, Nazhath (s Naz Ikramullah), b London 1938– , etch paint AKL IO

ASHTON, John, fl 1854–61, paint AKL H

ASKA, Warabe (b Takeshi Masuda), b Kagawa, Japan 1941– , paint CWW93 SAA56 T

ASKEVOLD, David Marius, b Conrad, Mont 1940– , Amer, con AKL CA3 WWA93

ASKIN, H.H., fl 1886, paint AKL H RCA

ASKREN, Patricia, b Seattle, Wash 1951– , wlhg SC

ASPELL, Peter Noel Lawson, b Vancouver 1918– , paint AKL CWW93 M NGC1,2 TB3

ASPENLIEDER, David, b 1947– , illus C

ASSELIN, Denis, b 1943– , paint AKL CAE1

ASTMAN, Barbara Anne, b Rochester, NY 1950– , mmed AKL CE1,2 DCA IO RCA WWA93

ATCHEALAK, Davie, b Cape Dorset, NWT 1947– , drw paint sculp CWW93

ATKINS, Ernest Caven, b London, Ont 1907– , paint prt AGO AKL GM Hu M MM NGC2 NGC68 WWA53

ATKINSON, Eric Newton, b W. Hartlepool, Eng 1928– , paint AKL CAE1 RCA TB3 WBA1 WWA93 WWB90

ATINSON, Florence, fl 1897–1909, paint AAA09 AKL B DWA H MM

ATKINSON, John, fl 1838–52, paint H

ATKINSON, Mary Helena Cass (m Alfred Atkinson), b Longueuil, Que c 1854, d c 1888, paint DFA DWA H

ATKINSON, Robert W., b London, Ont 1894, paint CWW58

ATKINSON, Sophia Mildred, b Newcastle-on-Tyne, Eng 1876, d 1972, paint AKL DBA DWA MM RCA WBA1

ATKINSON, Thomas Robert, Lt Col, b Ancaster Tp, Ont 1854, sculp Mo12

ATKINSON, William Edwin, b Toronto 1862 – d 1926, paint AAA06 AGO AKL B CWW10 H Hu M MM Mo12 NGC1,2 RCA TB1–3 W1–3 WBA2

ATMADJA, Handy, b Jakarta, Indo, fl 1980s, paint MFMS

ATWOOD, Margaret Eleanor (s Bart Gerrard[2], m Graeme Gibson), b Ottawa 1939– , illus AKL C CBC CE1,2 CWW93 Des[2] SAA50 WWC

AUBE/AUB/AUHE[2], Joseph, fl 1882–3, paint AKL H[2] K

AUBIN, Alma (Soeur Marie-de-Saint-Aubin), b Quebec 1885 – d 1967, paint K

AUBIN, Benjamin, fl 1902–5, paint K

AUBIN, Ernest (aka J.-B.-Ernest-Aubin[2]), b 1892 – d 1963, paint sculp K MM[2]

AUBIN, Napoléon (Aime-Nicholas, Nicolas-Narcisse[2]), b Chêne-Boueries, nr Geneva 1812, d Montreal 1890, paint AKL H[2] K LeJ[2] W1–3

AUBRY, Emile, b Sélif, Alg 1880, d 1964, Fr, paint AKL B K TB1

AUCLAIR, André, fl 1842–61, sculp K

AUCLAIR, Ferdinand, b Quebec c 1854, fl 1881–1908, d 1908, paint K

AUDET, Louis, fl 1903–4, sculp K

AUDET, O. (Bédard), fl 1920, paint K

AUDET dit LAPOINTE, Joseph, b Quebec 1819/20 – d 1854, carv K

AUDETTE, Madeleine Langlois, b 1925, des paint AKL CAE1

AUDLA/AULLAQ, Pee, E7-1043, b Cape Dorset, NWT 1920– , sculp DEA US

AUDUBON, John James (Jean-Jacques-Fougère), b Les Cayes, S Dom 1785, d New York 1851, Amer, paint AKL ANC App B DAA DAB DFP2 F G GW H J K L NCAB TB1 TCBA WWWA Y

AUDUBON, John Woodhouse, b Henderson, Ky 1812, d New York 1862, Amer, paint AKL B GW TB1 WWWA

AUDY, Jean Baptiste Roy. *See* ROY-AUDY, Jean-Baptiste

AUERBACH, Malca Rose, fl 1891–1910, paint AAA01 B DWA MM RCA

AUGOTOUTOK, Jonah, b Igloolik area, NWT, fl 1970s, sculp UG

AUGUSTIN, Frère. *See* QUINTAL, Augustin (Capt Joseph)

AUGUSTINE, Mary Staples, b New Jersey 1931– , gra paint AKL IO

AULT, Charles H., b Iroquois, Ont, fl 1877–81, paint AAA10 H

AUSTIN, B., fl 1886, paint H MM

AUSTIN, Dorothy. *See* STEVENS, Dorothy

AUSTIN, H.T., fl 1850–1, topog paint DFA H

AUSTIN, William Augustus, b Quebec 1829, d Ottawa 1896, topog paint AKL DeV6 DFA H

AVA MARIA. *See* KNICKLE, Ava Maria Sharon

AVERBUCH, Ilan, b Tel Aviv, Is 1953– , sculp WWA93

AVERY, Frances (m James Penney), b Kitchener, Ont 1911– , paint AKL IO WWA66

AVROM. *See* YANOVSKY, Avrom

AWAD, Macy, b W. Virginia 1946– , paint IO

AXANGAYUK. *See* AQJANGAJUK/AXANGAYUK, Shaa

AXLER, Gladis/Gladys[2], b Montreal 1928– , paint AKL[2] M

AYOT, Pierre, b Montreal 1943– , prt AKL NGC2

AYOTTE, Leo, b Ste-Flore, Que 1909,

d St-Hyacinthe, Que 1976, paint AKL M MM

AYOTTE, Robert, b Ste-Mélanie, Que, des paint AKL

AYRES, Charles Harold, b Toronto 1894, d 1977, paint Hu RCA

AZIZ, Philip (b John Andrew Ferris), b St Thomas, Ont 1923– , paint sculp CWW93 M

B

BAALAM, Arthur, b 1898, paint CAE1

BABCOCK, Stewart Lawrence, b 1941– , paint CAE2

BABCOCK, William Parkin, b Boston 1826, d France 1899, Amer, paint AKL B DAA F G GW H TB1 Y

BACHINSKI, Walter Joseph Gerard, b Ottawa 1939– , paint sculp AKL CAE1,2 CWW93 IO RCA UG WWA93

BACHMAN/BACHMANN[2], John, fl 1850–77, d New Orleans, La 1884, Amer, paint AKL DMA[2] GW H Y

BACK, Frédéric Henri, b Sarrebuick, Fr 1924– , anim des gra AKL CE1,2 CWW93 RCA WWC69

BACK, George, Adm Sir, b Stockport, Ches 1796, d London 1878, Eng, topog paint AKL CE1,2 DBLP DBWA DCB10 DMA DNB EC H H77 NGC2 NGC68 PNL ROM W1–3

BACON, Mary Ann. *See* WHITTLESEY, Mary Ann Bacon

BACSTROM, Sigismund, b Holland, fl 1763–1801, Dutch, paint EMA

BADEAUX, Guy (s Bado[2]), b Montreal 1949– , cart Des[2] Po86–88

BADEN, Mowry T., b Los Angeles 1936– , sculp AKL DCA WWA93

BADO. *See* BADEAUX, Guy

BAEB, Henry R. (s Hanks), b Nova Scotia 1922– , car WWA62

BAGA, Marie Sue (Mrs), b Montreal 1947– , paint ABC

BAGOT, Josceline Fitzroy, Sir, 1st Baron, b 1854, d England 1913, Eng, paint WWW

BAIG, Daisy, b Amherst, NS 1916, d Montreal 1965, paint CLA MA

BAIGENT/BAIGNET[2], Robert Richard, b Winchester, Eng 1830, d Toronto 1890, paint AKL DFA[2] H[2] Hu MM RCA ROM

BAILEY, Daisy (m Robert L. Bailey), b Toronto 1921, d 1972, paint AKL RCA

BAILEY, Diana, b Bremerton, Wash 1930– , gra paint AKL

BAILEY, Guy, b Cap-de-la-Madeleine, Que 1942– , illus AKL T

BAILEY, Jann Louise M., b Hamilton, Ont 1952– , prt AKL IO WWA93

BAILEY, Joseph, fl 1832–51, sculp K

BAILEY, Laurestine M., b Fredericton, NB, fl 1911–19, paint CLA MM

BAILLAIRGE, Flavien-Adolphe, b Quebec 1792 – d 1847, paint AKL K

BAILLAIRGE, Jean, b Blanzay, Fr 1726, d Quebec 1805, carv B CE1,2 DCB5 DFA K

BAILLAIRGE, Thomas, b Quebec 1791 – d 1859, carv AKL CE1,2 DCB8 K LeJ NGC2

BAILLA RGE, François, b Quebec 1759 – d 1830, carv paint ACA AKL B CE1,2 Co DCB6 DFA EC H H77 K LeJ MQ NGC2 NGC67 W1–3

BAILLA RGE, Pierre-Florent, b Quebec 1761 – d 1812, carv AKL DCB5 K

BAILLEUL, Jan, b Lille, Fr, fl 1901–29, sculp B K RCA

BAILLIE, Helen Phoebe Aird (m John R. Baillie), b London 1916– , paint AKL CAE1 IO RCA

BAILLY, Evern Earl, b Lunenburg, NS 1903 – d 1977, paint AKL M MM NGC2

BAIN, Freda Guttman[2], b Montreal 1934– , prt MM[2] NGC2

BAIN, Mabel A., b Prince Edward Isld 1880, paint AAW3 AC M WWNA

BAIN, Sophia Joyce, b Winnipeg 1903/8, paint MM O.My49

BAINBRIGGE, Philip John/James[2], b Lichfield, Eng 1817, d Blackheath, Eng 1881, Eng, paint AKL APH DFA GW H[2] PNL ROM WHC

BAINES, Henry Egerton, Lt, b Shrewsbury, Eng 1840, d Quebec 1866, paint AKL DFA ROM

BAINES, William Douglas, b Edmonton 1926– , drw CWW93

BAIRD, Ronald Arnott, b Toronto 1940– , sculp AKL CWW93 RCA

BAKER, Alice M.M. *See* DANIEL, Alice M.M. Baker

BAKER, Anna P., b London, Ont 1928– , etch paint AKL WWA78

BAKER, Edward M., b Orangeville, Ont 1927– , prt CAE1

BAKER, Joseph, Capt, b England 1767 – d 1817, Eng, paint EMA

BAKER, Ronald Seton, b Toronto 1951– , paint AKL IO

BAKER, Walter, fl 1880, d Montreal c 1912, paint AKL H

BAKER, William Henry, b London 1844, fl 1914, paint AKL Mo12

BAKER, William Robert, b London 1919– , paint IO

BAKES, Alan, b Toronto 1948– , drw paint AKL IO SC

BAKKE, Larry Hubert, b Vancouver 1932– , paint AKL WWA93

BAKKEN, Haaken, b Madison, Wis 1932– , sculp WWA93

BAKO, Louis Csaba/Czaba, b Hungary 1943– , prt AKL CAE2

BALBAR, George S., b Regina 1930– , paint AKL IO

BALBONI, Carlo, fl 1909–44, Amer, sculp B MM RCA

BALCH, Georgia W. (Mrs), b Toronto 1888, fl 1962, paint AKL DWA WWA62

BALFE, Louis Michael, b Long Beach, Calif 1950– , illus paint AKL IO

BALFOUR, Roberta (Mrs) (aka R. Thudicum/Thudichum), b Yarmouth, NS 1871, paint AAW2 AC DWA WWA40

BALHARRIE, James Watson, b Ottawa 1910– , paint CNS60 MM

BALJEU, Joost, b Middelburg, Neth 1925– , Dutch, sculp CA1

BALLACHEY, Barbara, b Edmonton 1949– , paint AA AKL SC

BALLANTYNE, Alexander J., fl 1865, d Gibraltar 1878, paint H

BALLANTYNE, Robert Michael, b Edinburgh 1825, d Rome 1894, paint DBA DNB H

BALLARD, Paul, b England 1947– , engr BB

BALLES, Mare-Liss, b Goteberg, Swe, des illus C

BALLON, Iris Shklar, b Montreal 1931– , paint CAE1 MM

BALLS, Herbert Ryan, b Winnipeg 1910– , paint CWW90

BALMAN, Ellen Bernice, b Windsor, Ont 1926– , paint O.Ag50

BAMFORD, Thomas, b Liverpool 1861, d Victoria, BC 1941, paint DFA H H77 WWNA

BANANA, Anna (b Anne Lee Long), b Victoria, BC 1940– , paint AKL WWA93

BANCROFT, William Henry, b Derby, Eng 1860, d Colorado Springs, Colo 1932, Amer, paint AAW1 AKL Sam

BANKS, J. Lisney, fl 1901–8, sculp AAA01 B RCA

BANKS, Peter, b Birmingham, Eng 1938– , cal paint AKL IO

BANKS, Robert, b Vancouver 1923– , paint AKL M

BANNERMAN[1], Frances M. Jones[2] (m Hamlet Bannerman), b Halifax 1855, d Eng 1940, paint AKL DBA[1,2] DFA DVP DWA G H H77 Hu Mo12 NGC67 WBA2

BANNISTER, Edward Mitchell, b St Andrews, NB 1828/33, d Providence, RI 1901, paint AAA28 AKL ANC App B F GW H TB1 TCBA WWWA Y

BANTING, Beatrice Aline Myles (m J. Maitland Banting, s Myles), b

Hamilton, Ont 1911– , paint M MM O.Ag49 RCA
BANTING, Frederick Grant, Sir, b Alliston, Ont 1891, d nr Musgrave Harbour, Nfld 1941, paint sculp AE AKL CE1,2 Co CWW38 DNB EC Hu M PMC S W1–3 WWW
BANTING, Gerald Thomas, b Bowmanville, Ont 1951– , paint IO
BANTING, Ida N., fl 1885–6, drw DWA H
BARABAS, Martin (b Marton Markosfalvi), b Transylvania, d Canada, fl 1950s, paint PHA
BARAN, Theodore, fl 1968, paint DFA
BARBEAU, Charles Marius, b Ste-Marie-de-Beauce, Que 1883, d Ottawa 1969, drw CC2 CE1,2 Co EC CWW64 RCA WWA70 WWC69
BARBEAU, Christian Marcel, b Montreal 1925– , paint sculp AKL CC2 CE1,2 CWW93 M MM MQ NGC2 NGC67 RCA WWA93
BARBEAU, Napoleon V., fl 1888–1903, paint K MM
BARBEAU, Suzanne Meloche. *See* MELOCHE, Suzanne
BARBER, Barbara Muir (m Fred Barber), b Brantford, Ont 1873, d Regina Beach, Sask 1966, paint BDSA
BARBER, Bruce Allister, b Auckland, NZ 1950– , drw AKL WWA93
BARBIER, Marie (Soeur Marie-Barbier, dite de l'Assomption), b Montreal 1673 – d 1739, paint AKL DCB2 DWA H H74 K KB
BARBIN (Raoul?), fl 1902–24, paint B K
BARBOUR, Carl, b 1905, fl 1974, paint DFA
BARDARUK, Michael, b c 1900, fl 1981, paint DFA
BARDWELL, Millicent Morgan (m John Alexander Eddie Bardwell), b Rosetown, Sask 1927– , paint BDSA
BARET, Jean-Baptiste, b St-Philippe, Que 1799 – d 1858, sculp K
BARKER, Charles F., b London 1875, fl 1941, paint AKL Sam WWNA
BARKER, Ernest Conyers, b Toronto 1909– , paint DBA Hu IO MM RCA WWA53
BARKER, George, fl 1851–81, paint H
BARKER, Henry Aston, b Glasgow c 1774, d Belton, nr Bristol, Eng 1856, Scot, panor AKL B Bry DBE DBWA DMA DNB DSP H Red TB1
BARKER, Sydney Herbert, b Brandon, Man 1893, d Saskatoon 1969, paint DFA NGC2
BARNARD, Henry William, Lt Gen, Sir (x William Henry), b Wedbury, Oxon 1799, d Delhi, India 1859, Eng, paint AKL APH DNB H ROM WHC
BARNARD, Julia Bingham (m H.J. Barnard), b London 1900, paint AKL M MM RCA
BARNES, Archibald George, b London 1887, d Toronto 1972, paint AGO AKL CC1 CWW70 DBA FCA M NGC1,2 NGC68 O.N47 RA RCA TB2 WBA1 WWA53 WWB34 WWC69
BARNES, Elias Paul, fl 1840–65, Amer, panor AKL GW H
BARNES, Wilfred Molson, b Montreal 1882 – d 1955, paint AKL CC1 CNS58 H77 Hu M MM NGC1,2 PMC RCA TB3 W2–3
BARNETT, David, b Cheltenham, Eng 1933– , drw paint AKL CAE1 IO
BARNETT, Madeleine Lorimer Jordan (m Leonard R. Barnett), b Manchester, Eng, fl 1917, paint sculp BDSA CLA RCA
BARNHOUSE, Dorothy Paul (m D.P. Barnhouse), b Burin, Nfld 1914– , paint AKL M MM
BARNJUM, Frederick S. (s F.S.B.), fl 1858–87, paint H
BARNSLEY, James MacDonald, b W Flamborough, nr Hamilton, Ont (x Toronto) 1861, d Verdun, Que 1929, paint AAA01 AKL B DBA DMA DSP EC H H77 Hu M MM Mo12 NGC1,2 RCA TB2 W1–3
BARNWELL, Leslie (Mrs), b Victoria, BC 1949– , paint ABC

BARR, Archibald M., fl 1856–9, engr ske AKL H

BARR, Patrick, fl 1860–80, paint DFA H

BARR, Robert Allan, b London 1890, d Toronto 1959, paint AGO AKL CWW55 M NGC1,2 O.F49 RCA TB3 W2–3 WWA59d62

BARRAUD, Alfred Thomas, b London 1849, d Brookline, Mass 1925, Amer, paint AKL B H

BARRAUD, Cyril Henry, b Barnes, Eng 1877, fl 1934, Eng, paint AGO AKL DBA NGC68 RA RCA TB3

BARRE, Louis, fl 1872–7, carv K

BARRE, Raoul (aka Raoul Barry), b Montreal 1874 – d 1932, paint AAA01 AKL B Des K MM RCA W2–3 WECa

BARRETT, Alfred T.B., b Gaspereaux, nr Wolfville, NS 1852, d Roxbury, Mass 1939, paint AKL DFA H Hu Mo12

BARRETT, Barbara, b Toronto 1920– , paint WWA80

BARRETT, Camille. *See* LEDUC-BARRETT, Camille

BARRETT-LENNARD, John Graham, b Cottesloe, Aus 1953– , drw paint IO

BARRIOS, Rafael, b 1947– , paint CAE1,2

BARRON, Sidney D. (Sid), b Toronto 1917– , cart Co Des Po86–88

BARROWMAN, James, b Muirkirk, Scot 1906– , paint AKL IO

BARRY, Anne Meredith, b Toronto 1932– , paint prt AKL IO SC WWA93

BARF.Y, Douglas Dennis, b Edmonton 1923– , mos paint AA AKL SC

BARRY, Francis Leopold (Frank), b London 1913– , paint sculp AKL CAE1 CWW93 MM NGC2 RCA WWA89

BARRY, John Joseph, b Hamilton, Ont 1885, d 1952, etch paint AAA31 AAW3 AC AKL B CWW52 F MM O.F49 RCA TB2 WWA53 Y

BARRY, Lily Emily Frances (Lillie, pseud Primrose), b Montreal 1863, d 1955, paint CNS40 DWA MM Mo98,12 RCA

BARRY, Raoul. *See* BARRE, Raoul

BART[1]-GERALD, Elizabeth (Mrs Gerald), b Cleveland, Ohio 1907– , paint AKL[1] RCA TB2 WWA40

BARTLETT, John Lawrence, b Toronto 1907– , paint MM O.Ag50 RCA

BARTLETT, William Henry, b Kentish Town, London 1809, d on *Egyptus*, nr Marseilles 1854, Eng, paint AKL B Bry CE1,2 Co DBLP DBWA DCB8 DeV2,3,5–9 DMA DNB DVLP DVP DWP EC G GW H MQ NGC2 NGC67 ROM TB1 W1–3 WHC WWWA

BARTOLINI, Mario, b Montreal 1930– , sculp NGC2

BARTON, Donald, b Oakville, Ont 1944– , tap IO

BARTON, Georgie Read. *See* READ, Georgie

BARTRAM, Edward John, b London, Ont 1938– , des prt AKL CAE1,2 CWW93 RCA S SC UG US

BASILI. *See* CHARLEBOIS, Joseph-Charles-Théophile

BASLAW, Morton, b Ottawa 1924– , paint AKL IO S

BASMADJIAN, Janet Kathleen Newcome, b Toronto 1943– , paint IO

BASTEDO[1], Hannah Elizabeth[1] (Miss L.[2]), b Hamilton, Ont 1850, fl 1900, paint AAA01 AKL B H[1,2] Hu

BASTIDE, J.H., fl 1745–58, Eng, topog AKL DBLP H PNL

BASTIEN, Gabriel, b Montreal 1923– , mur paint AKL M

BATAR, Samuel F., fl 1846–59, Amer, engr DeV1

BATCHELOR, Lawrence R., b Montreal 1887 – d 1961, paint NGC68

BATDORF, Thaya C. (m Luke Batdorf), b Boston, Mass 1927– , paint AKL M

BATEMAN, Robert McLellan, b Toronto 1930– , paint AKL CE1,2 CWW93 M WWA93 WWB92 WWC83

BATES, Catherine, b Windsor, Ont 1934– , paint sculp CAE1

BATES, Cornelius John Lighthall, b L'Original, Que 1877, d 1963, paint CWW61 Mo12

BATES, George W., b London 1930– , paint ABC

BATES, Gordon Anderson, b Burlington, Ont 1885, paint CWW70 MB

BATES, Maxwell Bennett, b Calgary 1906, d Victoria, BC 1980, paint AGO AKL B CAE1,2 CC2 CE1,2 CWW80 DBA DCA GM H77 M MM NGC1,2 RA RCA SC TB3 UG WWA80

BATES, Patricia Martin (m C.A. Bates), b Saint John, NB 1927– , prt sculp AKL B CAE1,2 CE1,2 M MM NGC2 RCA UG

BATES, Roy Elliott, b Connecticut 1882, paint MM Mo12

BATES, Wesley, b Whitehorse, YT 1952– , engr paint BB

BATISTE, Francis Olivier (Sis-Hulak), b Inkameep Res, Oliver, BC 1920– , paint WWNA

BATTERSBY, David McFarlane, b Toronto 1909 – d 1971, paint Hu

BATTISTA, Nicholas Ignatius, b Cornwall, Ont 1911– , paint CWW70

BATTY, Malcolm David, b India 1945– , paint CAE1 M

BATTYE, Edward W., Capt, b Kensington, London 1817, Eng, topog DFA H WHCp168

BATURA, Jurate, b 1948– , paint CAE1

BATUZ (Maar), Nicholas (Miklos), b Budapest 1933– , paint AKL PHA WWA80

BAUMAN, Bonnie, b London, Ont 1940– , mmed prt IO

BAUMAN, Joseph D., b 1815, d 1899, paint DFA

BAXTER, Bonnie Jean, b Texarkana, Tex 1946– , paint AKL CAE1 WWA93

BAXTER, Ingrid (m Joseph Wilson Iain Baxter, q.v.), b Spokane, Wash 1938– , paint RCA WWA78

BAXTER, Joseph Wilson Iain (aka N.E. Thing Co[2]) (m Ingrid Baxter, q.v.), b Middleborough, Eng 1936– , paint AKL CAE1,2[2] CE1,2 CWW85 DCA1,2[2] M MM NGC2 RCA WWA78

BAXTER, Judith Dianne Barnes (m Glendon Baxter), b Saint John, NB 1942– , paint CWW93

BAYARD, Alfred, fl 1878–1903, paint AKL H K

BAYEFSKY, Aba, b Toronto 1923– , mur paint AGO AKL CC1 CE1,2 CWW93 Hu IO M MM NGC68 RCA S TB3 WWA93

BAYFIELD, Fanny Amelia Wright[2] (m Henry Wolsey Bayfield, Adm, q.v.), b Kensington, London c 1813, d Charlottetown 1891, Eng, paint AKL DCB12[2] H PNL WHC

BAYFIELD, Henry Wolsey, Adm (m Fanny A.W. Bayfield, q.v.), b Kingston-upon-Hull, Eng 1795, d Charlottetown 1885, Eng, paint topog AKL APH CE1,2 DCB11 EC H LeJ W1–3 WHC

BAYNE, Frances Kirkpatrick Forbes (m Walter F. Bayne), b Halifax 1911– , paint CLA MA

BAYNES, Robert Lambert, Rr Adm, b England 1796, d Upper Norwood, nr London 1869, Eng, paint AKL DCB9 H

BAZSO, Sarah (Sarolta), b Hungary, fl 1977, paint AKL PHA

BEACH, Elizabeth Annie. *See* KNOWLES, Elizabeth Annie Beach

BEALE, Charles J., b England, fl 1871–98, des engr AKL H

BEALE, Henry B., b Cheltenham, Eng, fl 1871–85, engr AKL H

BEALL, George W., b Columbus, Ont 1851, d 1941, topog AKL DFA H

BEALL, Muriel, b Johannesburg, SA 1907– , paint Hu

BEALS, Helen Dorothy, b Canso, NS 1897, paint CLA MA WWA53 WWB72

BEAM, Carl, b W Bay, Manitoulin Isld, Ont 1943– , paint AKL CE1,2

BEAMENT, Thomas Harold, b Ottawa 1898, d Montreal 1984, paint AE AGO AKL CC2 CWW85 Hu M MM NGC1,2 NGC68 PMC RCA Sam TB3 WHC WWA84

BEAMENT, Thomas Harold (Tib), b Montreal 1941– , paint prt AE AKL CAE1 CWW93 M MM NGC2 RCA WWA93

BEAMIS, Ide C. (x J.), Jr, fl 1838, paint DeV9 H

BEANLANDS, Sophie Theresa Pemberton. *See* PEMBERTON, Sophie Theresa

BEAR, George Telfer, b Greenock, Scot 1874, Scot, paint AKL DBA RCA TB2 WBA1 WWB58

BEARDMORE, Helen Lissant, b Toronto, fl 1902, paint Mo12

BEARDY, Jackson (Quentin Pickering Jackson Beardy), b Garden Lake Res, Isld Lake, Man 1944– , paint AKL CAE1,2 CE Co DFA SC

BEASTALT/BEASTALL, William, fl 1795–7, paint GW H H77

BEATON, Al, b Vancouver 1923, d 1967, cart Des

BEATON, Carolyn Joan, b Toronto 1932– , paint prt AKL IO

BEATON, Mary Rodgers (m Reginald S. Houston), b Toronto 1902– , paint Hu

BEATTY, John William, b Toronto 1869 – d 1941, paint prt AE AGO AKL B CC1 CWW36 EC FCA H77 Hu M MM NGC1,2 NGC68 RCA S Sam TB2,3 TN UG W1–3

BEAU, Henri, b Montreal 1863, d Paris 1949, paint AKL B CE1,2 H H77 K MM Mo12 MQ NGC2 RCA

BEAU, Paul, b Montreal 1871 – d 1949, met AKL K MM RCA

BEAUCHEMIN, Micheline, b Longueuil, Que 1930– , paint stgl tap AKL CE1,2 CWW93 DCA M NGC2 NGC67 RCA TB3 WWA80

BEAUCLERK, Charles, Capt, Lord (son of 8th Duke of Saint Albans), b England 1813, d Scarborough, Eng 1861, Eng, paint topog AKL BPp2338 DBMP H H77

BEAUCOURS, Hyacinthe. *See* DUBOIS-BERTHELOT DE BEAUCOURS, Josue

BEAUCOURT, François Malepart[2] de, b Laprairie, Que 1740, d Montreal 1794, paint ACA AKL DCB4[2] EC GW H H77 Hu K LeJ M MQ NGC1,2 NGC67

BEAUCOURT, Paul Mallepart[2] de Grand Maison dit, b St-Eustache, Que 1700, d Quebec 1756, paint AKL B DCB3[2] H H77 K NGC67

BEAUDIN, Denise, b Montreal 1930– , tap AKL DCA

BEAUDIN, Jean Pierre, b Montreal 1935– , prt NGC2

BEAUDRY, Henry/Henri, b Poundmaker Res, nr Battleford, Sask 1921– , paint AKL

BEAUDRY, Jules A., fl 1869–81, paint AKL H K

BEAUDRY, Narcisse, b c 1839, d Montreal 1892, engr med AKL H K

BEAUFORT, Francis, Rr Adm, Sir, b 1774, d 1857, Eng, paint AKL DFA DNB ROM

BEAUFOY, Benjamin, Lt Col, fl 1814, d 1879, Eng, topog AKL DeV7 H MQ

BEAULIEU, Adolphe, fl 1897–1901, stgl K

BEAULIEU, Damase, b Montreal 1857 – d 1887, paint H K

BEAULIEU, Delphis-Adolphe/Delphisse[2], fl 1870s, d 1908, paint AKL H[2] K

BEAULIEU, Florent, b Montreal 1923– , paint AKL

BEAULIEU, Gustav, fl mid 19th cen, paint AKL DMA

BEAULIEU, Gustav de, b Aix-en-Provence, Fr 1801 – d 1860, Fr, paint AKL DMA TB1

BEAULIEU, Joseph-Alphonse, b

St-Sauveur-des-Monts, Que 1871, d 1958, paint K

BEAULIEU, Louis Jacques. *See* JAQUE, Louis

BEAULIEU, Olivier, fl 1918, paint K

BEAULIEU, Paul Vanier, b Montreal 1910– , paint prt AKL B M MM NGC2 NGC67 RCA TB3

BEAULIEU, Simone Aubry, b Montreal 1917– , paint AKL M

BEAULINCOURT, Comte de, fl 1886–7, Fr, paint K

BEAUMONT, fl 1833, dior H K

BEAUMONT, Henri, fl 1889–96, sculp K

BEAUMONT, Joseph, fl 1840–76, sculp K

BEAUPRE, Alfred, b 1884, d 1957, paint K MM RCA

BEAUPRE, Bernard, b Montreal 1914– , tap CWW88

BEAUPRE, Eugene Louis, b Kingston, Ont 1877/81, d Pasadena, Calif 1946, prt AAA24 K NGC2 RCA

BEAUPRE, Georges, b Quebec 1937– , illus paint AKL RCA WWGA2

BEAUREGARD, Charles G., b c 1856, fl 1880, paint H K

BEAUREGARD, Daniel, b St-Saturnin, Nantes, Fr 1682, d Quebec 1741, paint H K

BEAUVAIS dit SAINT-JAMES[2], René, b St-Philippe, Que 1785, d La-Prairie, Que 1837, carv AKL B DCB7 K MQ[2]

BEAVER, James, Chief, fl Six Nations Res, nr Brantford, Ont 1899, paint AKL H KB

BEAVON, Daphne. *See* ODJIG, Daphne

BECARD/BECART[2] de GRANVILLE et de FONVILLE, Charles (s Fonville), b Quebec 1675 – d 1703, crto drgt AKL DCB2[2] H H77 K

BECK, George, b Ellford, Eng 1748/50, d Lexington, Ky 1812, Amer, paint B DAA F G GW H WWWA Y

BECK, Helene, b Jonquière, Que 1930– , paint AKL CAE1

BECK, Ida, fl 1940+, paint pas CNS40 MM

BECKER, Carl Joseph, b Pottsville, Pa 1841, d Brooklyn, NY 1910, Amer, illus paint AAA10d28 AAW1 AC AKL B DeV3,4 H Sam

BECKER, Helmut Julius, b Castor, Alta 1931– , prt AKL IO WWA84

BECKETT, Charles E., b Portland, Me, fl 1844, d 1856, Amer, drw paint AKL DMA GW H Y

BECKLEY, Allan, b 1947– , paint CAE1

BECKWITH, James E., b Columbia, Me 1904/Mt Pleasant, Iowa 1907– , Amer, paint AKL MM RCA WWA62

BEDARD, Jean Thomas, b 1947– , paint prt AKL CAE1

BEDARD, Louis, b Quebec c 1849, fl 1881, engr K

BEDARD, Thomas, fl 1872–95, paint K

BEDDOE, Alan Brockman, b Ottawa 1893 – d 1975, paint AKL M NGC1p426 NGC68 RCA

BEDDOWS, Eric. *See* NUTT, Kenneth Eric

BEDER, Jack, b Opatow, Pol 1910– , paint CLA MM RCA

BEDFORD, Frederick George Denham, Adm, Sir, b 1838, d 1913, topog AKL DBMaP DBWA H WWW

BEDWASH, Richard, b Hillsport, Ont 1936– , paint UG

BEDWELL, Edward Parker, Lt, d England 1919, Eng, paint AKL DeV1 H

BEECH, Henry, fl 1875–90, engr AKL H

BEECHEY, Frances Ann. *See* HOPKINS, Frances Ann Beechey

BEECHEY, Frederick William, Rr Adm, b London 1796 – d 1856, Eng, prt AKL APH DCB8 DMA DNB EMA H

BEECHEY, Richard Brydges, Adm, b London 1808, d Southsea, Eng 1895, Eng, paint AC AKL B DBLP DBMaP DBWA DIA DMA DSP G PS TB1

BEEMER, Arthur Alexander, b London, Ont 1880, paint Hu

BEERBOHM, Marvin, b Toronto 1909– , mur paint AKL WWA62

BEETON, William, b Toronto 1935– , paint prt NGC2

BEEVOR, A.F. (Abraham F.?), fl 1882–1908, paint H MM RCA

BEHENNA, Katherine Arthur (pseud John Prendergast) (m Henry Carstairs Behenna), b Helensborough-on-Clyde, Scot c 1860, d 1920s, paint AAA13 AKL B DBA DWA Fo G H Mo12 WBA2

BEHNAN, Lynda Lapeer. *See* LAPEER, Lynda

BEHNAN, Michael Joseph (m Lynda Lapeer, q.v.), b Karache, Pak 1947– , paint AKL IO

BEIL/BIEL, Charles A., fl 1920s, d 1976, Amer, sculp AKL DAS Sam WWAd78

BELAND, Luc, b Lachine, Que 1951– , drgt paint prt AKL NGC2

BELANGER, Anaclet, b Quebec c 1843, fl 1901, engr sculp K

BELANGER, Denise Marie, b Montreal 1952– , stgl IO

BELANGER, Horace, b Rivière-Quelle, Que 1836, d Sea River Falls, Man 1892, paint DCB12 K

BELANGER, J. Ambrose, b Quebec 1830, fl 1910, sculp K

BELANGER, Louis Joseph Octave, b Montreal 1886 – d 1972, paint B CNS40 K MM RCA

BELCHER, Edward, Adm, Sir, b Halifax 1799, d London 1877, Eng, topog AKL DCB10 DMA DNB EMA H W1–3

BELCOURT, E. (Mlle), fl 1884, paint H K

BELFIELD, T.D. *See* BETFIELD/BELFIELD, T.D., Jr.

BELFIELD, William, fl 1850–1, paint DFA ROM

BELIVEAU, René-Charles, b Montreal 1872 – d c 1914, paint AKL H K MM RCA

BELL, Alister Macready, b Darlington, Eng 1913– , paint prt AKL BB CAE2 CC2 CWW93 DCA M MM NGC2 RCA S TB3 US WWA93

BELL, Charles Edward, b Portage La Prairie, Sask, fl 1948+, car Des

BELL, Delos Cline, b Beamsville, Ont, fl 1867–77, paint AKL H H77

BELL, Dorothy G. (m F.C. Bell), b Edinburgh 1893, d 1954, paint WWNA

BELL, Hilda Joyce Pocock. *See* STEWART, Hilda Joyce Pocock

BELL, J.E., fl 1871–3, paint H

BELL, James, fl 1827, d Saint John, NB 1877, paint AKL H

BELL, Mary Alexandra. *See* EASTLAKE, Mary Alexandra Bell

BELL, Peter Alan, b Grantham, Eng 1918– , gra paint AKL WWA80

BELL, Robin Charles Hungerford, b Seaforth, Ont 1949– , sculp AKL IO

BELL-IRVING, Jean M., b Vancouver 1923– , paint AKL

BELL-SMITH, Edward Llewellyn, b Morris, Man 1909– , paint Hu

BELL-SMITH, Eva, fl 1893, paint DWA H

BELL-SMITH, Frederick Marlett (Smith[2]), b London 1846, d Toronto 1923, paint ACA AE AGO AKL CC2 CE1,2 CWW10 DBA[2] DeV3,5,6,8 E Fo[2] G[2] H H77 Hu LeJ M MM Mo98,12 NGC1,2 NGC67 R2 RCA S Sam St TB3 W1–3 WBA2

BELL-SMITH, John, b Rotherite, Kent 1810, d Toronto 1883, paint H H77 Hu M NGC1,2 R2 RCA W1–3

BELL-SMITH, R. (Miss), fl 1885–93, paint DWA H

BELLARD, Maxim, b Canada c 1830, fl 1866, litho GW H

BELLE, Charles Ernest[2] de, b Budapest 1873, d Montreal 1939, paint AGO CWW36 DBA[2] H77 Hu K M[2] MM NGC1,2 PMC RA[2] RCA TB2,3

BELLEFEUILLE, Annette Sénécal[2] de (m Lionel de Bellefeuille), fl 1917–49, paint K[2] MM

BELLEFLEUR, Léon (Jean-Charles Rodrigue Léon), b Montreal 1910– , illus paint prt AGO AKL CC1 CE2 M MM MQ NGC1,2 NGC67 RCA S SC TB3 WWA76

BELLEFLEUR, Philippe. *See* LACELIN, Philippe

BELLEMARE, Raymond, b Nicolet, Que 1942– , gra CWW93 MM RCA

BELLERIVE, Marcel, b Grand-Mère, Que 1934– , paint prt AKL CAE1,2

BELLEROSE, Lorraine, b Richmond, Que 1935– , paint AKL

BELLEW, Frank Henry Temple, b Cawnpore, India 1828, d New York 1888, Amer, car illus AKL B DAB F GW H WECa WWWA

BELLIN, Jacques-Nicolas, b Paris 1703, d 1772, engr AKL K

BELLIOT, Roger, b St-Augustin-de-Desmaures, Que 1899 – d 1991, paint K

BELLIS, Daisy Maud, b Waltham, Mass 1887, Amer, paint AAA33 AKL DWA MM TB2 WWA62

BELLIVEAU, Philomène (Mlle), b 1853/8, fl 1893, paint K

BELLOWS, Albert Fitch, b Milford, Mass 1829, d Auburndale, Mass 1883, Amer, etch paint ANC App B DAB DBA F GW H NCAB TB1 WWWA Y

BELZILE, Charles-Henri, Lt Col, b Trois-Pistoles, Que 1933– , paint AKL CWW86

BELZILE, Louis, b Rimouski, Que 1929– , paint AKL H77

BENECKE, Herman, b Berlin, Ge c 1827, fl 1861, litho H

BENGOUGH[1], John Wilson (aka Côte[2]), b Toronto 1851 – d 1923, cart CE1,2 Co CWW10 Des[1] EC H LeJ M Mo98,12 R1 W1–3 WECa

BENGOUGH, William, b Whitby, Ont 1863 (x 1857), d Kiamesha Lake, nr Monticello, NY 1932, illus paint AAA31d32 B H RCA WWAd38

BENHAM, Mary Lile Love (m Hugh Avery Benham), b Winnipeg 1914– , paint CWW91

BENISTON, Susan, b Toronto 1953– , paint sculp DCA

BENJAMIN, Anthony, b Boarhunt, Eng 1931– , Eng, gra sculp UG

BENJAMIN, Kenneth Thomas. *See* CHEE CHEE, Benjamin

BENNER, Ronald William, b London, Ont 1949– , paint IO

BENNER, Thomas E., b London, Ont 1950– , paint sculp DFA IO

BENNER, Tony, b 1956– , paint sculp CAE2

BENNET, Edward, fl 1822–30, engr H

BENNETT, John Alfred Everest, b Diss, Norf 1919– , paint AGO CWW61 IO M MM O.My50 RCA UG

BENNETT, William James, b London 1787, d New York 1844, Amer, paint B DBLP DBWA DeV5 F GW H TB1 Y

BENOIT, Jean (m Mimi Parent, q.v.), b Quebec 1922– , paint CA77 CE1,2 TB2 WWA82

BENOIT, Lucien, fl 1875–1903, paint sculp H K

BENOIT, Mimi Parent. *See* PARENT, Mimi

BENOIT dit MARQUETTE, Paul-Salomon, fl 1935+, sculp K

BENOIT dit MARQUETTE, Pierre-Salomon, fl 1819–61, sculp K

BENOIT-DARVEAU, Jocelyne, b Montreal 1943– , paint CAE1

BENOLKEN, Leonore Ethel Williams[2] (m Irving Benolken), b Saskatchewan 1896, d Omaha, Nebr, paint AAW2 DWA[2] WWA40

BENSON, Leslie Langille, b Mahone Bay, NS 1885, paint AAA31 F TB2 WWA40

BENSON, Melvin (Mel), b Rama Indian Res, Ont 1952– , drw prt IO

BENSON, Susan (m Michael Whitfield), b Bexley Heath, Kent 1942– , des paint CWW93

BENTHAM, Douglas Wayne, b Rose-

town, Sask 1947– , sculp CAE2 RCA US WWA86
BENTHAM, Leonard, b Canada 1948– , paint DCA
BENTLEY, Dorothy May. *See* WILLIAMS, Dorothy May Bentley
BENTLEY, Lorna. *See* WREFORD, Lorna Bentley
BENTLEY, Robert Sidney, b Toronto 1928– , paint CWW70
BENTLEY, Wesley, D., fl 1901–4, drw H
BENTON, Margaret Maud Peake, b S Orange, NJ 1907, d 1975, Amer, paint Hu RCA WWA73d76 WWWA
BENY, Wilfrid Roy Roloff, b Medicine Hat, Man 1924, d Rome 1984, paint AGO CA1 CC2 CE1,2 Co CWW83 M MM NGC1,2 RCA TB3 UG WWA84
BERARD, Germaine (Soeur Marie-Philippine), b St-Barthélemy, Que 1891, d St Boniface, Man 1985, paint K
BERCIER, Etienne, b Montreal 1788, fl 1861, sculp K
BERCOVITCH, Aleksandre, b Cherson, nr Odessa, Rus 1893, d Montreal 1951, paint AGO MM RCA TB3
BERCZY, Charles Albert, b Newark, nr Niagara-on-the-Lake, Ont 1794, d Toronto 1858, paint DCB8 H
BERCZY, Jeanne Charlotte Allamand[2] (m William Berczy, q.v.), b Lausanne, Swi 1760, d Ste-Mélanie, Que 1839, min DCB7[2] DWA G H K[2]
BERCZY, Louise Amélie Panet[2] (m William Bent Berczy, q.v.), b Quebec 1789, d Ste-Mélanie, Que 1862, paint DWA H K[2]
BERCZY, William Bent (m Louise A.P. Berczy, q.v.), b London 1791, d Ste-Mélanie, Que 1873, paint AGO DCB10 H NGC2 WHC
BERCZY, William (Johann Albrecht Ulrich Moll) (s William von Moll Berczy) (m Jeanne C.A. Berczy, q.v.), b Wallerstein, Ge 1744, d New York 1813, paint ACA AGO APH BM CE1,2 Co DCB5 EC Fo G H H77 M MQ NGC1,2 NGC67 ROM W1–3 WHC
BERESFORD, R.F., fl 1818, paint H
BERG, Ronald J., b Niagara-on-the-Lake, Ont 1952– , des gra illus C CWW93
BERGE, Dorothy Alphena, b Ottawa 1923– , sculp DAS
BERGER, Jean, b St-Dizier-au-Mont-d'Or, nr Lyon, Fr c 1681, d after 1709, paint DCB2 H H77 K
BERGERON, Camille Léopold, b La-Reine, Que 1928– , carv paint CWW93
BERGERON, Jean-Claude, b St-Fortunat, Que 1941– , paint CAE1 IO
BERGERON, Ronald Ares, b Montreal 1946– , paint CAE1
BERGERON, Suzanne (m Jean Claude Suhit), b Causapscal, Que 1930– , paint prt AGO CC1 DCA M MM NGC1,2 RCA TB3
BERGMAN, Henry Eric, b Dresden, Ge 1893, d Winnipeg 1958, engr paint prt AGO BB CC2 GM M MM NGC2 RCA TB2,3 UG
BERKOVITZ, Martin, b Toronto 1944– , etch paint IO NGC2 RCA
BERLIN, Eugenia, b Kharkov, Rus 1905– , cer sculp Co M NGC1,2 O.Ag48 RCA TB3 WWA53
BERLIND, Robert, b New York 1938– , Amer, paint WWA93
BERLINGUET, François-Xavier, b Quebec 1830, d Trois-Rivières, Que 1916, sculp K MQ
BERLINGUET, Louis-Laurent-Flavien, b c 1821, fl 1877, sculp K
BERLINGUET, Louis-Thomas, b St-Laurent, nr Montreal c 1790, d Quebec 1863, sculp K MQ
BERLOTTE, Louis, fl 1842–3, sculp K
BERMAN, Michaele (s Jordana), b Winnipeg 1947– , paint IO NGC2
BERNATCHEZ, Michèle, b nr Matapedia, Que 1939– , tap CAE1 MQ
BERNHARDT, Sarah (Rosine Ber-

nard), b Paris 1844 – d 1923, paint B K TB1
BERNIER, Joseph, b Cap-St-Ignace, Que c 1835, fl 1861, sculp K
BERRINGTON, Adrian, b England c 1887, d London 1923, Eng, etch DBA RCA
BERRY, Wilson Reed (William R. Wilton[2]) b Cass Co, Ind 1851, Amer, engr litho paint AAA29 F H[2]
BERRYMAN, Edgar, b Queenston, Ont 1839, fl 1903, drgt DeV3 H Mo98
BERTEIG, Gary, b Swift Current, Sask 1946– , paint US
BERTHELOT, Amable, b Quebec 1777 – d 1847, paint DCB7 H K LeJ W1–3
BERTHELOT, Hector, b Trois-Rivières, Que 1842, d Montreal 1895, cart DCB12 Des K WECa
BERTHIAUME, Roland (Berthio[2]), b Montreal 1927– , cart Des[2] WECa
BERTHON, Claire/BERTHON[2], Sidonia Clara, b Toronto 1866, d 1953, paint DWA[2] H[2] K Mo12
BERTHON, Georges Theodore, b Royal Palace, Vienna 1806, d Toronto 1892, paint ACA AE AGO B CE1,2 Co DCB12 EC H H77 Hu K LeJ M NGC2 NGC67 R2 RCA W1–3
BERTON, Pierre, b Whitehorse, YT 1920– , paint ske CWW93
BERTRAND, Georges, fl 1885–1903, engr H K
BERTRAND, Joseph, fl 1837 76, sculp K
BERTRAND, Narcisse, b Cap-Santé, Que c 1842, d Quebec 1906/8, sculp K
BERTRAND, O.J., fl 1874–91, paint K
BERTRAND, Séraphin, fl 1817–31, sculp K
BERUBE, Jos. C., fl 1875–92, sculp K
BERVOETS, Hendrikus (Henk), b Heerlen, Limburg, Neth 1945– , paint sculp IO
BERZIN, Baiba, b Latvia 1944– , paint CAE1
BESANT, Derek Michael (m Alexandra Haeseker, q.v.), b Ft MacLeod, Alta 1950– , paint prt AA CAE2 CWW93 SC UG WWA93
BESNER, J. Jacques, b Vaudreuil, Que 1919– , sculp DMS WWA93
BESOLD, Bobbe, b 1950– , paint IO
BESSAU, Oscar (Oskar), b France, fl 1850–7, Fr, paint GW H K ROM
BESSEY, James William, b Toronto 1920– , paint IO
BESSONETTE, Cecilia Augusta, fl 1850s, paint H K
BEST, Arthur William, b Mt Pleasant, nr Peterborough, Ont 1859, d Oakland, Calif 1935, paint AAW1,2 AC B Sam
BEST, Harry Cassie, b Mt Pleasant, nr Peterborough, Ont 1863, d San Francisco 1936, paint AAA33 AAW1,2 AC B Sam WWA36d38
BEST, William Robert, fl 1851–60, illus APH DeV4 H ROM
BETFIELD/BELFIELD, T.D., Jr, fl 1858–64, paint H
BETHUNE, Charles James Stewart, b W. Flamborough, Ont 1838, d Toronto 1932, paint Co CWW10 H Mo98,12 R1 W1–3
BETHUNE, Henry Norman, b Gravenhurst, Ont 1890, d Huang Shiko, Chi 1939, paint CE1,2 Co EC Hu MM W1–3
BETTINGER, Hoyland B., b Lima, NY 1890, Amer, paint AAA33 TB2 WWA40
BETTINVILLE, Henri, b Belgium 1938– , illus CAE2 RCA
BEUG, Lorne Arthur, b Regina 1948– , sculp CWW93
BEULLAC, Raymond, b Brissac, Fr 1844, fl 1899, carv paint H K
BEUTEL, Josh, b Montreal, fl 1966– , cart Po86–8
BEUTHNER, Edward W., b Germany c 1849, d Montreal 1936, paint H
BEVAN, Oliver, b Peterborough, Eng 1941– , paint US

BEVELANDER, Annemarie Mieke, b Drachten, Neth 1945– , drw CAE1 IO

BEVERIDGE, Carole Bernice. *See* CONDE, Carole Bernice

BEVERIDGE, Karl John (m Carole Conde, q.v.), b Ottawa 1945– , prt sculp CAE1 CWW80 IO NGC2 WWA93

BEYNON, John Hubert, b Minnedosa, Man 1890, paint Hu M NGC1,2 TB3

BEZANSON, Thomas, Bro, b Halifax 1929– , cer DCA

BIANCHI, John Alan, b Rochester, NY 1947– , cart illus CWW90

BIBEAU, Fernand R., b Montreal 1931– , paint CWW93

BICE, Clare, b Durham, Ont 1909, d Saint John's, Nfld 1976, paint CBC CWW73 ICB2 M MM NGC2 O.N47 RCA S SAA22 UG WWA78d80 WWB77

BICKERSTAFF, Isaac. *See* EVANS, Don

BICKFORD, Nelson Norris, b Quebec 1846, d New York 1943, paint AAA17 F WWAd47

BIDNER, Thomas Michael (s Cloud), b London, Ont 1944– , prt CAE1,2 IO UG WWA86

BIDOT, Joseph, b St-Jacques, Que c 1834, fl 1861, paint H

BIEHN, Joshua (or Joseph), fl 1891–9, paint H

BIEL, Charles A. *See* BEIL/BIEL, Charles A.

BIELER, André Charles (m Jeannette Meunier, q.v.), b Lausanne, Swi 1896, d Kingston, Ont 1989, paint sculp AE AGO CC2 CE1,2 CWW89 EC GM H IO K M MM NGC1,2 O.My50 RCA SC St TB3 UG WWA89 WWB88

BIELER, André Charles Theodore (Ted), b Kingston, Ont 1938– , paint sculp AE B CC1 CWW93 IO M MM RCA WWA93

BIENVENUE, Marcella Jean, b Stettler, Alta 1946– , prt litho AA CAE2

BIERK, David Charles (s Bierkart), b Appleton, Minn 1944– , paint prt CAE2 IO WWA80

BIERMAN[1], Robert Maximillian (s Arem[2]), b Amsterdam 1921– , cart Des[1,2] Po86–8

BIERSTADT, Albert, b Solingen, nr Dusseldorf, Ge 1830, d New York 1902, Amer, paint AAAd28 AAW1 AC ANC App AW B BE Bry DAA DAB DMA DSP F G GW H L McC NCAB RCA Sam TB1 WHC WWWA Y

BIG BULL, William, Jr, b Peigan Res, nr Brocket, Alta 1954– , drw SC

BIGELOW, Dianne Mae, b Windsor, Ont 1938– , des prt IO

BIGELOW, Robert Clayton (Bob), b Los Angeles 1940– , paint sculp NGC2 WWA93

BIGGAR, Warren, b Hamilton, Ont 1931– , sculp CWW84

BIGGER, George Gordon, c 1856, d Vancouver 1905, paint H

BIGGER, Michael Dinsmore, b Waukegan, Ill 1937– , Amer, sculp WWA93

BIGSBY, John Jeremiah, b Nottingham, Eng 1792, d London 1881, Eng, ske DFA DNB H

BIKKERS, Rudolf, b Hilversum, Neth 1943– , etch paint IO

BILL, Edward B., fl 1885–1903, paint H MM

BILLAUX, Mary Jane Hélène (m Hugh Clifford[2]), b London 1903– , gra paint MM RCA WWNA[2]

BILODEAU, Ignace, b Quebec c 1841, fl 1920, sculp K

BILTON, Lance. *See* TAGGART, William Stuart

BING. *See* COUGHLIN, William Garnet

BINGHAM, William St Maur, fl 1858–62, paint GW H

BINKERT, G.A., fl 1863, illus H

BINKLEY, Michael, b Toronto 1960– , sculp ABC

BINKS, Thomas, b Hull, Eng 1799 –

d 1852, Eng, paint DBMaP DMA DSP PP

BINNEY, Herbert Newton, b 1766, d 1842, paint H

BINNING, Bertram Charles, b Medicine Hat, Alta 1909, d W Vancouver 1976, paint ACA AGO CC1 CE1,2 CLA Co CWW73 GM H77 M NGC1,2 NGC67 RCA S TB3 WWA76 WWB77

BIRCH, Thomas, b London 1779/87, d Philadelphia 1851, Amer, engr min paint ANC App B BE BM DAB DMA DSP F Fo GW H NCAB PP TB1 WWWA Y

BIRCHER, A.T., fl 1880, paint H

BIRD, Ernest Earle/Earl, b London 1869, paint Hu

BIRD, John Alexander Harrington, b England 1846, d Hammersmith, London 1936, Eng, paint B DBA DVP G M MM OELP RCA TB1,3 WBA1 WWB34 WWW

BIRIUKOVA, Yulia (Julie), b Petrograd, Rus 1897, d 1972, paint Hu RCA

BIRKS, Robert Morris, b 1848/68, d Ste-Anne-de-Bellevue, Que 1938, paint sculp H MM

BIRLEY, Patience (m S.P. Birley), b Bedfordshire, Eng 1905– , paint WWNA

BIRNIE, Elizabeth Annie, b Barrie, Ont 1851, fl 1914, paint H

BIRO, Geza Tibor, b Bene, Hu 1919, paint CAE1 PHA

BIRRELL, Ebenezer, b Scotland 1801–d 1888, paint DFA H H74 KB NGC67

BIRT, Christopher Richard, b England 1945– , drw IO

BIRTWHISTLE, Richard John, Col (aka Little Bobs), b Ottawa 1873, fl 1949, litho CWW49

BISHOP, George, Montreal c 1838, fl 1894, engr H

BISHOP, John Harold Gilbert, b Bathurst, NB 1908– , paint CLA

BISSON, Henri, b Ste-Marie, Beauce Co, Que, sculp CNS40 MM RCA

BISSON, Th., fl 1905, car illus K

BISWAS, Asit Kumar, b Balasore, India 1939– , paint CWW93

BLACK, Caroline (Martin) (Mrs), b St Catharines, Ont, fl late 19th cen, paint DWA H

BLACK, Donald, b Hamilton, Ont 1949– , prt IO

BLACK, Frank Charles, b Southall, Eng 1894, fl 1976, paint Hu RCA

BLACK, Malcolm Charles Lamont, b Liverpool 1938– , car drw CWW93

BLACK, Samuel, b Ardrossan, Scot 1913– , gra paint CWW93 M RCA S WBA1

BLACKELL, Margo, b Sackville, NB 1940– , mmed CAE2

BLACKWELL, Anne (Mrs), fl 1868–90, paint H RCA

BLACKWOOD, David Lloyd, b Wesleyville, Nfld 1941– , etch paint CE1,2 CWW93 DCA IO M NGC2 RCA S SC WWA93

BLACKWOOD, Frederick Temple. *See* DUFFERIN AND AVA, Frederick Temple Blackwood

BLADE, Mary Plumb (Mrs), fl 1960s, paint ABC

BLADEN, Ronald, b Vancouver 1918, d New York 1988, sculp BE CA1–3 DAS DCAA2–3 WWA86 WWWA

BLADES, Ann Sager (m David Morrison), b Vancouver 1947– , illus paint C CBC CE2 CWW93 SAA69

BLAGDON, John Locke, fl 1844, paint DFA

BLAHUT, John William, b Toronto 1950– , paint IO

BLAIN, Nicholas. *See* BLIN, Nicolas/BLAIN, Nicholas

BLAINE. *See* MacDONALD, Blaine

BLAIR, David, fl 1899, litho H

BLAIR, John/R. John², fl 1880–1920, Scot, paint B DBA DVP H² NGC1,2 Sam² SW

BLAIR, Robert Brown, fl 1880–1920, Scot, paint, H Sam

BLAKE, David Edward, b Montreal 1939– , etch paint IO
BLAKE, James, b London, Ont 1954– , paint IO
BLAKE, Robert Aldrich, fl 1875–6, Eng, paint H
BLAKE, Sarah Mary (Sara), b 1864, d 1933, paint DFA KB
BLAKEY, M. (Miss), fl 1840s, paint DFA
BLAKSTAD, Rolph Kenneth, b Vancouver 1929– , paint NGC2
BLANCHARD, F.G./G.F.[2], fl 1890–1, paint H[2] K
BLANCHET, François-Norbert, b St-François-de-Montmagny, Que 1795, d Oregon 1883, paint K
BLAND, James Alfred Anthony, b nr Isley, Yorks 1856/65, d Ottawa 1928, paint H MM
BLAND, James Fox, Lt (s J.F.B.), fl 1846, topog DeV9 H PNL
BLAND, Mavis Rose, b London 1927– , cer sculp IO
BLATCHLEY/BLATCHLY, William Daniel, b Bristol, Eng 1838, d Toronto 1903, paint B H Hu MM RCA US W1–3
BLAUVELT, Jabob L., fl 1915+, paint DFA
BLAZEJE, Zbigniew, b Barnaul, Sib 1942– , paint sculp AGO IO RCA WWA93
BLEAU, Delphis, b Montreal 1841 – d 1892, sculp K
BLENDERMAN, Robert A.J., b Germany 1934– , paint IO
BLENKHORNE, Donald MacMillan, b Pictou, NS 1923– , paint CWW80
BLIN, Claude, b Chambéry, Fr 1931– , paint CAE2
BLIN, Nicolas/BLAIN[2], Nicholas, fl 1688, engr H[2] K
BLODGETT, Stanford Earl, b Decorah, Iowa 1909– , paint M SC US
BLOIS, Charles-Theodore de. *See* DEBLOIS, Charles-Theodore
BLOIS, François-B. de[2], b Quebec 1829, d 1913, paint DMA F[2] GW[2] H[2] K
BLOIS, Josephine Marie de (Mrs Caron[2]), fl 1830–40, paint DWA[2] H[2] K
BLOM, Willem Adriaan, b Germiston, SA 1927– , paint prt NGC2
BLOMFIELD, James Jervis, b Maidenhead, Eng 1872, d 1951, paint Hu M
BLONDELA, Ozaine, fl 1788–9, Fr, drw EMA H
BLOOMFIELD, Henry, fl 1887–1900, paint stgl H
BLOORE, Ronald Langley, b Brampton, Ont 1925– , paint sculp AE AGO CAE1 CC2 CE1,2 Co H77 IO M MM NGC2 NGC67 O.My49 SC WWA76
BLOUET, Guillaume Abel, b 1795, d 1853, drgt H K
BLOUIN, Suzanne, b Quebec Prov 1938– , enam MQ
BLUM-SAMUEL, Juliette, b Victoria, BC, fl 1909–11, paint sculp B DWA
BLYTHE, Thomas A., fl early 1800s–1858, topog DeV5 H
BOAKE, George Elliot, b Toronto 1927– , paint CWW93
BOAKS, Ronald, b Newmarket, Ont 1952– , paint CWW93
BOBAK, Bruno Joseph (Bronislaw Josephus) (m Molly J.L. Bobak, q.v.), b Wawelowka, Pol 1923– , paint sculp AE AGO BB CC1 CE1,2 H77 M MM NGC1,2 NGC68 RCA TB3 US WWA93
BOBAK, Molly Joan Lamb (m Bruno Joseph Bobak, q.v.), b Vancouver 1922– , paint AE AGO CC2 CE1,2 DCA M MM NGC1,2 NGC68 RCA TB3 WWA59
BOBIER, Barbara Joan Symington (m David W.H. Bobier, q.v.), b London, Ont 1954– , paint IO
BOBIER, David William Henry (m Barbara J.S. Bobier, q.v.), b Dutton, Ont 1949– , prt IO
BODICHON[1], Barbara Leigh Smith[2] (m Eugene Bodichon), b Wathington, Sus 1827, d Scalands Gate, Sus 1891, Eng, paint DBA DBLP[2] DBWA[2]

DNB DVLP[2] DVP[1,2] DWA DWP[2] G[1,2]

BODMAN, Geoffrey Baldwin, b Barking, Eng 1894, Eng, etch US

BODMER, Karl (Carl, Charles), b Riesbach, nr Zurich, Swi 1809, d Barbizon, Fr 1893, Swiss, etch paint AAW1 AW B BE DAA DBA DeV5 DMA F GW H McC Sam TB1

BODOLAI, Joseph Stephen, b Youngstown, Ohio 1948– , sculp WWA78

BOIGON, Brian Joseph, b Toronto 1955– , con WWA93

BOILEAU, Philippe, b Quebec 1864, d New York 1917, paint AAAd28 B CWW10 F H K Mo12 WWWA

BOISBERTHELOT de BEAUCOURT, Hyacinthe. *See* DUBOIS-BERTHELOT de BECOURS, Josué

BOISSEAU, Alfred, b Paris 1823, d Buffalo, NY 1901, paint B DFA GW H K MM MQ RCA Sam Y

BOISVERT, Gilles, b Montreal 1940– , paint prt NGC2

BOIVIN, J.B., fl 1889–90, engr H K

BOIVIN, Jacques (s Jacques), b Quebec 1952– , gra CGA1

BOLDT, Barbara Hannellore (b Baerbel Hartmann), b Muelheim-Ruhr, Ge 1930– , paint ABC

BOLDUC, Blanche, b Baie-St-Paul, Que 1907– , paint DFA KB

BOLDUC, David Wayne, b Toronto 1945– , paint prt sculp CAE1,2 NGC2

BOLDUC, G.A., fl 1886–99, engr H K

BOLDUC, Yvonne, b Baie-St-Paul, Que 1905– , fl 1966, paint sculp DFA H74 KB M

BOLLEY, Andrea, b Guelph, Ont 1949– , paint CWW93 IO RCA

BOLLIGER, Thérèse, b Walde, Swi 1944– , paint IO

BOLLIVAR, Samuel, b Rhodes Corner, NS 1884, paint DFA KB

BOLT, Ronald William, b Toronto 1938– , etch paint prt CAE2 IO SC UG WWA93 WWC84

BOLTON, George S., fl 1843–80, engr H

BOLTON, George W., fl 1869–76, engr H

BOLVIN, Gilles, b St Nicolas-d'Avennes, Fr 1710, d Trois-Rivières, Que 1766, carv DCB3 K W1–3

BOLYER/BOLGER, Edward, b Ireland c 1831, fl 1861, glpt H

BOMPAS, George J., b Bristol, Eng 1822, d Lennoxville, Que 1889, paint DeV2 H

BON, Yee (aka Bon Yee), b China 1906– , paint Hu

BONATHAN, Kay, b Montreal 1943– , sculp ABC

BOND, Charles Herbert Acton, b England 1869, d Toronto 1924, paint H Mo12 RCA

BOND, Courtney Claude Joseph, b Toronto 1910– , illus topog CWW93

BOND, Marion, b Antigonish, NS, fl 1933+, paint M MA MM RCA

BONDERENKO, Richard, b London, Ont 1950– , paint IO

BONE, Charles Richard, b Belleville, Ont 1899, d 1974, paint M MM

BONE, Jerrold, b 1934– , paint CAE2

BONET, Huguette Bouchard. *See* BOUCHARD, Huguette

BONET, Jordi (m Huguette Bouchard, q.v.), b Barcelona, Sp 1932, d Montreal 1979, mur sculp CE2 M MM RCA TB3 WWA82

BONIFACHO, Bratsa, b Belgrade, Yu 1937– , paint CWW92

BONLI, Henry Thomas, b Lasburn, Sask 1927– , paint M MM US

BONNELL, Gordon, b 1947– , prt CAE2

BONNYCASTLE, Murray Carlow, b Campbellford, Ont 1909, d Toronto c 1962, paint O.F49 RCA WWA62d66

BONNYCASTLE, Richard Henry, Lt Col, Sir, b Woolwich, Eng 1791, d Kingston, Ont 1847, Eng, paint CE2 DCB7 DNB EC H LeJ W1–3

BONWELL, C.E.H., fl 1865–82, illus H

BOONE, Lillian Michiko (s Michi), b Coaldale, Alta 1945– , paint wlhg IO

BOONE, Susan, b London, Ont 1934– , paint pas prt IO
BOOSE, Helen Edith, b Windsor, Ont 1918– , paint sculp O.Ag50
BOOTH, Charles W., b Enterprise, Ont 1898, ske CWW58
BOOTH, Graham Charles, b London 1935– , illus IBYP SAA37
BOOTH, Ralph Edward, b Toronto 1927– , paint M
BOOTH, William, b England c 1747/8, d Bristol, Eng 1826, Eng, topog H WHC
BOOTHE[1], Jack Douglas (s Douglas[2]), b Winnipeg 1910, d Vancouver 1973, cart Des[1,2]
BORDEN, Marjorie Mary. *See* OBERNE, Marjorie Mary Borden
BORDUAS, Paul-Emile, b St-Hilaire, Que 1905, d Paris 1960, paint sculp ACA AE AGO B CA1 CC1 CE1,2 Co CWW58 H77 M MM MQ NGC1,2 NGC67 OC OCD P RCA TB3 W2–3 WWA62d66 WWB58
BORENSTEIN, Samuel, b Kalvariya, Lith 1908, d Montreal 1969, paint sculp MM NGC2 RCA W3
BORG, Carl Oscar (Oskar), b Grimstad, Swe 1879, d Santa Barbara, Calif 1947, Amer, etch paint AAA33 AAW1 AC B F NCAB39 Sam TB2 WWA36d47 WWWA Y
BORG, Dione, b Malta 1952– , paint MFMS
BORG, John Henry, b Msida, Malta 1948– , paint sculp IO
BORLAND, Doreen (Mrs), b Kamloops, BC, fl 1963, paint ABC
BORLAND, O., Lt, fl mid 19th cen, topog H
BORNSTEIN, Eli, b Milwaukee, Wis 1922– , paint sculp CC2 CE1,2 M MM NGC2 NGC67 US WWA93
BOROWSKY, Peter, b London, Ont 1948– , paint sculp IO
BOSQUI, Edouard A., b Montreal 1832, d San Francisco 1917, paint AAW1 AC GW H K
BOSSANGE, Hector, b France 1795 – d 1884, Fr, litho H K
BOSSE, Denise, b Montreal 1942– , sculp DCA
BOSSY, Walter J., b Jaslo, Pol 1899, coll DFA KB
BOSUSTOW, Stephen, b Victoria, BC 1911– , Amer, anim paint WECa
BOSWELL, Hazel May, b Quebec 1882, d 1979, illus ICB1
BOSWELL, Norman Gould, b Halifax 1882, illus paint AAA33 AAW1,2 AC TB2 WWA62
BOSZIN, Andrew/Endre, b Pilis, Hu 1923– , paint sculp CAE2 IO PHA WWA93 WWB90
BOTAR, Stephen (Istavan), b Elesd, Hu, sculp PHA
BOTHWELL, Mary, b Toronto, fl 1940s, paint CWW86
BOTT, Nicholas J., b Netherlands c 1941– , paint ABC
BOUCHARD, Edith-Marie, b Baie-St-Paul, Que 1924– , paint DFA M MM
BOUCHARD, Francine, b Montreal 1949– , sculp tap CAE1
BOUCHARD, George Lorne Holland, b Montreal 1913 – d 1978, paint M MM RCA SC WWA78d80
BOUCHARD, Huguette (m Jordi Bonet, q.v.), b Montreal 1933– , cer sculp M
BOUCHARD, Marie-Cécile (Soeur Marie-de-la-Sagasse), b Baie-St-Paul, Que 1920, d 1973, paint CC1 DFA KB M MM
BOUCHARD, Simone-Marie, b Baie-St-Paul, Que 1912 – d 1945, paint CC1 DFA H74 KB M MM NGC2
BOUCHER, Alexis-Charles, b Laprairie, Que 1808, d Montreal 1885, paint H K
BOUCHER, Ginette, b La Pocatière, Que 1944– , paint CAE1
BOUCHETTE, Jean-François, b Montreal 1803 – d 1833, des topog H K
BOUCHETTE, Joseph (Joseph Francis), Col, b Quebec 1774, d Montreal 1841,

paint topog APH DCB7 DeV2,5–9 H H77 K LeJ NGC67 PNL W1–3

BOUCHETTE, Joseph, b Montreal 1798 – d 1879, des topog DeV3 H K ROM

BOUCHETTE, Robert Shore Milnes, b Quebec 1805 – d 1879, paint APH DCB10 DeV2,6,7,9 DFA H K LeJ ROM W1–3

BOUDREAU, Catharine, b Sydney, NS 1922– , sculp B

BOUDREAU, Pierre de Ligny, b Quebec 1923– , paint M NGC1,2

BOUGHNER, Jacqueline, b Sarnia, Ont 1947– , prt IO

BOUILLON, Georges, Rev, b Rimouski, Que 1841, d Ottawa 1932, des K

BOUILLON, Joseph-Georges, b Bic, Que 1868, fl 1907, des K

BOUKER, fl 1807–14, sil DFA H H77

BOULANGER, Claudette (m Patrick McGuire), b Toronto 1940– , drw IO

BOULD, Kathleen Lawson (Kay) (m Cliff Bould), b Dumfrieshire, Scot 1901– , paint BDSA

BOULTBEE, Alfred Ernest, b Newmarket, Ont 1864 (x1863), d Toronto 1928, paint DFA H MM PNL RCA WHC

BOULTBEE, Constance Mary (m Alfred Ernest Boultbee[2], q.v.), fl 1890s, paint H MM RCA WHC[2]

BOULTON, Muriel Cameron Welsh, b Charlottetown 1881, d Barton-on-Sea, Eng 1957, paint Hu M MM NGC1,2 RCA TB3

BOUMA-PYPER, Marilyn Minke (m Ian Donald Pyper), b Meaford, Ont 1955– , des gra CWW93

BOURASSA, Napoleon, b L'Acadie, Que 1827, d Lachenaie, Que 1916, paint sculp CE1,2 EC H H77 Hu K LeJ M Mo98,12 MQ NGC1,2 RCA W1–3

BOURASSA, Samuel, fl 1875–92, paint H K

BOURDON, Jean, b Rouen, Fr c 1601, d Trois-Rivières, Que 1668, crto paint H K

BOURGAULT, Alphonse, b St-Jean-Port-Joli, Que c 1890, carv K

BOURGAULT, André, b St-Jean-Port-Joli, Que 1898, d 1957, carv DFA K KB

BOURGAULT, Harmonie, fl 1930s, carv K

BOURGAULT, Jean-Julien, b St-Jean-Port-Joli, Que 1910– , carv CWW93 DFA KB M S

BOURGAULT, Médard, b St-Jean-Port-Joli, Que 1897 – d 1967, carv CWW36 DFA K KB W3

BOURGAULT, Yvonne, b St-Jean-Port-Joli, Que c 1900, carv K

BOURGEAU, Victor, b Lavaltrie, Que 1809, d Montreal 1888, fl 1830s–1865, carv DCB11 K

BOURGEAULT, Victor, fl 1830s–1865, sculp K

BOURGEOIS[1], Aldéric (s Jacob[2], Passepoil[3]), b Montreal 1876 – d 1962, car illus paint Des[1,2,3] H K WECa

BOURGEOIS, Louis-Joseph, b St-Célestin, Que 1856, d Wilmette, Ill 1930, sculp K

BOURGEOIS, Marie (Soeur Marie-Louise-Gustave), fl 1895, paint K

BOURGEOIS, Ulric, b Fulford, Que 1874, d Manchester, NH 1963, carv K

BOURGET, Paul, fl 1893, illus K

BOURINOT, Arthur Stanley, b Ottawa 1893 – d 1969, paint CC2 CWW64

BOURKE, T. Larry, b Edmonton 1940– , des paint CWW93

BOURNE, Adolphus, fl 1820–54, engr, litho DeV7 H

BOUTAL, Pauline Le Goff (m Arthur Boutal), b France 1894, fl 1988, paint CLA K

BOUTHILLIER, C.C.A., fl 1885, paint H K

BOUTHILLIER, Nazaire-Frédéric, b Longueuil, Que 1867, d Nashua, NH 1943, paint K

BOUTILIER, Ralph, b 1906– , paint sculp DFA

BOUTILLIER, Douglas, b Niagara Falls, Ont 1947– , paint IO
BOWEN, Alexander Nicol, b North Bay, Ont 1920– , paint IO
BOWEN, Ashley, b Marblehead, Mass 1728 – d 1813, Amer, paint DMA
BOWEN, Natalie H., fl 1863–6, drw DeV7 H
BOWER, Perry Stafford, b Toronto 1903– , paint CWW67
BOWERING, Marilyn Ruthe, b Winnipeg 1949– , paint CWW93
BOWIE, Thomas Taylor, b Linlithgow, Scot 1905– , sculp DBA DVP M NGC2
BOWLES, Newton Rowell, b Chengtu, Chi 1916– , paint M MM
BOWMAN, James, b Allegheny Co, Pa 1793, d Rochester, NY 1842, Amer, paint DCB7 GW H
BOWMAN, Richard Irving, b Rockford, Ill 1918– , Amer, paint MM WWA53
BOY, Philibert-Michel, b 1673, d 1714, carv K
BOYANER, Mel, b Montreal 1924– , litho paint M
BOYD, Bruce Dickson (m Joan Boyd, q.v.), b Calgary 1926– , paint M TB3
BOYD, Henry N., fl 1867, d London 1871, Eng, paint B H
BOYD, James Henderson, b Ottawa 1928– , paint sculp AGO CWW93 DCA M MM NGC2 RCA TB3 WWA93
BOYD, Joan (m Bruce Dickson Boyd, q.v.), b New Westminster, BC 1925– , paint M
BOYD, John, b Spain 1926– , paint MF
BOYD, John (Jack), b London, Ont 1941– , paint sculp DCA
BOYD-WATERS, Frederick, b Guelph, Ont 1879, d nr Hawkshead, Eng 1967, min Fo
BOYER, Hubert, b Valleyfield, Que 1914– , sculp M
BOYER-BRETON, Marthe-Marie-Louise. *See* BRETON, Marthe-Marie-Louise
BOYES, J.J., b Bedfordshire 1865, fl 1907, paint H
BOYLE, John Bernard (Jack), b London, Ont 1941– , paint prt CAE2 CE1,2 CWW93 DCA IO MM NGC2 RCA UG
BOZAK, Robert Michael, b Hudson Bay Junction, Sask 1944– , paint sculp IO
BOZICKOVIC, Alex (Boz), b Sarajevo, Yu 1919– , Amer, paint WWA84
BRABANT, Gene, b Victoria, BC 1946– , carv SC
BRACE, Brad, b Toronto 1953– , paint prt IO
BRADFIELD, John Henry Warren, b Toronto 1909– , ske CWW73
BRADFORD, Elizabeth Mary. *See* HOLBROOK, Elizabeth Mary Bradford
BRADFORD, John Locke, b Windsor, NS 1897, carv CLA MM RCA
BRADFORD, Kenneth Raymond, b 1936– , paint CAE1
BRADFORD, Robert William, b Toronto 1923– , paint CWW93
BRADFORD, William, b New Bedford, Me 1823, d New York 1892, Amer, paint AAW1 AC App B BE DAA DAB DCB12 DMA DSP F G GW H H77 NCAB1 TB1 WWWA Y
BRADISH, Alvah, b Sherburne, NY 1806, d Detroit 1901, Amer, paint AAA03d28 F GW H H77 Y
BRADLEY, Robert, b Montreal 1957– , paint CWW90
BRADSHAW, Alan Bruce, b Toronto 1945– , engr BB
BRADSHAW, Alexandra Christine (m C.B. Hoag), b Nova Scotia, paint AAA33 AC WWA66
BRADSHAW, Alice, b Toronto 1916– , illus paint prt GM NGC2
BRADSHAW, Eva Theresa, b London, Ont 1871 – d 1938, paint Hu RCA
BRADSHAW, Nell Mary (m A. Brad-

shaw), b Ownyo, Calif 1904– , paint CAE1 M

BRADY, Cyril Patrick, b Toronto 1894, paint Hu

BRAGG, William Scott, b Chatham, Ont 1937– , paint prt IO

BRAINERD, Charlotte Blanche Mattison, b Rice Lake, Wis 1921– , paint prt IO NGC2

BRAITHWAITE, J.C., fl 1856–62, drgt drw H

BRAITSTEIN, Marcel, b Charleroi, Bel 1935– , sculp AGO CC2 CWW93 M MM RCA WWA93

BRAMS, Joan, b Montreal 1928– , Amer, sculp DAS

BRAND, Edythe. *See* HEMBROFF, Edythe

BRANDL, Eva, b Ste-Pétronille, Que 1951– , sculp CAE2

BRANDT, Guillaume (William[2]) R., b Germany, fl 1850–62, paint DFA H KB[2]

BRANDTNER, Fritz, b Danzig, Ge 1896, d Montreal 1969, paint prt AGO CC2 CE1,2 CLA GM H77 Hu M MM NGC1,2 RCA TB3 UG W3 WWA70

BRANNEN, Alison Jean, b Nova Scotia 1952– , paint prt IO

BRASSARD-TANQUAY, Thérèse (Mme), b Roberval, Que 1926– , enam MQ

BRAUBACH, Ida, fl 1867 72, paint H

BREEN, Faith Wood. *See* WOOD, Faith

BREEZE, Claude Herbert, b Nelson, BC 1938– , paint AE AGO CE1,2 Co IO M MM NGC2 RCA SC US

BREGENT, Ernest (E.A.), b France 1853/4, fl 1903, paint H K

BREKENMACHER, Jean-Melchior (Père François[2]), fl 1732–58, Fr, paint H[2] H77[2] K

BREMNER, Douglas, b Montreal 1893, pas CWW38 MM

BRENDER A BRANDIS, Gerard William, b Maarn, Neth 1942– , engr paint BB CAE1 IO WWA86

BRENER, Roland, b Johannesburg, SA 1942– , sculp CE1,2 DCA WWA93

BRENNAN, Patricia Lippert, b Kitchener, Ont 1931– , prt IO

BRENTON, Edward Pelham, R Adm, b Rhode Isld 1774, d England 1839, Eng, paint DNB DeV4 H ROM WHC

BRES, Hendrik, b The Hague, Neth 1932– , paint CAE1,2 SC

BRESDIN, Rodolphe, b Ingrandes, Fr 1825, d Sèvres, Fr 1885, Fr, des engr B K TB1

BRETON, André, b Tinchebray, Fr 1896, d Paris 1966, Fr, sculp K

BRETON, Marthe-Marie-Louise (b Boyer[2]), b Paris, fl 1879–1930, paint B DWA[2] K MM[2] TB2[2]

BRETT, Carl Eamon, b Cork, Ire 1928– , gra RCA WWGA2

BRETT, Katharine Beatrice Maw. *See* MAW, Katharine Beatrice

BRETT, Leonard, b 1944– , prt SC

BRETT, Melva Erickson (m Hap Day; m Gus Brett), b Medicine Hat, Alta 1925– , paint ABC

BRETT, Newton, b Dougald, Man 1890, d Winnipeg 1969, paint TB3

BREWER, Bessie Marsh, b Toronto 1883, d New York 1952, paint AAA32 DWA F WWA47d53

BREWER, George St P., b England 1814, d St Louis, Mo 1852, Amer, panor DFA GW H Y

BREWER, John S., b Canada c 1824, fl 1850, Amer, paint GW H

BREWER, Margit. *See* GATTERBAUER, Margit Brewer

BREWSTER, Catherine, b Owen Sound, Ont 1946– , sculp IO

BRIANSKY, Rita (m Joseph Prezament, q.v.), b Grajewa, Pol 1925– , illus paint M MM RCA SC T WWA93

BRICHER, Alfred Thompson, b Portsmouth, NH 1837, d New Dorp, NY 1908, Amer, paint AAA09d28 ANC App B DAA DMA DSP F GW TB1 WWWA

BRICKUS, Claire Marie Shoniker. *See* SHONIKER, Claire Marie
BRIDGEMAN, Charles Orlando, b England 1781, ret 1846, Eng, paint DMA
BRIDGMAN, George Brandt, b nr Byng, Ont 1864, d New Rochelle, NY 1943, paint AAA33 F H Hu Mo12 RCA WWA40d47
BRIDGMAN, John Wesley, b nr Smithville, Ont, fl 1861–1907, paint DFA H Hu NGC2
BRIEN, Louis, b Amos, Que 1941– , engr BB
BRIEN dit DESROCHERS, Jean-Baptiste, b Pointe-aux-Trembles, nr Montreal 1793/4, sculp K
BRIEN dit DESROCHERS[2], Pierre-Urbain, b Varennes, Que 1781, d Quebec 1860, carv B DCB8[2] K MQ NGC2
BRIGDEN, Corry William, b Toronto 1912– , paint AGO Hu MM RCA
BRIGDEN, Frederick, b Worthing, Eng 1841, d Toronto 1917, engr paint H H77 M NGC2
BRIGDEN, Frederick Henry, b London 1871, d Bolton, Ont 1956, paint prt AGO CC1 CNS40 CWW52 EC Hu M MM NGC1,2 O.F51 PMC RCA TB2,3 W2,3 WWA59
BRIGDEN, Guy Geldard, b Toronto 1900– , gra CWW67
BRIGHTON, Lee Anne, b 1951– , etch paint prt IO
BRINK, Anat, b Novosibirsk, USSR 1945– , paint IO
BRISEBOIS, Ephrem A., fl 1870s, paint DFA
BRISON, Mary J., b Rawdon, Que 1878, paint AAA25 TB2
BRISSON, Alberte, b Pointe-au-Père, Que 1938– , paint CAE1
BRITTAIN, Miller Gore, b Saint John, NB 1912, d 1968, paint CC2 CE1,2 Co M MA MM NGC2 NGC68 TB3 W3 WWA66d70
BRITTON, Harry (m Henrietta Hancock Britton, q.v.), b Cambridge, Eng 1878, d Toronto 1958, paint AGO CC1 Co CWW55 FCA Hu M MM NGC1,2 RCA TB2 WWA53d59
BRITTON, Henrietta Hancock[2] (m Harry Britton, q.v.), b Ealing, London 1869, d Toronto 1963, paint DWA H Hu M MM NGC2[2] RCA
BRITTON, Susan Kathleen, b Winnipeg 1952– , paint DCA NGC2
BROCK-SMITH, Mary. *See* PEPIN, Mary
BRODER, Steve, b Montreal 1906– , fl 1970, paint AC
BRODERICK, Diane, b 1947– , paint CAE1
BRODEUR, Albert Samuel, b Montreal 1862, d 1933, illus H K MM RCA
BRODEUR, Georges, fl 1900–4, car Des K
BRODIE, George Staunton, fl 1865, d 1901, topog DFA H
BRODIE, James Douglas (Jim), b Hamilton, Ont 1946– , prt AA CAE2 NGC2
BRODIE, William Woollcombe (Bill), b Ottawa 1931– , des sculp CWW93
BRODKIN, Steven, b 1950– , paint CAE1
BROMBERG, Maurycy-Moshe Bar-Am, b Piotrkow-Trybonalski, Pol 1920– , paint sculp CWW87
BROMLEY, Valentine Walter Lewis, b London 1848, d Fallows Green, nr Harpenden, Eng 1877, Eng, illus paint AAW1,3 AH ANC B Bry DAES DBWA DNB DVP DWP G H TB1
BRONFMAN, Phyllis. *See* LAMBERT, Phyllis Bronfman
BRONNUM, Winston, b New Denmark, NB 1929– , carv M
BRONSON, A.A. (aka Michael Wayne Tims, General Idea, q.v.), b Vancouver 1946– , mmed WWA93
BROOK, Eva. *See* DONLY, Eva Marie Brook
BROOK, Joan Madeline, b St Leonards-

on-the-Sea, Eng 1920– , illus prt O.Ag49

BROOK, Philip R., b Salmon Arm, BC 1919– , paint CWW93

BROOKER, Bertram Richard (pseud Richard Surrey Huxley Horne), b Croydon, Eng 1888, d Toronto 1955, paint AGO CC1 CE1,2 Co CWW52 EC H77 M MM NGC2 O.N47 OC P RCA TB3 UG W2–3 WWA53

BROOKS, Allan Cyril, b Etawah, India 1869, d Comox, BC 1946, paint CE1,2 M WWNA

BROOKS, Frank Leonard, b Enfield, London 1911– , paint prt AGO CWW93 M MM NGC2 NGC68 O.N47 RCA S UG WWA82

BROOKS, Maria Matilda, b Staines, Eng 1837, d New York 1913, Eng, paint AAAd28 B DBA DVP DWA G H MM NCAB8 RCA TB1

BROOKS, Mildred Beamish. *See* MANUEL, Mildred Beamish Brooks

BROOME, Isaac, b Valcartier, Que 1836, d Trenton, NJ 1922, Amer, sculp AAA22d28 B CWW10 DAS F GW Mo12 TB1,3 WWWA

BROOMFIELD, Adolphus George, b Toronto 1906– , paint CWW92 M MM NGC2 NGC68 O.N47 RCA S WWA91

BROSIUS/BROSIER, H., fl 1875, illus H

BROUCHOUD, Joseph F. (aka BROUCHON, Joseph[2] and S.[3]), b Switzerland 1814/15, fl 1875–1909, paint H[2,3] K MM[3]

BROUGHTON, Charles, b Peel Co, Ont c 1861, d c 1912, illus paint AAW2 AC H Mo98,12

BROUILLY, Louis (b Camille-Eusèbe-Marie), b La-Motte-en-Santerre, Fr 1878, d Quebec 1967, des illus K

BROUSSEAU, Napoléon (aka Mr Mxpltlzik), b Eastview, Ont 1954– , drw paint IO

BROUSSEAU, Raymond, b Montreal 1938– , paint sculp CAE1

BROWN, Andrew, Sr, Lt Col, b Edinburgh 1766, d Derry, Eng 1835, Eng, paint NGC2 WHC

BROWN, Andrew, Jr, b Colchester, Eng 1806, fl 1857, Eng, paint NGC2 WHC

BROWN, Archibald. *See* BROWNE, Joseph Archibald

BROWN, Arthur William, b Hamilton, Ont 1881, d 1966, illus AA32 CWW64 F IA1,2 Mo12 WWA66 WWWA

BROWN, Audrey Alexandra, b Nanaimo, BC 1904– , sculp CLA CWW64

BROWN, Brian E., b St Thomas, Ont 1951– , paint IO

BROWN, Clare Robert, b Woodstock, Ont 1932– , sculp IO

BROWN, Daniel Price Erichsen (Erichsen-Brown[2]), b Forrestville, Ont 1939– , paint prt CAE1,2 CE2 IO[2] MM

BROWN, George Blair, b Kinc, Scot 1878, d 1965, gra paint M

BROWN, Grafton Tyler, b Harrisburg, Pa 1841, d St Peter, Minn 1918, Amer, litho paint AAA13 AAW1,2 AC GW H Sam TCBA

BROWN, Harley, b Edmonton 1939– , pas SC

BROWN, Henry B. (aka Harrison Brown[2]), b Portland, Me 1831, d London 1915, Amer, paint ANC F GW[2] TB1

BROWN, Henry Harris (J. Harris[2]), b Northamptonshire 1864, d 1948, Eng, paint AAW B DBA G H[2] RCA TB1 WBA1

BROWN, J., fl 1813, min GW H

BROWN, Karen J., b Hillcrest, Alta 1945– , paint ABC

BROWN, Lily McEntee (Mrs), fl 1887–1904, paint AAA04 DWA H MM RCA

BROWN, Lynn Hutchinson, b Toronto 1946– , mmed CAE2

BROWN, Margaret Adeline Porter (m J.Y. Brown), b Huron Co, Ont 1867, paint CWW10 Mo12

BROWN, Newton, b Galt, re Cambridge Ont 1874, paint Hu

BROWN, Samuel E., fl 1840–60, Amer, engr GW H

BROWN, W., fl 1819–20, min GW H

BROWN, Warren, b 1950– , paint prt CAE2

BROWNE, Belmore, b Tompkinsville, Staten Isld, NY 1880, d Ross, Calif 1954, Amer, paint AAA33 AAW1,3 AC F NCAB Sam TB2 WWA53d56 WWWA

BROWNE, George R., fl 1831–54, drw H

BROWNE, Joseph Archibald, b Liverpool 1862, d Cornwall, Ont 1948, paint AE AGO CWW48 DBA FCA H M MM Mo12 NGC1,2 PMC RCA TB3 W2–3

BROWNE, William Henry James, Cdr RN, fl 1836, d Woolwich, Eng 1872, Eng, paint DFA DMA H H77

BROWNELL, Peleg Franklin, b New Bedford, Me 1857, d Ottawa 1946, paint AGO B CC2 CE1,2 CWW36 H H77 M MM Mo98,12 NGC1,2 O.My50 PMC TB3 W2,3

BROWNHILL, Harold, b Sheffield, Eng 1887, d Halifax c 1983, illus paint M WWA82

BROZE, Modris, b Toronto 1954– , sculp IO

BRUCE, Ada Mildred (m Thomas L. Torrance), b Grand Valley, Ont 1903– , paint Hu RCA

BRUCE, Alan J., b 1935– , drw ABC

BRUCE, Annie Priscilla (Mrs), b Jordan Ferry, NS 1868, paint DWA WWA62

BRUCE, Bella C. (m John Walden), fl 1890–1, d 1950, paint DWA H

BRUCE, Marjorie Mackenzie, b Shelbourne, NS 1895, des AAA30 WWA59

BRUCE, Robert Donald, b Grandview, Man 1911, d 1981, mur paint M

BRUCE, Robert Randolph, b St Andrews, Scot 1863, d Montreal 1942, cart CWW38 Des EC W1–3 WWW

BRUCE, William, b Uist, Scot 1833, fl 1898, drw illum paint H Mo98

BRUCE, William Blair, b Hamilton, Ont 1859, d Stockholm 1906, paint AGO B CE2 DCB13 DBA DVP EC G H H77 Hu LeJ M Mo98 NGC1,2 NGC67 R2 RCA TB1 W1–3

BRUENECH, George Robert, b St Malo, Fr 1851, d Toronto 1916, paint B DFA H Hu MM Mo12 RCA

BRUNEAU, Kittie Marguerite (m Serge Gilbert), b Montreal 1929– , paint prt sculp CAE1,2 CC1 M MM NGC2 RCA S WWA93

BRUNEL, Louis, b Montreal 1941– , paint CWW93

BRUNET, Jean-Emile, b Huntingdon, Que 1892/4/9, d Montreal 1977, sculp B K M MM RCA

BRUNET, Joseph, fl 1890–4, sculp K

BRUNET, Joseph-Olivier, b Ste-Martine, Que 1878, d St Boniface, Man 1950, sculp K

BRUNET, Louis Ovide[2], b Quebec 1827 – d 1876, paint DCB10 K[2]

BRUNET, Raymond Pierre, b St Boniface, Man 1948– , met CAE1

BRUNI, Umberto, b Montreal 1914– , gra paint M MM RCA WWA93

BRUNN, Margaret (May). *See* HOUGHTON, Margaret (May)

BRUNST, Stanley E. (Stanilus Ernst), b Birmingham, Eng 1894, d Vancouver 1962, paint CLA GM M

BRUSH, George De Forest, b Shelbyville, Tenn 1855, d Hanover, NH 1941, Amer, paint AAW1 DAA F H Y

BRUTE, Doctor. *See* METCALFE, Eric William

BRYMNER, William, b Greenock, Scot 1855, d Wallasey, Ches 1925, paint ACA AGO B CC2 CE1,2 Co CWW10 DBA EC H H77 Hu M MM Mo12 MQ NGC1,2 NGC67 R2 RCA TB1,3 W1–3

BUCHANAN, Ella, b Preston, Ont 1869, d Hollywood, Calif 1951,

Amer, sculp AAA33 AC F DAS DWA TB2 WWA53
BUCHANAN, Paul, b Toronto 1930– , paint UG
BUCHER, Carl (aka Carl Lander), b Zurich, Swi 1935– , paint sculp CA1
BUCK, William, fl 1840, paint H
BUCK, William M., fl 1872–4, paint H
BUCKLES, Susan Jane, b Toronto 1941– , fab IO
BUCKLEY, George E., b Saint John, NB, fl 1930s, paint CLA
BUDA, John (Janos), b Lajaskomarom, Hu, fl 1956, paint PHA
BUDAY, Leslie (Laszlo), b Budapest 1926– , gra PHA
BUELL, Katrina S.D., b Brockville, Ont, fl 1890–1926, paint B DWA H RCA
BUFF, Richard Eugene, b Chicago 1947 , sculp DCA IO
BUGDEN, Harold Barry, b England 1914– , paint MA
BUKAUSKAS, Romualdas, b Pakruojus, Lith 1929– , paint M MM
BULKELEY, Richard, Hon, b Dublin 1717, d Halifax 1800, paint DCB4 EC H LeJ W1-3
BULL, Edward Claxton, b England, fl 1847–51, Eng, panor H
BULL, Henry Osler (Hank), b 1949– , con WWA93
BULLEN, Annie Amelia Bushby (Mrs), b 1863, d 1956, paint H
BULLER, Audrey D. (Mrs Parsons), b Montreal 1902– , paint MM WWA62
BULLER, Cecil Tremayne (m John Joseph Aloysius Murphy), b Montreal 1886 (x1888) – d 1973, engr paint DWA Hu GM M MM NGC1,2 RCA TB2 WWA59
BULLET, Charles-Ferréal-Auguste, b Laval, Fr 1820, fl 1879, sculp K
BULLOCH, William, b London c 1831, fl 1867, stgl H
BULLOCK, Gaye Noel, b Kingston, Ont 1948– , paint sculp IO
BUNCE, Alan, b Ottawa 1951– , etch prt NGC2
BUNCE, Thomas Earl, b Toronto 1948– , paint IO
BUNNETT, Henry Richard Sharland, b England, fl 1881–9, Eng, paint DFA H MM RCA ROM WHC
BUOTE, Alma (m Joseph MacCormick), b Tignish, PEI 1894, d Alberton, NB 1966, paint K
BURBRIDGE, Kenneth Joseph, b Bathurst, NB 1911– , paint CWW93
BURCHELL, Henrietta. *See* CLARKE, Henrietta Burchell
BURDEN, Nancy Doris, b Ottawa 1923– , illus M
BURDOIN[1], Juliet Howson[2], b Toronto 1873, paint DWA[1,2] H[2] RCA[2] WWA62
BURFORD, Bella (m Dale Bertrand), b Saskatoon 1946– , illus C
BURFORD, Byron, b Jackson, Miss 1920– , Amer, paint AE
BURFORD, Robert, b England 1792, d London 1861, Eng, panor B Bry DBLP DNB G H OELP Red TB1
BURGESS, Cecil Scott, b Bombay, 1870, d 1971, paint DBA CWW67
BURGESS, George Henry, b London c 1831, d Berkeley, Calif 1905, Amer, illus paint AAW1 AC DeV1 GW Sam
BURGESS, Henry, fl 1845, paint H
BURGESS, J.A., fl 1886–98, paint H
BURGHERSH, Priscilla Anne Pole. *See* WESTMORLAND, Priscilla Anne Pole, Countess
BURGOYNE, Lorna Heywood[2] (m L. von Ritschl, Baron), b Plympton, Dev 1894, d Toronto 1961, illus paint B[2] DBA DWA MM RA RCA WBA1,2
BURGOYNE, Saint George, b England 1882, d Montreal 1964, paint prt Hu M NGC1,2 TB3
BURICH, Samuel Mario, b Crikvenica, Yu, fl 1965, sculp BCS M
BURKA, Jan, b Postelberg, Cz 1924– , paint M
BURKE, Lora Cantor (m Winston

Churchill Burke), b St Boniface, Man 1924– , paint BDSA

BURKE, Rebecca, b Kalamazoo, Mich 1946– , paint prt sculp CAE1,2 CWW93

BURKHART, Helen Sovereign (m Bruce Burkhart), b Quebec 1909– , paint WWNA

BURLAND, George Bull, b Wexford, Ire 1829, fl 1903, engr litho H Mo98

BURLEIGH, Ron, b Titusville, Pa 1941– , paint ABC

BURLING, Gilbert, b 1843, d 1875, Amer, paint ANC B F TB1

BURMAN, Irving, b Toronto 1928– , paint sculp AE AGO M

BURNES/BURNS[2], James, b Scotland c 1810, fl 1869, paint GW[2] H Y

BURNETT, Dorothy Alcorn, b Vancouver, fl 1935, illus illum CLA

BURNLEY, John Edwin, b Victoria, BC 1896, paint AAW3 WWA62 WWNA

BURNS, Milton J., b Mount Gilead, Ohio 1853, d New York 1933, Amer, paint B DeV4 DMA DSP TB1

BURNS, Robert John, b London 1942– , gra WWGA2

BURNS, S. Archie, b Ireland 1930– , drw paint ABC

BURNSIDE, John Thrift Meldrum, b Glasgow 1834/5, d Toronto 1900, paint DFA H NGC2

BURNSTEIN, James Arnold (s Burstein), b Toronto 1923– , sculp IO

BURON, Berthe (Mère Marie-Bernadette de l'Immaculée Conception), b St Boniface, Man 1887, d Buenos Aires 1986, paint K

BURR, William, b Fairfield, Conn 1810, fl 1875–6, Amer, panor DFA GW H

BURRELL, Louise H. Luker[2] (m P.H. Luker), b London 1873, d 1971, Eng, min paint AAA21 AAW2 AC DBA[2] DWA F Fo[2] G[2] RA[2] RCA

BURRELL, Raymond Alward, b Smiths Falls, Ont 1923– , paint prt IO

BURROWES, Thomas, b Wor, Eng 1796, fl 1846, Eng, topog DFA H

BURROWS, John (b John Burrows Honey), b Plymouth, Eng 1789, d Kingston, Ont 1848, paint ske DCB7 DeV6 DFA H ROM

BURROWS, Thomas Carl (Tom), b Canada 1940– , sculp WWA73

BURSTEIN, James Arnold. *See* BURNSTEIN, James Arnold

BURT, Charles Kennedy, b Edinburgh 1823, d Brooklyn, NY 1892, Amer, engr F GW H Y

BURT, Leonard, b Port Saunders, Nfld 1928– , paint DFA KB

BURTON, Dennis Eugene Norman (m Diane Fern Pugen, q.v.), b Lethbridge, Alta 1933– , paint sculp AGO B CAE1 CE1,2 Co CWW93 IO M MM NGC2 RCA TB3 US

BURTON, Diane Fern Pugen. *See* PUGEN, Diane Fern

BURTON, Edley Allen, b Walnut Cove, NC 1901– , paint M MM

BURTON, G. Allan, Lt Col, b Toronto 1915– , paint CWW93

BURTON, Ralph W., b Newsington, Ont 1905, d Ottawa 1983, paint M

BURY, Brenda, b Notts, Eng 1932– , paint CWW93 M

BURY, Jeanne Visart de[2], b Portland, NB 1871, paint H Mo12[2]

BUSCH, Leslie, b Los Angeles 1943– , paint CAE1

BUSH, Charles Robert (s Charles Robb[2]), b Toronto 1938– , paint IO[2] M[2] MM RCA WWA93[2]

BUSH, John Hamilton (Jack), b Toronto 1909 – d 1977, paint prt AE AGO B CA1–3 CC1 CE1,2 Co CWW73 M MM NGC2 NGC67 O.N47 OC OCD RCA TB3 UG WWA76d78

BUSH, Robin Beaufort, b Vancouver 1921– , des CWW82 RCA

BUSHBY, Annie. *See* BULLEN, Annie Amelia Bushby

BUSHNAN, John, fl 1818, d 1825, Eng, topog H

BUSNEL, Théophile, b St-Bréac-sur-Mer, Fr, fl 1904, d 1908, Fr, des illus K

BUTEAU, Augustin, b c 1830, d Longueuil, Que 1871, sculp K
BUTLER, J.W., fl 1837 8, Eng, topog H
BUTLER, Kenneth John (Jack), b Pittsburgh, Pa 1937– , paint M MM RCA
BUTLER, Ross, b Norwich, Ont 1907– , paint sculp CWW80
BUTLER, Sheila M., b 1938– , paint prt CAE2
BUTLER, William Francis, Lt Gen, Sir, b Suirville, Tipperary Co 1838, d Bansha Castle, Tipperary Co, Ire 1910, Irish, illus DNB H
BUTT, Sydney, b Carbonear, Nfld 1953– , paint DCA
BUTTERS, Edward, b England c 1843, fl 1861, glpt H
BUTTLE, John, b England, fl 1858–64, Eng, paint H
BUTTON, James Wilson, b Chicago 1917– , paint CWW64
BUYERS, Jane, b Toronto 1948– , etch paint IO
BY, John, Lt Col, b Lambeth/London 1779, d Frant, Sus 1836, Eng, paint topog CE1,2 Co DCB7 DNB EC H LeJ ROM W1-3
BYERS, John Robert Monk, b Brockville, Ont 1905– , paint M MM RCA
BYFORD, Josephine Gladys, b Toronto 1917– , drw paint IO
BYHRE, Dale, b New Westminster, BC 1956– , paint ABC
BYRNE, John L., b Ireland 1906– , fl 1940, paint M
BZDURRECK, Elke, b Minden, Ge 1946– , prt sculp CAE2

C

CABANE, Edouard-Louis-Lucien, b Paris 1857, fl 1899, Fr, paint B H K
CADDY, Edward C., b 1815, d 1897, paint DFA H WHC
CADDY, John Herbert, b Quebec 1801, d Hamilton, Ont 1883, paint topog CE2 DCB11 DeV5 DFA H ROM WHC
CADE, J.J., b Canada, fl 1890–1900, engr B F GW TB1 Y
CADOT, Mieke, b Amsterdam 1938– , mmed CAE1
CAHEN, Oscar, b Copenhagen 1916, d nr Oakville, Ont 1956, paint AGO CC2 CE1,2 H77 M NGC1,2 O.F51 RCA UG WWA59
CAHOON, Margaret Cecilia, b Hallowell Tp, PEI 1916– , paint CWW93
CAIBAIOSSI, Lloyd, b Spanish River Res, Ont 1947 – d 1975, paint Co
CAIN, Wendy J., b Ontario 1950– , prt IO
CAISERMAN, Ghitta (m Alfred Pinsky; m Maxwell W. Roth), b Montreal 1923– , paint prt AGO CA1 CC1 CE1,2 CLA CWW93 DCA M MM NGC1,2 RCA SC TB3 US WWA93
CAISSY, Richard, b Moncton, NB, fl 1976– , drgt DCA
CALDER, Art, b London 1893, paint WWNA
CALDWELL, Dorothy, b Bethesda, Md 1948– , drw paint IO
CALDWELL, Elizabeth A. (Mrs), fl 1894 1904, paint H MM RCA
CALDWELL, Robert Hampton, b 1945– , paint prt CAE1
CALDWELL, William Bletterman, Lt Col, b c 1798, d London 1882, Eng, paint DCB11 EC LeJ ROM W1-3
CALL, Frank Oliver, b W Brome, Que 1878, d Knowlton, Que 1956, paint Mo12 CWW52 MM
CALLEJA, Gina (m Joseph John Calleja, q.v.), b Lowestoft, Eng 1928– , illus C
CALLEJA, Joseph John (m Gina Calleja, q.v.), b Gozo, Malta 1924– , paint sculp IO M NGC2 RCA
CALLEN, Les, b Ignace, Ont 1905– , car Des
CALZETTA, Anthony (Tony), b Windsor, Ont 1945– , pas paint IO
CAM. *See* CARDOW, Cameron

CAMERON, A., fl c 1840s, Eng, car drw H KB
CAMERON, Alex, b 1947– , paint CAE2
CAMERON, Charles A., b Cornwall, Ont 1922– , paint ske CWW61
CAMERON, Donald Stewart, b Aberdeen, Scot 1866, fl 1941, paint H WWNA
CAMERON, Eric, b Leicester, Eng 1935– , paint DCA UG WWA93
CAMERON, Kenneth Aird, b Toronto 1919– , paint IO
CAMERON, Lilian T., fl 1897–1920, Eng, paint DBA H MM
CAMERON, Stewart, b Calgary 1912 – d 1970, cart Des
CAMILLE, Jean, b St-Jean-Port-Joli, Que 1920– , paint sculp M
CAML. *See* LYPCHUK, Camellia
CAMPBELL (of Campbell & Son), b Scotland, fl 1866–86, Scot, paint H
CAMPBELL, Alexander, b Victoria, BC 1853 – d 1943, paint H US
CAMPBELL, Alfred William, b Albion, Peel Co, Ont 1875, paint Hu
CAMPBELL, Archibald, Lord, b 1846, d 1913, Scot, illus paint BPp103 H WWW
CAMPBELL, Brenda, b Moose Jaw, Sask 1942– , tap AA
CAMPBELL, Colin Keith, b Reston, Man 1942– , sculp NGC2 WWA84
CAMPBELL, Daniel Edwin (Ted), b Fairville, NB 1904– , paint MA
CAMPBELL, David Alexander, b Victoria, BC 1918– , etch paint prt IO
CAMPBELL, David Owen, b Toronto 1949– , paint prt CAE1 IO
CAMPBELL, Dugald/Dougald, Lt, b Scotland 1758/9, d Fredericton 1810, drgt DCB5 H
CAMPBELL, Francis W., b Montreal 1837, fl 1903, ske H M98
CAMPBELL, Harriet Julia. *See* JEPHSON, Harriet Julia Campbell, Lady
CAMPBELL, Henriette Julie. *See* DUCHESNAY, Henriette Julie
CAMPBELL, James, b Glasgow 1907– , sculp ske CWW93
CAMPBELL, John, Gen, Sir, b 1807, d Crimea 1855, Eng, paint DNB H
CAMPBELL, John Douglas Sutherland. *See* ARGYLL, John Douglas Sutherland Campbell
CAMPBELL, Kathleen Louise. *See* PINKERTON, Kathleen Louise Campbell
CAMPBELL, Kathryn Isabelle (Kathy, Kay), b Windsor, Ont 1920– , etch paint IO
CAMPBELL, Leyda, b Vancouver 1949– , paint SC
CAMPBELL, Myfanwy. *See* PAVELIC, Myfanwy Spencer
CAMPBELL, Oreen Brown, b Des Moines, Iowa 1929– , paint UG
CAMPBELL, Paul, b 1949– , sculp DCA
CAMPBELL, Rosamond Sheila, b Bareilly, India 1919– , des paint MA WWA73
CAMPBELL, Sara Wendell, b Saint John, NB c 1886, d New York 1960, illus paint AAA32 DWA WWA59d62
CAMPBELL, Thomas Sebastian, b London 1951– , paint CWW93
CAMPBELL, Virginia A., b Saint John, NB 1930– , paint CWW93
CAMPBELL, William Allan, Maj, b Peterborough, Ont 1913– , paint CWW86
CAMPBELL-STARK, Laurel, b Toronto 1951– , illus paint DCA
CAMPING, Simon H., b Dockum, Neth, fl 1976– , paint SC
CANADA BANNER COMPANY. *See* RAPHAEL, Shirley; VENOR, Robert George
CANDILLE, Patrick, b Royan, Fr 1937– , paint CAE1
CANE, James, fl c 1837–41, ske H
CANN, Elizabeth Lovitt (Mrs), b Yarmouth, NS 1901– , paint CLA Hu M MA MM RCA
CANTELON, William Edgar, b 1866, d 1950, paint DFA

CANTERO, Antonio, b Ofena, It 1902– , paint CWW73
CANTIENI, Graham Alfred, b Albury, Aus 1938– , paint CAE1,2 WWA84
CANTIN, Pierre François Roland, b Mahebourg, Maur 1928– , paint CWW93
CANTINE, David, b Jackson, Mich 1939– , paint WWA93
CANTWELL, William, b Toronto 1845, fl 1893, paint H RCA
CAPE, Judith. *See* PAGE, Patricia Kathleen
CAPEL, Audrey. *See* DORAY, Audrey M. Capel
CAPEL, Reginald William Francis, b Bristol, Eng 1892, d 1962, paint Hu
CAPELLO/CAPPELLO, Luigi Giovanni Vitale (s Luigi G./Louis J. Capello), b Turin, It 1843, d Paris 1902, It, paint DCB13 H H77 MM RCA
CAPON, Inga, b England 1924– , sculp M
CAPREOL, Frederick Chase, b Bishops Stortford, Herts 1803, d Toronto 1886, paint DCB11 H
CAPUTO, Salvatore (Sam), b Italy 1950– , paint IO
CARBON, Jan, b Belgium 1942– , paint M
CARBONE, Frank J., b Thorold, Ont 1933– , sculp IO
CARBONNEAU, Alfred, b Quebec 1871, fl 1951, sculp K
CARBONNEAU, Joseph, fl 1890s, carv K
CARBONNEAU, Michel, b Quebec 1834/5, fl 1905, sculp K
CARBONNEAU, Paul-Emile, fl 1901, carv K
CARBONNEAU, Pierre, Capt, b Lévis, Que, fl 1880s, paint H K
CARDENAT, M. de, b Paris, fl 1675–85, Fr, paint H K
CARDERO/CORDERO[2], Manuel José (Josef/Joseph) Antonio, b Ecija, Sp 1766, d Sp c 1810, Sp, paint AC DCB5 EMA GW[2]
CARDIFF, M. Kathleen, b Edmonton 1913– , paint WWA62
CARDINAL, Jean Guy, Hon, b Montreal 1925– , paint CWW80
CARDINAL, Marcelin (Marcel), b Gravelbourg, Sask 1920– , paint WWA93
CARDOW, Cameron (Cam), b Ottawa 1960– , cart Po86–88
CAREY, Alice G. (Mrs), b Claresholm, Alta, fl 1930s, illus paint M
CAREY/CARY[2], Henry, fl 1879–88, Amer, paint F H[2] RCA
CAREY, Elizabeth. *See* FIELD, Elizabeth
CARIGNAN, Anatole, b Lachine, Que 1885, ske CWW49
CARIS, Jean, b 1934– , paint CAE1
CARLESS, Roy, b Swansea, Ont 1920– , cart Des
CARLETON, Edith, b Belfast, Ire 1900, paint M
CARLI, Alexandre, b Montreal 1861, d 1937, sculp K MM
CARLIE, Jacques (m Natcha Carlie, q.v.), b Bonnières-sur-Seine, Fr 1890, d Paris 1976, Fr, paint K
CARLIE, Natcha (m Jacques Carlie, q.v.), fl 1931, paint K
CARLISLE, Mary Helen, b Grahamstown, SA 1869, d New York 1925, Eng, paint pas AAAd28 AC B DBA DVP DWA F G MM RA RCA TB1,2
CARLISLE, William Ogle, Maj, fl 1870–86, Eng, car topog Des DeV3,7,9 H H77 RCA
CARLYLE, Florence, b Galt, re Cambridge, Ont 1864, d Crowborough, Sus 1923, paint AAA06 B CC2 DBA DFP3 DVP DWA G H Hu M MM Mo98,12 NGC1,2 NGC68 R1 RA RCA TB3 W1–3
CARMICHAEL, Emma Mildred, b Toronto 1907– , paint Hu
CARMICHAEL, Franklin, b Orillia, Ont 1890, d Toronto 1945, paint prt

AE AGO CC2 CE1,2 Co CWW38 EC GM H77 Hu M NGC1,2 NGC67 PMC RCA S TB3 TN UG W2–3

CARMICHEL, Robert Ralph, b Sault Ste Marie, Ont 1937– , des paint CAE1 CWW93

CARMIENCKE, Johann Hermann, b Hambourg 1810, d Brooklyn, NY 1867, Dan, paint B Bry F GW H TB1

CARON, Charles, fl 1857–82, paint H K

CARON, Josephine Marie de Blois. *See* BLOIS, Josephine Marie de

CARON, Marie, b 1947– , paint CAE2

CARON, Paul Archibald Octave, b Montreal 1874 – d 1941, paint prt CC1 CNS40 GM Hu K M MM NGC1,2 PMC RCA TB3

CARPENTIER, Hector, fl 1814–15, paint K

CARR, Donald F., b Toronto 1944– , drw paint prt IO UG

CARR, Emily, b Victoria, BC 1871 – d 1945, paint AAW2 ACA AGO B CC1 CE1,2 Co CWW48 Des DWA EC H77 Hu M NGC1,2 NGC67 OC OCD P RCA S Sam TB2,3 TN W2–3 WWNA

CARR-HARRIS, Ian Redford, b Victoria, BC 1941– , paint sculp CA3 CAE1,2 CWW93 DCA IO NGC2 WWA93

CARREAU-KINGWELL, Arlette, b Montreal 1917– , prt tap CAE1

CARRIE, Caroline. *See* HILLYARD, Caroline Learoyd Carrie

CARRIER, Joseph, b England, fl 1900–7, paint H

CARRIER, Louise (m André Garant, q.v.), b Lévis, Que 1925, d Quebec 1976, drgt paint NGC2

CARROLL, Barbara, b Toronto 1952– , paint sculp DFA KB

CARRUTHERS, Eleanor Ruthwell, b Peterborough, Ont 1908– , paint Hu MM RCA

CARSE, Margaret Ruth Pringle, b Edmonton 1916– , sculp CWW93

CARSON, Anita Pauline Jenner (Mrs), b Ottawa 1920– , paint M MM RCA

CARSON, Mary. *See* PACEY, Mary Elizabeth Carson

CARSWELL, Edward, b Ware, Eng 1832, paint Mo98

CARTER, Alexander Scott, b Harrow, Eng 1881, d Toronto 1968, des illum CC2 CNS40 CWW61 M NGC1,2 O.N48 PMC RCA WBA1

CARTER, Augusta Helene, b Toronto c 1887, d New York 1960, illus AAA32 DWA WWA59d62

CARTER, Don, b 1933– , paint ABC

CARTER, Dorothy Frances Colley (m A.M.W. Carter), b Stevenage, Herts 1903– , paint MM O.My50 RCA

CARTER, Dudley Christopher, b New Westminster, BC 1891, d Redmond, Wash 1992, sculp AAA33 AC BCS DAS TB2 WWA91d93 WWNA

CARTER, Elizabeth A., fl 1880–9, paint DWA H MM RCA

CARTER, George Ian, b Woodford, Essex 1942– , paint CWW93

CARTER, Harriet Estelle Manore (m John G. Carter), b Grand Bend, Ont 1929– , paint CAE1 CWW93 IO S WWA93

CARTER, Henry Thomas[2], b Belfast 1850, d Falmouth, Eng 1931, Irish, paint H[2] MM RCA WWB29

CARTER, Louisa C., fl 1891–9, paint DWA H

CARTER, Margaret H., b Vancouver 1911– , paint WWNA

CARTER, Robert P., b Sarnia, Ont 1950– , paint IO S

CARTER, Samuel John, b Des Moines, Iowa 1943– , paint sculp WWA93

CARTER, Thomas Henry. *See* CARTER, Henry Thomas

CARTMELL, Alban/Albin, b 1871, d 1957, paint DFA

CARTWRIGHT, Harriet Dobbs. *See* DOBBS, Harriet

CARTWRIGHT, Peggy (m Phil Baker), b Vancouver 1912, d 1953, paint CWW52

CARUSO, Barbara Ann, b Kincardine, Ont 1937– , paint CAE1,2 IO RCA

CARVER, Humphrey Stephen Mumford, b Birmingham, Eng 1902– , paint CWW93

CARY, Amelia Fitzclarence. *See* FALKLAND, Amelia Fitzclarence

CARY, Henry. *See* CAREY, Henry

CARY, William de la Montagne, b 1840, d Brookline, Mass 1922, Amer, illus AAW1 GW H McC Y

CASEY, Lucille C. (m Evender C. Kennedy; m John Adolphus Alexander MacArthur^2), b USA 1844, d 1902, bu London, Ont, paint DCB13 H^2 RCA^2

CASPROWITZ, George, b Los Angeles 1940– , paint prt CAE1,2

CASS, Mary Helena. *See* ATKINSON, Mary Helena Cass

CASSAN, Vival, fl 1876–83, engr DeV3 H K

CASSON, Alfred Joseph, b Toronto 1898 – d 1992, paint AE AGO B CC2 CE1,2 Co CWW91 DBA DCA EC FCA GM H77 IO M NGC1,2 NGC67 NGC68 O.My52 RCA S TB2,3 TN UG WWA62 WWC69

CASTAIGNE, J. André, b Angoulème, Fr 1861, d Paris 1929/30, Fr, paint B K TB1

CASTEL, Madeline, fl 1913–15, paint K MM

CASTLE & SON, fl 1879–1900, stgl H MM

CASTLE, Montague, b Montreal, d c 1949, paint stgl AAA21 F H MM RCA WWAd49

CASTONGUAY, Claude, b Quebec 1929– , paint CWW93

CATALOGNE, Gédéond (s Catalougne), b Arthez, Béarn, Fr 1662, d Louisbourg, NS 1729, crto DCB2 DeV3 EC LeJ W1–3

CATHCART, Charles Murray, 2nd Earl Cathcart, b Wolton, Essex 1783, d St Leonard-on-Sea, Sus 1859, Eng, paint BPp499 CE1,2 DCB8 DNB DP EC H W1–3

CATTELL, Raymond Victor, b Birmingham, Eng 1921– , paint CAE1 IO RCA S SC WWA93

CAUCHON, Olivier, fl 1875–89, paint K

CAUCHON, Robert, b c 1914, d 1969, paint DFA KB

CAUCHON dit LAVERDIERE, Charles-Honoré. *See* LAVERDIERE, Charles-Honoré

CAUDLE, Nancy Mary, b Cam, Glos, 1908– , paint O.My49 RCA

CAVAEL, Jackie, b Hamilton, Ont 1955– , paint prt CAE1

CAVALLI, Roger, b Liézey-Gerardmer, Fr 1930– , sculp CAE1

CAVALLO, Bruno, b Alberta 1913– , paint IO

CAVELTI, Peter Christian, b Switzerland 1948– , paint CWW91

CAWTHRA, Ann Mabel. *See* ADAMSON, Ann Mabel Cawthra

CAYLEY, Frank, b Russia, fl mid 19th cen, paint H

CAYLEY, William, b St Petersburg 1807, d Toronto 1890, paint DCB11 EC H W1–3

CELESTINO, Mary, b Windsor, Ont 1938– , paint IO

CERAT, Joseph, fl 1875, sculp K

CETIN, Anton, b Bojana, Yu 1936– , paint prt CAE1,2 CWW93 IO WWA93

CHABAUTY, Charles Ed, fl 1901–46, paint K MM RCA

CHABERT, Joseph, Abbé, b Lauris, Fr 1831, d Longue-Pointe, nr Montreal 1894, paint DCB12 H H77 K

CHABOULIE/CHABOILLEZ, Charles, b St-Rémi, Troyes, Fr c 1637/54, d Montreal 1708, carv DCB2 K NGC67

CHABOYER, Véronique (Soeur Marie-Cléonice de Saint-Sacrement), b St Laurent, Man 1880, d Ste-Anne-de-Beaupré, Que 1961, paint K

CHADWICK, Maurice, b Victoria, BC, fl 1968– , paint ABC
CHAKI, Yehuda Leon (b Sciaky), b Athens, Gr 1938– , paint CWW93
CHALIFOUX, J.B., fl 1826–8, des H K
CHALKE, John, b Glos, Eng 1940– , sculp AA DCA WWA93
CHALLENER, Frederick Sproston, b Whetstone, Eng 1869, d Toronto 1959, paint AGO B CC1 CWW55 FCA H77 M MM Mo12 NGC1,2 NGC68 O.Ag51 PMC RCA TB1 W2–3 WBA2 WWA59
CHALMERS, Audrey McEvers, b Montreal 1893, d Washington, DC 1957, illus ICB1
CHALMERS, Roland John Anderson, b Rochester, Kent 1884, drw etch MM PMC RCA
CHAMBERLAIN, Arthur B., b Kitchener, Ont 1860, paint AAA33 F Y
CHAMBERLIN, Agnes Dunbar Moodie (m Charles Fitz Gibbon; m Brown Chamberlin^2), b nr Cobourg, Ont 1833, d Toronto 1913, paint EC H H77 Mo98^2,12
CHAMBERS, Frank Pentland, b England 1900, Eng, sculp B DBA MM RA RCA TB2 WWB29
CHAMBERS, John Richard (Jack), b London, Ont 1931 – d 1978, paint AGO CA1 CC2 CE1,2 Co CWW70 H77 IO M MM NGC2 NGC67 RCA UG WWA78d80
CHAMBERS, Merton Francis, b Exeter, Ont 1929– , mur CAE1 IO
CHAMBERS, Robert William, b Wolfville, NS 1905– , cart Des WWA62
CHAMPAGNE, Fortunat, fl 1936+, cal illum K
CHAMPAGNE, Jean-Serge, b 1945– , sculp CAE1
CHAMPAGNE, Michel, b Montreal 1940– , engr paint CAE1 M
CHAMPLAIN, Samuel de, b Brouage (Saintonge), Fr c 1567, d Quebec 1635, Fr, drgt paint App CE1,2 DCB1 DeV9 DFA EC H K LeJ
CHAMPLAIN, Serge, b Montreal 1945– , cart Des
CHANDLER, Kenelm, fl 1784–1804, Eng, paint DFA H ROM
CHAPDELAINE, Flavien-Norbert, b St-François-du-Lac, Que 1859, d Montreal 1926, paint H K MM
CHAPDELAINE, Jacques, b Montreal 1932– , sculp DMS
CHAPLEAU, Serge, b Montreal 1945– , cart Des Po86–87
CHAPLIN, A.M. (Mrs), fl 1882–92, paint H MM
CHAPLIN, Carl, b 1946– , paint ABC
CHAPLIN, Millicent Mary (s MMC) (m Thomas Chaplin, Lt Col), fl 1838–44, paint DFA H PNL ROM WHC
CHAPMAN, Charles, b Norfolk, Eng 1827, d 1887, paint H
CHAPMAN, Cyrus Durand, b Irvington, NJ 1856 – d 1918, Amer, paint AAA18d28 B DFA F H
CHAPMAN, Ottis F. (Otto), fl 1880–92, paint AAW3 H
CHAPMAN, Walter, fl 1899–1915, paint H
CHAPPEL, Alonzo, b New York 1828, d Long Isld, NY 1887, Amer, paint GW WHC Y
CHAPPELL, Edward, Lt Col, b England 1792 – d 1861, Eng, paint DeV4
CHAPPELL, John L., b Yorkshire 1805, d 1878, carv DFA KB
CHAPPELLE, Margaret Morgan (m G.F. Chappelle), b Winnipeg 1919– , paint sculp M MM
CHARBONNEAU, Monique, b Montreal 1928– , paint prt MM NGC2 RCA
CHAREST, Elzéar, fl 1877–1914, cal paint H K
CHARETTE, Joseph, fl 1872–95, min paint K
CHARETTE, Luc A., b Edmundston, NB 1952– , sculp CAE1 CWW93

CHARLEBOIS, Charles-Théophile, fl 1877–93, paint H K
CHARLEBOIS, Joseph-Charles-Théophile (s Basili), b Montreal 1872 – d 1935, car illus Des K MM RCA
CHARLESON, Malcolm Daniel, b Manitoba 1880, illus paint AAA23 TB2
CHARLIE, Inukpuk, E9-906, b Port Harrison, Que 1941– , sculp DEA
CHARLIE, Kittosuck, E9-109, b Belcher Islds 1927– , sculp DEA
CHARLIE, Shegoapik (aka Sivuarapik), E9-1460, b Povungnituk, Que 1911, d 1968, sculp DEA
CHARLOT, Jean, b Paris 1898, d Honolulu 1979, Amer, illus paint sculp AAW1 B F IBYP K SAA8 TB2 WWA78d80 WWWA
CHARMOY, Cozette de, b London 1939– , paint prt MM NGC2
CHARNAY, Claude-Joseph-Désiré, b Fleurie, Fr 1828, d Paris 1915, Fr, drw K
CHARNETSKI, John A., b Edmonton 1935– , paint CAE1,2
CHARNEY, Melvin, b Montreal 1935– , sculp CE1,2 MM WWA93
CHARPENTIER, Louis, b Montreal 1947– , paint CAE1,2
CHARRON, Adélard Emile, b Ottawa 1878, fl 1891–1904, paint H K
CHARRON, Amable, b Varennes, Que 1785, d St-Jean-Port-Joli, Que 1844, carv DCB7 K
CHARTIER, Albert, b Quebec 1912– , illus WECo
CHARTIER, Eutrope, b 1831, fl 1861–77, sculp K
CHARTRAND dit VINCENNES, Vincent, b St-Vincent-de-Paul, Laval, Que 1795 – d 1863, carv paint DCB9 H K NGC2
CHASSEUR, Pierre Dangueusé dit le, b Beaumont, Que 1786, d Quebec 1842, sculp DCB7 K
CHASTELAIN, Alfred John Gardyne Drummond de[2], b Bucharest 1937– , paint CWW93[2]
CHATEAUVERT, Georges, fl 1890–1900, engr H K
CHATFIELD, Edward, b England 1802, d 1839, Eng, paint B G GW H TB1
CHATFIELD, Thomas Frederick Haig, b Toronto 1921– , paint IO SC
CHATILLON, Claude, b Ottawa 1917– , paint CWW82
CHAUCHETIERE, Claude, b St-Porchaire-de-Poitiers, Fr 1645, d Quebec c 1709, paint CE1,2 DCB2 H H77 K
CHAUSSEGNOS de LERY, Joseph Gaspard. *See* LERY, Joseph Gaspard Chaussegros de
CHAVEL, David James, b Woodstock, Ont 1942– , paint UG
CHAVIGNAUD, Christine, b Toronto 1897, paint Hu
CHAVIGNAUD, Georges, b Lanvéoc, nr Brest, Fr 1865, d Meadowvale, Ont 1944, paint AGO H Hu K M MM Mo12 NGC1,2 PMC RCA S TB3
CHEE CHEE, Benjamin (b Kenneth Thomas Benjamin), b Temagami, Ont 1944, d Ottawa 1977, paint CE1,2 Co
CHEESMAN, Elizabeth Steeves. *See* KETURAH, Elizabeth Steeves
CHEFF, Michel Vincent, b Ottawa 1950– , drw paint IO
CHENEY, Anna Gertrude Lawson (Nan) (m Hill Harrison Cheney), b Windsor, NS 1897, d Vancouver 1985, paint NGC2 WWNA
CHENIER, Richard (Rick), b Edmonton 1945– , paint AA
CHERRY, Aileen Alma, b Belleville, Ont 1896 – d 1957, paint Hu RCA
CHERRY, Edward J., b England 1886, d Vancouver 1960, etch US
CHESTER, Donovan T., b Saskatchewan 1940– , paint WWA76
CHESTER, Harry George, Capt, fl 1850s, paint topog DFA H
CHESTER, John William, b Liverpool 1884, d 1928, paint Hu

CHESTERTON, David, b Leicester, Eng 1930, d c 1980, gra WWA78d80
CHESTERTON, Walter, b London 1845, d Ottawa 1931, paint DFA H MM RCA
CHEVRE, Paul-Romain, b Brussels 1867, d 1914, sculp B K TB1
CHEVRETTE, Omer, Rev, b Fall River, Mass 1889, fl 1957, paint K
CHEWETT, Jocelyn, b Weston, Ont 1906– , sculp DMS
CHEWETT, William, Col, b London 1753, d Toronto 1849, paint H
CHIARANDINI, Albert, b Udine, It 1915– , paint WWA76
CHIASSON, Hermenegilde, b St Simon, NB 1946– , paint DCA
CHICOINE, Owen Alexander, b Belle-Anse, Que 1916, d Mont-St-Hilaire, Que 1982, paint CAE1 MM
CHICOINE, René, b Montreal 1905 – d 1981, paint MM RCA WWA78
CHILDS, Jeffrey Beaumont, b Long Isld, NY 1950– , sculp IO
CHIRIAEFF, Alexis, b Nice, Fr 1913, fl 1951– , paint B UG
CHIVERS, Denise May, b Winnipeg 1927– , paint M
CHIVERS, Ernest, b Newport, Eng 1894, paint M
CHISHOLM, Geraldine Major. *See* MAJOR, Geraldine
CHOATE, Richard F., b Warsaw, Ont 1880, paint CWW61
CHOUINARD, François, Père, b St-Patrice-de-la Rivière-du-Loup, Que 1830, d Ste-Marie-de-Beaverville, Que 1905, paint H K
CHOW, Raymond, b Vancouver 1941– , paint CAE1
CHRISTENSEN, Shirley Maureen, b Calgary 1955– , wlhg SC
CHRISTIANSEN, Liljan, b Aarhus, Dn, fl 1950s, paint ABC
CHRISTIE, Robert Duncan, b Saskatoon 1946– , paint US WWA93
CHRISTMAS, Henry, Rev, b 1811, d 1868, Eng, illus H
CHRISTOPHER, Ken, b Swift Current, Sask 1942– , paint CWW93 SC
CHRISTY, James Richard (b Christinzio), b Richmond, Va 1945– , paint sculp CWW93
CHRONES, Mary Louise Killey (Lou) (m John D. Chrones), b Saskatoon 1933– , paint BDSA
CHRONES, Matina Prassa (m James Chrones), b Swift Current, Sask 1932– , paint BDSA IO US
CHRYSTAL, Arthur, b Edinburgh 1904– , etch paint WWA62
CHU, Gene, b Kwongtong, Chi 1936– , paint prt CAE1 IO UG WWA93
CHUBB, Bryan, b Edmonton 1947– , paint prt DCA
CHUNG HUNG[2], Allan, b Canton, Chi 1946, d 1994, bu Vancouver, sculp BCS CWW93 RCA[2]
CHURCH, Elsie G., b Calgary 1897, paint AAW3 WWNA
CHURCH, Frederick Edwin, b Hartford, Conn 1826, d New York 1900, Amer, paint AAAd28 ANC App B BE Bry DAA DAB DMA DSP F G GW H L NCAB20 TB1,2 WWWA Y
CICANSKY, Frank (b Czekanski), b Romania 1900, d Regina 1982, paint DFA
CICANSKY, Victor, b Regina 1935– , sculp CAE1,2 CWW93 DFA US WWA93
CICCIMARA, Richard Matthew, b Vienna 1924, d Greece 1973, paint NGC2
CINQ-MARS, Alonzo, b St-Edouard-de-Lotbinière, Que 1881, d 1969, sculp K MM
CINQ-MARS, Clement, b 1918– , carv DFA KB
CINTRAT, A.R., fl 1886–95, sculp K
CIRIER, Antoine, b Montreal 1718, d Pointe-aux-Trembles, nr Montreal 1798, carv DCB4 K
CIRIER, Martin, b Pointe-aux-Trembles, nr Montreal 1678 – d 1751, sculp K

CLAQUE, John, fl 1897, paint H
CLAPP, Victor, b Cranbrook, BC 1942– , prt AA
CLAPP, William Henry, b Montreal 1879, d Oakland, Calif 1954, paint AAA33 AAW2 AC B F H77 Hu M MM NGC1,2 RCA TB2,3 WWA56 Y
CLARK, Brenda (m Robert J. Courtice), b Toronto 1955– , illus C CWW93
CLARK, Frank B., fl 1892–7, paint H
CLARK, Kelvin William David (Kelly), b St Boniface, Man 1935– , paint prt M NGC2
CLARK, Moira, b Toronto 1950– , etch IO
CLARK, Paraskeva Avdyerna Plistik (m Orestes Allegre; m Philip Clark), b St Petersburg 1898, d Toronto 1986, paint AGO CC1 CE1,2 Co DWA IO M MM NGC1,2 NGC68 O.My49 RCA TB2,3 TN WWA80
CLARKE, Ann (aka Darrah[2]), b Norwich, Eng 1944– , paint AA CAE1,2[2] DCA WWA93
CLARKE, B. Stanley, fl 1897–1902, paint H MM RCA
CLARKE, Collins[1]/Colin C.[2], b Nova Scotia c 1842, fl 1860–9, engr litho GW H[1,2]
CLARKE, Douglas Burns, b Montreal 1907– , paint sculp CWW80
CLARKE, Henrietta Burchell (m W.E. Clarke), b Sydney, NS 1886, paint MA
CLARKE, James Cummings, Lt Col, b 1827, fl 1877, topog H
CLARKE, Louise Waldorf, b Labrador c 1838, fl 1900, paint DWA H
CLARKE, Peter Merry, b 1940– , paint CAE1,2
CLARKE, Rigmor Ulla Tatty-Jana Widell (m John Frederick Clarke), b Lindsberg, Swe 1935– , paint BDSA
CLARKE, Ronald John Kennedy, b Toronto 1945– , paint CWW93
CLARKE, Stanley E., b Saint John, NB, fl 1930+, paint CLA
CLARKE, Sylvia Mary Lowther, b Cavendish, Eng 1911– , paint IO
CLARKE, William Pardoe, fl 1840s, paint DeV4 H
CLASS, Gerhard Hans, b Germany 1924– , sculp BCS
CLAVERT, François-Xavier, b Quebec 1830/1, fl 1861–91, paint K
CLAYTON, Charles O., b Canada c 1830, fl 1863, engr GW H
CLAYTON, V.G., Lt, fl 1868–70, Eng, topog H
CLEAVER, Elizabeth Ann Mrazik, b Montreal 1937 – d 1985, gra illus CBC CE2 ICB4 JAI4 RCA SAA23d43 WWA82
CLEFF, Ernest, fl 1874–80, paint sculp H K
CLEGG, J. (or T.) William, fl 1827–32, topog DFA H
CLEGHORN, James G.T., b Scotland 1844, d Winnipeg 1936, paint DFA
CLELAND, Isabel E., b New York 1908– , paint M UG
CLELAND, Mary Alberta, b Montreal 1876, d Cushing, Que 1960, paint sculp AAA01 DWA Hu M MM NGC1,2 RCA TB3
CLEMENS, Isaac, fl 1776–95, engr F GW H
CLEMENTI, Vincent, b London 1812, d Peterborough, Ont 1899, paint DFA H ROM
CLEMENTS, William Albert, b Toronto 1921– , sculp M RCA
CLEMES, Mary Bertha Williams[2] (m Walter Herbert Clemes), b Mitchell, Ont 1868, paint CNS36 Hu RCA[2]
CLEMES, Patricia (m Thomas La Pierre[2], q.v.), b Los Angeles 1935– , paint IO[2]
CLENCH, Harriet. *See* KANE, Harriet Clench
CLERK, Pierre Jean, b Atlanta, Ga 1928– , paint prt sculp DCAA2,3 NGC2 TB3 WWA86
CLERMONT, Monick, b Lévis, Que 1942– , paint CAE1
CLEVE, James Van, b Lawrenceville,

NJ 1808, d Sandwich, Ont 1888, paint DMA

CLEW, J.S. *See* CLOW/CLOWS/CLEW, Clephan J.

CLIFF, Denis Anthony, b Victoria, BC 1942– , paint CWW84 IO RCA WWA93

CLIFFORD, Henry, fl 1856–66, paint DBMaP DSP

CLIFFORD, Mary Jane Hélène. *See* BILLAUX, Mary Jane Hélène

CLIFTON, John Terrence, b Peterborough, Ont 1933– , des CWW93 RCA

CLIMO, Lindee Lawrence, b Norwood, Mass 1948– , illus paint CBC CWW93

CLINCH, Esther Leonora (Nora). *See* STREETON, Esther Leonora Clinch (Nora)

CLINE, C.H., fl 1882–5, paint H

CLOBAN, Clara MacGowan. *See* MacGOWAN, Clara

CLOTHIER, Robert Allan, b Prince Rupert, BC 1921– , sculp CWW93

CLOUGH, Gibson, b 1738, d 1799, Eng, ske DFA H74 KB

CLOUD. *See* BIDNER, Thomas Michael

CLOUTIER, Albert-Edouard, b Leominster, Mass 1902, d St-Hilaire, Que 1965, illus paint CC2 CNS40 CWW67 Hu M MM NGC1,2 NGC68 RCA TB3 W3 WWA62

CLOUTIER, L. Arsène, fl 1885–90, paint H K

CLOW/CLOWS/CLEW, Clephan J. John J.S., b Europe c 1790, fl 1831–50, min paint DeV9 Fo GW H H77

CLUTESI, George Charles, b Port Alberni, BC 1905, d Victoria, BC 1988, paint CBC CE1,2 Co

CLYMER, John Ford, b Ellensburg, Wash 1907– , paint Hu M MM RCA Sam WWA86

CMM. *See* MORGAN-McNEIL, Charlotte

COALLIER, Jean Pierre, b Montreal 1937– , cart Des

COAST, Oscar Regan, b Salem, Oreg 1851, d Santa Barbara, Calif 1931, Amer, paint AAA31 AAW1 AC B F H Sam TB3 Y

COATES, Edmund C. (aka Edward), b England 1816, d Brooklyn, NY 1871, Eng, paint DFA GW H NGC2 WHC

COATES, Richard, b Thornton, Yorks 1778, d Ontario 1868, paint DFA H H77 KB

COATES, Ross Alexander, b Hamilton, Ont 1932– , paint DCAA2,3 WWA93

COBURN, Frederick Simpson (m Malvina S. Coburn, q.v.), b Upper-Melbourne, Que 1871 – d 1960, paint AGO CC2 CE1,2 CNS40 CWW58 FCA H77 Hu ICB1 M MM Mo12 NGC1,2 RCA TB3 W2–3 WWA53

COBURN, Malvina Schiepers (m Frederick Simpson Coburn[2], q.v.), b Belgium, d 1933, paint CNS40[2] M[2] MM RCA

COBURN-DONNELLY, Kay, b Carman, Man 1935– , paint SC

COCHAND, Pierre-Henri, b Ste-Marguerite-Station, Que 1924– , paint NGC1,2 MM

COCHRANE, Bertha L., fl 1891–1915, paint AAA01 DFA DWA H MM RCA

COCHRANE, Josephine G., b Philadelphia, fl c 1912, Amer, paint AAA31 B DWA F MM WWA40

COCKAYNE, George, b 1906– , paint DFA

COCKBURN, Charles Frederick, Capt, b Quebec 1830, d 1908, Eng, paint DFA WHC

COCKBURN, James Pattison, Maj Gen, b New York 1779, d Woolwich, Eng 1847, Eng, paint topog B Bry CE2 Co DBLP DBMP DBWA DCB7 DeV5,7 DFA DMA DNB GW H H77 MQ NGC2 NGC67 PNL Red ROM TB1 UG WHC

COCKBURN, Jean Elizabeth. *See* MUNRO, Jean Elizabeth Cockburn

COCKBURN, John Henry (s J.H.C.), fl 1801–37, Eng, paint topog DFA H WHC

CODE, Ernva Willard (m F. Leslie), b Toronto 1900– , paint WWNA
CODY, Norman Redmond, b Saint John, NB 1914– , paint CLA MA
COFFIN, Irene (m Carl C. Coffin), b Russia 1909– , paint pas M
COGGINS, Dan, b Saskatoon 1954– , gra US
COGILL, Bobs (Zema). *See* HAWORTH, Zema Barbara Cogill (Bobs)
COHEN, Frederick E., b England, fl 1837 55, Eng, paint DFA GW H Y
COHEN, Nina Fried (m Harry Cohen), b Glace Bay, NS 1907– , paint CWW93
COHEN, Roslyn, b Montreal 1939– , enam paint IO
COHEN, Sorel, b Montreal 1936– , gra WWA93
COKE, Edward Thomas, b England 1807, d 1888, Eng, illus topog GW H
COLBECK, Edna Honeyford, b Grand Valley, Ont 1892, d Regina 1977, paint BDSA
COLBERT, Edouard-Charles-Victurnien, Count de Maulevrier, b Paris 1758, d France 1820, Fr, paint DMA GW H K
COLE, Joan Jeanette, b Chicago 1940– , paint IO
COLE, Florence Thompson Trenholme. *See* TRENHOLME, Florence Thompson
COLE, Thomas, b Bolton-le-Moors, Lancs 1801, d nr Catskill, NY 1848, Amer, paint ANC Bry DAB DBLP F G GW TB1 WWWA
COLEMAN, Arthur Philemon, b Lachute, Que 1852, d Toronto 1939, paint AE CWW38 H MM Mo98,12 RCA Sam
COLERIDGE, Francis George, Capt, b England 1838 – d 1923, Eng, cart paint APH DBA DVP G H
COLEMAN, Edward Thomas (aka Edmund), b England 1821, d London 1892, Eng, paint AAW1 B DVP G H ROM Sam TB1
COLIN/COLLIN[2], François, b 1818, d Ste-Rose, Que 1879, paint H[2] K NGC2
COLLACUT, Susan Elizabeth. *See* RIVAIT, Susan Elizabeth Collacut
COLLIER, Alan Caswell, b Toronto 1911, d North York, Ont 1990, paint AGO CC1 CWW90 IO M MM NGC1,2 O.Ag49 RCA S SC TB1 UG WWA91d93
COLLIER, Vincent. *See* COLYER/COLLIER, Vincent
COLLIN, Celia, fl 1969– , paint ABC
COLLINGS, Charles John, b Chudleigh, Dev 1848, d Seymour Arm, Shuswap Lake, BC 1931, paint B DBA DBWA DVP G H Hu M NGC1,2 RA Sam TB1,3
COLLINS, Bonita, b Detroit 1939– , paint sculp IO
COLLINS, Edna Gertrude, b Toronto 1885, paint AAW3
COLLINS, Fred L., b Prince Edward Isld 1876, paint AAA32
COLLINS, Heather (m Blair Kerrington), b Montreal 1946– , illus C
COLLINS, John Alton, b Washington, DC 1917– , cart CWW82 Des MM RCA
COLLINS, Norbert J., b Toronto 1909– , paint IO
COLLINSON, Richard, Adm, Sir, b Gateshead, Eng 1811, d Ealing, London 1883, Eng, paint DCB11 DMA DNB
COLLYER, Nora Frances Elizabeth, b Montreal 1898, d 1979, paint CLA DWA Hu M MM RCA
COLLYER, Robin John, b London 1949– , sculp CAE1,2 DCA IO NGC2 WWA93
COLMAN, Alfred Russell, b Lewes, Sus 1844, d Jarvis, Ont 1929, paint DFA UG
COLMAN/COLEMAN, Samuel, b Portland, Me 1832, d New York 1920,

Amer, etch paint AAAd28 AAW3 ANC App AW B BE DAB DMA F GW NCAB7 Sam TB1,3 WWWA Y
COLOMBIER, G. (1898 m Lucien Chevalier), fl 1891–5, paint DWA H K
COLONNA, Eugène/Edward/Edmond (b Klonne), b Mulheim-am-Rhein, Ge 1862, d Nice, Fr 1948, Ge, des paint H MM RCA TB1
COLOVIC, Misa, b Kragusevac, Yu 1944– , paint IO
COLSON, Frederick, b Shedfield, Hants 1854, d 1924, paint CWW10 H MM RCA
COLTON, Alfred Stanley, b Toronto 1921– , paint M
COLVILLE, Charles John, Baron, 1st Viscount Colville of Culross, b England 1818 – d 1903, Eng, paint BPp615 DP H ROM WWA
COLVILLE, David Alexander, b Toronto 1920– , paint ACA AGO B CA3 CC1 CE1,2 CLA Co CWW93 DCA L M MA MM NGC1,2 NGC67 NGC68 OC P RCA TB3 UG WWA91 WWC89
COLVILLE, William James, Col, Hon Sir, b Kensington, London 1827, d London 1903, Eng, paint BPp615 WHC WWW
COLWILL, Gary Russell, b Britain 1944– , paint IO
COLYER/COLLIER, Vincent, b Bloomingdale, NY 1825, d Contentment Isld, nr Darien, Conn 1888, Amer, litho paint AAW1 AC ANC B F GW H Sam TB1 Y
COMFORT, Charles Fraser, b Edinburgh 1900, d Ottawa 1994, paint ACA AE AGO APH B CC2 CE1,2 CWW93 DBA EC GM H77 Hu M NGC1,2 NGC67 NGC68 O.Ag49 RCA S TB2,3 TN WWA66 WWB72
COMINGO, Joseph Brown, b Lunenburg, NS 1784, d Nassau, Bah 1821, min paint DCB6 H H77
COMPTON, Anna Rockwell (m Carrier; m Charles Reid Compton), b Port Hope, Ont 1853, d 1928, paint H
COMPTON, P.M., b 1838, d 1897, paint DFA H
COMTOIS, Louis, b Montreal 1945, d New York 1990, paint sculp MQ
COMTOIS, Ulysse (m Rita Letendre, q.v.), b Granby, Que 1931– , paint sculp AE AGO CC1 CE1 M NGC2 NGC67 S TB3
CONDE, Carole Bernice (m Karl John Beveridge, q.v.), b Hamilton, Ont 1940– , paint sculp IO
CONDON, Kathryn E. Brown (Mrs), b Wolfville, NS, fl 1908+, paint AAA28
CONDON, Wanda Koop. *See* KOOP, Wanda
CONDY, Gordon Stanley, b Toronto 1928– , paint IO
CONDY, Roy, b Dagenham, Eng, fl 1968– , illus C
CONKLIN, George P. (s G.P.C.), fl 1848–56, engr paint H
CONNELL, William, fl 1834–7, engr paint H
CONNOLLY, Joseph Emile Reynald, b Montreal 1944– , paint prt NGC2 UG
CONNON, Thomas, b Udny, Scot 1832, d Elora, Ont 1899, paint DCB12 H UG
CONSTABLE, Mike, b Woodstock, Ont 1943– , cart Des Po86–88
CONSTANTIN-WEYER, Maurice, b Bourbonne-les-Bains, Fr 1881, d Vichy, Fr 1964, Fr, paint K
CONTANT, Edgar, b 1883, d 1944, paint K MM RCA
COOK, David, b Kingston, Ont 1947– , paint IO
COOK, Evelyn Margaret (Lyn) (m Robb Waddell), b Weston, Ont 1918– , paint CWW93
COOK, Louise Goota (m David Cook, q.v.), b Fir Ridge, Sask 1943– , paint BDSA
COOK/COOKE, Nelson, b nr Ballston Spa, NY 1817, d Saratoga Springs, NY 1892, Amer, paint AGO DFA GW H H74 H77 KB NGC2 Y
COOKE, Edwy Francis, b Toronto

1926– , paint AGO IO M MM O.F49 RCA TB3 WWA80

COOKE, Helen Agatha Becker (m John Cooke), b Macklin, Sask 1936– , mmed BDSA

COOKE, Jane Ann Millar (m John Valentine Cooke, Jr), d Drummondville, Que c 1885, paint DeV2 H

COOMBER, George, b Hagersville, Ont 1935– , prt IO

COOMBS[1], Edith Grace (m James Sharp Lawson[2]), b Hamilton, Ont 1890, d St Catharines, Ont 1986, paint stgl AE CC1 CNS40 CWW73 DWA[1,2] M MM O.N47 RCA S UG WWA66

COONAN, Geraldine Emily, b Montreal 1885 – d 1971, paint DWA NGC1,2 RCA TB3

COOPER, Barbara Ann, b Cuba 1935– , paint IO

COOPER, Colin Campbell (m Emma E.L. Cooper, q.v.), b Philadelphia 1856, d Santa Barbara, Calif 1937, Amer, paint AAA33 AAW1 AC B DBA F Sam WWA36 WWWA

COOPER, Emma Esther Lampert[2] (m Colin Campbell Cooper, q.v.), b Nunda, NY 1860, d Pittsfield, Mass 1920, Amer, paint AAAd28 AAW3 B DBA DWA F H[2] RCA[2] Sam TB1,3 WWWA Y

COOPER, Heather J., b Louth, Lincs 1945– , des illus CWW93 RCA WWC82

COOPER, Lynda Jane, b Windsor, Ont 1952– , etch paint IO

COOPER, Reed Talmage, b Hamilton, Ber 1931– , paint prt NGC2

COOPER, Sidney H., b London 1916– , paint CWW81

COOPER, Stanley Smith, b Leeds, Eng 1906– , paint O.My49 RCA

COOPER, Tony, b England 1950– , paint CAE1

COPE, Dorothy Walpole Stevens (m Clive A. Cope), b Vancouver 1915– (x 1925), paint CWW73 M MM WWA76

COPELAND, Ethel Ann Carson. *See* PLANTA, Ethel Ann Carson Copeland

COPELAND, Patrick Forbes, b London 1860, d Montreal 1933, illus paint H

COPPER, Wilhelmina Frederica. *See* SCHRYVERS, Wilhelmina Frederica Hendrika de Kan

COPPER THUNDERBIRD. *See* MORRISEAU, Norval

CORBEAU, Antoine, b Quebec 1778/9, d St-François, Lac-St-Pierre, Que 1839, sculp K

CORBEIL, Wilfred, Père, b St-Lin, Que 1893, d 1979, paint K MM

CORBY, John. *See* HOWARD, John George

CORKUM, Hilda Frances Corning (m Bertram K. Corkum), b Annapolis Royal, NS 1925– , paint M MA WWA66

CORMIER, Ernest, b Montreal 1885 – d 1980, paint sculp CE1,2 CNS36 CWW73 K MM NGC1,2 RCA

CORNEILLE, Mary, b 1917– , paint CAE1

CORNEIL, Samuel, fl 1851–64, paint H K

CORNELIUS, Louise, fl 1892, paint DWA H MM

CORNELL, Betty. *See* GALBRAITH, Elizabeth Roberta

CORNING, Hilda Frances. *See* CORKUM, Hilda Frances Corning

CORNU, Sophie (Mme), fl 1913–17, paint K MM

CORNWELL, Arthur Bruce b Victoria, BC 1920– , paint WWB92

COSGROVE, Stanley Morel, b Montreal 1911– , paint prt ACA AGO CC2 CE1,2 DCA M MM NGC1,2 NGC67 RCA SC TB3 WWA93 WWB68

COSGROVE, Theresa Lenore, b Port Arthur, Ont 1934– , paint IO

COTE. *See* BENGOUGH, John Wilson

COTE, Adélard, b Ste-Sophie, Que 1889, d Beddeford, Me 1974, sculp K

COTE, Alda, b Wottenville, Que 1900, d Edmonton 1962, paint K

COTE, Benoît, b Quebec Prov 1929– , paint M
COTE, Claude, b Quebec, fl 1922+, sculp K
COTE, Eugène, fl 1894, paint H K
COTE, Ferdinand, b Quebec 1842/4, fl 1871–1907, paint K
COTE, J.E., b c 1866, fl 1885, drgt paint H K
COTE, Jean-Baptiste (aka Grosperin[2]), b Quebec 1832 – d 1907, car engr illus paint sculp ACA DCB13 Des[2] DFA EC H H74 K KB MQ NGC1,2 NGC67 W1–3
COTE, Jean-Pierre, b Montreal 1926– , paint CWW93
COTE, Lucie, b Montreal, fl 1969– , paint sculp CAE1
COTE, Marc-Aurèle Suzor. *See* SUZOR-COTE, Marc-Aurèle de Foy
COTTET, Charles, b Puy, Fr 1863, d Paris c 1925, engr paint B K TB1
COTTON, John Wesley, b nr Dundas, Ont 1868/9, d Toronto 1931, etch paint AAA31d32 AAW1 AC AGO B F Hu MM NGC2 RCA Sam TB3
COTTON, W. Henry, b St Petersburg 1817, d Ottawa 1877, paint DFA H ROM
COUCILL, Irma Sophia Young (m Walter J. Coucill, q.v.), b London, Ont 1918– , paint CWW93
COUCILL, Walter Jackson (m Irma S.Y. Coucill, q.v.), b Camden, NJ 1915, d Toronto 1982, paint AGO CWW82 RCA
COUGHEY, Madeline Wood (1905 m Thomas J. Coughey), b Greenfield, Mass, fl 1940s, paint CLA
COUGHEY, Mary Wood. *See* HASHEY, Mary Wood Coughey
COUGHLIN, William Garnet (s Bing[2]), b Ottawa 1912– , fl 1982, car Des[2]
COUGHTRY, John Graham, b St-Lambert, Que 1931– , paint sculp AE AGO CAE1 CC1 CE1,2 Co DCA IO M MM NGC1,2 NGC67 RCA TB3 UG WWA86
COULING, Gordon Robert, b Guelph, Ont 1913, d 1984, paint O.Ag48 UG WWA76
COULON, Alphonse, fl 1859–70, drw H K
COULSON, Harry A., fl 1894, d 1897, paint H MM
COUPER, Charles Alexander, b Portsmouth, NH 1924– , paint WWA93
COUPER, William, fl 1862–5, paint H
COURCY, Michael John de, b Montreal 1944– , prt NGC2
COURMES, Alfred, b Bermes-les-Mimosas, Fr 1898, paint B K TB2
COURNOYER, Georges, b 1931– , paint sculp CAE1
COURSOLLES, J. Léandre, fl 1831–62, paint K
COURTEMARCHE, Adélard, b 1861, d 1957, sculp K
COURTICE, Rody Kenny Hammond (m Andrew Roy Courtice), b Renfrew, Ont 1895, d Toronto 1973, paint AGO CWW70 DWA M MM O.Ag42 RCA WWA73d76
COUSIN, Paul, b 1841, d 1895, illum H K
COUSINEAU, Alfred, fl 1913+, paint K MM
COUSINEAU, Sylvain P., b Arvida, Que 1949– , paint DCA
COUTELLIER, Francis, b Namur, Bel 1945– , paint CAE1,2 DCA
COUTTS, Lorne, b Toronto 1933– , paint IO
COUTURE, Guillaume, fl 1880s, paint H
COUTURE, Luc-André, b Ottawa 1920– , paint CWW83
COUTURIER, Marie-Alain, b Montbrison, Fr 1897, d Paris 1954, Fr, paint B K
COVENTRY, Alfred J., b London 1905– , paint CWW67
COVENTRY, Gertrude Mary McGowan (m E. Robertson[2]), b Glasgow c 1885, d 1964, Scot, paint DBA DScP DWA RA SW WBA1 WWB34[2]

COVERLY[1]-PRICE[2], A. Victor, b Winchester, Hants 1901– , Eng, paint DBA[1,2] MM RA WBA1 WWB

COUVILLON, Louis Amable. *See* QUEVILLON/COUVILLON/CUVILLON, Louis Amable

COWAN, Eric Charles, Brig Gen, b Ottawa 1921– , paint CWW67

COWAN, Harvey, b Toronto 1935– , paint IO NGC2

COWAN, Helen Aileen Hooper (s Aileen Hooper), b Windsor, Ont 1926– , paint sculp CAE1 IO WWA93

COWAN, Ralph Edward, b Saint John, NB 1897, d Halifax 1978, paint M

COWAN, Tillie, b Manchester, Eng, fl 1927+, paint O.My49

COWIN, Jack Lee, b Indianapolis, Ind 1947– , paint prt NGC2

COWLEY, Reta Madeline Summers (m Frederick Cowley), b Moose Jaw, Sask 1910– , paint BDSA CLA M SC US

COWLEY-BROWN, Patrick George, b Singapore 1918– , paint CLA M NGC68 RCA WWA53

COX, Arthur W., b England 1840, d Nottingham, Eng 1917, Eng, paint H Hu MM RCA TB1 W1–3

COX, Edwin James, b Montreal 1850, d c 1930, engr illum H MM RCA

COX, Elford Bradley, b Botha, Alta 1914– , sculp AGO CC2 Co IO M MM O.Ag47 RCA TB3 WWA62

COX, George, b Montreal 1834, engr H Mo98

COX, Palmer, b South Ridge, nr Granby, Que 1840, d Granby, Que 1924, cart illus AAAd28 AAW1 AC App B CWW10 DAB F H Mo98,12 NCAB NGC2 TB3 WECa WWWA

COXE, Judith, b Toronto 1937– , paint UG

COYNE, John Michael, b St Stephen, NB 1950– , paint CWW93 WWA93

COZENS, John, b Tottenham, Eng 1906– , des CWW93

COZIC, Yvon, b St Servan, Fr 1942– , paint sculp B CAE1,2 NGC2 RCA

COZZENS, Frederick Schiller, b New York 1846, d Livingston, Staten Isld, NY 1928, Amer, paint AAAd28 B DeV4 DMA DSP F H TB3

CRABTREE, Chris, b Ottawa 1948– , prt DCA

CRABTREE[1], Elvina Kennedy Greenham[2] (m Charles Archibald Crabtree), b London 1878, d Ottawa 1943, paint Hu MM RCA[1,2]

CRAIG, John, b Ireland 1804, d Toronto 1854, paint stgl DCB8 H

CRAIG, William Marshall, fl c 1765 – c 1834, Eng, min paint B BM Bry DBLP DBWA DIA DNB DWP Fo G H Red TB1

CRANE, Matilda Maud Muncy (m Chandler Crane), b Halifax 1830, d Bay Verte, NB 1901, paint DWA H

CRANMER, Douglas, fl 1958+, carv DFA

CRANSTON, Toller, b Hamilton, Ont 1949– , paint CE2 Co CWW93

CRANSTONE, Lefevre James, fl 1845–67, Eng, paint DFA G H PNL

CRAVEN, David, b London, Ont 1946– , drgt paint DCA IO S

CRAWFORD, Arthur, b Montreal 1867, d 1922, cart WECa WWWA

CRAWFORD, Catherine Betty, b Ingersoll, Ont 1910– , paint IO WWA93

CRAWFORD, Eugenia M./N., fl 1886–92, paint H MM

CRAWFORD, Georgie M. *See* WILCOX, Georgie M. Crawford

CRAWFORD, Julia Tilley, b Kingston, NB 1896, d Saint John, NB 1968, paint AGO DBA DWA M MA MM W3 WWA66

CRAWFORD, Robert Cree, b Govanbank, Scot 1842, d Glasgow 1924, Scot, paint DBA DScP DVLP DVP G RA SW WBA1

CRAWFORD, Walter John, b Toronto 1911– , paint Hu

CRAWFORD, William Henry, b Toronto 1865, fl 1929, paint H Hu

CRAWLEY, Frederick Sidney, b Ipswich, Eng c 1797, d Wolfville, NS c 1880, paint H

CREASE, Anthony R.V., Maj Gen, b England 1827, fl 1892, topog DFA H

CREASE, Barbara Lindley, b England 1857, d San Francisco 1883, paint DFA DWA H

CREASE, Josephine, b New Westminster, BC 1864, d Victoria, BC 1947, paint DFA DWA H

CREASE, Mary Maberly (m Frederick George Walker), b London 1854, d 1915, paint DFA DWA H

CREASE, Sarah Lindley, Lady (m Henry Pering Pellow Crease, Hon Sir), b Acton Green, nr London 1826, d Victoria, BC 1922, paint DFA DWA H

CREASE, Sarah Lindley, b Victoria, BC 1867 – d 1940, paint DFA DWA H

CREASE, Susan Reynolds, b Antron, Corn 1855, d Victoria, BC 1947, paint DFA DWA H

CREELMAN, Frieda I. Creighton (m Prescott A. Creelman), b Halifax 1900, d 1967, paint CLA MA

CREHEN/CRECKEN², Charles G., b Paris c 1829, fl 1891, litho paint B DeV3,7 GW H² K TB1

CREIGHTON, Frieda I. *See* CREELMAN, Frieda I. Creighton

CRESSWELL, Samuel Gurney, b King's Lynn, Eng 1827 – d 1867, Eng, topog DCB9 DFA DMA H

CRESSWELL, William Nicoll/Nichol, b Shoreditch, London 1818 (x1822), d nr Seaforth, Ont 1888, paint AAAW3 AGO H Hu MM NGC1,2 NGC67 RCA ROM W1–3

CRETAN, Tony. *See* KOTSIFOS, Anthony

CREVECOEUR, Jeanne de, fl 1909–25, pas K MM RCA

CREVIER, Hercule, fl 1877–81, paint K

CRIBB, Ada M., b Edinburgh 1931– , paint US

CRIBB, Marigold Lawrie (m Peter Cribb), b Edinburgh 1931– , mmed BDSA

CRICHTON, Robert Alexander, b Philadelphia, Pa 1931– , des gra CWW93

CRINCRIN. *See* JULIEN, Octave-Henri

CRISP, Arthur Watkins, b Hamilton, Ont 1881, d Biddeford, Me 1974, paint AAA33 CWW61 F Hu M NCAB NGC1,2 NGC68 RCA TB2 WWA66 WWWA Y

CRIST, Lela Gurnée, b Sheet Harbour, NS 1895, paint CLA

CRITTENDEN, John William Neil, b Brandon, Man 1939– , paint WWA82

CROASDALE, Henry S., fl 1879–90, paint H

CROCKART, James Bisset, b Stirling, Scot 1885, d Huntington, Que 1974, paint prt NGC2

CROCKER, James Sydney, fl 1876–86, paint H MM RCA

CROCKER-LEIGHTON, Alfred. *See* LEIGHTON, Alfred Crocker

CROCKETT, David, b USA 1944– , prt SC

CROCKETT, Robert, fl 1864–97, paint H

CROFT, Lewis Scott (m Mary E.G. Croft, q.v.), b Chester Basin, NS 1911– , paint CLA WWA80

CROFT, Mary Elizabeth Gillis (m Lewis Scott Croft, q.v.), b Montreal 1915– , paint CLA

CROKE, Alexander, Sir, b Aylesbury, Bucks 1758, d Studley Prior, Eng 1842, Eng, paint ske DCB7 DeV9 H LeJ ROM

CROMARTY, Margaret A., b Canada 1873, paint AAA33 DWA F TB2 WWA53

CROMBIE, Jonathan David, b Toronto 1966– , cart CWW93

CROMWELL, fl 1808, min H

CROMWELL, Larry D., b 1939– , drw CAE1

CRONYN, Hugh Verschoyle, b Vancouver 1905– , paint CWW93 DBA WBA1 WWB90

CROSBY, John Alexander, b Toronto 1925– , illus paint CWW93 IBYP M

CROSS, Frederick George, b Exeter, Dev 1881, d Lethbridge, Alta 1941, paint Hu M MM RCA Sam

CROSS, Nicolette, b England 1930– , paint ABC

CROSSEN-SARGENT, Sonia St Barbe (m Austin Underwood Sargent), b Montreal 1930– , paint BDSA

CROSSKILL, Herbert, b 1826, d 1902, paint DFA H

CROSSMAN, A.E., fl 1882–90, paint H

CROUCH, Robert Weir, b England, fl 1890s, d Lancaster, NH 1943, des etch H RCA

CRUIKSHANK, William, b Broughton Ferry, Scot 1848, d Kansas City 1922, paint AGO CE1 DBF1 DeV5,8 DFP3 EC G H H77 Hu LeJ M MM NGC1,2 NGC67 R2 RCA St TB1,3 W1–3

CRUISE, Stephen Patrick Christopher, b Montreal 1949– , drgt sculp DCA NGC2

CRYDERMAN, V. MacIntyre (Mackie) (m Clifford W. Cryderman), b Dutton, Ont c 1900, d London, Ont 1969, paint O.My50 R WWA70

CRYER, Bruce, b Calgary 1946– , paint SC

CSAPO, Heather Roxane, b Toronto 1951– , paint IO

CULBERT, Ronald J., b Sault Ste Marie, Ont 1953– , etch paint IO

CULINER, John William (Jack), b Hearst, Ont 1913– , sculp CWW93 IO

CULLEN, Maurice Galbraith, b Saint John's, Nfld 1866, d Chambly, Que 1934, paint ACA AE AGO B CC2 CE1,2 CNS40 EC H H77 Hu M MM Mo12 MQ NGC1,2 NGC67 NGC68 OCD PMC R2 RCA TB1–3 TN UG W1–3

CUMMING, Glen Edward, b Calgary 1936– , paint CWW93 WWA93 WWC89

CUMMINGS, Dale, b St Thomas, Ont 1948– , cart Des Po86–88

CUMMINGS, Jane Catharine, b Amherst Isld, nr Kingston, Ont c 1841, d Munich, Ge 1893, paint DWA H Hu M NGC1,2

CUNARD, Laura Charlotte Haliburton (1851 m William Cunard, q.v.) (x Samuel Cunard), b Windsor, NS, d Nice, Fr 1910, paint DBA DVLP DVP DWA G H Mo12

CUNARD, William S. (m Laura C.H. Cunard, q.v.), b Halifax 1825, d England 1908, paint BP DBA DVLP DVP

CUNEO, Cyrus Cincinnati, b San Francisco 1878/9, d London 1916, Amer, illus paint AAA16 AAW1 AC AH B DBA RA Sam TB1,2 WWW

CUNNINGHAM, F.C., b Ireland 1902– , paint WWNA

CURATOLO, Fred, b Toronto 1958– , cart CWW93 Po86–91

CUREL-SYLVESTRE, Roger, b Nice, Fr 1884, fl 1929, paint AAA29 B F K

CURLEY, Donald Houston, b Halifax 1940– , paint CAE1,2 WWA93

CURNOE, Gregory Richard, b London, Ont 1936, d nr London, Ont 1992, paint prt AGO CA1–3 CAE1 CC1 CE1,2 Co CWW92 IO M MM NGC2 NGC67 OC UG

CURRAN, Douglas Edward, b Seaforth, Ont 1952– , gra WWA93

CURRELLY, Judith (Judy), b Toronto 1946– , paint CAE1

CURREN, John D., b Scotland 1852, d Banff, Alta 1940, paint DFA KB

CURRIE, David Vivian, b Sutherland, Sask 1912– , paint CWW86

CURRIE, Emma Augusta Harvey (m Hon J.G. Currie), b Niagara Falls, Ont 1829, paint Mo12

CURRY, Elizabeth Eleanor, b Russell, Ont 1864, d Hamilton, Ont 1941, paint DWA H MM RCA

CURRY, Ethel Luella, b Irondale, Ont 1902– , sculp O.F49

CURRY, Ethel Marie Cartwright (s Peggy Curry) (m Stewart Curry), b Gosport, Eng 1885, paint CLA

CURTIS, Carolyn, b St Thomas, Ont 1903– , etch paint IO M

CUTHBERTSON, George Adrian, b Toronto 1900, d 1969, paint M RCA ROM

CUTTING, Lorna Muriel Russell. *See* RUSSELL, Lorna Muriel

CUTTS, Gertrude E. Spurr[2] (m William Malcolm Cutts, q.v.), b Scarborough, Yorks 1858, d Port Perry, Ont 1941, paint AAA01 AGO CWW38 DBA[2] DWA[2] H Hu M MM NGC1,2 RCA TB3

CUTTS, William Malcolm (m Gertrude E.S. Cutts, q.v.), b Allahabad, India 1857, d Port Perry, Ont 1943, paint CC1 CWW36 H Hu M MM NGC1,2 PMC RCA TB3 W1–3

CUVELIER, Léonce E., b Paris 1874, d Beauport, Que 1959, paint K MM

CUVILLON, Louis Amable. *See* QUEVILLON/COUVILLON/ CUVILLON, Louis Amable

CYOPEK, William, b Welland, Ont 1921– , paint sculp IO M MM RCA WWA70

CZEREWKO, Michael P., b Ontario 1949– , sculp IO

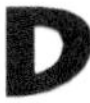

DABINETT, Diana, b Rhodesia 1943– , paint sculp CAE1

DABO, Ignace-Scott, d 1885, paint K

DABO, Léon, b Grosse Point, Mich 1868, d New York 1960, Amer, paint B F K TB1 WWA53

DAGLISH, Peter William, b Gillingham, Kent 1930– , paint prt sculp M MM NGC2 RCA TB3

DAGNEAULT, Josee (Jose Danio), b 1946– , paint CAE1

D'AGOSTINO, Anthony, b Locri, Reggio, It 1944– , paint IO

DAGYS, Jacob (b Jokubas Dags[2]), b Lithuania 1905– , paint sculp M[2] MM RCA WWA89

DAHL, Christopher, b 1948– , paint prt CAE1

DAHLSTROM, Eugene William, b Sandviken, Swe 1885, d Regina 1971, paint DFA KB NGC2

DAINIS. *See* MIEZAJS, Dainis

DAIR, Carl, b Welland, Ont 1912, d 1967, des CE1,2 Co

DALE, Archibald (s Archie), b Dundee, Scot 1882, d Winnipeg 1962, cart CWW55 Des EC W3 WECa

DALE, Marian. *See* SCOTT, Marian Mildred Dale

DALL, Bruce, b Montreal 1947– , paint ABC

DALLAIRE, Jean-Philippe, b Hull, Que 1916, d Vence, Fr 1965, illus paint ACA AE AGO B CC2 CE1,2 M MM MQ NGC1,2 NGC67 TB3 W3 WWA53 WWB66

DALLAS, Alexander Grant, b Br Guiana 1816, d London 1882, Eng, drgt DCB11 H

DALLAS, Jacob A., b Philadelphia, Pa 1825, d New York 1857, Amer, panor B GW H TB1

DALLEGRET, François, b Port Lyautey, Mor 1937– , paint prt sculp B NGC2 MM RCA

DALLIN, Norman, b 1948– , paint sculp CAE2

DALLISON, Ken, b Hounslow, nr London 1933– , illus paint CGA3

D'ALMAINE, George, b England, fl 1834–93, paint sil DFA GW H KB Y

DALTON, Ernest Alfred, b Brixton, Eng c 1887, d 1963, paint Hu

DALTON, John Joseph, b Toronto 1856, d 1935, topog ROM Sam

DALTON, Susanna Prescott (Mrs), fl 1796–1807, paint DFA KB

DALY, Charles, b Ireland 1808, d Toronto 1864, paint DFA H

DALY, Clive Anthony, b London 1936– , (x1916), des paint M
DALY, John Corry Wilson, b Liverpool 1796, d Stratford, Ont 1878, topog H
DALY, Kathleen Frances (m George Douglas Pepper[2], q.v.), b Napanee, Ont 1898, d Toronto 1994, paint AGO CE1,2 CWW93[2] DWA IO M MM NGC2 O.My48 RCA WWA93
DALZIEL/DALZEL, John Sanderson, b Edinburgh 1839, d Denver, Colo 1937, Amer, engr illus AAA1900 AAW3 DBBI H WWAd38
DAMASDY, Julius, b Hungary 1937– , paint sculp CAE1
DAME, G., fl 1809–11, min H K
DAMOREAU, Charles F., fl 1856–71, Amer, engr GW H K
D'AMOUR, Maurice, b 1949– , paint prt CAE1
DANA, James Dwight, b Utica, NY 1813, d New Haven, Conn 1895, Amer, drw App DAB EMA GW WWWA
DANBY, Kenneth Edison, b Sault Ste Marie, Ont 1940– , paint CAE1,2 CC2 CE1,2 Co CWW93 IO M MM NGC2 RCA SC TB3 UG WWA93
DANDURAND, G. (Miss), fl 1910+, paint K MM
DANGUEUSE dit LE CHASSEUR, Pierre. *See* CHASSEUR, Pierre Dangueusé dit le
DANIEL, Alice M.M. Baker (x S. Bancroft) (m George W. Daniel), b Burma 1882, paint DFA H Mo12
DANIEL KASUDLAK. *See* KASUDLUAK/KASUDLAK, Daniel
DANKS, Hilda Margaret Lawrence (m Walter F. Danks), b London 1893, d Niagara Falls, Ont 1969, paint MM RAC S
DANSEREAU, Gerard, b 1949– , paint CAE1
DANYLEWICH, Morris John, b Lachine, Que 1938– , des prt MM NGC2
DAOUST, Sylvia Marie Emilienne, b Montreal 1902– , fl 1993, sculp AGO CNS40 CWW93 M MM MQ NGC1,2 RCA TB3 WWA80
DARLING, Frank, b Scarborough, Ont 1850, d Toronto 1923, paint Co Mo12 NGC1,2 RCA R2 W1–3
DARLING, James (s Nemo), b Scotland 1836, d 1912, paint KB
DARRAH, Ann Clarke. *See* CLARKE, Ann
DARTNELL, Edward Taylor, b c 1820, d 1892, Eng, paint H
DARTNELL, George Russell, b 1798, d 1878, Eng, paint DFA H H77 MQ PNL ROM
DA SILVA, Ladis, b Zanzibar 1920– , drw paint MF
DAUDELIN, Charles, b Granby, Que 1920– , paint sculp B CE1,2 CWW93 M MM MQ NGC2 NGC67 TB3 WWA93
DAUDELIN, Fernand, b 1933– , tap MQ
DAUM, Leah Frey, b 1896, d 1979, paint DFA KB
DAUPHIN, Charles-Olivier, b Montreal 1807 – d 1874, paint K
DAUPHIN, Etienne, b c 1808, fl 1829, sculp K
DAVENPORT, Marie Crawley, b Hull, Eng 1898, d Saskatoon 1975, paint BDSA
DAUVERGRE, P., Lt, fl 1773, illus topog H
DAVEY, Alfred W., b Leics, Eng 1907– , paint US
DAVID, C., fl 1879–83, engr H K
DAVID, David-Fleury, b Sault-au-Récollet, Que 1780, d 1841, carv B K MQ
DAVID, Joe (Nuu-Chah-Nulth), b Opitsat, BC 1946– , sculp CE1,2 DFA
DAVID, Nantel, b Montreal 1912– , paint CWW67
DAVID, Stanilas, fl 1847–73, paint K
DAVID, Théophile, b Quebec Prov c 1799, fl 1861, paint H K

DAVIDEE, E7-1042, b Lake Harbour, NWT 1929– , engr sculp DEA
DAVIDIALUK, Alasua Amittuq[2], E9-824, b nr Povungnituk, Que c 1910 – d 1976, prt sculp AKL[2] CE1,2 Co DEA
DAVIDIE, Kagvik. *See* KAGVIK, Davidee/Davidie
DAVIDSON, Alexander, fl 1859–76, paint H
DAVIDSON, George, b Boston 1768, d c 1800, Amer, paint DMA EMA GW Y
DAVIDSON, Helen L. (m Frederic J.A. Davidson), b Belleville, Ont 1878, paint Hu RCA
DAVIDSON, Robert Charles, b Hydaburg, Alaska 1946– , sculp CE1,2 Co RCA
DAVIDSON, S. Kelso, b c 1848, d 1922, paint H
DAVIDSON, William C., fl 1880–92, engr litho H
DAVIES, Audrey, b Kingston, Ont 1916– , paint sculp IO
DAVIES, Gordon Albert, b Toronto 1890, paint Hu RCA
DAVIES, Haydn Llewellyn, b Rhymney, Wales 1921– , paint sculp CWW93 IO WWA93
DAVIES, Mary, b Truro, NS 1925– , paint CAE1,2
DAVIES, R., Capt, fl 1771–1806, Eng, paint DBLP G
DAVIES, Rose Leonard. *See* LEONARD, Rose
DAVIES, Sally J.K. (m Derrick Early), b Liverpool 1963– , illus C
DAVIES, Thomas, Maj Gen, b Shooter's Hill, nr Woolwich, Eng c 1737, d Blackheath, nr Woolwich, Eng 1812, Eng, topog ACA B Co DCB5 DFA DMA EC G GW H H77 KB M NGC2 NGC67 PNL ROM W2–3 WHC
d'AVIGNON, François, b nr Paris or St Petersburg 1813, fl 1870, Fr, litho engr B GW K TB1
DAVIS, Henry Samuel, Lt Col, b Marylebone, London 1809, ret 1851, Eng, paint DBWA DeV5 DIA H NGC2 ROM WHC
DAVIS, James Robert Leighton, b Winnipeg 1941– , paint prt CWW93
DAVIS, Joseph H. (aka Davies), fl 1877–82, drw paint H
DAVIS, Michael, b Toronto 1942– , con CAE1,2
DAVIS, Olea Marion Montgomery (m H.R.L. Davis), b Buffalo, NY 1899, sculp WWNA
DAVIS, Robert, b Wilts, Eng 1922– , paint IO
DAVIS, Theodore Russell, b Boston 1840, d Asbury Park, NJ 1894, Amer, illus DeV4,5 DMA GW H McC WI Y
DAVIS, William J., b 1876, d 1956, paint DFA H
DAVISON, Betty Young (m Richard Lewis; m Arthur Whitley Davison), b Ottawa 1909– , paint CWW92
DAVISON, Gertrude Elizabeth Mary (Betty), b Ottawa 1909– , paint prt IO NGC2
DAVISON, William, b Ontario c 1815, fl 1861, engr H
DAWSON, Charles F., fl 1889–93, engr litho H
DAWSON, F.A., fl 1880–1902, paint DFA H MM RCA
DAWSON, Fanny M., fl 1890–1905, paint H
DAWSON, G.W., fl 1887–93, engr H
DAWSON, George Mercer, b Pictou, NS 1849, d Ottawa 1901, paint CE1,2 DFA EC H Mo98 W1–3
DAWSON, Richard, Capt, fl 1748–58, topog DFA H KB ROM
DAWSON[1]-WATSON[2], Dawson (x John), b London 1864, d San Antonio, Tex 1939, Amer, paint sculp AAA33 AAW1 B DAS DBA[2] F H NCAB RCA Sam TB1[1,2],3 WWA38d40 WWWA Y
DAY, Fanny M. (Fannie), fl 1900–5, paint H MM
DAY, Forshaw, b London 1837, d King-

ston, Ont 1903, paint DeV9 EC H H77 Hu M MM Mo12 NGC1,2 RCA W1–3

DAY, Katherine, b Orillia, Ont 1889 – d 1976, paint prt NGC2

DAY, Mabel Killam (m Frank P. Day), b Yarmouth, NS 1884 – d 1961, paint AAA33 CLA DWA MA MM TB2 WWAA62

DAY, Richard W., b Canada 1896, d Los Angeles 1972, paint AAW2 AC

DAY, Shirley, b Toronto, fl 1950+, illus C

DAY, Stanley E., b Yakima, Wash 1933– , paint CAE2 US

DAY, W., fl 1810–24, drw H NGC67

DAYAN, Linda Spaner, b Barkerville, BC 1947– , paint ABC

DAZE, Louise, b Montreal 1943– , paint CAE1

DEACON, David Emmerson, b Toronto 1949– , illus paint CWW93

DEACON, Peter, b England 1945– , drw paint AA

DEAN, Ankaret, b England 1932– , tap IO

DEAN, Diana, b 1942– , paint CWW93

DEAN, Ernest Wilfrid, b London 1890, d Collingwood, Ont 1970, paint sculp WWA66d70

DEAN, Joan-Marie, b Ottawa 1934– , paint prt IO

DEAN, Max, b Leeds, Eng 1949– , prt sculp DCA NGC2

DEAN, Michael, b Manchester, Eng 1948– , paint CAE1

DEAN, Thomas G., b Canada 1947– , litho paint CAE1,2 MM RCA

DEANE, Lionel, b Canada 1861, paint AAA25 AAW3

DE ANGELIS, Joseph Rocco, b Providence, RI 1938– , sculp RCA WWA93

DEBASSIGE, Blair, b W Bay Res, Manitoulin Isld, Ont 1961– , paint IO

DEBASSIGE, Blake Randolph, b W Bay Res, Manitoulin Isld, Ont 1956– , paint CE1,2 Co IO WWA82

DEBENHAM, Guy P., b Scarborough, Eng 1923– , engr BB

DEBLOIS/BLOIS[2], Charles Théodore de, b Quebec Prov, fl 1862–88, engr paint H[2] K

DEBLOIS, François-B. *See* BLOIS, François-B. de

DEBLOIS, L. (Mme), fl 1859, paint DWA GW K

DE CAMILLIS, Laurie, b Vancouver 1951– , paint DCA

DECARIE, W., fl 1810–11, illus H K

DECARY, Louis Joseph Théophile, b St Jerome, Que 1882, d Montreal 1952, paint K MM

DE CLERCQ, Suzanne, b Antwerp, Bel 1928– , cer sculp IO

DE COURSEY, Inger Iversen (m William De Coursey), b Camrose, Alta 1931– , paint BDSA CAE1

DEFAUW, Jeanne (m Déseré Defauw), fl 1940s, Bel, paint K

DE FOREST, Henry Josiah, b Rothesay, NB 1860, d Calgary 1924, paint H PMC RCA Sam

DE FRANCESCO, Lorenzo, b Rome 1947– , sculp CWW93

DEGENHARDT, Germaine Mariaucourt (Mrs), b Vancouver 1932– , paint ABC

DEGGAN, Paul, b England 1932– , paint sculp M

DEGUIRE, Alphonse, b 1869, d 1942, paint K

DE HAAS, William Frederick, b Rotterdam 1830, d Fayal Azores 1880, Dutch, paint ANC GW

DEITCHER, Gloria Ann, b 1946– , prt CAE2

DE JONG, Beverly, b Calgary 1945– , met CAE1

DE JONG, Shirley Wales. *See* WALES, Shirley

DE KERGOMMEAUX[2], Duncan Robert Chassin, b Premium, BC 1927, paint CC1 CWW93 IO M[2] MM[2] NGC1[2],2 RCA[2] TB3[2] WWA93

DEKKERS, George, b Rotterdam 1892, paint DFA KB
DE LALL, Oscar Daniel, b St Petersburg 1903, d Montreal 1971, paint CLA CWW67 M MM NGC2 RCA
DELANEY, Edward, fl 1859–65, paint DeV4 H
DELATRI, Anthony (Tony), b Pennsylvania 1922– , car Des Po86–88
DELATTRE, Augustin Henri, b St Omer, Fr 1801, d Paris 1867, Fr, paint APH B GW H K TB1
DE LAURO, Joseph Nicola, b New Haven, Conn 1916– , Amer, sculp WWA93
DELAVALLE, Jean-Marie, b Clermont-Ferrand, Fr 1944– , sculp CAE1 NGC2
DEL BELLO, Egidio, b Italy 1951– , etch paint IO
DE LEEUW, Cateau Wilhelmina, b Hamilton, Ont 1903– , paint AAA33 WWA76
DELESSARD, Auguste-Joseph, b Paris 1827, fl 1891, paint B GW K TB1
DELFOSSE, Madeleine, b Montreal 1909– , paint CNS51 M MM
DELFOSSE, Marie Joseph Georges, b St-Henri-des-Mascouche, Que 1869, d Montreal 1939, paint CC2 CNS36 Hu M MM Mo12 MQ NGC1,2 PMC RCA TB3 W1–3
DELIGTISCH/DELIGTCH, Mani, b Germany 1934– , paint IO
DELISLE, Pierre G., fl 1865–88, engr litho H K
DELISLE, Urbain, fl 1851–67, carv K
DELL, Christine Louise, b Niagara Falls, Ont 1951– , cer sculp IO
DELOUCHERY, Marsha (m Brian Day), b Berwick, NS 1950– , paint BDSA
DELRUE, Georges, b Tourcoine, Fr 1920– , paint sculp M MM
DE LUCCA, Yargo Dieter Mueller, b Kassel, Ge 1925– , paint M MM NGC2
DELVIGNE, F., b France 1859/60, fl 1888, paint K
DE MATTEIS, Frank Alberto, b Avezzano, It 1952– , paint IO
DEMERS, Jean-Antoine, b Quebec Prov 1931– , paint M
DEMERS, Jean-Baptiste, b c 1857, fl 1875, drgt H K
DEMERS, Jérôme, Abbé, b St-Nichols, Que 1774, d Quebec 1853, des DCB8 H
DEMERS, Louis-Théophile, Abbé, b 1806, fl 1821–6, sculp K
DEMERS, Michel, b Quebec 1949– , cart WECa
DEMERS, Pierre, b Deal, Kent 1914– , paint CWW93
DEMIRLI, Oya, b Istanbul, Tur 1951– , litho prt IO
DEMPSEY, Paul Eugene, b Wolverhampton, Eng 1951– , sculp IO
DENECHAUD, Simone, b Montreal 1905 – d 1974, paint K MM RCA WWA53
DE NIKE, Michael Nicholas, b Regina 1923– , Amer, sculp DAS
DENIS, Louis N., fl 1868–75, paint H K
DENISON, George Taylor, b York, nr Toronto 1816, d Toronto 1873, paint DCB10 EC H W1–3
DENNIS, Claude W., fl 1880–1911, paint H MM RCA
DENNIS, Eva Aileen House (m Wesley C. Dennis, q.v.), b Gravenhurst, Ont 1904– , paint BDSA DFA KB
DENNIS, James B., Lt Col, Sir, b 1778, d 1885, Eng, paint DFA H KB
DENNIS, Wesley C. (m Eva A.H. Dennis, q.v.), b Wyoming, Lambton Co, Ont 1899, d 1989, paint DFA KB
DENNISTOUN, Mary Lydia. *See* KIRKPATRICK, Mary Lydia Dennistoun, Lady
DENNY, William, b 1804, d 1886, paint DFA PNL
DENTON, Francis William (Frank), b Toronto, fl 1919+, paint CWW84 MM RCA

DENTON, Kady MacDonald (m Trevor Davies Denton), b Winnipeg 1942– , illus C CWW93

DENYSE, David, b Red Bank, NJ 1952– , paint UG

DE PAOLI, Sergio, b Italy 1926– , paint O.My50

DE PEDERY[2]-HUNT[3], Dora (m Albert M. Hunt), b Budapest 1913– , med sculp AGO CC1 CE1,2 Co CWW93 IO M NGC1[2],2 PHA RCA[3] TB3[2] WWA93

DEPEW, Agnes Victoria, b Embro, Ont 1905, d Sarnia, Ont 1977, paint S

DEPEW, Verna Viola, b Stoney Creek, nr Hamilton, Ont 1894, paint DWA GM M UG WWA62

DEPPE, Horst, b Hanover, Ge 1929– , paint M

DERMAN, Alexander S., b Russia 1887, paint sculp M

DE ROS/DE ROOS[2], John Frederick Fitzgerald, Adm, Hon, b Boyle Farm, Sur 1804, d 1861, Eng, drw DeV3[2],9 GW H

DEROUIN, René, b Montreal 1936– , paint prt CAE1 MM NGC2

DE ROUSSAN, Jacques, b Paris 1929– , illus CBC SAA31

DEROY, Isidore-Laurent, b Paris 1797 – d 1886, Fr, paint B K TB1

DERRETH, Reinhard R., b Berlin, Ge 1928– , des gra CWW86 RCA

DERUM. *See* RUMPELMAYER, Denise

DERY, Hélène, b Tracey, Que 1956– , engr paint BB

DESANDROUINS, Jean-Nicolas, b Verdun, Fr 1729, d Paris 1792, Fr, des DCB4 K

DESAULNIERS, Louis, b Quebec 1935– , paint tap CAE1

DESAUTELS, André, fl 1861–76, sculp K

DESBARATS, Georges-Edouard-Amable, b Quebec 1838, d Montreal 1893, engr litho DCB12 DeV4,7 H K LeJ W1–3

DESBARATS, Guy Edouard André, b Montreal 1925– , sculp CWW93

DESBARATS, Peter, b Montreal 1933– , illus CWW92

DES BARRES, Joseph-Fréderic-Wallet, b Basel, Swi, or Paris 1722, d Halifax 1824, paint topog CE1,2 Co DCB6 DeV7,9 DFA DMA DNB H H77 K LeJ ROM W1–3

DESBIENS, Gérard, b Lévis, Que 1925– , sculp M RCA WWA62

DESCHENES, Alfred, b 1913, d 1975, paint DFA KB

DES CLAYES, Alice, b Aberdeen, Scot 1890, paint AGO CNS36 DBA DWA G Hu MM NGC1,2 RA RCA WWB56

DES CLAYES, Berthe, b Aberdeen, Scot 1877, d 1968, paint AGO CNS36 DBA DWA Hu MM NGC1,2 RA RCA

DES CLAYES, Gertrude, b Aberdeen, Scot 1879, d London 1949, paint B CNS36 DBA DWA Hu NGC1,2 RA RCA WBA1

DESJARDINS, Soeur (des Soeurs Grises), d Montreal 1879, paint H K

DESJARDINS, Isabelle, b Chicoutimi, Que 1948– , paint CAE1

DESJARDINS-FAUCHER, Huguette, b Montreal 1938– , paint prt NGC2

DESMARAIS, Oliva, fl 1864–78, des paint H K

DESMARAIS, Rose-Anna (Soeur Jérôme de la Croix), b St-Marc-sur-Richelieu, Que 1882, d Outremont, Que 1953, paint K

DESMARCHAIS, Andrée, b Ste-Anne-de-Bellevue, Que 1945– , prt tap CAE1

DESNOYERS, Charles, b St-Vincent-de-Paul, Que 1806, d 1902, sculp K MQ

DESPARD, Amy Constance, b London, Ont, fl 1940+, paint Hu

DESROCHERS dit BRIEN, Pierre-Urbain. *See* BRIEN dit DESROCHERS, Pierre-Urbain

DESROCHERS, Vital, fl 1836–45, carv paint H K
DESROSIERS, Yvon, b Quebec 1941– , sculp CAE1
DESSAILLIANT de RICHETERRE, Michel, dit de RISSETIERE, fl 1701–23, paint CE1,2 DCB2 H H77 K NGC67
DESVALLIERES, Georges-Olivier, b Paris 1861 – d 1950, Fr, paint B K TB1,2
DETWILER, J.D., b Roseville, Ont 1853, d Harrison, Ont 1910, paint H
DEUTSCH, Peter Andrew, b Trnava, Cz 1926– , paint NGC2 RCA WWA82
DEUTSCHER, Melbo Joyce Dew (m J. Adam Deutscher), b Riverhurst, Sask 1925– , paint BDSA CAE1
DEVELLANO, Joseph, b Hamilton, Ont 1945– , paint IO
DEVENYI, Ester S. (m Tibor Devenyi), b Budapest 1929– , paint pas IO MM
DEVER, Donald A., b Sudbury, Ont 1926– , paint CWW93
DEVILLE, Louis, fl 1854–63, Fr, des K
DEVLIN, Joyce, b Ft Fraser, BC 1932– , paint SC
DEVOS-MILLER, Kathryn, b Chicago, fl 1970– , paint prt CAE1
DEW, Keith G., b Owen Sound, Ont 1937– , paint IO
DEWAR, Susan, b Montreal 1949– , car Po86–88
DEWDNEY, Christopher, b London, Ont 1951– , illus sculp CE2
DEWDNEY, Selwyn Hanington, b Prince Albert, Sask 1909, d 1979, paint CLA CWW79
DEWHURST, Dorothy, b Blackpool, Eng 1916– , paint IO
DEWILDE, G.R., fl 1875–6, illus paint H
DEY-BERGMASER, Olga M., b Netherlands 1938– , drw MF
DIAMOND, Abel Joseph, b Piet Retief, SA 1932– , drw CWW93 RCA WWA82
DICK, David Brash, b Edinburgh 1846, d Eng 1925, paint H NGC1,2 RCA W1–3
DICKENSON/DICKINSON, Edgar A., fl 1871–1900, illus paint H RCA
DICKINSON, Anson, b Milton, nr Litchfield, Conn 1779 – d 1852, Amer, min AM DAB F GW H WWWA
DICKINSON, Preston, b New York 1891, d Spain 1930, Amer, min paint AAAd30 B BE DAB TB2 Y
DICKINSON, Doris Gillespie (Mrs), b Toronto, fl 1942+, paint prt? WWC69
DICKSON, Jennifer Joan (m Ronald Andrew Sweetman), b Piet Retief, SA 1936– , paint prt CAE1 CWW93 NGC2 RA RCA WWA93 WWB90
DIDIER, Ida Joy. *See* JOY, Ida
DIERKER, Louise Goueffic, b Marcelin, Sask 1933– , paint CAE1
DIERLAMM, M. Peter, b Shoenburg, Ge 1851, fl 1897, paint H
DIERNER, Eva, b Zurich, fl 1970– , paint CAE1,2
DIESPECKER, Richard Alan (Dick), b Adstock, Eng 1907– , paint CWW58
DIGNAM, Mary Ella Williams (m John Sifton Dignam), b Charlotteville, Ont 1860, d Toronto 1938, paint CNS40 CWW36 DWA EC H Hu MM Mo98,12 RCA TB2 UG WWB34
DIKEAKOS, Christos, b 1946– , con CAE1
DILLON, Richard, fl 1781–1811, paint topog DeV3 H
DILLON, William, fl 1871–86, paint H
DIMSON, Théo Aeneas, b London, Ont 1930– , des gra CWW93 ICB3 WWA93 WWGA1,2
DINER, Janis, b 1952– , pas SC
DINGLE, John Adrian Darley, b Barmouth, Wales 1911, d Mississauga, Ont 1974, paint CWW70 M NGC2 O.My49 S UG WECo WWA76
DINGLE, Ruth Marion (m Peter Hugh Douet[2]), b Calgary 1908, d Owen Sound, Ont 1980, paint CLA[2] MM RCA
DINGMAN, Dugald, fl 1890–7, paint H

DINSMORE, Edward Jackson, b Toronto 1885, d 1936, illus Hu

DION, Charles, b Canada c 1833, fl 1867, paint H K

DION, Louis, b Lévis, Que 1809/10 – d 1894, sculp K

DI PETTA, Angelo. *See* PETTA, Angelo di

DIPPY, Rhobena. *See* MAILLET, Corinne Dupuis

DIRCKINCK-HOLMFELD, Helmuth. *See* HOLMFELD, Helmuth Emanuel Bernhard Edwin

DISBROWE, F.A., b 1852, d 1943, paint DFA

DIVIDIAN, Sosy, b Jerusalem 1948– , paint MFMS

DIX, Wakeford G., b Garden Isld, Ont 1888, paint Hu MM RCA

DIXEE, Thomas, fl 1828–65, Eng, paint B DVLP DVP G H TB1

DIXON Brian, b Winnipeg 1930– , sculp CWW93

DIXON, George, Capt, fl 1785–8, d c 1800, Eng, paint DeV1 DNB EMA GW H

DIXON, Jane F., fl 1864–8, drw H

DLUGOPOLSKA, Zofia, b Zakopane, Pol, fl 1972– , tap IO

DMYTRUK, Ihor R., b Ukraine 1938– , drw paint AA CAE1,2 WWA93

DOBBS, Harriet (x Henrietta) (m Robert David Cartwright[2]), b Dublin 1808, d Portsmouth, nr Kingston, Ont 1887, paint DCB11 DWA[2] H[2] PNL[2]

DOBELL, Sybil Octavia Robertson. *See* ROBERTSON, Sybil Octavia

DOBEREINER, John Philip, b 1920– , paint prt CAE1

DOBEREINER, Wendy, fl 1970– , prt CAE2

DOBUSH, Peter, b Winnipeg 1908– , drw CAE1

DOCTOR, Antonio P., b Dagopan, Phil 1931– , paint WWC82

DOCTOR BRUTE. *See* METCALFE, Eric William

DODD, Eric Maxwell, b Canada 1923– , sculp WWA93

DODD, Robert, b London 1748, d England 1815/16, Eng, engr paint B Bry DBHP DBLP DBMaP DeV9 DMA DNB DSP DWP H OELP PP Red TB1

DODDS, Nancy, b High River, Alta 1953– , prt AA

DOERRIE, Waltraud Markgraf. *See* MARKGRAF, Waltraud/Traudle

DOIRON, Joseph Aubin, Hon, b N Rusteco, PEI 1922 , paint CWW90

DOMOKOS, Alex (Sandor), b Szabadka, Hu 1921– , illus sculp PHA

DOMVILLE, Paul, b Hamilton, Ont 1893, paint AAA33 F TB2 WWA62

DONAHUE, James. *See* DONOAHUE, James Thomas (Jim)

DONALDSON, Marjory Rogers (m Allan Donaldson), b Woodstock, NB 1926– , paint MA WWA91

DONATO, Andrew (Andy), b Toronto 1937– , cart paint CAE2 Des IO Po86–88

DONEY, Thomas, b France, fl 1840s, Fr, engr B F GW H K TB1 Y

DONGES, Langley Thomas, b Toronto 1901– , paint Hu RCA

DONLY, Eva Marie Brook (Ava Maria) (m Augustine William Donly; m A. Williams[2]), b Simcoe, Ont 1867 – d 1941, paint AAA33 DWA F H[2] Hu M MM NGC1,2 RCA TB3 WWA40 Y

DONOAHUE, James Thomas (Jim), b Walkerton, Ont 1934– , des gra CWW93 WWGA2

DONOVAN, John Ambrose, b Hamilton, Ont 1871, d Los Angeles 1941, paint AAW3 AC

DORAY, Audrey M. Capel (m Victor Doray), b Montreal 1931– , gra paint M MM NGC2 WWA93

DORE, Joseph, fl 1771–2, sculp K

DORION, Alexandre, b Quebec 1855/6, fl 1881–90, sculp K

DORION, C.A., fl 1882, paint H K RCA

DORION, Joseph-Hercule, Abbé, b Ste-

Anne-de-la-Pérade, Que 1820, d Yamachiche, Que 1889, paint H K

DORION, Robert Bernard Joseph, b Montreal 1944– , paint sculp CWW93

DORN, Peter Klaus, b Berlin 1932– , des gra CWW93 RCA WWA93

DORRANCE, David, b Sault Ste Marie, Ont 1946– , sculp AA

DORSEY, John, b Nova Scotia c 1827, fl 1860, paint GW H

DORVAL, Georges-S., b Quebec 1861/2, fl 1924, paint H K

DOUBBLE, Dorothy Evelyn, b Cataroque, Ont 1886/7, d 1974, illus paint AAA28 DWA

DOUCET, Emmanuel Arthur, b Massachusetts 1888, d Montreal 1960, des K MM

DOUBT, William George, b Trail, BC 1926– , car paint CLA

DOUDIET, Jacques-Frédéric, b Basel, Swi 1802, d Montreal 1867, paint APH B K

DOUET, Ruth Dingle. *See* DINGLE, Ruth Marion

DOUGHTIE, William, b Edinburgh 1846, d Orlando, Fla 1882, paint H RCA

DOUGLAS. *See* BOOTHE, Jack Douglas

DOUGLAS, Bloomfield, Capt, b 1832, d 1906, paint DFA H MM RCA

DOUGLAS/DOUGLASS, Eleanor, b Port Elgin, Ont, fl 1894–1917, paint AAA03 DWA H RCA

DOUGLAS, Howard, Gen, Sir, b Gosport, Eng 1776, d Tunbridge Wells, Eng 1861, Eng, paint CE1,2 DCB9 DNB EC H W1–3

DOUGLAS, Martha. *See* HARRIS, Martha Douglas

DOUGLAS, Thomas. *See* SELKIRK, Thomas Douglas

DOUGLAS, William, b Scotland c 1841, fl 1861, paint H

DOULL, Mary Allison, b Wilmot Creek, nr Summerside, PEI 1866, d 1953, min paint AAA31 DFA DWA F H PMC

DOW. *See* NIEUWENHUIS, Douwe

DOW, Adrian, b Regina 1946– , paint CAE1 IO

DOWLER-GOW, Isobel Elizabeth, b 1933– , fl 1970s, gra sculp CAE2

DOWNES/DOWNS, J.F., fl 1830–47, illus H

DOWNING, Frances Page, b 1943– , wlhg IO

DOWNING, Robert James, b Hamilton, Ont 1935– , paint sculp CAE1 CWW93 MM RCA WWA84

DRAHANCHUK, Walter. *See* DROHAN, Walter

DRAKE, John Poad, b Stoke-Damerel, Dev 1794, d Fowey, Corn 1883, Eng, paint B DMA DNB GW H H77 NGC2 RCA TB1

DRAKE, William Alexander, b Toronto 1891, d Bergenfield, NJ 1979, paint prt AGO Hu MM NGC2 RCA WWA62

DRAPPEL, Josef (Joseph), b Humpolec, Bohemia, Cz 1940– , paint CAE1,2 CE1,2 DCA IO WWA93

DRAYTON, Reginald, b c 1849, fl 1934, paint H

DREANY, Edward Joseph, b N Bay, Ont 1908– , paint Hu MM RCA

DRENTERS, Andreas, b Poppel, Bel 1937– , sculp MM RCA UG

DRENTERS, Yosef Gertrudis, b Poppel, Bel 1929, d Guelph, Ont 1983, paint sculp AE CC2 Co CWW84 DFA KB M RCA S UG

DREWERY, Thomas. *See* DRURY/DREWERY, Thomas

DROHAN, Walter (b Drahanchuk), b Calgary 1932 , paint sculp AA CWW93 RCA

DROLET, Philippe, b Quebec 1812/13, fl 1876, sculp K

DROPE, McCleary Herbert (aka Swami Bodhi Anando, c 1979), b Detroit 1931– , paint sculp H77 MM NGC2 RCA

DRUE, Juconde, b Paris 1664, d c 1739, Fr, paint DCB2 H K

DRUM, Sydney Maria (m Frank De Salvo), b Calgary 1952– , drgt prt CWW93 DCA IO

DRUMMOND, Arthur Alexander, b Toronto 1891, d c 1977, illus paint AAA29 MM RCA WWA76d78

DRUMMOND, Harriet O./D., fl 1896–1908, min H RCA

DRUMMOND, I.G., b Edmonton 1923– , Amer, sculp DAS WWA80

DRUMMOND, Jeanie Redpath (Jeanne), fl 1891–1906, paint H MM

DRUMMOND, Kenneth Whitney, b Toronto 1905– , paint Hu

DRUMMOND, Sophie Theresa Pemberton. *See* PEMBERTON, Sophie Theresa

DRUMMOND-DAVIES (Mrs), b 1862, d 1949, paint DFA DWA H

DRURY / DREWERY, Thomas, fl 1820s – 1833, paint H

DRUTZ, June, b Toronto 1920– , paint prt IO NGC2 RCA S UG WWA93

DRYDEN, Robert Stephen, b Cambridge, Ont 1947– , sculp IO

DUANE, James, b Canada c 1810, fl 1850, engr G W H

DUBE, Louis-Théodore, b St-Roch-des-Aulnaies, Que 1862, d Paris 1937, paint B H K MM RCA Sam

DUBERGER, Jean-Baptiste dit SANS-CHAGRIN, b Detroit 1767, d St-Thomas, Montmagny, Que 1821, drgt engr DCB6 H K

DUBERGER, Jean-Baptiste, b Quebec c 1795, fl 1826, drgt H K

DUBOIS, André, b Quebec 1947– , paint CAE1

DUBOIS, J., fl 1929–37, illus K

DUBOIS, Macy, b Baltimore, Md 1929– , des RCA WWW93

DUBOIS, Marius, b 1949– , paint CAE1

DUBOIS BERTHELOT DE BEAUCOURS[2], Josué (Jean-Marie-Josué) (aka Boisberthelot[3] de Beaucourt, Hyacinth), b Le-Bodéo, Bretagne, Fr c 1662, d Montreal 1750, paint DCB3 H[3] K LeJ[2]

DUBREUIL, Jules, fl 1885–1903, litho H K

DUCHARME, Georges, fl 1861–83, sculp K

DUCHARME, Maurice, fl 1942+, sculp K

DUCHARME, Noel, b Nipigon, nr Ft William, re Thunder Bay, Ont 1921, d Thunder Bay, Ont 1988, paint Co IO

DUCHARME, Raoul, drw K MM

DUCHESNAY, Henriette Julie (m Thomas Edmund Campbell), b Beauport, Que 1813, d St-Hilaire, Que 1873, paint DCB10 DWA H K

DUCHESNE, Christophe (aka Chrysôstome Perrault[2]), b St-Jean-Port-Joli, Que 1793 – d 1829, paint sculp H[2] K

DUCK, Adele Lillian, b Windsor, Ont 1948– , prt IO UG

DUCLOS, J., fl mid 19th cen, paint H K

DUDAS, Frank Edward, b Strathroy, Ont 1928– , des CWW80

DUDLEY, Robert, fl 1857–93, Eng, paint B DBA DBMaP DeV4 DMA G H ROM TB1

DUDOWARD, Charles, fl 1873, paint H H77

DUFAULT, Joseph Ernest Nephtali. *See* JAMES, William Roderick

DUFF, Ann MacIntosh, b Toronto 1925– , paint AGO CWW93 IO M MM NGC2 RCA S WWA93

DUFF, Annie Elexey, b nr Carleton Place, Ont 1873 – d 1955, paint NGC2

DUFF, Walter Raymond, b Hamilton, Ont 1879, d Toronto 1967, paint prt Hu NGC2

DUFFERIN AND AVA, Frederick Temple Blackwood[2], 1st Marquis, Gov-Gen 1872 8, Earl of Ava, b Florence 1826, d Clandeboye, Ire, Irish, paint BP[2]p848 CE1,2 DNB[2] DP EC H W1–3 WWW

DUFFY, Aileen Anne Plaskett. *See* PLASKETT, Aileen Anne

DUFLOCQ, fl 1862, Fr, panor B H K TB1
DUFLOT de MOFRAS, Eugène, b Toulouse, Fr 1810, d Paris 1884, Fr, paint K
DUFOUR, André, b La-Malbaie, Que 1939– , paint prt NGC2
DUFOUR, Claude, b Chicoutimi, Que 1925– , paint sculp CAE1
DUFOUR, Gilles, b Jonquière, Que 1941– , paint sculp NGC2
DUFRESNE, Honorius Philip^2, fl 1876–89, paint H^2 K
DUFRESNE, Jean, b Quebec 1844/5, fl 1881, carv K
DUFRESNE, L.N.R., fl 1883–7, paint H K
DUFROST de LAJEMMERAIS, Joseph, b Varennes, Que 1706, d Ste-Famille, Que 1756, paint K
DUGAL, Charles-Olivier, b St-Michel, nr Quebec 1796, d Terrebonne, Que 1829, sculp DCB6 K
DUGAL, François, b 1796, d 1862, carv K
DUGAS dit LABRECHE, François, fl 1861–9, paint K
DUGGAN, Frank, b Montreal 1904, cart Des
DUGUAY, Rodolphe, b Nicolet, Que 1891 – d 1973, illus paint prt CE1,2 CWW70 GM Hu K MM MQ NGC2
DUKES, Caroline, b Ujpest, Hu 1929– , Amer, paint sculp CAE1 WWA93
DULINO, M. *See* MARTIN DE LINO, Antoine
DULMAGE, William Z., b 1830, d 1913, cal paint DFA KB
DULONGPRE, Louis, b St-Denis, nr Paris 1754/9, d St-Hyacinthe, Que 1843, paint pas APH DCB7 DFA GW H H77 K KB MQ NGC1,2 NGC67 W1–3
DULUDE, Claude, b Montreal 1931– , paint CWW93 MM RCA
DUMA, William (Bill), b Calgary 1936– , paint SC
DUMAIS-BERUBE, Yvette, b St-Joseph-de-Lepage, Que 1930– , paint WWW93
DUMAIS, Pascal-Horace, fl 1876–8, illus H K
DUMAIS, Réal, b 1947– , paint CAE1,2
DUMAS, Antoine, b Quebec 1932– , gra paint CWW93 DCA RCA WWA93
DUMAS, Jean-Romain, fl 1834, sculp K
DUMAS, Michael Godfrey, b Whitney, Ont 1950– , paint IO
DUMKE, Susan Noble, b Pittsburg, Pa 1942– , sculp IO
DUMOUCHEL, Albert, b Bellerive, nr Valleyfield, Que 1916, d St-Antoine-sur-Richelieu, Que 1971, paint prt sculp ACA AGO B CC1 CE1,2 M MM MQ NGC1,2 NGC67 TB3
DUMOUCHELLE, Henry, fl 1884, litho H K
DUNBAR, Daphne French, b Port Colban, Ont 1883, litho paint DWA WWA62
DUNBAR, Leslie Alexander, b Blackpool, Eng 1902– , paint CWW58
DUNBAR, Ulric Stonewall Jackson, b London, Ont 1862, d Washington, DC 1927, Amer, sculp AAAd28 B CWW10 DAS F Mo12 NCAB RCA TB1,3 WWWA Y
DUNCAN, Alice McLaren, b Colborne, Ont 1879, paint Hu MM
DUNCAN, Alma Mary, b Paris, Ont 1917– , illus paint IO MM NGC2 NGC68 O.F51 RCA
DUNCAN, Dorothy (m Hugh MacLennan), b E Orange, NJ 1903, d Montreal 1957, paint CLA CWW55 MM W2–3
DUNCAN, James D., b Coleraine, Ire 1806, d Montreal 1881, paint B Co DCB11 DeV3,7 H H77 MQ NGC2 NGC67 ROM W1–3 WHC
DUNCAN, Oliver, b Canada c 1825, fl 1850–60, litho GW H
DUNCAN, Wilfrid Eben Pinkerton, Maj, b Glasgow 1891– , paint CWW58
DUNCANSON, Robert Stuart/Scott,

b NY 1817/21, d Detroit 1872, Amer, paint BE DAA DCB10 GW H NGC2 Sam TCBA WWA Y
DUNIERE, Louis, fl 1789–99, drw paint H K
DUNLAP, Clarence R., b Sydney Mines, NS 1908– , paint CWW86
DUNLAP, William, b Perth Amboy, NJ 1766, d New York 1839, Amer, min paint AM App B BE BM Bry DAA DAB F Fo GW H NCA6 TB1 WWWA Y
DUNLOP, Alexander Francis, b Montreal 1842 – d 1923, paint H MM Mo98,12 NGC1,2 RCA
DUNMORE, Charles Adolphus Murray[2], 7th Earl, b London 1841, d Frimley, nr Camberley 1907, Eng, paint BPp875 DNB[2] DP H[2] WWW
DUNN, Thomas W., b Newfoundland c 1836, fl 1863, litho GW H
DUNN, William, Maj Gen, fl 1800–62, drw H
DUNNING, George, b Toronto 1920, d 1978, cart Co WECa
DUNNING, William Dale Morris, b Ottawa 1946– , sculp IO
DUNSMORE, Henry Y., b Grangemouth, Scot 1947– , prt CAE1,2 IO
DUPLESSIS, Marie-Andrée Regnard[2] (Mère de Sainte-Hélène), b Paris 1687, d Quebec 1760, paint DCB3[2] K
DUPRAS, Pierre, b Montreal 1938– , cart illus Des WECa
DUPUIS, Corinne. *See* MAILLET, Corinne Dupuis
DUPUIS, François, fl 1841–5, sculp K
DUPUIS, Luce, b Ste-Marthe, Que 1940– , sculp CAE1
DUQUET, Georges-Henri, b 1887, d 1967, paint sculp K MM
DURANCEAU, Suzanne, b Saint-Laurent, Que 1952– , paint sculp CAE1
DURANGEL, Leopold, fl 1853, paint H K
DURAND, L.J., fl 1878–80, engr H K
DURHAM, Michael, b Leeds, Eng 1944– , paint CAE1 IO
DURIE, Alex, fl 1860s, illus DeV7 H
DURIE, Sally Ann, b Coburg, Ont 1929– , paint IO
DURNFORD, Jane, fl 1830–60, Eng, paint DWA H WHC
DUROCHER, Urbain, fl 1843–8, sculp K
DURR, Patricia Beth Goldberg (m Laurence Durr), b Kansas City 1939– , paint prt IO RCA WWA93
DURRANT, Marjorie Helen Cook (m E. Frederick Durrant), b Herbert, Sask 1926– , paint BDSA
DUSHKA. *See* AREZINA, Dushka
DUSSAULT, Jean (John), fl 1902, sculp K
DUSSAULT, Madeleine, b Montreal 1920– , paint CAE1
DUSSAULT, Monique, b Montreal 1943– , paint prt CAE1
DUTACEL, b France, fl 1860–77, paint H K
DUTZI, Julius J., b Karlsruhe, Ge 1920– , paint ABC
DUVAL, Jean-René, b France 1706, fl 1758, Fr, paint H K
DUVERNET, Henry Abrahams, Col (c 1842 Henry Abrahams Du Vernet Grosset Muirhead), b 1787, d Bredisholm, nr Coatbridge, Scot 1843, Eng, topog DCB7 H
DUVERT, Paul-Léon, fl 1876–84, paint K
DYCK, Graydon, b Leamington, Ont 1946– , drw paint prt CAE1 IO
DYCK-KOLENICK, Jan (s Jan Kolenick), b Los Angeles 1942– , paint BDSA
DYENS, Georges Maurice, b France 1932– , drgt sculp DCA WWA93
DYER, C.J. (aka E.G.), fl 1874–7, illus DeV5 H
DYER, Marilyn, b Alberta 1933– , paint SC
DYNELEY, Amelia Frederica, b Leeds, Eng 1830, fl 1860, Eng, paint ROM WHC
DYNELEY, Mary Frederica Law (1827

m Thomas Dyneley[2], Lt Gen), b England, fl 1827, d Bytown, re Ottawa 1851, Eng, paint DFA DNB[2] ROM WHC

DYNES, Joseph, b Burlington, Ont 1825 – d 1897, paint DeV7 H H77

DYONNET, Edmond, b Crest, Fr 1859, d Montreal 1954, paint B CC2 CE1,2 CNS40 CWW53 EC H H77 K M MM Mo12 MQ NGC1,2 NGC68 RCA W2,3 WWA53 WWB56

DYONNET, Eugenie, b France, d Montreal 1875, paint H K

DYSON, John Holroyd, b Folkestone, Eng 1910– , paint WWA89

DZENIS, Eduard A., b Latvia 1907, d Toronto 1999, illus paint IO M MM RCA

DZIDRA, b 1926– , paint CAE1

DZIEMBOWSKA, Irena T., b Poland, fl 1970– , tap IO

E

EADE, Wallace Cotman, b Ipswich, Suf 1872, d Vancouver 1916, paint DFA

EAGER, William, b Ireland c 1796, d Saint John, NB 1839, litho paint ACA DCB7 DeV4,9 DFA H H77 NGC67 ROM

EARLE, Paul Barnard, b Montreal 1872 – d 1955, paint Hu M MM NGC1,2 PMC RCA TB3 WWA56

EAST, Benoît, b St-Augustine, Portneuf, Que 1915– , paint M

EASTCOTT, Robert Wayne, b Trail, BC 1943– , paint CAE2 CWW93 RCA WWA93

EASTLAKE, Charles Herbert (m Mary Alexandra Bell Eastlake, q.v.), fl 1889–1940, Eng, paint DBA DVP G MM RA RCA TB1 WBA1

EASTLAKE[1], Mary Alexandra Bell[2] (m Charles Herbert Eastlake, q.v.), b Douglas, Ont 1864, d Ottawa 1951, paint AE AGO B DBA DBWA DVP[2] DWA G[1,2] H Hu M MM Mo98 NGC1,2 RA[2] RCA TB1–3, WWB34

EASTMAN, Antonia Larribe (m D. Mack Eastman), b Paris 1886, d Vancouver 1972, paint BDSA

EASTMAN, Harrison, b New Hampshire c 1822, d San Francisco 1890/1, Amer, paint AAW1 AC DeV1 GW Sam Y

EATON, Charles Henry (Harry), b Akron, Ohio 1850, d Leonia, NJ 1901, Amer, paint AAAd28 AAW1 B F H McC MM TB1 WWWA Y

EATON, Charles Warren, b Albany, NY 1857, d Leonia, NY? 1937, Amer, paint AAA33 AAW3 B DBA DBLP DVLP F G H RA TB1,3 WWA36d38 WWWA Y

EATON, Charles Wyatt (m Charlotte Amelia Collin Eaton, q.v.), b Philipsburg, Que 1849, d Middletown, nr Newport, RI 1896, paint AGO ANC App B BE CE1,2 DAB DCB12 F H M MM MQ NCAB8 NGC1,2 R2 TB1 W1–3 WWWA Y

EATON, Charlotte Amelia Collin (1887 m Charles Wyatt Eaton[2], q.v.), Eng, paint DAB[2] DCB12[2] Mo12 R2[2]

EBSEN, Alfred Karl, b Berlin 1908– , cal des CWW93 WWA93

ECCLES, Ronald Kenneth, b Canada 1944– , paint IO

ECCLESTON, Pegi, b 1935– , drw CAE2

ECHALOOK, Noah, b Elsie Isld, NWT 1946– , carv prt CWW93

ECHEVERRIA y GODOY, Atanasio, fl 1792–1804, Sp, paint EMA

EDA-NSA. *See* EDENSHAW, Albert Edward

EDE, Charles, fl 1850–2, Eng, paint sculp topog H

EDE, Frederick Vipond/Vipont, b Nottawa, Ont 1865, fl 1911, Amer, paint B H MM RCA TB1 Y

EDELL, Nancy, b Omaha, Nebr 1942– , paint prt WWA93

EDEMA, Gerard van, b Friesland, Neth c 1652, d Richmond, Sur c 1700,

Dutch, paint B Bry DBLP DNB H H77 OELP Red TB1

EDENSHAW, Albert Edward (Eda-Nsa[2]), b Gatlinskun, Queen Charlotte Islds, BC 1810, d Masset, BC 1894, carv DCB12[2]

EDENSHAW, Charles, b Skidigate, Queen Charlotte Islds, BC c 1839 – d 1920, carv CE1,2 Co DFA

EDGAR, Percival James, b Toronto 1888, d Cloguet, Minn 1946, paint prt NGC2

EDMONSON, Joe, b Windsor, Ont 1952– , paint IO

EDMUNDS, Philip J., fl 1882–90, engr H

EDOUART, Augustin-Amand-Contant-Fidèle, b Dunkerque, Fr 1789, d Guines, nr Calais, Fr 1861, Fr, sil APH B BSA DFA DIA GW H J K TB1

EDSON, Aaron Allan, b Stanbridge, Que 1846, d Glen Sutton, Que 1888, paint ACA AGO B CE1,2 DCB11 DeV1,2 EC H H77 LeJ M MM MQ NGC1,2 NGC67 RCA TB1 W1–3

EDSON, William, fl 1894–7, paint H MM

EDWARDS, Allan Whitcombe, b Edmonton 1915– , illus paint WWA82 WWNA

EDWARDS, Frank A., b Belleville, Ont 1940– , cart Po86–88

EDWARDS, Gordon Lewis, R Adm, b Medicine Hat, Alta 1931– , stgl CWW85

EDWARDS, Henrietta Muir (m O.C. Edwards), b Montreal 1849, d Ft Macleod, Alta 1931, min paint DFA DWA H MM Mo12 RCA

EDWARDS, O.E. (Mrs), fl 1899–1900, min H RCA

EDWARDS, Robert Chambers (Bob), b Edinburgh 1864, d Calgary 1922, cart CE1,2 Des EC W1–3

EDWARDS, Roger Glenn, b Barbados 1948– , paint sculp IO

EEGYVUDLUK, Ragee, E7 865, b Ikerrasak (camp nr Cape Dorset, NWT) 1920, d Cape Dorset 1983, prt NGC2

EGAN, Alice Mary. *See* HAGEN, Alice Mary Egan

EGAN[1], J. Hugh (F. Hugh[2]), fl 1892–1929, paint H MM RCA[1,2]

EGAR, Stanley Ernest, b Montreal 1913– , paint CWW80

EGERTON, Francis (b Francis Granville), 1st Earl Ellesmere of Ellesmere, Viscount Brackley of Brackley, b Picadilly, London 1800, d London 1857, Eng, paint BPp2587 DNB DP

EGERTON, Rowland Philip, b Lahore Punjab, India 1891, paint M

EGNATOFF, Peter George, b Perdue, Sask 1912– , paint O.My50

EGYEDI, Bela Ferenc, b Esztergom, Hu 1913, d 1982, gra prt CAE2 PHA

EHLERT, Una Mavis, b Bristol, Eng 1922– , sculp CAE1 IO

EISENHAUER, Collins, b 1898, d 1979, carv DFA

EITEL, George Edward, b Preston, Ont 1906, d Kitchener, Ont 1961, paint AGO M MM O.Ag50 RCA

EKOOTA, David, E2-349, b Baker Lake, NWT 1929– , sculp DEA

EKOOTAK, Victor, b Holman Isld, NWT 1916– , prt DEA

EL MAHDY, Wadie. *See* MAHDI, Wadie

ELDER, David Morton, b Windsor, Ont 1936– , Amer, sculp DAS WWA93

ELDRIDGE, Charles William, b New London, Conn 1811, d 1883, Amer, min F GW H

ELEESHUSHEE/ELISHUSHI, E7-1023, (m Parr, E7-1022, q.v.), b Cape Dorset, NWT 1896, d 1975, prt DEA

ELGIN, Mary Louisa Lambton, Countess (m James Bruce[2], 8th Earl of Elgin, 12th Earl of Kincardine), b England 1819, d Broomhall, Scot 1898, Eng, paint BPp322 DCB9[2] DNB[2] DP EC H LeJ W1–3 WHC[2]

ELIAS, André, b Banyuwangi, Indo 1952– , paint sculp MF

ELIAS, Arthur Edward, b Llansadwrn, N Wales 1872, paint Hu MM RCA

ELIASSON, Gissur, b Winnipeg 1912– , des paint M

ELIOT, Charles Graham, b Ottawa 1912, d 1940, paint Hu

ELIOT, Ruth Mary (aka Mary R.), b Ottawa 1913– , paint AGO MM

ELIZABETH, E9-1139, b Sugluk, Que, fl 1970s, sculp S

ELLERHUSEN, Florence Cooney (m Ulric Henry Ellerhusen), b Norwood, Ont 1888, d Towaco, NJ 1950, paint AAA33 DWA F WAA47d53 WWWA

ELLICE, Katherine Jane Balfour (m Edward Ellice), b 1814, d 1864, Eng, paint H PNL

ELLIOT, Arthur, b Taunton, Dev, fl 1881–2, Eng, paint topog H

ELLIOT/ELLIOTT, Joseph H., fl 1871–99, litho H

ELLIOTT, Douglas Ferguson, b Woodstock, Ont 1916– , paint IO

ELLIOTT, Emily Louise Orr (m John Ephraim Elliott[2]), b Montreal 1867, d Toronto 1952, paint AAA01 CWW49[2] DWA H Hu RCA

ELLIOTT, Gillian (Mrs), b Barrie, Ont 1940– , paint ABC

ELLIOTT, Glen Curtis, b Regina 1944– , paint IO

ELLIOTT, John David, b Niagara, Ont 1953– , paint IO

ELLIOTT[1], William (x Robert[2]), Capt, fl 1774, d Leeds, Eng 1792, Eng, paint topog Bry[2] DBHP DBLP DMA DNB DSP DWP G GW H Red[1,2]

ELLIS, Ada Leslie Withrow (m W.H. Ellis), b Saint John, NB c 1862, d Victoria, BC 1939, paint H

ELLIS, Dean, fl 1970– , con CAE1,2

ELLIS, Francis Wilson, fl 1778–1810, paint DFA

ELLIS, John[1]/John George[2], fl 1845–66, d 1888, des engr DeV8[1] H[1,2] RCA[1]

ELLIS, Owen William, b Swindon, Eng 1888, paint CWW67

ELLIS, Roy Gilmore, b Peterborough, Aus 1906– , paint CWW89

ELLIS, Salathiel, fl 1824–64, d New York, Amer, med paint B F GW H TB1

ELLIS, William, b London 1747 – d 1810, Eng, paint DBWA DMA DWP EMA

ELLISON, John, b Hamilton, Ont 1912, d 1957, paint M MM RCA

ELLWOOD, William James Howard, Col, b Cottesmore, Eng 1893, paint CWW58

ELOUL, Kosso (m Rita Letendre, q.v.), b Mourom, USSR 1920– , sculp CE1,2 CWW93 IO SC WWA93

ELPHICK, Gertrude Jean Hanson. *See* HANSON, Gertrude Jean

ELSTON, Dave, b 1958– , car Po86–88

EMODI, Arnold Ignace, b Tokay, Hu 1860, paint H Hu RCA

EMOND, Pierre, b Quebec 1738 – d 1808, carv DCB5 K

EMORI, Eiko, b Dairen, Japan 1938– , des gra CWW93 RCA WWA82

ENGEL, Howard (s Foo), b Toronto 1931– , cart CE2 CWW93

ENGELHART, Lou, b Campbellton, NB 1915– , car paint ABC

ENGLEHEART, Gardner D., fl 1860, Eng, paint DeV9

ENNECKER, Louis, b Germany c 1818, fl 1866, litho H

ENNS, Maureen, b Chilliwack, BC 1943– , paint sculp AA SC UA

ENSE, Donald Orion Henry, b Mindemoya, Manitoulin Isld, Ont 1953– , illus paint CE1,2

ENSOR, Arthur John, b Llanishen, Wales 1905– , des paint CWW93 NGC1,2 RCA Sam WBA1 WWB92

ENTZ, Anne Marie, b 1952– , paint CAE2

EPERJESSY, Ferdinand (Nandor), b Percel, Hu 1905– , paint PHA

EPOO, Lazarusie. *See* LAZARUSIE LAGUNUSIL, Epo/Epoo

EPP, Edward, b Saskatoon 1950– , paint CWW93
EPP, Paul, b Sexsmith, Alta 1949– , sculp IO
EPP, William Harold, b Glenbush, Sask 1930– , mur sculp MM US
EPSTEIN, Max, b on SS *Bremen* 1932 , paint prt CAE2 IO
EPSTEIN, William, b Calgary 1912– , sculp CWW91
ERICHSEN-BROWN, Daniel Price. *See* BROWN, Daniel Price Erichsen
ERICHSEN-BROWN[2], Frank, b Galt, re Cambridge, Ont 1878, d Toronto 1967, paint CWW64 MM Mo12[2] W3
ERICKSON, Arthur Charles, b Vancouver 1924– , paint CE1,2 Co CWW93 NGC2 RCA WWC89
ERICKSON, Bryce, b N Battleford, Sask 1948– , engr paint BB
ERKEL, John, fl 1970– , prt CAE2
ERKOOLIK, Toona, E2-167, b Baker Lake, NWT 1935– , sculp DEA
ERNETTE, Victor (aka Adolphe?), b France, fl 1842–4, paint H K
ESAR, Joan, b Montreal 1943– , prt sculp CWW93
ESLER, Annemarie Schmid. *See* SCHMID, Annemarie
ESLER, John Kenneth (m Annemarie Schmid, q.v.), b Pilot Mound, Man 1933– , etch litho paint AA AGO CAE1,2 CWW93 M MM NGC2 RCA S UG US WWA93
ESTCOURT, Caroline Pole Crew (1837 m James Bucknall Bucknall Estcourt, q.v.), d The Priory, Tetbury, Eng 1886, Eng, paint M PNL
ESTCOURT, James Bucknall Bucknall, Sir (m Caroline P.C. Estcourt, q.v.), b Glos, Eng 1802, d nr Sevastopol, Crimea 1855, Eng, paint topog DCB8 DNB H H77 PNL
ETIENNE, Errol Herbert Russell, b Edinburgh 1941– , des paint CWW93 RCA
ETROG, Sorel, b Jassy, Rom 1933– , paint prt sculp AGO CA1 CC1 CE1,2 Co CWW93 M MM NGC2 NGC67 RCA SC US WWA93
ETUNGAT. *See* ISHUHUNGITO/ ETUNGAT, E7-726
ETUNGAT/ETUNGET[2], Abraham, E7-809, b Cape Dorset, NWT 1911– , sculp DEA[2] RCA
EVALUARJUK/EVALUARDJUK[2], Henry, b nr Igoolik, NWT 1923– , paint prt sculp CE2 CWW93[2]
EVANS, Andrew Fitzherbert, R Adm, fl 1780, d Jersey Channel Islds 1826, Eng, paint DFA H WHC
EVANS, Anne Cynthia Marsh[2] (m James Alexander Evans, q.v.), b Nottingham, Eng 1923– , paint IO M[2]
EVANS, Blanche B., fl 1891–1906, paint H MM RCA
EVANS, Dennis J., b Hamilton, Ohio 1942– , sculp AA
EVANS, Don (s Isaac Bickerstaff[2]), b Toronto 1936– , car illus Co Des[2]
EVANS, Elizabeth Anne, b 1944– , paint IO
EVANS, Ford William (s Ford), b London, Ont 1952– , sculp IO
EVANS, James Alexander (m Anne Cynthia M. Evans, q.v.), b London, Ont 1918– , paint prt IO CWW93
EVANS, Jane Turnbull. *See* TURNBULL, Jane Mildred
EVANS, Lindsay A., b Chelsea, Mass 1891, d 1976, paint CAE1
EVANS, M.A. (Miss), fl 1862–6, paint H
EVANS, Owen Norton, b Toronto 1864, fl 1936, paint H Hu MM RCA
EVANS, Richard Charles (Ric), b Toronto 1946– , paint IO
EVANS, Sarah, b Brussels, Ont 1870, fl 1918, paint AAA05 B DWA
EVASCHESEN, Christine (m Kent Lynn), b Regina 1946– , paint BDSA
EVELEIGH, Henry, b Shanghai 1909– , paint AGO CLA MM WWA70
EVERETT, Florence Harris[2], b Thorold, Ont, fl 1913+, paint AAA13[2],33 DWA[2] F WWA40

EVERETT, Herbert D. (Mrs), fl 1880–1912, paint H

EVERMON, Robert (Bob), b 1941– , prt CAE2

EVES, Walter Graham, b Regina 1924– , paint CWW86

EVOY, Arthur, b Saskatchewan 1924– , paint SC

EWAN, Gladys Kathleen Mackintosh (1941 m George Ewan), b Victoria, BC, fl 1940s+, paint CLA M

EWART, Peter, b Kisbey, Sask 1918– , paint SC

EWEN, Thomas, b Vancouver 1949– , tex IO

EWEN, William Paterson (m Françoise Sullivan, q.v.), b Montreal 1925– , paint prt CAE2 CC2 CE1,2 CWW93 DCA IO M MM MQ NGC2 RCA TB3 WWA93

EWERT, fl c 1824, paint topog DMA

EYRE, Ivan Kenneth, b Tulleymet, Sask 1935– , paint sculp CAE2 CE1,2 CWW93 MM NGC2 RCA SC UG US WWA93

F

FABIEN, Henri-Zotique, b St-Cunégonde, Montreal 1878, d Ottawa 1935, paint B CNS36 H Hu K M MM RCA

FAFARD, Joseph Yvon (Joe), b Ste Marthe, Sask 1942– , sculp CAE2 CE1,2 DCA DFA M NGC2 SC WWA86

FAHRLAND, Théophile, b France 1825, d 1870, engr H K

FAILLE, Charles Arthur (Carl), b Detroit 1883, d Newport, RI 1956, Amer, paint AAA33 AAW2 AC B F K TB2 WWA53

FAILLON, Etienne-Michel, b Tarascon, Fr 1799, d Paris 1870, Fr, carv sculp DCB9 K

FAINMEL, Marguerite Paquette[2] (m Charles Fainmel), b Montreal 1910, d Nuns' Isld, nr Montreal 1981, paint AGO MM NGC2 WWA53[2]

FAINT, Johnny B., fl 1866–8, paint H

FAIRBAIN, Archibald, b Cape of Good Hope, SA, fl 1930+, paint WWNA

FAIRBAIRN, Robert Edis, Rev, b Sunderland, Eng 1880, d c 1956, carv engr CWW52

FAIRBAIRN, Sandy, b 1947– , paint CAE1

FAIRCHILD, G.M., Jr, b Quebec 1854, fl 1890, paint H

FAIRFIELD, Robert C., b St Catharines, Ont 1918, d Thornbury, Ont 1994, paint CWW91

FAIRHEAD, Patricia Mary Wiley (m Robert Fairhead), b Hull, Yorks 1927– , paint CWW93 IO

FAIRLEY, Barker, b Barnsley, Yorks 1887, d Toronto 1986, paint AGO CE1,2 Co CWW86 EC MM RCA TB3

FALARDEAU, Antoine-Sébastien, b Petit-Bois-de-l'Ail, nr Cap-Santé, Que 1822, d Arno River, nr Florence 1889, paint DCB11 EC H H77 K LeJ M NGC2 R2 W1–3

FALCONER, Alan Graham, b Edmonton 1943– , paint sculp IO

FALCONER, John M., b Edinburgh 1820, d New York 1903, Amer, etch paint AAAd28 ANC B F GW H TB1 Y

FALK, Gathie (Agatha) (m Dwight Swanson), b Alexander, Man 1928– , paint sculp CAE1 CE1,2 CWW93 MM NGC2 WWA82

FALKENBERG, Edward George, b Edmonton 1936– , sculp CAE1 IO

FALKENBERG, William, b Germany 1929– , sculp CAE1 IO

FALKLAND, Amelia Fitzclarence (m Lucius Bentick Cary[2], 10th Viscount Falkland), b Busby Park, nr London 1807, d 1858, Eng, paint APH BPp981 DCB11[2] DP DWA EC H W1–3

FANAIS, George Sarras (b Katsafanas), b Windsor, Ont 1922– , paint sculp M O.My50 RCA

FANE, Francis A., fl 1853, Eng, paint MQ

FANE, Priscilla Anne Pole. *See* WESTMORLAND, Priscilla Anne Pole, Countess

FANIEL, Jean-Alfred/Alfred-Jean-Joseph[2], b Verviers, Bel 1879, d Montreal 1950, paint K MM[2] RCA[2]

FANSHAW, Hubert Valentine, b Sheffield, Eng 1878, d Winnipeg 1940, paint GM Hu M MM NGC1,2 RCA Sam TB3

FARAGO, Kathleen Barbara, b Budapest 1952– , paint prt IO

FARAUD, Henri, b Gigondas, Fr 1823, d St Boniface, Man 1890, paint stgl K

FARBOTKO, George M., fl 1970– , paint sculp CAE2

FARLEY, Lilias Marianne Ar De Soif, b Ottawa 1907, d Whitehorse, YT 1989, sculp M RCA WWA70 WWNA

FARLOW, Harry MacNaughton, b Chicago 1881, d W Hartford, Conn 1956, Amer, paint B F Hu RCA TB2 WWA59

FARNCOMB, Caroline, b Newcastle Ont 1858, d Sheldon, Ont 1951, paint DWA H Hu MM RCA

FARNELL, Clyde, b 1919, d 1986, paint sculp DFA

FARNSWORTH, Alfred Villiers, b England c 1858, d San Francisco 1908, Eng, paint AAW3 AC

FARNUM, Suzanne. *See* SILVERCRUYS, Suzanne

FARNY, Henry/Henri-François, b Ribeauville, Alsace, Fr 1847, d Cincinnati 1916, Amer, illus paint AAA17d28 AAW1 AC AW B DAA F H K McC Sam TB1,3 WWWA Y

FARRAR, Michael, Rev, fl 1813–76, ske H KB

FARRELL, Sidney Baynton, b Malta 1829, d Barbados 1879, Eng, paint topog WHC

FASSIO/FASCIO[2], Gérôme (x Guiseppe), b Bonifacio, Corsica 1789, d Bytown, re Ottawa 1851, paint DCB8 H[2] K MQ NGC2

FAUCHER, Jean-Charles, b Montreal 1907– , paint B MM NGC2 RCA TB3 WWA62

FAUCHER, Pierre, b Montreal 1931– , paint prt CAE1

FAUCHOIS, Michel, fl 1675–8, sculp K

FAULKNER, Norman, b Edmonton 1944– , cer sculp AA

FAULKNER, Philippa Mary Burrows (m George Vermilyea Faulkner), b Belleville, Ont 1917– , paint sculp CAE1 CWW93 IO MM RCA

FAUNT, Jessie, b Doncaster, Eng, fl 1913–46, paint WWNA

FAUTEAUX, André-Lucien, b Dunnville, Ont 1946– , sculp CE1,2 IO NGC2

FAUTEUX, Henriette (m Jules T. Massé), b Coaticook, Que 1924– , paint M MM NGC2 RCA

FAUTEUX, Marie-Claire-Christine, b Montreal 1890, fl 1980s, paint CNS40 K MM RCA

FAVRE, M., fl 1913, med K MM

FAVREAU, Marcel, b 1922– , paint CAE1

FAVRO, Murray Carl, b Huntsville, Ont 1940– , paint sculp CA1–3 CAE1,2 CE1,2 DCA NGC2 WWA93

FAWCETT, Edgar, b New South Wales, Aus 1847, fl 1912, paint H

FAWCETT, George, b London 1877, d Miami, Fla 1944, paint prt AAA32 B F NGC2 RCA TB2 WWA36d47 Y

FAZAN, Juliet Sylvia. *See* McMASTER, Juliet Sylvia Fazan

FAZEKAS, Ilona Juhasz (Mrs), b Mezatur, Hu 1907– , paint PHA

FEATHERSON, William, b 1927– , paint sculp CAE1,2

FEDIOW, Pauline Hazel Daisy Redsell. *See* REDSELL, Pauline Hazel Daisy

FEIST, David, b 1909– , paint CAE2

FEIST, Harold Elmer, b San Angelo, Tex 1945– , paint sculp WWA93

FIELD, Robin W., b 1945– , paint prt CAE1,2
FIELD, Saul (m Dorothy Jean Townsend, q.v.), b Montreal 1912, d 1987, paint prt IO M MM WWA86d89
FIELDING, Edward, b San Diego, Calif 1943– , paint sculp CAE1
FIERTEL, Neil, b New York 1941– , sculp AA
FILER, Mary Harris (m Antonio Romo), b Edmonton 1920– , paint sculp stgl AGO CLA MM NGC2
FILIATRAULT, Jean, b Montreal 1919– , paint CWW82
FILIAU dit DUBOIS, François, b 1761/2, d Montreal 1831, sculp K
FILION, Armand, b Montreal 1910– , sculp M MM MQ RCA
FILION, Gabriel, b Montreal 1920– , paint M MM TB3
FILION, Jean-Paul, b nr St-André-Avellin, Que 1927 , paint CC2 MM
FILION, Pierrette, b Arvida, Que 1935– , paint MM TB3
FILIPOVIC, Augustin, b Davor, Yu 1931– , paint sculp AGO CAE1 Co M WWA93
FILLION, John, b Little Current, Ont 1933– , sculp B RCA
FINCH, Robert Duer Claydon, b Freeport, Long Isld, NY 1900– , paint prt CC2 CWW93 Hu NGC2
FINDLAY, Jean Ness[2] (m John A. Findlay), b Montreal 1901– , paint M MM[2]
FINDLEY, Allan Y., b Toronto 1902– , paint CWW64
FINE, Phyllis Kurtz, b Toronto 1924– , etch sculp IO MM
FINES, Anne (m C. Welch), b Toronto 1946– , paint prt CAE1
FINLAY, George E., Lt, b 1819, fl 1837–50, Eng, topog DFA H
FINLAY, Samuel Stevenson, b Lisburn, Ire 1888, d Toronto 1938, illus Hu RCA
FINLAYSON, Isobel Graham Simpson[2] (m Duncan Finlayson), b London 1811 – d 1890, Eng, paint DCB11[2] DWA H
FINLAYSON, Ken, fl 1975– , prt sculp CAE1
FINLEY, Frederick James, b New Castle, Aus 1894, d Toronto 1968, etch paint CWW64 M MM NGC1,2 O.N47 RCA S TB3 US W3 WWA66
FINLEY, Gerald Eric, b Munich, Ge 1931– , paint CWW93 MM RCA S WWA93
FINN, Henry James William, b Sydney, NS 1787, d Long Isld Sound, NY 1840, Amer, min BM F Fo GW H WWWA Y
FINSTERER, Daniel, b Sainte-Marguerite-de-Blairfindie, Que c 1791, fl 1811–27/30, sculp K
FINSTERER, Georges, fl 1788–1824, sculp K
FIORE, Giuseppe, b Mola di Bari, It 1931– , paint sculp CAE1
FISCHER, George, b St Petersburg 1903– , sculp M
FISCHER, Trudy, b Basel, Swi 1917– , paint prt US
FISCHL, Eric, b New York 1948– , Amer, drw paint DCAA3 NGC2 WWA93
FISH, Robert. *See* FIELD, Robert James
FISHER, Alvan T., b Needham, Mass 1792, d Dedham, Mass 1863, Amer, paint B BE DAA F GW H TB1 Y
FISHER, Amy, fl 1892–1905, paint H MM
FISHER, Arthur John, b London 1913– , paint CWW84
FISHER, Benjamin, Maj Gen, fl 1785–96, Eng, paint WHC
FISHER, Brian Richard, b Uxbridge, Eng 1939– , paint prt AE CAE1 CC2 MM NGC2 RCA S SC
FISHER, George Bulteel, Maj Gen, b Peterborough, Eng 1764, d Woolwich, Eng 1834, Eng, paint topog B DBLP DBWA DCB6 DeV7 G GW H OELP ROM TB1 WHC
FISHER, Orville Norman, b Vancouver

1911– , paint CLA GM M MM NGC68 TB3 WWA62

FISHER, Robert William[2], b Bainsville, Ont 1923– , etch paint IO RCA[2]

FISHER, Roy, b Toronto 1890, fl 1935, paint Hu

FISI, Judit (Mrs), b Budapest 1949– , paint ABC

FITCHES, Williams, b Oshawa, Ont 1945– , mmed DCA

FITLER, William Crothers, b Philadelphia 1857, d 1915, Amer, paint B H TB1

FITZCLARENCE, Amelia. *See* FALKLAND, Amelia Fitzclarence

FITZGERALD, Clara Du Bois Osler[2] (1896 m Frederick William Gerald Fitzgerald[3]), fl 1890–7, paint DWA[2] H MM[2] Mo12[3]

FITZGERALD, Lionel Le Moine, b Winnipeg 1890 – d 1956, paint ACA AE AGO CC1 CE1,2 Co EC GM H77 Hu M NGC1,2 NGC67 OC RCA S Sam SC TB2,3 TN UG US W2,3 WWA53

FITZGERALD, Thomas, fl 1858–60, paint H

FITZGIBBON, Agnes Dunbar Moodie. *See* CHAMBERLIN, Agnes Dunbar Moodie

FITZJAMES, James, Capt, fl 1845, Eng, topog H

FITZMAURICE, J.B. (Fitz), b England 1873, d Vancouver 1974, cart Des

FITZMAURICE, M. Douglas, b Liskard, Eng 1902– , paint CWW70

FLAKEY ROSE HIP. *See* LEWIS, Glen Alun

FLANCER, Ludwig, b 1902, d 1980, paint DFA KB

FLECK, Margaret H. *See* AHEARN, Margaret Howit Fleck

FLEISHER, Patricia, b Toronto 1930– , prt IO WWA93

FLEMING, Alexander M., b Chatham, Ont 1876, d Guelph, Ont 1929, paint Hu MM RCA

FLEMING, Allan R., b Toronto 1929 – d 1977, gra APH Co RCA WWA78 WWGA1

FLEMING, John Arnot, b Kirkcaldy, Scot 1835, d Toronto 1876, paint topog DCB10 H Sam

FLEMING, Sandford A., Sir, b Kirkcaldy, Scot 1827, d Halifax 1915, des CE1,2 Co CWW10 DeV8 DNB EC H LeJ Mo98,12 W1–3

FLETCHER, Ed, b 1900, d 1980, paint DFA KB

FLETCHER, Frederick Ernest, b Toronto 1923– , paint CWW93 RCA

FLETCHER, George, b Toronto 1914– , paint IO

FLEURY, Henriette H. Krentel (m Théodore Fleury[2]), fl 1928–9, sculp K[2]

FLEWELLING, Dorena, b Lacombe, Alta 1909– , paint M

FLEWELLING/FLEWWING[2], Charles H., fl 1876–90, engr H RCA[2]

FLINN, Wesley Robson, b Toronto 1906– , paint Hu

FLODBERG, Gilbert Allan, b Calgary 1938– , prt SC

FLOOD, Edward Alison, Lt Col, b Saint John, NB 1904– , paint CWW79

FLORES, Gerri, fl 1970– , paint sculp CAE2

FLOUD, Phyllis Allen Ford, Lady (1909 m Sir Francis Lewis Casile Floud[2]), Eng, paint MM WWW[2]

FLOWER, Anthony, b London 1794, d 1867, Eng, paint H

FOLEY, Wilma, b 1938– , paint IO

FOLINGSBY, George Frederick, b Wicklow Co, Ire 1828/30, d Melbourne, Aus 1891, Irish, paint B DBHP DBWA DIA G GW H TB1

FONES, Robert John, b London, Ont 1949– , prt sculp CAE1,2 NGC2

FONKIN, Laza, b Nis, Yu 1939– , sculp ABC

FONS. *See* WOERKOM, Fons van

FONVILLE, Charles. *See* BECARD/BECART de GRANVILLE et de FONVILLE, Charles

FOO. *See* ENGEL, Howard
FOO FAT, Dulcie, b London 1946– , paint SC
FOOTNER, Wilhelm, b Germany 1799, d Montreal 1867, drgt H
FORBES[1], Elizabeth Adela Armstrong[2] (m Stanhope Alexander Forbes), b Kingston, Ont 1859, d Newlyn, Corn 1912, paint B DBA DBWA DVP DWA G[1,2] H M MM Mo12 NGC1,2 RA RCA TB1 WBA1 WWW
FORBES, Frances Kirkpatrick. *See* BAYNE, Frances Kirkpatrick Forbes
FORBES, Jean Mary Edgell (m Kenneth Keith Forbes, q.v.), b Karachi, Pak 1897, paint Hu MM RCA
FORBES, John, b Scotland c 1807, fl 1861, paint H
FORBES, John Allison, b Evansburg, Alta 1922– , paint WWA93
FORBES, John Colin, b Toronto 1846 – d 1925, paint B CWW10 EC H H77 Hu LeJ M MM Mo98,12 NGC1,2 R2 RCA ROM S TB1,3 W1–3 WBA2
FORBES, Kenneth Keith (m Jean M.E. Forbes, q.v.), b Toronto 1892, d North York, Ont 1980, paint AGO CC2 CWW80 DBA FCA M NGC1,2 NGC68 PMC RA RCA TB2 US WWA62 WWC66
FORBES, Laura June. *See* McCORMACK, Laura June Forbes
FORBES, W.F., b Canada, fl 1848–68, paint DFA H
FORCIES, François A., b St-François-du-Lac, Que 1888, fl 1951, sculp K
FORD. *See* EVANS, Ford William
FORD, Charles Erskine, Maj Gen, fl 1848–53, ret 1868, Eng, ske DFA H
FORD, Harriet Mary, b Brockville, Ont 1859, d England 1938, paint AGO DBA DVP DWA H Hu M MM NGC1,2 RCA TB3 WWB29
FORD, Susan, b El Reno, Okla 1944– , prt SC
FORGIE, George Patrick, b Toronto 1932– , paint sculp IO RCA S UG
FORGUES, Michel Alain, b Lauzon, Que 1945– , prt CAE1
FORREST, Charles Ramus, Lt Col, b England c 1787, d Bath, Eng 1827, Eng, paint topog APH H H74 NGC2 ROM WHC
FORREST, Nita Osborne, b Quesnel, BC 1926– , drgt paint DCA
FORRESTAL, Thomas De Vany, b Middleton, NS 1936– , paint CAE1 CC1 CE1,2 CWW93 DCA M MA MM RCA WWA93
FORRESTER, Ellen Brooks, b New York 1950– , paint IO
FORSTER, Francis Michael, b Calcutta 1907– , drgt paint AGO B CC2 M MM NGC2 NGC68 TB2 WWA53
FORSTER, John Wycliffe Lowes, b Norval, Ont 1850, d Toronto 1938, paint AGO B CC1 CE1,2 CNS36 DBA EC H H77 M MM Mo98,12 NGC1,2 PMC RCA TB1,3 US W1–3 WWB34
FORSTER, Terry, b England 1936– , prt NGC2
FORSTER, William Charles, b Dublin 1816, d Hamilton, Ont 1902, drw paint DIA H
FORSYTH, Mina Mabel McDonald (m Basil Forsyth), b Estevan, Sask 1920, d 1987, paint BDSA US
FORTIER, Ivanhoe, b St-Louis-de-Courville, Que 1931– , paint sculp M MM MQ
FORTIER, John Des, b Demorestville, Ont 1851, d 1923, paint H K
FORTIER, Joseph, fl 1882–1900, litho H K
FORTIER, Michael, b Montreal 1943– , paint prt AGO NGC2
FORTIN, Célyne, b La-Sarre, Que 1943– , paint CWW93
FORTIN, Flora (Soeur Marie-Jean-du-Calvaire), b 1874, d Outremont, Que 1927, paint K
FORTIN, Marc-Aurèle, b Ste-Rose, Que 1888, d St-Jean-de-Macamic, Que 1970, paint AE AGO B CC2 CE1,2 CWW61 EC H77 Hu K M MM MQ

NGC1,2 NGC67 RCA TB2 TN W1–3 WWA53
FOSBERY, Ernest George, b Ottawa 1874, d Cowansville, Que 1960, paint AGO B CNS40 CWW53 DBA EC H77 M MM Mo12 NGC1,2 NGC68 PMC RA RCA TB2 US W2,3 WWA53 WWB62
FOSBERY, Lionel Gooch, b Ottawa 1879, d Wakefield, Que 1956, sculp M MM NGC2 PMC RCA
FOSTER, Benjamin (Ben), b North Anson, Me 1852, d NY 1926, Amer, paint AAA25d28 AAW1,3 B DAB F H NCAB11 Sam TB1,3 WWWA Y
FOSTER, Doreen, b Sault Ste Marie, Ont 1956– , paint IO
FOSTER, Evelyn R. *See* WRIGHT, Evelyn R. Foster
FOSTER, Frederick Lucas, fl 1842–1900, paint H Hu ROM
FOSTER, Harold, b Halifax 1892, d Spring Hill, Fla 1982, illus CE1,2 WECo
FOSTER, Hilda Vincent, b W Bridgeford, Notts 1896, paint M RCA
FOSTER, Laura Barter (m James Frink Foster), b Hartland, NB 1919– , paint pas CWW70
FOSTER, Malcolm Burton, b Montreal 1931– , paint CWW93
FOSTER, Robert Gibbons, b Hamilton, Ont 1888 – d 1948, prt NGC2
FOSTER, Velma Alvada, b Maidstone, Sask 1938– , paint prt BDSA CAE1
FOTHERGILL, Charles, b Yorks, Eng 1782, d Toronto 1840, paint DCB7 H H74 H77 KB ROM W1–3
FOUCHARDIERE, Marie-Noelle de la, b 1946– , paint tap CAE1
FOUGERAT, Emmanuel, b Rennes, Fr 1869, d Paris c 1958, Fr, paint B K RCA TB1,2
FOULDS, Donald Miles, b Saskatoon 1953– , paint sculp US
FOULGER, Richard F., b Kamloops, BC 1949– , paint prt CAE1,2 WWA86
FOULIS, Robert, b Glasgow 1796, d Saint John, NB 1866, paint DCB9 H H77
FOURDRINIER, Emily Louise, b Waterloo, Que 1870, d Ottawa 1896, paint H K MM RCA
FOUREUR dit CHAMPAGNE, Jean-Louis, b Montreal 1745 – d 1822, sculp K
FOUREUR dit CHAMPAGNE, Louis, b Montreal 1720 – d 1789, carv DCB4 K
FOURNELLE, André, b Montreal 1939– , prt sculp CAE1 MM NGC2
FOURNIER, Alexander Paul, b Simcoe, Ont 1939– , paint DCA IO MM NGC2 UG WWA80
FOURNIER, Ambrose, fl 1847–76, sculp K
FOURNIER, Arthur, b St-Jean-Port-Joli, Que c 1866 – d 1935, carv K
FOURNIER, Claude, b 1799/1800, fl 1817, sculp K
FOURNIER, François-Marie, b Cap-St-Ignace, Que 1790, d Montmagny, Que 1864, sculp K NGC2
FOURNIER, Thomas, b St-Charles-de-Bellechasse, Que 1825, d 1898, carv paint H K
FOWLER, Daniel, b Champion Hill, Comberwell, Sur 1810, d Amherst Isld, Ont 1894, paint ACA AE AGO B CE1,2 DCB12 DBLP EC H H77 LeJ M MM NGC1,2 NGC67 R2 RCA ROM St TB1 W1–3
FOWLER, Graham, b Halifax 1952– , paint CWW93
FOWLER, J.O., fl 1871–9, paint H
FOWLER, Joseph Ades, b 1850, d 1921, paint H
FOX, Charles Harold, b Clarks Harbour, NS 1905, d 1979, cer WWA78d80
FOX, Frances Galbraith (m W. Claude Fox), b Concord, NH 1895, paint Hu
FOX, John Richard, b Montreal 1927– , paint AE B CC1 CE1,2 CWW93 M MM NGC1,2 RCA TB3 WWA93
FOX, Robert Atkinson, b Toronto 1860, fl 1900, paint AAA01 H RCA Sam

FOX, Winnifred Grace McGill (m Charles H. Fox), b Avondale, NS 1909– , illus paint CLA M MM WWA80

FOX-PITT[2], Douglas, b London 1864, d Chertsey, Sur 1922, Eng, illus paint B[2] DBA DBWA[2] DVP[2] TB1[2],2 WBA WWW

FOXCROFT, David, b Calgary 1953– , paint sculp AA

FRACAS. *See* POIRIER, Normand

FRAME, Margaret Josephine Geraldine Fulton (m H.S. Beatty), b Oxford, NS 1903– , paint M MM RCA US

FRAME, Statira Elizabeth Wells (m William Frame), b Waterloo, Que 1870, d Vancouver 1935, paint AAW3 WWNA

FRANCE, Anna, b N Ireland 1948– , tap IO

FRANCE, Eurilda Loomis (m Jessie Leach France, q.v.), b Pittsburg, Pa 1865, d New Haven, Conn 1931, Amer, paint AAA29d31 DWA H MM RCA

FRANCE, Jessie Leach (m Eurilda Loomis France, q.v.), b Cincinnati, Ohio 1862, d New Haven, Conn 1926, Amer, paint AAA26d28 B F MM RCA TB3

FRANCEY, Jeannette Hanna (m Peter Francey), b Rochester, NY 1952– , gra CWW93

FRANCHE, Don, b Grand Forks, BC, fl 1949+, illus paint M

FRANCHERE, fl 1862, Fr, panor B H K TB1

FRANCHERE, Joseph Charles, b Montreal 1866 – d 1921, paint CC2 CE1,2 H H77 Hu K MM MQ NGC1,2 RCA TB3 W1–3

FRANCIS, Britton M., b 1947– , paint CAE1

FRANCIS, Dorothy Delores Leonard (m Harold Reid Francis), b Dinsmore, Sask 1923– , paint CWW93

FRANCIS, Harold Carleton, b Culloden, Ont 1919– , engr paint M WWA76

FRANCIS, Mary, b 1900, d 1979, paint KB

FRANCIS, Tim, b Hamilton, Ont 1949– , paint SC

FRANCIS, Vincent, b London 1912– , paint O.Ag49 RCA

FRANCK, Albert Jacques (m Florence Gertrude Vale, q.v.), b Middleburg, Neth 1899, d Toronto 1973, paint AGO CE1,2 Co M MM RCA UG WWA76

FRANCK, Florence Gertrude Vale. *See* VALE, Florence Gertrude

FRANCOIS, Père. *See* BREKENMACHER, Jean-Melchior

FRANCOIS, Claude, dit LUC[2], Frère, b Amiens, Fr 1614, d Paris 1685, Fr, paint ACA[2] B CE1,2[2] Co[2] DCB1 EC[2] H[2] H77[2] K M[2] MQ NGC67[2] TB1

FRANCOISE, Annette (Mrs Zeldin[2]), b California, fl 1960s, tex IO[2]

FRANK, J. Peter, b St Gallen (x St Gall), Swi 1903– , gra paint WWNA

FRANKENSTEIN, Godfrey N., b Germany 1820, d Springfield, Ohio 1873, Amer, paint DAA GW H Y

FRANKENSTEIN, John Peter, b Germany c 1816, d New York 1881, Amer, paint sculp B DAA DAS GW H TB1 Y

FRANKLIN, Edward Livingstone, b Texas 1921– , cart Des Po86–88

FRANKLIN, Hannah, b Poland 1937– , sculp CAE1 WWA93

FRANKS, Christopher Ralph, b Bombay, India 1937– , sculp CWW93

FRANKS, Frederic, Capt, d 1844, Eng, paint H

FRANQUELIN, Jean-Baptiste-Louis, b St Michel de Villebernin, Fr c 1651, d France 1718, Fr, paint topog DCB2 H K LeJ W1–3

FRASER, A. McLeod, fl 1856, litho H ROM

FRASER, Carol Lucille Hoorn (m John

Fraser), b Superior, Wis 1930– , paint CC2 DCA MM NGC2 RCA WWA89

FRASER, Charles Malcolm, b Montreal 1868, d Orlando, Fla 1949, illus paint AAA33 B CWW48 F NCAB TB1 WWA47d53 WWWA Y

FRASER, Edward D., b Toronto 1946– , paint IO

FRASER, Elizabeth A. *See* McLEOD, Elizabeth A. Fraser

FRASER, Frederick Alexander, b Toronto 1897, paint O.F49

FRASER, Gregory G., b Oshawa, Ont 1949– , paint CAE2 IO

FRASER, Isabel Evelyn, b Charlottetown 1890, paint MA

FRASER, James (Jim), b Toronto 1950– , paint IO

FRASER, Janny, b Zwolle, Neth 1943– , tex IO

FRASER, John, b Tomnac Loch, Scot 1750, d London 1811, Scot, paint DNB GW

FRASER, John Arthur, b London 1838, d New York 1898, paint AAW1 ACA AE AGO CE1,2 DBA DCB12 EC H H77 M MM Mo98 NGC1,2 NGC67 RCA Sam TB1 W1–3

FRASER, John Keith, b Ottawa 1922– , paint CWW93

FRASER, Malcolm. *See* FRASER, Charles Malcolm

FRASER, William Lewis, b London 1841, d New York 1905, illus paint AAAd28 B DFA H H77 Y

FRAZER, George Alexander, Capt, b pre 1817, d c 1863, Eng, paint APH

FRECHETTE, Archille, b Lévis, Que 1847, d San Diego, Calif 1927, paint CWW10 H K Mo12 RCA

FRECHETTE, Célina (Soeur Marie-de-Saint-Jean-Berchmans), b 1853, d 1942, paint K

FRECHETTE, Louis-Honoré, b Pointe-Lévy, Que 1839, d Montreal 1908, paint CE1,2 Co EC H K LeJ Mo98 W1–3

FRECHETTE, Marie-Marguerite, b Ottawa 1878 (x 1884), d San Diego, Calif 1964, paint AAA25 AC DWA F H K MM RCA Y

FREDERICK/FREDERICKS, Alfred, fl 1853 81, Amer, paint GW H

FREEDMAN, Harry, b Lodz, Pol 1922– , paint CWW93

FREEDY, Constance Elizabeth (m George Glenn), b Cutknife, Sask 1944– , paint BDSA

FREEMAN, George, b Bolton, Spring Hill, Conn 1787/9, d Hartford, Conn 1868, Amer, min paint AM BM F Fo GW H WWWA Y

FREEMAN, James Edward, b Grand Passage, NS 1808, d Rome 1884, paint ANC B DAB F GW H TB1 Y

FREEMAN, Richard Audley, b Leicester, Eng 1932– , paint ABC SC

FREER, J.H., fl 1833–51, paint H

FREIFELD, Eric, b Saratov, USSR 1919, d 1984, drw paint CAE1 CWW85 DBA IO M NGC2 RCA UG WWA84d86 WWC82

FREIMAN, Lillian (Lilly), b Guelph, Ont 1908, d New York 1986, paint AE B CC1 Hu M MM NGC1,2 NGC67 S TB3 UG

FREMONT, John Charles, b Savanna, Ga 1813, d New York 1890, Amer, panor topog K

FRENCH, Betty M. *See* McCAUGHEY, Betty M. French

FRENCH, Maida Doris. *See* KNOWLES, Maida Doris Parlow

FRENCH, Michael Peter, b Chilliwack, BC 1951– , paint IO

FRENIERE, F. Daunais, fl 1833–43, paint H K

FRENKEL, Vera, b Bratislava, Cz 1938– , prt sculp CE1,2 NGC2

FRENZENY, Paul, b France c 1840, d c 1902, Fr, illus AAW1 AC DBA H K McC Sam WWWA

FREY, Christle Norman, b Morriston, Ont 1886, d c 1950, paint DFA KB

FREY, Hey, b Berne, Swi 1938– , sculp IO

FRICK, Joan, b Toronto 1942– , drw paint CAE1,2 DCA IO WWA93

FRIED, Emily Mary Gunn. *See* GUNN, Emily Mary

FRIEDEL. *See* WASHCHUK, Friedel

FRIEDMAN, Sydney M., b Montreal 1916– , paint CWW93

FRIEND, Washington Frederick, b Washington, DC c 1820, d Littlehampton, Eng 1891, Eng, paint AAW2 AC B H NGC2 RCA ROM Sam WHC

FRIESEN, Victor, b Lyesnoye, Ukr 1911– , paint M

FRIPP, Charles Edwin, b Hampstead, London 1854, d Montreal 1906, bu London, Eng, illus paint AAW1,3 AH B DBA DBHP DBMP DBWA DVP DWP G H Sam TB1 WBA1 WI

FRIPP, Thomas William, b St John's Wood, London 1864, d Vancouver 1931, paint CC2 CE1,2 DBA DVLP EC H H77 Hu MM NGC1,2 RCA Sam TB3 WBA2 WWNA

FRISE, James Llewellyn, b Scugog Isld, nr Port Perry, Ont 1890, d 1948, illus Co CWW48 WECo

FROME, Edward Charles, Lt, b 1802, d 1890, Eng, paint DFA H

FRONTINI, Gian F., b Milan, It 1936– , paint IO

FROST, Arthur Burdett, b Philadelphia 1851, d Pasadena, Calif 1928, Amer, paint AAA27d28 AAW1 AC B DAB F H NCAB Sam TB1,3 WWAd38 WWWA Y

FROST, George Albert (Charles^2), b Boston 1843, fl 1906, Amer, paint AAA05 AAW1 AC B H^2 TB1

FROST, John Ings Crawford, b Merrick, NY 1894, Amer, sculp CWW38

FROST, Teresa (m David Frost), b Sault Ste Marie, Ont 1961– , illus C

FROWDE, Lola Marie. *See* MOULD, Lola Marie Frowde

FRY, Beatrice Adelaide (Bessie) (m Richard Symons), b Farringdon, Berks 1884, d Victoria, BC 1976, paint GM RCA UG WWNA

FRY, Brian Jeffrey, b Brighton, Sur 1944– , paint IO

FRYER, Bryant Wilkins, b Galt, re Cambridge, Ont 1897, d Toronto 1963, paint Hu RCA

FRYER, John Leslie, b London 1938– , cal CWW93

FUGLER, Grace (m Leonard Hutchinson, q.v.), b Hamilton, Ont 1915–, engr AGO GM MM RCA

FULFORD, Alice Mary (1858 m Henry Martin Lower), b England – d 1922, Eng, paint WHC

FULFORD, Patricia Naomi (m Raymond Spiers, q.v.), b Toronto 1935– , sculp B CWW93 RCA

FULLER, Charles S., b London c 1835, fl 1861, litho H

FULLER, Thomas, b Bath, Eng 1822, d Ottawa 1898, paint ACA App CE1,2 Co DeV6,8 H Mo98 NGC1,2 RCA

FULLERTON, Frederick Charles (Ted), b Ottawa 1953– , paint prt IO

FULLONTON, Evelyn M., b Canada 1853, d Laguna Beach, Calif 1931, paint AAA24 AC

FUNNEKOTTER, Jan, b Netherlands 1929– , paint SC

FUREY, Conrad Stephen, b Baie Verte, Nfld 1954– , paint DFA IO

FUROY, Gill (s Gill), b Notre-Dame-du-Nord, Que 1951– , drw paint CAE1,2 IO

FYSHE, Aviss Selina, b Halifax 1886, illum AAA30 MM

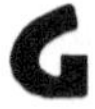

GABANKOVA, Maria, b Czechoslovakia 1951– , paint MFMS

GABE, Ron. *See* PARTZ, Felix

GABLE, Brian, b Saskatoon 1949– , cart Po86–88

GABO/GABORIAU, Pierre. *See* LA PALME, Pierre

GABOURY, Serge, b Quebec 1954– , car Po86–89
GADBOIS, Denyse (Mme Chaput), b Montreal 1921– , paint sculp M MM NGC2 WWA53
GADBOIS, Louis V., fl 1876–1904, paint DFA H K
GADBOIS, Marie-Marguerite-Louise-Landry[2] (m Emilien Gadbois), b Montreal 1896 – d 1988, paint DWA K[2] M MM MQ NGC1,2 RCA WWA53
GAGE, Frances Marie, b Windsor, Ont 1924– , sculp CWW93 IO M RCA UG WWA93
GAGEN, Caroline S., fl 1879–85, paint H RCA
GAGEN, Robert Ford, b London 1847, d Toronto 1926, paint AGO B CC1 EC H H77 Hu LeJ M MM NGC1,2 NGC68 R1 RCA TB1,3 US W1–3
GAGNE, Michel, fl 1890–1, sculp K
GAGNE, Rosaire, fl 1913+, paint K
GAGNER, Yvon, b Montreal 1946– , paint CAE1
GAGNIER, Charles S., fl 1873–89, paint K
GAGNIER, Jacques, b Montreal 1917 – d 1978, car Des
GAGNIER, Perpétue, fl 1880–96, paint K
GAGNON, Aristide (Arist), b Amqui, Que 1930– , paint sculp M
GAGNON, Cécile (m Michel Bergeron), b Quebec 1936– , illus SAA58
GAGNON, Charles, b Montreal 1934– , paint B CC2 CE1,2 DCA M MM MQ NGC2 NGC67 S UG WWA93
GAGNON, Clarence-Alphonse, b Ste-Rose, nr Montreal 1881, d Montreal 1942, paint AAA25 ACA AGO B CC1 CE1,2 Co CWW38 FCA H77 Hu M MM Mo12 MQ NGC1,2 NGC67 RCA TB1,2 TN W1–3
GAGNON, Elizabeth (Liz, aka Liz Ingram), b Buenos Aires 1949– , prt AA UG
GAGNON, Joseph, fl 1930+, paint K
GAGNON, Maurice, b Ottawa 1904– , paint WWA53
GAGNON, René, b Chicoutimi, Que 1927– , paint M
GAIRDNER, James Arthur, b Toronto 1893, d c 1969, paint CWW67 WWC68d71
GAITSKELL, Charles Dudley, b Kent, Eng 1908– , paint O.N49
GAKOVIC, Maria Bogdanov (m Caslaw Gakovic), b Osijek, Yu 1918– , paint BDSA
GAL, Laszlo, b Hungary 1933– , illus CBC SAA32,52
GALARNEAU, Léopold, fl 1882–92, paint H K MM
GALAVARIS, George, b Greece 1926– , paint CWW93
GALBRAITH, Clara E., fl 1895–1900, paint H
GALBRAITH, Elizabeth Roberta (Betty) (m C.D. Cornell), b Montreal 1916– , paint M MM RCA
GALBREATH, Janet M., b Glasgow 1927– , paint M
GALE, Denis, b Quebec 1828, d 1903, paint H WHC
GALE, Goddard Frederick, b England 1857, d Oakland, Calif 1938, paint AAA09 AAW2 AC DBA H
GALEA, Edward Zarb, b Valletta, Malta 1893, sculp CNS40 MM
GALLANT, Yvon, b Moncton, NB 1950– , con paint DCA
GALLI, Saverio, b Ceccano, It 1921– , paint M
GALLIE, Tommie J., b Halifax 1946– , sculp AA CAE2 SC
GALLOWAY, Kenneth Murray, b Salmon Arm, BC 1927– , paint M
GALLOWAY, Margaret, b Rochester, Kent 1915– , paint BDSA
GALLWEY, Thomas Lionel John, Lt Gen, Sir, b Farm Hill, Killarney, Ire 1821, d Eastbourne, Eng 1906, Eng, paint H WHC WWW
GALPER, Devora, b Toronto 1954– , prt IO

GALT, Jean, b 1928– , paint CAE1
GALT, Jocelyn (m George Galt), b Montreal 1927– , paint M MM
GAMACHE, Jeannine/Janine (m Philippe Paquette), b Quebec 1931– , paint M MM
GAMBIOLI, Joan, b Vancouver 1920– , sculp BCS M
GAMBLE, Eric/Erik, b Toronto 1950– , paint pas IO
GAMBOLI. *See* HARPS, Tony
GAME, Robert, b Edmonton 1944– , etch paint IO SC
GARANT, André (m Louise Carrier, q.v.), b Lévis, Que 1923– , paint M TB3
GARDINER, Frederick, fl 1878–9, illus H
GARDINER, John Rawson, b London 1866, d Montreal 1956, paint H MM RCA
GARDNER, James Martin, b Toronto 1884, paint Hu
GARNEAU, Elzébert, b 1891, paint K
GARNEAU, Hector de Saint-Denys, b Montreal 1912, d Ste-Catherine-de-Fossambault, Que 1943, paint CE2 MM
GARNEAU, Michael (s Garnott), b Montreal 1951– , car Po86,88
GARNER, Alec John, b S Hampton, Eng 1897, d Kootenay Bay, BC 1995, paint M RCA
GARNER, Bruce Graham, b Toronto 1934– , paint sculp IO M
GARNERAY, Ambrose-Louis, b Paris 1783 – d 1857, Fr, paint ANC B G W K TB1
GARNOTT. *See* GARNEAU, Michael
GARRIOCH, Ian, b 1936– , paint CAE1,2
GARRISON, Benjamin, b 1757, topog H ROM
GARSIDE, Thomas Hilton, b Duckinfield, Ches 1906, d 1980, paint M MM RCA
GARSTANG-HODGSON, Wilfred, b Barrington Hall, Scot 1885, d 1971, carv M
GARTH, William Edward de[2], b Kasko, Fin 1907, d Etobicoke, Ont 1983, paint sculp CLA[2] M[2] MA WWA82
GARWOOD, Audrey Elaine (m Herb R. Hosie), b Toronto 1927– , paint CWW93 M MM RCA WWA93
GASCARD, G., fl 1873–6, cart illus DeV2,3,7,8 H K
GASCON, Carmel, b Shawinigan, Que 1924– , paint tap CAE1
GASKING, fl 1851–60, engr G W H
GASS, Mabel McCulloch. *See* McCULLOCH, Mabel
GASS, Marjorie Earle, b Saint John, NB 1889, d Montreal 1928, paint DWA Hu M MM NGC1,2 RCA TB3
GATIEN, Felix, b Quebec 1776, d Cap-Santé, Que 1844, sculp DCB7 K
GATTERBAUER, Margit Brewer (Mrs), b Gablonz, Cz 1934– , paint M
GAUCHER, Yves, b Montreal 1934– , paint AE AGO B CA1–3 CC2 CE1,2 Co M MM MQ NGC2 NGC67 RCA UG US WWA93
GAUDARD, Pierre-Raymond, b Marvelise, Fr 1927– , gra WWA93
GAUDAUR, Jacob Gill, b Orillia, Ont 1920– , paint CWW93
GAUDET, Antoine, fl 1890–1908, paint K
GAUDREAU, Amédée, b St-Damase, Que 1932– , sculp S
GAUDREAU, Maurice, b Rimouski, Que 1907, d 1980, engr sculp M
GAUGEL, Heinz, b Germany 1928– , paint sculp M
GAUSE, Joseph Ernest, b Split, Yu 1910– , sculp M
GAUTAMA, Nirmana (Nirmala) (s Nym), b Nairobi, Kenya 1929– , paint IO
GAUTHIER, A., fl 1897+, paint H K
GAUTHIER, Amable, b St-Jean-Baptiste-de-Nicolet, Que 1792, d Maskinongé, Que 1875, sculp DCB10 K

GAUTHIER, Félix-Norbert, fl 1898+, sculp K
GAUTHIER, Joachim George, b N Bay, Ont 1897, d Minden, Ont 1988, paint pas CNS40 CWW88 K M NGC2 O.F48 RCA UG WWA82
GAUTHIER, Joseph, b Quebec 1844/5, fl 1891, paint H K
GAUTHIER, Joseph, b St-Marc-des-Carrières, Que, fl 1906–37, sculp K
GAUTHIER, Louis-Zéphirin, b 1842, d 1922, sculp K
GAUTHIER, Ovide, b Quebec 1845/6, fl 1871–81, paint K
GAUTHIER, Paul F., b Toronto 1937– , paint IO
GAUTHIER, Pierre, b France, fl 1849–50, paint H K
GAUTHIER, Suzanne Anita, b St Boniface, Man 1948– , paint prt sculp CAE1,2 WWA93
GAUTHIER, T.A., fl 1890–1900, paint K
GAUTTIER, P., fl 1865–76, sculp K
GAUVIN, Claude E., b Bathurst, NB 1939– , paint WWA93
GAUVIN, François-Pierre, b Quebec 1866 – d 1934, sculp K
GAUVIN, Hervé A., b Lewiston, Me 1900– , paint CWW64 K
GAUVREAU, Claude, b Montreal 1925 – d 1971, paint CC2 CE1,2
GAUVREAU, Gilles, b Quebec 1924– , paint M MM
GAUVREAU, Pierre, b Montreal 1922– , prt CE1,2 M MM MQ NGC2 TB2,3
GAVAN, Frank, fl 1960– , paint M
GAVILLER, Maurice, b 1842, d 1928, prt Mo98,12 PNL
GAY, Marie-Louise (m David Toby Homel), b Quebec 1952– , illus CBC88 CWW93
GAY, Ruth A., b Ontario 1911– , sculp DAS
GEBHARDT, Berthiaume, fl 1885–91, engr litho H
GEBHARDT, C. Keith, b Cheboygan, Mich 1899, paint Hu
GEBHARDT, George J., fl 1866–84, des engr H
GECIN, Sindon (b Gerard Sindon[2]), b Montreal 1907– , paint AE AGO M MM[2] NGC2 NGC67
GEDDES, Frances Mildred (Mrs), b Tring, Oxon 1888, paint Hu MM RCA
GEDEN, Dennis, b N Bay, Ont 1944– , paint prt CAE1,2 IO
GEGARGEWSKOL, Louis, b Warsaw, fl 1820–30s, drw paint H
GELLER, Manly, b 1928– , paint SC
GELY, Gabriel Joseph, b Paris 1924– , paint sculp M SC
GEMMEL, J. (Miss), fl 1871–3, paint H
GENDREAU, Marcel, b c 1930– , paint sculp M
GENDRON, Arthur, fl 1879–88, des H K
GENDRON, Ernest, b Arntfield, nr Rouyn, Que 1912 (x 1922), d 1985, paint DFA M WENA
GENDRON, Pierre, b Montreal 1934– , engr paint AE CC1 M MM NGC2 RCA TB3
GENERAL, David M. (Tawit), b Six Nations Res, nr Brantford, Ont 1950– , carv paint prt IO
GENERAL IDEA (*see also* A.A. Bronson, Felix Partz, Jorge Zontal) CA3 CAE1,2 IO NGC2
GENEREUX, Onésime, fl 1861–71, paint H K
GENEST, Louis, b Quebec 1852/3, d Detroit 1895, paint H K
GENEST, Paul-Emile, b Sherbrooke, Que 1940– , paint M
GENEST, Pierre M.A., b St-Joseph-de-la-Pointe, Que 1844, d Quebec 1901, paint sculp H K RCA
GENN, Robert Douglas, b Victoria, BC 1936– (x 1916), paint CWW93 M SC
GENNER, Samuel, b France, fl 1675–8, sculp K
GENOT, Jean-Etienne-Achille, b 1823, d Montreal 1879, paint H K
GENSONNET, Catherine Lybia Exar-

chou (Mrs), b Athens, Gr 1921– , paint M

GENUSH, Luba (m Peter Bloor), b Odessa, Ukr 1924– , paint prt CAE1,2 M MM NGC2 RCA TB3

GEORGE, Nellie Harriet, b Springfield, Man 1892, fl 1965, paint DWA M

GEORGE, Richard Morgan, b Galt, re Cambridge, Ont 1909– , paint Hu

GERAGHTY, Paul Anthony, b England 1941– , drw paint IO

GERMAIN. *See* PERRON, Germain

GERMAN, Mischa Maria Van Eck (Mrs), b Netherlands 1919– , paint M

GERMUSKA, Andrey, b Toronto 1933– , paint IO

GERRARD, Bart. *See* ATWOOD, Margaret Eleanor

GERSON, Wolfgang, b Hamburg, Ge 1916– , paint CWW91 RCA

GERSOVITZ, Sarah Valerie Gamer (m Benjamin Gersovitz), b Montreal 1920– , prt CWW93 M MM NGC2 RCA WWA93

GERVAIS, Eugène, b Quebec 1862/3, fl 1881–1919, paint K

GERVAIS, J. Etienne Leo[2], b Quebec 1917 carv, M[2] MM

GERVAIS, Lise, b St-Césaire, Rouville Co, Que 1933– , paint sculp AE B CC1 M MM NGC2 RCA

GERVAIS, Raymond, b Montreal 1943– , paint NGC2

GESNER, Gladys Mary, b Halifax 1906– , paint M MA MM

GEUER, Juan W. (The Truth Seeker Co.), b Netherlands 1917– , paint IO M

GHADIALLY, Feroze Novroji, b Bombay, India 1920– , sculp CWW93

GIARD, Adélard, fl 1894–8, paint K

GIBB, David Alexander, b Galt, re Cambridge, Ont 1884 – d 1971, paint M MM PMC RCA

GIBBON, H./Amelia F.H. (Miss), fl 1859–65, paint H

GIBBON, John Murray, b Udewelle, Ceylon 1895, paint CWW49

GIBBONS, Charles, fl 1880–1914, paint DFA

GIBBS, Eric L., b Edmonton 1912– , car Des

GIBBS, Leonard James, b Cranbrook, BC 1929– , paint CAE2 CWW93 SC

GIBSON, Dick (s Teasdale), b Sault Ste Marie, Ont 1934– , car Po86,87

GIBSON, George, b 1912– , paint M

GIBSON, Goodwin, b Toronto 1926– , paint CWW87

GIBSON, Richard R., b Maryland c 1795, fl 1855, Amer, paint GW H Y

GIBSON, Susan, b Colingbourne, Kingston, Wilts 1894, paint WWNA

GIBSON, Thomas Kent Hamilton, b Edinburgh 1930– , paint CE1,2 MM

GIBSON, William Hamilton, b Sandy Hook, Conn 1850, d Washington, DC 1896, paint F H Y

GIFFARD, Alexandré S., fl 1863–80, paint H H77 K

GIFFEN, Perry Tudson, b Goldboro, NS 1885, paint CWW36

GIFFORD, Robert Swaine, b Nonamesset Isld (x Naushon), Mass 1840, d New York 1905, Amer, paint AAAd28 AAW1,3 AC ANC App B DAB DMA DSP F GW H McC Sam TB1 WWWA Y

GIFFORD, Sanford Robinson, b Greenfield, NY 1823, d New York 1880, Amer, paint AAW1,3 AC ANC App AW B Bry DAA DAB DMA F GW H McC NCAB2 Sam TB1 WWWA Y

GIFFORD, William Brent, b New Westminster, BC 1940– , paint M

GIGNAC, Louise, fl 1908–37, paint K

GIGNOUX, Régis-François, b Lyon, Fr 1816, d Paris 1882, Fr, paint B K TB1 Y

GIGUERE, E. Louise. *See* MONTIGNY-GIGUERE, E. Louise de

GIGUERE, Roland, b Montreal 1929– , paint prt CC2 CE1,2 DCA M MM NGC2 NGC67 TB3

GILBERT, George A., fl 1864–71, paint H

GILBERT, Grove Sheldon, b Clinton, NY 1805, d Rochester, NY 1885, Amer, paint F GW H H77 Y
GILBERT, Helen Mar, fl 1888, paint H MM
GILBERT, Herbert, b Moose Jaw, Sask 1926– , paint prt NGC2 TB3
GILBERT, Ina Elaine, b Toronto 1932– , sculp IO
GILBERT, Kittie Marguerite Bruneau. *See* BRUNEAU, Kittie Marguerite
GILBERT, William Herbert, b Regina 1926– , paint CC2 M RCA TB3
GILHOOLY, David James, b Auburn, Calif 1943– , sculp CA1 CAE1,2 Co CWW93 IO MM NGC2 RCA WWA93
GILL. *See* FUROY, Gill
GILL, Arthur B., b W Calder, Scot 1909, d 1972, paint CWW70
GILL, Charles-Ignace-Adélard, b Sorel, Que 1871, d Montreal 1918, paint CC1 CE1,2 EC H77 K LeJ M MM RCA W1–3
GILL, Mary C. (Minnie), b Pierreville, Que, fl 1897–1920, paint AAA01 DWA H MM RCA
GILL, William, fl 1881–90, paint H RCA
GILLAM, William Charles Frederick, b Brighton, Eng 1867, d 1962, etch paint AAA33 AAW2 AC DBA G RA TB3 WWA40
GILLEN, Denver L., b Vancouver 1914– , illus paint Sam
GILLES, Albert Marschner, b Paris 1895, fl 1948+, sculp K M
GILLESPIE/GELLESPIE, J.H., b England 1793, fl 1810–49, Eng, min sil BSA DFA Fo GW H H77 J NGC2
GILLESPIE, John, fl 1841–9, paint DeV8 H
GILLETT, Violet Amy, b Liverpool 1898, d New Brunswick 1996, paint sculp CLA CWW80 M MA
GILLIES, James (Jim), b London, Ont 1951– , paint sculp CAE2 IO
GILLILAND, Jillian Hulme (m James Gilliland), b Natal, SA 1943– , illus C
GILLING, Lucille, b Hamilton, Mo 1905– , prt IO M WWA93
GILLIS, Mary Elizabeth. *See* CROFT, Mary Elizabeth Gillis
GILMAN, Harold, b Rode, Som 1876, d 1919, Eng, paint NGC68
GILMAN, Phoebe, b New York 1940– , illus paint C SAA58
GILMORE, A., fl 1871, ske DeV9 H
GILMOUR, Mary E. Hallen[2] (May) (m George Gilmour), b Hairleybury, Worc 1819, d England 1907, paint DWA H ROM[2]
GILPIN, Eliza. *See* MILLIDGE, Eliza Gilpin
GILPIN, John Bernard, b Newport, RI 1810, d Annapolis Royal, NS 1892, drgt DCB12 H
GILSON, Jacqueline Marie Charlotte, b Melun, Fr 1912– , paint AE TB3 WWA62
GILVERSON, Queenie Viola (m C.H. Sorley[2]), b Toronto 1890, paint Hu RCA[2]
GINGRAS, Gilles Emmanuel, b Magog, Que 1932– , paint M
GINSBERG, Jerry Donald, b Toronto c 1943– , paint IO
GIRARD, Claude, b Chicoutimi, Que 1938– , paint CAE1 CWW93 M MM RCA
GIRARD, Ernest, b Trois-Rivières, Que 1873, d 1897, paint K
GIRARD, Joseph-Basil, b Courpière, Fr 1846, d Texas 1918, paint AAW3 K
GIRARD, Suzanne R., b Montreal 1936– , prt CAE1
GIRERD, Jean-Pierre (s Girerd), b Algeria 1931– , cart Des Po86–88 WECa
GIROUARD, Jean-Joseph, b Quebec 1794, d St-Benoît, Que 1855, min sculp APH DCB8 H K MQ
GIRSCH, Frederick, b Bijdingen, nr Darmstadt, Ge 1821, d Mount Vernon, NY 1895, engr paint B DeV4 F GW TB1 Y
GIROUX, Alfred, fl 1857–88, sculp K
GIROUX, André-Raphaël, b Charles-

bourg, Que 1815, d St-Casimir, Que 1869, sculp DCB9 K
GIROUX, Eugène, fl 1869, sculp K
GISSING, Roland, b Broadway, Eng 1895, d Okotoks, Alta 1967, paint KB M MM RCA Sam W3
GITE. *See* TURGEON, Jean
GLACKMEYER, Michel, b c 1795, fl 1828, paint H
GLADSTONE, Charles, b Skidegate, Queen Charlotte Islds, BC 1877, d 1947, carv Co
GLADSTONE, Fowler Shelly, b Toronto 1944– , paint IO
GLADSTONE, Gerald, b Toronto 1929– , sculp AE AGO B CC2 Co IO M MM NGC2 NGC67 RCA TB3
GLADWIN, George E., fl 1876–7, drw DeV4
GLANVILLE, Sally, b 1938– , prt IO
GLASS, Alain, b Montreal 1932– , mmed M
GLASSCO, Ivan, d 1941, cart Des
GLASSER, Penelope. *See* MacPHERSON, Penelope Glasser
GLASSEY, John, b Truro, NS 1936– , paint M
GLAZ, Kazimierz/Kazimir, b Borkiniz, Pol 1931– , paint prt IO UG
GLAZEBROOK, Hugh de Twenebrokes, b Hampstead, London 1855, d London 1937, Eng, paint B DBA G H RA RCA TB1–3 WBA1 WWW
GLEN, Edward Randolph, b London, Ont 1887 – d 1963, paint AGO Hu MM RCA
GLOSTER, Barney, fl 1880–1909, drgt H
GLOVER, Edwin S., b Michigan 1845, d Tacoma, Wash 1919, Amer, drgt AAW3 DeV1 H Sam
GLOVER, Lyle, b Peterborough, Ont c 1921– , illus paint M
GLYDE, Henry George, b Luton, Beds 1906– , gra paint AGO CC2 CE1,2 CLA CWW93 GM M MM NGC1,2 NGC68 RCA SC TB3 WWA93 WWC73
GOBERT, Thomas M., fl 1873–5, paint H
GODFREY, Marcel, b London 1893, paint WWNA
GODFREY, William Frederick George, b London 1884, d Toronto 1971, paint AGO CWW70 GM Hu M MM NGC2 RCA
GODIN, Raymonde, b Montreal 1930– , paint AGO B CAE2 DCA NGC1,2 TB3
GODKIN, Celia, b London 1948– , illus CWW93
GODOY. *See* ECHEVERRIA y GODOY, Atanasio
GODWIN, Edward William (Ted) (m Phyllis Godwin, q.v.), b Calgary 1933– , paint AGO CAE2 CC1 CWW93 M MM NGC2 RCA SC TB3 UG
GODWIN, Karl, b Walkerville, Ont 1893, illus paint AAA33 AC TB2 WWA40 Y
GODWIN, Phyllis Wanda Goota (m Edward William Godwin, q.v.), b Fir Ridge, Sask 1930- , paint sculp BDSA M SC
GOETZ, Othon Marne, b Berne, Swi 1899, paint sculp CWW38
GOETZ, Peter Henry, b Slavgorod, Sib 1917– , paint CWW93 IO M MM RCA S UG WWA93
GOFFIN, Rodolphe, b Sprimont, Bel 1890, sculp K
GOGAN, Dorothy Jean, b Nova Scotia 1926– , paint CWW93
GOGUEN, Georges-Henri, b Moncton, NB 1934– , paint M
GOGUEN, Jean, b Montreal 1927 – d 1989, paint B NGC2
GOING[1], Margaret Hamel[2] (Mrs), b 1860, d 1936, paint DWA H[1,2] Hu[2]
GOLD, Charles Emilius, Lt Gen, b 1803, d Dover, Eng 1871, Eng, paint DMA
GOLDBERG, Eric (m Regina Seiden Goldberg, q.v.), b Berlin 1890, d Mon-

treal 1969, paint CC2 CLA M MM NGC1,2 TB2,3 W3 WWA62

GOLDBERG, Regina Seiden[2] (m Eric Goldberg, q.v.), b Rigaud, Que 1897, d Montreal 1991, paint DWA Hu[2] M MM[2] NGC1,2 RCA[2] TB3 WWA62

GOLDENBERG, Ester, b c 1929– , paint M

GOLDHAMER, Charles, b Philadelphia, Pa 1903, d Toronto 1985, paint AGO CE1,2 CNS40 CWW84 IO M MM NGC1,2 NGC68 O.F48 RCA TB2 WWA82

GOLDMAN, Saul, b Toronto 1954– , sculp IO

GOLDSMITH, Sidney Charles Joseph, b Toronto 1922– , paint M MM NGC1,2 O.Ag50 RCA TB3

GOLFMAN, Eleanor R., fl 1970– , paint prt CAE1

GOMES, John Joseph, b Port of Spain, Tri 1948– , paint prt CAE2 IO

GOMES, Mark, b Sarnia, Ont 1949– , sculp DCA IO

GOMEZ, Ricardo, b San Francisco 1942– , sculp SC

GOODALL, Edward, b Wells, Som 1909– , paint M

GOODELL, Mary Elizabeth, b Kirkville, NY 1888, paint DWA WWA62

GOODIE, Scott William, b Saint John's, Nfld 1955– , paint CWW93

GOODIER, Marina (m Norman Goodier), b Petrograd 1906– , paint Hu

GOODMAN, George Samuel, b Toronto 1919, d New York 1967, paint AGO

GOODMAN, Russell C., b c 1926– , stgl M

GOODMAN, Trevor G., b Montreal 1923– , paint CWW61

GOODRIDGE, Harold Berwick, b St John's, Nfld 1901– , paint M

GOODSIR, Robert Anstruther, fl 1849, topog DFA H

GOODWIN, Betty Roodish (m Martin Goodwin), b Montreal 1923– , paint CAE1 CE1 CWW93 DCA M MM NGC2 RCA

GOOTA, Alexandria. *See* SAFRUK, Alexandria Goota

GOOTA, Louise. *See* COOK, Louise Goota

GOOTA, Phyllis Wanda. *See* GODWIN, Phyllis Wanda Goota

GORANSON, Paul Alexander, b Vancouver 1911– , paint GM M NGC68 RCA WWA53 WWNA

GORDANEER, James Edward, b Toronto 1933– , paint CAE1,2 M MM RCA S UG

GORDON, Frederick Charles S., b Coburg, Ont 1856, d High Orchard, NJ 1924, illus paint AAA24d28 B F H RCA TB1 WWWA Y

GORDON, Geoffrey David, b London, Ont 1944– , paint sculp IO NGC2

GORDON, Hortense Crompton Mattice (m John Sloan Gordon, q.v.), b Hamilton, Ont 1877 – d 1961, paint AGO CC2 CWW58 Hu DWA M MM NGC2 RCA W3

GORDON, J. (Miss), fl 1866–78, paint DFA H

GORDON, John King, b Winnipeg 1900– , paint CWW88

GORDON, John Sloan (m Hortense C.M. Gordon, q.v.), b Brantford, Ont 1868, d Hamilton, Ont 1940, paint CWW52 Hu M MM NGC1,2 PMC RCA TB3

GORDON, Russell Talbert, b Philadelphia, Pa 1936– , paint WWA93

GORE, Graham, fl 1845, paint ske DFA H

GORE, John, b Boston 1718 – d 1796, Amer, paint GW H

GORE[1], Millicent (m P.H. Anderson[2]), fl 1893–1930, paint AKL[2] B DBA[1,2] DWA[2] G MM[2] RA[2] RCA

GORE, Ralph, Lt Col, fl 1809–21, paint DFA GW H ROM

GOREY, Christopher, b 1950– , paint DCA

GORMAN, Richard Borthwick,

b Ottawa 1935– , paint AE AGO M MM NGC2 RCA

GORMLEY, Anna, fl 1894–1907, paint DWA H MM RCA

GOSBEE, Chuck, b British Columbia c 1939– , paint M

GOSLING, William Gilbert (aka Wilfred^2), b Bermuda 1863, fl 1914, paint H MM^2 Mo12

GOSS, Geoffrey, b London, fl 1940s, paint M

GOSSAGE, Eve Laws. *See* LAWS, Eve

GOSSE, Philip Henry, b Worcester, Eng 1810, d St Marychurch, Eng 1888, Eng, paint DNB H

GOSSE, William, b Worcester, Eng 1806, fl 1822–45, Eng, paint DeV4 H

GOSSELIN, Felix, fl 1875–6, des engr litho K

GOSSELIN, Gabriel, b 1690, d 1769, sculp K

GOSSELIN, Guy, b Belgium 1932– , paint M

GOSSELIN, Lucien-Hippolyte, b Whitefield, NH 1883, d Manchester, NH 1940, Amer, sculp AAA33 B F K

GOSSELIN, Marie-Scholastique (Soeur), b Ste-Famille, Que 1806, d St Boniface, Man 1876, sculp DCB10 K

GOTTSCHALK, Fritz, b Zurich, Swi 1937– , gra CWW91 RCA WWA93

GOUIN, Judith Mary (Judy), b Farnborough, Hants 1947– , prt CAE2 IO NGC2

GOULD, John Howard, b Toronto 1929– , paint AE CWW93 IO M MM NGC2 RCA S WWA93

GOULD, Stella Evelyn Grier. *See* GRIER, Stella Evelyn

GOULET, Claude, b Montreal 1925– , paint B DCA NGC2 RCA WWA93

GOULET, Joseph (x Goulette^2), b 1792, fl 1811, carv paint H^2 K

GOULET, Michel, b Asbestos, Que 1944– , sculp MQ

GOULIN, Judith, b Farnborough, Hants 1947– , prt IO

GOURLAY, Mrs E.C./E.E.E. (m E.C. Gourlay, Col), fl 1860–8, paint H

GOW, Isobel Elizabeth Dowler. *See* DOWLER-GOW, Isobel Elizabeth

GOWARD, Elizabeth Remington (m Owen Goward), b Indianapolis, Ind 1910– , paint US

GOWDY, Ruth. *See* McKINLEY, Ruth Gowdy

GOYET, Joseph, b 1789/90, d Saint-Constant, Que 1882, carv K

GRABE, Margaret, fl 1957– , sculp M

GRADOWSKI, Michael Willard (s Michael White), b 1946– , drw paint IO

GRAF, Christa, b Germany 1934– , paint MFMS

GRAFF, Leslie Fredrick, b Camrose, Alta 1936– , paint M SC

GRAFF, Tom, fl 1970– , con CAE1

GRAHAM, Albert W., fl 1858–80, engr H

GRAHAM, Arthur J., fl 1881–4, ske H

GRAHAM, Charles, b Rock Isld, Ill 1852, d New York 1911, Amer, topog AAW1 AC DeV4 Sam

GRAHAM, Donna, b Saskatchewan 1929, d 1971, paint M

GRAHAM, Ineka Felderhof (m Keith Graham), b Netherlands 1937– , paint M

GRAHAM, James Lillie, b Belleville, Ont 1871/3, fl 1965, paint AGO H Hu M MM NGC1,2 RCA TB3

GRAHAM, Kathleen Margaret Howitt (m J. Wallace Graham), b Hamilton, Ont 1913– , paint CAE2 CWW93 IO RCA SC WWA93

GRAHAM, Payson (Miss), b London, Ont 1878, illus sculp AAA21 DAS DWA F

GRAMMAT, George, b Paris c 1931– , illus M

GRANCHE, Pierre, b Montreal 1948– , sculp CAE1

GRANDMAISON, Nickola de (Nicolas) (m Sonia de Grandmaison, q.v.), b Moscow 1892, d Calgary 1978, paint AAAW1 M RCA Sam US WWA70

GRANDMAISON, Orestes Nicholas de (Rick), b Calgary 1932, d 1985, paint M SC

GRANDMAISON, Sonia de (m Nicholas de Grandmaison, q.v.), b Moscow, fl 1967– , sculp M

GRANGER/GRAINGER, Francis Hincks/Hicks, b Toronto 1829, d 1906, paint GW H

GRANGER, Napoléon, fl 1876–84, paint H K

GRANKOWSKA, Denise (Mrs), fl 1959– , paint M

GRANSOW, Helmut Wilhelm, b Rottluff, nr Chemnitz, Ge 1921– , paint prt CWW93 IO M MM

GRANT, Beatrice Liechenstein, b Halifax 1909– , paint M RCA

GRANT, Brigid Toole, b 1938– , prt DCA

GRANT, Donald, b Toronto c 1934– , des paint M

GRANT, Duncan Edmund, b Roseneth, Scot 1846, d Montreal 1937, paint DFA H MM NGC2 RCA

GRANT, F.A., Lt, fl 1829–54, Eng, topog H

GRANT, John, fl c 1825–45, paint H

GRANT, Kathleen. *See* MORRISON, Kathleen Grant

GRANT, Lewis John Mason, b Bhagulpur, India 1881, fl 1913, Eng, paint DBA DVP G Hu MM RCA

GRANT, Mary, b Huntington, Que 1870, d Montreal 1957, paint Hu MM NGC1,2 RCA TB1

GRANT, Mary Jane, b 1941– , des stgl M

GRANT, Neil Anthony, b W Kirby, Ches 1927– , sculp M

GRANT, W., Rev, fl 1862–90, paint H

GRANVILLE, Charles Bécard de. *See* BECARD/BECART de GRANVILLE et de FONVILLE, Charles

GRANZIN, Horst Willy, b Crossen, Ge 1935– , paint prt NGC2

GRASSET de SAINT-SAUVEUR, Jacques, b Montreal 1757, d Paris 1810, paint B K TB1

GRASSICK, Bert, b Victoria, BC 1909– , cart Des

GRASTON, Mike, b Montreal 1954– , cart Des Po86–87,90

GRATER, Lindsay, b Cambridge, Eng 1952– , illus prt C

GRATTON, Joseph-Olindo, b Ste-Thérèse-de-Blainville, Que 1855 – d 1941, sculp K

GRAUER, Gay Sherrard (Sherry) (m John William Keith-King), b Toronto 1939– , sculp CAE2 CWW93 DCA M NGC2 RCA WWA93

GRAVEL, Francine, b 1944– , paint prt CAE1

GRAVEL, Raymonde, b Montreal 1913– , paint M MM RCA

GRAVES, Shelley, b Toronto 1938– , paint prt CAE2 IO

GRAY, Benjamin Gerrish, fl 1803–5, topog H

GRAY, Claude W., b c 1880, d c 1940, Eng, paint DBA G RCA

GRAY, Corbett Moffat, b Winnipeg 1913, d Fergus, Ont 1991, paint IO M UG

GRAY, Francis William, b Yorkshire 1877, sculp CWW38 MM

GRAY, Gordon, b Windsor, Ont 1906– , paint CWW67

GRAY, Henry Alfred, Maj, b Birmingham, Eng 1843, paint H Mo98

GRAY, Jack Lorimer, b Halifax 1927, d W Palm Beach, Fla 1981, paint M MM

GRAY, James, fl 1828–33, paint G H

GRAY, John Warren, b England 1824, d Maissonneuve, nr Montreal 1912, paint H MM RCA

GRAY, Scott William Alfred Hamilton, Cdr RN, b Saint John, NB 1855, drw paint H Mo98

GRAYSON, Ellen Vaughan Kirk (m A.J. Mann[2]), b Moose Jaw, Sask 1894, paint BDSA DWA M WWA80[2] WWNA

GRAYSON, Joseph Henry Lee. *See* LEE-GRAYSON, Joseph Henry

GREASON, William, b St Mary's, Ont 1884, d 1945, paint AAA33 F PMC WWA40 Y

GREAVES, E.L., b Nova Scotia, fl 1866–71, paint DMA

GREAVES, Robert Lewis, b Leicestershire 1949– , drw IO

GREAVES, Theodore W., b Nowgong, Assam, India 1878, paint WWNA

GREBZE, Otto N., b Latvia 1910, d Parry Sound, Ont 1992, paint M

GRECO, Christina, b New York 1913– , sculp AA

GREEN, Arthur Nelson, b Frankfort, Ind 1941– , paint prt CAE2 DCAA3 IO NGC2 WWA93

GREEN, Barbara, b Hamilton, Ont 1927– , paint CAE1

GREEN, Betty (Mrs), b Toronto 1908– , paint sculp M

GREEN, Doreen, b Vancouver, fl 1970– , paint ABC

GREEN, Elizabeth Piers (m William G. Green), b Canada 1814 – d 1839, paint H

GREEN, Harold Abbott, b Montreal 1883, paint AAA33 F TB2

GREEN, Hiram Howard, b Paris, NY 1865, d Fort Erie, Ont 1930, Amer, etch paint AAA29d30 AAW2 F Sam TB2

GREEN, Mildred C., b Paris, NY 1874, illus paint AAA33 F DWA TB2 WWA40

GREEN, Richard, b Barrie, Ont 1946– , sculp IO

GREEN, William, b Manchester, Eng c 1760, d Ambleside, Westm 1823, Eng, paint B Bry DBLP DBWA DNB G H Red TB

GREENAWAY, Roy, b Toronto 1891 – d 1972, paint M MM RCA

GREENE, Barbara Louise, b Hamilton, Ont 1917– , paint IO M

GREENE, Evan Loren Robert, b Edmonton 1910, d 1961, paint Hu M RCA

GREENE, Richard Waddilve Eustace, b Roseland, Port Nelson, Ont 1848, d Islington, Ont 1934, paint H

GREENE, Thomas Garland, b Toronto 1875, d Orillia, Ont 1955, paint AGO CNS40 M MM NGC1,2 O.F49 RCA TB3

GREENE-MERCIER, Marie Zoe (m Wesley H. Greene; m L.J. Mercier), b Madison, Wis 1911– , sculp DAS M MM RCA TB3 WWA93

GREENSTEIN, Anne (m Sam Greenstein), b Warsaw 1914– , paint M MM

GREENSTONE, Marion (m Myron Greenstone), b New York 1925– , paint M MM RCA TB3 WWA93

GREENWOOD, Charlotte, fl 1895–7, paint H RCA

GREER, John Sydney, b Amherst, NS 1944– , con sculp CAE1,2 NGC2 WWA93

GREER, William Newton, b Kingston, Ont 1925– , ske CWW93

GREG, Rada, b Yugoslavia 1941– , paint DFA KB

GREGOR, Helen Frances Lorenz (m Tibor P. Gregor), b Prague, Cz 1921, d Seoul, Kor 1989, tap CAE1 CWW89 DCA IO NGC2 RCA WWA89

GREGORY, Hardy, fl 1856–65, paint DeV5

GREGORY, Mary Frances. *See* PATTULLO, Mary Frances

GREGORY, Scott, b Windsor, Ont 1942– , paint IO

GREGORY/GREGOR[2], Thomas A./A.T.[3], fl 1887–95, paint H MM[2] RCA[3]

GREIG, William, fl 1887–1916, illum H MM

GRENKIE, Hazel Jensen (m Percy Charles Grenkie), b Zealandia, Sask 1916– , paint sculp BDSA CAE1,2

GRESHAM, Arthur, b Sheffield, Eng 1891, fl 1953, paint Hu MM RCA

GREY, Jerry, b Vancouver 1940– , paint prt IO RCA

GREY, William, Rev, b England 1819, d Exeter, Eng 1872, Eng, paint DCB10 DeV4 H

GRIER, Edmund Geoffrey, b Toronto 1899, d Ottawa 1965, paint M MM RCA

GRIER, Edmund Wyly, Sir, b Melbourne, Aus 1862, d Toronto 1957, paint AGO B CC2 CNS40 CWW53 DBA DVP EC FCA G H H77 Hu M MM Mo98,12 NGC1,2 NGC67 NGC68 PMC RCA TB1,3 W2,3 WBA2 WWA53

GRIER, Eldon Brockwill, b London 1917– , paint CC2 M MM

GRIER, Louis Monro, b Melbourne, Aus 1864, d St Ives, Eng 1920, paint B DBA DVP G RA TB1 WBA1 WWW

GRIER, Stella Evelyn (m A.E. Gould), b Toronto 1898, d Ottawa 1994, paint DWA M MM O.N48 RCA TB2

GRIFFIN, Catherine Norah, b Toronto 1910– , paint Hu

GRIFFIN, Francis John, Lt Col, b Greenwich, Kent 1809, d Torquay, Dev 1858, Eng, paint WHCp221

GRIFFIN, George Henry, b Uckfield, Sus 1898, d 1974, paint Hu RCA

GRIFFITH, Julius Edward Lindsay, b Vancouver 1912– , engr paint AGO BB CWW93 GM M NGC2 O.F49 RCA S WWA70

GRIFFITHS, Deirdre E., fl 1970– , paint CAE2

GRIFFITHS, James, b Newcastle-under-Lyme, Eng 1825, d London, Ont 1896, paint ACA DFA EC H M MM NGC1,2 NGC67 RCA W1–3

GRIFFITHS, John Howard, b Newcastle-under-Lyme, Eng 1826, d London, Ont 1898, paint DFA H H77 NGC2

GRIFFITHS, William Gordon, b Port Aubert(?), Wales 1885, d Saskatchewan 1955, paint US

GRIGNON, V.J./V.L. (Mme), fl 1900–6, paint DWA H K MM

GRINDLEY, Heather, b Montreal 1931– , paint SC

GRINSTED, Edgar, Cdr, b London 1897, paint CWW64

GRIPS, Carel Joseph/J.C., b Grave, Neth 1825, d Vught, Neth 1920, Bel, paint B H TB1,3

GRISON, Brian, b Toronto 1947– , drgt paint DCA IO

GROOT, Andrée de, b Bourgogne, Fr 1908– , paint sculp CAE1

GROOTELAAR, Angela Jean Alexandria (m John Grootelaar), b Vlissingen, Neth 1936– , paint BDSA

GROSE, D.C., fl 1860–80s, Eng, paint H Sam

GROSPERIN. *See* COTE, Jean-Baptiste

GROSS, E.M., fl 1879, ske H

GROSS, Peter Alfred, b Schnecksville, nr Allentown, Pa 1849, d Chicago 1914, Amer, paint AAAd28 B DBA DeV4 H TB1 Y

GROSS, Richard Emil Frank, b Lodz, Pol 1943– , paint M NGC2 SC

GROSSMAN, Milton H., b British Columbia 1908– , sculp AAA33 DAS TB2 WWA40

GROUARD, Emile-Jean-Baptiste, Bishop, b Brulon, La Sarthe, Fr 1840, d Grouard Mission, Alta 1931, paint CWW10 H LeJ K W1–3

GROVES, Naomi Catherine Adair Jackson. *See* JACKSON, Naomi Catherine Adair

GRUBBE, W.H., Capt, fl 1840–54, paint H

GRUMIEUX, Emile-Jacques, b Gosslies, Bel 1897, d Chicago 1954, Amer, paint AAA33 F K

GRUPPE, Charles Paul, b Picton, Ont 1860, d Rockport, Mass 1940, paint AAA33 B CWW36 F H Hu M MM NCAB30 NGC1,2 TB1–3 WWA40d47 WWWA Y

GRYMONPRE, Jean, b France, fl 1916–46, paint K RCA

GUARD, Marie Cecilia (m J. Kenneth

Phillips), b Toronto 1908– , paint Hu M
GUDERNA, Ladislav, b Nitra, Cz 1921– , paint prt CAE1 IO WWA84
GUDERNA, Martin, b Cz 1956– , paint prt IO
GUENET-VARIN, Marie-Anne (Soeur), fl 1755, sculp K
GUENETTE, Léonidas, fl 1884–99, paint H K
GUENTHER, Pearl Harder, b Winnipeg 1882, paint AAW1 AC DWA WWA62
GUERIN, Alphonse, fl 1861–73, paint K
GUERIN, Gus, fl 1970– , prt CAE2
GUERIN, Thomas, fl 1920+, sculp K RCA
GUERNEY, Eric, b Winnipeg c 1920– , Amer, cart WECa
GUERNON dit BELLEVILLE, François, b Paris c 1740, d nr St-Jacques, Que 1817, carv DCB5 K
GUEST, Marie Olivia Hewson[2] (m H. Benson Guest), b Oxford, NS 1880, d 1966, paint CLA DWA Hu M MM[2] RCA[2]
GUEST, Robert, b Beaverlodge, Alta 1938– , drw paint AA
GUIBORD, Charles, b 1800/1, fl 1816, sculp K
GUIBORD, Pierre, b 1798/9, fl 1816–29, sculp K
GUIGNON, Eugene, fl 1910+, paint K MM
GUILLET, Glenn, b Prince Rupert, BC 1949– , sculp AA CAE1
GUILLET dit TOURANGEAU, Emilie, b Quebec 1829, fl 1844, paint K
GUILLET dit TOURANGEAU, Flore (Soeur Saint-Joseph), b Quebec 1821 – d 1850, drw K
GUILLET dit TOURANGEAU, Joséphine (Soeur Sainte-Marguerite), b Quebec 1833 – d 1866, paint K
GUILLET dit TOURANGEAU, Marie-Mathilde (Soeur Sainte-Anne), b Quebec 1823 – d 1902, drw K
GUINAN, Tom, b Halifax 1936– , paint SC
GUINDON, Pierre-Adolphe-Arthur, Rev, b St-Polycarpe, Que 1864, d Montreal 1923, paint H H77 K
GUITE, Suzanne (m Alberto Tommi), b nr Percé, Gaspé, Que 1927– , sculp B M MM RCA WWA82
GUNDRY, Thomas, b 1830, d Toronto 1869, paint DeV8
GUNDY, Henry Pearson, b Toronto 1905– , paint CWW93
GUNN, Bessie, fl 1893–7, drw H
GUNN, Emily Mary (m John Fried), b London, Ont, fl 1893–1914, paint DWA H RCA
GUNN, Patricia O'Brien. *See* O'BRIEN, Patricia Dorothy Gunn (Paddy)
GUNTHER, R.M. (Mrs), fl 1890–7, paint H
GURD, Fraser Baillie, b Montreal 1883, paint CWW48 MM Mo12
GURR, Albert Frederick, b S Shields, Eng 1898, paint CWW61
GUSE, Donna, b Schreiber, Ont 1953– , paint IO
GUSH, William, fl 1832–74, Eng, paint B BM Fo G H TB1
GUSTAFSON, Anna, b 1952– , mmed CAE2
GUSTIN, Paul Morgan, b Fort Vancouver, Wash 1886, d Seattle, Wash 1974, Amer, paint AAA33 B F TB1 WWA40 WWNA
GUTTMAN, Freda. *See* BAIN, Freda Guttman
GUY, Clovis-Edouard, b Ste-Anne-de-la-Pocatière, Que 1819, d Frenchville, Me 1910, sculp K
GUY, Francis, b Burton-in-Kendal, nr Keswick, Eng c 1760, d Brooklyn, NY 1820, Eng, paint B DAA DMA F GW TB1 WWWA Y
GUYART, Marie (m Claude Martin), Mère Marie[2] de l'Incarnation, b Tours, Fr 1599, d Quebec 1672, paint CE2[2] DCB1 EC[2] H[2] K W1–3[2]
GUYON, Jean, Abbé, b Château-Richer,

Que 1659, d Paris 1687, paint CE1,2 DCB1 H H77 K NGC67

GYORE, Emese Kover (Mrs), b Kovaszna, Hu, paint PHA

HAANEL, Florence Eugenie, b Leslie Ridge, Mich c 1867, d 1950, paint DWA H RCA

HABERER, Eugene, b Switzerland 1837, d 1921, engr illus DeV1–7,9 H

HADDOCK, A.T., fl 1835–40, paint GW H

HADDOCK, William Richard, b Birmingham, Eng 1909– , paint Hu M MM RCA

HAESEKER, Alexandra (Sandy) (m Derek Michael Besant, q.v.), b Breda, Neth 1945– , paint AA CAE2 DCA SC UG

HAG, Gunnel Margareta Elisabeth, b Sweden 1946– , prt IO

HAGAN, Robert Frederick, b Toronto 1918– , paint sculp IO M MM NGC2 O.F49 RCA UG WWA93

HAGARTY, Beatrice (m Percy Robertson[2]), b Toronto 1879, paint Hu[2] M[2] MM[2] RCA

HAGARTY, Clara Sophia, b Toronto 1871 – d 1958, paint AGO CNS40 CWW55 DWA M MM Mo12 O.F48 PMC RCA

HAGELL, Edward Frederick (Teddy), b Lethbridge, Alta 1895, d Alberta 1964, paint DFA M RCA

HAGEN, Alice Mary Egan (m John C. Hagen), b Halifax 1872, d 1972, paint CLA DWA M WWA62

HAGGERSTONE, Wyn, fl 1970– , paint ABC

HAGGERTY, Cheryl Elizabeth, b Kingston, Ont 1953– , paint prt IO

HAGUE, Mary Elizabeth (Libby), b St Thomas, Ont 1950– , paint prt IO RCA WWA62

HAHN, Elizabeth Wyn Wood. *See* WOOD, Elizabeth Wyn

HAHN, Emanuel Otto (m Elizabeth Wyn Wood, q.v.), b Reutlingen, Ge 1881, d Toronto 1957, sculp AGO CC1 Co CWW55 EC M MM NGC1,2 O.N48 RCA TB2,3 W2,3 WWA56d59

HAHN, Gustave (Gustavus), b Reutlingen, Ge 1866, d Toronto 1962, paint B CC1 CWW58 H M NGC1,2 O.F48 RCA W3 WWA56

HAHN, Sylvia, b Toronto 1911– , engr paint BB GM M NGC2 O.F48 RCA WWA62

HAID, Sara Helen (Mrs), b Winnipeg 1902– , paint sculp M

HAIG, H. de H., Capt, fl 1885, illus H

HAILSTONE, Harold William, b London 1897, Eng, illus paint WBA2

HAINAULT, J.M., fl 1876–80, engr illus H K

HAINES, Bowen Aylesworth, b Canada 1858, illus paint AAA31 F

HAINES, Dorothy. *See* HOOVER, Dorothy Haines

HAINES, Frederick Stanley, b Meaford, Ont 1879, d Thornhill, Ont 1960, paint AAA31 AGO CC2 CWW58 EC F GM H77 M MM NGC1,2 O.F48 PMC RCA TB2 UG W3 WWA62

HAISOCH, H., b Lachine, Que 1910– , paint SC

HAISOCH, Hubert, b Milwaukee, Wis 1933– , col etch paint IO

HAIST, Reginald Evan, b Hamilton, Ont 1910– , paint CWW87

HAJDU, Philippa, b England 1937– , prt IO

HAKA. *See* QAQAQ/HAKA/KAKA/QAKA, Ashoona

HALCHUK, Carl, b Ottawa 1936– , paint M

HALE, Barbara. *See* PERRIN, Barbara Hale

HALE, Elizabeth Frances Amherst[2] (m John Hale), b England 1774, d Quebec 1826, Eng, paint DCB6[2] DWA H KB NGC2 PNL WHC

HALES, Gwendolyn, b Wolfville, NS 1901, d 1976, paint sculp CLA MA

HALFORD, Josiah, fl 1868–74, paint H

HALIBURTON, Laura Charlotte. *See* CUNARD, Laura Charlotte Haliburton

HALIBURTON, Robert Grant, b Windsor, NS 1831, d Pass Christian, Mo 1901, paint H Mo98 RCA W2,3

HALKETT, John (b John Weddeburn), Baron, b Pitfirrane, Scot 1768, bu Petersham/London 1852, Scot, paint DCB8 DFA H

HALL, Barbara B., b New York 1942– , drw prt CAE1,2 IO

HALL, Basil, Capt, b Dunglass, Scot 1788, d London 1844, Scot, paint B DBE DBLP DMA DNB GW H H77 ROM TB1

HALL, Charles Francis, Capt, b 1821, d 1871, topog H

HALL, Cyrenius, b 1830, fl 1878, paint AAW1 H Sam

HALL, Edward, Lt, fl 1861–6, topog DeV1 H

HALL, Francis, Lt, fl 1813–17, topog H

HALL, Harry, b nr Hull, Eng 1893, d Toronto 1954, cart Des

HALL, J., Rev, fl 1798–1802, drw DeV4

HALL, Jeanne Patricia, b Toronto 1922– , paint M

HALL, John Alexander, b Toronto 1914– , paint AGO CWW93 IO M MM NGC2 O.Ag48 RCA WWA93

HALL, John Scott, b Edmonton 1943– , illus paint AA CAE1,2 CE1,2 DCA NGC2 RCA WWA93

HALL, Joice (m John Scott Hall), b Edmonton 1943– , paint AA RCA

HALL, Margaret Mary Turner (Peggie) (m John D. Hall), b Torquay, Dev 1922– , paint BDSA

HALL, Mary G. (Mrs), b England, fl 1831–6, paint DeV9 DFA DWA H ROM

HALL, Pam, b Kingston, Ont 1951– , illus paint CBC

HALL, Pauline Hooton, b Shirebrook, Eng 1931– , engr BB

HALL, Robert, b Winnipeg 1925– , paint O.Ag49

HALL, Sydney Prior, b Newmarket, Eng 1842, d London 1922, Eng, illus paint AAW1 AH ANC B DBA DBHP DBMP DBWA DVP G H ICB1 PNL RA RCA Sam TB1 WBA1 W1 WWW

HALL, Thomas Herbert, b Ackworth, Yorks 1885, d Pointe Claire, nr Montreal 1972, paint M MM RCA

HALLAM, Joseph Sydney, b Manchester, Eng 1899, d Toronto 1953, paint AGO CWW49 Hu M MM NGC1,2 NGC68 O.F48 RCA Sam TB3 UG WWA56

HALLAM, Lindsay, b Ottawa 1947– , paint IO

HALLE, Marie-Joseph (Soeur Saint-François d'Assisi), b Quebec Prov 1762, d Quebec 1818, carv K

HALLEN, Eleanor, b England 1822, d Toronto 1846, paint DWA H

HALLEN, George, fl 1882, paint H

HALLEN, Mrs George, fl 1878–82, paint H

HALLEN, Mary E. (May). *See* GILMOUR, Mary E. Hallen

HALLETT, Vera Elizabeth Taplin (Mrs), b Bracebridge, Ont 1906, d 1979, paint M

HALLEWELL, Edmund Gilling, Cdr, fl 1839, d Sandhurst, Eng 1869, Eng, paint DBWA H NGC2 ROM WHC

HALLIDAY, Richard Stuart, b Vancouver 1939– , paint M

HALLMAN, H. Theodore, b Bucks Co, Pa 1937– , des paint WWA93

HALSTEAD, Richard Stewart, b Lafayette, Ind 1947– , paint IO

HAMASKI, Kazuo, b Prince Rupert, BC 1925– , paint IO

HAMBIDGE, Jay (x Hambridge[2]), b Simcoe, Ont 1867, d New York 1924, illus paint AAA23 B DAB F[2] H Mo12 Sam Y

HAMBLETON, John (Jack), b Preston, Lancs 1916– , paint M SC
HAMBLETON, Josephine (m Gilbert Tessier), b Ottawa 1919– , illus paint M
HAMEL, Gustave, b 1867, fl 1917, drw K
HAMEL, Joseph-Arthur-Eugène, b Quebec 1845 – d 1932, paint EC H H77 Hu K M MM NGC1,2 NGC67 RCA TB3
HAMEL, Margaret. *See* GOING, Margaret Hamel
HAMEL, Pierre-Narcisse[2], fl 1879, paint H[2] K
HAMEL, René, b c 1938– , paint M
HAMEL, Théophile (François Xavier), b Sainte-Foy, nr Quebec 1817, d Quebec 1870, paint ACA B CE1,2 DCB9 EC H H77 Hu K LeJ M MQ NGC1,2 NGC67 TB1 W1–3
HAMELIN, Ella, b 1867, fl 1914, paint H
HAMELIN, Pierre, fl 1890–3, sculp K
HAMER, Betty (m Jack Hamer, q.v.), b England 1917– , paint IO
HAMER, Jack (m Betty Hamer, q.v.), b Brighouse, Yorks 1914– , paint IO M MM RCA
HAMILL, Doris Vivian Pickup (Mrs), b Winnipeg 1924– , paint M
HAMILTON, Augustus Terrick, Capt, fl 1835–8, Eng, topog H WHC
HAMILTON, Hamilton, b Oxford, Eng 1847, d Norwalk, Conn 1928, Amer, paint AAA27d28 AAW1 App B F H RCA TB1,3 WWWA Y
HAMILTON, Henrietta Martha Drummond, Lady (m Charles[2] Hamilton, Sir), b England c 1780 – d 1857, Eng, min APH DCB7[2] DNB[2] EC[2]
HAMILTON, Henry, Brig Maj, b Dublin/England c 1734, d Antigua 1796, Irish, topog App DCB4 DFA H LeJ W1–3 WWWA
HAMILTON, Ida Gertrude, b St Mary's, Ont 1887, paint Hu MM RCA
HAMILTON, James, b England 1810, d London, Ont 1896, paint DCB12 DFA H H77 NGC2 WHC
HAMILTON, James, b Etrien, nr Belfast 1819, d San Francisco 1878, Amer, paint AAW1 AC BE DAA DeV5 DIA DMA DSP GW Sam Y
HAMILTON, Jane, fl 1876–87, paint DWA H
HAMILTON, John, Capt, fl 1753, d 1777, paint DBLP G H PNL
HAMILTON, Kathleen Anita, b Vancouver 1931– , paint M MM
HAMILTON, Kenneth Morrison, Rev, b Worthing, Eng 1917– , des paint M
HAMILTON, Lauchlan Alexander, b Penetanguishene, Ont 1852, d Toronto 1941, paint DFA H Mo98,12
HAMILTON, Mary Riter (m Alexander H. Hamilton), b Teeswater, Bruce Co, Ont 1873, d Vancouver 1954, paint B DWA Hu MM Mo12 WWNA
HAMILTON, S. (Mrs), fl 1876–86, paint DWA H
HAMILTON-SMITH, Joan, b Toronto 1925– , paint CAE1 M
HAMMEL, Agnes Agatha (m Ernest Keene Robinson[2]), fl 1929–72, paint CWW48 WWB72[2]
HAMMER, Alfred Emil, b New Haven, Conn 1925– , paint WWA93
HAMMERECHTS, August, b Belgium, fl 1950s, sculp M
HAMMOCK, Virgil Gene, b Long Beach, Calif 1938– , paint WWA93
HAMMOND, Charlotte Emily. *See* WILSON-HAMMOND, Charlotte Emily
HAMMOND, Frances Long (m William Hammond), b Varency, Norfolk Co, Ont 1834, d Port Dover, Ont 1921, paint DWA H
HAMMOND, John A., b Montreal 1843, d Sackville, NB 1939, paint AE AGO B CWW36 DBA G H M MM Mo98,12 NGC1,2 PMC Sam St TB3
HAMMOND, Rody Kenny. *See* COURTICE, Rody Kenny Hammond

HAMPSON, Beatrice Mary Stephen Cantlie (m Robert Hampson), b Montreal 1897, d 1976, paint CLA

HANCE, James Busik, b England 1847, d 1915, paint AAA1900 CWW10 H MM

HANCOCK, Henrietta. *See* BRITTON, Henrietta Hancock

HANCOCK, Herbert, b 1836, d 1882, paint H

HANDFORTH, Thomas Schofield, b Tacoma, Wash 1897, d Los Angeles 1948, Amer, illus paint AAA1,3 B TB2 WWA47d53 WWNA Y

HANDY, Arthur, b New York 1933– , sculp AGO CAE2 Co IO M MM NGC2

HANEQUAND, Daniel. *See* HANNEQUAND/HANEQUAND, Daniel

HANES, Ursula Ann (m David John Fry; m D. Peter Guthrie), b Toronto 1932– , paint sculp CWW93 M RCA WWA73

HANFORD, Charles (Mrs), fl 1834–9, paint H

HANKO, Gilmore, b c 1934, d 1969, paint M

HANKS. *See* BAEB, Henry R.

HANKS/HANKES, Jarvis F. (aka Jervis, Jerois), b Pittsfield, NY c 1799, fl 1852, Amer, sil B BSA DBHP F GW H H77 J TB1

HANLEY, William H., b Canada, fl 1843–69, paint F GW H Y

HANNA, Charles G., b Alexandria, Egy 1952– , paint CWW93

HANNAFORD, Michael, b Stoke Gabriel, Dev 1832, d Toronto 1891, paint H Hu MM RCA W1–3

HANNAM, Herbert Henry, b Swinton Park, Ont 1898, d 1963, paint CWW61

HANNEQUAND/HANEQUAND[2], Daniel, b France 1938– , drgt prt DCA IO[2]

HANSCOMBE, Arthur Randell, b Toronto c 1866, d Vancouver 1953, engr H

HANSEN, Frances, b Prince Albert, Sask 1918– , paint KB

HANSEN, James Colin, b Warren, Ohio 1939– , paint prt CAE2 UG

HANSEN, Thorkild Conrad, b Gevno-Lyderslev, Dn 1903, d 1976, paint sculp M O.Ag49

HANSLOW, Ralph Arthur, b Chichester, Sus 1918– , paint M

HANSON, Gertrude Jean (m John A. Elphick), b Toronto 1933– , paint CWW84 M MM RCA WWA86

HANSON, John William, b 1920– , paint IO

HANZALEK, George (Jiri), b Velkalhota, Cz 1926– , paint sculp IO M

HARBISON, Cathy. *See* SENITT-HARBISON, Cathy

HARBUZ, Ann Alexandra Napastuk (m John Bilawich; m Mike Harbuz), b Winnipeg 1908, d N Battleford, Sask 1989, paint BDSA DFA KB

HARCSAR, Frank (Ferenc), b Szatmar, Hu 1910– , paint PHA

HARDCASTLE, J.W., fl 1854–82, paint H

HARDCASTLE, Jack W., b at sea, nr Whitby, Yorks c 1881, d 1973, paint M

HARDER, Rolf Peter, b Hamburg, Ge 1929– , des CWW93 RCA WWA93 WWGA2

HARDING, Beatrice Louise Lewis (m William McAra Harding), b Morden, Man 1913– , paint BDSA

HARDING, Chester (aka Charles[2]), b Conway, Mass 1792, d Boston 1866, Amer, min paint ANC App B BM Bry DAA DAB DVP[2] F Fo G[2] GW H TB1 WWA Y

HARDING, Noel Robert, b London 1945– , sculp WWA93

HARDMAN, Jack Nelson, b New Westminster, BC 1923– , sculp M MM NGC2

HARDWICK, Melbourne Havelock, b Digby, NS 1857, d Belmont, nr

Waverly, Mass 1916, paint AAAd28 B F H TB1 Y

HARDY, Campbell, Maj Gen, b Norwich, Eng 1831, fl 1914, paint DeV9 H

HARDY, Gregory, fl 1856–65, litho paint H

HARDY, Jane Coulson, fl 1980– , paint sculp MFMS

HARDY, Jean-Baptiste, b Quebec 1731, fl 1770s, carv K

HARDY, Pierre, b Quebec 1737, fl 1772, sculp K

HARDY, Xavier, b Quebec 1856/7, fl 1881, sculp K

HARGITT/HARGIT[2], George F., b Edinburgh c 1838, d c 1928, paint H[2] M

HARISCH, William, b Czechoslovakia 1917 , paint sculp M

HARLANDER, Susan Michel (Suzanne) (m Théodore Harlander, q.v.), b Stuttgart, Ge 1920– , sculp IO M RCA

HARLANDER, Théodore (Ted) (m Susan M. Harlander, q.v.), b Bavaria, Ge 1920– , sculp IO M RCA

HARLEY, Harry George, b St Catharines, Ont 1929– , crto WWA73

HARLEY, James Kimball, b Canada 1828, d 1889, paint GW H Y

HARMAN, Jack Kenneth, b Vancouver 1927– , sculp BCS Co M MM RCA WWA80

HARNESS, Laura, b Alysham, Sask 1928– , paint BDSA DFA KB

HAROLD, Alexander, b Scotland c 1846/56, d Montreal 1924, paint H Hu MM NGC1,2 TB3

HAROLD, Hans, b Germany, fl 1958– , paint M

HARPE, Gerhard, b Poland 1943– , sculp DCA

HARPE, Sophie Elaine, b Quebec Prov 1895, d California 1981, des paint AAW3 AC

HARPER, Archie S., b New Brunswick c 1925– , paint M

HARPER, George Robinson, b 1843, d 1910, paint H

HARPER, John Russell, b Caledonia, Ont 1914, d Cornwall, Ont 1983, paint CE2 CWW83 RCA WWA82

HARPER, Lillian (Mrs), b Ontario, fl 1961– , paint M

HARPER, William Allen, b nr Cayuga, Ont 1873, d Mexico City 1910, paint AAA10d28 AAW2 WWWA

HARPS, Tony (s Gamboli[2]), b Montreal 1937– , cart Des[2]

HARRINGTON, Anna Lois Dawson (1876 m Bernard James Harrington[2]), fl 1882–1915, paint CWW10[2] H MM Mo98[2] RCA

HARRINGTON, Conrad F., b Montreal 1912– , paint CWW93

HARRINGTON, Nola Dawn Harris (m Joseph John Harrington), b Saskatoon 1931– , paint BDSA

HARRINGTON, Rebecca Christina (m E.A. Harrington), b Toronto 1869, d 1930, paint DWA M MM RCA

HARRIS, Alfred Peter, b Toronto 1932– , paint IO M MM RCA S WWA93 WWC82

HARRIS, Anne, b Woodstock, Ont 1928– , sculp IO

HARRIS, Bess Larkin (m Frederick B. Housser; m Lawren Stewart Harris, q.v.), b Brandon, Man 1890, d Vancouver 1969, paint CLA DWA M MM RCA

HARRIS, Clara Isabella (m Frederick William Harris), b King, Ont 1887, paint Hu M

HARRIS, Dora. *See* WECHSLER, Dora Harris

HARRIS, Edward Alexander, fl 1920–31, paint DFA

HARRIS, Florence. *See* EVERETT, Florence Harris

HARRIS, Frederick William, b Toronto 1890, paint Hu

HARRIS, James Edward, b Charlottetown 1886 – d 1954, paint CLA PMC WWA53d56

HARRIS, Jean Mildred. *See* HORNE, Jean Mildred Harris

HARRIS, John, b 1830, d 1861, engr H

HARRIS, Joyce Kathleen, b 1946– , prt CAE2

HARRIS, Lawren Phillips, b Toronto 1910, d Ottawa 1994, paint prt AGO CC1 CWW73 DCA H77 IO M MA MM NGC1,2 NGC67 NGC68 O.F48 RCA TB3 WWA89 WWB72

HARRIS, Lawren Stewart (m Bess Larkin Harris, q.v.), b Brantford, Ont 1885, d Vancouver 1970, paint AAW3 ACA AE AGO CC2 CE1,2 CLA Co CWW67 EC FCA H77 Hu M MM NGC1,2 NGC67 OC OCD RCA S Sam TB2 TN UG US W3 WWA70

HARRIS, Martha Douglas (Mrs), b Victoria, BC 1854, d 1933, paint H

HARRIS, Mary. *See* FILER, Mary Harris

HARRIS, Michael, b Winnipeg 1945– , paint CAE1

HARRIS, Peter. *See* HARRIS, Alfred Peter

HARRIS, Philip N., b Toronto 1945– , paint IO

HARRIS, Robert, b Ty'n-y-Groes, Wales 1847, d Montreal 1919, paint ACA AGO B CC1 CE1,2 Co CWW10 DBA DVP EC G H H77 Hu L LeJ MM Mo98,12 NGC1,2 NGC67 R1 RA RCA TB1,3 W1–3 WWW

HARRIS, Walter, b Kispiox, BC 1931– , carv prt CE1,2

HARRISON, Allan. *See* HARRISON, William Allan

HARRISON, Birge Lovell. *See* HARRISON, Lovell Birge

HARRISON, Edith Elizabeth (m W.E.C. Harrison), b London 1907– , paint DFA M MM RCA

HARRISON, Edward Hardy (Ted), b Wingare, Dur 1926– , illus paint C CBC CE2 CWW93 M T SAA56

HARRISON, Fred, b Toronto 1947– , paint CAE1

HARRISON, Harriet N., fl 1863–7, paint DWA H

HARRISON, J.P., fl 1850, dior paint H

HARRISON, Jennie, b Kentville, NS, fl 1960– , paint Mp384

HARRISON, Lawrence Victor, b Portage la Prairie, Man 1941– , paint Mp385 WWA76

HARRISON, Lovell Birge[2], b Philadelphia 1854, d Woodstock, NY 1929, Amer, paint AAAd29 AAW1,3 AC[2] B DAB F H[2] NCAB[2] Sam[2] TB[2] WWWA[2] Y

HARRISON, Mark Robert, b Hovringham, Yorks 1819, d Fond du Lac, Wis 1894, Amer, dior paint DCB12 GW H WWWA Y

HARRISON, Ted. *See* HARRISON, Edward Hardy

HARRISON, Thomas C., b c 1825, d Quebec 1846, dior paint H

HARRISON, Tom, b England 1926– , illus T

HARRISON, William Allan, b Montreal 1911 – d 1988, paint CWW88 M MM RCA WWA86d89

HARROD, Frank Stanley, b Leeds, Eng 1881, d Newmarket, Ont 1954, prt NGC2 RCA

HARRY, Philip, fl 1833–57, paint GW H Y

HART, Charles, fl 1866, topog H

HART, Ernest Percival Tudor. *See* TUDOR-HART, Ernest Percival

HART, Patricia Ann, b Lethbridge, Alta 1928– , paint IO

HART, William M., b Paisley, Scot 1823, d Mount Vernon, NY 1894, Amer, paint ANC App B DAA DAB F GW H TB1 WWWA Y

HARTAL, Paul Zev, b Szeged, Hu 1936– , paint CWW93 WWA93

HARTLEY, Marsden, b Lewiston, Me 1877, d 1943, Amer, paint AAA33 DFA OC WWA40

HARTMAN, John, b Midland, Ont 1950– , paint UG

HARTVIKSEN, Ronn, b Port Arthur, Ont 1947– , drw IO

HARTY, Dwayne John, b Shaunavon, Sask 1957 , paint sculp CWW93
HARVEN, Hélène de, b Belgium, fl 1891–2, paint K
HARVEY, Donald, b Walthamstow, nr London 1930– , paint CAE1,2 CWW93 M MM NGC2 RCA S WWA93
HARVEY, George, b Tottenham, London c 1800, d Soho, London c 1878, Eng, paint B BE DAA DMA DVP F Fo G GW H Sam WWWA Y
HARVEY, George H. (m Priscilla Harvey, q.v.), b Torquay, Dev 1846, d England 1910, paint H RCA WBA2
HARVEY, James V., b Toronto 1929, d New York 1965, paint DCAA1 WWA66
HARVEY, Phyllis Nelson (m Cecil Richards), b Montreal 1906– , paint Hu M MM RCA
HARVEY, Priscilla (m George H. Harvey, q.v.), fl 1883–6, paint H RCA
HARVEY, Reginald Llewellyn, b Southampton, Eng 1888, d Victoria, BC 1973, paint M MM
HARVEY, Sydenham Parker, b Cobden, Ont 1914– , sculp M MM RCA
HARVIE, Bettina (Mrs), b England c 1900, d 1971, paint M
HARVISON, Clifford W., b Montreal 1902– , paint CWW64
HARWOOD, Ida Alberta Shantz (1934 m Frank Caister Harwood[2]), b Winnipeg, d Victoria, BC 1952, paint CWW38[2]
HASEMANN, Sylvia, b Vancouver c 1942– , paint M
HASHEY, Mary Wood Coughey (m Lawrence F. Hashey), b McAdam, NB 1910– , paint CLA MA
HASKELL, Hiram Betts, b Fredericton 1823, d Newburyport, Mass 1873, paint GW H Y
HASPEL-SEGUIN[2], Tutzi (Bertha) (m Georges Seguin), b Bucharest, Rom 1911– , paint IO MM RCA WWA70[2]
HASS, John, b Renfrew, Ont 1925– , paint M MM
HASSAN, Jamelie, b London, Ont 1948– , paint sculp IO
HASSELFELDT, Edgar (m Elva Hasselfeldt), fl 1971– , paint sculp MFMS
HASSELFELDT, Elva (m Edgar Hasselfeldt), tap MFMS
HASSELL, Hilton Macdonald, b Lachine, Que 1910, d Port Credit, Ont 1980, paint CWW93 IO M MM NGC2 RCA UG
HASTENTEUFEL, Dieter, b Krefeld, Ge 1939– , sculp WWA93
HATCHER, James Donald, b St Thomas, Ont 1923– , paint CWW90
HATCHER, John Joslyn, b Winnipeg 1931– , paint M MM
HATHAWAY, Norman Blasdell, b New Hamburg, Ont 1924– , des gra CWW93
HATTON, W.S. (s W.S.H.), fl 1855–64, topog H H77 WHC
HAUFSCHILD, Lutz, b Germany, fl 1969– , stgl ABC
HAUKANESS/HAUKNESS, Lars Jonson, b Hardanger, Nor 1862, d nr Lake Louise, Alta 1929, paint CE2 DFA H Hu M PMC
HAUSER, Gordon, fl 1971– , paint sculp M
HAVELL, Robert, b Reading, Eng 1793, d Tarrytown, NY 1878, Amer, paint B DAB F GW H NCAB Red TB1 WWWA Y
HAVERFIELD, John T., fl 1848, d 1885, Eng, topog H
HAWKEN, George, b Owen Sound, Ont 1946– , prt IO UG
HAWKINS, O. John, b Oregon City, Oreg 1935– , paint CWW93
HAWKSETT, Samuel C., b London 1827, d Montreal 1903, paint GW H NGC2 RCA
HAWKSLEY, J. Frederick, fl 1882–5, Eng, paint H MM RCA
HAWLEY, Wilhelmina D., fl 1898–1908, paint AAA05 DWA H RCA

HAWORTH, Bobs. *See* HAWORTH, Zema Barbara Cogill

HAWORTH, Colin Reid, b Ottawa 1916– , paint M MM

HAWORTH, Peter (m Zema B.C. Haworth, q.v.), b Oswaldtwistle, Lancs 1889, d Toronto 1986, paint AGO CC2 CNS40 CWW86 IO M MM NGC1,2 NGC68 O.F50 RCA S SC TB2,3 WWA86d89

HAWORTH, Zema Barbara Cogill (Bobs) (m Peter Haworth, q.v.), b Queenstown, SA 1904, d Toronto 1988, paint AGO CC1 CNS40 CWW88 IO M MM NGC1,2 NGC68 O.My50 RCA TB3 UG WWA86d89

HAWTHORNE, Marion McClure (Miss), b Montreal 1897, paint CNS40 Hu MM RCA

HAXBY, Francis J., b Dundee, Scot c 1905, d 1976, paint M

HAY, Darlene Gladys Busch (m James Robert Hay), b Gravelbourg, Sask 1945– , paint BDSA

HAY, Norman Kyle, b Ottawa 1883, paint Hu RCA

HAY, Norman Mackenzie, b Vancouver 1924, d 1988, des CWW58

HAY, Pierre, b France 1661, d Montreal 1708, sculp K

HAY, William, b Peterhead, Scot 1818, d Edinburgh 1888, paint DeV8

HAYCOCK, Maurice Hall, b Wolfville, NS 1900– , paint M US

HAYDEN, Michael, b Vancouver 1943– , sculp CAE1 CE1,2 IO M NGC2 RCA UG

HAYDON, Harold Emerson, b Ft William, re Thunder Bay, Ont 1909– , Amer, paint CWW91 DAS WWA93

HAYDON, Margot (m H.H. Haydon), fl 1950– , paint M

HAYES, Isaac Israel, b Chester Co, Pa 1832, d New York 1881, Amer, paint topog App DAB DCB11 DMA H NCAB3 WWWA

HAYES, Margaret Clarissa. *See* TOULMIN, Margaret Clarissa Hayes

HAYLETT, Malcolm John, b Montreal 1923– , paint TB3 WBA2 WWB86

HAYMAN, Stanley, b Toronto 1910– , engr M MM RCA

HAYNES, Douglas Hector, b Regina 1936– , paint AA CAE2 CE1,2 M RCA SC WWA93

HAYWARD, Alfred Frederick William (m Edith B. Hayward, q.v.), b Ravenscourt, nr Port Hope, Ont 1856, d Hemingford Grey, nr St Ives, Cambs 1939, paint B DBA DBF DFP3 DVP G H Hu NGC1,2 RA RCA TB1,3 WBA1 WWB34

HAYWARD, Caroline (m Alfred Hayward, Capt), fl mid 19th cen, paint DWA H

HAYWARD, Chris, b London 1938– , paint CAE1,2 SC

HAYWARD, Edith Burrowes (m Alfred F.W. Hayward, q.v.), fl 1897–1933, paint DBA DFA DWA G H RA WBA

HAYWARD, Gerald Sinclair, b nr Port Hope, Ont 1845, d New York 1926, min paint AGO B DBA Fo G H M Mo12 RCA ROM

HAYWARD, John, fl 1884–90, illus DeV4

HAYWARD, Octavia Elizabeth Tyler. *See* MARR, Octavia Elizabeth Tyler Hayward

HAZARD, William Garnet, b Wallaceburg, Ont 1903– , paint M

HAZELAND, Mary, fl 1969– , paint M

HAZELGROVE, Nancy Ann, b Montreal 1945– , paint prt IO

HAZELL, Eileen Long (m Stanley G. Hazell), b Richmond, Sur 1903– , sculp M RCA

HAZELL, Frank, b Hamilton, Ont 1883, d c 1957, illus paint AAA33 F MM TB2 WWA56d59

HAZEN, Bessie Ella, b Waterford, NB 1862, d Los Angeles 1946, paint AAA33 AAW2 AC DWA F TB2 WWA40d47

HEACOCK, Rebecca M. (m K.E. Heacock), b Minnesota, 1890, paint M

HEAD, Anna Maria Yorke, Lady (m Edmund Walker Head, 8th Baron, q.v.), b England c 1808, d London 1890, Eng, paint DWA Hp153

HEAD, Edmund Walker, Sir, 8th Baron (m Anna Maria Yorke Head, q.v.), b Wiarton Place, nr Maidstone 1805, d London 1868, Eng, paint BPp1297 CE1,2 DCB9 DNB EC H W1–3

HEAD, George Bruce, b St Boniface, Man 1931– , paint sculp CAE2 CC1 CWW93 M MM NGC2 RCA S TB3 WWA93

HEAD, Horatio Nelson, b Palermo, It 1799, fl 1825, Eng, topog DFA DMA H

HEADE, Martin Johnson, b Lumberville, Pa 1819, d St Augustine, Fla 1904, Amer, paint AAW1 ANC App B BE DAA DMA DSP F GW H TB1 WWWA Y

HEALY, Julia Schmitt, b 1947– , paint CAE2

HEALY, Sinclair Davis, b Moncton, NB 1925– , paint M MM TB3

HEAPS, Frank N., b Toronto 1941– , paint CWW93

HEARN, R. Jock, b Scotland 1926– , paint M

HEARNE, Samuel, b London 1745 – d 1792, Eng, topog CE1,2 Co DCB4 DNB EC H W1–3

HEASLIP, Ann (Mrs), fl 1876–97, paint DWA H

HEASLIP, William, b Toronto 1898, d Morristown, NJ 1970, illus paint IA2

HEATH, Mel, b Saskatoon 1930– , paint SC

HEAVEN, Ethel R., fl 1897–1906, paint H MM RCA

HEAVISIDE, Mary. *See* LOVE, Mary Heaviside, Lady

HEBBLETHWAITE, Walter Benson, b Ridgetown, Ont 1929– , paint M MM

HEBERT, Adrien, b Paris 1890, d Montreal 1967, paint B CC2 CE1 CNS51 CWW61 K M MM MQ NGC1,2 PMC RCA TB2 W3 WWA53

HEBERT, Artémise (Soeur Marie-Eustochium), b St-Michel, Que 1862, d Outremont, Que 1934, paint K

HEBERT, Godfrey, b c 1906– , paint M

HEBERT, Henri, b Montreal 1884 – d 1950, sculp ACA AGO B CC2 CE1,2 CNS40 Co CWW48 K M MM MQ NGC1,2 NGC67 PMC RCA TB2 WWA53d68

HEBERT, Julien, b Rigaud, Que 1917– , sculp M RCA TB3 WWA78

HEBERT, Louis-Philippe, b Ste-Sophie-de-Megantic, Que 1850, d Westmount, Que 1917, sculp ACA B CC1 CE1,2 Co CWW10 EC K LeJ M MM Mo98,12 MQ NGC1,2 NGC67 R1 TB1,3 US W1–3

HEBERT, Pierre, b Montreal 1944– , anim engr CC2 CE1,2 CWW93

HECHT, Estelle, b Montreal 1900 – d 1971, paint M MM RCA

HECHT, Mary S., b New York 1931– , sculp CAE1 IO WWA86

HEDDINGTON, Thomas, b Chatham, Eng c 1777, d England 1860, Eng, illus AC EMA

HEDLEY, Robert Wesley, b Ontario 1871, paint CWW49 M WWA62

HEDRICK, Robert Burns, b Windsor, Ont 1930– , paint sculp AE AGO IO M MM NGC2 RCA S TB3 UG

HEER, Louis-Chrétién de, b Bouxwiller, Fr 1760, d France pre-1808, Fr, paint DCB5 H H77 K MQ

HEGGTVEIT, Bruce Allen, b Maidstone, Sask 1917– , paint M

HEIDERSDORF, Ernest, b Westphalia, Ge 1901– , paint M

HEILIG, Lee Leibl. *See* LEIBL, Lee

HEIM, Guenter/Guenther, b Nuremberg, Ge 1935– , paint IO M SC

HEIMANN, Helmar, b Liegnitz, Silesia, Ge 1931– , paint US

HEIMLICH, Herman, b Setoraljaujehely, Hu 1904– , paint M MM RCA

HEINE, Harry, b Edmonton 1928– , paint ABC DSP M SC WWA93

HEINE, Minnie B., b Norton, NB 1869, paint AAW1

HEINE-BAUX, Manfred, b Munich, Ge 1940– , paint CWW93 WWA93

HEINE-KOEHN, Lala Henryka, b Zuromin, Pol 1936– , paint BDSA

HEISLER, Franklyn, b Bridgewater, NS 1949– , sculp CAE1

HELLER, Jules, b New York 1919– , Amer, prt CWW85 WWA76

HELLER, Mary Ida Clair, b Toronto 1909– , sculp M RCA

HELLER, Susanna, b New York 1956– , paint CWW93 WWA93

HELME, James Burn, b Smiths Falls, Ont 1897, d State College, Pa 1945, paint CWW36 WWA40d47

HEMBROFF, Edythe (m Frederick J. Brand; m J. Schleicher), b Moose Jaw, Sask 1906, d Victoria, BC 1994, paint WWNA

HEMING, Arthur Henry Howard, b Paris, Ont 1870, d Hamilton, Ont 1940, paint AAA31 AAW1 B CC2 CNS40 CWW36 EC F Hu M McC Mo98,12 NGC1,2 RCA Sam TB1,3 W1–3 WWA40 Y

HEMMING, Edith, fl 1894–1911, Eng, min paint AAA03 DBA DWA Fo G H MM RA RCA RSA

HEMSTED, Margaret J. (Mrs), b England, fl 1896–1900, paint AAA01 DWA H RCA

HENAUT, Monique, b France 1933– , paint CAE1

HENDERSHOT, Janet Carol, b New York 1945– , paint prt IO

HENDERSHOT, Rae (m Thomas Reid MacDonald, q.v.), b Hamilton, Ont 1921– , drw paint IO M

HENDERSON, Bert, b Owen Sound, Ont, fl 1959– , paint sculp M

HENDERSON, D'Arcy Stuart, b 1940– , fl 1963– , paint sculp CAE2 M

HENDERSON, Edmund Yeamans Walcott, Lt Col, Sir, b Muddeford, nr Christchurch, Eng 1821, d London 1896, Eng, paint topog DFA DNB H H77 KB

HENDERSON, James, b Glasgow, Scot 1871, d Regina 1951, paint EC H77 Hu M MM NGC1,2 RCA Sam TB3 UG US W2–3 WBA2

HENDERSON, Marg, b 1945– , fl 1967– , paint M

HENDERSON, Nickolas, b Jones Falls, Ont 1862, d Portsmouth, Ont 1934, paint H KB

HENDERSON, W.R., fl 1898–1900, paint H

HENDRIE, Betty Lillian Scale, b England 1916– , paint IO

HENDRY, Charles Eric, b Ottawa 1903– , ske CWW79

HENDRY, Linda, b Nokomis, Sask 1961– , illus C

HENNEPIN, Louis, b Ath, Bel 1626, d Netherlands c 1705, Bel, paint Co DAB DCB2 DeV5 H K LeJ W1–3

HENNESSEY, Frank Charles, b Ottawa 1893 – d 1941, paint AGO CC1 EC Hu M MM NGC1,2 RCA S TB2 W1–3 WHC

HENNESSY, William John, b Thomastown, Ire c 1839, d Rudgwick, Sus 1917, Irish, illus paint AAAd28 ANC App B DAB DBA DVLP DVP F G GW TB1 WWWA

HENRICKSON, Martha, b New York 1942– , con CAE1,2

HENRICKSON, Thomas, b New York 1944– , con CAE1,2

HENRIQUEZ, Richard G., b Jamaica 1941– , sculp CWW93

HENRY, Dennis, b Portsmouth, Eng 1919– , paint M

HENRY, Frank, b c 1947– , sculp CAE1

HENRY, Myra E. (m R.H. Henry, q.v.), b Oakville, Ont 1852, d Pasadena, Calif 1949, paint DWA H

HENRY, Pierre, b Bonaventure, Que 1932– , paint CAE1

HENRY, R.H. (m Myra E. Henry, q.v.), b Oshawa, Ont 1848, d Los Angeles 1906, paint H

HENRY, Robert Brian, b 1834, d 1911, paint DFA
HENSCHEL, Gordon, b Manitoba, fl 1979– , paint ABC
HENSHAW[1], Arthur N. / S.[2], fl 1885–1901, paint H MM[1,2] RCA
HENSHAW, Ruth Beatrice, b Montreal c 1893, paint Hu
HENSON, Percy Henry Edgar, b Sussex, Eng 1890, d 1975, paint M
HENZELL, Dorothy Gwendolyn. *See* WILLIS, Dorothy Gwendolyn Henzell
HEON, Oscar, b 1901, d 1976, carv DFA KB
HEPPELL, Denis, b St-Jean-Port-Joli, Que 1944/5– , sculp M
HERARD, L.J., fl 1876–81, carv K
HERBERT, William Beverley, b Medicine Hat, Alta 1916– , paint M RCA
HERIOT, George, b Haddington, Scot c 1759, d Chelsea, London 1839, Scot, paint ACA B CE1,2 Co DBLP DBMaP DBWA DCB7 DMA DWP G H H77 LeJ M NGC2 NGC67 PNL SW UG W1–3 WHC
HERMES, Gertrude Anna Bertha (m Blain Hughes-Stanton), b Bromley, Kent 1901, d c 1984, Eng, engr sculp DBA MM RA TB2 WBA1 WWB82
HEROLD, Hans, b Munich, Ge 1925– , paint SC US
HERREILERS, John, b Edmonton 1924– , paint SC US
HERRY, Célestine de Neyer, Baroness, b Belgium 1879, d 1952, paint K WWNA
HERTZBERG, Phyllis Armour. *See* ARMOUR, Phyllis
HESS, Walter William, b 1910– , paint DFA
HESSAY, Carl/Carle, b Shanghai, Chi c 1911, d 1978, paint M
HESSE, Emma, b Niagara Falls, Ont, fl 1975– , des illus M
HEUPERMAN, Frederick Justinus, b 1887, d 1946, paint DFA
HEUSCH, Lucio de[2], b Sherbrooke 1946– , paint MQ RCA WWA93[2]
HEWARD, Efa Prudence, b Montreal 1896, d Los Angeles 1947, paint AGO CC1 CE1,2 Co DWA EC H77 Hu M MM NGC1,2 RCA TB2 UG W2–3 WWA53
HEWARD, Ross, b Montreal 1937– , paint CAE1,2
HEWETT / HEWITT, John, Lt, fl 1814–15, Eng, topog DMA H
HEWETT, Garnet, b N Bay, Ont, fl 1964– , paint M
HEWITT, Jean Edith, b Ottawa, fl 1947+, paint M
HEWITT, Minnie C., b Lunenberg, NS 1868, carv paint CLA WWA62
HEWKO, Michael (Mike), b St Catharines, Ont 1945– , sculp UG
HEWLETT, Annie Elizabeth May (Mrs), b Sutton-on-Hull, Yorks 1887, fl 1958, paint M
HEWSON, Frances Mary. *See* MacLAREN, Frances Mary Hewson
HEWSON, Marie Olivia. *See* GUEST, Marie Olivia Hewson
HEWTON, Randolph Stanley, b Maple Grove, Megantic, Que 1888, d Trenton, Ont 1960, paint AGO CC1 CE1,2 CWW58 Hu M MM NGC1,2 PMC RCA TB2 WWA59
HEYBROEK, Sandy (m William H. Heybroek), fl 1960– , paint M
HEYMANN, Gunter, b Berlin, Ge 1908, d 1960, paint M MM RCA
HEYVAERT, Pierre, b Lebbeke, Bel 1934, d Montreal 1974, sculp M MM MQ NGC2
HEYWOOD, John Carl, b Toronto 1941– , des gra CAE2 CWW93 IO M NGC2 RCA UG WWA93
HIAMAS. *See* SEAWEED, Willie
HIANVEU dit LAFRANCE, Etienne-Joseph, b Quebec 1756 – d 1838, des K
HICKLIN, Barbara Roe (m H. Hicklin), b Toronto 1918– , paint AA M SC
HICKLING, Walter Robert, b Delhi,

Ont 1924– , paint sculp IO M MM RCA WWA62
HICKMAN, William, fl 1857–60, Eng, topog DeV9 H UG
HICKS, Edward, Lt Col, fl 1778–82, d London 1787, Eng, topog DeV9 H
HICKS, Morley, b Picton, Ont 1877, d 1959, paint AAA33 TB2 WWA40
HICKS, Richard Percival Daniel, Rev, b Sussex, Eng 1903, d London, Ont 1973, paint M RCA S
HICKSON, A. Beatrice, b Montreal, fl 1916+, paint CNS36
HIDE, Peter Nicholas (m Elizabeth H. Prince, q.v.), b Carshalton, Sur 1944– , sculp CE1,2 CWW93 WWA93
HIDER, Arthur H., b 1870, d 1952, illus H
HIDER, Russell John, b Toronto 1899, paint AC AGO
HIESTER, Mary Augusta. *See* REID, Mary Augusta Hiester
HIGGINS, Elizabeth (m Wilham Pickering Jones), b Toronto 1960– , paint CWW93
HIGGINSON, Thomas Tweed, b Hawkesbury, Ont 1828 – d 1903, sil H
HIGHMAN, Sydney, fl 1890–1905, Eng, illus paint AH Sam
HILL, Albert J., fl 1869–77, paint DeV9 H
HILL, Derek, b Southampton, Eng 1916– , Eng, paint RA TB2 WBA1 WWB90
HILL, Donald Richings, b Buffalo, NY 1900, d Toronto 1939, paint M MM RCA
HILL, Eleanor Caroline. *See* FELLOWS, Eleanor Caroline Hill
HILL, George William, b Shipton, Que 1862, d Montreal 1934, sculp CC2 M MM Mo12 NGC1,2 PMC RCA TB2 W1–3
HILL, Harold Gordon, b Saskatoon 1913– , sculp CAE1 IO M
HILL, James Thomas, b Hamilton, Ont 1930– , paint M RCA
HILL, John William, b London 1812, d W Nyack, NY 1879, Amer, paint topog B DeV9 DMA F GW H TB1 Y
HILL, Kate Foss, b Halifax 1846, d Windsor, NS 1936, paint H RCA
HILL, Peter Gordon, b Toronto 1948– , drw paint IO
HILL, Thomas, b Six Nations Res, nr Brantford, Ont 1943– , drw prt Co IO
HILL-BUCHAR, Olive Cynthia, b Markdale, Ont 1951– , paint IO
HILLIARD, Margaret Burkholder (m Foster Hilliard), b Ottawa, fl 1930+, paint CLA
HILLYARD, Caroline Learoyd Carrie, b St Mary's, Ont, fl 1895–1940, paint AAA1900 H Hu RCA
HILLYER, William, fl 1832–64, paint F GW H
HILPERT, Joseph (Jozsef), b 1893, d Bacska-Kulut, Hu 1975, paint CWW36 PHA
HILTON, Charles, b Melville, Sask 1937 , sculp AA
HILTS, Alvin, b Newmarket, Ont 1908– , sculp IO M RCA UG WWA93
HIME, Ainslie Barron (Mrs), fl 1899–1922, paint H
HIND, Henry Youle, b Nottingham, Eng 1823, d Windsor, NS 1908, paint APH App CE1,2 Co DNB H LeJ Mo98 Sam W1–3
HIND, William George Richardson, b Nottingham, Eng 1833, d Sussex, NB 1889, paint APH CE1,2 Co DCB11 H H77 M NGC2 NGC67 PNL ROM Sam W1 3
HINDS, Cletus Frederick, b Barrie, Ont 1914– , paint M
HINE, Henry George, b Brighton, Eng 1811, d Hampstead, Eng 1895, Eng, engr illus paint ANC B DBA DBLP DBWA DVP G H ROM TB1
HINES, Robert Frederick, b Toronto 1925– , paint M
HINGSTON, Lillian Isabel Peterson (m Donald Alexander Hingston), b Montreal 1881 – d 1967, paint DWA M MM RCA

HINSCHELWOOD, Robert (Hinshelwood²), b Edinburgh 1812, d after 1875, engr paint B DeV7 F GW H² TB1

HINTZMAN, William Albert, b Berlin, Ge 1893, sculp M

HIRSCHBERG, Martin, b Toronto 1937– , paint sculp CAE1 IO M MM RCA

HLAVINA, Rasto (Rastislav), b Topolcany, Cz 1943– , paint sculp WWA93

HOBBS, Isabel (Mrs), b Norfolk, Eng 1885, paint WWNA

HOBBS, Robin A., b Oldham, Eng 1945– , sculp IO

HOBDAY, Phyllis M. (Mrs), b c 1907, fl 1964+, paint M

HOBSON, Norman C., b Woodstock, Ont 1897, paint CWW58

HOCH, James, b St Kitts, BWI 1827, d Toronto 1878, paint AGO H Hu W1–3

HOCHBAUM, Hans Albert, b Greeley, Colo 1911– , paint CWW80 M

HOCHSTETTER, L.G., b Germany, fl 1791–6, engr DeV7 DFA H

HODGINS, Aimée Gertrude Burgess (s Ai le Moncy/A. de Moncy) (m C.R. Hodgins), b India 1866, paint CWW38 H MM

HODGKINS, Arnold Benjamin, b Silverdale, Ont 1911– , paint M

HODGKINSON, Edward Allen, b Windsor, Ont 1918– , paint Hu

HODGSON, Barbara L., b Edmonton 1955– , des CWW93

HODGSON, John Joseph Trevor, b Bradford, Eng 1931– , paint CAE1 IO WWA80

HODGSON, Marjorie Jane Botting (m Joshua Hodgson), b Hamilton, Ont 1932– , paint CWW93 IO

HODGSON, Thomas Sherlock, b Toronto 1924– , paint AGO CAE1 CC2 M MM NGC1,2 O.Ag48 RCA TB3

HODGSON, Trevor. *See* HODGSON, John Joseph Trevor

HOENIGAN, Henry, b Zarnowiec, Pol 1917– , paint CAE1,2 IO M WWA76

HOFFI, Anna M. (s M. Hoffi), b Timmins, Ont 1952– , prt IO

HOFFMAN, Gaston, b Paris 1883, fl 1926, Fr, car paint B K

HOGAN, J., fl 1882–90, drw etch DeV4,6 H

HOGBIN, Stephen James, b Tolworth, Sur 1942– , sculp CAE2 IO WWA93

HOGENKAMP, Claire Florence (m Alfred Pinsky, q.v.), b The Hague, Neth 1940– , gra sculp M MM

HOGG, George C., b Kimberly, BC 1929– , paint ABC

HOGG, Grace Mary Isabel MacKenzie (m James D. Hogg), b Oxbow, Sask 1900, d Saskatoon 1989, paint BDSA M MM US

HOGG, Isobel, b Montreal 1887, sculp DBA DWA RA TB2 WBA1 WWB34

HOGLUND, Betty. *See* HOWE, Betty Hoglund

HOHNDORF, Eric, b Krefeld, Ge 1938– , paint ABC

HOIT, Albert Gallatin, b Sandwich, NH 1809, d W Roxbury, Mass 1856, Amer, min paint BM Fo GW H RCA

HOLBROOK, Elizabeth Mary Bradford (m John J. Holbrook), b Hamilton, Ont 1913– , sculp CWW93 IO M MM NGC2 O.My49 RCA WWA89

HOLDEN, Sarah/Sara Baldwin (Mrs Hunter²), b Belleville, Ont, fl 1886–1907, paint AAW1 B DWA² H² MM RCA

HOLDSTOCK, Alfred Worsley, b Bath, Eng c 1819, d Montreal 1901, paint AGO H H77 NGC2 ROM W1–3 WHC

HOLDSWORTH, Geoffrey Leigh, b London, Ont 1952– , paint CAE1 IO

HOLGATE, Edwin Headley, b Allandale, Ont 1892, d Montreal 1977, paint AGO CC1 CE1,2 CLA CNS40 Co CWW36 DCA EC FCA GM H77 M MM MQ NGC1,2 NGC67 NGC68

PMC RCA S Sam TB2 UG WWA76d78

HOLLAND, Kiff, b S Africa, fl 1970– , paint ABC

HOLLAND, Miriam Ramsay, b Montreal 1904 – d 1953, paint Hu M MM RCA

HOLLAND, Samuel Johannes, b Nijmegen, Neth c 1728, d Quebec 1801, topog CE1,2 DCB5 EC H LeJ W1–3

HOLLENBACK, William Grant, b Canada 1919– , paint IO

HOLLENBERG, Morley Donald, b Winnipeg 1942– , cal CWW93

HOLLIDAY, Charles William, b London 1870, paint WWNA

HOLLOWAY, Frederick H., fl 1840–53, ske DFA H ROM

HOLLOWAY, Geoffrey, b London, fl 1945+, paint M

HOLMAN, Donald R., b Kansas City 1946– , prt CWW85 RCA

HOLMAN, James Henry, b London/Plymouth, Eng 1821, d Boston 1891, paint DCB12 Hp460 RCA

HOLMAN, Louis Arthur, b Summerside, PEI 1866, d 1939, etch illus AAA13 F Y

HOLMDEN, Kenneth Hensley, b Ottawa 1893, d Montreal 1963, paint MM NGC2 RCA

HOLMES, Betty Marion Ruth, b Winnipeg 1914– , paint sculp M

HOLMES, David Bryan, b Harrowsmith, Eng 1936– , paint prt CWW93 WWA93

HOLMES, Reginald, b Calgary 1934– , gra paint CAE2 IO M RCA UG WWA80

HOLMES, Robert H., b Cannington, Ont 1861, d Toronto 1930, paint AGO CC2 EC H H77 Hu M MM NGC1,2 R1 RCA St TB2 W1–3

HOLMES, William W., b Belfast, N Ire 1924– , paint ABC

HOLMFELD, Helmuth Emanuel Bernhard Edwin, Baron de Holmfeld, Baron Dirckinck[2]-Holmfeld, b Schwarzenbeck, Holstein, Dn 1835, d Seattle, Wash 1912, Dn, paint B[2] H MM RCA TB1[2],3

HOLMSTED, Marie H. (Mrs), b Toronto 1857, d Moose Jaw, Sask 1911, paint AAA01 DWA H MM RCA

HOLMSTEN, Olle Werner, b Uppsala, Swe 1915– , sculp M

HOLOWNIA, Thaddeus, b Bury St Edmunds, Eng 1949– , paint CWW93

HOLT, Edwin Albert, b Toronto 1921– , paint O.F50

HOLYOAK, Don, b Toronto 1952– , paint CAE1

HOMER, Merlin, b USA 1943– , drw paint IO

HOMES, Verna Georgie Leonard[2] (Vera) (Mrs), b Sydney, NS 1927– , paint M[2] MA

HONE, John Ramsey McGregor (m Mary E.S. Hone, q.v.), b Prince Albert, Sask 1920– , engr paint BB CAE1 M

HONE, Mary Elizabeth Springer (Beth) (m John R. McGregor Hone, q.v.), b Halkirk, Alta 1918– , sculp BDSA CAE1 M

HONEY, John Burrows. *See* BURROWS, John

HONGWORTH, Doris (Dodi). *See* MORRIS, Doris Hongworth (Dodi)

HONSA, Marlene, b Germany 1933– , tap IO M

HOO SING[2] (Hoo Sing Yuen), b Canton, Chi 1909– , sculp CWW93 IO M MM O.F48 RCA WWA93[2]

HOOD, Harry (Henry), b Cupar, Scot 1876, d Vancouver 1956, paint Sam WWNA

HOOD, Robert, Lt, b Portarlington, Ire c 1797, d nr Lake Providence, NWT 1821, Irish, topog DCB6 CE1,2 H PNL WHC

HOOK, Anne Smith, b Ireland 1900, fl 1965+, paint IO M

HOOKER, Marion Hope Nelson[2] (m Frank W. Hooker), b Richmond,

Va 1866, d St Catharines, Ont 1946, paint AGO DWA H H77 MM[2] RCA[2]
HOOLE, Kate Adeline Smith. *See* SMITH, Kate Adeline
HOOPER, Edward, b London 1829, d Brooklyn, NY 1870, gra illus DeV8 F GW H
HOOPER, Helen Aileen. *See* COWAN, Helen Aileen Hooper
HOOPER, John (m Katharine B. Hooper, q.v.), b Southampton, Eng 1926– , sculp M MM
HOOPER, Katherine B. Furse (Kathy) (m John Hooper[2], q.v.), b 1935– , paint DCA M[2]
HOOPER, Samuel, b Devon, d London 1911, sculp Mo12
HOORN, Carol Lucille. *See* FRASER, Carol Lucille Hoorn
HOOTON, Pauline, b Shirebrook, Derb 1931– , paint M
HOOVER, Dorothy Haines (m G.L.J. Hoover), b Toronto 1904– , paint Hu M RCA
HOPE, James, b Drygrange, Roxborough, Scot 1818/19, d Watkins Glen, NY 1892, Eng, paint DMA F GW H ROM Y
HOPE, James Archibald, Gen, Sir, b England 1785, d Cheltenham, Glos 1871, Eng, topog DNB H
HOPE, James E., b England, fl 1864–87, Eng, engr litho H
HOPE, William R., b Montreal 1863 – d 1931, paint H Hu M MM Mo12 NGC1,2 RCA TB2 W1–3
HOPE-WALLACE, James (b James Hope, 1844 Lord Hope-Wallace of Asholme), b England 1807, d Featherstone Castle, N'land 1854, Eng, topog BPp1625 PNL ROM WHC
HOPKINS, Elizabeth Margaret, b Gilkicker, nr Portsmouth, Eng 1894, d Saltspring Isld, BC 1991, paint KB
HOPKINS, Frances Ann Beechey (m Edward Martin Hopkins), b England 1838, d London 1919, Eng, paint APH B DBA DVP DWA G H H77 M RA ROM Sam St TB1
HOPKINS, John William, b Liverpool 1825, d Montreal 1905, drw NGC1,2 RCA
HOPKINS, Tom, b Summerside, PEI 1934– , paint CWW93
HOPKINSON, Peter, fl 1950+, paint M
HOPKINSON, William John, b London 1887, d York Co, Ont 1970, paint M RCA
HOPPNER, Henry Parkyns, Capt, b London 1795, d Lisbon 1833, Eng, paint DCB6 DMA H
HOREIS, William Richard, b New York 1945– , prt WWA86
HORNBROOK, Thomas Lyde, Lt, b Plymouth, Eng c 1780 – d 1850, Eng, paint topog B DBLP DBMaP DeV3 DMA DSP DVP G H TB1
HORNE, Arthur Edward Cleeve (m Jean Horne, q.v.), b Jamaica 1912– , paint CC1 Co CWW93 M NGC1,2 O.F48 RCA TB3 WWA93 WWB90
HORNE, Arthur William, b Vancouver 1945– , sculp IO
HORNE, Huxley. *See* BROOKER, Bertram Richard
HORNE, Jean Mildred Harris (m Arthur Edward Cleeve Horne, q.v.), b Toronto 1914– , sculp M RCA
HORNE, Joicey Mary, b Carnduff, Sask 1906– , paint CWW84 O.N49
HORNE, Mercédès Deely (m David Ernest Horne), b Birmingham, Eng 1925– , paint CWW90 M RCA S
HORNE, Nesta Bowen (m Thomas A. Horne), b West Indies, fl 1946+, paint M
HORNER, Keith Reginald James, b Buxton, Eng 1909– , paint CWW52
HORNYANSKY, Nicholas (Nicholaus), b Budapest 1896, d Toronto 1965, etch paint AGO APH CWW61 M MM NGC2 O.F48 PHA RCA TB3 UG W3 WWA70d73
HORSFALL, Arthur, b Winnipeg 1915– , paint CAE2 SC

HORTON, John M., b Poole, Dor c 1935– , paint ABC

HORVATH, George A., b Hungary 1933– , paint CAE1 SC

HORWOOD, H., fl 1862–90s, stgl DFA H KB

HOSKINS, Ruby, b Cardiff, Wales 1909– , paint CAE1

HOSKINSON, Catherine Ann, b Vancouver 1949– , prt CAE1,2

HOUDE, Alphonse, b Notre-Dame-du-Sacré-Coeur, Que 1889, d 1973, sculp K

HOUGH, Michael, b Nice, Fr 1928– , paint CWW93

HOUGHTON, Arthur Boyd, b Bombay 1836, d Hampstead, London 1875, Eng, illus AAW13 AH B Bry DVP G Red Sam TB1

HOUGHTON, Frank, b Montreal 1862, paint H MM PMC RCA

HOUGHTON, Margaret (May) (m Jules Brunn), b Montreal 1865, fl 1922, paint B DWA H Hu MM Mo12 RCA TB1

HOULAHAN, Kathleen, b Winnipeg 1887, d 1964, paint AAA33 AAW2 AC DWA F WWA40

HOULE, Robert James, b St Boniface, Man 1947 , paint Co WWA86

HOUPT, Angela Miriam, b England 1939– , sculp IO

HOUSE, Joan Mary (m Walter K. House), b Wales 1913– , paint M

HOUSSER, Bess Larkin. *See* HARRIS, Bess Larkin

HOUSSER, Muriel Yvonne McKague[2] (m Frederick Broughton Housser), b Toronto 1898 – d 1996, paint AGO APH CC2 CWW73 DWA Hu[2] M NGC1,2 TB2 UG WWA86

HOUSTON, Deryk, b Scotland 1954– , paint ABC

HOUSTON, James Archibald, b Toronto 1921– , illus paint CBC CE1,2 CWW92 Co ICB3 JAI4 M SAA13

HOUSTON, Mary Rodgers Beaton. *See* BEATON, Mary Rodgers

HOUSTOUN, Donald MacKay, b Stevensville, Ont 1916– , paint AGO IO M MM NGC2 RCA S

HOVADIK, Jaroslav, b Cz 1935– , paint sculp CAE2

HOVENDEN, Richard J., b Ireland, fl 1867–99, paint H

HOVEY, Lorraine Bruce-Robertson (m Frederick Lucas Hovey), b Toronto 1923– , paint O.Ag48

HOVINGTON, Gaetan, b Tadousac, Que c 1947– , sculp M

HOWARD, Alfred Harold, b Liverpool 1854, d Toronto 1916, des paint AGO H Hu M NGC1,2 RCA W1–3

HOWARD, Helen Barbara (m Richard Daley Outram), b Long Branch, Ont 1926– , engr paint AGO BB CWW93 M NGC2 RCA WWA93

HOWARD, Jemima Frances Meikle (1827 m John George Howard, q.v.), b England, d Toronto 1877, paint DWA H

HOWARD, John George (b John Corby) (m Jemima F.M. Howard, q.v.), b Bengeo, Herts 1803, d Toronto 1890, paint AGO CE1,2 Co DCB11 H H77 RCA W1–3

HOWARD, Norman Douglas, b Nottingham, Eng 1899, d 1955, Eng, paint DBA MM RA WBA1 WWB54d56

HOWARD, R. Vivien, b Glencoe, Ont 1891, d London, Ont 1965, paint S

HOWARD, Robert Boardman, b New York 1896, d Santa Cruz, Calif 1983, Amer, paint sculp AAW1 AC DAS Sam TB2 WWA82d84 WWWA

HOWARTH, Glenn Edward, b Vegreville, Alta 1946– , paint CAE2 RCA SC

HOWDEN, Robert T., fl 1839–47, paint H

HOWE, Betty Hoglund (m Maurice Howe), b Kimberley, BC 1933– , paint ABC

HOWE, Richard, b Rosebank, NB 1912, d 1988, paint MA

HOWELL, Alfred, b Oldbury, Eng 1889, d Cleveland, Ohio 1978, sculp M NGC1,2 RCA

HOWELL, J. Constance E., fl 1878–95, Eng, paint DBA DWA H MM

HOWITT, Kathleen Margaret. *See* GRAHAM, Kathleen Margaret Howitt

HOWLAND, Henry Stark, Jr, b Kleinburg, Ont 1855, fl 1925, etch paint AGO DBA H NGC2 RCA

HOWLETT, Leslie Ernest, b London 1903– , paint CWW93

HOWLIN, John, b London 1941– , paint prt IO

HOWORTH, George, b England c 1791, fl 1860, Eng, paint GW H

HOWS, John Augustus, b New York 1832 – d 1874, Amer, illus paint ANC App B Bry F GW H TB1

HOWSON, Juliet. *See* BURDOIN, Juliet Howson

HOYT, Edith, b W Point, NY 1894, d Washington, DC c 1971, Amer, paint AAA33 DWA F MM TB2 WHC WWA66

HRUBY, Malenka Eleonora, b Prague, Cz 1930– , paint M MM

HUBEL, Vello, b Tallin, Est 1927– , des paint CWW93 RCA

HUDON, Louise, fl 1963– , paint M

HUDON, Normand, b Montreal 1929– , cart APH Des M MM WECa

HUDON, Simone-Marie-Yvette (x Hudson) (m Henri Beaulac), b Quebec 1905, d 1984, etch M MM WWA53

HUDSON, Andrew, b Birmingham, Eng 1935– , paint M MM NGC2

HUDSON, Michael K. (Mike), b England 1946– , paint prt IO

HUDSPETH, Robert Norman, b Caledonia, Ont 1862, d Concord, Mass 1943, paint sculp AAA33 DAS F H Hu RCA TB1 WWA40

HUEBNER, Dieter, b W Germany 1946– , sculp MF

HUESTIS, Doris Louise. *See* SPEIRS, Doris Louise Huestis

HUET, Jacques, b Montreal 1932– , sculp M MM

HUFFMAN[1], Isobel Mary Knox[2] (m Percival Huffman), b Toronto 1895, fl 1952, paint DBA MM RA[1,2] RCA WWB34

HUGGARD, Leonard Roy, b Norton, NB 1920– , paint M RCA

HUGGINS, Ross, b Toronto 1916– , paint M MM

HUGHES, Andrew Ross, b 1904– , paint Hu RCA

HUGHES, Edward John, b N Vancouver 1913– , paint ACA AGO B CC1 CE1,2 CLA CWW93 DFA GM M MM NGC1,2 NGC68 RCA SC TB2,3 WWA93

HUGHES, George H., fl 1832–78, paint H NGC2 WHC

HUGHES, Jean Eleanor. *See* PARTRIDGE, Jean Eleanor Hughes

HUGHES-STANTON, Gertrude. *See* HERMES, Gertrude Anna Bertha

HUGHSON, Maxine Williams (m Horace G. Hughson), b Kentville, NS 1910– , gra paint MA

HULL, Evelyn, fl 1970– , paint CAE1

HULL, Mae (Mrs), fl 1940s, d 1971, paint sculp M

HULME, George, b Manchester, Eng 1913– , paint sculp CWW70

HUME, Isabel Clara Burbidge (m A. Claire Hume), b Kindersley, Sask 1914– , paint BDSA

HUME, James Nairn Patterson, b Brooklyn, NY 1923– , paint CWW93

HUMEN, Gerald, b Ukraine 1935– , paint AGO IO M NGC2 S UG

HUMME, Joseph Julius, b Prussia 1825, d Point Ideal, Lake of Bays, Ont 1889, paint H RCA

HUMPHREY, Jack Weldon, b Saint John, NB 1901 – d 1967, paint ACA AGO APH CC2 CE1,2 Co CWW64 H77 M MA MM NGC1,2 NGC67 NGC68 RCA S TB2,3 UG W3 WWA66d70 WWB68

HUMPHRIES/HUMPHRYS, Harry,

fl 1790, d Pacific Ocean, Eng, paint AC DeV1 EMA
HUMPHRIES, John, b Blockley, Glos 1882, d Lachine, Que 1958, paint CNS40 M MM RCA
HUNG CHUNG, Allan. *See* CHUNG HUNG, Allan
HUNGERFORD, Sophia, b Guelph, Ont 1907– , sculp UG
HUNKLER, Dennis French, b Oakland, Calif 1943– , drw paint WWA93
HUNSBERGER, David Peter, b Waterloo, Ont 1950– , prt IO
HUNT, D. Earl, b Honeywood, Ont 1915– , cal CWW93
HUNT, Dora De Pedery. *See* DE PEDERY-HUNT, Dora
HUNT, Henry, b Port Rupert, BC 1923– , carv DFA CE1,2 SC
HUNT, Jessie Doris, b Southampton, Eng 1909– , paint CLA M
HUNT, Joan Emily Gladys, b Dartmouth, NS 1893, paint M MA
HUNT, John Powell, b St Mary's, Ont 1854, d London, Ont 1932, paint H MM RCA
HUNT, Katherine J., b Toronto 1945– , etch prt CAE1 IO SC
HUNT, Thomas Lorraine, b London, Ont 1882, d Santa Anna Valley, bu San Bernardino, Calif 1938, paint AAA25 AAW1 AC WWAd40
HUNT, Tony, b Alert Bay, BC 1942– , sculp CE1,2 Co CWW93 DFA S
HUNT, William Henry, fl 1823–34, Scot, litho GW H
HUNTEN, Janet, fl 1960– , gra M
HUNTER, George Leslie, b Rothesay, Isle of Bute, Scot c 1877, d Glasgow 1931, Scot, paint AC DBA DBF2 DFP3 WBA1
HUNTER, Gordon (Gorde), b Winnipeg 1925– , cart Des
HUNTER, James, Lt, fl 1766–99, topog H PNL
HUNTER, Jane Proud James (m John Donald Hunter), b Sarnia, Ont 1939– , paint CWW93 IO S
HUNTER, Raoul, b St-Cyrille-de-l'Islet, Que 1926– , car sculp Des M MM Po86,89
HUNTER, Samuel, b Milbrook, Ont 1858, d Toronto 1939, cart CWW36 Des H M Mo98,12
HUNTER, Sarah/Sara Baldwin Holden. *See* HOLDEN, Sarah/Sara Baldwin
HUNTER, Wilhelmina Blewett Elliott (Mrs), b Hamilton, Ont 1893, paint Hu RCA
HUNTER, William Stewart, b St-Jean, Que 1823, d Stanstead, Que 1894, illus paint AGO DeV2,3,6,8 DFA H
HUNTLEY, Walter Edwin, b Newark, NJ 1887, d Toronto 1931, paint Hu M MM RCA US
HUOT, Charles-Edouard-Masson, b Quebec 1855, d Sillery, Que 1930, paint B CC1 H Hu K LeJ M MM MQ NGC1,2 NGC67 PMC RCA TB3 W1–3
HUOT, Joseph, Abbé, fl 1841, paint H K
HURD, L.P., fl 1863–73, paint H ROM Sam
HUREL, Jules, b France 1856/9 – d 1915, Fr, sculp K
HURLBATT, Ethel, b Bickley, Kent, fl 1890s–1936, Eng, ske Mo12 CWW36
HURLBUT (Mrs), fl 1848–60, paint H
HURLEY, Robert Newton, b London 1894, d 1980, paint CLA Co DFA M US
HURST, George Leopold, Rev, b London 1868, carv CWW52
HURST, Patrick Russell, b Vulcan, Alta 1947– , sculp AA
HURTUBISE (Mlle), fl 1893, paint DWA H K
HURTUBISE, Jacques, b Montreal 1939– , illus paint AGO CA1 CAE1 CC2 CE1,2 Co M MM MQ NGC2 NGC67 RCA SC US WECo WWA93
HUSBAND, Vicky/Vicki, b Victoria, BC 1940– , paint DCA
HUSER, Glen Anton, b Elk Point, Alta 1943– , paint CWW93

HUSHLAK, Gerald Marshall, b Edmonton 1944– , paint prt CAE2 CWW93 RCA SC WWA93

HUSVETI, Alexander S., b Eger, Hu 1927– , engr BB

HUTA, Jaroslav F., b Czechoslovakia 1940– , paint sculp MF

HUTCH, B., b Iowa 1915– , sculp M

HUTCHINS, Ernest J., fl 1900–12, paint DFA ROM

HUTCHINSON, Frederick William. *See* HUTCHISON, Frederick William

HUTCHINSON, George, b Colchester, NS, fl 1884–7, min paint DBA Fo G H

HUTCHINSON, Grace Fugler. *See* FUGLER, Grace

HUTCHINSON, Leonard (m Grace Fugler, q.v.), b Manchester, Eng 1896, d Thornhill, Ont 1980, prt CE1 GM IO M MM NGC2 RCA

HUTCHINSON, Lynn. *See* BROWN, Lynn Hutchinson

HUTCHISON, Alexander Cowper, b Montreal 1838 – d 1922, drgt CWW10 EC H MM Mo98,12 NGC1,2 RCA W1–3

HUTCHISON, Bruce. *See* HUTCHISON, William Bruce

HUTCHISON, Frederick William (x Hutchinson[2]), b Montreal 1871, d Hudson Heights, Que 1953, paint AAA33[2] AGO CWW48d49 F[2] M MM NGC1,2 RCA TB3[2] WWA53

HUTCHISON, John Mason, b Toronto, fl 1954– , paint MA

HUTCHISON, William Bruce (s Pentridge[2]), b Prescott, Ont 1901– , car CE1,2 CWW91 Des[2]

HUTNER, Paul, b Toronto 1948– , paint CWW93

HUTTER, Erich, b Innsbruck, Au 1927– , paint M

HUTTON, Gwendolen Kortright. *See* LAMONT, Gwendolen Kortright Hutton

HUYGHUE, Samuel Douglas Smith, b Charlottetown 1816, d Melbourne, Aus 1891, paint DCB12 Ke

HUYSHE, G.L., Capt, fl 1870–1, illus H

HYAMS, Hannah (Mrs), b 1918– , paint M

HYDE, Laurence Evelyn, b Kingston-on-Thames, Eng 1914, d 1987, paint AGO BB GM IO M NGC2 TB3 WWA82

HYNDMAN, Robert Stewart, b Edmonton 1915– , paint M MM NGC68 RCA WWA62

HYRCHENUK, Mary, b Ft Frances, Ont, fl 1937+, drw paint M

I

IACURTO, Francesco (Frank), b Montreal 1908– , paint CWW93 M MM NGC2 RCA WWA93

IBING, Donna Marie, b Windsor, Ont 1947– , paint IO

IDDESLEIGH, 1st Earl. *See* NORTHCOTE, Stafford Henry

IHRIG, Robert, b c 1934– , illus paint M

IKRAMULLAH, Naz. *See* ASHRAF, Nazhath

IKSIKTAARYUK/IKSEETARKYUK[2], Luke, E2-45, b nr Baker Lake, NWT 1909– , prt sculp Co DEA[2] US

ILGACS, Valdis Leo (s Valdis), b 1951– , sculp IO

ILIGLIUK, fl c 1824, drw DMA

ILIU, Joseph, b Romania 1914– , paint M

IMHOF, Joseph, b Brooklyn, NY 1871, d Taos, NM 1955, Amer, litho paint AAW1 Sam

IMHOFF, Berthold von, b Karlsruhe, Ge 1886, d St Walburg, Sask 1939, paint M

IMREDY, Elek, b Budapest 1912, d Vancouver 1994, sculp BCS M PHA RCA

INCE/INCH, Capt, fl 1758, paint H

INDERJEET, Sahdev, b 1938– , carv M

INGALLS, Walter, b Canterbury, NH 1805, d Oakland, Md 1874, Amer, paint DFA GW H Y

INGELS, Kathleen Beverley Robinson[2]

(m Frank Lee Ingels), b Aurora, Ont 1882, d San Bernardino Co, Calif 1958, paint sculp AAA09[2] AC DAS[2] DWA RCA[2] WWA40

INGLE, Bertha Maylaw, b Nassagaweya, Ont 1878, d nr Guelph, Ont 1962, paint Hu RCA

INGLEFIELD, Edward Augustus, Adm, Sir, b Cheltenham, Glos 1820, d London 1894, Eng, topog B DBMaP DMA DNB DSP DVP G H H77 TB1

INGLIS, John Noel, b Toronto 1931– , paint M WWA62

INGRAHAM, Joseph, b Boston 1762, Amer, topog EMA

INGRAM, Douglas, fl 1950+, paint M

INGRAM, Elizabeth. *See* GAGNON, Elizabeth

INNES, Alice Amelia, b Brooksdale, Oxford Co, Ont 1890, d St Thomas, Ont 1970, paint Hu M MM RCA

INNES, John, b London, Ont 1863, d Vancouver 1941, paint CC1 Des H H77 Mo12 RCA Sam W2–3 WWNA

INNES, Thomas W. (Tom), b Salem, Oreg 1923– , cart Des Po86

INNESS, George, b Newburgh, NY 1825, d Bridge of Allan, Scot 1894, Amer, etch paint App B Bry DAB F GW NCAB2 TB1 WWWA Y

INNUTSIAK, E7-603, b Frobisher Bay, NWT 1886, d c 1965, sculp Co DEA

INUKPUK, Johnnie[2]/Johnny, E9-904, b Inouchjuac, nr Port Harrison, Que 1911, fl 1987, sculp AGO CE1,2 Co CWW93 DEAp91[2] RCA S

INVERARITY, Robert Bruce, b Seattle, Wash 1909– , carv paint AAA33 M WWA WWNA

IOLA, E7-923, b Lake Harbour, NWT 1936– , sculp DEA

IPEELEE, Osuitok. *See* OSHAWEETOK/OSHOOWEETOOK, 'B'

IRANYI, Judith Rosengarten (Mrs), b Latvia, fl 1960– , paint M

IRELAND, Denise, b Manchester, Eng 1949– , paint CWW93

IRELAND, Ian, b England c 1939– , paint M

IRELAND, James Arthur, b Yorkshire 1945– , des paint CWW93

IRELAND, Myrtle (m W. Ireland), fl 1960– , paint M

IRELAND, Samuel John, b Barnstable, Eng 1854, d Hamilton, Ont 1925, paint H

IRELAND, Thomas, b c 1824, d Montreal 1896, engr litho H

IRISH, Margaret Holmes, b Blenheim, Ont 1878, paint AAA33 DWA F WWA36

IRO, George, b Hungary, fl 1950+, gra M

IRTON, Richard, b Irton Hall, Cumb 1798, d England 1847, Eng, paint WHC

IRVIN, Emily Dorothy. *See* McAVITY, Emily Dorothy Irvin

IRVINE, Donald Frederick, b Vancouver 1934– , cal CWW93

IRVINE, Maureen (Mrs), fl 1954– , paint M

IRVINE, Robert, fl 1812–20, paint H

IRVING, Daphne Butler (m Ronald Ian Irving), b Elizabeth, NJ 1931– , paint CWW81 RCA

IRWIN, Benoni, b Newmarket, Ont 1840, d S Coventry, Conn 1896, paint AAW2 AC B F H Hu TB1 W1–3 Y

IRWIN, M. Eleanor[2], fl 1898–1910, paint AAA28 DWA H MM RCA[2]

IRWIN DE LA CHEROIS, Thomas, Col, b Armagh Co, Ire 1843, d Carnagh, Armagh, Ire 1928, Eng, paint sculp CWW10 DFA H Mo98,12 RCA ROM Sam WWW

ISAAC, Amiktok, E9-1, b Belcher Islds, NWT 1916– , sculp DEA

ISHUHUNGITO/ETUNGAT, E7-726, b Cape Dorset, NWT 1947 , prt US

ISKOWITZ, Gershon, b Kielce, Pol 1921, d Toronto 1988, paint AGO B CA1 CAE1,2 CE1,2 CWW88 IO M MM NGC2 RCA WWA86d89

ISLEY, Velma Elizabeth, b Edmonton 1918– , illus paint IBYP ICB2
ITALIANO, Carlo, b Montreal 1920– , illus paint CBC M T TB1
ITUKALLA, Juanisi (aka Joanassie, Jack), b nr Povungnituk, Que 1949– , prt sculp CWW93
IVAN, Agnes. *See* TAN, Agnes Ivan
IVAN, Edit Zilahi (m Leslie P. Ivan), b Debrecen, Hu 1920, d Saskatoon 1962, paint BDSA M
IVES, Antoinette, fl 1882–9, paint H MM RCA
IRWIN, P.K. *See* PAGE, Patricia Kathleen
IYAITUK, Matiusie, b nr Cape Smith, NWT 1950– , sculp CWW93
IYOLA, Kingwatsiak, E7-914 (m Pootogook, E7-864, q.v.), b Cape Dorset, NWT 1933– , prt sculp Co DEA NGC2
IZZARD, Daniel, b London 1923– , paint ABC M

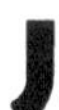

JACK, Marion Elizabeth, b Saint John, NB 1866, d 1954, paint DBA DWA MM Mo12 RCA
JACK, Martha Sharpe Forrester (Patti), b Gatehouse of Fleet, Kirc c 1850, d St Andrews, Scot 1908, Scot, paint DBA DWA G H MM RCA
JACK, Richard, b Sunderland, Eng 1866, d Montreal 1952, prt B DBA DVP G H Hu M MM NGC2 NGC68 RA RCA TB1–3 WBA1 WWB50 WWW
JACKMAN, Ted, b Paris, Ont 1947– , cart Des
JACKS, Robert, b Melbourne, Aus 1943– , paint CWW70 IO MM
JACKSON, Alexander Young, b Montreal 1882, d Kleinburg, Ont 1974, paint ACA AE AGO B CC2 CE1,2 Co CWW70 DBA EC FCA H77 M MM MQ NGC1,2 NGC67 NGC68 O.F.My.Ag54 OC OCD RA RCA Sam TB1,2 TN UG US W3 WBA2 WWA76
JACKSON, Andrew Sander, b Winnipeg 1925– , paint CWW93
JACKSON, Brian Henry, b London 1926– , des CC1 M
JACKSON, David E., b Kirkland, NB 1874, paint AAW3 WWNA
JACKSON, Edward Boyd, b Harriston, Ont 1933– , paint prt M
JACKSON, Edwin Falder, b Penrith, Cumb 1904– , paint M
JACKSON, Erna Nook, b Petrolia, Ont 1886, paint Hu MM RCA
JACKSON, Harry Browne, b Waltham, Mass 1871, d Monroe, Mich 1952, Amer, illus paint NGC2
JACKSON, Henry Alexander Cameron, b Montreal 1877, d Manotick, Ont 1961, paint M MM NGC2 RCA
JACKSON, Kenneth William, b London, Ont 1944– , paint IO
JACKSON, Mason, b Ovingham, Eng 1819, d London 1903, Eng, engr paint DeV1 DNB DVP G
JACKSON, Nancy Ruth, b Elmer, NJ 1952– , engr BB
JACKSON, Naomi Catherine Adair (m J. Walton Groves[2]), b Montreal 1910– , paint M[2] MM RCA WWA93[2]
JACKSON, Ronald Threlkeld, b Hamiota, Man 1902– , paint ABC M
JACKSON, Sarah Jeanette (m Anthony Jackson), b Detroit, Mich 1924– , paint sculp CAE1 CWW93 IO M MM NGC2 TB3 WWA93
JACKSON, William Henry, Capt, b Keesville, NY 1843, d New York 1942, Amer, paint MM WWA40d47
JACMAIN, Jacques, b Montreal 1940– , paint CAE1
JACOB. *See* BOURGEOIS, Aldéric
JACOBI, Otto Reinhold, b Königsberg, Pru 1812, d Ardoch, ND 1901, paint AE AGO B DCB13 EC H H77 LeJ M MM Mo98 NGC1,2 NGC67 R2 RCA ROM TB1 W1–3

JACOBS, Arnold, b Six Nations Res, nr Brantford, Ont 1942– , paint IO

JACOBS, Joseph, b Cayuga Band, Six Nations Res, nr Brantford, Ont c 1934– , sculp Co IO

JACOBS, Michel, b Montreal 1877, d Rumson, NJ 1958, Amer, paint sculp AAA33 B CWW61 DAS F MM RCA TB1 WWA56d59 WWB34 WWWA

JACOBS, Peter (aka Pahtahseg, A.), b nr Belleville, Ont c 1807, d Rama Res, nr Simcoe, Ont 1890, paint CE2

JACOBSON, Sybil Atkinson (m Peter Henley; m Johann Sigurdir Jacobson), b London 1881, d Vancouver 1953, paint BDSA

JACOBY, Ella May. *See* WALKER, Ella May Jacoby

JACQUES. *See* BOIVIN, Jacques

JACQUETTE, Yvonne Helene Burckhardt, b Pittsburg, Pa 1934– , Amer, paint prt CA1 WWA93

JACQUIER/JACQUIES[2] dit LEBLOND, Jean (b Jan Jaques Bloem), b St Catherine parish, Brussels 1688, fl 1724, d Que Prov, paint sculp DCB2[2] H K

JACSON, Antoine, b Paris c 1720–30, d Quebec 1803, carv DCB5 K

JAENICKE, Beulah Irene (m Edward J. Rosen), b Leader, Sask 1918– , paint M MM WWNA

JAKOVAC, Nikolette Marie, b St Louis, Mo 1940– , etch paint pas IO

JALAVA, Erkki, b Finland, fl 1950+, paint M

JAMASIE, E7-977 (m Angotigulu, q.v.), b Cape Dorset, NWT 1910– , prt sculp Co DEA

JAMES, Ann, b Hove, Sus 1925– , paint sculp CAE2 M

JAMES, Cecil E., b Manchester, Eng 1908– , paint US

JAMES, Frank, b Peru, Que 1845, d 1907, paint AAAd28 B Y

JAMES, John, b New York, fl 1811–45, Amer, paint G W H

JAMES, William Roderick (b Joseph Ernest Nephtali Dufault[2]), b St-Nazaire-d'Acton, Que 1892, d Hollywood, Calif 1942, paint AAA33 AAW1 AC DAB F K[2] NCAB35 Sam TB2 WWA40d47 WWWA

JAMESON, Anna Brownell Murphy[2] (m Robert Sympson Jameson, q.v.), b Dublin 1794, d Ealing, Eng 1860, Irish, paint Bry CE2 Co DCB8[2] DNB EC H KB Red W1–3

JAMESON, Lionel B., b Regina c 1908– , paint M

JAMESON, Robert Sympson (m Anna Brownell Murphy Jameson, q.v.), b Harbridge, Eng 1796, d Toronto 1854, paint DCB8 EC H W1–3

JAMIESON, Martha Greening, b Calgary 1918– , paint M MM RCA

JAMISON, Cecillia Viets Dakin (m George Hamilton; m Samuel Jamison), b Yarmouth, NS 1837, d Roxbury, Mass 1909, Amer, paint DAB DWA F WWWA

JANES, Phyllis Hipwell (m Henry F. Janes), b Alliston, Ont 1905, d London, Ont 1990, paint M MM NGC2 RCA S WWA62

JANG, Alvin, fl 1970– , etch paint CAE2

JANISS, Eugene, b Latvia 1911– , sculp CWW91

JANITCH, Mary, b Belleville, Ont 1949– , mmed sculp CAE2 IO NGC2

JANITSCH, Marguerite D., b Quebec, fl 1950+, paint M MM

JANOWSKY, Béla, b Budapest 1900, d New York 1982, sculp AAA33 DAS RCA WWA80

JANSONS, Inese, b Oldenburg, Ge 1949– , illus C

JANVIER, Alex Simeon, b Le Goff, nr Bonnyville, Alta 1935– , paint AA CAE1 CE1,2 Co CWW93 DFA M SC UG

JAQUE, Louis (b Louis-Jacques Beaulieu), b Montreal 1919– , paint M MM NGC2 RCA SC WWA93

JARAIN. *See* RAINVILLE, Jacques

JARDINE, Alex, fl 1870–96, paint H

JARDINEL, Emile-Jean-Marie, b France 1832/3, fl 1871–81, sculp K

JAREMA, Tom, b 1952– , con CAE1

JARNUSZKIEWICZ, Wocjiec, b Poland 1927– , sculp M

JARSKY, Paul Howard, b 1950– , sculp CAE1 IO

JARVIS, Alan Hepburn, b Brantford, Ont 1915, d Toronto 1972, sculp CE2 Co CWW70 M NGC2 T3 W3 WWB72

JARVIS, Donald Alvin, b Vancouver 1923– , paint AE CC1 M NGC1,2 RCA TB3 WWA93

JARVIS, Kenneth Phillips, b Toronto 1926– , sculp CWW93 RCA

JARVIS, Lucy Mary Hope, b Toronto 1896, d 1986, paint CLA DCA DWA M MA MM RCA

JASMIN, André, b Montreal 1922– , paint CC2 M MM NGC2 TB3

JASMIN, Edouard, b Bois-Franc, Que c 1905– , sculp KB M

JAURAN. *See* REPENTIGNY, Rodolphe de

JAWORKSA, Tamara Jankowska (m Tadeusz Jaworski), b Archangelsk, USSR 1928– , tap CWW93 DCA IO RCA WWA91

JEAN, Charles, b 1949– , paint CAE1

JEAN, David, b Toronto 1938– , paint IO

JEAN, Marcel, b Quebec 1937– , paint sculp M MM MQ

JEAN dit LATOUR, Jean, b Lagny-sur-Marne, Fr 1631/2, d Quebec 1677, sculp K

JEAN-LOUIS, Donald Charles, b Ottawa 1937– , sculp AGO IO M MM NGC2 RCA WWA93

JEBB, Joshua, Maj Gen, Sir, b Chesterfield, Derb 1793 – d 1863, Eng, paint APH DCB9 DNB EC H

JEFFERIES, Gerald F., b Halifax 1914– , paint M MM

JEFFERIES, Gloria, b Toronto 1923– , sculp M O.F49 RCA

JEFFERY, A.A. (Miss), fl 1836–49, drw DeV9

JEFFERYS, Barbara Alice West, b Toronto 1916– , paint Hu RCA

JEFFERYS, Charles William, b Rochester, Kent 1869, d York Mills, Ont 1951, illus paint AE AGO CC2 CE1,2 Co CWW49 Des EC FCA M MM Mo12 NGC1,2 NGC68 O.F49 PMC RCA Sam St TB2 TN US W2,3 WHC WWA47d53

JEFFERYS, Jean F.M. Adams (m Charles William Jefferys[2], q.v.), d New Jersey 1899, paint AAA03 DWA M[2] MM WHCp131

JEFFRIES, Donald Clark, b Sussex, NB 1914– , paint M

JEFFRIES, Lulu Rita/Zita Roderick[2] (m H.P. Jeffries), b Nova Scotia, fl 1916+, paint AAA29 DWA[2] F

JEKYLL, Robert, b Montreal 1933– , stgl IO

JEMMETT, Mary Ella Maud Martineau (m Douglas M. Jemmett), b Cermisce, It 1892, d 1986, paint AE MM

JENEY, Eva, b Esztergom, Hu 1950– , paint PHA

JENICEK, Jana, b Prague, Cz 1941– , paint CAE1

JENKINS, A. *See* AITKEN, Ross

JENKINS, Anthony (Tony), b Toronto 1951– , cart Des Po86–88

JENKINS, George, b Wilkie, Sask 1920– , paint M

JENKINS, John George, b 1920– , paint CAE2

JENKYNS, Kenneth Mark, b Winnipeg 1950– , drw CAE1

JENNINGS, Lorna Karen, b Camrose, Alta 1936– , wlhg IO

JENSEN, LeRoy Hackett, b Vancouver 1927– , paint M

JEPHSON, Harriet Julia Campbell, Lady (m Sir Alfred Jephson), b Quebec 1854, d 1930, Eng, paint DBA DVP DWA H Mo98, 12 WWW

JEROME (Frère). *See* PARADIS, Jérôme

JEROME, Jean Paul, b Montreal 1928– , paint M MM MQ RCA TB3
JEROME de la CROIX (Soeur). *See* DESMARAIS, Rose-Anna
JESENKO, Anna C., b Austria 1925– , paint CAE1
JETTEN, Doreen (Mrs), b Kampali, Ug, fl 1953– , paint M
JEWELL, Milton Walker, b Toronto 1938– , paint IO
JIRAR, Claude, b Quebec 1944– , paint CAE1
JOANASSIE, E7-1171, b Cape Dorset, NWT 1938– , sculp DEA
JOBERT, Paul C.F., b Tlemcen, Alg 1863, fl 1925, paint B K TB1
JOBIN, Achille, b Quebec 1847/8, fl 1875–81, sculp K
JOBIN, Ferdinand, b Quebec 1813/17 – d 1871, sculp K
JOBIN, Ivan/Yvan[2], b Montreal 1885, d France c 1975, paint sculp K[2] M MM
JOBIN, Louis, b St-Raymond, Que 1845, d Ste-Anne-de-Beaupré, Que 1928, sculp AGO CC2 CE1,2 EC K KB M MQ NGC1,2 NGC67 TB3 W1–3
JOBIN, Theodore, b Quebec 1873, fl 1955, engr paint K
JOE, David Wing On, b Toronto 1952– , paint IO
JOE, Mendelson. *See* MENDELSON, Joe
JOEL, Jack, b Reading, Eng 1940– , drw paint IO
JOHN, Alex. *See* JONES, Alice
JOHNASSIE, E7-981 (m Mary Pitseolak, E7-982, q.v.), b Cape Dorset, NWT 1923, d 1984, sculp DEA
JOHNASSIE KAVIK, E9–56 (m Sarah Kavik, E9-57, q.v.), b Belcher Isld, NWT 1916– , sculp DEAp88
JOHNASSIE KAVIK, Sarah. *See* KAVIK, Sarah
JOHNNIE, Inukpuk. *See* INUKPUK, Johnnie/Johnny
JOHNNIEBO (aka ASHEVAK, Johnnibo), E7-1034 (m Kenojuak, E7-1035, q.v.), b Cape Dorset, NWT 1923– , prt sculp DEAp90
JOHNNY, Meeko, E9-68, b Belcher Isld, NWT 1933– , sculp DEAp92
JOHNSON, Anne McAllister, b Prince Rupert, BC 1916– , paint S
JOHNSON, Arthur, b Droylsden, Eng 1918– , paint sculp AE
JOHNSON, Brian R., b Victoria, BC 1932– , paint SC
JOHNSON, Bruce Henderson, b Toronto 1926– , illus M MM RCA T
JOHNSON, Catherine C. (m Carl E. Johnson), b Nova Scotia 1883, sculp AAW3 WWNA
JOHNSON, Douglas, b Smithville, Ont c 1924– , paint M
JOHNSON, Edwin J., b Brigden, Ont 1889, fl 1971, paint M
JOHNSON, Frederick Murray Godshall, b Montreal 1882, d c 1942, paint CWW36
JOHNSON, Helen Dorothy, b Toronto 1899, paint Hu
JOHNSON, Helen G., fl 1893-4, paint DWA H MM RCA
JOHNSON, John Oswald, b c 1880, d 1964, paint DFA
JOHNSON, Kathleen Beatrice, b York Tp, Ont 1917 , paint CAE2 IO M RCA
JOHNSON, Natalie Gordon Wilson (m Fred W. Johnson), b Durban, Natal, SA, paint CLA
JOHNSON, Philippa, b Cheshire, Eng, fl 1949+, prt sculp IO
JOHNSON, Terence L., b Baltimore, Md 1940– , sculp CWW93
JOHNSON, W.A., Rev, b England, fl 1835–79, paint H
JOHNSON, William, Sir, b Smithstown, Ire c 1715, d Johnstown, NY 1774, Irish, drw App DAB DCB4 DNB H NCAB10 W1–3 WWWA
JOHNSON, William James, b Windsor, Ont 1927– , paint M
JOHNSTON, David Skelton, b Rotherham, Eng 1948– , paint CAE2 IO

JOHNSTON, Dorothy Paine Dunn (Mrs), b Harcourt, NB 1925– , sculp M

JOHNSTON, Frances Anne (m George Franklin Arbuckle[2], q.v.), b Toronto 1910 – d 1987, paint AKL[2] CLA CWW88 Hu IO[2] M MM NGC2 RCA S Sam

JOHNSTON, Francis Hans (Franz), b Toronto 1888 – d 1949, paint AGO CC1 CE1,2 Co CWW48 EC H77 Hu M MM NGC1,2 NGC67 NGC68 PMC RCA Sam TB2,3 TN

JOHNSTON, Gordon, b Tillsonburg, Ont 1920– , cart Co

JOHNSTON, Hugh, fl 1881–90, paint H

JOHNSTON, Iris (s Peggy Johnston), b Bristol, Eng 1918– , paint IO

JOHNSTON, James Dalzell, b Birnie, Man 1918– , paint M

JOHNSTON, Lloyd Vernon, b Sault Ste Marie, Ont c 1906– , paint IO

JOHNSTON, Lynn, b Collingwood, Ont 1947 , cart CE2

JOHNSTON, M./M.A., fl 1896–7, paint H

JOHNSTON, P.T. Hamilton (Mrs), b Brighton, Eng 1842, d c 1926, paint H

JOHNSTON, Patricia Wilson, fl 1970– , paint CAE2

JOHNSTON, Paul. *See* RODRIK, Paul

JOHNSTON, Peggy. *See* JOHNSTON, Iris

JOHNSTON, Peter, b England 1949– , sculp CWW93

JOHNSTON, Randolph Wardell, b Toronto 1904– , etch sculp CWW92 DAS RCA WWA62

JOHNSTON, Robert Edwin, b Toronto 1885, d Leonia, NY 1933, cart paint AAA33 B M RCA TB2 WWA36d38

JOHNSTONE, John Young, b Montreal 1887, d Havana, Cuba 1930, paint Hu M MM NGC1,2 RCA TB2,3 W1–3

JOHNSTONE, William, b Edinburgh 1866, d 1928, paint DBA G PMC

JOLICOUER, Michel, b St-Laurent, Que 1946– , paint CAE1

JOLIVET/JOLINET[2], Albert, fl 1869–79, paint H[2] K

JOLLIET, Louis, b Quebec 1645, d nr Anticosti Isld, Que 1700, crto CE1,2 Co DCB1 EC LeJ W1–3

JOLLIFFE, Susan Margaret Rennick. *See* RENNICK, Susan Margaret

JONE, Wing, b Toronto 1922– , des paint M

JONES, Alfred, b Liverpool 1819, d New York 1900, Amer, engr illus AAAd28 ANC App B DeV7 DAB F GW H NCAB12 TB1 WWWA Y

JONES, Alice (aka Alex John), b Halifax, fl 1902+, illus Mo12

JONES, Arthur James, Capt, fl 1838–49, paint DFA ROM

JONES, Bill (William), b Antioch, Calif 1946– , paint CAE1 NGC2 WWA78

JONES, Brian Rendel, b Chatham, Ont 1950– , paint prt CWW93 DCA IO

JONES, Chilion, b Brockville, Ont 1835, d Bermuda 1912, des H W1–3

JONES, Daniel Herbert, b Stourbridge, Eng 1875, d Guelph, Ont 1954, paint CWW38 UG

JONES, David Thomas[2], b Llangoedmor, Wales c 1796 – d 1844, topog DCB7 H NGC67

JONES, Dennis Gordon, b London 1932– , gra paint M MM NGC2

JONES, Edith Victoria (Mrs), b 1918– , fl 1953, gra paint M

JONES, Elizabeth (Eliza) Field. *See* FIELD, Elizabeth (Eliza)

JONES, Frances M. *See* BANNERMAN, Frances M. Jones

JONES, Frances Martha (m Robert Victor Rosewarne), b Smiths Falls, Ont 1916– , prt IO M MM

JONES, Garry Jablonski, b Edmonton 1949– , paint sculp AA

JONES, H. *See* JONES, David Thomas

JONES, Harry Ernest, b Bracknell, Eng 1892, paint M RCA

JONES, Helen Isabel (m H.M. Jones), b Arkona, Ont 1909– , drw paint M S

JONES, Henry Wanton, b Waterloo,

Que 1925– , paint sculp M MM RCA T3 WWA93

JONES, Hugh Bolton, b Baltimore, Md 1848, d New York 1927, Amer, paint AAA25 DBA F G H Y

JONES, Hugh Griffith, b Randolph, Wis 1872, d Montreal 1947, paint CE1,2 CWW36 M MM NGC1,2 PMC RCA

JONES, Ida C., fl 1850–7, paint DWA H

JONES, Imogene, fl 1857–9, paint DWA H

JONES, J.L., b London 1850, fl 1893, engr H

JONES, Jacobine. *See* JONES, Phyllis Jacobine

JONES, Jim, b Toronto 1942– , prt NGC2

JONES, John, fl 1869–97, paint H

JONES, John (Jack), b England 1873, d 1963, drw GM

JONES, Llewellyn Petley. *See* PETLEY-JONES, Llewellyn

JONES, Lulu, fl 1882, d 1920, paint DWA H

JONES, Marvin Harold, b Flora, Ill 1940– , paint sculp CAE1

JONES, Myron, b Kitchener, Ont 1949– , paint CAE2

JONES, Phyllis Jacobine, b London 1898, d Niagara-on-the-Lake, Ont 1976, sculp CWW73 DBA DWA M NGC1,2 RA RCA TB3 UG WWA78d80

JONES, Rupert, b Sandys Parish, Ber 1924– , paint sculp M MM

JONES, Sam M., fl 1887–99, paint stgl H

JONES, Sidney, b Montreal 1875, paint AAA33 WWA40

JONES, W.H., fl 1829–30, paint H

JONES, William. *See* JONES, Bill

JONGERS, Alphonse, b Mézières, Fr 1872, d Montreal 1945, paint AAA33 B CC1 F K M MM NGC1,2 RCA TB1,3 WWAd47 Y

JOPLING, Frederic Waistell, b Kensington, London 1859/60, d Toronto 1945, etch illus sculp AAA25 AGO DAS H Hu MM NGC2 NGC68 RCA WHC

JORDAN, Patricia Jane Laidman (m Laurance Theodore Jordan), b Vernon 1931– , paint CWW91

JORDAN, Robert Lionel (Bob), b Toronto 1941– , paint prt CAE1,2 IO

JORDANA. *See* BERMAN, Michaele

JORGE. *See* OLNEY, Georges L.

JORGENSEN, Flemming, b Aalborg, Dn 1934– , paint CAE2 M MM NGC2 RCA WWA93

JORSTAD, Arthur, b Lloydminster, Alta 1936– , paint US

JOSIN, Patti, b Regina 1952– , paint SC

JOSLIN/JOSELIN, James, b England c 1814, fl 1873, engr H

JOST, Edward R., fl 1864, paint DFA H H74

JOST, Josef (m Ottilie Palm, q.v.), b 1875, sculp B RCA TB1,2

JOST, Ottilie Palm. *See* PALM, Ottilie

JOUBERT, Léon, b Quimper, Fr, fl 1876–1920, Fr, paint B K MM TB1

JOUBERT, Suzanne (s Joubert), b Montreal 1933– , paint IO

JOUBIN, Franc R. (Francis), b San Francisco 1911– , paint CWW93

JOURDAIN, Jacques, b Trois-Rivières, Que 1931– , paint M MM

JOURDAIN, Roger, b Montreal 1914– , paint M

JOURDAIN dit LABROSSE, Denis, b La Rochelle, Fr 1671, d Montreal 1743, sculp K

JOURDAIN dit LABROSSE, Dominique, b Montreal 1730, fl 1755, sculp K

JOURDAIN dit LABROSSE^2, Paul Raymond, b Montreal 1697 – d 1769, carv AGO^2 CE1,2^2 DCB3 K M^2 NGC2 NGC67^2

JOY, Ida (m M. Nicholas August Didier), b Tilsonburg, Ont 1858, paint Mo98

JOY, John, b Toronto 1925– , paint IO M

JOY, Nancy Jean Hannah Grahame, b Toronto 1920– , illus CWW93 WWA82

JOZIASSE, Ann, b Netherlands 1943– , wlhg SC

JUANISIALUK, E9-1407, b Povungnituk, Que 1912– , prt sculp DEA

JUDAH, Doris Minette Trotter (m E. Lionel Judah), b Montreal 1887 – d 1965, sculp CNS40 DWA M MM RCA

JUDD, Helen. *See* KINGHORN, Helen Judd

JUDD, Marguerite. *See* TAYLOR, Marguerite Judd

JUDGE, Marguerite (Maggie) (Mrs), b India 1941– , illus paint ABC

JUDGE, Mary Edith Perceval, b Surbeton, nr London 1875, d N Vancouver 1966, paint CWW64

JUDSON, William Lees, b Manchester, Eng 1842, d Los Angeles 1928, paint AAAd29 AAW1 AC B F H MM RCA Sam WWWA

JUHASZ, Paul, b Györ Hu 1911– , des M

JUHASZ, Peter, b Olahszentgyorgy, Transylvania, Rom 1921– , paint sculp M

JULE, Walter, b Seattle, Wash 1940– , drw prt AA NGC2 RCA

JULIEN[1], Octave-Henri (aka Crincrin; Octavo[2]), b St-Roch, nr Quebec 1852, d 1908, cart paint CC2 CE1,2 Co DCB13 Des[1,2] DeV3,8 EC H H77 Hu K M MM MQ NGC2 R2 RCA ROM W1–3

JUMP, Edward, b France c 1831/2, d Chicago 1883, Amer, cart illus AAW1 AC Des DeV3,5,8 GW H K Sam WECa Y

JUNEAU, Denis, b Verdun, Que 1925– , paint sculp B CAE1,2 CWW93 M MM NGC2 RCA TB3 US

JUNGKIND, Walter, b Winterthur, Swi 1923– , gra paint WWGA2

JURSEVSKIS, Zigfrids, b Ceresy, Pol 1910, d Toronto 1989, sculp IO WWA93

JUTRAS, Joseph, b Montreal 1894, d 1972, paint K M MM

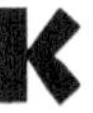

KADLEC, Dusan, b Czechoslovakia c 1942– , paint M

KAGAN, Samuel Lazar, b Russia 1906– , sculp IO

KAGIGE, Francis, b Wikwemikong, Manitoulin Isld, Ont 1929– , paint Co IO

KAGVIK, Davidee/Davidie[2], E9–130, b Great Whale River, Que 1915– , sculp DEAp46[2] M

KAHANE, Anne (m Robert Langstadt), b Vienna 1924– , sculp AE AGO CC1 CE1,2 CLA Co M MM NGC1,2 NGC67 RCA TB3 WWA80 WWB80

KAHRS, C.H., fl 1896–8, cart Des

KAJANUS, Johanne (m Kaare Hultgreen), b Oslo, Nor, fl 1937+, sculp M

KAKA. *See* QAQAQ/HAKA/KAKA/QAKA, Ashoona

KAKATUK. *See* QUATUTU, Makusi Angasa

KAKEGAMIC, Goyce, b Sandy Lake, Ont 1948– , paint prt IO

KAKEGAMIC, Joshim, b Sandy Lake, Ont c 1953– , paint prt Co IO

KAKINUMA, Thomas, b Tochigi-Ken, Japan 1908– , sculp M MM RCA

KALDOR, Ingrid Svenning (m Harold Kaldor), b Davidson, Sask 1919– , paint BDSA

KALLAI, Vary Valerio (Mrs), b Ozd, Hu 1930– , paint PHA

KALLMEYER, Minnie, b Detroit 1882, d Toronto 1947, paint DWA Hu M NGC1,2 RCA TB2

KALSNER, Stanley, b New York 1936– , paint CWW91

KALVAK, Helen, W2-428, b Victoria Isld, NWT 1901, d Holman Isld, NWT 1984, prt CE1,2 Co DEA M RCA

KAMIENSKI, Jan Jacob, b Poland 1923– , cart illus Des M Po86,87

KAMPMANN, Dürten, b Berlin 1941– , sculp M

KANANGINAK POOTOOGOOK[2], E7-1168, b nr Cape Dorset, NWT 1935– , prt sculp CE1,2 Co CWW93[2] DEAp101 M NGC2 RCA

KANAYOOK, E9-1434, b Povungnitung, NWT 1937– , prt DEA

KANBARA, Bryce, b Hamilton, Ont 1947– , paint prt IO

KANE, Elisha Kent, b Philadelphia 1820, d Havana, Cuba 1857, Amer, topog DAB H NCAB WWWA

KANE, Harriet Clench (m Paul Kane, q.v.), d 1892, paint DFA DWA H

KANE, Paul (m Harriet Clench Kane, q.v.), b Mallow, Cork Co, Ire 1810, d Toronto 1871, paint ACA AE AGO APH App CE1,2 Co DCB10 DFA EC GW H H77 LeJ M McC NGC1,2 NGC67 ROM Sam TB2 W1–3

KANN, Isabel, b Bangalore, Ind 1921– , paint CWW93

KANTAROFF, Maryon, b Toronto 1933– , sculp Co CWW93 M

KAPELL, Alana, b Canora, Sask 1948– , paint IO

KARACSONY, Ilona (Mrs Pucser), b Tet, Hu 1920– , des PHA

KARATSON, Edvin, b Csaprendek, Hu 1934– , paint CAE1 IO PHA

KARDOS, Ladislas, b Budapest 1909– , paint M

KARLIK, Pierre, b Ranklin Inlet, NWT c 1931– , sculp M

KARMAN, Robert, b Montreal 1933– , paint CWW93 M MM RCA

KAROO, Ashevak. *See* ASHEVAK, Karoo

KASHETSKY, Hertzl, b Saint John, NB 1950– , paint DCA

KASHETSKY, Joseph, b Saint John, NB 1941, d 1974, paint M

KASSIAN, Olena, b Munich, Ge 1947– , paint UG

KASUDLUAK/KASUDLAK, Daniel[2], E9-1699, b Port Harrison, Que, sculp DEAp43[2] S

KASUDLUAK, Davidee, E9-1552 (m Lizzie Kasudluak, q.v.), b Port Harrison, Que 1913– , sculp S

KASUDLUAK, Lizzie, E9-1553 (m Davidee Kasudluak, q.v.), b Port Harrison, Que 1914– , sculp DEAp132

KASYN, John, b Winnipeg 1926– , paint IO RCA SC

KATZ, Robert, b Tirgu-Mures, Rom 1952– , paint sculp CWW93

KATZ, Ronni, b Toronto 1936– , paint CAE1

KAUFMAN, C. Marty, b Regina 1954– , stgl CWW93

KAUFMAN, Helen/Helena, b Poland c 1963– , paint M

KAUFMANIS, Rusins (s Rusins[2]), b Riga, Lat 1925– , car Des[2] M

KAUFMANN, William/Wilhelm, b Winnipeg 1901– , paint SC

KAVANAGH, Robert, b Montreal 1942– , sculp IO

KAVIK. *See* JOHNASSIE KAVIK

KAVIK, John/Johnnie, E2-290, b Gjoa Haven, NWT 1897–1993, sculp CAE1 CE1,2 DEA

KAVIK, Sarah, E9-57 (m Johnassie Kavik, E9-56, q.v.), b Belcher Isld, NWT 1924– , sculp DEAp207

KAY, Louis (Lajos), b Kissziget, Hu 1919– , paint PHA M

KAYE, David Haigh, b Kingston, Ont 1947– , des tap DCA IO RCA WWA93

KEAGEY, James William, b W Flamborough, Ont 1878, d Dundas, Ont 1956, drgt paint prt NGC2 RCA

KEARNS, Celia Bruce, fl 1890–1923, paint H RCA

KEARNS, Murray William, b Toronto 1929– , etch paint M

KEATING, Frank, b St John's, Nfld 1892, d 1970, paint M

KEATING, Harriette (m C.L.W. Wors-

ley), b Seattle, Wash 1898, paint BDSA RCA
KEDDIE, Kate M. Wilson (m Philip Keddie), b Sept-Isles, Que 1887, paint DWA M
KEEASH, Magnus, b Weagamow Lake, Ont 1948– , paint prt IO
KEEFER, Nini. *See* MacDOUGALL, Nini Keefer
KEEHN, Nancy Luxmore, b 1926– , engr prt IO
KEELAN, Margaret Florence, b Regina 1948– , sculp US
KEELE, Paul, d 1973, prt CAE2
KEELEY, Shelagh Evelyn, b Oakville, Ont 1954– , drw prt IO
KEENE, Caleb, b Stourbridge, Eng c 1862, d Oakville, Ont 1954, paint M MM RCA
KEENE, Christopher Brooke, b London, Ont 1948– , sculp IO
KEENE, Louis, b London 1888, paint Hu M MM NGC68 RCA
KEENE, Susan Warner, b Toronto 1942– , tap CWW93
KEEVIL, Roland, b nr London c 1887, d Saskatoon 1963, paint DFA M NGC2
KEIRSTEAD, James Lorimer, b Saint John, NB 1932– , paint CWW93 IO M
KEITH-COOK, David, b Chatham, Ont 1948– , sculp IO
KELLER, Terrence John, b Edmonton 1947– , paint sculp CWW93 DCA
KELLETT, Edith, b Yorkshire 1877, d Brantford, Ont 1932, min DWA M RA TB2
KELLINGER, John A., b Canada c 1822, fl 1850, engr GW H
KELLY, Beverley Ann Lambert[2] (m Alex Kelly), b Biggar, Sask 1943– , paint BDSA[2] CAE1,2[2] M
KELLY, Donna, b Winnipeg 1941– , prt IO
KELLY, Elizabeth May, b Clarkson, Ont 1888, paint Hu
KELLY, Ethel Knight Mollison (1903 m T.H. Kelly), b Saint John, NB, paint Mo12
KELLY, Hannah Rusk (m Samuel L.P. Kelly), b Elderslie, Ont (Elmslie, Ont[2]) 1860, d 1935, paint DWA H[2] Hu MM RCA
KELLY, John David, b Gore's Landing, Ont 1862, d Toronto 1958, paint AGO H Hu M MM RCA W2–3
KELLY, Norman, b 1939– , paint ABC
KELLY, Patrick, b England c 1937– , paint sculp M
KELLY, Thomas, b Dublin c 1795, d New York c 1841, min B F GW H TB1 Y
KELMAN, Harry (m Olga Kelman, q.v.), b 1911, d 1970, paint M
KELMAN, Olga (m Harry Kelman, q.v.), b France c 1925– , carv paint M
KELSEY, Charles William, b London 1877, d Montreal 1975, paint stgl DBA M MM PMC RA RCA
KELSEY, Leonard Edgar, b London 1883, d W Vancouver 1975, paint M MM RCA
KEMBALL, Patrick Charles (s Manwoman), b Cranbrook, BC 1938– , paint M
KEMP, Elmore G., b Innisfail, Alta 1898, sculp WWNA
KEMP, Florence Evelyn. *See* PROCTOR, Florence Evelyn Kemp
KEMP, James Alexander, b Toronto 1914, d 1983, paint CWW70 IO M MM RCA S UG
KEMP, Robert G., b Toronto 1928– , paint M
KEMPKES, Jim, b Buffalo, NY 1947– , car Po86–88
KENDALL, Edward Nicholas, b England 1800, d S Hampton, Eng 1845, Eng, paint topog DMS DSP H
KENDERDINE, Augustus Frederick Lafosse, b nr Blackpool, Eng 1870, d Saskatoon 1947, paint CC2 CE1,2 DBA EC G H77 Hu M NGC1,2 RCA Sam TB2 US W47d53
KENDRICK, C., b England, fl 1871 3, illus DeV5,7 H

KENDRICK, Matthew, b Dublin c 1797, d London 1874, paint DIA

KENMURE, Adam Gordon, Viscount of, b Dumfries, Scot 1792, d Kenmure Castle, Kirc 1847, Scot, topog H ROM

KENNEDY, Alex, b 1934– , fl 1965, paint M

KENNEDY, Catherine, b Isle of Lewis, Scot, fl 1959– , gra paint M

KENNEDY, David Johnston, b Port Mullin, Scot 1816, d Philadelphia 1898, paint DFA GW UG

KENNEDY, Donald, b 1804, d Nepean, nr Ottawa 1888, paint DeV6

KENNEDY, Frederick Dawson, b Peterborough, Ont 1906, d 1967, paint M O.My49 RCA

KENNEDY, Garry Neill, b St Catharines, Ont 1935– , paint CE1,2 DCA M MM NGC2

KENNEDY, John de Navarre, b London 1888, paint CNS36 CWW79 M O.My50 RCA

KENNEDY, Joseph, b 1945– , fl 1966, paint M

KENNEDY, Kathleen Cooley, b Kingston, Sur 1908– , fl 1932, paint M

KENNEDY, Mary L., b Ft Garry, Winnipeg 1861, d St Boniface, Man 1945, paint DFA H

KENNEDY, Sybil, b Quebec 1899, d Montreal 1986, prt sculp CLA CWW73 DAS DWA M MM NGC1,2 RCA TB2,3 WWA62 WWB66

KENNEDY, William, b Toronto 1944– , paint prt IO

KENOJUAK (aka ASHEVAK[2], Kenojuak), E7-1035 (m Johnniebo, E7-1034, q.v.), b Ikerasak, nr Cape Dorset, NWT 1927– , prt sculp AKL[2] CC1 CE1,2 Co CWW93[2] DEA M NGC2 RCA UG WWA93

KENT, Valerie, b 1947– , paint CAE1

KENYON, J.J., b Washington, nr Drumbo, Ont 1862, d 1937, paint DFA H74 KB

KERGOMMEAUX, Duncan Robert Chassin de. *See* DE KERGOMMEAUX, Duncan Robert Chassin

KERNERMAN, Barry, b Toronto 1932– , paint AGO M

KERR, Estelle Muriel, b Toronto 1879, d 1971, paint sculp DWA M MM Mo12 O.F48 RCA

KERR, Illingworth Holey (Buck), b Lumsden, Sask 1905, d Calgary 1989, paint AA CC1 CE1,2 CWW89 H77 M MM NGC1,2 RCA S SC TB2,3

KERR, Mark Henry James, Lord (s of 5th Marquis of Lothian[2]), b England 1802 – d 1855, Eng, paint Bp1654[2] H

KERR-LAWSON, James (b James Kerr Lawson[2]), b Anstruther, Scot 1862, d London 1939, Scot, paint B CC1[2] DBA DScP DVP H[2] H77 Hu[2] MM[2] NGC2 NGC68 RCA[2] SW UG WBA1[2] WWB34

KERSHAW, Joe, b Rossland, BC 1932– , paint ABC

KERTESZ-RACZ, Maria, b Környe, Hu 1922– , paint M

KERTZER, Anita Elizabeth, b Ottawa, paint sculp WWA93

KERWIN, Claire Roland (m George Kerwin), b Chatelet, Bel 1921– , paint prt CWW93 IO RCA

KETTLE, Horace Garnard, b London 1906– , paint M MM O.Ag51 WWA53

KETURAH, Elizabeth Steeves (m Fred John Cheesman), b Meadow Lake, Sask 1916– , paint M

KEVER, Honor Elizabeth (aka Honor Rogers), b Boise, Idaho 1948– , paint BDSA

KHALSA, Dayal Kaur, b New York 1943– , illus CWW89

KHANBEGIAN, Jean MacNeil (Mrs), b Glace Bay, NS, fl 1967– , paint M

KHAZANOV, Igor, b Moscow 1943– , paint WWA86

KHENDRY, Janak Kumar, b Amristar, India 1935– , sculp WWA89

KHOUBESSERIAN, Hagop G., b Egypt 1931– , drw IO

KIAKSHUK, E7-1057, b Ungava, Que

1886, d Cape Dorset, NWT 1966, prt sculp Co DEA NGC2

KIAWAK/KIUGAK[2], Ashoona[3], E7–1103 (m Sorosilutoo, E7–1172, q.v.), b Tariugajak Camp, NWT 1933– , prt sculp CE1,2[2] CWW93[3] DEA NGC2 US

KIDD, Joseph M., b Athlone, Ont, fl 1892–1905, paint H MM RCA

KIDDER, Jack, b Little Sioux, Iowa 1925– , fl 1969– , sculp M

KIDSTON, William Quigley, b Hamilton, Ont 1926– , paint UG

KIEFFER, Thomas Kemp, b Jamaica 1921– , paint IO

KIERAN, Philip Peter, b Dublin 1888, etch paint Hu MM RCA

KIERSTEAD, Karl, b S Africa, fl 1943+, paint M

KIHN, Wilfred Langdon (aka William), b Brooklyn, NY 1898, d Hadlyme, Conn 1957, Amer, paint AAA33 AAW1 B F NCAB Sam TB1–3 WWA56d59 WWWA

KIKAUKA, Talis, b Riga, Lat 1929, d Meaford, Ont 2000, paint IO

KIKUCHI, Mitsugi (s Shinran), b Japan 1933– , paint IO

KILBOURN, Rosemary Elizabeth, b Toronto 1931– , engr paint BB IO M RCA UG

KILBURN, Samuel S., Jr, fl 1830s – c 1881, Amer, illus topog DeV7 GW H WHC

KILGOUR, Andrew Wilkie, b Kirkcaldy, Scot 1868, d Strathmore, Que 1930, paint Hu M MM NGC1,2 RCA TB3

KILLALY, Alicia/Alice Margaret (m Christopher Hatton Turnor), b London, Ont 1836, d Stoke Rochford, Grantham, Eng 1916, paint DeV7 DWA H ROM WHC

KILLAM, Mabel. *See* DAY, Mabel Killam

KILLINS, Ada Gladys, b Caistor To, Lincoln Co, Ont 1901, bu Smithville, Ont 1963, paint M O.My50 W1–3

KILLMAN, Murray, fl 1960– , paint M

KILPATRICK, Aaron Edward, b St Thomas, Ont 1872, d San Luis Obispo, Calif 1953, paint AAA33 AAW1 AC CWW48 F WWA40 Y

KILPIN, Leigh Mulhall, b Ryde, I of W 1853, d Montreal 1919, paint DBA DVP G H Hu M MM NGC2 RCA

KILVERT, Benjamin Sayre Cory, b Hamilton, Ont 1879, d New York, cart paint F Mo12 TB2 WECa WWA40d47

KIM, Carole, b Korea 1955– , paint ABC

KIMBEL, Richard M., b New York 1865, d 1942, Amer, paint AAA33 Y

KIMBER, Hetty Donne, b Oxford, Eng c 1854, d Sydney, NS 1946, paint AAA01 DFA DWA H MM RCA

KIMPTON, Allan, b Toronto 1921– , paint M

KING, Alan, b Belfast, N Ire 1947– , car Po86–88

KING, Byron Lance, b Sacramento, Calif 1948– , paint ABC

KING, Harold S., b Toronto 1904 – d 1949, paint AGO

KING, Jimmy (Chief Ka-Kwa-Ga-La of Kingcome Inlet), b British Columbia c 1900, fl 1969, carv M

KING, John, b Vancouver 1949– , paint sculp DCA

KING, Laurence F., b Toronto 1913– , paint IO M S

KING, Richard Henry, R Adm, b England 1790 – d 1862, Eng, paint DMA WHC

KING, William, fl 1785–1809, Amer, sil BSA DFA GW H H77 J TB1

KING, William Ross, Lt Col, b England 1822, fl 1880, Eng, illus H

KINGAN, Edward Nathan (Ted), b Lytham St Anne's, Lancs 1927– , paint CWW93 M RCA

KINGHORN, Helen Judd (1910 m John Burpee Kinghorn), b Lindsay, Ont, paint MA

KINGSCOTE, Anthony A., b Manchester, Eng 1902– , paint M UG

KINGSFORD, Winnifred, b Toronto 1880 – d 1947, sculp DWA M NGC2 RCA

KINGSLAND, Alan Malcolm, b England 1933– , paint IO

KINGWATSIAK. *See* IYOLA, Kingwatsiak

KINNEAR, John H., b England c 1920– , paint M

KINNIS, William Gilbert, b Trail, BC 1921– , paint M

KINSMAN, Katharine Nixon Bell (m Ronald Desmond Lewis Kirkpatrick[2]), b Los Angeles 1909– , paint CWW61[2] M MM

KINTON, Ada Florence, b Battersea, London 1859, d Huntsville, Ont 1905, paint ske DCB13

KINTON, Jerrine Wells (Mrs), b Waterloo, Ont 1892, paint M MM RCA

KIPLING, Barbara Ann (m Leonard Epp), b Victoria, BC 1934– , drgt paint DCA M NGC2 RCA S

KIPLING, Brian M., b Edmonton 1953– , drgt prt CAE2 IO

KIPPS, A(rthur) K., b c 1834, fl 1859–60, paint GW H

KIRBY, Luther Henry, b Oshawa, Ont 1882, paint M RCA

KIRKHAM, Richard A., b Switzerland c 1850, d 1930, Eng, paint AAW3 AC H

KIRKPATRICK, Marianne Elizabeth, b Kingston, Ont 1831, d 1877, paint DWA H

KIRKPATRICK, Mary Lydia Dennistoun, Lady (1896 m Sir George Macaulay Kirkpatrick[2]), b Peterborough, Ont , fl 1940+, paint prt CWW48[2] DNB[2] RCA WWW[2]

KIRKWOOD, Alevade/Alwilda/Hilda, b Kemptville, Ont, fl 1886–92, paint DFA H

KIRWIN, Brian, fl 1960– , paint M

KISS, Steven Joseph, b Calgary 1933– , paint M

KITCHEN, William, fl 1820, paint H

KITSCO, John Phillip, b 1947– , paint CAE1

KITSCO, Margaret Rose, b Edmonton 1938– , paint M

KITTLITZ, Friedrich Heinrich Von, b Breslau, Pru 1799, d c 1874, paint EMA

KITTOSUCK. *See* CHARLIE, Kittosuck, E9-109; LUCASSIE Kittosuck, E9-103; LUCASSIE Kittosuck, E9-174

KIYOOKA, Harry Mitsuo (m Dorothy K. van der Ohe, q.v.), b Calgary 1928– , paint AA CC2 M MM RCA SC

KIYOOKA, Roy Kenzie, b Moose Jaw, Sask 1926, d Vancouver 1994, paint sculp AE AGO CC1 CE2 Co H77 M MM NGC1,2 NGC67 RCA TB3 UG US

KLAASSEN, Jean (m William Klaassen), fl 1960– , paint M

KLASSEN, Alvina (Mrs), fl 1960– , paint ABC

KLASSEN, Jacob Frank, b Donskoi, Rus 1904, d 1978, paint CLA M

KLASSEN, John, fl 1969– , sculp M

KLAUSNER, Leo, b USSR 1920– , sculp CAE1 IO

KLAYMAN, Al, b Toronto 1934– , prt CAE2 IO

KLEIN, Lillie V. O'Ryan (Mrs), b Quebec, fl 1900, paint AAA15 AAW2 DWA

KLEMMING, Maria Elisabeth (Maj-Lis) b Uleaborg, Fin 1901– , paint M

KLIMEK, Lylian, b Humbolt, Sask 1942– , sculp AA BDSA

KLIMOFF/KLIMHOFF, Eugene, b Mitau, Rus 1901– , paint prt M

KLOEZEMAN, Gijsbertus (Bert), b Ipoh, Malay 1921– , paint CAE1 IO M WWA62

KLOPPENBURG, Ann, b Dublin, fl 1970– , paint IO

KLUCKNER, Michael John, b Vancouver 1951– , illus paint CWW93

KLUNDER, Barbara, b c 1949– , fl 1970s, car illus Po87

KLUNDER, Harold, b Deventer, Neth 1943– , paint NGC2
KLUTSCHALK, Henry W., b Austria, fl 1878–9, paint DMA
KNAPP, Stanley C., b Devon 1912– , paint M
KNEELAND, Stillman Foster, Hon, b S Stukeley, Que 1845, paint CWW89
KNICKLE, Ava Maria Sharon (s Ava Maria), b Beardmore, Ont 1947– , sculp IO
KNIGHT, Charles, fl 1947, cart M
KNIGHT, Jack Thomas, b Welland, Ont 1949– , paint CAE1,2
KNOFT, Ernestine, b Toronto, fl 1925, d 1976, paint M MM RCA
KNOTT, Arthur Harold, b Toronto 1883, d Morro Bay, Calif 1977, paint AAA29 AAW2 AC F
KNOTT, Norman, b Curve Lake, Ont 1944– , paint IO
KNOWLES, Dorothy Elsie (m William Perehudoff, q.v.), b Unity, Sask 1927– , paint AGO BDSA CAE1 CE1,2 Co M MM RCA SC UG US WWA82
KNOWLES, Elizabeth Annie Beach[2] (m Farquhar M.S.S. Knowles, q.v.), b Ottawa 1866, d Riverton, NH 1928, paint AAA29 AE AGO CWW10 DWA F H Hu M MM Mo12 NGC1,2 R2[2] RCA TB1 W1–3
KNOWLES, Farquhar McGillivary Strachan Stewart (m Elizabeth A.B. Knowles, q.v.; m Lila C.T. Knowles, q.v.), b Syracuse, NY 1859, d Toronto 1932, paint AAA31d32 AE AGO B CWW10 DBA DVLP F H M MM Mo12 NGC1,2 R2 RCA TB1,2 W1–3 Y
KNOWLES, John, b 1932– , fl 1958, paint M
KNOWLES, Lila Caroline Taylor (m Farquhar M.S.S. Knowles, q.v.), b Granton, Ont 1886, d 1967, paint DWA Hu M MM RCA
KNOWLES, Maida Doris Parlow[2] (m Arthur Raymond Knowles; m Donald French[3]), b Toronto 1891, d 1977, paint CC1[3] CWW73[3] DWA M RCA[2]
KNOWLES, Winnifred Ann. *See* MacLACHLAN, Winnifred Ann Knowles
KNOWLTON, Jonathan, b New York 1937 , paint CAE1 MM WWA93
KNOX, David Lindsay, b Toronto 1942, d Vancouver 1987, gra NGC2
KNOX, Isobel Mary. *See* HUFFMAN, Isobel Mary Knox
KNUDSEN, Niels Christian, b Denmark 1945– , paint prt WWA93
KOBAYASHI, Reimi, b 1951– , prt CAE2
KOCEVAR, Frank J., b nr Metlika, Au 1899, d 1982, paint DFA KB SC
KOCHANSKI, Vera (Mrs Worling), b Oshawa, Ont 1928– , paint M MM
KODDO, Galina Kuprijanov (Mrs), b St Petersburg, Rus 1916– , paint M
KOEHLER, Marie, b Manchester, NH 1939– , illus paint M
KOEHN, Lala Henryka. *See* HEINE-KOEHN, Lala Henryka
KOENIG, John Franklin, b Seattle, Wash 1924– , paint NGC2 WWA91
KOENIG, Kurt, b Austria, fl 1960– , paint M
KOFLER, Ernest H., b Austria, fl 1947, paint M
KOHLUND, Hans, b Freiburg, Ge 1915– , fl 1962, anim gra M
KOHUSKA, Helen, b Sioux Lookout, Ont 1929– , paint M
KOKS, Endel, b Estonia 1912– , mmed paint S
KOLACZ, Jerry, b Czeladz, Pol 1938– , illus paint CWW93
KOLAUT[1] / KALOUT[2], Pacome, b nr Igloolik, NWT c 1926 – d 1968, sculp M[1,2]
KOLENICK, Jan. *See* DYCK-KOLENICK, Jan
KOLISNYK, Peter Henry, b Toronto 1934– , paint sculp CAE1 CWW93 IO M MM RCA WWA93
KOLLNER, Augustus, b Dusseldorf,

Ge 1812, d Philadelphia 1906, engr paint DeV3,8 DMA GW H TB1 WHC Y

KOMINERK/KRAMINERK, Philip, E5-902 (m Paneeloo, E5-244, q.v.), b Arctic Bay, NWT 1933– , sculp DEAp114

KONDZIELEWSKI, Zygmont, b Scott, Sask 1933– , paint US

KONG, Shiu Loon, b Hong Kong 1934– , paint CWW93

KONING de BOURBON, Amelia Marie Antoinette, b Surabaya, Indo 1936– , paint IO

KONIUSZY, Edward, b Poland 1919– , sculp IO

KONTSKI, Stefan, b Poland c 1898, mur paint M

KOOCHIN, William, b Brilliant, BC 1927– , sculp BCS DCA M MM RCA WWA91

KOOKEEYOUT/KUKIIYAUT, Myra, E2-210 (m Luke Agnaknak, E2-365, q.v.), b Baker Lake, NWT 1929– , prt DEA US

KOOMWARTOK/KUMWARTOK[2], Ashoona, E7-1102, b Nettiling Lake, NWT 1930, d Cape Dorset, NWT 1984, sculp DEAp126[2] NGC2

KOOP, Wanda (Mrs Condon[2]), b Vancouver 1951– , gra paint DCA[2]

KOPAK/KUPAK, Felix, E3-904, b Repulse Bay, NWT 1918– , sculp US

KOPERQUALOOK/QUPIRQUALUK, Isa, E9-801, b Povungnituk, Que 1916– , sculp DEAp119

KOPMANIS, Augusts Arnold, b Riga, Lat 1910, d Genoa 1976, sculp CWW73 M MM RCA WWA78

KOPPEL, Charles W., b Germany, fl 1853–1903, engr AAW1 AC GW H Sam

KORDA, Evee, b Budapest, fl 1970– , sculp CAE1

KORDIUK, Stefan Ihor, b W Germany 1946– , paint IO

KORNER, John Michael Anthony, b Novy Jicin, Cz 1913– , paint AE AGO CC2 M NGC1,2 TB3 WWA82

KOROKNAY, Imre (Emery), b Hungary 1920– , paint PHA

KORT, William Thomas, b 1943– , paint prt CAE1,2

KORTES, Catherine Walyor (m Achilles Kortes), b Revenue, Sask 1908, d Saskatoon 1977, paint BDSA

KORTRIGHT, Reginald Guy, b Clifton, Glos c 1877/8,Eng, paint CWW36 DBA RA WBA1 WWB34

KORTT, Mikola, b Poland, fl 1960– , carv M

KOSEBA, Eddy, fl 1959– , paint M

KOST, Robert Theodore, b Lac Du Bonnet, Man 1936– , paint CAE2 M SC

KOSTIUK, Lena, b McRae, Alta 1930– , paint CAE1 KB

KOSTYNIUK, Ronald Peter, b Wakaw, Sask 1941– , sculp AA CAE1,2 CWW93 M RCA S WWA93

KOSUTH, Joseph, b Toledo, Ohio 1945– , Amer, con CA1–3 DCAA2,3 WWA93

KOTSIFOS, Anthony (s Tony Cretan), b Greece 1922– , paint IO

KOTTMAN, Donald D., b St Louis, Mo 1946– , paint AA SC

KOUSAL, Matthew F., b Czechoslovakia 1903– , paint CNS59 M

KOVACH, Rudy, b Yugoslavia 1929– , gra paint M

KOVALIK, Peter Paul, b Bratislava, Cz 1956– , paint prt IO

KOVALIK, Tibor F., b Poprad, Cz 1935– , paint CAE2 CWW93 IO

KOVALSKI, Maryann (m Gregory Sheppard), b New York 1951– , illus C CWW92 SAA58

KOVER, Emese. *See* GYORE, Emese Kover

KOVER, Mathilda Kasas (m John/Janos Kover), b Elopaktak, Hu 1900, tap PHA

KOVINATILLIAK, 'B,' E7-1024,

b Cape Dorset, NWT 1930– , prt DEA

KOWAL, Ivan, b Ukraine, fl 1960– , paint sculp stgl M

KOWALLEK, Hele, b Detmold, Ge 1951– , paint prt CAE1

KOWALSKY, Elaine, b London 1948– , prt CAE2

KOZO, Margit, b Mak, Hu 1920– , paint PHA

KRAEMER, James Joseph, b Kitchener, Ont 1928– , paint pas IO

KRALKA, Suzanne Ranger (Mrs), b Quebec Prov, fl 1984– , paint sculp MFMS

KRAMER, Burton, b New York 1932– , des gra CWW93 RCA WWA93 WWGA2

KRAMER, Richard, b Germany 1936– , sculp IO

KRAMINERK. *See* KOMINERK KRAMINERK, Philip

KRAMOLC, Theodore Maris (Ted), b Ljubljana, Yu 1922– , etch paint AGO IO NGC2 S WWA82

KRASHUDLUAK, Angela, E2-187 (m Makpa Arnasungnark, E2-120, q.v.), b Baker Lake, NWT 1925– , sculp DEA

KRASNER, Joanna Vanterpool (m Oscar Krasner), b Saskatoon 1930– , paint BDSA US

KRAUSE, Jerome Clark, b Columbus, Ohio 1943– , paint CWW93

KRAUSZ, Peter Thomas, b Brasov, Rom 1946– , paint CWW93

KREGER, Hank. *See* SENGGIH

KREYES, Marielouise Bodewein (Mrs), b Lobberich, Ge 1925– , sculp CAE2 M

KRIEGER, Jim, b Biloxi, Miss 1946– , sculp ABC

KRIEGHOFF, Cornelius David, b Amsterdam 1815, d Chicago 1872, paint ACA AGO B CE1,2 Co DCB10 DeV3,7 DFA EC H H77 L LeJ M MQ NGC1,2 NGC67 OCD ROM Sam TB1 US W1–3

KRIEKLE, Donna Lynne (aka Donna Peters) (m Richard Diener), b Regina 1945– , paint BDSA

KRISTMANSON, Lawrence William, b 1932– , etch paint M

KRIZAN, Samuel Jan, b Windsor, Ont 1939– , paint IO M

KRONBERGS, Charles, b Latvia 1923– , paint prt IO S

KROSNICK, Julie, b 1947– , sculp CAE1

KROUPA, Bohuslav/Bohsular, fl 1872–80, Au-Hu, engr illus AAW3 DBA DeV1,3–7,9 DFA H

KRUPP, Susan, b Toronto 1962– , illus C

KRYKORKA, Vladyana, b Prague, fl 1970– , illus paint C MFMS

K.T. *See* TOBIN, Kevin Joseph Michael

KUBOTA, Nobuo, b Vancouver 1932– , sculp CAE1 IO M NGC2 RCA

KUCH, Peter, b Winnipeg 1917– , cart paint Des M

KUCHANSKY, Norman, b c 1915– , fl 1944, gra paint M

KUCHARSKI, Zig, b Hamilton, Ont 1929– , paint M

KUCHMIJ, Nicholas, b Montreal 1936– , prt M MM

KUCZER, Michael J., b Winnipeg 1910– , paint CAE1 M

KUEBER, Eleanor, b Flin Flon, Man 1935– , tap SC

KUEHNER, Albert Lincoln, b Kitchener, Ont 1902– , paint CWW64

KUHNER, Manfred R.W., b Calicut, India 1902– , paint CWW64

KUJUNDZIC, Zeljko Desider, b Subotica, Yu 1920– , paint sculp BCS M

KULBACK/KULBACH, René L., b Russia, fl 1930+, paint M MM

KULHA, Pauline Holancin, b Gatineau, Que 1933– , paint IO

KULIK, Sharon, b Saugus, Calif 1951– , con CAE1,2

KULMALA, George Arthur, b Pori, Fin 1896, d Toronto 1940, paint AGO Hu M RCA

KULYK, Karen Gray, b Toronto 1950– , paint IO CWW93
KUMMER, Julius Hermann, b Dresden, Ge 1817, fl 1850–69, Amer, paint DeV6 GW H TB1 Y
KUMWARTOK. *See* KOOMWARTOK/KUMWARTOK, Ashoona
KUNDZINS, Pauls, b Smiltene, Lat 1888, d Halifax 1983, fl 1952, paint M
KUPAS, Dennis, fl 1970– , prt CAE2
KUPESIC, Rajka, b Yugoslavia 1952– , paint KB
KURELEK, William (Wasyl), b nr Whitford, Alta 1927, d Toronto 1977, paint AE AGO CA1 CAE1,2 CBC CC1 CE1,2 Co DFA KB JAI5 M MM NGC2 NGC67 RCA SAA8d27 SC T UG WWA78
KURKURSKI, Robert, b on board RMS *Queen Elizabeth* 1944– , prt sculp IO
KUTHAN, George, b Klatovy, Cz 1916, d 1966, engr etch prt M
KUUNNUAQ/KOUNOOAK, Marie, E2-126 (m Thomas Quqimat/Kakimut, E2-240), b nr Baker Lake, NWT 1933– , sculp US
KUYPERS, Francine, b Semarang, Indo, fl 1970– , paint IO
KUZELA, Miroslav, b Czechoslovakia, fl 1967– , paint DFA H74 KB
KWARTLER, Alexander, b Hungary 1924– , paint sculp M PHA WWA78
KWAXITOLA. *See* SEAWEED, Willie
KWO, Chin Charles, b Loyang, Honan, Chi 1926– , paint CWW93
KYBA, Angeline Vera, b Le Pas, Man, fl 1969– , etch paint IO
KYLE, James Fergus, b Hamilton, Ont c 1876, d Toronto 1941, cart illus paint Des M
KYLE, Joseph, b Ohio 1815, d New York 1863, Amer, paint F GW H TB1 Y

L

LABA, Victor, b Grimsby, Ont 1936– , paint M
LABBE, Françoise, b Baie-St-Paul, Que 1934– , enam paint M
LABBE, Michel, b Vallée Junction, Que 1944– , paint M
LABELLE, Henri-Sicotte, b Montreal 1896, fl 1979, carv CNS40 CWW70 K MM RCA
LABELLE, Joseph-Arthur-Pierre, b Montreal 1857 – d 1939, illus litho H K MM
LABELLE-OUELLET, Lise (m Jean Ouellet), fl 1968– , paint sculp M
LABERGE, Marie (Mrs), b Quebec 1923– , paint M
LABERGE, Paul, b Cap-de-la-Madeleine, Que 1945– , paint tap CAE1
LA BORIE, Phillip E., b Rochester, NY 1939– , paint CAE1
LABOUREUR, Jean-Emile, b Nantes, Fr 1877, d France 1943, Fr, engr paint B K TB1
LABOURIERE/LABOURRIERE[2], Charles-Emile, Abbé, b Kamouraska, Que 1863, d Santa Cruz, Tri 1893, paint H[2] K
LABRECQUE, Nathalie. *See* PERVOUCHINE, Nathalie
LABROQUERIE, b France, fl 1757, Fr, topog H K
LABROSSE, Paul Jourdain. *See* JOURDAIN dit LABROSSE, Paul Raymond
LA BRULERIE[2], Bernard de, fl 1913, paint K MM[2]
LACAS, Emile, b Canada, fl 1890, paint H K
LACELIN, Philippe (b Philippe Bellefleur), b Montreal 1938– , engr paint CAE1 M
LACELLE, Beatrice, fl 1969, paint M
LACELLE, Florence, fl 1969, paint M
LACELLE, William, fl 1969, paint M

LACHAPELLE, Edouard, b Montreal 1943– , paint prt CAE1

LACK, Stephen H., b Montreal 1946– , etch paint CAE1 CWW93

LACROIX, Alfred E., fl 1888, sculp K

LACROIX, Jacques, b Chicoutimi, Que 1944– , sculp M

LACROIX, Joseph Samuel Richard, b Montreal 1939– , paint sculp AGO B CAE1 CC1 CE1,2 CWW93 M MM MQ NGC67 RCA US WWA89

LACROIX, Paul, b Ste-Marie-de-Beauce, Que 1929– , drw paint sculp M TB3

LADDS, Elizabeth, b Dartmouth, NS 1922– , paint DFA H NGC67

LAFFIN, W.M., fl 1882, paint H RCA

LAFITAU, Joseph-François, b Bordeaux, Fr 1681 – d 1746, Fr, des DCB3 K

LAFLAMME, Hélène, fl 1960– , engr M

LAFLAMME, Roger, b Montreal 1925– , paint M

LAFLEUR, Claude, b Montreal, fl 1960– , paint sculp M

LAFONTAINE, François, fl 1818 28, sculp K

LAFONTAINE, Marguerite de Montigny[2] (m Georges Lafontaine), b Montreal 1890, d 1982, sculp CNS40[2] K[2] MM RCA

LAFONTAINE, Yvan, b 1943– , engr paint M MM

LAFORCE, Pierre, b Quebec 1829/30, fl 1861–81, sculp K

LAFORD, John Eric, b Wikwemikong, Manitoulin Isld, Ont 1955– , paint IO

LAFORGE, Jean-Marie, b Belgium 1946– , paint Des M

LA FORTUNE, Douglas, b Bellingham, Wash 1953– , sculp S

LAFRAMBOISE, Benjamin, b Ottawa, fl 1957– , paint K

LA FRANCE, Louise, b Medicine Hat, Alta 1960– , illus C

L'AFRICAIN, Eugène, b 1859, d 1892, paint H K

LAGACE, Jean-Baptiste, b 1868, d 1946, paint H K MM

LAGRAVE, Marie-Marguerite-Eulalie (Soeur), b St-Charles-sur-Richelieu, Que 1805, d Red River, nr St Boniface, Man 1859, sculp K

LAGUNUSI. *See* LAZARUSIE/LAGUNUSI, Epo/Epoo

LA HONTAN, Louis-Armand de Lom[2] d'Arce, Baron de, b Lahontan, Fr 1666, d Hanover, Ge 1716, Fr, drw illus DCB2[2] K

LAIDLAW, Archibald Malloch, b Ottawa 1913– , paint CWW81

LAIDLAW, Frieda, b Toronto 1904– , paint Hu

LAIDLER, Keith James, b Liverpool 1916– , paint CWW91

LAING, John Wood, b Edinburgh 1871, paint WWNA

LAING, Marion, b Quebec 1849, d Montreal 1932, paint H MM RCA

LAING, Shayna (m Frederick Michaels), b Montreal 1933– , paint sculp CAE2 M SC

LAING, William (Bill), b Glasgow 1944– , drgt paint AA CAE2 DCA SC

LAJAMBE, Denise (Mrs), b Montreal 1928– , paint M

LAJEUNIE, Jean-Claude, b Eaubonne, Fr 1943– , sculp M

LAJOIE, Paul, b Montreal 1932– , paint IO

LALANDE, Edith. *See* PATTERSON, Edith Lalande Ravenshaw

LALIBERTE, Alfred, b Ste-Elizabeth, Que 1878, d Montreal 1953, paint sculp B CC2 CE1,2 CNS40 Co CWW49 EC K M MM MQ NGC1 PMC RCA TB1–3 WWA53d56

LALIBERTE, Joseph-Laurent-Guy, b Hull, Que 1930– , paint M

LALIBERTE, Madeleine, b Victoriaville, Que 1922– , paint CAE1 M NGC1 TB3

LALIBERTE, Norman, b Worcester, Mass 1925– , illus paint F M WWA80

LAMARCHE, Ulric E., b Oakland,

Calif 1867, d Montreal 1921, cart paint H K M MM RCA

L'AMARRE, Pierre, b Germany 1915– , cart paint M

LAMARSH, Rhoda (m W. Clayton Lamarsh), b c 1892, d 1960, paint M

LAMARTINE, Gert Louis, b Uiffingen, Baden, Ge 1898, d 1965, paint sculp CNS59 M MM

LAMB, Charles Cowan, b Toronto 1904– , paint Hu RCA

LAMB, Harold Mortimer (m Vera Olivia Weatherbie, q.v.), b Leatherhead, Eng 1872, d Vancouver 1970, paint M MM Mo98, 12

LAMB, Molly Jean. *See* BOBAK, Molly Jean Lamb

LAMB, Vera Olivia Weatherbie. *See* WEATHERBIE, Vera Olivia

LAMBE, Annie M., fl 1897–1903, paint H MM

LAMBE, Elizabeth Haines (Libbie[2] H.), fl 1888–1903, paint H[2] MM

LAMBE, Lawrence Morris (aka Laurence), b Montreal 1863, paint CWW10 H MM Mo12 RCA

LAMBE[1], Sarah M. (Zaidee[2]), fl 1887–8, paint H[1,2] MM RCA

LAMBE, William Busby, b Montreal 1826, paint H MM Mo98 RCA

LAMBERT, Beverley Ann. *See* KELLY, Beverley Ann Lambert

LAMBERT, Jacques, b Que Prov 1928– , paint M

LAMBERT, Jane, b c 1950– , paint M

LAMBERT, John, b England c 1777, fl 1806–16, Eng, paint DCB5 DeV3,7 DNB G W H

LAMBERT, Phyllis Bronfman[2] (m Jean Lambert), b Montreal 1927– , sculp CWW93 MM[2] RCA WWA91 WWC

LAMBERT, Pierrette, b Montreal 1948– , paint sculp CAE1

LAMBERT, Richard Tullie, b London 1923– , paint M RCA

LAMBERT, Ronald M., b Oshawa, Ont 1927– , paint AGO M MM RCA

LAMBTON, Gwenda, b Wilhelmshaven, Ge 1914– , engr illus M

LAMBTON, Mary Louisa. *See* ELGIN, Mary Louisa Lambton, Countess

LAMER, Gilles, b 1928– , paint M

LAMONT, Gwendolen Kortwright Hutton (m J.M. Lamont), b Ft Macleod, Alta 1909, d Kelowna, BC 1979, paint M MM WWNA

LAMONT, Laura A. Shannon (m A. Lamont), b Tara, Ont 1880, d Regina 1970, paint BDSA

LAMONTAGNE, Blanche-Beauregard (Mme), b Escoumins, Que 1889, d Montreal 1959, illus K

LAMPE, Walter, fl 1967– , paint M

LAMPERT, Emma Esther. *See* COOPER, Emma Esther Lampert

LAMPITOC, Rolando Ponce, b Laoag City, Phil c 1926– , paint prt WWA93

LAMPMAN, Helen Winifred MacKenzie (m Archibald Otto Lampman), b Lakefield, Ont 1898, fl 1958, paint DWA M

LAMPRECHT, Gisela Helene von Eicken (Mrs), b Munich 1899, sculp DWA M MM

LANARY, Jean, b Quebec 1927– , cart Des

LANC, Paul (b Lancz), b Hungary c 1919– , sculp M

LANCEMAN, Audrey, b London, fl 1957– , paint M

LANCTOT, C.B., fl 1878–9, paint H K

LANDER, Carl. *See* BUCHER, Carl

LANDMAN, George Thomas, Lt Col, b Woolwich, Eng 1779, d Shacklewell, nr London 1854, Eng, paint DBMP DMA DNB

LANDORI, Eva (m Rudolf Hoffman), b Budapest 1912– , paint CAE1 M MM PHA

LANDRIAU, Lawrence Alfred, b L'Original, Que? 1894, paint CWW64

LANDRY, Jean, b Quebec 1937– , cart Des

LANDRY, Marie-Marguerite-Louise.

See GADBOIS, Marie-Marguerite-Louise Landry

LANDRY, Napoléon, fl 1889–97, engr H K

LANDRY, Paul, b Halifax 1933– , paint M

LANDRY, Pierre, b Trois-Rivières, Que 1939– , sculp M

LANDRY, Yvan, b Quebec 1932– , cer mur M

LANDSLEY, Patrick Alfred, b Winnipeg 1926– , paint CAE1 CC2 M MM RCA

LANDWEER, Els, b Netherlands, fl 1959– , paint ABC

LANE, Fitz Hugh (b Nathaniel Roger Lane), b Gloucester, Mass 1804 – d 1865, Amer, litho paint DAA DMP DSP F GW H Y

LANE, Henry Bowyer Joseph, b Corfu, Gr c 1817/18, fl 1851, paint DCB8

LANE, William Bowyer, b London 1787 – d 1853, Eng, drw paint DeV8

LANG, Byllée Fay, b Didsbury, Alta 1908, d Bermuda 1966, sculp M MM RCA W3

LANGDALE, Stella, b Scotland, fl 1910–40, Scot, illus paint sculp DBA DWA M WBA2

LANGE, Detta B., b 1923– , paint prt M

LANGENBACH, Clara Emma, b Sebringville, Ont 1871, paint AAA33 DWA WWA62

LANGEVIN, Claude, b Montreal 1942– , paint M

LANGEVIN, Roger, fl 1960– , paint sculp M

LANGHAM, E., Hon (Mrs), fl 1879–92, Eng, paint DBA DVP H MM RCA

LANGLAMENT, Louis, b Saint-Brieuc, Fr, fl 1911+, Fr, paint K

LANGLEY, Henry, b London 1836, d Toronto 1907, drw paint Co DeV8 NGC1

LANGLOIS, Claude, b Montreal 1918– , paint M

LANGLOIS, Jean, b Montreal 1916– , paint M MM RCA

LANGLOIS, Sheila (Mrs), fl 1967– , paint M

LANGMAID, Rowland John Robb, Lt Cdr, b Esquimalt, BC 1897, d Malaga, Sp 1956, paint DBA DBMaP DSP RA TB1 WBA1 WWB34 WWW

LANGS, Mary Metcalfe, b Burford, Ont 1887, sculp DAS DWA WWA62

LANGSDORFF, Georg Heinrich von, b Wollstein, Ge 1774, d Freiburg, Ge 1852, Ge, paint AAW1 AC EMA

LANGSTADT, Anne Kahane. *See* KAHANE, Anne

LANGSTADT, Robert (m Anne Kahane, q.v.), b 1912– , prt CAE1

LANGTON, Anne, b Bolton Abbey, York 1804, d Toronto 1893, paint DCB12 H

LANGTON, William, b Peterborough, Ont 1854, d Toronto 1933, paint DeV8 H RCA W1–3

LANKAU, Hans Gottfried Edita, b Berlin, Ge 1897, sculp M

LANMAN, Charles, b Monroe, Mich 1819, d Georgetown, DC 1895, Amer, paint AAW3 App B DAB F GW H NCAB TB1 WWWA Y

LANSDOWNE, James Fenwick, b Hong Kong 1937– , paint Co CWW93 M RCA SC WWA93

LAPALICE, Joseph-Hengard, b Rivière-du-Loup, Que 1817, d St-Aimé, Que 1889, sculp K

LA PALME, Pierre (s Pierre Gaboriau[2]; Gabo), b New York 1935– , paint M[2] MM NGC2[2]

LA PALME, Robert, b Montreal 1908– , car CGA1 Co CWW93 Des M RCA TB3 WECa

LAPENSE, Michel, b 1947– , paint DFA

LAPEER, Lynda (m Michael Joseph Behran, q.v.), b 1949– , paint DFA KB

LAPERLE, Marie-Philippe-Richard Banlier, dit, b La Prairie, Que 1860, d Montreal 1934, paint sculp H K

LA PIERRE, Patricia Clemes. *See* CLEMES, Patricia

LA PIERRE, Thomas (m Patricia

Clemes, q.v.), b Toronto 1930– , paint CAE2 CWW93 IO M MM RCA UG WWA93

LAPINE, Andreos Christian Gottfried (Andre) (b Andrejs Lapins), b Shujen, Riga Prov, Rus 1866, d Minden, Ont 1952, paint AE AGO CC1 CWW49 H Hu M MM NGC1 RCA TB2,3

LAPOINTE, C. (Mlle), b St-Gervais, Que, fl 1884, paint H K

LAPOINTE, Epiphane, b Ile-aux-Coudres, Que 1822, d Rimouski, Que 1862, paint H K

LAPOINTE, Frank, b Port Rexton, Nfld 1942– , paint prt DCA RCA WWA93

LAPOINTE, Gaetan, b 1950– , paint CAE1

LAPOINTE, Jean. *See* MIHALCHEON, Jean Lapointe

LAPOINTE, Joseph, b 1820/1, fl 1847–51, sculp K

LAPOINTE, Marc C., b Montreal 1923– , paint CWW93

LAPORTE, Denis, fl 1960– , paint M

LAPORTE, Paul Carmel, b Verchères, Que 1885, fl 1971, sculp K M

LAPRE, Leopold, b Montreal 1933– , prt CAE1

LAPTUTA, Christine, b Toronto 1951– , etch paint IO

LARCHEVEQUE, André Robert, b Montreal 1923– , paint M WWA93

LARIVEE, Francine, b 1942– , sculp CAE1

LARIVIERE, Roger, b Ottawa 1917– , paint M RCA

LARK. *See* POLLOCK, Florrie

LARKIN, Bess. *See* HARRIS, Bess Larkin

LARKING, Patrick Lambert, b Rudgwick, Sus 1907, d 1981, paint DBA Hu RA RCA TB3 WBA1 WWB82

LARMOUR, William Gardham, b Brantford, Ont 1870, d 1943, paint DMA

LAROCQUE, Sylvio, b c 1935– , paint M

LAROSE, Ludger, b Montreal 1868 – d 1915, paint ACA CC2 CE1 K M MM MQ NGC67 RCA

LAROSE, Louis, fl 1866–74, paint K

LARSENEUR, Charles, fl 1842–50, paint sculp K

LARSENEUR, Pierre, b Montreal 1813/14, d California 1867, sculp K

LARSON, Doris Wall, b Aberdeen, Sask 1939– , paint sculp BDSA

LARTER, John, b Swift Current, Sask 1950– , cart Des Po87–88

LASBY, William Walter, b Ariss, Ont 1911– , paint CWW70

LASNIER, Raymond, b Quebec 1924, d Trois-Rivières, Que 1968, paint M MM W3

LASSZNER, Gabor, b Hungary, fl 1961– , paint M

LATCHOLASSIE, E7-1055, b Cape Dorset, NWT 1919– , sculp Co DEA US

LATOUR, Georges, b Valleyfield, Que 1877, d 1946, illus K RCA

LATOUR, Jacques. *See* LEBLOND de LATOUR, Jacques

LATTA, Samuel John, b London, Ont 1866, d 1946, paint CWW52

LAU, Tin Yum, b Hong Kong 1941– , paint prt CAE1

L'AUBINIERE, C.A. de (m Georgina M.S. de L'Aubinière, q.v.), b France, fl 1880–8, paint AC H K

L'AUBINIERE, Georgina M. Steeple[3] de[2] (m C.A. L'Aubinière, q.v.), b England 1844, d 1925, paint DBA[2] DWA[3] G[2] H M RA[2]

LAUDA, Georges Jiri, b Prague, Cz 1925– , drw M MM

LAUDER, James (Jim), b Toronto 1936– , paint sculp M

LAUFER, Murray Bernard, b Toronto 1929– , des Co

LAUGHLIN, J.E., fl 1895–1900, illus H

LAUNDERS, James B., fl 1858–63, d Nanaimo, BC 1878, drgt H

LAUR, Edgar Lee, b nr Aylmer, Ont

1867, d Woodbridge, Ont 1943, paint AGO H M
LAURE, Pierre-Michel, b Orleans, Fr 1686, d Les Eboulements, Que 1738, paint DCB2 H H77 K
LAURENCE, Henry Buckton, fl 1860s, Eng, illus H
LAURENDEAU, Simon D., fl 1884–1910, engr H K
LAURENT, Brigette, b Montreal 1961– , sculp CWW93
LAURENT, Robert, b Concarneau, Fr 1890, d Cape Neddick, Me 1970, Amer, sculp AAA33 B DAS DCAA2,3 F K TB1,3 WWA70 Y
LAUSSUCQ, Henri L., b Bordeaux, Fr 1882, d Pittsburgh, Pa 1947, paint K
LAUTERMAN, Dinah, b Montreal 1889 – d 1945, drw sculp M MM RCA
LAUZON, Larry, b 1947– , paint M
LAUZON, Normand, b Montreal 1925– , drw paint M MM
LAUZON, Real, b Montreal 1945– , sculp CAE1
LAVANOUX, Maurice, b New York 1894 – d 1974, Amer, des K
LAVERDIERE, Auguste, fl 1870s, illus paint H K
LAVERDIERE, Charles-Honoré (CAUCHON dit LAVERDIERE), b Château-Richer, Que 1826, d Quebec 1873, drw DCB10 K
LAVERTY, Samuel George, b Watford, Herts 1922– , paint AE RCA
LAVIGUEUR, Roch, fl 1876–86, paint H K
LAVOIE, Onésime-M., fl 1868–94, paint H K
LAVOYE, Marie Ann Juliette (b Lavoie), b Montreal 1903– , min M MM
LAW, Charles Anthony Francis, b London 1916– , paint CWW70 M MA MM NGC68 RCA WWA93
LAW, Frederick Charles, b Brent, Som 1841, d Toronto 1922, paint CWW10 H Mo98,12 RCA
LAW, Gordon, b 1914– , carv DFA KB
LAW, Ivan, b c 1885, d 1979, carv DFA KB
LAW, Sidney George, b England 1901– , paint CWW64
LAWDER, James T., fl 1873–80, des paint H RCA
LAWLEY, John Douglas, b Glace Bay, NS 1905, d 1971, paint CWW67 M MM
LAWRENCE, Mary C. (Mrs), b Isld of Mull, Scot 1899, fl 1950+, paint M
LAWRENCE, Mollie Cruickshank, b Regina 1920– , paint BDSA M
LAWS, Eve (b Eva Maria Huldschinsky) (m Stevenson Milne Gossage[2]), b Berlin, Ge c 1919– , paint CWW84[2] M
LAWSON, Arthur Wendell Phillips, b Toronto 1898, d Columbus, Ohio 1952, drw paint Hu M MM RCA
LAWSON, Edith Grace Coombs. *See* COOMBS, Edith Grace
LAWSON, Ernest, b Halifax (x San Francisco) 1873, d Miami, Fla 1939, paint AAA33 AAW1 ACA AGO BE CC2 DAA DAB DCAA2 DMA F H M NCAB31 NGC1 NGC67 OCD P RCA S Sam TB1,2 WWA38d40 WWWA Y
LAWSON, Gertrude, b Donald, BC 1892, paint WWNA
LAWSON, James Kerr. *See* KERR-LAWSON, James
LAWSON, M.T., fl 1882–5, paint H
LAWSON, Wendell. *See* LAWSON, Arthur Wendell Phillips
LAWSON-SHANKS, Jennifer, b England 1949– , paint prt IO
LAWTON, Alfred V., b 1848, d 1929, paint DFA
LAWTON, Pierre, b Chicoutimi, Que c 1933– , paint M MM
LAX, David, b New York 1910– , Amer, paint WWA89
LAX, Tomas (Thomas), b Ostrava, Cz 1948– , prt IO
LAXTON, Harold McLean, b Hamilton, Ont 1922, d 1986, mur paint M

LAYCOCK, Brent H., b Lethbridge, Alta 1947– , paint SC

LAYNE, Barbara J., b Seattle, Wash 1952– , sculp WWA93

LAZAR, Patricia, fl 1968– , prt sculp M

LAZARE, Gerald John (Jerry), b Toronto 1927– , illus paint IBYP ICB3 IO SAA44

LAZARUS, Ian, b Toronto 1951– , paint SC

LAZARUSIE/LAGUNUSIL, Epo/Epoo[2], E9-1619, b Port Harrison, Que 1932– , sculp DEA S[2]

LAZEAR, Ann Tarantour (m Art Lazear), b Montreal 1927– , paint M

LEA, Allan, b c 1941– , paint M

LEACH, John, b Toronto c 1938– , drw paint M

LEACH, Prudence, b England 1932– , sculp BCS

LEACH, William, b Crewe, Eng 1891, paint CWW70

LEADBEATER, Roy, b Ashbourne, Derb 1928– , sculp M SC

LEADBETTER, Murray David, b Toronto 1949– , paint IO

LEADBETTER, Noble W., b Wardsville, Ont 1875, paint AAW3 WWNA

LEAF, June, b Chicago 1929– , paint sculp WWA93

LEANING, John Dalton, b London 1926– , paint M

LEARY-POSNICK, Muriel, fl 1960– , paint ABC

LEATHER, Ethel Armine, b 1861, d 1957, paint DWA H

LEATHERS, Audrey Riller. *See* RILLER, Audrey

LEATHERS, Winston Lyle (m Audrey Riller, q.v.), b Miami, Man 1932– , paint prt CAE2 CWW93 M MM RCA S SC WWA93

LEAVERS, William W., b Brighton, Eng, fl 1920+, paint AC

LEBEL, Maurice, b Montreal 1898 – d 1963, engr illus paint CNS36 K M MM RCA

LEBER, Pierre, b Montreal 1669, d Pointe-St-Charles, nr Montreal 1707, paint CE1,2 DCB2 DFA EC H H77 K KB W1–3

LE BEUF, C. (Mrs), fl 1918, min K MM

LE BEUF, Jean Guy, b Quebec 1932– , paint M

LEBLANC, Augustin, b Yamachiche, Que 1799, d St-Hugues, Que 1882, carv DCB11 K

LEBLANC, Jeanne (m Gerald Rhéaume[2]), b Montreal 1915– , paint B M[2] MM MQ[2] NGC1[2] RCA TB2[2]

LEBLANC, Zacharie, b Quebec Prov 1876, fl 1891, paint K

LEBLOND, Jean. *See* JACQUIER/JACQUIES dit LEBLOND, Jean

LEBLOND de LATOUR, Jacques, b Bordeaux, Fr 1671, d Baie-St-Paul, Que 1715, carv paint DCB2 H H77 K MQ NGC67

LEBOW, Julius Leonard, b Toronto 1920– , paint M

LEBRUN, E., fl 1879, des H K

LEBRUN, Roland, b Quebec Prov 1923 – d 1973, paint M

LE CHAUDELAC, fl 1840, drw H K

LE CLAIR, Ester Deak/Esther, b Tiszasederkeny, Hu 1921– , pas paint IO

LE CLAIRE, Alphonse, b Montreal 1843, fl 1926, carv K MM

LECLAIRE, Irene, fl 1915, paint K MM

LE CLEAR, Thomas (aka LE CLAIR), b Oswego, NY 1818, d Rutherford Park, NJ 1882, Amer, paint App B Bry DAA DAB GW H NCAB WWWA Y

LECLERC, Eugène, b Quebec Prov 1886, d 1968, sculp K

LECLERE, Jean-Olivier, fl 1822, paint sculp K

LE COCQ, Doris Roosmale (m Fred T. Tabuteau), b Blackheath, London, fl 1930+, sculp CLA DBA M MM RA

LECOMTE, Pierre, b Magog, Que 1935– , paint M

LECORRE, Paul (Tex Lecor), b St-Michel-de-Wentworth, Que 1937– , paint M

LE DAIN, Bruce, b Montreal 1928– , paint CWW93 M MM RCA
LEDIEU, Léon, fl 1887–8, illus H K
LEDINGHAM, Sandra M. (Sandy), b Midale, Sask 1948– , mmed BDSA
LE DRU, Pierre, fl 1808, paint K
LEDSON, Sidney Albert James, b London 1925– , paint pas M RCA
LEDUC, Fernand, b Montreal 1916– , paint CAE1 CC2 CE1,2 M MM MQ NGC1 TB3
LEDUC, Ozias, b Mont-St-Hilaire, Que 1864, d St-Hyacinthe, Que 1955, paint ACA B CA1 CC1 CE1,2 Co CWW48 DFP3 H H77 K M MM MQ NGC1 NGC67 OCD PMC RCA TB1,3 UG WWA53d56
LEDUC-BARRETT, Camille (s Camille Barrett), b 1932– , fl 1964– , paint M
LEE, Abel Alexander, b Estonia 1918– , sculp M
LEE, Byng, fl 1960– , paint M
LEE, Eu Jeanne Park (m John Lee), b Seoul, Kor 1940– , paint M
LEE, Frederick Walter, b London 1863, d Chilliwack, BC 1941, paint AAA1900 DBA Fo G H M RCA WWNA
LEE, J.T., fl 1873, paint H
LEE, Raymond Man, b Canton, Chi 1935– , des WWA82
LEE-GRAYSON, Joseph Henry, b Harrogate, Yorks 1875, d Summerland, BC 1954, paint M MM Sam
LEE-NOVA, Gary (b Gary Nairn), b Toronto 1943– , paint sculp M US
LEE-SMITH, Marianne, b Sutton-on-Hull, Eng 1872, paint Hu MM RCA
LEESON, William Ernest (Bill), b Walsall, Eng 1894, paint IO
LE FEBVRE, Jean, b Montreal 1930– , paint M MQ
LEFEBVRE, Marie-Elmina (Soeur Marie-de-l'Eucharistie[2]), b Quebec 1862 – d 1946, paint H[2] K
LEFEBVRE, Henri, b 1874, d 1965, des paint K M
LEFEBVRE, Marcel Victor, b Ottawa 1914, d 1978, sculp M
LEFEVRE/LEFEBVRE[2], Charles A., b 1855/6, d Montreal 1923, des paint H[2] K
LEFKOVITZ, Sylvia, b Montreal 1924– , paint sculp M MM
LEFORT, Elizabeth, b Point Cross, NS 1914– , tap M
LEFORT, Marie-Agnès, b St-Rémi, Que 1891, d Montreal 1973, prt DWA Hu K M MM RCA WWA62
LEFOUREUR, Pierre, fl 1792, des paint H K
LEGARE, Joseph, b Quebec 1795 – d 1855, paint ACA B CE1,2 Co DCB8 DFA EC H H77 K KB M MQ NGC1 NGC67 W1–3
LEGARE, Juliette, b Montreal 1937– , mur paint M
LEGATE, P. Lister, b Montreal 1911– , paint S
LEGAULT, Jean-Onésime, b Ste-Justine-de-Newton, Que 1882, d Montreal 1944, paint K M
LEGENDRE, Irene, b Fall River, Mass 1904– , paint M MM RCA
LEGER, Caroline, b Paquetville, NB, fl 1894–1919, sculp K
LEGER, Fernand, b Argentan, Fr 1881, d Gif-sur-Yvette, Fr 1955, Fr, paint B K TB1,2
LEGER, J.A., fl 1908–19, paint sculp K MM RCA
LEGER, Jeanne, b Ste-Marie-de-Kent, NB 1895, d 1978, paint K
LEGER, Léon, b Barachois, NB 1848, d Moncton, NB 1918, sculp K
LEGER, Onésime-Aimé (x Onésime-André[2]), b Quebec 1881 – d 1924, paint sculp K MM[2] RCA[2]
LEGGE, Elizabeth, b Toronto 1952– , car sculp CWW93
LEGGO, William Augustus, Jr, b Quebec 1830, d Lachine, Que 1915, engr H

LE GOFF, Jean François, b Lanhouarneau, Fr 1864, d Winnipeg 1919, paint K

LE GOFF, Pauline. *See* BOUTAL, Pauline Le Goff

LEHMANN, Henry, b 1945– , prt CAE2

LEHTO, Joyce (m Robert J. Kaiser), b Sudbury, Ont 1928– , tap M

LEIBL, Lee (m Philip Heilig), b Plzen, Cz, fl 1963– , drw paint M

LEIBOVITCH, Norman, b Montreal 1913– , paint sculp M MM

LEIER, Grant W., b Lloydminster, Sask 1956– , illus paint ABC M

LEIGH, David Leroy, b Toronto 1927– , paint stgl M

LEIGHTON, Alfred Crocker (Crocker-Leighton[2]) (m Barbara Leighton, q.v.), b Hastings, Sus 1901, d Calgary 1965, paint CC2 CWW36[2] DBA H77 Hu M NGC1 RA RCA Sam SC W3 WBA1,2 WWA62d66 WWB29

LEIGHTON, Barbara Barleigh (m Alfred Crocker Leighton, q.v.), b Plymouth, Eng 1911– , prt GM SC

LEIGHTON, Thomas Charles, b Toronto 1909– , paint M RCA

LEITCH, Margaret Cartwright (Peggy) (m John D. Leitch), b Toronto 1920– , paint sculp IO M

LEITCH, Richard Principal, b Glasgow, fl 1840-60, Eng, illus DBLP DBWA DeV1 DVP G H TB1 WHC

LEITH, James Andrews, b Toronto 1931– , paint CWW93

LE JEUNE, James George, b Saskatoon 1910– , paint WBA1 WWB90

LE JEUNE (LE JEUNE[2]), Paul, b France 1591 – d 1664, Fr, paint DCB1 K[2]

LELIEVRE (Mlle), fl 1785–7, paint DWA H K

LE MAN, Stephanie Alexandra (Mrs Lindsay[2]), b Toronto 1951– , paint IO[2]

LEMAY, Arthur, b Nicolet, Que 1900, d 1944, car paint K WECa

LEMAY, Marcien, b 1926/7– , sculp M

LEMAY, Rodolphe, b Lotbinnière, Que 1875, fl 1945, sculp K

LE MESSURIER, Ernest-Carl, b Hamilton, Ont 1894, d Montreal 1932, cart AAAd32 Des K R2 WWAd38

LEMIEUX, Emile, b Montreal 1889, d 1967, paint K M MM RCA

LEMIEUX, Irene, b Quebec 1931– , gra CAE2 WWA93

LEMIEUX, Jean-Paul (b Marie-Joseph-Jean-Paul), b Quebec 1904, d Laval, Que 1990, paint ACA AGO B CC1 CE1,2 Co CWW89 DFA H77 M MM MQ NGC1 NGC67 P RCA S TB2,3 WWA91d93

LEMIEUX, Lucienne. *See* MARTINEAU, Lucienne Lemieux

LEMIEUX, Marguerite, b Montreal 1899, d 1971, paint sculp CNS40 DWA K M MM RCA

LEMIEUX, Maurice, b 1932– , sculp CAE1 M

LEMIEZ, Armand, b Belgium 1894, d Ste-Anne-des-Chênes, Man 1984, paint sculp K

LEMIRE, Marie-Florida-Melina (Soeur Marie-Léonille), b Nicolet, Que 1894, d St Boniface, Man 1959, paint K

LEMOINE/LE MOYNE[2], Berthe, b 1884, d 1958, illus paint K MM[2]

LEMOINE, Edmond, b Quebec 1877 – d 1922, paint K M MM MQ NGC1 RCA

LEMOINE, J., fl 1850, paint K

LEMON, Charles, b c 1843, fl 1871, illus H

LEMONDE, Serge, b 1945– , paint M

LE MOYNE, Berthe. *See* LEMOINE/LE MOYNE, Berthe

LENDVAY, Istvan Stephen, b Csorna, Hu 1929– , paint CAE1 M MM

LENEY, William Satchwell, b London 1769, d Longue Pointe, nr Montreal 1831, Eng, engr B Bry DAB DeV3 DNB F GW H Red TB1 WWWA Y

LENHARDT, Molly Stefanie Bassaraba (m Joseph Francis Lenhardt), b nr

Lake Winnepegosis, Man 1920– , paint BDSA DFA KB
LENNARD, John Barry, b Barrie, Ont 1937– , drw paint M RCA
LENNARD, John Graham Barrett. *See* BARRETT-LENNARD, John Graham
LENNIE, Edith Beatrice Catharine, b Nelson, BC 1904 (x 1906), d W Vancouver 1987, sculp M MM RCA WWA86 WWNA
LENNOX, Jean Alexandra Luella, b Toronto c 1905– , drw mur sculp IO O.F50
LENNOX, Sarah Erma. *See* SUTCLIFFE, Sarah Erma Lennox
LENT, Doris Geneva, b Elmvale, Ont 1904– , paint Hu M
LEON, Pierre R.A., b Ligré, Fr 1926– , drw gra paint CWW93
LEONARD, Bernard, fl 1877–89, paint H
LEONARD, John Charles, b Oxted, Sur 1944– , paint CWW85 M MM RCA S
LEONARD, Reginald Haviland (Ted[2]), b Toronto c 1913– , paint M[2]
LEONARD, Rose (m R.D. Davies), b nr St Paul, Alta, fl 1950+, paint M
LEONARD, Verna Georgie (Vera). *See* HOMES, Verna Georgie Leonard (Vera)
LEPAGE, fl 1871–5, drw H K
LE PAGE, Denis, b Vancouver 1934– , sculp M
LE PAGE, Edwin Brian (Eddie), b Dundas, Ont 1948– , paint pas IO
LE PAGE, Jean-Baptiste, fl 1890, drw H K
LE PAGE, Marc, b c 1947– , paint M
LE PAGE, Terrance D., b 1934– , paint MM S
LE PREVOST, Pierre-Gabriel, b Quebec Prov 1674 – d 1756, paint sculp K
LEPROHON, Etienne-Alcibiade, fl 1866, sculp K
LEPROHON, Jules, b Quebec 1877, d 1949, sculp K
LEPROHON, Louis, fl 1842–62, carv K
LEPROHON, Louis-Xavier, b Montreal 1795, d Ottawa 1876, sculp K
LEPSENYI, Ellinidha, b Alap, Hu c 1921– , paint MFMS
LEQUESNE, Donald Corbel, b Montreal 1932– , paint M MM
LERCH, Tosca, b Bohemia, Cz, fl 1960– , paint M
LEROUX, A./Adolphe (aka A. Lerouc), b St-Eustache, Que 1833, fl 1858–80, cart paint Des H K
LEROUX, Antonio, b 1880, d 1940, paint sculp K
LE ROUX, Edgar Joseph, b Ottawa 1922– , paint sculp CWW93
LEROUX, Georges-Paul, b Paris 1877, d Meudon, Fr 1957, Fr, paint B K TB1–3
LEROUX-GUILLAUME, Janine, b St-Hermas, Que 1927– , paint prt DCA M
LEROY, Bacqueville de la Potherie, Claude-Charles, b Paris 1663, d Guadeloupe 1736, Fr, illus DCB2 K
LE ROY, Hugh Alexander Côté, b Montreal 1939– , sculp B CAE1 CWW91 M MM RCA WWA93
LERY, Joseph Gaspard Chaussegros[2] de, b Toulon, Fr 1682, d Quebec 1756, drgt DAB DCB3[2] H K W1–3
LESHYK, Tonie, b Toronto 1950– , sculp WWA93
LESLIE, Ernva Willard Code. *See* CODE, Ernva Willard
LESLIE, Robert Charles (C.R.[2]), b London 1826, fl 1888, Eng, paint ANC B DBA DBLP DBMaP DMA[2] G GW H TB1
L'ESPERANCE, Alphonse, b Montreal 1914– , paint M
L'ESPERANCE, Marie-Cécile-Christine Talon (Soeur Youville), b Dorval, Que 1828, d St Boniface, Man 1902, drw K
LESSARD, Emile, b 1909– , paint sculp DFA KB
LESSORE, Frederick, b Brighton, Eng 1879, d London 1951, Eng, paint

sculp CWW49 DBA RA RCA TB2 WBA1 WWB34d52 WWW

LESTER, Barbara (Mrs), fl 1965– , paint M

L'ESTRANGE, fl 1832–4, Eng, min paint H

LESUEUR, Peter, fl 1853, paint DeV3 H K

LESYNSKI, Loris, b Sweden 1949– , illus C

LETARTE, Jean-Paul, b Montreal 1933– , paint M MM

LETELLIER, André, b c 1944– , sculp M

LETENDRE, Rita (m Ulysses Comtois, q.v.; m Eloul Kosso, q.v.), b Drummondville, Que 1928– , paint AGO B CAE1,2 CC2 CE1,2 Co CWW93 DCA IO M MM RCA SC TB3 UG WWA93

LEVASSEUR, Charles (Charly), b Pointe-aux-Trembles, nr Montreal 1723, fl 1744, sculp K

LEVASSEUR, François-Noël (aka Vasseur), b Quebec 1703 – d 1794, carv DCB4 K M MQ

LEVASSEUR, Jacqueline, fl 1965– , paint M

LEVASSEUR, Noël, b Quebec 1679 – d 1740, carv sculp ACA DCB2 K M NGC67

LEVASSEUR, Pierre-Noël, b Quebec 1690 – d 1770, carv sculp DCB3 K M MQ NGC67

LEVASSEUR, Pierre-Noël, b Quebec 1719, fl 1769, carv sculp K

LEVASSEUR, René-Michel, b Boucherville, Que 1724, fl 1758, des K

LEVASSEUR, Stanilas, b Quebec 1732, fl 1784, sculp K

LEVASSEUR dit DELORS, Jean-Antoine (aka Vasseur), b Quebec 1717 – d 1775, carv DCB4 K

LEVENTHAL, Ian, b Toronto 1951– , sculp IO

LEVER, Harry, b England 1920– , fl 1963, paint M

LEVESQUE, Gérald, b Woonsocket, RI 1926– , paint CWW93

LEVESQUE, Isabel, b Castor, Alta 1919– , paint AA

LEVESQUE, Leon, b Pincher Creek, Alta 1931– , sculp SC

LEVESQUE, Solange, b Quebec 1946– , paint M

LEVI SMITH. *See* SMITH, Levi

LEVINE, Leslie Leopold, b Dublin 1935– , Amer, sculp AGO BE CA1–3 CAE1,2 Co CWW93 DAS DCA DCAA2,3 NGC67 WWA93

LEVINE, Marilyn Anne Hayes (m Sidney Levine), b Medicine Hat, Alta 1935– , sculp CA1–3 CAE1 DAS DCA M MM US WWA93

LEVINGE, Richard George Augustus, Lt Col, Sir, 7th Baron (x Levigne[2]), b 1811, d Westmeath, Ire 1884, Eng, paint BPp1599 DBWA DeV5 DNB GW H[2] H77 PNL ROM

LEVINSOHN, Lisl, b Vienna 1924, d 1983, drw M

LEVITT, Marvin Richard (Dick), b Macklin, Sask 1915– , sculp M

LEW, Fon T., b China c 1942– , paint M

LEWICKI, Walter (Wladimir), b Tuapse, USSR 1921– , paint M

LEWIS, Everett (m Maude D. Lewis, q.v.), b 1893, d 1980, paint DFA KB

LEWIS, Glenn Alun (Flakey Rose Hip), b Chemainus, BC 1935– , mur sculp AE DCA M MM WWA93

LEWIS, Harriet, b Montreal c 1941– , paint M

LEWIS, Ivor Rhys, b Wales c 1882, d Toronto 1958, paint sculp CWW55 M RCA

LEWIS, Marion, b Poland 1910– , sculp IO M

LEWIS, Maude Dowlet (m Everett Lewis, q.v.), b Ohio, Yarmouth Co, NS c 1903, d Digby, NS 1970, paint DFA KB M

LEWIS, Percy Wyndham (Wyndham-Lewis[2]), b on yacht 'Wanda,' nr Amherst, NS 1882, d London 1957, Eng, paint ABH[2] B1 CA1,2 DBA

DNB NGC68 OC OCD P TB1 3 WBA1

LEWIS, Robin Baird, b Brantford, Ont 1951– , illus paint C IO

LEWIS, Roy C., b Ottawa, fl 1953– , sculp BCS

LEWIS, Stanley, b Montreal 1930– , des etch gra paint sculp AE CAE1 M MM WWA93

LEWORTHY, John Vernon, b Ft William, re Thunder Bay, Ont 1910– , paint CWW67

L'HERAULT, Jos, fl 1874–95, paint H K

LHERITIER, Régine (m Jean Noel Lavoie), b Paris 1935– , paint prt CWW93

LI, Chi Hung Tam (Mrs), b Shanghai, fl 1960– , paint M

LICASTRO, Joseph, b Toronto 1918– , paint Hu M

LICENSE, R.J., fl 1889–94, d 1896, paint H RCA

LICUSHINE, Dimitry Semenoff, b Rostoff, Rus 1896, paint M MM RCA

LIEBERT, Philippe Pierre (aka Leber), b Nemours, Fr 1733, d Montreal 1804, paint sculp DCB5 H K M MQ NGC67

LIEBICH, Kathleen Chipman Sweeny (Mrs), b Toronto 1892, paint M MM

LIGHT, Richard H., fl 1867 97, drw H

LIGHTBODY, Maya (b Maria Antoinette Smodlibowski) (m Russell N. Lightbody), b Lwow, Pol 1933– , paint sculp M MM

LIGHTMAN, E.J., b Toronto 1952– , sculp IO

LIGNY-BOUDREAU, Pierre de. *See* BOUDREAU, Pierre de Ligny

LIM, John, b Singapore 1932– , paint sculp IO M SAA43

LIM, Sing, b Vancouver 1915– , illus T

LIMA, Thomas (Tom), b Toronto c 1925– , paint M

LIN, Chien Shih, b 1918– , paint CAE2

LIND, Carl Werner, b Sweden 1891, d St Walburg, Sask 1961, paint M W1–3

LINDE, Louise Van der. *See* VAN DER LINDE, Louise

LINDEMERE, Gladys (m Richard Lindemere, q.v.), b Yorks, Eng c 1887, fl 1968, paint DWA M

LINDEMERE, Richard (m Gladys Lindemere, q.v.), b London 1881, d Ladysmith, BC 1956, paint M US

LINDGREN, Charlotte (m Edward Lindgren), b Toronto 1931– , tap CWW93 DCA M RCA WWA91

LINDNER, Degen, b Saskatoon 1943– , paint BDSA

LINDNER, Ernest, b Vienna 1897, d Saskatoon 1988, paint AGO CAE1 CC1 CE1,2 Co CWW88 GM M MM RCA St US WWA89

LINDOE, Luke Orton, b Bashaw, Alta 1913– , paint AO M MM RCA

LINDSAY, Bertrand, fl 1969– , paint sculp M

LINDSAY, Doreen (m Gabor Szilasi), b London, Ont 1934– , paint CWW93 M UG

LINDSAY, Ellen Trider, b Saint John, NB 1900, d Halifax 1964, paint CLA CWW61 M MA MM

LINDSAY, Fanny Lord, b Collingwood, Ont, fl 1895–1936, paint CNS36

LINDSAY, Isobel, fl 1958– , paint M

LINDSAY, Robert Henry, b Prescott, Ont 1868, d Brockville, Ont 1938, paint H Hu M MM PMC RCA

LINDSAY, Stephanie. *See* LE MAN, Stephanie Alexandra

LINDSTROM, Matt, b Finland 1890, d Calgary 1974, paint M SC

LINDZON, Rose, b Poland, fl 1972– , paint CAE2 IO

LINEN/LINNEN, John, b Greenlaw, Scot c 1802, d New York 1888, Amer, paint GW H H77 Y

LINES, Beryl Jones (Mrs), b Port Arthur, re Thunder Bay, Ont, fl 1942+, paint M

LINNELL, Lilian B., b Fredericton 1894, paint AAW3 WWNA

LINSSEN, Benedict Johan Marie, b 1936– , paint prt CAE2
LINTON, Ian, b Hamilton, Ont 1948– , paint CAE1
LIPARI, François Amedeo Angeli (Frank), b Montreal 1927– , des gra illus paint M MM RCA
LIPPERT, Jane Elizabeth, b Kitchener, Ont 1924– , etch mur M
LISHMAN, William (Bill), b Pickering Tp, Ont 1940– , sculp M
LISIANSKI, Yur Fedorovich, b Negin, Rus 1773, d 1837, Rus, paint EMA
LISMER, Arthur, b Sheffield, Eng 1885, d Montreal 1969, paint ACA AE AGO B CC2 CE1,2 Co CWW64 EC H77 M MM NGC1 NGC67 NGC68 PMC RCA S TB2 TN UG US WWA62
LITTLE, Carol, b Calgary, fl 1977– , wlhg SC
LITTLE, James, b Calgary c 1932– , paint sculp M
LITTLE, John Geoffrey Caruthers, b Montreal 1928– , paint M MM NGC1 RCA SC TB1
LITTLE, Margaret, b 1929– , paint prt CAE1
LITTLE BOBS. *See* BIRTWHISTLE, Richard John
LITZGUS, Hazel C. (Mrs), b Lloydminster, Alta 1927– , paint AA M SC
LIVERNOIS, Paul, b Montreal 1948– , paint sculp CAE1 M
LIVESAY, J., fl 1882, paint H
LIVEY, Lorna Jean, b Quebec 1951– , etch paint IO
LIVING, Marion A., fl 1894–1900, paint DWA H MM RCA
LIVINGSTON, Alice, fl 1891–7, paint DWA H MM RCA
LLOY, Arthur George, b Halifax 1929, d 1986, paint M
LLOYD, A. Thomas, b Ireland c 1828, fl 1861, paint H
LLOYD, Patrick A., b Sydney, BC 1942– , paint SC
LLOYD, Thomas Daniel, b Wexford, Ire 1803, fl 1886, paint H
LOARING, David Charles, b Windsor, Ont 1948– , paint sculp IO
LOATES, Martin Glen, b Toronto 1945– , paint CWW93 M RCA
LOBCHUK, William Harry (Bob), b Neepawa, Man 1942– , prt CAE2 SC
LOBO, Fernandes Jose, b Mozambique 1921– , paint MFMS
LOCAS, Serge, b 1960– , car paint M
LOCHHEAD, Douglas Grant, b Guelph, Ont 1922– , paint CC2
LOCHHEAD, Kenneth Campbell, b Ottawa 1926– , paint ACA AE AGO CC1 CE1,2 CWW93 DCA H77 M MM NGC1 NGC67 RCA SC TB3 UG WWA73
LOCHNER, Ellen Sigrid (Mrs), b Dresden, Ge 1925– , paint prt CAE1 IO M
LOCK, Frederick William, fl 1842–71, Eng, min paint B BM DVP Fo G GW H ROM TB1
LOCKE, F.D., fl 1950+, paint M
LOCKERBY, David William, Lt Col, b Montreal 1869, paint H Mo12
LOCKERBY, Mabel Irene, b Montreal 1887 – d 1976, paint AGO DWA Hu M MM NGC1 RCA TB2
LOCKWOOD, Alvira, b Madrid, NY 1845, fl 1923, paint DWA H
LOCKWOOD, William, b England c 1803, d Quebec 1866, min DFA H H77
LOCKYER, Elizabeth Prat Nixon (m Frank Sabbin Lockyer), b Kentville, NS 1890, paint CLA
LODGE, Jeanine, b Paris, Fr 1937– , sculp IO
LODGE, Judith, b 1941– , paint CAE2
LODOEN, Jeanette Posnikoff, b Blaine Lake, Sask 1935– , paint BDSA KB
LOEFFLER, Charles (Karl Frederich), b c 1823, d Vienna 1905, paint B GW H TB1
LOEHNDORF, Christine, b Allan, Sask 1941– , paint BDSA
LOEMANS, Alexander Francis/Alexandre François, b France, fl 1864–94, paint AAW2 H K MM RCA Sam

LOEWE, Eric, b Munich, Ge 1892, paint M

LOFFLER, J., b Germany c 1814, fl 1861, paint H

LOGAN, Archibald David (Dan[2]), b St Catharines, Ont 1918– , paint sculp M[2]

LOGAN, Martha Alexander (Mrs), b Hartford, Conn 1863, d Toronto 1937, paint DWA H M MM RCA

LOGAN, Robert Fulton, b Lauder, Man 1889, d Boston 1959, etch paint AAA33 CWW48 F M TB1,2 WWA62 WWWA

LOGAN, Stan, fl 1940+, paint M

LOGAN, William Edmond, Sir, b Montreal 1798, d Gilgerran, Wales 1875, crto drgt CE1,2 DCB10 DNB EC H LeJ W1–3

LOGGIE, John Millar, b Langside, Scot 1896, paint CNS36 MM RCA

LOH, Joseph Sinn Kuen, b Canton 1948– , paint IO

LOHN, George, b Natal, BC 1934– , paint M

LOHNES, Jeannette Ross (Mrs), b Stellarton, Picton Co, NS 1915– , paint M

LOISELLE, Miche, b Roberval, Lac St-Jean, Que, fl 1963– , paint M

LOISELLE, Yvonne, fl 1960– , paint M

LOIZIDES, Marios, b Cyprus c 1931– , paint M

LOM d'ARCE, Louis-Armand de. *See* LA HONTAN, Louis-Armand de Lom d'Arce, Baron

LOMER, Lorna Gertrude (m Robert R. Macaulay[2]), b Montreal 1881, fl 1949, paint DWA[2] M[2] MM RCA

LONDON, Peter, b 1939– , paint M

LONEY, William Glenworth, b 1878, d 1956, carv paint DFA H74 KB

LONG, Anna Lee. *See* BANANA, Anna

LONG, Beatrice Mary Carter (Mrs), b Kirton, Eng 1877, paint DWA M MM

LONG, Joy Zemel (m Jack Long), b Vancouver, fl 1959– , paint M

LONG, Marion, b Toronto 1882 – d 1970, paint AGO CWW67 DWA FCA M MM NGC1 O.F50 RCA TB2,3 US W3 WWA66

LONG, Victor Albert, b Ft Erie, Ont 1866, d Vancouver 1938, paint H M US

LONG, Wilfrid Elvin, b Regina 1912– , paint M

LONGHURST, William Belsey, b Canterbury, Eng 1847, carv Mo12

LONGMAN, John B., b Toronto 1860, paint AAA06

LONGTIN, J. Oswald, fl 1945+, paint M

LONGUL, Ross, b c 1945– , fl 1969, car paint M

LONN, George, b Rocanville, Sask 1914– , paint M

LONSDALE, 5th Earl. *See* LOWTHER, Hugh Cecil

LOOKER, Lorne, b Kitchener, Ont, fl 1954– , sculp M

LOOMIS, Clarence Ainslie, b Toronto 1917– , paint M RCA

LOOMIS, William Andrew, b Syracuse, NY 1892, d 1957/9, Amer, paint AAA33 AAW1,2 APH IA1,2 WWA53

LOOS, Walter, b Saskatchewan, fl 1917+, paint M

LORAIN, Richard, b France 1929– , des paint M

LORANGER, Georges, b Sherbrooke, Que 1931– , paint DCA M MM

LORCINI, Gino, b Plymouth, Eng 1923– , sculp B Co CWW93 IO M MM RCA US WWA93

LORD, Shirley (Mrs), b Hanley, Sask 1938– , paint ABC

LORENZ/LORENS, Frederick William, b Stuttgart, Ge 1827, d Montreal 1913, paint H

LORENZ, Helen Frances. *See* GREGOR, Helen Frances Lorenz

LORIMER, Amy McClellan (m Frederick Lorimer), b Toronto 1893, d c 1950, paint DWA WWA47d53

LORING, Beth Rogers McLaughlin (m Thomas J. Loring), b Toronto 1919– , paint M

LORING, Frances Norma, b Wardner, Idaho 1887, d Newmarket, Ont 1968, sculp AGO CC2 CE1,2 Co CWW64 DWA EC M MM NGC1 NGC68 O.N48 RCA St TB2 UG W3 WWA62 WWC68

LORION, Louis, fl 1823–7, sculp K

LORNE, Louise Caroline Alberta, Marchioness of. *See* LOUISE, Caroline Alberta, HRH Princess

LORNE, Marquis of. *See* ARGYLL, John Douglas Sutherland Campbell

LORT, John Cecil Rolston, b Victoria, BC 1914– , ske CWW88

LORT, Ross Anthony, b Birmingham, Eng 1889, d Vancouver 1968, paint CWW64 M

LORTI, François. *See* NISKA

LOTH, Cedric, b St-Jerome, Que 1955– , cart Des

LOTT, Isiah, b Buffalo, NY 1938– , paint IO

LOTT, Sheena (Mrs), b Glasgow 1950– , paint ABC

LOU. *See* SKUCE, Thomas Louis

LOUCH, Anne Ethelyn, b Ontario 1898, fl 1975, etch paint IO

LOUDON, Isabel Mary, b Toronto 1884, des paint DWA M MM RCA

LOUDON, John Samuel, b Armagh, Ire 1851, d Toronto 1933, paint R2

LOUGHEED, Deborah Sinclair, b Edmonton, fl 1970– , paint MFMS

LOUGHEED, Margaret, b British Columbia, fl 1929+, paint M

LOUGHEED, Robert Elmer, b Massey, Ont 1910– , illus paint M MM RCA Sam WWA82

LOUISE Caroline Alberta, HRH Princess (m John Douglas Sutherland Campbell, Marquis of Lorne, 9th Duke of Argyll[2], q.v.), b Windsor Castle 1848, d Kensington Palace 1939, Eng, paint sculp AKL[2] BPp103 DBA DBWA DNB H Mo12p1197 RCA

LOUISE DE SAVOIE (Soeur). *See* TELLIER, Antoinette

LOUISON, Maurice, b nr Broadview, Sask 1945– , paint KB

LOUVIN. *See* VINEBERG, Louise

LOVAS, Leslie (Laszlo), b Kapasvar, Hu 1915– , gra paint PHA

LOVE, Elisabeth (Lisa) (m Paul Love), b Delbourne, Alta, fl 1944+, paint M

LOVE, Mary Heaviside[2], Lady (m Lt Col Sir James Frederick Love), b Halifax 1806, fl 1866, paint DCB9[2] DNB DWA H M

LOVEJOY, Margot MacDonald (m Derek Lovejoy), b Campbellton, NB 1930– , paint M

LOVER, Samuel, b Dublin 1797, d Jersey, CI 1868, Eng, min paint B BM Bry DBLP DIA DNB DVLP DVP Fo G Red TB1

LOVEROFF, Frederic Nicholas (b Postnikoff), b Tiflis, Rus 1894, d Redwood City, Calif 1959, paint AGO CC2 Hu M MM NGC1 PMC RCA TB2 US

LOVETT, W. Norman, b c 1888, fl 1930–66, paint M

LOW, Colin Archibald, b Cardston, Alta 1926– , drw M

LOW, Thomas, b Glasgow 1875, fl 1934, paint M RCA

LOWE, Frederic C., fl 1843–56, engr DeV8 H

LOWE, Nellie Keillor (m Kenneth Lowe), b Baggot, Man c 1917, d Sudbury, Ont 1967, paint M MM

LOWE, Stephen Won H., b Taoshien, Kwangtung Prov, Chi 1938, d 1975, paint M

LOWELL, Orson Byron, b Wyoming, Iowa 1871, d New Rochelle, NY 1956, Amer, cart paint AAA33 F Sam WECa WHC WWA56d59 WWWA

LOWENTHAL, Myra, b Belgrade, Yu 1947– , paint CWW93

LOWER, Alice Mary Fulford. *See* FULFORD, Alice Mary

LOWERY, Richard, b Newcastle-on-Tyne, Eng 1910– , paint CWW93

LOWN, John H., b Waterford, Ont, fl 1968– , paint M

LOWREY, John D., fl 1935+, d St-Sauveur, Que 1945, paint M

LOWTHER, Hugh Cecil, 5th Earl of Lonsdale[2], b London 1857, d Barley Thorpe, Eng 1944, Eng, paint BPp1652[2] DNB H WWB29

LUBBERS, Theodore, b Netherlands 1922– , stgl M

LUBOJANSKA, Janina (Mrs), b Poland 1934– , paint M

LUC, Frère. *See* FRANCOIS, Claude, dit LUC, Frère

LUCAS, Helen Billie Geatros (m Derek Fuller), b Weyburn, Sask 1931– , paint BDSA IO M

LUCAS-TROWELL, Ian Douglas. *See* TROWELL, Ian Douglas Lucas

LUCASSIE Kittosuck, E9-103, b Belcher Isld, NWT 1908– , sculp DEA

LUCASSIE Kittosuk, E9-174, b Belcher Isld, NWT 1949– , sculp DEA

LUCIANI, Tony, b Toronto 1956– , paint CWW93

LUCKOCK, Charles Warren, b Toronto 1915– , paint sculp AGO M MM O.Ag49

LUCOW, Marion (m Maurice Lucow), b Winnipeg 1918– , paint M RCA

LUCY QINNUAYUAK, E7-1068 (m Tikitok, E7-1067, q.v.), b nr Sugluk, Que 1915, d Cape Dorset, NWT 1982, prt CE1,2 DEAp138

LUDLAM, Mary Ann Mason (m Arthur W. Ludlam), b Oshawa, Ont 1933– , paint CWW93

LUDLOW, Gregory Charles, b Brampton, Ont 1954– , paint IO

LUKACHKO, Andreas Leonard (Andrew), b Czechoslovakia 1927– , paint M RCA

LUKAS, Dennis Brian, b Hamilton, Ont 1947 , paint sculp IO M WWA93

LUKE, Jane Corbus (m E.B. Luke), b Chicago 1881, fl 1922–45, paint M MM RCA

LUKE, Margaret Alexandra (m Marcus Everett Smith; m Clarence Ewart McLaughlin), b Montreal 1901, d Oshawa, Ont 1967, paint CWW64 M MM RCA TB3 WWA70

LUKEMAN, Edward Arthur, b Toronto 1924– , paint M NGC1 O.My50 RCA TB3

LUKER, Louise H. *See* BURRELL, Louise H. Luker

LUKTA/LUKTAK[2]/QIATSUK[3], E7-1060, b nr Cape Dorset, NWT 1928– , prt sculp CWW93[3] DEAp139 S[2]

LUMBERS, James Richard, b Toronto 1929– , paint M WWA93

LUMSDEN, Ernest Stephen (m Mabel A. Royds, q.v.), b London 1883, d Edinburgh 1948, Eng, etch paint DBA DScP RA SW WBA1 WWB34 WWW

LUMSDEN, Mabel Alington Royds. *See* ROYDS, Mabel Alington

LUND, Carl Christian, b Newcastle-on-Tyne, Eng 1874, paint M MM RCA

LUND, Knut, b Norway c 1909– , sculp M MM

LUNDBERG, Sten, fl 1965– , paint M

LUNEAU, Claude Pierre, b Paris 1935– , sculp CWW93 WWA93

LUNN, Gwendolen Carlton (Mrs), b England 1920– , paint M

LUPPEN, François-C. Van[2], b Antwerp 1838, d St-Josse-Ten-Noode, Bel 1899, Bel, sculp B K[2] RCA TB1

LUSSIER, Pierre, b 1945– , paint CAE1

LUTHI, Ernest (Ernie), b Zurich, Swi 1906– , paint US

LUTKENHAUS, Almuth Katrina Wirsing (m Klaus Muthing; m Arthur Lackey), b Hamm, Ge 1927– , sculp IO M

LUTYENS, Charles August Henry, b 1829, d 1915, Eng, paint B DBA DVP G H TB1 WBA1 WHC

LUTZ, Jurgen, b Germany, fl 1965– , paint M

LUZ, Virginia Erskine, b Toronto 1911– , paint CWW93 IO M O.F51 RCA WWA93

LUZNY, Thomas A., b Inwood, Man c 1924– , paint M

LYALL, Laura Adeline Muntz[2] (m Charles W.B. Lyall), b Radfork, War 1860, d Toronto 1930, paint AGO B[2] CC1 DWA H H77 Hu M MM[2] Mo12[2] NGC1 RCA[2] TB3 W1–3

LYLE, Florence Lorraine Newby (m Alexander Lyle), b Chilliwack, BC, fl 1940+, paint CNS44

LYLE, John MacIntosh, b Connor, Ire 1872, d Toronto 1945, paint CE1,2 Co NGC1 RCA TB3

LYMAN, John Goodwin, b Biddeford, Me 1886, d Barbados 1967, paint ACA B CC2 CE1,2 CLA Co CWW64 H77 Hu M MM MQ NGC1 NGC67 OC RCA TB2 TN W3 WWA66d70

LYMAN, Roswell Corse, b Montreal 1850 – d 1892, paint H

LYMAN, Walter Kenneth Gordon, b Montreal 1897 – d 1951, paint MM PMC RCA

LYNCH, James O'Connor, b Sydney, NS 1908– , drw MM RCA WWA62

LYNCH, Kathleen R., b Cornwall, Ont, fl 1972, paint ABC

LYNN, James, b Canada 1855, d Port Huron, Mich 1924, paint DMR

LYNN, Washington Frank, b Chelsea, London 1827/37, d London 1906, Eng, paint DCB13 H H77

LYON, George Francis, Capt (x Lyons), b 1795, d 1832, fl 1808–32, Eng, paint topog DMA DNB Hp203

LYON, Harold Lloyd, b Windsor, Ont 1930– , paint CAE1 M WWA82

LYON, N.T., fl 1880–90, paint stgl H RCA

LYONS, Catherine, fl 1848, paint AGO H

LYONS, Jamie Joseph, b Minneapolis, Minn 1946– , paint IO

LYPCHUK, Camellia (Caml), b Chilliwack, BC 1939– , paint IO

LYSAK, Adriana, b Ukraine 1930– , prt CAE1,2

LYSONS, Daniel, Gen, Sir, b Rodmarton, Glos 1816, d England 1898, Eng, paint DNB H

LYTLE, William, b Toronto, fl 1963– , mur paint M

LYTTLETON, Westcott Witchurch, Capt, b c 1818, d Keswick, Eng 1879, Eng, topog DeV9 H H77 ROM

LYWOOD, Ken, b 1935– , paint M

MAARTENSE, Gertrude Jacoba (Mrs), b Leerdam, Neth 1918– , paint sculp CAE1 M

MABIE, Donald Edward, b Calgary 1947– , drw mmed AA CAE1 M WWA80

McADAM, Gerald Victor, b Oshawa, Ont 1941– , paint AGO M US

McADAM, Josiah Wilson, b Brantford, Ont 1858, d Vancouver 1941, paint H

McANSH, Joan Regina Brough-Bayley (m Andrew McAnsh), b London 1920– , paint BDSA

McARTHUR, Betty Marie, b 1923– , paint IO RCA

McARTHUR, John C., fl 1876–86, paint H MM

MacARTHUR, Lucille Casey. *See* CASEY, Lucille C.

McAULAY, Anthony, b Macclesfield, Eng 1947– , paint IO

McAULIFFE, James J., b St John's, Nfld 1848, d Midford, Mass 1921– , paint AAA18d28 F H Y

McAVITY, Catharine (m J. Patrick McAvity), b Moncton, NB 1915– , paint CAE1 M

McAVITY, Emily Dorothy Irvin (m Harry Haddon McAvity), b Halifax 1876 – d 1958, paint DWA M

MacBEAN, Clara Sophia, b Coburg, Ont 1841, fl 1911, paint DFA DWA H M MM RCA

McBEAN, F.M., Lt Col, fl 1840–4, paint topog H

McBRIDE, Donald, b St Catharines,

Ont c 1923, d Niagara Falls, Ont 1971, paint M MM RCA

McBRYAN, Evy, fl 1960– , paint M

McCAFFREY, John Allan, b Liverpool, NS 1904– , paint M MM

McCALL, Alice Howe (m F.J. McCall), b Exeter, Dev 1882, paint WWNA

McCALL, Ann, b Toronto 1941– , paint prt RCA SC US WWA93

McCALLUM, Donald (Mrs), b Baltimore, Md c 1885, fl 1965, paint DWA M

McCANN, Joan. *See* SPENCER, Joan McCann

McCARA, Marianne. *See* McCLAIN, Marianne McCara

McCARGAR, William C., b Newcastle, Ont 1906, d 1980, paint CAE1 DFA KB

McCARROLL, Bill J., b USA 1937– , paint SC

McCARTER, John Alexander, b Wareham, Eng 1918– , paint CWW93

McCARTHY, Barry, b Deep River, Ont 1951– , paint prt IO

MacCARTHY, Coeur de Lion, b London c 1881, d Montreal 1979, sculp MM PMC RCA

McCARTHY, Doris Jean, b Calgary 1910– , paint sculp AGO CWW93 DCA Hu IO M MM RCA SC UG WWA93

MacCARTHY, Hamilton Thomas Carleton Plantagenet, b London 1846, d Ottawa 1939, sculp B CWW36 DBA EC G M MM Mo98,12 NGC1 PMC RCA TB1,3 W1–3

McCARTHY, Roderick Leon Ottoman (Rick), b Montreal 1941– , paint sculp IO

McCARTHY, S. (Mrs), fl 1866–78, paint sculp H

McCAUGHEY, Betty M. French[2] (m Lloyd O. McCaughey), b London, Ont 1921– , paint M MM[2] RCA S

MACAULAY, Catherine Marsha, b Swift Current, Sask 1949– , paint BDSA

MACAULAY, John Philip Rankin, b Montreal 1912– , paint M MM RCA

MACAULAY, Lorna Gertrude Lomer. *See* LOMER, Lorna Gertrude

McCAUSLAND, Joseph, b Armagh Co, Ire 1828, d Toronto 1905, stgl DCB13 H M

McCAUSLAND, Robert, b Toronto 1856 – d 1923, stgl H M Mo12

McCLAIN, Helen Charleton L., b Toronto 1884 (x1887), d 1960, paint AAA33 DWA F M O.F48 RCA WWA40

McCLAIN, Marianne McCara (m William C. McClain), b Edmonton 1920– , sculp ABC

McCLELLAN, Norma Harriet (m Douglas McClellan), b Windsor, Ont 1913– , paint M

McCLELLAND, Jeannette E., b Calgary, fl 1977, pas SC

McCLELLAND, John, fl 1964– , paint M

McCLURE, Dorothy Clark (Mrs), b Guelph, Ont, fl 1967– , paint M

McCOMB, Eleanor (Mrs), b Toronto, fl 1968– , paint M

McCONNELL, Brian Douglas, b Gaspé, Que 1836, fl 1860–80, paint DFA Mo12 ROM

McCONNELL, Clyde S., b Los Angeles 1944– , paint AA M

McCONNELL, Elisha Newton, b Lakeview, Ont 1877, cart Mo12

McCONNELL, James (Jim), b Belfast, Ire, fl 1968– , paint M

McCONNELL, John, b Ireland 1937– , paint M

McCONNELL, M. Cary (Miss), b Blyth, Huron Co, Ont, fl 1890–1939/40, paint H Hu MM RCA

McCONNELL, Newton, b Elgin Co, Ont 1872, d Toronto 1940, cart Des

McCORD, Anne Ross (m John Samuel McCord), fl 1841–52, paint H

McCORD, David Ross, b Montreal 1844 – d 1930, drw DFA EC H Mo12 W1–3

McCORD, George Herbert, b New

York 1848/9 – d 1909, Amer, paint AAA09 ANC App F

MacCORMACK, Jamie, b Ottawa 1951– , drw sculp M

McCORMACK, Laura June Forbes (m Edward McCormack), b London 1921, d Toronto 1961, paint M

McCORMACK, M. (Miss), fl 1891–2, paint H

McCORMICK, Arthur David, b Coleraine, Ire 1860, d London 1943, Eng, illus paint B DBA DBWA DWP G H RA TB1,3 WBA1 WWB34 WWW

McCORMICK, Robert, b Runham, Eng 1800, d Wimbledon, nr London 1890, Eng, topog DCB11 DNB H

McCORMICK, Stuart, b nr Alexandria, Ont c 1900, fl 1968, paint M

McCRACKEN, Thea (Mrs), b Glasgow 1950– , paint M

MacCRAE, George, b Edinburgh, fl 1783–1802, Scot, paint H H77

McCREA, Harold Wellington, b Peterborough, Ont 1887, d Toronto 1969, paint AGO M NGC1 O.F48 RCA TB1

McCREA, Stanley James, b Lethbridge, Alta 1929– , paint M

McCREADY, Warren Thomas, b New York 1915– , paint CWW93

McCROW, William Frederick Jon, b Princeton, Ont 1913– , paint M

McCUE, John Arthur Wilson, b Toronto 1943– , paint IO M

McCULLAGH, Lavoine, b Kitchener, Ont 1945– , tap SC

McCULLOCH, Mabel (m Donald M. Gass[2]), b New Glasgow, NS 1889, d 1977, paint CLA DWA MA[2] MM WWA62

McCULLOUGH, Kay (m John McCullough), b Thunder Bay, Ont, fl 1958– , paint M

McCURDY, Patricia Ann, fl 1954– , paint M

MacDERMID, Margaret Vickers (m Fred J. MacDermid), b Chicago 1899, paint BDSA

McDERMOTT, Arthur, b Ireland, fl 1969– , paint M

McDERMOTT, Dennis, b Portsmouth, Eng 1922– , paint CWW93

MacDIARMID, John Duncan/L.D., fl 1838–48, topog H ROM

MacDONALD, Albert Angus, b Bristol, Eng 1909, d 1986, paint sculp CWW86 Hu M MM O.F48 RCA

McDONALD, Alexander A., fl 1886–91, paint H

MACDONALD, Archibald St Aubyn, b Verdun, Que 1931– , paint M MM

MacDONALD, Blaine (s Blaine[2]), b Glace Bay, NS 1937– , cart Des[2] M Po[2]86–88

MacDONALD, Charles William, b 1874, d 1967, paint sculp DFA KB

MacDONALD, Cim, b Ardrossan, Scot, fl 1970– , paint ABC

MacDONALD, Colin Somerled, b Ottawa 1925– , paint M WWA93

MacDONALD, D. Claude, fl 1951– , paint M

MACDONALD, Elsie Amy (m N.S. Macdonald), b Camberwell, London 1906– , paint M MM

MacDONALD, Errol David, b Halifax 1924– , paint M RCA

MacDONALD, Evan Weekes, b Guelph, Ont 1905 – d 1972, illus paint CNS40 CWW73 M MM O.My48 RCA UG

MACDONALD, Grant Kenneth, b Montreal 1909, d Kingston, Ont 1987, illus paint AE AGO CC1 CWW87 EC IO M MM O.F51 RCA S TB2 WWA86

MacDONALD, Harriett J. *See* MacDONNELL, Harriett J.

MACDONALD, James Alexander Stirling, b Abbey, Sask 1921– , paint sculp CC1 M MM NGC1 RCA TB3

McDONALD, James B., b Sudbury, Ont 1932– , paint sculp IO M

MACDONALD, James Edward Hervey, b Durham, Eng 1873, d Toronto 1932, paint ACA AE AGO CC2 CE1,2 Co EC G H77 Hu L M MM

NGC1 NGC67 OC R2 RCA S Sam TB2 TN UG W1–3

MACDONALD, James Williamson Galloway (Jock), b Thurso, Scot 1897, d Toronto 1960, paint AE AGO CC2 CE1,2 Co CWW58 GM H77 Hu M MM NGC1 NGC67 O.Ag49 OC OCD RCA Sam TB2 W2,3 WBA2 WWA59d62 WWB60 WWNA

MACDONALD, Jock. *See* MACDONALD, James Williamson Galloway

MACDONALD, Malcolm Philip, b Stornoway, Scot 1879, d Toronto 1965, etch paint AGO RCA

MacDONALD, Manly Edward, b Point Anne, Ont 1889, d Toronto 1971, gra paint AE AGO CC2 CWW67 Hu M MM NGC1 NGC68 RCA TB2 UG WWA70

MacDONALD, Margaret Ellis (m Douglas M. MacDonald), b Toronto 1919– , paint M

McDONALD, Mary, b Toronto, fl 1971– , paint M

MacDONALD, Murray William, b Baddeck, NS 1898, d Edmonton 1989, paint CLA M

MacDONALD, Myles J., b New York 1941– , paint CWW93 SC

MacDONALD, Neil, b Vancouver 1943– , paint ABC

MACDONALD, Norman, b c 1941– , fl 1966– , paint M

MacDONALD, Rae Hendershot. *See* HENDERSHOT, Rae

MacDONALD, Ronald B., b Amherst, NS 1948– , drw paint sculp IO

MacDONALD, Rose/Rosa. *See* WILLIS, Rose/Rosa MacDonald (Rosa)

McDONALD, Rosemary Lavinia (m Arthur H. McDonald), b Saint John, NB 1924– , pas M

MacDONALD, Thomas, fl 1825–37, litho paint DFA KB NGC67

MacDONALD, Thomas Reid (m Rae Hendershot, q.v.), b Montreal 1908, d Paris 1978, paint CWW73 M MM NGC1 NGC68 O.Ag49 RCA TB3 WWA78d80

MacDONALD, Thoreau, b nr Toronto 1901– , illus paint AGO CC1 CE1,2 Co GM Hu M NGC1 RCA TB2 WWA78

McDONALD, Veronica Pridham (m Keith McDonald) (s Vie McDonald; Veronica), b Kelowna, BC, fl 1957– , paint M

MacDONALD, Wallace B., b Espanola, Ont 1919– , cart Des

MACDONALD, Wilson Pugsley, b Cheapside, Ont 1880, etch CWW64 PMC

McDONIC, Henry Reed (Harry), b W Hartlepool, Eng 1902, d Toronto 1982, paint Hu MM RCA

McDONNELL, Doolee Merry, b W Kootenays, BC, fl 1976– , paint ABC

MacDONNELL, Harriett J. (x MacDonald[2]), fl 1882–1922, paint H[2] MM RCA

McDOUGALL, Clark Holmes, b St Thomas, Ont 1921, d 1980, paint IO M MM O.Ag50

McDOUGALL, George F., fl 1850–4, d 1870, Eng, topog DMA H

MacDOUGALL, James Ian, b Toronto 1936– , engr BB

McDOUGALL, Katharine E. *See* WILSON, Katharine E. McDougall

MACDOUGALL, Ken, b Sault Ste Marie, Ont c 1933– , paint M

MacDOUGALL, Marianne Adelaide Miles, Lady (1860 m Patrick Leonard MacDougall[2], Gen, Sir), b England, fl 1881, Eng, paint DCB12[2] DNB[2] H RCA

MacDOUGALL, Nini Keefer (m Peter MacDougall), b Ottawa 1915– , paint M

McDOWALL, Catherine, b Scotland, fl 1956– , paint M

McELCHERAN, William Hadd, b Hamilton, Ont 1927– , sculp CAE1 M RCA WWA86

McELHERON, James Thomas, b Vancouver 1935– , paint M MM
McELROY, George Eldon, b Richmond, Ont c 1878, d Ottawa 1945, illus paint M
MacELWAIN, Peter Brown, b Windsor, Ont 1948– , sculp IO
McEVOY, Bernard (s Thomas Redbarn), b Birmingham, Eng 1842, d Vancouver 1932, paint CWW10 H Mo12 R2 W1–3
McEVOY, Henry Nesbitt (Harry), b Birmingham, Eng 1828, d Detroit 1914, paint AAA14d28 GW H MM RCA Y
MacEWEN, Christina Jean, b Toronto 1946– , cer sculp IO
McEWEN, Jean Albert, b Montreal 1923– , paint AE AGO B CC1 CE1,2 Co CWW93 M MM MQ NGC67 P RCA TB3 US WWA93
McEWEN, John Alan, b Toronto 1945– , sculp CWW93 IO
McFADDEN, Mary (Mrs), b London, Ont 1930– , paint M
McFADDEN, Mary Josephine, b Ekfrid Tp, Ont 1900– , paint M
McFADDIN, Charles Eugene, b Millbank, Ont 1910– , paint O.Ag49
McFARLAND, Constance M., b Nardin, Okla 1897, paint M
MacFARLANE, David Huron, b Montreal 1875, d Mont-St-Hilaire, Que 1950, paint M MM PMC RCA
McFARLANE, Jan (Mrs), b 1925– , fl 1952– , paint M
MacGEE, Chris, b Peterborough, Ont 1951– , paint DCA
McGEOCH, Lillian Jean McKittrick (m Rae McGeoch), b Sundridge, Ont 1903/4, paint sculp CLA M WWA82
McGIFFIN, Norah, b Ottawa 1905 – d 1960, paint M
McGILL, Harold, b Yarmouth, NS, fl 1894–1912, cart Mo12
McGILL, Marie, b Vancouver 1926– , paint wlhg CAE1,2
McGILL, Winnifred Grace. *See* FOX, Winnifred Grace McGill
MacGILLIVRAY, Dougald John, b Windsor, Ont 1905– , paint M
McGILLIVRAY, Florence Helena, b Whitby, Ont 1864, d Ottawa 1938, paint AAA33 AE AGO B CWW36 DBA DWA F H Hu M MM NGC1 RCA ROM TB2 Y
MacGILLIVRAY, John William, b Toronto 1927– , paint M
McGILLIVRAY, Margaret, b Meaford, Ont, fl 1906–28, paint AAA28
McGIVERIN, Harold MacKintosh, b Ottawa 1900, d Victoria, BC 1937, paint M MM RCA
McGIVNEY/McGIVENY, Jean Margaret, b Toronto 1949– , paint IO
McGOUN, Lachlan, b Scotland 1837, d Napanee, Ont 1896, paint EC
McGOVERN, Beatrice Hatfield (m Albert D. McGovern), b Derbyshire, d Saint John, NB 1967, paint M
MacGOWAN, Clara (m Edward Cloban), b Montreal 1895, paint AAA33 DWA WWA53
McGRATH, Joan Margaret, b Great Britain 1932– , prt IO
MacGREGOR, Charles, b Edinburgh 1893, paint AGO Hu M RCA UG
McGREGOR, Edward/Edwin, fl 1847–72, paint GW H H77
McGREGOR, Hone, b Prince Albert, Sask 1920– , paint prt M
MacGREGOR, James Gamble, b Glasgow 1898, paint M MM RCA
MacGREGOR, John Boyko, b Dorking, Eng 1944– , drw paint sculp CAE2 CWW93 IO M MM UG WWA86
MacGREGOR, Larry, b 1945– , sculp M
McGREGOR, Robert, b Saskatoon 1933– , drw US
MacGREGOR, William Firth, b Edinburgh 1896, paint Hu
McGUIRE, Claudette Boulanger. *See* BOULANGER, Claudette
McGUIRE, Patrick Samuel, b 1943, d 1970, paint IO M
MACHAR, Agnes Maule (pseud Fidelis), b Kingston 1837, d Gananoque,

nr Kingston 1927, paint CWW10 DWA H Mo98,12 R1

McILWRAITH/McILLWRAITH, William Forsyth, b Galt, Ont 1867, d Fishkill, NY 1940, etch illus paint AAW1 Sam WWNA

McILWORTH, Thomas, b Scotland, fl 1757–70, paint GW H

McINDOE, Marion C. (m Fred C. McIndoe), fl 1897–1914, paint H MM

McINNES, Harvey A., b 1904– , paint DFA

McINNIS, Robert Francis Michael, b Saint John, NB 1942– , paint CWW93 M

McINTOSH, Don, b Vancouver 1927– , paint M

McINTOSH, Ian William (m Sylvia H.S.G. McIntosh, q.v.), b Vancouver 1931– , prt sculp M

McINTOSH, Sylvia Helen Scott Golman (m Ian William McIntosh, q.v.), b N Vancouver 1930– , etch paint M

McINTYRE, Edgar, b Charlo Station, NB, fl 1966– , sculp M

McINTYRE, Iona, b Bowen Isld, BC 1930– , illus paint M

MACINTYRE, Marjory Shives, b Saint John, NB 1898, paint CAE1 MA MM

MACK, Mary Agnes, b Cornwall, Ont 1899, paint DWA M MM RCA

McKAGUE, Muriel Yvonne. *See* HOUSSER, Muriel Yvonne McKague

McKALE, Daniel, b Pointe-aux-Chênes, Que 1951– , cart Des

MACKAY, Ailsa Margueritte, b Manitoba 1918– , paint CAE1

McKAY, Arthur Fortescue, b Nipawin, Sask 1926– , paint AGO CC2 CE1,2 H77 M MM NGC67 SC TB3 UG US WWA93

MACKAY, Barry Kent, b Toronto 1943– , paint M

MACKAY, Bill, b Edmonton 1953– , cart Po88

MACKAY, Donald Cameron, b Fredericton 1906, d 1979, paint CLA GM M MA NGC68 RCA WWA78 WWB80

MACKAY, Donald Ian, b Jahnsi, India 1937– , paint prt IO

McKAY, Gladys (m Harold McKay), fl 1949+, paint M

McKAY, Ian, b Maryport, Cumb 1949– , paint UG

MACKAY, J.R., fl 1862–4, topog DFA

MacKAY/McKAY, James G., b Hamilton, Ont, fl 1873–85, cart engr Des DeV5 H

McKAY, James William, b Port Alice, BC 1939– , paint US

MacKAY, Jean V. (Mrs Heinrich), b Halifax 1909– , sculp DAS WWA53

McKAY, Joseph William, b Rupert House, James Bay, Que 1829, d Victoria, BC 1900, paint DCB12 H W1–3

MACKAY, Marion Florence S. *See* NICOLL, Marion Florence S. Mackay

McKAY, Mary Muriel, b Collingwood, Ont 1906– , paint M

MacKAY, Tom, fl 1963– , paint M

McKAY, William, fl 1864–79, paint stgl H

McKEAN, Janet Cordelia, b Pictou, NS 1887, paint CLA MM

McKECHNIE, Neil Kenneth, b England 1873, d Birch Cliff, Ont 1951, paint W2–3

McKEE, John Robert, b Sudbury, Ont 1941– , paint CWW93

MacKEEMAN, Karl Douglas, b Halifax 1948– , prt CAE1,2

McKELVEY, Marianne O'Dell, b London, Ont 1891, paint DWA

McKENNY, Rosalie McQueen (m John McKenny; m Arthur Setterington), b Olunder, nr Kingsville, Ont 1856, fl 1898, paint DWA H

MacKENZIE, Alice Beirne Sawtelle (m Hugh MacKenzie), b Ft Riley, Kans 1898, illus paint O.Ag50 RCA

McKENZIE, Charles, b Inverness, Scot 1933– , paint sculp M

MACKENZIE, Frank J., b London 1865,

d San Francisco 1939, Amer, paint AC M WWA38d40

MacKENZIE, Helen Winifred. *See* LAMPMAN, Helen Winifred MacKenzie

MACKENZIE, Hugh Seaforth, b Toronto 1928– , etch paint IO M MM RCA WWA93

MacKENZIE, Landon, b Boston 1954– , paint CWW93

MACKENZIE, Percival Molson. *See* RITCHIE, Percival Molson Mackenzie

McKENZIE, Robert Tait, b Almonte, Ont 1867, d Philadelphia 1938, paint sculp AAA33 AGO B CC2 CE1,2 Co CWW36 DAS DBA EC F G H M MM Mo98,12 NCAB NGC1 RA RCA TB2 W1–3 WWA36d40 WWWA Y

MacKENZIE, Robin, b Pickering Tp, Ont 1938– , sculp CAE1,2 IO M MM US

McKENZIE, Ruth Tye, b Edmonton 1929– , etch paint IO

MACKERETH, Elaine Louise Muth. *See* MUTH, Elaine Louise

MacKEY, Eleanor Dorothy Johnston (Mrs), b Port Colborne, Ont 1932– , paint M

MACKEY, J.R., fl 1862–4, topog H

MACKIE, Catherine M., b Montreal 1943– , paint M

MACKIE, Helen, b Ontario 1926– , prt SC

McKIE, Mary R. (x MacKie), fl 1840–62, paint APH DFA H PNL

McKIEL, Christian (Mrs), b Pictou, NS 1889, paint pas DWA M MA MM RCA

McKIM, Irene (m James McKim), b Kingston, Ont, fl 1965– , paint CAE2 IO M RCA

McKINLAY, Duncan E., b Orillia, Ont 1862, fl 1911+, Amer, paint CWW10 Mo12 WWWA

McKINLEY, Donald Lloyd, b Bartlesville, Okla 1932– , des IO WWA82

McKINLEY, Ruth Gowdy (m Donald Lloyd McKinley), b Brooklyn, NY 1931, d 1981, des IO RCA WWA82

MacKINNON, Bruce, b Nova Scotia, fl 1955– , cart Po87

MacKINNON, Frank, b Charlottetown 1919– , paint CLA

McKINNON, John Charles, b Brantford, Ont 1953– , sculp IO

McKINNON, Shirley B. *See* RUSSELL, Shirley B. McKinnon

MacKINNON-PEARSON, Ella Cecilia (m Ian MacKinnon-Pearson, q.v.), b St Catharines, Ont 1882/7/9, paint AAA31 DWA M MM

MacKINNON-PEARSON, Ian (m Ella Cecilia MacKinnon-Pearson, q.v.), b Bearsdon, nr Glasgow 1896, etch paint M MM UG WWA53

MACKINTOSH, Gladys Kathleen. *See* EWAN, Gladys Kathleen Mackintosh

McKITTRICK, Lillian Jean. *See* McGEOCH, Lillian Jean McKittrick

MACKLIN, Edith, b nr Fenella, Ont 1871, fl 1963, paint M

MACKNIGHT, Dodge, b Providence, RI 1860, d 1950, Amer, paint AAA33 AAW2 B F TB1,2 WWA40

MacLACHLAN, Graham Martin, b Winnipeg 1914– , paint CWW82

MacLACHLAN, Winnifred Ann Knowles (m Peter N. MacLachlan), b Winnipeg 1913– , paint M

MacLAGAN, David, b 1932– , paint ABC

McLAREN, Alex, b Lisbon, Port 1892, fl 1969, illus paint M

MacLAREN, Frances Mary Hewson (m George Edward Gordon MacLaren, q.v.), b Baddeck, NS 1918– , paint M

MacLAREN, George Edward Gordon (m Frances M.H. MacLaren, q.v.), b Pictou, NS 1909– , carv M

McLAREN, John Wilson (Jack), b Edinburgh 1896, paint AGO GM M RCA

McLAREN, Norman, b Stirling, Scot 1914, d Montreal 1987, anim paint prt sculp CA1 CAE1 CC1 CE1,2

CGA2 Co CWW86 M MM RCA WECa WWA86 WWGA1,2

MacLAUGHLAN, Donald Shaw, b nr Charlottetown 1876, d c 1938, Amer, etch paint AAA33 F M TB1 WWWA Y

McLAUGHLIN, Agnes, b c 1920– , paint DFA KB

McLAUGHLIN, Beth Rogers. *See* LORING, Beth Rogers McLaughlin

McLAUGHLIN, Isabel Grace, b Oshawa, Ont 1903– , paint AE AGO CE1,2 CWW84 Hu M MM NGC1 RCA TB3

McLAY, Peter Milton, b 1952– , engr etch IO

MacLEAN, Donna, b 1914– , paint tap CAE1

MACLEAN, Donna (Mrs), b 1918– , paint M

McLEAN, George Elson, b Toronto 1939– , paint CWW93 M

McLEAN, Jack Lee, b Vancouver 1924– , paint M

McLEAN, Robert, b Wahamun Lake, Man 1933– , paint CAE1

MACLEAN, Sarah Jean Munro (m Lachlan A. Maclean), b Pictou, NS 1873, d Montreal 1952, paint CNS40 DWA Hu M MM NGC1 RCA TB3

MACLEAN, Susan, b Manitoba 1880, paint BDSA

McLEAN, Terry, b Virden, Man c 1935– , paint M

McLEAN, Thomas Wesley, b Kendal, nr Port Hope, Ont 1881, d Toronto 1951, paint AGO M RCA

MacLEAY, Rosanna MacLeay Stewart (m Stewart MacLeay), b Wakarusa, Kans 1887, fl 1945, paint M MM RCA

MacLELLAN, Charles Archibald, b Trenton, Ont 1885, illus paint AAA33 F TB2 WWA62

McLELLAN, James, b Edinburgh 1899, gra illus Hu M

MacLELLAN, John Borland, b Stevenston, Ayrs 1913– , paint M RCA

MacLELLAN, Morna Isabelle, b Pictou, NS 1905– , paint CLA MM

MacLENNAN, Dorothy Duncan. *See* DUNCAN, Dorothy

McLENNAN, Louise Ruggles Bradley (m John S. McLennan), b Chicago 1860, d Sydney, NS 1912, paint H MM RCA

McLENNAN, S.B., fl 1882, paint H RCA

MacLENNAN, Toby Chapman, b Detroit 1939– , sculp CAE1

MacLEOD, Alexander Samuel, b Orwell, PEI 1888, d c 1961, etch paint AAA31 AAW1 AC F TB2 WWA62

McLEOD, Donald Ivan, b Owen Sound, Ont 1886, d 1967, paint CWW64 Hu M RCA WWA40

McLEOD, Elizabeth A. Fraser (Mrs), b Point de Bute, NB 1875, d Sackville, NB 1963, paint MA MM RCA

MacLEOD, Grace (Mrs Roberts[2]), b MacCrimmon, Glengarry Co, Ont 1899, d 1982, paint DWA H[2] M MM[2]

MacLEOD, Hazel A. Parks (m D.J. MacLeod), b Napanee, Ont, fl 1957–, paint M MA MM

MacLEOD, Ian, fl 1976– , des paint M

McLEOD, Pauline Margaret (s P. McLeod), b Owen Sound, Ont 1954– , paint IO

MacLEOD, Pegi Nicol[2] (Margaret Kathleen Nichol; m Norman MacLeod), b Listowel, Ont 1904, d New York 1949, paint ACA AGO CC1 CE1,2 EC H77 Hu[2] M MM[2] NGC1 NGC68 RCA[2] Sam TB2 WWA47

McLEOD, Susan Duplan, b London, Ont 1953– , paint sculp IO

McLORN, Devona Lorraine Paquette. *See* PAQUETTE, Devona Lorraine

McLOUGHLIN, Bernard, b Ft William, re Thunder Bay, Ont 1925– , mur paint M RCA

MACLURE, Margaret Catherine (m M.C. Maclure), b Greenock,

Scot 1869, d Victoria, BC 1938, paint WWNA

McLURE, Samuel, b Sapperton, nr New Westminster, BC 1860, d Victoria, BC 1929, paint CE1,2 Co H PMC RCA

McMASTER, Juliet Sylvia Fazan (m Rowland Douglas McMaster), b Kisumu, Kenya 1937– , sculp CWW93

MacMELLON, Jack, b Yarmouth, NS 1911, cart Des

MacMILLAN, Duncan Park, b Cornwall, Ont 1873, fl 1908, paint H MM RCA

MacMILLAN, Ruth F. Hall (m William MacMillan), fl 1965– , paint M

McMULLEN, Ralph Spencer, b Picton, Ont 1885, paint Hu M

McMURRAY, William, b New Westminster, BC, fl 1980– , paint ABC

McMURRICH, Norman Hay, b Toronto 1920– , ske CWW93

McMURTRIE, William Birch, b Philadelphia 1816, d 1872, Amer, paint AAW1 AC DFA GW H Y

McMURTRY, Roland Roy, b Toronto 1932– , paint CWW93

McNAIR, Marguerite, b Victoria Co, NB, fl 1965– , paint M

McNALLY, Edwin Dean, b Ft William, re Thunder Bay, Ont 1916, d Franklin Centre, nr Montreal 1971, cart paint Des M

McNALLY, Lorne William, b Port Colborne, Ont 1942– , paint M MM RCA

MacNAMARA, Gordon Robertson, b Toronto 1910– , paint M MM WWA62

McNAMEE, Donald Keith, b Assiniboia, Sask 1938– , paint M

McNAUGHT, Kenneth, b Toronto 1918– , ske CWW93

McNAUGHT, William Carlton, b Toronto 1888, paint CWW58

McNAUGHTON, Audrey Watts, b Toronto, fl 1957– , paint M

MacNAUGHTON, John H., fl 1876–99, paint H MM RCA

McNEALY, Robert, b Twin Falls, Idaho 1942– , paint sculp IO WWA93

McNEELY, Thomas Ross, b Toronto 1935– , paint M

McNEIL, David Keith, b Chatham, Ont 1952– , paint IO M

McNEIL, Joan Elsie, b Jonquière, Que 1941– , drw sculp BDSA

McNEILL, Denise Elena Therrien. *See* THERRIEN, Denise Elena

McNEILL, Richard John, b Northampton, Eng 1946– , paint sculp IO

McNEILLEDGE, Alexander, b Greenock, Scot 1791, d nr Port Dover, Ont 1874, paint DFA KB

McNICOLL, Helen Galloway, b Toronto 1879, d Swanage, Eng 1915, paint CC1 DBA DWA Hu M MM NGC1 RCA TB3 W1–3

McNIFF, Peggy E., b Chatham, Ont 1950– , drw pas sculp IO

MacNUTT, Glenn Gordon, b London, Ont 1906, d 1987, paint WWA86d88

McNUTT, H.R. (Miss), fl 1890–2, paint H RCA

MacPHEE, Medrie (m Harold Crooks), b Edmonton 1953– , drw paint CWW93

McPHERSON, Aileen McGeer (Mrs), fl 1961– , paint M

MACPHERSON, Annie A.H. (m D.B. Macpherson), fl 1887–96, paint H MM RCA

MACPHERSON, Duncan Ian, b Toronto 1924, d Beaverton, Ont 1993, cart paint AGO CE1,2 Co CWW93 Des M Po86–88 RCA WECa

MACPHERSON, Kenneth Rose, b Montreal 1860 – d 1916, paint H MM RCA

MacPHERSON, Margaret Campbell, b St John's, Nfld, fl 1885–1907, paint B DBA DVP DWA G H Mo12 TB1

McPHERSON, Murdoch, b Canada 1841, d 1915, paint DMA DSP

MacPHERSON, Penelope Glasser

(Mrs), b Kitchener, Ont 1943– , paint IO

MacPHERSON, Robert L., b Greenwood, NS 1952– , paint SC

McPHERSON, Ruth Patric. *See* PATRIC, Ruth

MACREDIE, Alice Clarke, b Calgary 1913– , paint BDSA

McRITCHIE, Donald, b Englishtown, NS 1881, d Halifax 1948, cart CWW38 Des

McTAGGART, Ernest Royal, b Kempville, Ont 1889, d Vancouver 1958, cart paint Des

McTAVISH, Robert, b 1888, d 1966, carv DFA M

McTIGHE, Anne, b Canada, fl 1900+, paint AAA27 DWA WWA40

MacVICAR, Anna. *See* RUSSELL, Anna MacVicar

MacVICAR, Annie, fl 1895–1900, paint H M

MacVICAR, Donald Norman, b Montreal 1869 – d 1929, paint MM PMC RCA

McVICAR, Mervin E.B., fl 1943+, paint M

McVITTIE, Robert, b England c 1935– , paint M

MacWILLIAM, David Charles, b Halifax 1951– , paint CWW93

McWILLIAMS, Allan J., b Vancouver 1944– , sculp CAE2 RCA

MACY, W.S., fl 1882, illus H

MADAY, Hélène Julia (Mrs), b Hungary 1916– , sculp IO M

MADDEN, Orval Clinton, b Napanee, Ont 1892, d Toronto 1971, paint Hu M MM RCA

MADSEN, Aage, b Riersley, Dn 1898, sculp M WWA62

MADSEN, Britta, fl 1964– , paint M

MADSEN, Katy/Katie (Mrs), fl 1964– , paint pas M

MAGAR, Ralph, b Richmond, BC, fl 1967– , paint M

MAGGS, Arnaud Cyril Benvenuti, b Montreal 1926/7– , gra TB3 WWA93

MAGOON, Ida May, b Mansonville, Que 1901– , paint AAA28

MAGOR, Elizabeth (Liz), b 1948– , sculp CAE2 DCA

MAGRILL, Cyril, b Dublin c 1908– , paint DFA

MAGUIRE, Thomas, fl 1807–23, paint H

MAH, Peter, b China 1946– , drw paint IO UG WWA82

MAH, Ping, b Kwantung, Chi 1946– , paint M UG

MAHDI, Wadie (El Mahdy[2], Wadie), b Cairo 1921– , paint CWW84[2] M

MAHIAS, Robert, b Brussels 1890, fl 1925, Fr, paint B K MM TB2

MAHON, Charles Augustus, b Montreal 1867, fl 1931+, paint H MM RCA

MAIBAUER, Ulli Gerhard Max, b Berlin, Ge 1929– , paint M

MAILLARD, Charles, b Tiaret, Alg 1887, d Montreal 1973, paint K M MM RCA

MAILLARD, Charles-Adrien, Msgr, b Montreuil-sur-Mer, Fr 1873, d Montreal 1939, paint B K M

MAILLET, Corinne Dupuis[2] (s Rhobena Dippy, Colin Martel), b Montreal 1895, paint DWA K [2] M MM RCA[2]

MAILLY, Jules, b Noray-l'Archevèque, nr Besançon, Fr 1828, d Paris 1884, Fr, paint sculp K

MAITLAND, H.B., b Port Perry, Ont 1895, paint CWW58

MAITLAND, Peregrine, Sir, b Hampshire 1777, d London 1854, Eng, topog CE1,2 DCB8 DNB EC H LeJ W1–3

MAJOR, Charlotte Ruth, b Sarnia, Ont 1893, paint AAA30 DWA WWA40

MAJOR, Geraldine (m Baron Wrangel; m H. Chisholm), fl 1922–50, paint DBA MM RCA

MAJOR, Laure, b Montreal 1930– , paint M MM

MAJOR, Richard Walter, b Toronto 1899, paint Hu M MM RCA

MAJUMDER, Khaletun (m Soumen Majumder), b Rajskami, Ban 1942– , des illus MF
MAKA, Jahan, b Lithuania 1900– , paint DFA KB
MAKI, Sheila Anne, b Sudbury, Ont 1932– , paint prt CAE2 IO M WWA93
MAKPA ARNASUNGNARK, Vital, E2-120 (m Angele Krashudluak, E2-187, q.v.), b Baker Lake, NWT 1922– , prt sculp DEAp142
MALACH, Josephine Lorraine, b Regina 1933– , mur paint BDSA M
MALCHI, Bezalel, b Simno, Lith 1902– , sculp CNS40 M MM RCA
MALCOLM, Bess Hull (Mrs), b Dutton, Ont 1909– , paint M
MALCOURONNE, Kathleen Delacour, b Montreal 1855 – d 1951, illus paint M MM
MALCZEWSKI, Rafal, b Crakow, Pol 1892, paint M MM
MALEPART de BEAUCOURT, François. *See* BEAUCOURT, François Malepart de
MALER, Miroslav, b Horni Becva, Cz 1946– , sculp S
MALHAME, Violette (Mrs), b nr Geneva, Swi, fl 1959– , paint M
MALIKTUNUK. *See* NALUKTURUK/MALIKTUNUK, Josephie
MALISH, Miro, b Bratislava, Cz 1944– , drw paint CAE1,2 IO
MALKIN, Louise Walters. *See* WALTERS, Louise
MALLANDAINE, Edward, b Singapore 1827, d Victoria, BC 1905, ske topog DCB13 H
MALLEPART de GRAND MAISON, Paul. *See* BEAUCOURT, Paul Mallepart de Grand Maison dit
MALLET, Denis, b Alençon, Fr c 1670, d Montreal 1704, carv DCB2 K
MALLETTE, Phil, b Sault Ste Marie, Ont 1955– , cart Des Po86–88
MALO, Pierre-Aimé, b Montreal 1859/60 – d 1924, sculp K
MALONE, Richard Sankey, Brig, b Owen Sound, Ont 1909– , paint CWW85
MALTAIS, Marcelle, b Chicoutimi, Que 1933– , paint M MM TB3
MALTWOOD, Katherine Emma Sapsworth (m John Maltwood), b England 1878, d Victoria, BC c 1961, sculp DBA DWA RA WBA2 WWB34
MAMCHURE, Kenneth Christopher, b Toronto 1947– , paint IO
MANAREY, Thelma Alberta (m C.H. Manarey), b Edmonton 1913, d 1984, etch paint AA M SC WWA84
MANCUSO, Fred, b Lachine, Que 1925– , paint MF
MANDAGGIO, Eddie, b Lorne, Man 1927 , carv paint CWW93
MANGOLD, Carl, b Trimback, Swi 1901– , mur paint M MM RCA
MANGULINS, Shanie, b England 1943– , etch paint IO
MANIAS, Grace, b Milan, It 1942– , sculp IO RCA
MANIGAULT, Edward Middleton, b London, Ont 1887, d San Francisco 1922, paint AAA22d28 F TB1
MANLEY, Elizabeth Alberta (m Donald Manly), b Winnipeg 1938– , paint sculp CAE1 IO M
MANLY, Charles MacDonald, b Englefield Green, Sur 1855, d Toronto 1924, gra paint AE AGO CC2 CE1 DVLP DVP EC H H77 Hu M MM NGC1 RCA Sr TB3 W1-3 WBA2
MANN, Cy (b Glicksman), b Toronto 1928– , anim cart CWW93
MANN, Ellen Vaughan Kirk Grayson. *See* GRAYSON, Ellen Vaughan Kirk
MANN, Margaret (m Nick Butuk), b Eatonia, nr Kindersley, Sask 1913– , paint CAE1 M
MANN, Norman Whitefield, b Shoeburyness, Eng 1882, d 1953, paint PMC
MANNGUQSUALUK, Victoria, b nr Back River, NWT 1930– , drw paint sculp CWW93

MANNING, Joan Elizabeth, b Sidney, BC 1923– , etch paint CAE2 CWW93 IO M RCA SC UG WWA93
MANNO, E7–887, b Frobisher Bay, NWT 1923– , sculp DEA
MANNY, Nicolas, b St-Luc, Que 1811/12, d Beauharnois, Que 1883, sculp K
MANORE, Harriet Estelle. *See* CARTER, Harriet Estelle Manore
MANSARAM, Panchal, b Mount Abu, India 1934– , etch paint IO RCA WWA93
MANSELL, Victoria, b London 1951– , drw etch paint prt IO
MANUEL, Evelyn, fl 1963– , paint M
MANUEL, Leon W.L., b Lulu Isld, nr Vancouver 1903– , paint M
MANUEL, Mildred Beamish Brooks (m Charles Edward Manuel), b Liverpool, NS 1899, paint CLA DWA M
MANWOMAN. *See* KEMBALL, Patrick Charles
MARA, E.A., fl 1862–3, paint H
MARACLE, Clifford Lloyd, b Tyendingo Res, nr Deseronto, Ont c 1944– , paint Co IO
MARANGONI, Christine (m Aldo Marangoni), fl 1960– , paint M
MARATTA, Hardesty Gillmore, b Chicago 1864 – d 1924, Amer, paint AAAd28 AAW2 H
MARCEL IDEA, MARCEL DOT. *See* MORRIS, Michael William
MARCH, Herrat, b Angola, Port, fl 1962– , paint M
MARCH, Peter, fl 1846–51, paint H
MARCHAK, Maureen Patricia Russell (m William Marchak), b Lethbridge, Alta 1936– , paint CWW93
MARCHAND, Andrée, b Montreal 1935– , sculp tap DCA
MARCHAND, Gilles, b Shawinigan, Que 1949– , paint M
MARCHAND, Jean-Omer, b Montreal 1873 – d 1936, paint K
MARCHAND, Lauren Margaret, b Kerobert, Sask 1949– , paint BDSA
MARCHAND, Nicole (Mrs), b Ottawa, fl 1965– , paint M
MARCHANT, Christopher L., b Montreal 1944– , sculp M
MARCHESSAULT, Jovette, b Montreal 1938– , paint M
MARCHIORI, Carlos, b Italy 1937– , illus paint M
MARCIL, Joseph, b 1941– , carv M
MARCIL, René, b Montreal 1917– , paint pas IO
MARCOE, Leonard, fl 1972– , prt M
MARCOTTE, Edouard, b 1884, d 1957, sculp K
MARCOTTE, Pauline, b St-Raymond-Portneuf, Que 1920– , paint CAE1 M
MARCOU, Jules, b Salins-les-Bains, Fr 1824, d Cambridge, Mass 1898, Fr, drw K Sam
MARCOUX, Joseph, b Quebec 1791, d Caughnawaga, Que 1855, paint DCB8 H K LeJ
MARCOUX, Omer, fl 1930–41, sculp K
MARCUS, Ella, fl 1957– , paint M
MARCUS, Richard (b Miskiewicz), b Barquismeto, Ven 1951– , des sculp CWW93
MARDON, Allan, fl 1931+, illus IA2 M
MARDON, John, fl 1967– , illus paint M
MARE, John (s Jno Mare), b New York c 1739, fl 1795, Amer, paint DAA F GW H TB1
MAREGA, Charles (Carlos), b Lucinico Trieste, It 1871, d Vancouver 1939, sculp M WWNA
MARI, Paul, b USSR c 1919, fl 1951– , paint M
MARICH, Geza (Gordon), b Budapest 1913– , paint M MM
MARIE-ANASTASIE (Soeur), b Mont-Laurier, Que 1909– , paint sculp CAE1
MARIE-ANDREE-de-SAINTE-HELENE (Mère). *See* DUPLESSIS, Marie-Andrée Regnard
MARIE BARBIER dite de L'ASSOMPTION (Soeur). *See* BARBIER, Marie

MARIE-BERNARDETTE de L'IMMACULEE CONCEPTION (Mère). *See* BURON, Berthe
MARIE-CLEONICE de SAINT-SACREMENT (Soeur). *See* CHABOYER, Véronique
MARIE de JESUS (Soeur). *See* ANGER/ANGERS, Marie-Elmina
MARIE-de-LA-GARDE (Soeur), fl 1931+, paint K
MARIE-de-L'EUCHARISTIE (Soeur). *See* LEFEBVRE, Marie-Elmina
MARIE de L'INCARNATION (Mère). *See* GUYART, Marie
MARIE-de-SAINT-AUBIN (Soeur). *See* AUBIN, Alma
MARIE de SAINTE-CROIX (Soeur). *See* VANDER HEYDEN, Louise
MARIE-de-SAINT-JEAN-BERCHMANS (Soeur). *See* FRECHETTE, Célina
MARIE-de-SAINTE-VIRGINIE. *See* RHEAUME, Marie-Elmina
MARIE-EUSTOCHIUM (Soeur). *See* HEBERT, Artémise
MARIE-HELENE-de-la-CROIX. *See* MARTIN, Elisabeth
MARIE-IRMA (Soeur). *See* SAINT-PIERRE, Marie-Blanche
MARIE-LEONILLE (Soeur). *See* LEMIRE, Marie-Florida-Melina
MARIE-LOUISE-GUSTAVE (Soeur). *See* BOURGEOIS, Marie
MARIE-MADELEINE-de-SAINT-LOUIS (Soeur). *See* MAUFILS, Marie-Madeleine
MARIE-PHILIPPINE (Soeur). *See* BERARD, Germaine
MARIE-SAINTE-VERONIQUE (Soeur). *See* NOLIN, Géraldine Montgomery
MARION, Gilbert, b Montreal 1933– , gra paint AGO M MM
MARION, Israel, fl 1886, drw H K
MARION, Jules, fl 1851, d Montreal 1878, engr DeV3 H K
MARION, Rachel Potvin (m Ulysse Marion, q.v.), b Richelieu Valley, Que, paint M
MARION, Salomon/Sozoman, b c 1783, d 1832, sculp M
MARION, Ulysse (m Rachel P. Marion, q.v.), b Lyon, Fr, fl 1942+, paint M
MARKELL, Jack Harold, b Winnipeg 1919, d N Vancouver 1979, paint M MM NGC1 RCA TB3 WWA62
MARKEN, Joslin Robertson (s Marken Joslin) (m M. Marken), fl 1968– , paint M
MARKGRAF, Peter Franz, b Munich, Ge 1924– , gra M
MARKGRAF, Waltraud/Traudl[2] (m Gerhard Doerrie), b Hanover, Ge 1937– , paint AGO Mp1112[1,2] MM
MARKHAM, David H., fl 1850–1, ske H
MARKHAM, Michael J., b 1946– , paint M
MARKHAM, Peggy (Mrs), b Montreal 1932– , paint M
MARKIEWICZ, William (s Wilek), b Cracow, Pol 1935– , paint pas IO
MARKLE, Edna E., b Weyburn, Sask 1907 , paint BDSA
MARKLE, Jack M., b Winnipeg 1939– , sculp CAE1 WWA93
MARKLE, Robert Nelson, b Hamilton, Que 1936, d nr Holstein, Ont 1990, paint AE AGO CAE1 CC1 DCA IO M MM
MARKLE, Sam, b Winnipeg 1932– , mmed sculp CAE1 M WWA93
MARKS, Esther (m Malcolm Marks), b Glasgow, fl 1965– , sculp M
MARKSTEIN, Aurelia (s Ora), b Hungary 1924– , sculp IO
MARLAY, Thomas George, Lt, b Scotland 1809, d Saint John, NB 1937, engr H
MAROIS, A., fl 1882–6, drw H RCA
MAROIS, Joseph C./A., fl 1882–90, paint H K
MAROIS, Lauréat, b St-Euphrem-de-Beauce, Que 1949– , gra prt CAE1,2 M SG

MAROIS, Marcel, b Quebec 1949– , prt wlhg CAE1 MQ
MAROK, John (Jack), b Nanaimo, BC 1930– , paint M
MAROSAN, Julius, b Budapest 1915– , paint sculp AGO M PHA
MARQUETTE, Hilda Sophia. *See* RUSTON, Hilda Sophia Marquette
MARQUIS, Lyse D'Amours (m Robert Marquis), b c 1941– , paint M
MARR, Octavia Elizabeth Tyler Hayward (m Bertram Henry Marr), b Waverly, NS 1891, paint CLA DWA M
MARRYAT, Frederick, Capt, b London 1792, d Langham, Norf 1848, Eng, car paint DMA DNB
MARSEILLE, Jean Natte dit. *See* NATTE dit MARSEILLE, Jean-Sébastien
MARSH, Anne Cynthia. *See* EVANS, Anne Cynthia Marsh
MARSH, Annette, b Victoria Co, Ont, fl 1926+, paint M
MARSH, Bessie Thomson, b Toronto 1883, paint pas Mo12
MARSH, Peter, fl 1965– , paint sculp M
MARSH, Winnifred Florence Petchey. *See* PETCHEY, Winnifred Florence
MARSHALL, David Franklin, b Islay, Alta 1928– , sculp BCS M
MARSHALL, Lois C., b Toronto 1924– , paint CWW93
MARSHALL, Patricia J., b Granby, Que 1951– , sculp IO
MARSHALL, Victoria (Vicky), b England 1952– , paint CWW93
MARSIGLIA, Gerlando/Gherlando, b Italy 1792/7, d New York 1850, Amer, paint B F G W H TB1 WWWA
MARSOT, Jacques, b St-Jean, Que 1944– , cer M
MARSTON/MARSDEN, Benjamin, b Salem, Mass 1730, d Bolama, Portuguese Guinea 1792, Eng, topog DCB4 H
MARTCHENKO, Michael, b Carcassone, Fr 1942– , illus CBC CWW93 SAA50
MARTEL, Colin. *See* MAILLET, Corinne Dupuis
MARTEL, Elisée (s A.E. Martel[2]), b 1881, d 1965, paint K MM[2]
MARTEL, Gisèle, b Montreal c 1942– , etch paint M
MARTEL, Jacqueline Panneton (m Paul-Emil Martel), b Trois-Rivières, Que 1922– , paint M
MARTEL, Joan Frances (s Joan Willsher-Martel), b Victoria, BC 1925– , paint IO
MARTEL, Joseph, fl 1792, drw H K
MARTEL, Raymond, b France, fl c 1900, d 1915, Fr, drw K
MARTEL, Richard, b Bagotville, Ont 1950– , cer sculp WWA93
MARTEL, William T., fl 1961– , paint M
MARTELL, I. Arleigh (m Peter Armstrong), fl 1936+, paint M
MARTEN, Thomas Henry Oake, b Leamington, Ont 1880, d Toronto 1950, gra illus M Mo12
MARTENS, Cornelius, b Ukraine 1918– , sculp AA
MARTIAL, Lucien Raoul Jean, b Paris 1892, fl 1937, paint B K M MM TB2
MARTIN, b Quebec Prov 1862, fl 1899, paint H K
MARTIN, Agnes Bernice Fenwick, b Macklin, Sask 1912– , Amer, paint BDSA CA3 DCAA3 M WA WWA91
MARTIN, Annie D., fl 1885–94, paint H RCA
MARTIN, Bernice Fenwick (m Langton Martin, q.v.), b Shelbourne, Ont 1912– , paint RCA WWA82
MARTIN, David, b c 1917, d at sea nr Vancouver Isld 1959, sculp M
MARTIN, Dorothy Murray (m James Ellis Martin), b St Peters, NS 1909, d Oak Ridge, Tenn 1984, paint BDSA
MARTIN, Douglas William, b Toronto 1948– , paint prt CAE1,2 M
MARTIN, Elisabeth (Soeur Marie-

Hélène-de-la-Croix), b St-Jacques, Que 1861, d 1956, paint K
MARTIN, Emma May, b Toronto 1865, d Montreal 1957, paint CNS40 DWA H MM O.F50 RCA
MARTIN, Felix (François-Marie), b Auray, Fr 1804, d Paris 1886, Fr, paint DCB11 H K LeJ
MARTIN, H. George, b London 1921– , paint CWW84
MARTIN, Henry (Hy), b Painswick, Glos c 1832, d Toronto 1902, paint H MM RCA
MARTIN, J. Ronald, b Glace Bay, NS c 1930– , paint Mp1130
MARTIN, Jacques, b Edmundston, NB 1952– , paint sculp CAE1
MARTIN, James M., b Yorkshire, fl 1969– , paint M
MARTIN, Jane (m Ewan Duncan McCuaig), b Montreal 1943– , paint CAE2 CWW93 DCA IO M WWA93
MARTIN, John (Jack), b Nuneaton, War 1904, d Ayr, Ont 1965, engr paint CWW61 DFA M MM O.F48 RCA WWA70
MARTIN, John Henry, b Toronto 1941– , paint prt IO M
MARTIN, Kenneth F., b Winnipeg 1914– , paint M
MARTIN, Langton (m Bernice Fenwick Martin, q.v.), b Toronto 1903– , paint WWA82
MARTIN, Lise, b Montreal 1966– , sculp M
MARTIN, Mungo, b Ft Rupert, BC c 1879, d Victoria, BC 1962, carv CE1,2 Co CWW58 DFA M W3 WWA78
MARTIN, Nancy, b England 1906– , fl 1970s, paint AC
MARTIN, Ronald Albert, b London, Ont 1943– , paint sculp CA1–3 CAE1,2 CE1 CWW93 DCA IO M MM WWA86
MARTIN, S.W., fl 1842+, paint DFA H74 KB
MARTIN, Ted, b Blackpool, Eng 1938– , cart Des
MARTIN, Thomas Mower, b Inner Temple, London 1838, d Toronto 1934, paint AGO App CC2 CWW10 H Hu M MM Mo98,12 NGC1 PMC RCA ROM S Sam TB3 UG W1–3
MARTIN, W.W. (Mrs), fl 1948+, paint M
MARTIN DE LINO, Antoine (Guillaume) (Père Antoine) (s M. Dulino), b Quebec 1690 – d 1773, paint DCB2 H K
MARTINEAU/MARTINO, E., fl 1873–4, paint H K
MARTINEAU, H. (Lt[2]), fl 1876, illus H[2] K
MARTINEAU, Lucienne Lemieux[2] (m Alphonse Martineau), b Montreal 1890, fl 1955, paint DWA K[2] M
MARTINEAU, Mary Ella Maud. *See* JEMMETT, Mary Ella Maud Martineau
MARTINEAU, Michel, b 1956, fl 1978– , paint prt M
MARTINEAU, Paul, b Bryson, Que 1921– , paint CWW93
MARTINEAU, Rolande (Mrs Vaillancourt), fl 1966– , paint M
MARTINEAU, W. Stanley, b Montreal 1915– , sculp M
MARTON, Jirina Kakubuv (Mrs), b Liberec, Cz 1946– , des illus MFMS
MARTON, Joseph, b Hungary c 1930– , sculp M
MARTUCCI, Carmen William, b Montreal 1922– , paint M MM
MARTYN, Carol, b Stratford, Ont 1916/18– , paint pas CAE1 IO RCA
MARX, May (m Karl Marx), b Toronto 1928– , prt sculp IO M RCA
MASCIUCH, John Edward. *See* NEON, John
MASON, Ambrose Wilcock, b Bickleigh, nr Plymouth, Eng 1851, fl 1883–6, paint H
MASON, David, fl 1964– , paint M
MASON, Michelle, fl 1971– , paint M
MASON, Patrick, b Ottawa 1948– , paint M

MASON, William Clifford, b Winnipeg 1929, d Meech Lake, Que 1988, paint CWW88 RCA WWA89

MASSAM, Bryan Hazelwood, b England 1940– , paint CWW93

MASSE, Bob, fl 1970– , drw CAE2

MASSE, Georges-Sévère, b Montreal 1918– , paint MM RCA WWA76

MASSELOTTE, Antonio, b Quebec Prov, fl 1911–37, paint K MM

MASSELOTTE, Paul-Gaston, b Paris c 1848, d Quebec 1895, paint H K

MASSEY, Hart Parkin Vincent (s Clayton Norfield), b Toronto 1918– , met CWW93

MASSEY, John, b Toronto 1950– , paint DCA

MASSEY, John B., fl 1830–1, sil H

MASSEY, Pixie Mudge, b Toronto 1944– , sculp IO RCA

MASSICOTTE, Edmond-Joseph, b Ste-Cunégonde, Montreal 1875, d Sault-au-Récollet, Que 1929, illus paint CE1,2 K M Mo12 W1–3

MASSON, Francis, b Aberdeen 1741, d Montreal 1805, Scot, paint DBF DNB

MASSON, Henri Leopold, b Namur, Bel 1907– , paint ACA AE AGO B CC2 CE1,2 CWW93 DCA M MM MQ NGC1 O.Ag49 RCA S SC TB2 WWA80 WWB91

MASSON, Margaret, b Peterborough, Ont, paint AAA33 WWA38

MASSON, Marik, fl 1964– , sculp M

MASSON, Mary, fl 1964– , sculp M

MASSON, Raymond, b Terrebonne, Que 1860, d 1944, sculp K MM

MASSON-APPS, William, b Kent, Eng 1929– , paint sculp CAE1

MASSOT, Andrée, b Provence, Fr, fl 1957– , paint M

MASSY, Auguste, fl 1877–8, des H K

MATHESON, Audrey, fl 1966– , paint M

MATHESON, Roderick Darey, b Ottawa 1897, paint M MM

MATHEWS/MATTHEWS, George, b England c 1816, fl 1864, engr litho DeV3 H

MATHEWS, Ralph Godard, b Toronto 1888, paint NGC68

MATHEWS, Richard George, b Montreal 1870, paint pas CWW10 MM Mo12 RCA WWB34

MATHEWS, Thomas Edward, b Montreal 1920– , paint IO M

MATHEY, Jean, b Switzerland, fl 1824, paint K

MATHIES, J.L.D., fl 1816–48, paint GW H

MATHIEU, Philippe, fl 1880s, paint H K

MATHIEU, Pierre, b Montreal 1933– , paint CWW93

MATHUR, Florence, b 1934– , paint CAE1 RCA

MATHUSIE, Peter[2], E9-1316, b Povungnituk, Que 1936– , sculp AGO DEAp190[2]

MATROSOVS, Ursula, b Kassel, Ge 1941– , tap DCA IO M

MATSON, Graham, b London 1934– , paint WWA82

MATSUBARA, Naoko, b Tokushima, Japan 1937– , prt IO WWA93

MATTAR, John Soloman, b Haifa, Is 1935– , paint IO M RCA

MATTE, François, b Les-Ecureuils, Que c 1808 – d 1839, paint H K NGC67

MATTE, Jacques Denys, b Cap-Santé, Portneuf, Que 1930– , drw paint CAE2 M MM TB3

MATTE, Madeleine (Mimi). *See* PACKHAM, Madeleine Matte (Mimi)

MATTEAU, Philippe (s Matto[2]), b Trois-Rivières, Que 1921– , min paint M[2]

MATTHEWS, John Edmund, b Ottawa 1942– , sculp IO M

MATTHEWS, Marmaduke, b Barchester, Eng 1837, d Toronto 1913, paint AGO CC1 EC H Hu LeJ M MM Mo98,12 NGC1 R2 RCA ROM Sam TB3 W1–3

MATTHEWS, Peter Allan, b Montreal 1931– , paint M MM
MATTICE, Hortense Crompton. *See* GORDON, Hortense Crompton Mattice
MATTO. *See* MATTEAU, Philippe
MATTOCK, Donald, fl 1967– , paint M
MAUFILS, Marie-Madeleine (Soeur Marie-Madeleine-de-Saint-Louis), b Ste-Anne-de-Beaupré, Que 1671, d Hôtel-Dieu, Quebec 1702, paint DCB2 DWA H H77 K
MAUNDER, John, fl 1962– , paint M
MAUPAS, Emile, b Evreux, Fr 1874, d 1948, sculp K MM
MAURAULT, Thomas-Marie-Olivier, Abbé, b L'Isle-Verte, Que 1839, d Nicolet, Que 1887, paint H K
MAURIN. *See* MORIN, Maurice
MAUSER-BAIN, Lynn, b Oakland, Calif 1944– , gra AA
MAW, Katharine Beatrice (Betty) (m Gerard Brett[2]), b Hull, Eng 1910– , paint CWW89[2] Hu MM RCA
MAW, Samuel Herbert, b Needham Market, Suf 1881, d Toronto 1952, paint AGO M MM PMC RCA
MAXFIELD, James E., b Detroit 1848, fl 1904, Amer, paint AAA04 B H MM RCA TB1 Y
MAXWELL, Edward, b Montreal 1867 – d 1923, paint CE1,2 Co MM Mo12 NGC1 RCA
MAXWELL, William Sutherland, b Montreal 1874 – d 1952, paint CE1,2 CNS36 Co CWW52 MM Mo12 NGC1 PMC RCA TB3
MAY, Derek John, b London 1932– , paint MM TB3
MAY, Henrietta Mabel, b Westmount, Que 1884, d Vancouver 1971, paint AGO CC1 CWW67 DWA Hu M MM NGC1 RCA TB2,3 WWA70
MAY, Karl, b Reinowitz, Au 1901, d 1975, paint M S
MAY, Margaret, b Galahad, Alta 1951– , prt AA
MAY, Percy Moreland, b Birkenhead, Eng 1886, paint CNS36 CWW49 MM NGC68 RCA
MAY, Samuel Passmore, b Truro, Corn 1828, fl 1887, des H Mo98
MAY, Walter, b Edmonton 1950– , sculp AA
MAY, Walter William, Cdr, b England 1831 – d 1896, Eng, paint topog B DBA DBMaP DBWA DMA DSP DVP G H RCA TB1
MAYCOCK, Bryan John, b Newmarket, Eng 1944– , paint prt CAE1,2 CLA M
MAYCOCK, Gillian Margaret Cameron (Jill) (m Bryan John Maycock), b England 1945– , paint IO
MAYDANYK, Jacob, b 1892, carv paint M
MAYER, Anka, b Prague, Cz, fl 1956– , paint M
MAYER-GUNTHER, Werner, b Nuremberg, Ge 1917– , paint M
MAYEROVITCH, Harry (Mayo[2]), b Montreal 1910– , cart etch paint Des[2] M MM RCA
MAYHEW, Elza Edith Lovitt (m C. Alan Mayhew), b Victoria, BC 1916– , sculp BCS CWW93 Co M RCA WWA93
MAYHEW, Robert, b Montreal 1905– , paint M
MAYNARD, Max, b India 1903, d Victoria, BC 1982, paint M
MAYNE, Richard Charles, Adm, b England 1835 – d 1892, Eng, illus DNB H H77
MAYO. *See* MAYEROVITCH, Harry
MAYOR, Malcolm, b Edmonton 1962– , cart Po86–88
MAYRS, Charles Alexander, b Winnipeg 1940– , paint CWW93 M MM
MAYRS, David Blair, b Winnipeg 1935 , paint CAE2 CWW93 M WWA93
MAYRS, Frank Black, b Winnipeg 1934, d Aylmer, Que 1994, paint M MM
MAYRS, William John Black (Bill), b Winnipeg 1932– , paint M MM
MAYS, Douglas Lionel, b London

1900– , Eng, illus paint DBA Hu RA WBA1 WWB90
MAZUREK, Michel Z., b Poland 1940– , prt sculp CAE1
MAZZOCCHI, Rico Bruna (Mrs), b Trail, BC, fl 1968– , paint M
MEAD, Ray John, b Watford, Herts 1921– , gra paint M O.Ag50 TB3 WWA56
MEADE, Frederick Vincent, b N Sydney, NS 1905– , paint CWW64
MEADOWS, Christian, fl 1873–5, des engr H
MEADOWS, Donna Beth (m James W. Meadows, q.v.), b Brooklyn, NY 1949– , paint sculp M
MEADOWS, James Willock (m Donna B. Meadows, q.v.), b Regina 1943– , paint sculp M
MEADOWS, Robert A., b Calgary 1946– , paint SC
MEAGHER, Aileen Alethea, b Edmonton 1910– , paint CC2 M MA MM
MEAGHER, George Alfred, b Kingston, Ont 1867, paint H MM RCA
MEARES, Hermina (Ina), b Greys, Essex 1921– , paint M MM RCA
MEARES, John, Cdr, b England c 1756 – d 1809, Eng, topog DCB5 DeV1 DMA DNB EMA GW
MECH, Zdzislaw Romuald, b Poland 1930– , paint IO
MECHAM, George Frederick, Cdr, b Cobh, Co Cork, Ire 1828, d Honolulu 1858, Irish, paint topog H
MEDD, Scott Ackerman, b Peterborough, Ont 1911– , paint M
MEECHAM, James Patrick, b Glasgow 1930– , gra paint M
MEEKIS, Johnson, b Red Lake, Ont 1954– , paint IO
MEEKO. *See* JOHNNY, Meeko
MEERES, George A., b Grimsby, Eng 1878, paint WWNA
MEERTS, Michael Robert, b Belgium 1923– , paint M
MEGE, Salvador, b Bayonne, Fr 1853, fl 1878-98, Fr, paint B K
MEGGITT, Anne E. Williams (Mrs), b Florida 1930– , paint BDSA
MEIKAR, Arendt, b Odessa, Rus c 1910– , fl 1970, paint M
MEINTJIES, Jane Ellen, b London 1944– , cart gra Des M
MEISTER, Alfred Ernest. *See* ALFRED, Paul
MEISTERMAN, Ken, b Vancouver 1953– , paint DCA
MELCHIOR, Norman, b 1930– , fl 1965– , illus M RCA
MELENDY, Tony (Hi), fl 1963– , sculp M
MELIKI/MELICHI (aka Aussar), b Southampton Isld, NWT c 1909– , drw ske DCB13
MELIS, Johannes Eduard (Hans), b Tilbury, Neth 1925, d 1978, sculp M MM
MELLES, Henk, b Netherlands 1943– , paint sculp CAE1
MELNICK, Linda White (Mrs), b Arkansas 1943– , paint sculp IO
MELOCHE, François-Xavier-Edouard, b Montreal 1855 – d 1914, paint H K MM
MELOCHE, Suzanne (m Christian Marcel Barbeau), b Ottawa 1926– , paint M MM TB3
MELVILLE, Clare Gladys, b Ottawa 1897, fl 1964, paint DWA M MM
MELVIN, Grace Wilson, b Glasgow c 1892, d Vancouver 1977, paint CLA DScP DWA M RCA TB2 WWA76d78 WWB32 WWNA
MELVIN, Hattie G., fl 1887, paint H RCA
MELVIN, Philip, b Lamanche, Nfld 1928– , carv DFA KB
MENARD, Felix, fl 1865–77, sculp K
MENARD, Jean-Baptiste, fl 1868–87, carv K
MENARD, Louis, fl 1860, d Philipsburg, Que 1874, sculp K
MENDEL, Eva (m Max Miller[2]), b Recklinghausen, Ge 1919– , paint BDSA[2] M

MENDELSON, Joe[2], b Toronto 1944– , paint KB[2]
MENDES, Allan Ross, b Toronto 1927– , paint M
MENELAWS, William, b Edinburgh, fl 1913–65, paint M WWNA
MENO, Stanley J., fl 1972– , paint M
MENSES, Jan, b Rotterdam 1933– , paint prt CAE1,2 CWW93 M MM NGC67 RCA WWA93
MENZIES, Archibald, b Weem, Scot 1754, d Notting Hill, London 1842, Scot, paint DCB7 DNB
MENZIES, Don, fl 1972– , paint M
MENZIES, Sheena Lilian, b Regina 1921– , illus M
MERCER, Alexander Cavalie, Lt Gen, b Hull, Yorks 1783, d Exeter 1868, Eng, topog DCB9 H H77 PNL
MERCER, Barbara, b 1933– , paint M
MERCER, Malcolm Smith, Maj Gen, b Etobicoke, nr Toronto 1859, d Sanctuary Wood, Bel 1916, paint R2
MERCIER, Madeleine, b Ham-Nord, Que 1930– , gra paint M MM
MERCIER, Monique (Soeur), b Nicolet, Que 1934– , paint tap M WWA80
MEREDITH, John (b John Meredith Smith), b Fergus, Ont 1933– , paint AE AGO B CA1–3 CAE2 CC2 CE1,2 Co CWW91 IO M MM RCA TB3 WWA93
MERES, James S., fl 1786–1835, paint topog DFA PNL
MERINO, Luis, b Mexico 1944– , paint M
MERKUR, Sharon, b Toronto 1932– , prt IO SC
MEROLA, Mario Virgilio, b Ahuntsic, nr Montreal 1931– , paint sculp CAE1 CC1 CWW93 M MM RCA TB3 WWA93
MEROZ, Jean, b Montreal 1911– , sculp M RCA
MERRICK, John, b Halifax c 1756, d Horton, NS 1829, paint DCB6
MERRIFIELD, Maria Luisa, b Mexico City 1941– , paint IO
MERRILL. *See* PECK, Pamela Merrill
MERRILL, Grace, b Toronto 1910– , paint Hu RCA
MERRITT, C.M. (Miss), fl 1893–6, paint H
MERRITT, Catherine Rodman Prendergast (1816 m William Hamilton Merritt), fl 1810–50s, paint H
MERRITT, E.L. (Miss), fl 1893, paint H
MESSNER, Rudolph Anton, b Germany c 1912– , paint M
MESTEROM, Gerald, b Netherlands, fl 1951– , stgl M
METCALF, Eliab, b Franklin, Mass 1785, d New York 1834, Amer, min sil B F Fo GW H H77 J TB1 Y
METCALFE, E. Belle, fl 1897–1902, paint H RCA
METCALFE, Eric William (Doctor Brute), b Vancouver 1940– , gra paint M WWA93
METCALFE, Wharton, fl 1861–7, Eng, paint G H
METIVIER, Louis, fl 1828–34, sculp K
METSON, Graham, b London 1934– , paint WWA82
METZGER, Henry, Father, b Grendelbroock, Fr 1877, d Kronau, Sask 1949, paint M
MEUNIER, Claire, b St-Denis-sur-Richelieu, Que 1928– , paint CAE1 MM
MEUNIER, Jeannette (m André-Charles Biéler, q.v.), fl 1934, des K MM
MEUX, Gwendolyn D., fl 1920+, Amer, paint AAA33 DWA MM RCA WWA40
MEYER, H. (m Hoppner Francis Meyer, q.v.), fl 1859, paint H M
MEYER, Henry, b S Africa c 1948– , illus prt M
MEYER, Hoppner Francis (m H. Meyer, q.v.), b London, fl 1832–62, paint H H77 M W1–3
MEYERS, Arnold, b c 1919– , paint M
MEYERS, Betty (m John W. Warnock), b Alexandria, Va 1938– , paint BDSA

MEZEI, Rozsa (m Stephen Mezei), b Pecs, Hu, fl 1970– , drw paint IO
MICHALOWSKA, Bronislawa Chadzynska (Bronka), b Poland c 1915/22– , enam paint IO M
MICHALOWSKI, Jon Peter (Jan), b Oakville, Ont c 1954– , enam paint IO
MICHAUD, William, b nr Key Harbour, Georgian Bay, Ont 1919– , paint M
MICHAUX, François-André, b Versailles, Fr 1770, d Pontoise, Fr 1855, Fr, drw DAB K
MICHENER, Patricia Rae (m Ted Michener, q.v.), b Sudbury, Ont 1946– , paint M
MICHENER, Robert, b Preston, Minn 1935– , paint SC
MICHENER, Ted (m Patricia Rae Michener, q.v.), b Hamilton, Ont 1941– , illus paint M
MICHELOT, A.-Alexis, b France, fl 1855–7, sculp K
MICHI. *See* BOONE, Lillian Michiko
MICHON, Guy, b Montreal 1925– , mur paint M S TB3
MICKLE, Alfred Ernest, b Guelph, Ont 1869, d Hamilton, Ont 1966, paint CWW52 M MM NGC1 O.Ag49 RCA TB3
MICKUNAS, Irene (m Osvald Mickunas), b Lithuania 1931– , paint MM S
MIDDLESTAT, Larry, b Toronto 1935– , paint IO
MIDDLETON, Allan, b c 1942– , fl 1967 , carv sculp M
MIDDLETON, Bernard, b Derbyshire 1909– , paint M RCA
MIDDLETON, Janet Holly Blench (m J.M. Churchill), b Vernon, BC 1922– , paint sculp AO CAE1 M MM SC UG
MIDDLETON, Michael J., fl 1970– , illus M
MIDMORE, Bessie Helen Isabelle Stevens (m J.F. Midmore), b Davidson, Sask 1913– , paint BDSA
MIEZAJS, Dainis (s Dainis), b Kaucminde, Lat 1929– , paint M S UG WWA93
MIGNOSA, Santo, b Priolo, nr Siracusa, It 1934– , cer sculp BCS CAE2 M WWA93
MIHALCEAN, Gilles, b Montreal 1946– , sculp M
MIHALCHEON, George J. (m Jean Lapointe Mihalcheon, q.v.), b Boian, nr Vegreville, Alta 1924– , paint AA CWW93 M
MIHALCHEON, Jean Lapointe (m George J. Mihalcheon, q.v.), b Domremy, Sask 1929– , mmed mur AA BDSA SC
MIHOK, Tony, b 1949– , paint M
MIKELSON, Arnold, b Latvia 1922– , paint sculp M
MIKKANEN/MIKKALEN, Raili Marjatta (m Robert Richard), b Valkeakoski, Fin 1953– , paint CAE1 M
MIKUSKA, Frank Peter, b Winnipeg 1930– , gra paint M MM RCA
MIKUSKA, Vincent, b Winnipeg 1956– , paint CWW93
MILBERT, Jacques Gerard, b Paris 1786 – d 1840, Fr, paint B GW H K TB1
MILBURN, Oliver, b Toronto 1883, d Los Angeles 1932, paint AAA33 AAW2 AC
MILBOURNE/MILLBOURNE, John/C. (aka Charles C; Cotton), b England 1745, d Montreal 1823, paint F GW H
MILES, Anthony, b London 1932, d 1986, paint M
MILES, Frederick H.C., b Saint John, NB 1863 – d 1918, paint H RCA
MILES, John Christopher, b Saint John, NB 1837 – d 1911, paint AAA06 EC H Hu M MM Mo12 RCA W1-3
MILES, Victor, b London 1929– , paint M MM
MILETTE/MILLETTE, Alexis, b Yamachiche, Que 1793 – d 1869, carv DCB9 K
MILINKOVICH, Egon, b Budapest 1925– , paint sculp M

MILL, Richard, b 1949– , paint CAE2 MQ

MILLAIS, John Guille, b London 1865, d England 1931, Eng, paint sculp DBA DVP WBA WWW

MILLAR, Alexander Samuel, b Toronto 1921, d Cedar Valley, nr Aurora, Ont 1978, paint IO M MM NGC1 RCA S TB3

MILLAR, Clara Louise Neads (m T. Bonne Millar), b Bowmanville, Ont c 1888, fl 1940s, paint AAW3 DWA Hu M RCA WWNA

MILLAR, Diane Margaret, b Hamilton, Ont 1949– , paint IO

MILLAR, J.H.R., b 1893, fl 1945, paint M

MILLAR, Jane Anne. *See* COOKE, Jane Anne Millar

MILLARD, Charles Stuart, b nr Weston, Ont 1837, d Cheltenham, Eng 1917, paint B DVLP DVP H Hu M MM NGC1 RCA

MILLARD, Colleen, fl 1958– , paint M

MILLER, Alfred Jacob, b Baltimore, Md 1810 – d 1874, Amer, paint AAW1 ANC App AW B Bry DAA F GW H McC Sam TB1 WWWA

MILLER, Archibald McArthur, b Shawinigan Falls, Que 1930– , sculp M MM

MILLER, Cecilia J., fl 1892–1909, paint H MM

MILLER, Elva (m Lloyd Miller), fl 1963– , paint M

MILLER, Eva Mendel. *See* MENDEL, Eva

MILLER, Francis John, b London 1929– , mur paint M WWA93

MILLER, Germaine, b France, fl 1968– , paint M

MILLER, Helga Arnasson (m T.M. Miller), b Winnipeg 1911– , paint M

MILLER, Harriet S. (m Milton H. Miller), b 1926– , fl 1962– , paint sculp M

MILLER, Herbert McRae, b Montreal 1895, d nr Ste-Agathe, Que 1981, paint sculp CWW81 M MM NGC1 RCA TB3 WWA78

MILLER, J. Crosby, fl 1838, paint GW H

MILLER, John, b 1929– , fl 1970s, paint CAE1

MILLER, John Arthur (s John Nold), b St Thomas, Ont 1951– , paint IO

MILLER, John Melville, b Montreal 1875 – d 1948, paint M MM NGC1 PMC RCA

MILLER, Keith Richard, b Chatham, Ont 1949– , drw DSP IO

MILLER, Margaret L. (m Henry Miller), fl 1897–1903, paint H MM

MILLER, Maria Frances Ann Morris. *See* MORRIS, Maria Frances Ann

MILLER, Mary Elizabeth Palmer (m Otto V.B. Miller), b Saint John, NB 1903– , paint MA MM

MILLER, Paul, b Hamilton, Ont 1946– , paint M

MILLER, Richard, b Windsor, Ont 1930– , paint M

MILLER, Robert Gary (s R.G. Miller), b Simcoe, Ont 1950– , paint IO

MILLER, William Rickarby, b Staindrop, Dur 1818, d New York 1893, drgt AAW3 GW H WWWA Y

MILLET, Jean-Marie, b Longueuil, Que 1931– , paint M

MILLIDGE, Eliza Gilpin (m A.W. Millidge), b 1819, d 1856, paint H

MILLIGAN, Edward L., fl 1883–1901, paint H

MILLIGAN, Florence Margaret, b Cardinal, Ont 1890, paint SC

MILLIKEN, Leonard Moncrief (Len), b Six Nations Res, nr Brantford, Ont c 1949– , paint M

MILLMAN, Michael, b Montreal, fl 1942– , paint M

MILLNER, Charles Blisset, b Bristol, Eng 1805, d St Catharines, Ont 1895, paint AE H

MILLNER, George W., fl 1850s, carv paint H

MILLS, Doris Louise Huestis. *See* SPEIRS, Doris Louise Huestis

MILLS, Elizabeth Ann Newdigate. *See* NEWDIGATE, Elizabeth Ann

MILLS, Gray Hoye, b Cleveland, Ohio 1929– , mur paint M MM RCA

MILLS, Helen (Mrs), b 1900– , fl 1960s, gra paint M

MILNE, Bruce Lane, b Toronto 1910– , gra sculp M RCA

MILNE, David Brown (x Bruce), b nr Paisley, Ont 1882, d Toronto 1953, gra paint AAA29 ACA AE AGO APH B CC1 CE1,2 Co EC F H77 M MM MQ NGC1 NGC67 NGC68 OC P S TB1,2 TN UG US W2,3 WWA53

MILNE, Margaret E., b Keyes, Man 1920– , paint M

MILNE, Rose Eleanor[2], b Saint John, NB 1925– , sculp CWW93[2] M[2] RCA

MILNE, W.B., fl 1949– , paint M

MILOR De[2], fl 1789, paint H[2] K

MILROY, William, fl 1887–97, paint H

MINARD, Asa Raymond, b Port Medway, NS 1873, engr Mo12

MINOT, Michael, b London 1923– , sculp BCS M

MINTO. *See* PURVITIS, Mentauts Dennis

MIOLEE, Anna Louise (s Anna), b Asmara, Eritrea 1943– , prt IO

MIRCK, Jan Peter, b Schozen, nr Antwerp 1920– , fl 1962, paint M MM

MIRON, Claire, b Belgium 1923– , des paint M

MIRVISH, Ann (m Ed Mirvish), fl 1962 , sculp M

MITCHELL, Beresford Strickland, b Hamilton, Ont 1921– , des illus WWA80

MITCHELL, Constance Aileen (m George Joseph Mitchell), b Calgary 1929– , paint BDSA

MITCHELL, David Alexander, b Regina 1930– , paint CWW93

MITCHELL, Edward Michael/Michael Edward[2], b Toronto 1921– , paint AGO[2] M

MITCHELL, Hutton, b Dundee, Scot 1872, d Braintree, Essex 1935, paint DBA MM PMC RCA

MITCHELL, Janet, b Medicine Hat, Alta 1912 (x 1915)– , paint AA CC2 CWW93 DFA KB M NGC1 RCA S SC TB3

MITCHELL, Jocelyn Taylor. *See* TAYLOR, Jocelyn

MITCHELL, Laura M.D. (m Arthur A. Tennyson), b Halifax 1883, d Alhambra, Calif 1965, min AAA33 AAW1 AC DBA DWA F TB1,2 WWA62 Y

MITCHELL, Marjorie Chambers, b Draycott, Glos 1884, paint M

MITCHELL, Michael Edward. *See* MITCHELL, Edward Michael

MITCHELL, Molly Greene (m John A. Mitchell), b c 1923– , fl 1950s, paint ske M

MITCHELL, Raymond, b Malartic, Que 1942– , fl 1966– , sculp M MQ

MITCHELL, Thomas, b c 1833, fl 1875–6, d 1925, paint topog DFA H PNL

MITCHELL, Thomas Wilberforce, b Clarksburg, Ont 1879, d Barrie, Ont 1958, paint CWW55 M MM NGC1 O.N48 RCA TB2,3 WWA62

MITCHELL, Willard Morse, b Saint John, NB 1879, d Montreal 1955, paint M MM

MITCHELL, William, b Detroit, fl 1969– , drw M

MITCHELL, Winifred Laura (m George Mitchell), b Fernie, BC 1917– , fl 1961– , paint ABC M RCA

MITRIS, Laimon, b Latvia, fl 1964– , paint M

MITTON, Ross, b Truro, NS, fl 1968– , paint M

MIYAUCHI, Haruo, b Japan 1943– , fl 1971– , paint M

MOAK, Allan Edward, b Kingston, Ont 1946– , illus paint IO T

MOCHIZUKI, Betty Ayako, b Vancouver 1929– , gra paint M S WWA80

MOCIORNITZA, Lorscue Rosette

(m Ion Mociornitza), b Romania, fl 1969– , paint M
MOCZORODYNSKI, Mario, b Poland 1923– , fl 1950s, paint M
MODDLE, Roland, fl 1940s, paint M
MOEN, Douglas, b Rosetown, Sask 1945– , sculp US
MOESTL, Leo, b Austria, fl 1972– , sculp M
MOFFAT, John F., b Inverness, Scot 1947– , paint M
MOFFAT, John William, b Copenhagen 1932– , paint CWW93
MOGRIDGE, Marjorie Good (m James Leslie Mogridge), b Didsbury, Alta 1906– , paint M
MOHAMED, Nur-Jehaan, b Cape Town, SA 1926– , paint sculp CAE1
MOHANDAS. *See* PILLAI, Mohandas
MOHR, Jurgen Klaus (s Ama), b Theisenort, W Ge 1948– , sculp IO M
MOHRMANN, John Henry, b San Francisco 1857, d Alberta 1916, Amer, paint DMA DSP PP SP
MOIR, Lydia Maitland McLaughlin (s Lily M.) (m John Moir), b Quebec 1847, d Los Angeles 1941, paint AC H M RCA
MOIR, Madeleine Fanais, b Manchester, Eng 1918– , coll paint IO M
MOISAN, Gatien, b St-Raymond-de-Portneuf 1939– , paint M
MOISAN, Laurent, b Quebec 1849, d Ste-Anastasie, Que 1913, carv K
MOISEIWITSCH, Carel, b England, fl 1970– , illus M
MOISEIWITSCH, Tanya (m Felix Krish), b London 1914– , des CC2 Co
MOISEYER, George, fl 1969– , paint M
MOL, Jakob (Jake), b Netherlands 1935– , paint pas prt IO
MOL, Leo (b Leonid Molodoshanin/Molodizhanyn), b Ukraine 1915– , paint sculp stgl AGO M MM RCA WWA78
MOLINA, Valentino, b Savannah, Ga 1880, Amer, paint AAA21 MM RCA TB2
MOLINARI, Carla, b Medolla, It 1945– , sculp M
MOLINARI, Guido, b Montreal 1933– , paint prt AGO B CA1–3 CAE1 CC2 CE1,2 Co DCA M MM MQ NGC67 OC P RCA TB3 US WWA93
MOLL, Corinne-Martha (Soeur Louis-Arthur Moll), b Massachusetts, fl 1925–72, paint sculp K
MOLL, Ela, b 1950, d 1969, paint M
MOLLER, Shirlee Sarah Klein (m Arne Moller), b Montreal, fl 1968– , paint M
MOLLISON, Ethel Knight. *See* KELLY, Ethel Knight Mollison
MOLLOT, Fortuné, b Lyon, Fr 1845, d St Boniface, Man 1925, paint B K
MONAGHAN, Philip Johnston, b Hamilton, Ont 1931– , paint M
MONAHAN, Hugh C., b Ireland 1914, d Delta, BC 1970, paint M WBA2
MONCY, Ai de/le. *See* HODGINS, Aimée Gertrude Burgess
MONDOR-MORACHE, Yolande, fl 1959– , paint M
MONGEAU, A., fl 1884–91, engr H K
MONGEAU, André, b 1947– , paint sculp CAE1
MONGEAU, Jean-Guy, b Verdun, Que 1931– , paint CC1 M MM
MONGRAIN, Claude, b Shawinigan, Que 1948– , sculp DCA MQ WWA93
MONGRAIN, Henri, b Trois-Rivières, Que 1934– , paint M RCA
MONKS, Robert (Bob), b Michigan 1927– , cart Des
MONOGHAN, Tela. *See* PURCELL, Tela Monoghan
MONREN, Marguerite, b Winnipeg 1920– , carv paint M
MONRO, William (x Munroe[2]), b Edinburgh 1815, fl 1851+, Scot, paint H[2] WHC
MONTCASTLE, Clara H. *See* MOUNTCASTLE, Clara H.
MONTCOMBROUX, Michael, b England 1936– , engr BB
MONTE. *See* WRIGHT, Monte M.

MONTGOMERIE, Stewart, b Newfoundland 1941– , paint sculp M
MONTGOMERY, Gladys Eleanor, b Jarvis, Ont, fl 1934+, paint M RCA
MONTGOMERY, Joan (Mrs) (s Monty), b England, fl 1962– , paint M
MONTGOMERY, M. (Miss), fl 1894, paint H
MONTGOMERY, Sheila Ann (Mrs), b Victoria, BC 1935– , gra paint CAE2 M
MONTIGNY, Marguerite de. *See* LAFONTAINE, Marguerite de Montigny
MONTIGNY[1]-GIGUERE[2], E. Louise de (Mme de Montigny), b La-Prairie, Que 1878, d 1969, paint sculp DWA K[1] M MM RCA[2]
MONTIZAMBERT, Beatrice Blanch, b Quebec 1874, fl 1927, min paint AAA19 B DWA K M MM RCA TB1 Y
MONTMIGNY, Charles S., b 1850, fl 1878–93, carv engr H K
MONTMOLIN, Jacques de, fl 1785–8, des engr H K
MONTOUR, Nathan, b Six Nations Res, nr Brantford, Ont c 1892, d Brantford, Ont 1969, sculp M
MONTPETIT, André, b Montreal 1943– , gra AGO M
MONTPETIT, Guy, b Montreal 1938– , gra mur paint M MM MQ
MONTRESOR, John, Capt, fl 1759, drw H
MONTREUIL, Roméo, b 1877, d 1967, sculp K
MONTY, Louis Eustache, b St-Césaire, Que 1873, d Montreal 1933, paint H K
MOODIE, Agnes Dunbar. *See* CHAMBERLIN, Agnes Dunbar Moodie
MOODIE[1], Susanna Strickland[2] (m John Wedderburn Dunbar Moodie[3]), b Bungay, Suf 1803, d Toronto 1885, paint AGO App[1,2,3] CE1,2 Co DCB11[2] DWA EC H PNL R2 ROM W1–3
MOODY, David William, fl 1844–51, litho topog GW H
MOODY, Hampden Clement Blamire, b pre-1813, d Belfast, Ire 1869, paint DFA PNL ROM
MOODY, Rufus, b Skidegate, BC c 1923– , sculp Co M
MOONEY, Craig McDonald, b Lloydminster, Sask 1913– , engr BB
MOORE, Annie E., fl 1895–7, paint H MM
MOORE, Arthur W., b 1850, fl 1872–7, illus DFA H
MOORE, Cecil Gresham, b Kingston, Ont 1880, illus paint AAA33 F Y
MOORE, David, b 1943– , paint prt CAE1
MOORE, Doug, fl 1969– , des drw mur M
MOORE, Eva Constance, b Bowmanville, Ont, fl 1923+, paint CNS40
MOORE, Jeremy, b Norwich, Eng 1939– , drw sculp M
MOORE, Macleod, Lt Col, fl 1883, topog H
MOORE, Margaret (Mrs), fl 1954, paint M
MOORE, Penny, b London, Ont c 1950– , gra paint M
MOORE, Richard William, b Glechien, Alta 1893, gra M MM
MOORE, Samuel, fl 1808, sil H
MOORHOUSE, Ashleigh Edward, b Winnipeg 1924– , paint IO
MOORSAM, William Scarth, Capt, b 1804, d 1863, Eng, paint DeV9
MOPPET, Carroll May Lindoe (m Ronald Benjamin Moppet, q.v.), b Calgary 1948– , sculp AA RCA
MOPPET, Ronald Benjamin (m Carroll M.L. Moppet, q.v.), b Woking, Sur 1945– , paint AA CAE2 M RCA
MORAN/MORON[2], J. fl 1831–2, drw paint GW H[2]
MORAN, John Leon[2], b Philadelphia 1864, d Watchung, NJ 1941, Amer, paint F H[2] Y
MORAN, Mary Nimmo (m Thomas Moran, q.v.), b Strathaven, Scot 1842, d E Hampton, Long Isld, NY 1899,

Amer, etch AWW2 App B DAA DBA DWA F McC NCAB

MORAN, Thomas (m Mary N. Moran, q.v.), b Bolton, Lancs 1837, d Santa Barbara, Calif 1926, Amer, etch paint AAAd28 AAW1 AC ANC App AW B DAA DAB DBA DeV1 DMA DSP F G GW H McC NCAB RCA Sam TB1 WWWA Y

MORAND, Joseph, b St Jerome, Que 1786, d Montreal 1816, paint H K

MORANG, Giselle, b Australia, fl 1971– , sculp M

MORAVEC, Hella (m Julian Street), b Czechoslovakia, fl 1973– , sculp M

MORDOWANEC, Halyna (Mrs Regenbogen[2]), b Germany 1945– , sculp IO[2]

MORE, David John, b Aberdeen 1947– , cart paint CWW93

MOREAU, Charles-Henri, b Paris 1835, d France 1867, Fr, car des paint Des H K W1–3

MOREAU, Diane, b Montreal 1946– , gra paint M

MOREAU-PERRAULT, Henry, b Montreal 1899, paint Hu K

MOREL, Jeanne, fl 1972– , paint M

MOREL, Octave, b Quebec 1837, d Ste-Anne-de-Beaupré, Que 1918, carv DFA K KB

MORELL, Egon O. *See* OGYALLAY-MORELL, Egon

MORENCY, André, b Montreal 1910– , paint CNS40 M MM RCA

MORENCY, Jacqueline, b Ste-Anne-de-Beaupré, Que, fl 1951– , paint M

MORENCY, Louis, b Quebec 1853/4, fl 1879–99, paint H K

MORENCY, Mireille, fl 1969– , tap M

MORESBY, Matthew F. (s MFM), b c 1824, fl 1853, Eng, topog DFA H

MORETON, Julian, b Chelsea, London 1825, d London 1900, paint DCB12 H

MOREY, Charles T., b Cummington, Mass 1927– , drw paint M RCA

MORGAN, Judith Phillis, b Kitwanga, BC 1930– , paint M

MORGAN, Liliane, b 1932– , fl 1962– , paint sculp M

MORGAN, Marion L. (m J.R. Morgan), b Minneapolis, Minn 1875, gra GM WWNA

MORGAN, Mary Vernon (m Walter Jenks Morgan), b Birmingham, Eng, fl 1880–1930, Eng, paint DBA DVP G H RCA WBA1

MORGAN, Nicola (m David W. Tupper), b Victoria, BC 1959– , illus paint C CWW93

MORGAN, Sybil Andrews. *See* ANDREWS, Sybil

MORGAN, Wayne, b Dunnville, Ont c 1943– , paint M

MORGAN-McNEIL, Charlotte (s CMM), b Toronto 1948– , paint M

MORHAM, Marion A. (m A. Dance), b London 1902– , gra WWNA

MORIN, Jacques, b c 1951– , paint M

MORIN, Jean-Marc, fl 1958– , carv M

MORIN, Lucien, b Montreal 1918– , paint M MM

MORIN, Maurice (s Maurin[2]), b St-Victor-de-Beauce, Que 1929– , paint CWW93[2] M

MORIN, Pierre-Louis, b Nonancourt, Fr 1811, d St-Henri-de-Mascouche, Que 1886, drw H K

MORISSET, Denys, b Paris 1930, paint sculp M MM TB3

MORISSET, Gerard, b Cap-Santé, Que 1898, d Quebec 1970, paint CWW67 K M

MORIZIO, Antonio, b Casamassima, It 1926– , drw paint M

MORLEY, Patricia F. (Pat), b Summerside, PEI 1952– , paint IO

MORLEY, Rita, b Lac-St-Jean, Que, fl 1969– , paint M

MOROSAN, Vojislav, b Belgrade, Yu 1941– , paint IO

MOROSOLI, Joelle, b France 1951– , sculp CWW93

MORRELL, Charlotte Mount Brock. *See*

SCHREIBER, Charlotte Mount Brock Morrell

MORRELL, Clarence Allison, b Rochester, NY 1899, paint CWW82

MORRELL, Joyce, fl 1970– , paint CAE2

MORRICE, David Rousseaux, b Toronto 1903– , paint M

MORRICE, James Wilson, b Montreal 1865, d Tunis 1924, paint ACA AGO B CC2 CE1,2 CNS36 Co DBA DVLP EC H H77 L M MM Mo12 MQ NGC1 NGC67 NGC68 OC OCD P R1 RCA S TB1 TN W1–3 WBA2

MORRIS, Andrew, b Kilmarnock, Scot, fl 1844–52, Scot, litho paint DeV3 GW H

MORRIS, David, b Toronto c 1945– , gra paint M

MORRIS, Doris Hongworth (Dodi) (m Harry Morris), b Madrid, NY 1917– , paint M

MORRIS, Edmund Montague, b Perth, Ont 1871, d nr Portneuf, Que 1913, paint AGO CC1 CWW10 H77 Hu LeJ M MM Mo12 NGC1 RCA ROM TB3 W1–3 WBA2

MORRIS, Jones Fawson, fl 1830–40, paint GW H

MORRIS, Karyn, b Toronto 1950– , sculp stgl IO

MORRIS, Kathleen Moir, b Montreal 1893, d Rawdon, Que 1986, paint CC2 CNS40 CWW81 DWA Hu M MM NGC1 RCA TB2 WWA82

MORRIS, Lincoln Godfrey, b Newport, Mon 1887, prt M MM RCA

MORRIS, Maria Frances Ann (m Garret Trafalgar Nelson Miller[2]), b Halifax 1813 – d 1875, paint DCB10 DWA[2] EC[2] H[2] H77[2] M[2] W1–3[2]

MORRIS, Michael William (aka Marcel Idea, Marcel Dot), b Saltdean, Sus 1942– , gra paint sculp CA1–3 M MM US WWA80

MORRIS, Robert, fl 1850, litho H

MORRIS, Roy, fl 1972– , paint M

MORRIS, Wanda Kondzielewski (Mrs), b Nipawin, Sask 1936– , des paint US

MORRISEY, Patience, b Alberta 1921– , paint IO

MORRISON, Alfred L., b Pleasant Grove, PEI 1909– , paint DFA KB

MORRISON, Ann K. Spencer (Mrs), b Saskatoon 1929– , paint BDSA

MORRISON, G.W.B., fl 1880, illus H

MORRISON, Hal A.C., b Prince Edward Island c 1853, d Atlanta, Ga 1927, Amer, paint H

MORRISON, Irene Elaine (m Donald M. Morrison), b Jefferson, Okla 1906– , paint M

MORRISON, Kathleen Grant (m F.C. Morrison), b New Glasgow, NS 1913– , paint M MA

MORRISON, Mildred (Mrs), fl 1967– , cer sculp M

MORRISSEAU, Norval (Copper Thunderbird), b Sand Point Res, nr Beardmore, Ont 1931– , paint AGO CE1,2 Co DCA M NGC67 UG

MORROW, Harold, fl 1965– , paint M

MORROW, Lynn, fl 1969– , paint M

MORROW, Thorn, fl 1971– , paint M

MORSE, Susan Mary Peters (m Charles Morse), b St John, NB 1862, d c 1939, paint DWA H Hu M MM RCA

MORTIMER, Alexander, fl 1880–5, litho DBA H RCA

MORTIMER, Florence Maud (m Percival Barling Mortimer), b Wakkerstrom, SA 1879, d Edmonton 1959, paint M RCA

MORTON, Bill, b Alberta, fl 1967– , paint M

MORTON, Douglas Gibb, b Winnipeg 1926– , paint CC1 CWW93 IO M MM NGC67 RCA SC US

MORTON, Edith Alice. *See* POWER, Edith Alice Morton

MORTON, Gary, b England 1945– , drw paint M

MORTON, H. (m George Morton), fl 1886–9, paint H MM

MORTON, Ruth. *See* RIDEOUT, Ruth Morton
MORTON, Sylvia, fl 1964– , paint M
MOSCHINSKY, Volodimir, b Kiev, Ukr c 1896/1904, mur paint M
MOSCRIP, Mary D., b Galt, re Cambridge, Ont 1848, d 1930, paint H
MOSDOSSY, Imre Von, b Hungary, fl 1934+, paint M
MOSER, James Henry, b Whitby, Ont 1854, d Washington, DC 1913, illus paint AAA14d28 B F H TB1 Y
MOSER, Joseph, b Baden, nr Toronto 1832, fl 1864, paint H
MOSES, Michel, fl 1837–66, paint H K
MOSHER, Terry (s Aislin[2]), b Ottawa 1942– , cart APH[2] Co CWW93 Des[2] M Po86–8[2] WECa
MOSNA, Tony, b c 1948– , paint M
MOSONYI, Eva N., b Budapest 1935– , paint M
MOSS, Charles Eugene, b Pawnee City, Nebr 1860, d Ottawa 1901, paint AAA01 AAW1 H Hu M MM NGC1 RCA ROM W1–3
MOSS, Edward Lawton, fl 1862–76, Eng, topog H
MOSS, Helen Betty, b Ameliasburg, Ont 1921– , sculp IO
MOSS, Mary Helen (Mrs Weatherston[2]), b Hamilton, Ont 1916– , paint IO[2] M
MOSSIERE, Eva Jana Newman. *See* NEWMAN, Eva Jana
MOSSOP, Ronald Herbert, b Toronto 1925– , paint M
MOTT, Michael, b London 1948– , paint AA
MOTTER, Dean Roger, b Berea, Ohio 1953– , Amer, car illus WWA82
MOTTER, Francis Douglas, b Chicago 1913– , mmed paint M SC
MOULD, Dorothy Mary, b Cainsville, Ont 1924– , paint IO
MOULD, Lola Marie Frowde (m William Mould), b Sydney, NS 1908– , paint M MA WWA80
MOULD, Vernon, b Toronto 1927– , illus paint M
MOULDING, Fred, b 1894, carv CAE1 DFA
MOULTON, Donn, b Ravenna, Ohio 1929– , Amer paint AE
MOUNT, Rita, b Montreal 1885/8 – d 1967, paint CWW64 DWA Hu M MM NGC1 RCA TB3 WWA62
MOUNTAIN, Kate A.P., paint DWA H
MOUNTAIN, William Harry, b Nova Scotia 1947– , sculp IO
MOUNTCASTLE, Clara H. (aka Caris Sima), b Clinton, Ont 1837 – d 1908, paint DCB13 DWA H Mo98 RCA
MOUNTCASTLE, Eliza, fl 1880s, paint H
MOUNTFORT, Julia Ann, b Coaticook, Que 1888, paint AAA33 DWA WWA62
MOUSSEAU, Jean-Paul-Armand, b Montreal 1927, d 1991, mur sculp CC2 CE1,2 DMS M MM NGC1 NGC67 TB3
MOWAT, Alexander Sutherland, b Bonnybridge, Scot 1905– , paint CWW67 M WWA70
MOWAT, Grace Helen, b St Andrews, NB 1875, d 1964, paint CLA DWA M
MOYER, Harry, b Beamsville, Ont 1884, cart Des
MOYER, Stanley Gordon, b Mildmay, nr Walkerton, Ont 1887, d 1968, paint Hu M RCA
MRAZOVA, Hana Malik (s Mraz), b Ostrava, Cz 1941– , paint BDSA
MROCZKOWSKI, James Albert, b Windsor, Ont 1950– , paint IO
MUCKLE, Robert, b Jonquière, Que 1942– , mur paint M
MUDGE, Zacharie, Adm, b Plymouth, Eng 1770, d Plympton, Eng 1852, Eng, topog AAW1 DeV1 DMA DNB EMA GW H
MUELLER/MULLER, Ernst/Ernest, fl 1876–96, paint H MM RCA
MUELLER, Helmut, b Germany, fl 1952– , paint M
MUELLER/MULLER, Henry, fl 1850–2, paint GW H Y
MUELLER, John Gilbert Charles,

b Kitchener, Ont 1935– , paint IO M
MUGFORD, David, b 1952– , paint M
MUHLSTOCK, Louis, b Narajov, Pol 1904– , paint AGO CC1 CE1,2 DCA H77 Hu M MM MQ NGC1 RCA S TB2,3 WWA82
MUIR, Francis Reed, b London 1898, paint M MM
MUIR, Henrietta. *See* EDWARDS, Henrietta Muir
MUIRHEAD, Henry Abrahams. *See* DUVERNET, Henry Abrahams
MUIRHEAD, Marguerite. *See* PARKINSON, Cathy
MULAIRE, Bernard-René-Joseph, b St Pierre Jolys, Man 1945– , drw engr M
MULCASTER, Wynona Croft (Nonie), b Prince Albert, Sask 1915– , paint BDSA M MM UG US
MULLER, Robin, b Toronto 1953– , illus C CBC
MUNAMEE, 'B,' E7-1063 (m Paunichea, E7-1064), b Cape Dorset, NWT 1919– , sculp DEA
MUNCLINGER, Ludmila, b Czechoslovakia 1944– , paint IO S
MUNCY, Maitland. *See* CRANE, Maitland Maude Muncy
MUNDER, Weldon, b Leduc, Alta 1934– , prt M
MUNDY, Elizabeth (Betty) (Mrs), b Alberta, fl 1951– , paint M
MUNGITUK/MUNGITOK[2], E7-999, b Cape Dorset, NWT 1935– , prt sculp AGO DEA[2]
MUNN, Kathleen Jean, b Toronto 1887, drw paint AGO DWA H77 Hu M MM RCA
MUNNOCH, John, b Wallacestone, Scot 1855, d killed in action WW1 1914, paint M WBA2
MUNRO, Jean Elizabeth Cockburn (m Gordon Munro), b Orillia, Ont 1869, d 1945, paint CNS40 DWA Hu M MM RCA
MUNRO, Sarah Jean. *See* MacLEAN, Sarah Jean Munro
MUNROE, George, b England 1907– , carv DFA KB
MUNTZ, Elizabeth L.G., b Toronto 1894, paint sculp DBA DWA WBA1 WWB77d80
MUNTZ, Laura Adeline. *See* LYALL, Laura Adeline Muntz
MURATA, Catherine Pentland. *See* PENTLAND, Catherine
MURCH, Walter Tandy, b Toronto 1907, d New York 1967, Amer, paint DAA DCAA2–3 M WWA66d70
MURDOCK, Greg, b Saskatoon 1954– , sculp WWA93
MURILLO, Ivor, b Scotland c 1919– , paint M
MURPHY, Anna Brownell. *See* JAMESON, Anna Brownell Murphy
MURPHY, Cecil Tremayne Buller. *See* BULLER, Cecil Tremayne
MURPHY, John, fl 1870–92, paint H
MURPHY, John Francis, b Oswego, NY 1853, d New York 1921, Amer, paint AAA21d28 B DAA F H TB1 Y
MURPHY, Rowley Walter, b Toronto 1891 – d 1975, paint AGO CWW73 M NGC1 NGC68 O.My48 RCA SA WWA73d76
MURPHY, Sean Buller, b London 1924– , paint CWW93
MURRAY, Alexander Hunter, b Kilmun, Argyl 1818/19, d Lower Ft Garry, nr Winnipeg 1874, paint DCB10 EC H W1–3
MURRAY, Amelia Matilda, Lady (m Alexander Lindsay of Evelick, Sir), b England 1795, d Glenbarrow, Herts 1884, Eng, paint BPp1748 DBWA DNB
MURRAY, Charles Adolphus. *See* DUNMORE, Charles Adolphus Murray, 7th Earl
MURRAY, Doris, b Princeton, NJ 1916– , paint IO M
MURRAY, Frederick William, b Scotsburn, NS 1916– , paint M
MURRAY, Ian Stewart, b Pictou, NS 1951– , sculp WWA93
MURRAY, John, b Ireland 1810, fl 1868, illus paint DeV3 DFA H

MURRAY, Killman, b c 1930– , paint M
MURRAY, Robert Gray, b Vancouver 1936– , paint sculp AGO B CA1–3 CC1 CE1,2 Co DAS DCAA2,3 IO M MM OC RCA WWA93
MURRAY-WEBER, Kathleen. *See* WEBER, Kathleen Nichol Murray
MURRAYGREEN, Ryan, b Toronto 1947– , paint WWA82
MUSGRAVE, Frances (m Herbert Dodson), b Antigua c 1840, d Victoria, BC 1904, paint BCA NAC
MUSGROVE, Alexander Johnston (Alec), b Edinburgh 1882, d Winnipeg 1952, paint CC2 GM H77 M MM RCA WBA2 WWA47d53
MUSICK, Florence (m B. Musick), b Winnipeg, fl 1969– , paint M
MUTH, Elaine Louise (aka Mackereth), b Lafleche, Sask 1948– , paint BDSA
MUTHING, Almuth. *See* LUTKENHAUS, Almuth Katrina Wirsing
MUYSSON, Bill, b Netherlands 1940– , paint M
MUYSSON, Hertha Kirchner (Mrs), b Netherlands 1898, d 1984, paint DWA DFA KB
MXPLTLZIK (Mr). *See* BROUSSEAU, Napoléon
MYERS, Anna, b Toronto 1953– , drw etch IO M
MYERS, Edna Aaron (m Bernard Myers), b Brandon, Man 1917– , paint M
MYLES, Beatrice. *See* BANTING, Beatrice Aline Myles
MYLES, Joan (m Robert G. Myles), b Ottawa, fl 1967– , paint M
MYREN, Ronald L., b Galloway, BC 1937– , paint SC

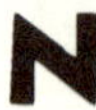

NADEAU, Albert, b St-François-de-Madawaska, NB 1915– , carv DFA KB M
NADEAU, Joseph, b Canada 1698, fl 1743, sculp K
NADEAU, Joseph, b Beaumont, Que 1726, fl 1780, paint K
NADEAU, Marc Antoine, b Montreal 1943– , gra sculp M
NADON, Robert, b Montreal 1938– , paint CAE1
NAGEL, Arturo, b Mexico City 1945– , paint prt IO
NAGY, Elena, b Hungary, fl 1963– , paint M
NAGY, George Charles (Gyorgy Karoly), b Gyergyoremete, Hu 1932– , paint PHA
NAHANEE, David, b c 1939– , carv M
NAHL, Hugo Wilhelm Arthur, b Kassel, Ge 1833, d San Francisco Bay 1889, Amer, illus paint AAW1 AC DeV1 GW Sam WWWA Y
NAIRN, Gary. *See* LEE-NOVA, Gary
NAKAMURA, Kazuo, b Vancouver 1926– , paint ACA AGO CAE2 CC2 CE1,2 Co CWW93 M MM NGC1 RCA S TB3 WWA93
NALUIYUK, Jonasi, E9-1155, b Sugluk, Que 1917– , sculp S
NALUKTURUK/MALIKTUNUK, Josephie, E9-1735, b Port Harrison, Que 1936– , sculp S
NAMER, Rosalie, b Montreal 1925– , paint sculp M
NANE-PIROCHE, Setsuko, b Japan 1933– , paint M
NANOGAK, Agnes, W2-473, b Holman, Baillie Isld, NWT 1925– , drw gra CE1,2 Co DEA M
NANTEL, Arthur, b Montreal 1874, d 1948, paint NGC1p430 NGC68
NAPARTUK, Henry, E9-1652, b Great Whale River, Que 1930– , prt sculp DEAp65
NAPHEGYI, Emery/Imre, b Kolozsvar, Hu 1912– , paint sculp PHA
NAPIER, William Henry Edward, b Montreal 1829, d Edinburgh 1894, topog DFA H PNL ROM UG

NARANG, Saran A., b Agra, India 1930– , paint sculp CWW93

NARBONNE, Louis, b St-Rémi, Que 1809, d Montreal 1869, sculp K

NARBONNE, Pierre-Rémi, b St-Remi, Que 1806, d Montreal 1839, paint H K W1-3

NASH, John E., fl 1862–81, paint H

NATTE dit MARSEILLE[2], Jean-Sébastien, b Marseille, Fr 1734, d Quebec 1803, paint DCB5 H[2] H77 K

NAZER, Marjorie, b Kent, Eng 1905– , paint IO

NEADS, Clara Louise. *See* MILLAR, Clara Louise Neads

NEASE, Stephen Richard, b Woodbridge, Ont 1955– , cart Po88

NEAVITT, Richard Barrington. *See* NEVITT/NEAVITT, Richard Barrington

NEDDEAU, Donald Frederick Price, b Toronto 1913– , gra paint CWW93 IO M MM O.My49 RCA WWA93

NEEDHAM, Alfred Carter, b Beachville, nr London, Ont 1872, paint AAA33 F

NEEL, Ellen Newman (m Edward [Ted] Neel), b Alert Bay, BC 1916, d Vancouver 1966, sculp M MM

NEESHAM, Robin Kenneth George, b Bristol, Eng 1934– , paint M

NEGIN, Louis Mark, b London 1932– , des CC1 M

NEIL, Frances Barbara, b Wolverhampton, Eng 1909– , paint O.Ag50 RCA

NEILSON, Henry Ivan, b Cap-Rouge, Que 1865, d Quebec 1931, paint AGO H Hu M MM Mo12 NGC1 PMC RCA TB3 W1-3

NEILSON, Jean-Louis-Hubert (John), Lt Col, b nr Quebec 1845, d 1925, drw paint K Mo98,12

NEILSON, Samuel, fl 1790–1827, illus H

NEISON, Adrian, b England, fl 1877, paint H ROM

NELLES, Arthur Douglas, b Ottawa 1917– , illus M

NELSON, Freida, b Duluth, Minn 1940– , drw paint IO

NELSON, Marion Hope. *See* HOOKER, Marion Hope Nelson

NELSON, Mary I. Murphy (m Blair Nelson), b Saskatoon 1920– , paint BDSA

NELSON, Robert Allen, b Milwaukee 1925– , Amer, paint MM WWA86

NEMETH, Stephen (Istvan), b Hungary 1936– , paint PHA

NEMETHY, Louis (Lajos), b Csikszent Marton, Hu 1904– , sculp PHA

NEMISH, Bryan, b Winnipeg 1944– , paint AA M

NEMO. *See* DARLING, James

NEON, John (b John Edward Masciuch, s John Neon), b Ottawa 1944– , sculp M

NERON, Gertrude, b Chicoutimi, Que, fl 1952+, paint M

NESBIT, Douglas Charles, b London 1926– , paint CWW93

NESBITT, Matthew John, b Montreal 1928– , paint sculp CAE2 M MM MQ RCA

NESBITT, Prynce, b St Catharines, Ont, fl 1968– , paint M

NESFIELD, William Andrews, b Chester-le-Street, Dur 1793, d London 1881, Eng, paint B DBWA DNB DVLP DVP TB1

NESIC, Miroslav, b Yugoslavia 1945– , paint IO

NESS, Helen Louise, b Galt, re Cambridge, Ont 1931– , etch paint IO

NESS, Jean. *See* FINDLAY, Jean Ness

NESTEL, Jeannette, b Poland 1923– , paint sculp CAE1 IO SC

NESTOREL, Monyo Simon Mihaelesque, Prince, b Bucharest, Rom, fl 1966– , paint sculp M

N.E. THING CO. *See* BAXTER, Joseph Wilson Iain

NEUENDORFF, Wilhelm, b Altwerpel, Est 1897, d 1977, paint M

NEUFELD, Woldemar/Woldeman, b Ukraine 1909– , prt DFA MM

NEUHOF, Jean, b Maastricht, Neth 1934– , paint CAE1
NEUMANN, Ernst, b Budapest 1907, d Vence, Fr 1955, prt APH M MM NGC1 RCA TB3 UG
NEVEROFF, Alexander, b Yugoslavia 1937– , paint IO
NEVERS, Lorenzo de, b St-Elphège, Que 1883, d Woonsocket, RI 1967, paint K
NEVILLE, G. Douglas, b Toronto 1931– , ske CWW93
NEVILLE, Maureen (Mrs), b Hereford, Eng 1921– , paint M
NEVITT, Richard, b Montreal 1936– , paint M WWA84
NEVITT/NEAVITT[2], Richard Barrington, b Savannah, Ga 1850, d Toronto 1928, paint H[2] Mo98 R1
NEWBOLD, Brian T., b Manchester, Eng 1932– , paint CWW93
NEWBY, Florence Lorraine. *See* LYLE, Florence Lorraine Newby
NEWCOMBE, William John Bertram, b Victoria, BC 1907, d London 1969, paint M MM O.My49 RCA TB3 WWA59 WWB72
NEWCOME, Janet Kathleen. *See* BASMADJIAN, Janet Kathleen Newcome
NEWDIGATE, Elizabeth Ann (m John Mills), b Grahamstown, SA 1934– , paint BDSA
NEWFELD, Frank (b Neufeld), b Brno, Cz 1928– , des illus CBC Co CWW93 M RCA
NEWMAN, Barnett, b New York 1905– d 1970, Amer, paint BE CA1–3 DAA DCAA2,3 L OC P TB3 WA WWA70d73 WWWA
NEWMAN, Brian, b Victoria, BC 1943– , sculp US
NEWMAN, Ernest. *See* NEUMANN, Ernst
NEWMAN, Eva Jana (m Gilles-Jean Mossière), b Prague 1948– , paint BDSA
NEWMAN, H.J., Maj, fl 1959+, paint M
NEWMAN, Jean Dorothy Reading (m T. Campbell Newman), b El Paso, Tex, fl 1950s, paint M WWC71
NEWMAN, John Beatty, b Toronto 1933– , paint CWW93 IO M MF RCA WWA93
NEWMAN, Sydney, b Toronto 1917– , paint sculp CWW93
NEWMAN, Winifred M. (Freda), b London 1915– , paint sculp BDSA
NEWTON, Ada, b 1861, d 1934, paint H
NEWTON, Alison Houston Lockerbie (m Stanley Newton), b Leith, nr Edinburgh 1890, d Toronto 1967, paint GM M MM RCA
NEWTON, Garry, b York, Eng 1939– , paint sculp M
NEWTON, Gilbert Stuart, b Halifax 1794, d Chelsea, London 1835, illus paint App B Bry DNB F G GW H Hu NCAB Red ROM TB1 W1–3
NEWTON, John Neil, b Montreal 1933– , prt IO WWA93
NEWTON, Lilias Torrance (m Francis G. Newton), b Montreal 1896, d Cowansville, Que 1980, paint AGO CC1 CE1,2 CNS40 CWW73 DWA EC FCA M MM NGC1 NGC67 NGC68 RCA TB2 WWA53d76
NEWTON, W. Parker, fl 1885–93, paint H
NEWTON, William Henry, b England, fl 1851–70, d British Columbia 1875, topog H
NEWTON-WHITE, Muriel Elizabeth, b Robillard Tp, Ont 1928– , mur paint M
NEYLAND, Harry A., b McKenzie, Pa 1877, d 1958, Amer, paint AAA33 B MM RCA TB1 WWA40
NG, Betty Shuet-Wah, b Hong Kong, fl 1960s, paint M
NGAN, Wayne, b China 1938– , paint sculp ABC M
NIBLOCK, Hugh, b Toronto, fl 1950s, drw mur paint M

NICE, Ken, b Toronto 1949– , sculp CAE1

NICHOL, Pegi. *See* MacLEOD, Pegi Nicol

NICHOL, Peter, b Slavgored, Sib c 1912– , carv M

NICHOLAS, Joseph George Frederick, b Windsor, Eng 1891, fl 1950s, paint CLA M MA

NICHOLLS, Herbert C., b Whitstable, Eng 1890, ske CWW61

NICHOLLS, Josephine Lewis (m Burr H. Nicholls), b Hamilton, Ont 1865, paint AAA33 DWA F WWA40

NICHOLLS, Ken E., b St Catharines, Ont 1949– , paint sculp DCA

NICHOLS, Frederick B., b Bridgeport, Conn 1824 – d 1906, engr F GW H TB1

NICHOLS, Jack, b Montreal 1921– , paint ACA AE AGO B CC2 CE1,2 CWW70 M MM NGC67 NGC68 RCA S TB3 UG WWA53

NICHOLS, William Dale, b David City, Nebr 1904– , paint M TB2 WWA62

NICHOLSON, Christian Martin, b Saint John, N B 1948– , paint CWW93 IO M

NICKELL, Ruth, fl 1970s, paint M

NICKERSON, Forrest C., b Richfield, NS 1929– , paint M

NICKERSON, Vivian, b Yarmouth, NS, fl 1971– , paint M

NICKLE, Lawrence, b Toronto 1931– , paint M

NICOL, Almira E., b Toronto 1923– , paint SC

NICOL, Nancy, b 1951– , fl 1970s, paint M

NICOL, Pegi. *See* MacLEOD, Pegi Nicol

NICOLAS, Louis, b Aubenas, Fr 1634, d 1678, drw K

NICOLETTI, Rodolfo (Rudi), b Toronto 1914– , paint M MM RCA

NICOLL, James McLaren (Jim) (m Marion F.S.M. Nicoll, q.v.), b Ft MacLeod, Alta 1892, d 1986, paint AA M MM SC RCA

NICOLL, Marion Florence S. Mackay (m James McLaren Nicoll, q.v.), b Calgary 1909, d 1985, paint AA CC1 CWW83 M MM RCA S SC

NIDENOFF, Michele, b London, Ont 1959– , illus C

NIELSEN, Kaj, b Copenhagen 1909– , carv M

NIEMANN, Friedrich C. (Fritz), b Duisburg, Ge 1936– , paint M

NIEMININ, Jorma, b Finland 1940– , paint M

NIEMININ, Martti, b Finland 1943– , paint M

NIESSEN, Wolfram F., b Krefeld, Ge 1923– , sculp M MM

NIEUWLAND, Arend, b Dirksland, Neth 1946– , sculp IO

NIEUWENHUIS, Douwe (Dow), b Netherlands, cart illus M

NIFFELER, Max, b Lucerne, Swi 1934– , sculp CAE1

NIGNUIK, Davidee, b 1925– , fl 1963– , sculp M

NILSSON, Toby, b 1951– , paint prt CAE2

NILSSON, William, b Barry, Wales 1930– , paint prt IO S

NINCHERI, Guido, b Florence, It 1887, d 1973, paint stgl CNS40 M

NIND, Jean Helen Marriott (m Thomas Eagleton Westwood Nind), b Miri, Sarawak, Borneo 1930 , paint prt BDSA IO M WWA93

NINGEWANCE, Patricia, fl 1971– , paint M

NISBET, Florence Alma (Mrs), b Toronto 1913– , paint M

NISHIMURA, Mikko Barbara, b Canada, fl 1967– , paint M

NISKA (b François Lorti), b Montreal 1940– , paint CAE1 M

NIVERVILLE, Georges Hector de, b Ottawa 1928– , paint M MM

NIVERVILLE, Louis de[2], b Andover, Eng 1933– , paint AE CAE1,2[2] CC1

CE1,2 Co[2] IO[2] M MM RCA S[2] UG

NIVIAKSIAK, b Cape Dorset, NWT 1908 – d 1959, prt sculp AGO Co DEA

NIXON, Andrew William (Andy), b Toronto 1931– , paint IO M

NIXON, Donald Allan, b Hamilton, Ont 1928– , drw paint M

NIXON, Elizabeth Prat. *See* LOCKYER, Elizabeth Prat Nixon

NIXON, Gary Laird, b Sarnia, Ont 1945– , paint IO S

NIZAMI, Harris M., b Pakistan 1943– , paint M

NOAH, E7-877, b Frobisher Bay, NWT 1900– , sculp DEA S

NOAH, Kenourak, E9-848, b Povungnituk, Que 1914– , sculp DEA S

NOAH, William, E2-391, b Baker Lake, NWT 1943– , prt sculp Co DEA S

NOBBS, Percy Erskine, b Haddington, Scot 1875, d Montreal 1964, paint CE1,2 CNS27 CWW61 MM Mo12 NGC1 PMC RCA TB3 WWC21

NOEL, Edouard-Auguste, b Paris 1845, d Palaiseau, Fr 1909, Fr, paint H K

NOEL, Jean-Guy, b Montreal 1940– , paint sculp CAE1 M WWA93

NOEL, Marie-Josée, b Montreal 1954– , paint CAE1

NOEL, Richard, b Gaspé area, Que, fl 1970s, paint M

NOESTHEDEN, John Theodore M., b Netherlands 1945– , paint sculp CWW93 IO WWA93

NOHR, Niels, fl 1970– , sculp CAE2

NOKONY, Denis Wesley, b Oxbow, Sask c 1951– , cart paint Des US

NOLAND, Kenneth, b Asheville, NC 1924– , Amer, paint BE CA1–3 DAA DCAA2,3 L OC OCD P TB3 WA WWA93 WWB80

NOLD, John. *See* MILLER, John Arthur

NOLIN, Alice, b Sorel, Que 1896, d Montreal 1967, paint sculp K MM RCA

NOLIN, Géraldine Montgomery (Soeur Marie-Sainte-Véronique), b Winnipeg 1896, d St Boniface, Man 1976, paint K

NOLTE, Gunter, b Germany 1938– , sculp CAE1,2 M WWA93

NONCOURT, Michel de, b Grand-Mère, Que 1941– , sculp M

NONNAST, Paul, b Philadelphia, Pa 1948– , paint sculp M

NONNECKE, Karen, b Lethbridge, Alta 1947– , drw UG

NOOEELARLIK, Josiah, E2-385, b Baker Lake, NWT 1928– , sculp DEA

NOORDHOEK, Harry Cecil, b Moers, Ge 1909– , sculp CAE1 CWW92 M MM RCA

NOR, Jana K., b Prague, Cz 1948– , tap IO

NORBURY, Frank Herbert, b Liverpool, Eng 1871, d Edmonton 1965, sculp M

NORFIELD, Clayton. *See* MASSEY, Hart Parkin Vincent

NORGATE, Robert Maxwell, b Toronto 1920 – d 1956, sculp M O.F49 RCA

NORMAN. *See* RITCHIE, William Norman

NORMAND, Auguste/Augustin, b Trois-Rivières, Que 1836/7, fl 1876, sculp K

NORMAND, Nicolas François, b Charlesbourg, Que 1779, d Trois-Rivières, Que 1854, carv DCB8 K

NORMAND, François, fl 1837–57, carv K

NORMANDEAU, Pierre-Aimé, b Outremont, Que 1906, d Montreal 1965, sculp M MM RCA

NORMANDIN, Richard, b Shawinigan, Que 1934– , paint prt CAE1 M

NORRINGTON, Harold V., b Toronto 1940– , prt IO

NORRIS, George Alexander, b Victoria, BC 1928– , sculp BCS M RCA

NORRIS, Joseph (Joe), b Halifax 1924– , paint DFA KB

NORRIS, Leonard Matheson (Len),

b London 1913– , cart Co CWW83 Des Po86–88 WECa WWA93

NORRIS, Marieanne, b New York, fl 1944+, wlhg SC

NORTH, Diana Thorne. *See* THORNE, Diana

NORTHCOTE, Stafford Henry, 1st Earl of Iddesleigh[2], b London 1818 – d 1887, paint BPp1407[2] DNB H

NORTHCOTT, Ruth J., b Solina, Ont 1913– , paint CWW64

NORTHEY, Rodney, b Toronto 1902– , paint CWW64

NORTON, William Edward, b Boston 1843, d New York 1916, paint AAA15 ANC B F G H MM TB1

NORWELL, Graham Noble, b Edinburgh 1901, d Val-David, Que 1967, paint AGO Hu M MM NGC1 RCA TB2

NORWELL, John Craigie, b Elie, Fife, Scot 1903– , paint M

NOSEWORTHY, George, b 1929, d 1985, paint M

NOTTEBROCK, Pat, b nr Barrhead, Alta c 1941– , paint M

NOURRY-BARRY, Joan P., b Kingston, Ont 1927 , paint sculp AA CAE2

NOVAK, Yozef, b Yugoslavia c 1940– , car paint M

NOVOTNY, George Milos, b Prague 1929– , paint CWW93

NOWAKIWSKA, Halyna, b Ukraine, fl 1966– , paint M

NOWLAN, Emery, b 1887, d 1982, carv DFA KB

NOYES, George Loftus, b Bothwell, Ont 1864, d 1954, paint AAA33 AAW2 F H TB1 WWA40 WWWA

NUDDS, Ralph Arnold James, b Blenheim, Ont 1921– , sculp CAE1 M

NUDDS, Wallace Albert John, b Blenheim, Ont 1919– , cart paint sculp CAE1 M

NUGENT, John Cullen, b Montreal 1921– , sculp CE1,2 M RCA WWA84

NULF, Frank Allen, b Lima, Ohio 1931– , paint WWA86

NULITIS, Arnolds, b Latvia 1896, d Toronto 1988, paint M MM TB2

NUTT, Elizabeth Styring, b Oucham, I of M 1870, d Sheffield, Eng c 1946, min paint CWW38 DBA DWA Fo Hu M MM NGC1 RA RCA TB2 WWB34

NUTT, Kenneth Eric (aka Eric Beddows), b Woodstock, Ont 1951– , illus paint CBC CWW93 IO

NUTTING, Benjamin F., b c 1801, d 1887, Amer, paint DeV9 GW

NYILASI, Tibor, b Kesztolc, Hu 1936– , paint IO M PHA

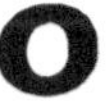

OAD, Jan, b Kihno Isld, Est 1889, carv DFA WENA

OAKLEY, Fred, fl 1963– , illus paint M

OAKLEY, George, b England 1793, d 1869, Amer, paint B F GW H TB1 Y

OBERGFELL, Richard, b Germany 1921, d 1971, paint M

OBERNE, Marjorie Mary Borden[2] (Mrs), b Montreal 1911– , paint M MM[2] RCA[2]

OBREAU, Gabrielle, b Bucharest, Rom 1917– , paint IO

O'BRIEN, D.C., fl 1846–62, drw H

O'BRIEN, Hazel, b Alberta, fl 1960s, paint sculp M

O'BRIEN, Henry Higgins Donatus, b 1801, d 1868, paint DFA PNL

O'BRIEN, J. Leonard, b New Brunswick 1895, paint CWW70 M

O'BRIEN, John Daniel O'Connell, b Saint John, NB 1831, d Halifax 1891, paint ACA DCB12 DMA DSP H H77 NGC1 NGC67 PP

O'BRIEN, Lucius Richard, b The Woods, Kempenfelt Bay, re Shanty Bay, Ont 1832, d Toronto 1899, paint ACA AE AGO App B CE1,2 Co DBA DCB12 DeV1,8 DMA EC G H H77 LeJ M MM Mo98 NGC1 NGC67 PNL RCA ROM Sam TB1 UG W1–3

O'BRIEN, Mary Elizabeth, b Kingston, Ont 1956– , paint IO

O'BRIEN, Michael David Joseph, b Ottawa 1948– , drw sculp M

O'BRIEN, Patricia Dorothy Gunn[2] (Paddy) (Mrs), b Surrey, Eng 1929– , paint IO M[1,2] MM RCA

O'BRIEN, Sylvia B., b Halifax 1952– , sculp IO

OBROTZA, Lydia, b 1939– , paint M

OCHS, Peter Paul, b Tilset, Pru 1931, d Gibsons, BC 1994, sculp BCS CAE1 M WWA82

O'CONNOR, Harry, b Ottawa 1892 – d 1963, carv M

OCTAVO. *See* JULIEN, Octave-Henri

ODDY, Allan Colman, b Eriksdale, Man 1923– , paint M

O'DETTE, John Herbert, b Brockville, Ont 1920– , paint CWW93

ODJIG, Daphne (m Chester Beavon), b Wikwemikong, Manitoulin Isld, Ont 1919– , paint CE1,2 Co CWW93 DFA M WWC85

O'DONNELL, Daphne Lee, b Quebec, fl 1971– , paint M

O'DONNELL, Paul, b Aylmer, Que c 1940– , sculp M

OELSCHTEGER, Gustavus, b Canada c 1833, fl 1860, engr GW H

OESTERLE, Leonhard Friedrich, b Bietigheim, Ge 1915– , sculp CAE1 CWW93 IO M MM RCA WWA93

O'FLYNN, Claudia Yvonne, b Kitchener, Ont 1938– , sculp wlhg CAE1

OGDEN, Henry Alexander (Harry), b Philadelphia, Pa 1856, d Englewood, NJ 1936, Amer, illus AAA33 AAW1 B F H Sam TB1,2 WWA36d38 WWWA Y

OGILVIE, Jessie Aird, b London 1908– , paint M

OGILVIE, Willa Margaret, b Montreal 1933– , paint M MM

OGILVIE, William Abernethy, b Stutterheim, nr Cape Town, SA 1901, d Toronto 1989, paint ACA AGO CC2 CE1,2 CWW89 H77 M MM NGC1 NGC67 NGC68 O.My48 RCA S TB2 UG WWA91

OGILVY, Carol Cole (Mrs), b Rossland, BC, fl 1957+, paint M

OGILVY, Isabella Ewan Laurie (m John Ogilvy), b Montreal 1863, fl 1936, paint CNS40 D WA H MM

O'GORMAN, Mabel (1913 m Constantine A. O'Gorman), paint CNS40 MM

OGYALLAY-MORELL, Egon (s Egon O. Morell), b Budapest 1924– , paint IO

O'HAGAN, Margaret S. Peterson. *See* PETERSON, Margaret S.

O'HANLON, Harry, b Edmonton 1915– , paint sculp DAS

O'HARA, James Frederick, b Ottawa 1904, d 1980, Amer, paint Sam WWA78d80

O'HARA, Pat (m Richard Schneider), fl 1970s, paint CAE1 M

OHASHI, William Ken, b Canada 1934– , mur sculp M

OHE, Dorothy Katie Minna von der (m Harry Kiyooka, q.v.), b Peers, Alta 1937– , sculp AA M RCA SC WWA93

O'HENLY, John Donald, b Toronto 1923– , drw paint IO M MM

OHI, Ruth, b Toronto 1964– , illus C

OILLE, Ethel Lucille (m Kenneth McNeill Wells), b Toronto 1912– , engr illus M RCA

O'KEEFE, Judith, fl 1970– , paint prt CAE2

OKEY, Ronald N., b Northampton, Eng 1921– , paint M

OLASSON, B., fl 1885, paint H MM

OLDFIELD, Clifford Thomas, b Montreal 1923– , paint M

OLDRICH, Robert (Bob), b Ostrava, Cz 1920– , paint sculp M

OLDRING, Joanne. *See* SYDIAHA, Joanne Oldring

OLITSKI, Jules, (b Jules Demikovsky), b Snovsk, USSR 1922– , Amer, paint sculp BE CA1–3 DAA DCAA2,3 OC P TB3 WA WWA93

OLIVER, Bobbie, b Windsor, Ont c 1945– , paint IO

OLIVER, John, b Scotland 1807/8, fl 1863, paint GW H Y

OLIVER, Thomas Craig, b St Catharines, Ont 1949– , prt IO

OLIVIER, Suzanne, b Montreal 1943– , paint CWW93

OLNEY, Georges L. (s Jorge), b c 1933– , paint M

OLSANSKY, Klement, b Brno, Cz 1909– , paint M

OLSEN, Andreas V., b Copenhagen, fl 1967– , paint M

OLSON, Gary G., b Minneapolis, Minn 1946– , drw prt AA CAE2 SC

OLSON, Jeff, b Cloris, NM 1946– , sculp CAE2

OLTEAN, Eleanor June Lloyd (m Dean C. Oltean), b Calgary 1924– , paint BDSA US

OLTHUIS, Stanley Lorne, b Barrhead, Alta 1951– , paint IO

OMAN, Nelda, b Michigan 1948– , paint CAE1

ONDAATJE, Betty Jane Kimbark (m D.G. Jones; m Michael Ondaatje), b Toronto 1928– , paint prt IO M MM

O'NEIL, Bruce William, b Winnipeg 1942– , paint AA M SC WWA93

O'NEILL, Helen (Mrs), fl 1958, d 1977, paint M

ONGMAN, Marlene (Mrs), b c 1933– , paint M

ONLEY, Norman Antony (Toni) (x Antonio), b Douglas, I of M 1928– , paint AE AGO B CAE1,2 CC1 CE1,2 Co CWW93 DCA M MM RCA S SC TB3 UG US WWA93

OOMEN, Susan Antoinette, b Smiths Falls, Ont 1953– , paint IO

OONARK, Jessie Seekanik, E2-284, b nr Black River, Keewatin, NWT 1906, d Churchill, Man 1985, prt CE1,2 Co DEA M RCA SC US

OOSTERHOFF, William Frederic Karel, b Delft, Neth 1895– , sculp M

OOSTERMAN, Pierre, b Netherlands, fl 1967– , wlhg M

OPERTI, Albert Jasper Ludwig Roccabigliera, b Turin, It 1852, d 1927, It, car paint AAAd1929 DMA F TB1

OPPENHEIMER, Joseph, b Wurtzburg, Ge 1876, d 1966, paint M

ORA. *See* MARKSTEIN, Aurelia

ORAM, Barry Spence, b Birmingham, Eng 1936– , paint sculp IO

ORBELIANI, Mary (m Alexis Orbeliani, Prince), b Russia 1873, paint DWA M

OREMBA, Krystyra, b Poland 1949– , paint pas IO

ORENSTEIN, Henry, b Midland, Ont 1918– , gra M O.Ag50 RCA

ORLEANS, François-Ferdinand d', Prince-de-Joinville, b Neuilly, Fr 1818, d 1900, paint K

ORLOWSKI, Stanislaw Tadeusz, b Skarzysko, Pol 1920– , paint CWW93

ORTIZ, Arthur Donald, b Toronto 1925– , paint O.N48

ORTON, Ann, fl 1971– , enam M

O'RYAN, Lillie V. *See* KLEIN, Lillie V. O'Ryan

OSBORN, Sherard, R Adm (x Osborne), b London 1822 – d 1875, Eng, topog DNB H

OSBORNE, Dennis Henry (m Jean Osborne, q.v.), b Portsmouth, Eng 1919– , paint M MM RA WBA1 WWB84

OSBORNE, Jean (m Dennis Henry Osborne, q.v.), b Antrim Co, N Ire 1926– , des M

OSBORNE, John, fl 1965– , paint M

OSBORNE, Lyndal, b Newcastle, Aus 1940– , drw prt AA CAE2

OSBORNE, Rosalynde Fuller, b Hamilton, Ont, fl 1924+, paint Hu M MM RCA

OSCAR, Arthur, fl 1967– , paint sculp M

OSGOOD, Ross Reverdy (s R.R. Osgoode), b Dereham, Ont 1867, d St

Thomas, Ont 1946, paint AGO H Hu M PMC

OSHAWEETOK/OSHWEETUK[2], 'A,' E7-932, b Cape Dorset, NWT 1918– , sculp DEAp177 MM[2]

OSHAWEETOK/OSHOOWEETOOK, 'B,' E7-1154 (aka Osuitok Ipeelee[2]), b Cape Dorset, NWT 1923– , prt sculp AGO CE2[2] CWW93[2] DEAp177 RCA

OSICKA, Peter, b Prague, Cz 1950– , paint prt CAE1 IO

OSINCZUK, Michael, b Ukraine c 1890, fl 1949+, Amer, paint M

OSLER, Clara Du Bois. *See* FITZGERALD, Clara Du Bois Osler

OSTED, Hans, b Denmark 1916– , paint M

OSTELL, John, b London 1813, d Montreal 1892, paint H

OSTIGUY, Jean-René, b Marieville, Que 1925– , paint CWW93 WWA93

O'TOOLE, Nancy (m Eric O'Toole), b Saskatchewan 1930– , paint ABC

OTT, Philip A., fl 1855–7, paint GW H

OTTENBRITE, Philip, b Windsor, Ont 1951– , paint pas IO

OTTO, Guttorn, b nr Lodz, Pol 1919– , paint M

OTTOCHIE, Ashoona, E7-1105, b Cape Dorset, NWT 1942– , prt sculp DEA

OUCHI, Eugene Masahiko, b Vernon, BC 1943– , paint prt CAE1,2 M SC

OUDEMANS, Michiel, b Fredericton 1950– , engr BB

OUDENDAG, Egbert, b Raalte, Neth 1914– , paint M WWC75

OUELLETTE, Alain, b St-Pascal, Que c 1939– , paint M

OUELLET, David, b 1844, d 1915, carv K

OUTHET, Rickson A., b Montreal 1874, paint MM PMC RCA

OVENS, Fran Reid (Mrs), b Vancouver 1935– , paint prt ABC

OUTRAM, Helen Barbara Howard. *See* HOWARD, Helen Barbara

OVEREND, William Heysham, b Coatham, Yorks 1851, d 1898, Eng, illus paint B BA DBMaP DBWA DMA DSP G H TB1 Y

OWEN, Frederick Howard, b Jasper, Alta 1934– , sculp M

OWEN, James G., fl 1873–90, illum litho H

OWEN, John, fl 1874–80, paint H RCA

OWEN, Violet (m Peter Owen), b Edmonton 1930– , drw paint AA CAE1 M

OXBOROUGH, Dorothy Marie (m H.A. Johnson), b Calgary, Alta 1922– , paint pas M

OZARD, Elmore George, b Victoria, BC 1914– , gra paint M

OZERDEM, Ulker, b Turkey 1926– , sculp M

OZOLS, Arija, b Latvia, fl 1970s, paint CAE1

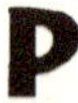

PACEY, Mary Elizabeth Carson (m Desmond Pacey), b Ottawa 1915– , paint M MA

PACHTER, Charles, b Toronto 1942– , prt IO M

PACKARD, Peggy Walton, b Victoria, BC 1914– , paint sculp M

PACKHAM, Madeleine Matte[2] (Mimi) (m James Packham), b Regina 1929– , paint CWW93[2] IO

PAESIDE, Adrian, b Dunedin, NZ 1957– , car Po1–3

PAGE, Andrée, b Baie-Comeau, Que 1951– , drw sculp CAE1

PAGE, Frederick Rowden, fl 1820–60, drw DeV4

PAGE, J.R., fl 1864–5, paint H

PAGE, Lewis, b Quebec 1931– , sculp M

PAGE[1], Patricia Kathleen (s P.K. Irwin[2], pseud Judith Cape) (m William Arthur Irwin, q.v.), b Swanage, Dorset 1916– , paint CC1 CE1,2 Co CWW93 M[1,2] NGC2[2]

PAGE, Robin, b London 1932– , paint sculp M WWA82

PAGET, Henry Marriott, b London 1856, d 1936, Eng, illus paint B1 DBA DBHP DVP G RA WBA1 WWW

PAGET, James (Jim), b Port Perry, Ont 1943– , paint M

PAGET, Maude Lumb (Mrs), b England c 1873, d Victoria, BC 1967, min paint M

PAGINTON, George Alfred, b Swindon, Eng 1904– , paint M MM

PAGNUELO, Françoise, b Westmount, Que 1918, d 1957, paint M MM

PAINCHAUD, Julie (Soeur Saint-François de Borgia[2]), b Ile-aux-Grués, Que 1799/1800, d Quebec 1834, paint H[2] K

PALARDY, Jori. *See* SMITH, Marjorie Thurston (Jori)

PALARDY, Joseph-Jean-Albert (m Marjori T. [Jori] Smith, q.v.), b Fitchburg, Mass 1905– , paint Hu M MM RCA

PALCHINSKI, John (m Sylvia Scott Palchinski, q.v.), b Cudworth, Sask 1940– , paint prt IO M UG

PALCHINSKI, Sylvia Scott (m John Palchinski, q.v.), b Regina 1946– , prt sculp BDSA CAE1,2 M

PALEY, R.L., fl 1886–8, paint H RCA

PALETTE. *See* PARKER, John Frederick Delisle

PALFREEMAN, Elizabeth Patricia Mary, b Braintree, Essex 1929– , sculp M MM

PALIN, Ethel, fl 1888–95, paint H RCA

PALKO, Helga Maria Jandaurek (m Michael Palko), b Linz, Au 1928– , drw M US

PALL, (Moricz) John (Janos), b Bajot, Hu 1914– , paint PHA

PALM, Ottilie (Palm-Jost[2]) (m Josef Jost, q.v.), b Hamilton, Ont 1878, d Munich, Ge 1961, paint B DWA Mp1476[2] MM RCA TB[2]

PALMER, Herbert Franklin (Frank), b Calgary 1921– , paint AGO CC2 M MM NGC68 RCA SC TB3

PALMER, Herbert Sidney, b Toronto 1881 – d 1970, paint AGO CC2 CNS40 CWW64 Hu M MM NGC1 RCA S TB2 UG US WWA62

PALMER, J.E. Lynwood, fl 1891–2, paint H

PALMER, Mary Elizabeth. *See* MILLER, Mary Elizabeth Palmer

PALMER, Samuel, fl 1834–45, paint H H77 M

PALMER, Valerie, b Toronto 1950– , paint CWW93

PALMER, W.J., fl 1873, illus H

PALUMBO, Jacques-Gaëtan, b Philippeville, Alg 1939– , paint sculp M RCA WWA93

PAN, Marta (m André Wogensky), b Budapest, Hu c 1923– , sculp M

PANABAKER, Frank Shirley, b Hespeler, Ont 1904, d Ancaster, Ont 1992, paint AE CWW92 M MM O.F49 PMC RCA S Sam UG WWA80

PANAGAPKA, Edward Patrick, b Kapuskasing, Ont 1933– , sculp IO

PANCHAL, Mansaram. *See* MANSARAM, Panchal

PANEELOO/PANELOO[2], E5-244 (m Philip Kominerk, E5-902, q.v.), b Clyde River, Baffin Isld, NWT 1935– , sculp DEA M[2]

PANET, Louise Amélie. *See* BERCZY, Louise Amélie Panet

PANGNARK, John, E1-104, b Windy Lake, NWT 1920, d Rankin Inlet, NWT 1980, sculp CAE1 CE1,2 Co DEA M

PANICHELL, Achille, b France, fl 1924–6, des paint K

PANKO, Daniel Duane, b Fir Mountain, Sask 1937– , paint CAE1

PANKO, Don, b Fir Mountain, Sask 1937– , paint CAE1

PANKO, William, b Tulukow, Au 1892, d Edmonton 1948, paint CC1 DFA H74 H77 KB M PNL

PANNETON, Jacqueline. *See* MARTEL, Jacqueline Panneton

PANNETON, Louis-Philippe, b Trois-Rivières, Que 1906– , drw paint M MM RCA

PANNETON, Louise de Cotret (Mrs), b Trois-Rivières, Que 1926– , paint tap CAE1 DCA M
PANTER-DOWNES, Edward D., Lt, fl 1857–9, Eng, topog DFA H PNL
PANTON, Lawrence Arthur Colley, b Engremont, Ches 1894, d Toronto 1954, paint AGO CC2 CNS40 CWW52 EC GM Hu M NGC1 O.F50 RCA S TB2,3 UG W2,3 WWA53d56 WWB54d56
PANTON, Paul Ramus, b Melita, Man 1935– , paint M
PAPIALU, Aisa/Isa, E9-1413, b Povungnituk, Que, sculp S
PAPIAULUK, Josie Pamiuto, b nr Issuksiuvi, NWT 1918– , drw prt CWW93
PAPP, Joseph Sulyokde, b Savjhely, Hu 1897, paint CNS36 MM RCA
PAQUET, François-Xavier, b Quebec 1845, fl 1869–91, illus paint K
PAQUET, Jean-Baptiste, b St-Charles, Que 1828, d 1912, carv H K
PAQUET dit LAVALLEE, André, b St-Charles, Que 1799, d Charlesbourg, Que 1860, sculp DCB8 K
PAQUETTE, Devona Lorraine (m Philip McLorn), b Woodstock, Ont 1930– , gra paint M
PAQUETTE, Joy, b Ottawa 1922– , paint M MM
PAQUETTE, Marguerite. *See* FAINMEL, Marguerite Paquette
PAQUETTE, Suzanne Marie Cécile, b Valleyfield, Que 1949– , gra paint M
PAQUETTE-GAMACHE, Jeannine/Janine. *See* GAMACHE, Jeannine/Janine
PAQUIN, Roger, b Deschambault, Que 1941– , sculp M
PARADIS, C.A.M., Abbé, b Canada, fl 1882–7, paint H K
PARADIS, Guy, b nr Lévis, Que 1930– , paint M
PARADIS, Jérôme (Frère Jérôme), b Charlesbourg, Que 1902– , paint M
PARADIS, Jobson Emilian Henri, b St-Jean-sur-Richelieu (St-Johns), Que 1871, d Guelph, Ont 1926, paint H K MM RCA W1–3
PARANT, Alexis, b Quebec 1832/3, fl 1871–6, sculp K
PARANT, Ulderic, b Quebec 1854/5, fl 1871, sculp K
PARAY, Michael, b Calgary 1911– , paint M
PARCEHIAN, Duffy, b Sofia, Bul, fl 1947+, gra WWA82
PARE, Alexandrine, b St-Bruno, Que 1840, d Montreal 1906, drw H K
PARE, Anne, b Quebec 1938– , paint prt M MM
PARE, Clement, b Deschambault, Que 1918– , sculp M
PARENT, Léandre, b Quebec 1809 – d 1889, carv K
PARENT, Louis Joseph, b Montreal 1908– , sculp M MM
PARENT, Louise, b St-Jerome, Que 1930– , gra paint M MM
PARENT, Michel, b Charlesbourg, Que 1938– , paint M MM
PARENT, Mimi (m Jean Benoit, q.v.), b Outremont, Que 1924– , paint M MM
PARENT, Omer, b Quebec 1907– , paint CWW93 M MM
PARENT, Pierre-Ovide-Lucien, b Montreal 1893 – d 1956, illus paint K MM
PARFITT, Gilbert, b England 1886, d 1966, paint DFA
PARISO, Narcisse, b Quebec 1823/4, fl 1856, sculp K
PARIZEAU, Marcel-B., b Montreal 1898 – d 1945, paint CNS44 K RCA
PARK, Asa/Aza, fl 1815, d Lexington, Ky 1827, Amer, paint F GW H TB1
PARKER, Arthur Henry, b Newcastle-under-Lyme, Eng 1874, paint MM PMC RCA
PARKER, Delisle. *See* PARKER, John Frederick Delisle
PARKER, Elmo Elizabeth, b Strathroy, Ont 1915– , paint IO
PARKER, Gretchen, b Montreal 1915– , paint M

PARKER, Harley Walter Blait, b Ft William, re Thunder Bay, Ont 1915, d Vancouver 1992, paint M MM O.Ag50 RCA

PARKER, Jessie Cecilia Alward (m Benjamin Cronyn Parker), b Courtland, Ont 1891, fl 1963, paint DWA M MM

PARKER, Jessie Maretta, b Prince Edward Island 1943– , gra prt M

PARKER, John Frederick Delisle (aka Palette), b New York 1884, d Vancouver 1962, paint AAA25 CLA F M MM TB1 Y

PARKER, Lewis, b Toronto 1926– , cart illus Des M

PARKER, Robert, Jr, fl 1842, d c 1865, min paint H

PARKER, William, b Calgary 1946– , paint AA SC

PARKINSON, Cathy (b Marguerite Muirhead), b Regina, fl 1964– , paint M

PARKINSON, Patricia Anne Cleary (Pat) (m David K. Parkinson), b London 1938– , prt M

PARKS, Hazel A. *See* MacLEOD, Hazel A. Parks

PARKYNS, George Isham, b Nottingham, Eng c 1750, d Cambridge, Eng c 1820, Eng, paint DBLP DBMaP DeV9 DFA DMA F G GW H NGC67 TB1

PARLANE, William George, b Prince George, BC 1914– , illus paint M

PARLOW, Maida Doris. *See* KNOWLES, Maida Doris Parlow

PARR, E7-1022 (m Eleesushee, E7-1023, q.v.), b Baffin Isld, NWT 1893, d Cape Dorset, NWT 1969, prt sculp CE1,2 Co DEA UG US

PARR, Thomas Roworth, Hon Lt Col, b Geneva, Swi 1836, fl 1890, Eng, topog H WHC

PARRIS, Mary Delmege (m J.E. Parris), b Edmonton 1914– , paint M

PARRISH, Stephen, b Philadelphia, Pa 1846, d Windsor, Vt 1938, Amer, paint AAA33 App B DBA F H NCAB RCA TB1 WWA38d40 WWWA

PARSONS, Bruce. *See* PARSONS, William Bruce

PARSONS, Charles, b Rowlands Castle, Hants 1821, d Brooklyn, NY 1910, paint DeV4 F GW TB1 Y

PARSONS, Helen Somerton. *See* SHEPHERD, Helen Somerton Parsons

PARSONS, William, b Toronto 1909, d 1982, paint M

PARSONS, William Bruce, b Montreal 1937– , paint M MM UG

PARTHENAIS, Louis-Etienne-Anatole, b St-Paul d'Industrie, Que 1839, d Joliette, Que 1864, sculp K

PARTRIDGE, David Gerry, b Akron, Ohio 1919– , paint sculp AE AGO CA89 CC1 CWW93 M MM O.My49 RCA S TB3 UG WWA93

PARTRIDGE, Donald Warren (m Jean E.H. Partridge, q.v.), b Cincinnati, Ohio 1900– , paint CWW64 M MM WWC66

PARTRIDGE, Jean Eleanor Hughes (1949 m Donald Warren Partridge, q.v.), fl 1945+, paint M

PARTRIDGE, Joseph E., b England 1792, fl 1830, drw min paint DMA F GW H

PARTZ, Felix (aka Ron Gabe, General Idea, q.v.), b Winnipeg 1945, d Toronto 1994, mmed WWA93

PARZYBOK, Christine Currlin, b USA 1948– , paint sculp M

PARZYBOK, Stephen M., b 1944– , coll drw sculp M

PASSEPOIL. *See* BOURGEOIS, Aldéric

PASSILLE-SYLVESTRE de, Micheline, b Montreal 1936– , enam M MQ

PASSILLE-SYLVESTRE, Yves de, b Montreal 1932– , enam M MQ

PASSMORE, J., fl 1845–50, paint H

PASTERNAK, Eugenia Nowakiwsky (m Eugene Pasternak), b Halychyna, Ukr 1919– , paint CWW93

PATEL, Mahen, b Dar-es-Salaam, Tan 1939– , paint M

PATERSON, Alexander, b Isle of Whithorn, Scot 1887, paint WWNA

PATERSON, Alice Pringle (Mrs), b Hamilton, Ont, fl 1950s, paint M

PATERSON, Robert Allen, b Unity, Sask 1936– , etch paint M RCA

PATKAU, Karen Anne, b Winnipeg 1951– , gra illus C CWW93

PATON, David, b Fernie, BC 1921– , paint sculp M MM

PATON, Richard, b London 1717 – d 1791, Eng, engr paint B Bry DBHP DBLP DBMaP DeV9 DMA DNB DSP G H OELP Red TB1 WHC

PATRIC, Ruth (Mrs McPherson), b Winnipeg 1897, paint DWA M MM

PATRICIA, HRH Princess Victoria, Patricia Helena Elizabeth, Lady Patricia Ramsay[2] (m Hon Sir Alexander Robert Maule Ramsay), b Buckingham Palace 1886, d Windlesham, Sur 1974, Eng, paint BPp721/ Dalhousie DBA[2] DNB[2] DWA[2] MM RA[2] RCA TB2[2] WBA[2]1,2 WWW[2]

PATRICK, James H., b Cranbrook, BC 1911, d Los Angeles 1944, paint AC WWA41d47

PATRICK, Martha A., fl 1898–1900, paint H RCA

PATRY, Edmond (de Patrie), b Quebec 1856/7, fl 1927, sculp K

PATSTONE, Alfred Cyril, b Bentley, Alta 1908– , paint M

PATTEN, Edmund, fl 1838–50, Eng, illus DVP G H

PATTEN, Thomas, fl 1760–2, topog DeV3 H ROM

PATTERSON, Andrew Dickson (m Edith L.R. Patterson, q.v.), b Picton, Ont 1854, d Montreal 1930, paint AGO DeV8 EC H Hu M MM Mo12 NGC1 RCA ROM TB3 W1–3

PATTERSON, Clyde Rodier, b Portage la Prairie, Man 1914– , paint CWW93

PATTERSON, Daniel, b 1884/6, d 1968, sculp DFA KB

PATTERSON[1], Edith Lalande[2] Ravenshaw[3] (m Andrew Dickson Patterson, q.v.), b Eastsheen, Sur, fl 1896–1924, paint DBA[1,3] DVP[3] G[3] MM RA[1,2] RCA

PATTERSON, George E., b Frontenac Co, Ont 1862, fl 1889+, engr H

PATTERSON, Glen/Glenn, b Victoria, BC 1953– , des sculp M

PATTERSON, Joyce Isobel, b London, Ont 1930– , prt M

PATTERSON, Nancy Lou (m E. Palmer Patterson), b Worcester, Mass 1929– , paint sculp IO M

PATTERSON, Russel, b Omaha, Nebr 1890, d 1977, cart des Des IA1,2

PATTERSON, Sascha Jane, b Toronto 1912– , paint Hu

PATTERSON, William John, b Belfast, Ire 1916– , paint AGO Hu RCA

PATTISON, Albert Mead, b Clarenceville, Que 1887, d Hudson, Que 1957, paint M MM RCA

PATTON, Andrew John (Andy), b Winnipeg 1952– , paint WWA93

PATTON, Harold Preston, b Calgary, 1929– , paint sculp CWW93 M

PATTULLO, Mary Frances (m W. D. Gregory[2]), fl 1889–90, paint DWA[2] H[2] MM RCA

PAUL, Awana G. (m Norman Fraser Paul), b Winnipeg 1932– , sculp M

PAUL, Gregory Preston, b Toronto 1933– , paint M WWA62

PAUL, Leonard, b Halifax 1953– , drgt DCA

PAUL, Louise, b Ft William, re Thunder Bay, Ont, d Oakville, Ont 1961, paint sculp M RCA

PAUL, Pijush Kanti, b Seremba, Malaya c 1934– , paint M

PAULING/PAULDING/PAULIN/ PALIN, Richard A., fl 1841–70, paint GW H

PAULOOSIE, E9-1540, b Port Harrison, Que 1915– , sculp DEA

PAULS, Henry, b Khortitza, Rus 1904– , paint DFA KB

PAULS, Mary Funk (Mrs), b Morden, Man, fl 1967– , paint M

PAUNICHAA (aka Pannichiak), E7-1064 (m Munamee 'B,' E7-1063, q.v.), b Cape Dorset, NWT 1920– , prt DEA

PAUTA (aka Pauta Saila[2]), E7-990 (m Pitalouisa, E7-1006, q.v.), b Kilaparutua Isld, NWT 1916– , drw prt sculp CE1,2 Co CWW93[2] DEA M US

PAVELIC, Myfanwy Spencer (m Donald Campbell; m Nikola Pavelic), b Victoria, BC 1916– , paint CE1,2 RCA WWNA

PAWCZUK, Eugene, b Germany 1946– , paint sculp M

PAWSON, Ruth May, b Stratford, Ont 1908– , paint BDSA M

PAXY, Charles, b Hungary c 1916– , sculp M

PAYNE, David H., b England c 1885, d 1954, paint M S

PAYNE, Emma Lane, b Canada 1874, paint AAA33 B DWA F TB1 WWA40 Y

PAYNE, Emma Solvason (m Gordon Eastcott Payne, q.v.), b Nova Scotia 1899, paint AAA33 M WWA40

PAYNE, Frances Emily Travers (m John Payne, q.v.), b Toronto 1864, d 1923, paint H

PAYNE, Gordon Eastcott, b Payne's Mills, Ont c 1890, paint AGO M MA O.F48 PMC RCA

PAYNE, Gordon MacEwan, b Ashcroft, BC 1933– , paint DCA M

PAYNE, John (m Frances E.T. Payne, q.v.), fl late 19th cen, paint H

PAYNE, Reginald A., b Montreal 1915– , paint M

PAYTON, Evlyn Beatrice Eaton (m Russel T. Payton), b Sidcup, Eng 1920– , paint prt CAE1 IO M

PAZ, Hilda I., b Ottawa 1951– , paint IO

PAZUKAITE, Vanda, b Lithuania 1911– , paint prt M

PEABODY, Franklin Winchester, b Whitehall, NY c 1826, fl 1870, Amer, engr GW H Y

PEACHEY, James, fl c 1773, d 1797, Eng, etch paint CE1,2 DBLP DCB4 DeV3,7 G H H77 PNL ROM WHC

PEACOCK, Graham, b London 1945– , paint AA CAE1,2 M

PEACOCK, Wilbur Kells, b Canton, Ont nr Port Hope, Que 1898, d Canton, Ont 1990, paint M MM O.N48

PEARCE, Deborah A. (s D. Pearce), b 1952– , paint IO M

PEARL, Sonia (Mrs), b Ottawa 1938– , paint IO M

PEARLE, Harold Abraham, b 1891, d 1977, etch illus paint APH

PEARN, Maxwell Clark, b Sussex, NB 1909– , paint M

PEARRON, Jean. *See* PIERRON / PEARRON, Jean

PEARSE, B.W., fl 1853+, d 1902, topog H

PEARSON, Charles Gordon, b Toronto 1907 , paint Hu M

PEARSON, Ella. *See* MACKINNON-PEARSON, Ella Cecilia

PEARSON, Freda Canellakos (Mrs), b Ottawa 1902– , paint M MM

PEARSON, Ian Mackinnon. *See* MACKINNON-PEARSON, Ian

PEARSON, Leo Earl, b Lawrence, Kans 1883, d 1952, paint Hu M NGC1 TB3

PECK, Hugh A., b Montreal 1888 – d 1945, paint M MM RCA

PECK, Miriam Louise, b New Westminster, BC 1900– , paint M

PECK, Pamela Merrill (s Merrill) (m Esmond H. Peck), b 1918– , paint M MM

PECK, Robin, b Alberta 1950– , sculp M

PEDDER, John (s J.P.), b Liverpool 1850, d Maidenhead, Eng 1929, Eng, paint B DBA DBWA DVLP DVP DWP G H PNL RA TB1,2 WBA1 WWB29 WWW

PEDERSEN, Paul Aleksander, b Vadso, Nor 1906– , paint M

PEDERSON, Tilde, b Denmark 1917– , paint CAE1 IO M

PEDNEAULT, Joachim (s Pedno[2]),

b Isle-aux-Coudres, Que 1930/2– , paint CAE1[2]

PEDRALBA, Rodrigo, b Philippines 1953– , paint ABC

PEEL, John R., b England, fl 1856–70, paint M

PEEL, Mildred, Lady (m Sir George William Ross[2]), b London, Ont 1856, d 1920, paint DWA H M MM Mo98,12[2] RCA

PEEL, Paul, b London, Ont 1860, d Paris 1892, paint AE AGO B CE1,2 Co DCB12 EC H H77 Hu LeJ M MM NGC1 NGC67 RCA St TB1 W1–3

PEGY, W., fl 1885, paint H RCA

PEHAP, Erich Konstantin (Eric), b Viljandi, Est 1912– , paint prt IO M RCA WWA82

PELHAM, Richard, b London 1941– , illus T

PELL, Augustus J., fl 1859–85, paint H MM RCA

PELLAN, Alfred (b Pelland), b Quebec 1906, d Laval, Que 1988, paint ACA AGO B CA1 CAE1 CC2 CE1,2 Co CWW88 H77 M MM MQ NGC1 NGC67 OC P RCA S TB2 WWA89 WWC66

PELLETIER, André, b Quebec 1943– , paint CAE1 M

PELLETIER, Andrée, b Montreal 1951– , sculp CWW93

PELLETIER, David, b Toronto 1950– , sculp IO

PELLETIER, Regina (m Paul A. Pelletier), b Claire, NB 1898, fl 1962, carv DWA M

PELLETIER, Robert, fl 1938+ , sculp M MM

PELLUS, G.E., fl 1921–30, illus paint K

PELTOMAA, Arthur Matti, b Finland 1922– , sculp M

PEMBERTON, Augustus Frederick, fl 1855–71, topog H

PEMBERTON, John Tudor, b Toronto 1937– , paint IO

PEMBERTON, Joseph Despard, b Dublin 1821, d Victoria, BC 1893, paint DCB12 H

PEMBERTON, Sophie Theresa (m Arthur John Beanlands[2]; m Deane Drummond), b Victoria, BC 1869 – d 1959, paint CC1 DBA DBF2 DFP3 DVP DWA G H77 M MM Mo12[2] RCA

PEMBERTON-SMITH, Frederica Augusta (Freda), b Montreal 1902, d Vankleek Hill, Ont 1991, paint M

PENCE, Eileen, b Ogden, Utah 1944– , engr BB

PENFOLD, Catherine/Katherine[2] S., fl 1892–6, paint H MM RCA[2]

PENNELL, Joseph, b Philadelphia 1857/60, d Brooklyn, NY 1926, Amer, etch paint AAA26d28 AAW3 AC B B1 DAA DAB F H NCAB TB1 WBA1 WWW WWWA Y

PENNEY, Millicent, b Newfoundland 1907 , paint M

PENSON, Seymour R.G., fl 1880–91, paint H RCA

PENTLAND, Catherine (Mrs Murata[2]), b Toronto 1948– , paint pas IO[2] M

PENTRIDGE. *See* HUTCHISON, William Bruce

PENTZ, Donald Robert, b Bridgewater, NS 1940– , paint CWW93 M MM RCA WWA93

PEPER, Ernest August Wilhelm, b Hamburg, Ge 1883, d Waterloo, Ont 1969, sculp M

PEPIN, Arthur, b Hartford, Conn 1928– , engr paint M

PEPIN, François, b 1805, fl 1819–33, sculp K

PEPIN, Georges, b 1809, fl 1881, d Montreal 1892, sculp K

PEPIN, Jean-Paul, b Montreal 1894, d 1983, paint K M

PEPIN, Jérôme, b c 1795, d St-Jacques-le-Mineur, Que 1862, sculp K

PEPIN, Joseph, b Sault-au-Récollet, Que 1770, d St-Vincent-de-Paul, Que 1842, sculp K

PEPIN, Louis, b Quebec 1761/2, d Pointe-du-Lac, Que 1840, sculp K

PEPIN, Mary (b Sheila Mary Brock-Smith) (m Jean-Luc Pepin), b Bellingham, Wash 1929– , paint M

PEPIN, Yves, b Canada 1943– , paint M

PEPPER, George Douglas (m Kathleen F. Daley, q.v.), b Ottawa 1903, d Toronto 1962, paint AGO CC1 CE1,2 CWW58 GM Hu M MM NGC1 NGC68 O.My49 RCA S TB2 UG WWA62

PEPPER, John Robert (Jack), b Prescott, Ont 1905– , paint Hu M

PEPPER, Kathleen Frances Daly. *See* DALY, Kathleen Frances

PERCIVAL, Phyllis M. Reynolds[2] (m Albert C. Percival), b USA, fl 1918+, paint CNS40 MM[2] RCA

PERCIVAL, Robert, b Chesterfield, Eng 1924– , paint sculp M

PERCY, Henry Hugh Manvers, Gen, Lord, b Cobham, Sur 1817, d London 1877, Eng, topog BP DNB H

PEREHUDOFF, Catherine Anne, b Saskatoon 1958– , paint CWW93

PEREHUDOFF, Dorothy Elsie Knowles. *See* KNOWLES, Dorothy Elsie

PEREHUDOFF, William W. (m Dorothy Elsie Knowles, q.v.), b Langham, Sask 1919– , paint CAE1 CE1,2 M MM RCA SC US WWA93

PERELMA, Ossip/Ossy de, b Russia, fl 1906-25, paint B MM

PERKINS, Arthur Alan, b Toronto 1915– , prt IO M WWA93

PERKINS, David William, b 1938– , sculp IO

PERKINS, Donald, b Scarborough, Ont 1933– , paint M

PERLIN, Rae, b St John's, Nfld, fl 1950– , paint M WWA93

PERRAULT, Chrysostome. *See* DUCHESNE, Christophe

PERRAULT, Suzanne Parent (Mrs), b Montreal 1924– , paint M MM RCA

PERRE, Henri, b Strasbourg, Fr c 1828, d Toronto 1890, paint AGO DCB11 DeV7,8 EC H H77 K M MM NGC1 RCA W1–3

PERREAULT, Gabriel Henri Joseph, b Ste-Sophie, Que 1932– , paint M MM

PERREAULT, Pierre, b Montreal 1955– , paint M

PERRIER, Gordon B., b Saskatchewan 1935– , paint M

PERRIGARD, Hal Ross, b Montreal 1891 – d 1960, paint CLA Hu M MM NGC1 PMC RCA TB2

PERRIN, Barbara Hale (Mrs), b Detroit, fl 1960s, paint M

PERRIN, Michel, b Lyon, Fr 1932– , paint CAE1 M

PERRIN, Nicolas, b 1806/7, fl 1841, sculp K

PERRIN, Pierre, b 1804/5, fl 1820s, sculp K

PERRON, Germain (s Germain), b Montreal 1943– , paint M MM

PERRON, Louis Paul, b Rivière-du-Loup, Que 1919– , mur paint M

PERRON, Marie Louise, b nr Spalding, Sask 1943– , paint BDSA M

PERROT, Ferdinand, b Paimboeuf, Fr 1808, d St Petersburg 1841, Fr, paint topog B H K TB1

PERROTT, James Stanford, b Claresholm, Alta 1917– , paint AA M WWA76

PERRY, Frank, b Vancouver 1923– , sculp BCS CWW93 DCA M MM RCA WWA93

PERRY, John S. (Jack), b England 1898, paint M

PERRY, Raymond W., b Natick, Mass 1883, paint AAA29 WWA53

PERVOUCHINE, Nathalie (m Pierre Labrecque), b Berlin, Ge 1923– , sculp M

PERZ, Walter G., b Vienna 1929– , paint M

PESTICH, Bruno, b Zadar, Yu 1937– , paint prt CAE1 M

PETCHEY, Winnifred Florence (m Donald B. Marsh[2]), b London 1905– , paint M RCA[2]

PETEL, Pierre, b Montreal 1920– , paint M MM

PETER, Friedrich Gunther, b Dresden, Ge 1933– , des paint CWW93 RCA WWA93

PETER, Margaret Ann (Mrs), b Leamington, Ont 1943– , prt IO M

PETER, Nori, b Hungary c 1935– , sculp M

PETERS, Barry, b Pikangikum Res, Ont 1958– , paint prt IO

PETERS, Donald Burpee, b Saint John, NB 1919– , paint M

PETERS, Donna. *See* KRIEKLE, Donna Lynne

PETERS, Gordon, b Edinburgh 1920– , paint IO M RCA

PETERS, John P., b England 1876, fl 1957, paint M

PETERS, Kenneth M., b Regina 1939–, paint CAE1 M MM

PETERS, Lawrie/Laurie, b Pioneer Mine, BC 1942– , paint M

PETERS, Lloyd A., b c 1912– , fl 1939+ , etch paint M MM RCA

PETERS, Paddy, b Pikangikum Res, Ont 1956– , paint IO

PETERSMANN, Brigitte, b Danzig 1943– , paint M

PETERSON, Margaret S. (m Howard O'Hagan), b Seattle, Wash 1902– , paint M MM WWA66

PETERSON, Norman, b Narol, Man 1924– , carv M

PETERSON, Roy Eric, b Winnipeg 1936– , cart Co CWW93 Des M Po86–88 WECa

PETERSON, Warren H., b Salina, Kans 1935– , paint US

PETHICK, Jerry, b London, Ont c 1936– , sculp M

PETIT, Joseph Gérard Gaston Ignace, b Shawinigan, Que 1930– , paint sculp M SC

PETITJEAN, Etienne-Charles, b Fouquières-sur-Bièvre, Fr 1906– , paint M O.Ag49

PETITOT, Emile-Fortune-Stanilas-Joseph, Frère, b Grancey-le-Château, nr Marseilles, Fr 1838, d Mareuil-les-Meux, Fr 1917, Fr, paint H H77 K KB LeJ M

PETLEY, Robert, Maj, b Gibraltar 1812, d Royal Military College, Sandhurst, Eng, Eng, topog DeV9 H ROM WHC

PETLEY-JONES[2], Llewellyn, b Edmonton 1908, d 1986, paint AGO CWW87[2] GM M RCA

PETRALIA, George, b Catania, It 1936– , paint sculp M

PETREVAN, Charles Carl, b Aljmas, Yu 1919– , paint M

PETRISKA, Josef, b Arad, Rom 1930– , paint sculp M

PETROFF, Nathan (Natand), b Poland 1916– , paint M NGC1

PETRY, Nancy (Mrs Wargin), b Montreal 1931– , paint M

PETTA, Angelo di, b Calle d'Anchise, It 1948– , cer IO M

PETTERSON, Andre, b Rotterdam 1950– , paint CWW93

PETTI, Mario Airomi, b Rome 1892, paint M

PEVERLEY, Harold M., b Ottawa, fl 1970s, paint ABC

PEYRAUD, Frank Charles, b Bulle, Swi 1858, d Highland Park, Ill 1948, Amer, paint AAA33 AAW3 B F K TB1 WWA WWWA

PEZZANI, Gino, b Glasgow 1927– , paint M

PFEIFER, Bodo, b Dusseldorf, Ge 1936– , paint sculp AE M MM RCA WWA78

PFEIFFER, Gordon Edward, b Quebec 1899, d Rosemère, Que 1983, paint CNS36 M MM RCA

PFEIFFER, Harold Samson, b Quebec 1908– , sculp IO M MM RCA

PFEIFFER, Walter M., b Quebec 1896, paint M

PFLIGER, Terry Lee, b St Joseph, Mich 1947– , paint sculp CAE2 DCA IO M

PFLUG, Christiane Sybille Schutt (m Michael Pflug, q.v.), b Berlin, Ge

1936, d Hanlan's Point, Toronto Isld, Ont 1972, paint AE Co M MM RCA
PFLUG, Michael (m Christiane S.S. Pflug, q.v.), b Kassel, Ge 1929– , paint M MM
PHELPS, Elizabeth Campbell (Mrs), b Edmonton, 1924– , paint US
PHENIX, Louis Serge, b Outremont, Que 1924– , paint M MM
PHILIBERT, André, b Quebec 1944– , paint M
PHILIPPOTEAUX, Paul-Dominique, b Paris 1845 – d 1923, Fr, paint panor B F K TB1
PHILLIPPS, Frederick, b Padstow, Corn c 1860, Eng, paint DFA
PHILLIPS, Douglas, b Willowdale, Ont c 1941– , sculp M
PHILLIPS, Edward Openshaw, b Montreal 1931– , paint CAE1 M
PHILLIPS, Harriet Ann Dougall (m John Philpot Curran Phillips[2]), fl later half 19th cen, paint H Mo12[2]
PHILLIPS, John Kenneth (Ken), b Toronto 1909– , paint AGO Hu M R
PHILLIPS, Mary Martha, b Montreal 1856, d 1937, paint DWA H MM Mo12 RCA
PHILLIPS, Myfanwy, b Dehra Dun, India 1945– , paint M
PHILLIPS, Timothy Adair, b Toronto 1929– , paint CWW93 IO M
PHILLIPS, Walter John Herbert, b Salisbury, Wilts 1912– , anim ske M
PHILLIPS, Walter Joseph, b Barton-on-Humber, Eng 1884, d Victoria, BC 1963, engr etch paint prt AAA31 AGO B BB CC1 CE1,2 CWW61 EC GM H77 Hu M MM NGC1 NGC67 PMC RCA Sam SC TB1,2 UG W3 WBA2 WWA53 WWB74
PHILLIPS, William H., fl 1882–98, engr H
PHILLIPSON, Gillian Saward[2] (Mrs), b Maidstone, Kent 1934– , paint IO[2] M
PHILP, Donald F., b Montreal 1900– , paint CWW64
PIC. *See* PICKERSGILL, Peter
PICARD, Claude, b Edmunston, NB 1932– , paint M
PICARD, Françoise, b W Shefford, Que 1923– , paint M MM NGC1 RCA TB3
PICARD, François-Xavier (Tagourenché), fl 1879, paint H K NGC1
PICARD, Raymond R., b Montreal 1925– , paint M
PICHE, Reynald, b Rock Isld, Que 1929– , paint sculp CAE1 M
PICHE-WHISSEL, Aline Marie Blanche Marguerite (m Percy Whissel), b Trois-Rivières, Que 1919– , paint stgl M
PICHER, Claude, b Quebec 1927– , paint AE AGO B CC2 M MM NGC1 NGC67 RCA TB3 WWA93
PICHER, Joseph George, b Ste-Sophie-de-Megantic, Que, fl 1892, d Montreal 1942, sculp K
PICHET, Roland (b Pichette), b Verdun, Que 1936– , paint prt M MM RCA
PICKEL, Patricia, b New Jersey 1931– , paint M
PICKERING, Bernard, b Toronto 1903– , paint M RCA
PICKERSGILL, Peter (Pic), b Ottawa 1945– , cart paint Des M
PICKETT, Frederick Albert, b Oak Point, NB 1868, d Newport, RI 1904, engr paint M
PICKETTS, Marcia, b Asquith, Sask 1913– , paint BDSA M
PICOTTE, Michel-François, b Montreal 1947– , paint sculp M
PIDDINGTON, Helen Vivian, b Victoria, BC 1931– , carv prt AGO M S
PIENOVI, Angelo (Angello Pianovi), b Genoa, It c 1773, d Montreal 1845, paint DCB7 GW H
PIER, Roland, b France 1936– , cart Des M Po86–88
PIERCE, Elizabeth R. (m Vernon L. Pierce), b Brooklyn, NY 1898, paint WWA91
PIERCE, Gordon, b 1883, d Kingston, Ont 1975, sculp M

PIERCE, M., fl 1834–48, paint H
PIERIE/PIERRIE, William, Capt, fl 1759–77, Eng, topog DBLP DeV5 GW H WHCp158
PIEROWAY, Percy, b Newfoundland 1921– , paint DFA KB
PIERRON/PEARRON, Jean (Père), b Dun-sur-Meuse, Fr 1631, d Pont-à-Mousson, Fr 1700 (x New York State), Fr, paint ske DCB1 H H77 K
PIERS, Elizabeth. *See* GREEN, Elizabeth Piers
PIERS, Harry, b Halifax 1870, paint CWW38 Mo98,12
PIERS, Henry, Maj, b England c 1781, d Cape Colony, SA 1872, Eng, drgt drw H
PIERS, Henry, Jr, fl 1830–1, drgt H
PIERS, William Bevil Thomas, b St John's, Nfld 1808, d USA 1855, paint H
PIESINA, Raymond, b Germany 1945– , paint M
PIFKO, Ted L., b Budapest, Hu 1935– , paint sculp M
PIGEON, Alfred J., fl 1865–84, carv H K
PIGOTT, Arthur, Capt, fl 1835–50, topog DFA H
PIGOTT, Marjorie, b Yokohama 1904– , paint CWW89 IO M MM RCA S WWA84
PIKE, Alfred Leonard (m Gladys Pike, q.v.), b London 1890, d Ottawa 1977, stgl M
PIKE, Gladys (m Alfred Leonard Pike, q.v.), b England c 1904– , fl 1980s, paint M
PIKE, Pauline M., b Lancashire, fl 1977– , paint ABC
PILKINGTON, Robert, Col, b Chelsfield, Kent 1765, d London 1834, Eng, paint topog DBWA DCB6 DNB H ROM W1–3
PILLAI[1], Mohandas (s Mohandas[2]), b Penang, Malay 1936– , paint M[1,2]
PILON, Paul, b Hull, Que 1909– , drw paint M
PILOT, Robert Wakeham, b St John's, Nfld 1898, d Montreal 1967, paint AGO CC1 CE1,2 CNS36 CWW64 EC Hu M MM MQ NGC1 NGC68 RCA TB2 UG W2–3 WWA53 WWB68
PILSWORTH, Graham, b Toronto 1943– , cart Des
PIM, Bedford Chapperton Trevelyan, Lt RN, b Bideford, Dev 1826, d Deal, Eng 1886, Eng, topog DNB H
PINDER, W.G., fl 1879–81, topog H
PINE, John Michael, b Wolverhampton, Eng 1928– , paint sculp M MM
PINHEY, Donald McNab, fl 1890s, paint H
PINHEY, John Charles, b Ottawa 1860, d Montreal 1912, paint CWW10 EC H Hu M MM Mo12 NGC1 RCA TB3 W1–3
PINKERTON, Harriet Jane Taylor (m Robert Pinkerton), b Toronto 1852, d 1936, paint DWA H MM
PINKERTON, Kathleen Louise Campbell Ward (m Horace H. Ward; m George McGill Pinkerton), b Toronto 1902– , fl 1973, paint prt IO MM
PINNEO, Georgiana Paige, b Waterville, NS 1896, fl 1974, paint M MM RCA
PINNIE (SENNY) NUKTIALUK, E9-937, b Port Harrison, Que 1930, d 1969, sculp DEA
PINSENT, Gordon Edward, b Grand Falls, Nfld 1930– , paint CWW93
PINSKY, Alfred (m Ghitta Caiserman, q.v.; m Claire Florence Hogenkamp, q.v.), b Montreal 1921– , paint CLA DCA M MM NGC1 RCA WWA82
PINSKY, Claire Florence Hogenkamp. *See* HOGENKAMP, Claire Florence
PINSKY, Ghitta Caiserman. *See* CAISERMAN, Ghitta
PIOTROW, Roger, b Nottingham, Eng 1945– , drw M
PIOTROWSKI, Adolph, b Toronto 1931– , paint sculp IO M
PIPER, Audrey Jean Smith (m George W. Piper), b London 1925– , paint BDSA M

PIQTOUKUN, David Robert, b Paularuk, NWT 1950– , paint prt sculp CWW93

PIRLOT, Paul L., b Metter, Bel 1920– , sculp CWW90

PIROCHE, Setsuko, b Tokyo 1933– , paint M

PIROT, Jean-Marie, b France 1926– , paint sculp M

PIROTTON, Nicolas, b Liège, Bel 1882, d St Boniface, Man 1943, sculp K

PISKO, Michael, b Lethbridge, Alta 1913– , paint M

PISKUNOWICZ, Paul, b Poland c 1914– , paint M

PISSUYUL, Martine (Mrs), b McConnell River, NWT 1933– , sculp M

PITALOUISA/PITALOOSIE[2] (aka Pitaloosie Saila[3]), E7-1006 (m Pauta, E7-990, q.v.), b nr Cape Dorset, NWT 1942– , drw prt CWW93[3] DEA M[2]

PITCHFORD, Roger Watkins, b Northampton, Eng 1905– , paint O.My50

PITRE, James A., b Bathurst, NB 1918 – d 1969, paint M

PITSEOLAK, E7-1100 (m Ashoona), b Tugjak, Nottingham Isld, NWT c 1900, d Cape Dorset, NWT 1983, prt CE1,2 DEA M RCA WWGA2

PITSEOLAK, Mary[2], E7-982 (m Johanassie, q.v.), b Cape Dorset, NWT 1925– , prt DEAp147[2]

PITSEOLAK, Peter[2], b Nottingham Isld, NWT 1902, d Cape Dorset, NWT 1973, prt sculp CE1,2 Co DEAp191[2] M WWGA

PITSIULAK, Lipa/Lypa, b Pangnirtono, NWT 1941– , paint sculp CWW93 M

PITT, Douglas Fox. *See* FOX-PITT, Douglas

PLAINWOMAN, Percy (Two Gun), b c 1895, d 1961, paint DFA

PLAMONDON, Antoine (x Sebastien), b L'Ancienne-Lorette, Que 1804, d Neuville, Point-aux-Trembles, Que 1895, paint ACA AGO B CE1,2 Co DCB12 EC H H77 K LeJ M MQ NGC1 NGC67 OC RCA W1–3

PLAMONDON, Ignace, b Ancienne-Lorette, Que 1796 – d 1835, paint H K

PLAMONDON, Marius Gérald, b Quebec 1919 – d 1976, sculp stgl M RCA WWA78

PLANT, Stafford Donald, b Georgetown, Ont 1914– , paint M

PLANTA, Ethel Ann Carson Copeland (m Clive Planta), b Newcastle, NB 1896, paint M MM

PLANTE, Louis, fl 1866–82, paint K

PLANTE, Pierre, b nr Ste-Victoire-de-Sorel, Que 1853 – d 1930, sculp K

PLANTENGA, Stansje, b Netherlands 1947– , paint prt CAE1 M

PLASKETT[1], Aileen Anne (Mrs Duffy[2]), b London 1905– , paint Hu M[1,2] RCA

PLASKETT, Joseph Francis, b New Westminster, BC 1918– , paint AGO CC2 CLA CWW93 DCA NGC1 RCA S SC TB3 UG

PLATNER, Rae Katz (m Israel Platner), b Poland 1905– , sculp M

PLATT, Charles Adams, b New York 1861, d Cornish, NY 1933, Amer, etch paint AAA31d33 App B DAB F H NCAB TB1,2 WWWA

PLATT, Les, b Entwhistle, Alta 1951– , paint prt sculp SC

PLAW, John, b Putney, London 1746, d Charlottetown 1820, paint DCB5 H

PLAYFAIR, Charles Gregory Paul, b Hagersville, Ont 1917– , paint M MM O.Ag49 RCA TB3

PLEAR, Scott Edward, b Vancouver 1952– , paint WWA93

PLETZER, George Arnold, b Orangeville, Ont 1907 , paint Hu MM RCA

PLEWES, Doris Willard, b Wallaceburg, Ont 1898, paint CWW48

PLEWMAN, Veronica Ann, b Vancouver 1948– , paint CWW93

PLIMSOLL, Ellen J., fl 1892+, paint H

PLIMSOLL, Fanny Grace, b London,

fl 1891–1916, Eng, min paint DBA DWA H MM RCA TB3
PLIOPLYS, Audrius, b Toronto 1951– , mmed paint CWW93
PLOMTEUX, Léon (m Raymonde Plomteux, q.v.), b Belgium 1905– , paint M
PLOMTEUX, Raymonde (m Léon Plomteux, q.v.), b Liège, Bel 1905– , paint M
PLOMTEUX, Tiziana Tabbia, b Turin, It 1938– , paint M
PLOSKER, Oscar, b Regina, Sask 1953– , paint M
PLOTEK, Leopold, b Moscow 1948– , paint WWA93
PLUNGUIAN, Mrs (b Rosner) (m Mark Plunguian), b Germany c 1905, d Newark, NJ 1962, Amer, sculp DAS M
POCOCK, Hilda Joyce. *See* STEWART, Hilda Joyce Pocock
POCOCK, Nicholas, b Bristol, Eng 1740, d Maidenhead, Eng 1821, Eng, paint B Bry DBHP DBLP DBMaP DBWA DeV5 DMA DNB DSP DWP G H MP MPE OELP PS Red TB1 WHC
PODESKVA/PODESVA, Yehuda, b Poland 1926– , paint IO M
PODGRABINSKI, Miet (Mieczyslaw), b Lublin, Pol 1901– , gra sculp IO M
POINT, Nicolas, Père, b Rocroi, Fr 1799, d Quebec 1868, paint AAW1 GW K Sam WWWA
POIRIER, Elizabeth, b Trois-Rivières, Que 1945– , paint prt M
POIRIER, J. Gérard, b Ste-Elizabeth, Que 1912– , paint M
POIRIER, Marcel, b c 1948– , paint M
POIRIER, Narcisse, b St-Félix-de-Valois, Que 1883, d 1983, paint K M MM RCA
POIRIER, Normand (s Fracas), b c 1942– , fl 1967– , drw M
POIRIER-McCONNELL, Edmonde, b St-Cléophas, Que 1940– , tap DCA
POISSON, Christiane (m Robert Van der Hilst), b France 1941– , des prt M
POISSON, Joseph, b Ste-Elisabeth-de-Warwick, Que 1873, d Montreal 1951, sculp K
POKLEN, Jeffrey Ervin, b Carmel, Calif 1934– , paint sculp CAE1 M MM UG
POKRANT, Luther, b Rosenfeld, Man 1947– , paint M SC
POL, Ebel H., b Netherlands c 1930– , paint M
POLDAAS, Jaan Aare, b Kristjanstad, Swe 1948– , paint IO M
POLGAR, Vladimir, b Zagreb, Yu 1941– , mur paint sculp M
POLIQUIN, Jean-Noel, b Trois-Rivières, Que 1927– , paint sculp M
POLL, Frank, b Austria 1932– , sculp M
POLLAK, Ludo, b Romania 1914– , illus paint M
POLLARD, Alice Blair. *See* THOMAS, Alice Blair Pollard
POLLARD, Irene, fl 1970s, illus paint M
POLLOCK, Allan D., b c 1906, d 1978, paint M
POLLOCK, Allan L., b China 1918– , des paint M
POLLOCK, David Raymond, b Toronto 1926– , paint M MM
POLLOCK, Florrie (aka ANISMAN, Rosalyn) (s Lark), fl 1972– , paint sculp M
POLLOCK, Jack Henry, b Toronto 1930 – d 1992, paint prt IO M
POLLOCK, Lou, fl 1970s, drw illus MFM S
POLLOCK, R.G., b Martintown, Ont 1915– , paint M
POLUJAN, Alexandra Lecia. *See* PRITZ, Alexandra Lecia Polujan
POLUTNIK, Jose, b Yugoslavia c 1938– , paint sculp M
POMMIER, Hugues, Abbé, b Vendôme, Fr c 1637, d France 1686, Fr, paint DCB1 H K NGC67
POMMINVILLE, Louise b Montreal 1941– , enam M

POMROY, M.A., fl 1884–6, paint H
PONTONI, Andrea, b Italy c 1914– , paint M
POOLE, Franklin Dayton, b Keewatin, Ont 1904, d 1972, paint M
POOLE, Frederick Victor, b Southampton, Eng, fl 1890–1910, Eng, paint B DBA DVP F G H RA RCA TB1 Y
POOLE, Jacqueline Lynda, b 1944– , paint IO M
POOLE, Judith (m Don Buckle), b Tunbridge, Eng 1943, d Saskatoon 1973, drw gra paint BDSA M US
POOLE, Leslie Donald, b Halifax 1942– , paint CAE1 M SC WWA93
POOLEY, H., Lt, fl 1840s, topog H
POOLMAN, Al, b Peterborough, Ont c 1913– , paint M
POOTAGOOK/POOTAGOK, b Cape Dorset, NWT c 1889 – d 1959, prt sculp AGO DEAp196
POOTOGOOK, E7-864 (m Iyola, E7-914), b Cape Dorset, NWT 1936– , prt DEAp197
POOTOOGOOK, Kananginak. *See* KANANGINAK POOTOOGOOK, E7-1168
POPE, Franklin Leonard, Maj, b Great Barrington, Mass 1840 – d 1895, Amer, topog App DAB DeV1 H NCAB WWWA
POPE, Maud Mary, b Watertown, NY c 1867, fl 1916, paint DWA H MM
POPE, Robert, b Windsor, NS c 1957, d Halifax 1992, drw illus M
POPE, William, b Maidstone, Kent 1811, d Port Ryerse, Ont 1902, paint H M
POPESCU/POPESCO, Cara, b Munich 1922– , engr paint sculp IO M WWA91
POPESKI, Jessie Liss (Mrs), b Kowal, Pol 1926– , paint M
POPLONSKI, Alexander Jan, b Warsaw, Pol 1933– , paint sculp IO M
POPOFF, Alicia Dawn (m Leslie Potter), b Saskatoon 1950– , paint BDSA US
POPOV, Vassil, b Sofia, Bul, fl 1973– , paint sculp ABC M
POPOVIC, John, b Yugoslavia 1938– , paint M
POPPLETON, Marjorie, b London 1895, illus CWW48
POPPLEWELL, John, fl 1833–41, engr illus paint H
PORCHER, Edwin A., Capt, fl 1865, topog H
PORTELANCE, Joseph Eugene Donald, b Vancouver 1938– , paint prt CAE2 M
PORTEOUS, Cameron John, b Rosetown, Sask 1937– , des CWW93
PORTEOUS, Charles, E.L./B., fl 1880–96, paint H MM RCA
PORTEOUS, Frances Esther Dudley, b Ste-Petronille, Que 1896, d Montreal 1946, paint M MM RCA
PORTEOUS, Piercy Evelyn Frances (m George Robert Younger), b Montreal 1907– , paint M MM RCA
PORTER, Ann Pearson McCurdy (Mrs), b Halifax 1929– , paint M WWA62
PORTER, Brian, b Yarmouth, NS 1948– , paint M
PORTER, C.G., b Kent, Eng c 1872, d Victoria, BC 1957, paint M
PORTER, Edward Clark, b Bronxville, NY 1935– , engr BB M
PORTER, Irene Cattelle (m Robert Samuel Alexander, q.v.), b Montreal 1922– , paint sculp CLA
PORTER, Margaret Adeline. *See* BROWN, Margaret Adeline Porter
PORTER, Mary Marguerite. *See* ZWICKER, Mary Marguerite Porter
PORTER, Yolande (Mrs), b Jamaica 1917– , paint IO M
PORTLOCK, Joseph Ellison, Maj Gen, b Gosport, Hants 1794, d Blackrock, nr Dublin 1864, Eng, paint DNB
PORTLOCK, Nathaniel, Capt, b c 1748, d Greenwich, Eng 1817, Eng, topog DCB5 DMA DNB EMA GW H
PORTNALL, Francis Henry, b Cater-

ham Valley, Sur 1886, d 1976, paint CNS29 M RCA
PORUBSZKY, Istvan J., b Kispest, nr Budapest, Hu 1927– , paint M
POSA, Andrew, b Budapest, Hu 1938– , sculp M
POSTMA, Robert, b Akron, Ohio 1939– , Amer, paint UG
POTEMPKA, Joe, b Germany c 1926– , paint M
POTTER, Alicia Dawn Popoff. *See* POPOFF, Alicia Dawn
POTTER, Geoffrey Gilbert, b Saskatoon 1944– , paint prt M
POTTRUFF, Richard Phillip, b Hamilton, Ont 1945– , paint M
POTVIN, Daniel, b Metabetchoan, Que 1946– , paint stgl WWA80
POTVIN, Rachel. *See* MARION, Rachel Potvin
POULIN, Bernard Aimé, b Windsor, Ont 1945– , paint CWW93 M
POULIN, Robert, b Quebec c 1949– , sculp M
POULIN, Roland L., b St Thomas, Ont 1940– , sculp CAE1 CWW93 M WWA93
POULIOT, André, b Quebec 1919, d Montreal 1953, paint sculp M
POULIOT, Mario, b Sherbrooke, Que 1949– , engr paint M
POULIOT, Nadeau, b 1930– , paint CAE2
POULIOT, Paul R., b Joliette, Que 1909– , paint M
POULTON, Michael, b Winnipeg 1948– , paint prt IO M
POUSSIELGUE, Achille, b France, fl 1848–69, Fr, illus K
POW, Robert, b Montreal 1942– , paint M
POWE, Lawrence Wilfred (Larry), b Montreal, fl 1936+, paint M MM
POWELL, Frederick Y., b Toronto 1924 – d 1992, sculp CWW84 IO M
POWELL, J.T., b Canada c 1823, fl 1850s, litho G W H
POWELL, Jeannette M., b Kingston, NS c 1871, d New York 1944, paint prt AAA33 AAW2 DWA F WWAd47
POWELL, William Benjamin, b Hamilton, Ont 1938– , paint IO M
POWER, Edith Alice Morton (m Joseph William Power), b Brockville, Ont 1854, fl 1909, paint DFA DWA H MM RCA
POWER, Florence, fl 1892, paint H MM
POWLESS, Bill, b Six Nations Res, nr Brantford, Ont 1952– , paint pas IO
PRACK, Karen Lesley, b Hamilton, Ont 1949– , sculp IO
PRAGER, Eva Oppenheimer (m Richard Prager), b Berlin, Ge 1912– , paint M
PRAGNELL, Bartley Robilliard, b Moose Jaw, Sask 1908, d Calgary 1966, paint M RCA
PRANISHNIKOFF, J./L.J., fl 1873–9, illus H
PRANKE, Walter W., b Czechoslovakia 1925– , paint M
PRAT, Annie Louisa, b Paradise, Nfld 1860, d Nova Scotia 1960, min paint H M
PRATT, Christopher. *See* PRATT, John Christopher
PRATT, Claire. *See* PRATT, Mildred Claire
PRATT, George Forbes, b Minden, Ont 1939– , carv M
PRATT, James C., b St John's, Nfld 1880, d 1956, paint M
PRATT, John Christopher (m Mary F.W. Pratt, q.v.), b St John's, Nfld 1935– , paint B CAE2 CC1 CE1,2 Co CWW93 M RCA SC UG
PRATT, Mary Frances West (m John Christopher Pratt, q.v.), b Fredericton 1935– , paint CE1,2 CWW93 M RCA UG WWA86
PRATT, Mildred Claire, b Toronto 1921– , prt IO M
PRATTE, Fernande, b Montreal 1938– , paint CAE1 M
PRATTE, Noël, fl 1866–81, sculp K
PREFONTAINE, Leonard, b Sher-

brooke, Que 1897, carv paint CWW61

PRENDERGAST, Catherine Rodman. *See* MERRITT, Catherine Rodman Prendergast

PRENDERGAST, Murray, fl 1894–8, paint H MM

PRENDERGAST, John. *See* BEHENNA, Katherine Arthur

PRENT, Mark George, b Lodz, Pol 1947– , sculp CA1–3 CAE2 CE1,2 CWW93 M MM RCA WWA93

PRESCOTT, Ken, b London, Ont 1938– , coll paint ABC M

PRESCOTT, Yves, b Drummondville, Que 1957– , paint M

PRESTON, Annette Dorothy (Mrs), b Huddersfield, Yorks 1918– , paint BDSA

PRETTY, Lloyd, b Chapel Ann, Nfld 1944– , paint M

PREVOST, Alyre, b 1880/1, d Quebec 1937, carv K

PREVOST, Antoine, b Quebec 1930– , paint M

PREVOST, Robert, b 1928, d 1982, des CC1 RCA

PREVOT, Edith, fl 1918+, paint K RCA

PREVOT, Marie, fl 1915–17, paint K MM RCA

PREYSS, Witold Ludwick, b Danzig 1919– , paint M NGC1

PREZAMENT, Joseph (m Rita Briansky, q.v.), b Winnipeg 1923, d 1983, drw paint M MM RCA WWA80

PREZAMENT, Rita Briansky. *See* BRIANSKY, Rita

PRICE, A. Victor Coverly. *See* COVERLY-PRICE, A. Victor

PRICE, Addison Winchell, b Port Credit, Ont 1907– , paint M O.My48 RCA UG

PRICE, Arthur Donald, b Edmonton 1918– , paint sculp AE Co IO M MM O.N49 RCA WWA66

PRICE, Caroline, b Ottawa 1948– , gra paint M

PRICE, Daniel, b Keswick, NB c 1947– , paint M

PRICE, G.F., fl 1850–2, paint H

PRICE, Julius Mendes, b London 1857/60 – d 1924, Eng, illus AH B DBA DVP G H RA Sam TB1 WBA1 WWW

PRICE, Norman Mills, b Brampton, Ont 1877, d New York 1951, Amer, illus AAA32 IA1,2 IBYP ICB1 Sam TB1 WWA47d53

PRICE, Ralph Morton, b Montreal 1939– , paint CWW93

PRICE, Winchell. *See* PRICE, Addison Winchell

PRIDDAT, Fritz, b Germany c 1924– , paint M

PRIEST, Hartwell Wyse (Mrs), b Brantford, Ont 1901– , Amer, gra paint AAA32 TB2 WWA93

PRIEST, Margaret Diane (m Tony Scherman), b Tyringham, Bucks 1944– , paint prt CWW93 DCA

PRIMEAU, Claude, fl 1960– , sculp M

PRIMROSE, Clarence Stewart, b Annapolis Royal, NS 1896, paint AAA30

PRINCE, Elizabeth Hilary (m Peter Nicholas Hide, q.v.), b Johannesburg 1945– , paint CWW93

PRINCE, James Hubert, b Toronto 1935– , paint ske M

PRINCE, Richard Edmund, b Comox, BC 1947– , sculp CAE1,2 CE1,2 CWW93 M RCA WWA93

PRINGLE, Alice. *See* PATERSON, Alice Pringle

PRINGLE, Annie White Greive (m James B. Pringle), b Leith, Scot 1867, d Smiths Falls, Ont 1945, paint CNS40 H M MM RCA

PRINS, Nick, b Breukelen, Neth 1927– , paint SC

PRIOR, Melton, b London 1845 – d 1910, Eng, illus AAW1 AH B DBMP DeV1 DNB H ROM Sam TB1 WBA2 WI WWW

PRITCHARD, Denny, b Hamilton, Ont 1935– , cart Po86–88

PRITCHARD, George Thompson, b Havelock, NZ 1878, d Reseda, Calif 1962, paint AAW3 AC
PRITTIE, Mary Elizabeth (Mrs), b St Catharines, Ont 1908– , gra paint M
PRITZ, Alexandra Lecia Polujan (Mrs), b Austria 1945– , paint M
PRIVETT, Molly, b Streatham, Eng 1905– , paint M MM
PRIZEK, Mario Henry Dominique, b Edmonton 1922– , paint CLA
PROCH, Donald, b Inglis, Man 1944– , drw prt sculp CAE1,2 DCA DFA M SC US
PROCTOR, Alexander Phimister, b Bosanquet, Ont 1862, d Palo Alto, Calif 1950, paint sculp AAA33 AAW1 AC BE CWW36 DAS EC F H McC Mo12 NGC1 Sam TB1,2 WWA47d53 WWNA WWWA
PROCTOR, Edward D'Arcy, b Toronto 1919– , paint M
PROCTOR, Florence Evelyn Kemp (m Albert Henry Courtney Proctor), b Montreal 1886, paint Hu M MM RCA
PROKOP, George, b Czechoslovakia 1925– , paint M
PROSSER, Harvey Thomas, b Ottawa c 1930– , paint M
PROUDLOCK, Sarah Maloney Murphy (s Sarah Murphy), b New York 1946– , paint sculp IO
PROULX, Anne, b Timmins, Ont 1923– , paint M
PROULX, Carol, b Jonquière, Que c 1946– , sculp M
PROULX, Joseph-Onésime, b Boston 1890, d 1970, paint K MM RCA
PROULX, Rolland E., b Ottawa 1944– , paint M
PROUSE, Rod, b England 1945– , drw pas M
PROUSE, William, b England c 1914– , paint M
PROVOST, Aurette, b Montreal 1915– , paint TB3
PROVOST, Jean, b Montreal c 1926– , paint M
PRUD'HOMME, André, b Montreal 1928– , sculp M
PRYCE, Campbell Knollys, fl 1862, Eng, paint H
PRYDE, Ian, b Toronto c 1949– , sculp M
PRYNE, Rolf Edmund, b Toronto 1914– , paint IO M RCA
PUCHTA, Siegfried Rudolf (Siggy), b 1933– , sculp IO M
PUDLAT, E7-1173, b Cape Dorset, NWT 1919– , prt sculp DEA
PUDLO/PUDLAT/PADLOO, E7-899, b Kamadjuak Camp, Baffin Isld, NWT 1916– , paint prt sculp CE1,2 CWW93 DEA
PUFAHL, John Kenneth, b Urbana, Ill 1942– , prt IO WWA93
PUGEN, Diane Fern (m Dennis Eugene Norman Burton, q.v.), b Toronto 1943– , etch paint IO M
PULEY, Geraldine Mae Dicken (Gerry) (Mrs), b Summerland, BC 1925– , paint IO M
PULFORD, Edward Berwyn (Ted), b Saskatoon 1914– , paint M
PULLEN, Dorothy (m Ed Pullen), b England, fl 1950s, paint M
PULVER, William A., b Hamilton, Ont 1922– , paint M
PUNDLEIDER, Heinz V., b Salzburg, Au 1925– , paint IO M
PUPLETT, Terence, b England c 1940– , paint M
PURA, William Paul, b Winnipeg 1948– , litho prt M WWA93
PURCELL, Joseph Douglas (m Tela M. Purcell, q.v.), b Halifax 1927– , paint CLA M MM RCA
PURCELL, Tela Monoghan (m Joseph Douglas Purcell, q.v.), b Halifax c 1932– , paint M
PURDY, Bernice, b Lockhartville, NS 1940– , drgt paint DCA
PURDY, Henry Carl, b Wolfville, NS 1937– , paint prt CWW93 M RCA WWA93

PURDY, Richard, b Ottawa c 1953– , paint M
PURGINA, Emil, b Czechoslovakia 1937– , gra paint M
PURVITIS, Mintauts Dennis (Minto), b Latvia c 1942– , drw paint M
PUTMAN, Amy Elsie Violet, b Brockville, Ont 1893, paint M
PUTMAN, Gerald (Gerry), b Belleville, Ont c 1938– , paint M
PYE, Thomas, fl 1866, illus H

Q

QAQAQ/HAKA[2]/KAKA/QAKA, Ashoona, E7-1101, b nr Cape Dorset, NWT 1928– , sculp CE1,2 DEAp63[2]
QIATSUK, Lukta. *See* LUKTA/LUKTAK/QIATSUK, E7-1060
QUACKENBUSH, Diane, b California c 1951– , drw paint prt M
QUAN, Elizabeth (Mrs), b Toronto 1921– , paint IO M
QUATUTU, Makusi Angasa (aka Kakatuk), E9-1369, b Povungnituk, Que 1919– , sculp S
QUENTIN, René Emile, b Paris c 1854/60, d Providence, RI 1914, paint H K MM
QUEVILLON/COUVILLON/CUVILLON, Louis Amable, b St-Vincent-de-Paul, Que 1749 – d 1823, sculp CE1,2 DCB6 EC K LeJ W1–3
QUINN, Hugh Summerville, b Ottawa c 1872 – d 1948, paint M MM RCA
QUINNEY, Gerrard Joseph, b Vancouver 1913– , paint M
QUINTAL, Augustin (Capt Joseph), Frère Augustin, b Boucherville, Que 1683, d Montreal 1776, paint sculp DCB4 H K
QUINTAL, Dorothy, b Manitoba 1922– , paint CAE1 M
QUINTIN, Thomas James, b Harbour Grace, Nfld 1903– , paint CWW70
QUMALU, Jusi/Josie, E9-837, b Povungnituk, Que, sculp S
QUPIRQUALOOK. *See* KOPERQUALOOK/QUPIRQUALOOK, Isa
QURESHI, Abdur Rehman, b Karachi, Pak 1927– , paint CAE1 M

R

RAAB, Ernest (x Rabb), b Komarno, Cz 1926– , sculp M RCA
RAAB, George, b c 1948– , paint M
RAADE, Wilhelm, b Norway 1893, paint M
RABINOWITCH, David George, b Toronto 1943– , sculp B CAE1,2 CE1,2 CWW93 DCA IO M RCA WWA93
RABINOWITCH, Royden Leslie, b Toronto 1943– , sculp B CAE1 CE1,2 CWW93 IO M WWA93
RACETTE, E., fl 1890–1, paint H K
RACEY, Arthur George, b Quebec 1870, d Montreal 1941, cart illus CWW36 Des Mo98,12 M
RACICOT, Camille, b Valcourt, Que 1935– , paint sculp M
RACICOT, Denyse, b Montreal 1937– , mur paint M
RACINE, Robert, b Montreal 1956– , paint sculp DCA
RACKUS, George Keistutis, b Kalvarija, Lith 1927– , paint prt AGO CWW93 IO M MM S WWA93
RADFORD, Edward, b Plymouth, Eng 1831, d Southwick, nr Brighton, Eng 1920, Eng, paint ANC B DBA DBWA DVP G TB1 WBA1 WWW
RADFORD, Edward Joseph, b Winnipeg 1953– , paint CWW93
RADFORD, Gary Charles, b St Thomas, Ont 1952– , paint prt IO M
RADFORD, John A., b Devonport, Eng 1860, d Vancouver 1940, paint H M RCA
RADFORTH, Norman William, b Barrow-in-Furness, Lancs 1912– , paint CWW93
RAE, John, b Orkney Isld, Scot 1813,

d London 1893, Scot, paint CE2 DCB12 DFA DNB H W1–3

RAESIDE, Adrian, b Dunedin, NJ 1957– , cart Po86–88

RAICUS, Ethel, b Toronto 1901– , des paint IO M RCA

RAINE, Herbert, b Sutherland, Dur 1875, d Montreal 1951, etch AGO DBA G M MM MQ NGC1 RA RCA TB2

RAINE, John Michael, b 1932– , fl 1967– , paint sculp CAE1 M

RAINEY, Paul, b Winnipeg 1949– , paint M

RAINEY, Tim, b Winnipeg 1946– , paint M

RAINNIE, Hedley Graham James, b London 1914, d England 1961, illus paint pas M NGC68 RCA WWA53

RAINS, Malcolm, b Bristol, Eng 1947– , sculp DCA M

RAINVILLE, Jacques (s Jarain[2]), b St-Jean, Que c 1934– , paint M[2]

RAINVILLE, Réal, b Berthierville, Que 1949– , paint M

RAJOTTE, Yves, b Montreal 1932– , paint M MM

RAKINE, Boris (m Marthe Rakine, q.v.), b Russia 1905– , sculp M

RAKINE, Marthe (m Boris Rakine, q.v.), b Moscow c 1906– , paint AE AGO CC2 M MM NGC1 RCA TB2 UG

RALE, Sébastien. *See* RASLES, Sébastien

RAMAGE, John, b Dublin c 1748, d Montreal 1802, paint AM BE BM DCB5 DIA Fo GW H TB1 Y

RAMAUT, Louis, b France 1916, d 1973, paint M MM

RAMER, Noah Hubert, b Markham, Ont 1860, d Hamilton, Ont c 1931, paint H Hu M RCA

RAMMELL, George, b Cranbrook, BC 1952– , sculp M

RAMPEN, Leo, b Surabaya, Java 1928– , anim des gra illus M

RAMSAY, Colin Cameron, b Bridge of Allon, Scot 1891, d N Vancouver 1966, paint WWNA

RAMSAY, Patricia, Lady. *See* PATRICIA, HRH Princess Victoria Patricia Helena Elizabeth

RAMUNNO, Pasquale, b Italy 1937– , sculp M

RAND, Paul (b Otto Schellenberger), b Bonn, Ge 1896, d Vancouver 1970, paint CLA M MM RCA WWNA

RANDLE/RANDALL[2], Charles, Capt, fl 1775–1813, Eng, topog DBWA DFA H PNL[2] ROM

RANEY, Edgar Fraser, b Saco, Me 1888, ske CWW70

RANEY, Suzanne Bryant (Mrs), b London 1918, d 1967, engr paint sculp M MM RCA S WWA66

RANGER, A.F., b Nanaimo, BC c 1936– , paint M

RANGER, Henry Ward, b Syracuse, NY 1858, d New York 1916, Amer, paint AAA17d28 B DAA F H TB1 Y

RANGER, Réal, b Alexandria, Ont 1924– , sculp M

RANIA, Rachhpal S., b Punjab, India 1938– , paint IO M

RANKIN, Elizabeth Eugenie, b Glen Burnie, nr Kingston, Ont 1872, d Saskatoon 1960, paint BDSA M US

RANKIN, Joan Melvin (m John Sargent Rankin), b Calgary 1927– , paint BDSA M

RANKIN, John A., b nr Cobden, Ont 1931, d Vancouver 1968, paint M

RAPAPORT, Lester, b Brooklyn, NY 1947– , paint pas M

RAPHAEL, Shirley (aka Canada Banner Company), b Montreal 1937– , paint sculp CAE1,2 M RCA

RAPHAEL, William, b Prussia 1833, d Montreal 1914, paint ACA CE1,2 EC H H77 Hu M MM Mo98,12 NGC1 NGC67 RCA UG W1–3

RAPIN, François Xavier Aldéric, b St-Timothée, Que 1868, d Montreal 1901, paint H K M W1–3

RAPP, Otto, b Austria 1944– , paint CAE1 M
RAPPAPORT, Aron M., b Sereth, Au 1904– , sculp CWW92
RASLES, Sébastien (Rale[2], Rales[3]), b Pontarlier, Fr 1657, d Narantsouak, nr Norridgewock, Me 1724, Fr, paint App DCB2[2] EC H H77[3] K LeJ W1–3[2]
RASTO, Hlavina (Ratislav), b Topolcany, Cz 1943– , sculp WWA84
RATCHFORD, Douglas, b Caledonia, Ont 1937– , drw paint M
RATEL, Albert, fl 1889–98, paint H K
RATHE, Thomas Ignace, b Ayr, Ont, fl 1958– , paint M MM
RATTRAY, Alexander, fl 1859–62, topog DFA H ROM
RATTRAY, Dawn Amelia McCracken, b Fredericton 1935– , paint M MM
RATTRAY, Robert W., b c 1839, fl 1861–73, paint H
RAVAL, Pallavi, b India 1948– , paint M
RAVARY, Marcel (s Ravy), b Montreal 1940– , paint M
RAVAUX, Damase, b Ai, nr Epernay, Fr 1827, d Montreal 1896, des illus H K
RAVENSHAW, Edith Lalande. *See* PATTERSON, Edith Lalande Ravenshaw
RAVY. *See* RAVARY, Marcel
RAWBON, Joseph Loxton, b South Africa 1855, d 1942, paint H M
RAWLYK, Mary E. (m George Rawlyk), b Toronto 1934– , prt IO M SC UG
RAWSTRON, Alice Delphine, b Montreal 1924– , des paint M MM
RAY, Carl, b Sandy Lake Res, Ont 1943, d Sioux Narrows, Ont 1978, drw paint CAE1 CE1,2 Co IO M
RAY, Gail (Mrs Hyndman), b Ottawa c 1940– , paint M
RAYBOULD, Eileen Shannon (m H.N. Raybould), fl 1970s, paint M
RAYCROFT, Jessie (Mrs), fl 1886, paint H MM
RAYMOND, Jean-Baptiste, b St-Denis, Que 1873, d 1943, paint K
RAYMOND, Kelsey Ogden, b Brooklyn, NY 1926– , paint M
RAYMOND, Maurice, b Montreal 1912– , paint M MM NGC1 RCA TB2 WWA62
RAYMOND, Thomas, fl 1880–1913, carv K
RAYNER, Gordon, b Toronto 1935– , paint prt AE AGO CAE1 CC1 CE1,2 Co CWW93 DCA IO M MM RCA WWA93
RAYNER, Gordon Wesley, b Wesleyville, nr Port Hope, Ont 1911– , illus M
READ/REED, Clement L., fl 1877–85, paint H
READ, Georgie (m George Barton[2]), b Summerside, PEI 1902– , paint AKL[2] MM RCA WWA91[2]
READ, Horace Emerson, b Port Elgin, NB 1898, paint CWW70
READ, John F., b Reading, Eng 1940– , stgl CWW93
READ/REED/REID, Walter, b Guelph, Ont, fl 1877–89, litho paint Hpp261,263
READY, Alfred, b Quebec 1851/2, fl 1871–81, sculp K
REAL, Sue, b Chicago 1950– , drgt paint DCA M
REBRY, Gaston, b Wevelgem, Bel 1933– , paint M
RECHENBERG, Horst Dieter, b Hamburg, Ge 1936– , paint M
REDBARN, Thomas. *See* McEVOY, Bernard
REDBIRD, John, b Ojibwa Res, Ont 1932– , paint sculp M
REDDIE, Bernard J., b Toronto 1913– , gra M
REDFERN, Charles Kinghorn, b Toronto 1919– , paint M S
REDFERN, Thomas Lincoln, b Rotherham, Eng 1895, paint CWW58
REDGRAVE, Helen Felicity Fox (m Patrick Redgrave), b England 1920– , paint M WWA93

REDGRAVE, Julia, b Montreal 1949– , paint M
REDINGER, Walker Fred, b Wallacetown, Ont 1940– , sculp B CA1–3 CAE1 Co M MM RCA UG US WWA93
REDSELL, Pauline Hazel Daisy (m William Fediow), b Toronto 1908 – d 1980, sculp M MM O.F49 RCA
REED, Alice Mary, b Toronto 1957 , paint CWW93
REED, Egbert Charles (Bert), b Toronto 1886, d Norval, Ont 1957, paint M
REED, Hayter, b L'Original, Que 1849, d 1939, topog CWW10 H Mo98,12
REED, Torquil Arnold Sargent, b Quebec 1920– , paint M MM RCA
REEDER, Joseph, b Ohio 1944– , paint M
REES, Christopher, b Reading, Berks 1947– , sculp M
REESE, Peter Joseph, b New York 1944– , drw M
REESON, Cecil, b Toronto 1926– , sculp M
REEVE, Alan, b New Zealand 1910, d 1962, cart Des
REEVE, Gordon, b Chatham, Ont, fl 1968– , paint sculp M
REEVE, William Gordon, b Clarksburg, Ont 1898, fl 1972, paint M RCA
REFORD, William, fl 1881+, d 1895, paint H RCA
REGAMEY, Felix Elie, b Paris 1844, d Juan les Pins, Fr 1907, Fr, illus AAW1 AH B K Sam TB1
REGENBOGEN, Halyna Mordowanec. *See* MORDOWANEC, Halyna
REGNARD, Marie-Andrée. *See* DUPLESSIS, Marie-Andrée Regnard (Mère de Sainte-Hélène)
REGNIER, Sylvia Johanna Lucia Geisler (m Robert Regnier), b E Berlin 1948– , illus paint BDSA M
REIBER, Eileen, b Calgary 1917– , etch paint M
REIBESTIJN, Joseph, b Netherlands 1946– , paint sculp M
REICHARDT, Joachim Ferdinand. *See* RICHARDT/REICHARDT, Joachim Ferdinand
REICHARDT, Rudi, b nr Black Forest, Ge 1929– , paint M
REICHERT, Donald Karl, b Libau, Man 1932– , paint AGO CWW92 M MM RCA SC US WWA93
REID, Barbara Jane (m Ian Robert Crysler), b Toronto 1957– , illus paint C CBC CWW93
REID, Barbara Wagner, b USA 1945– , paint IO
REID, Bill. *See* REID, William Ronald
REID, Daniel Leigh, b Oshawa, Ont 1951– , prt sculp IO M RCA
REID, George Agnew (m Mary A.H. Reid, q.v.; m Mary Evelyn Wrinch, q.v.), b nr Wingham, Ont 1860, d Toronto 1947, paint AE AGO B CC2 CE1,2 Co CWW36 DBA EC FCA H H77 M MM Mo98,12 NGC1 NGC67 NGC68 PMC RA RCA TB1,2 UG W2,3 WBA2 WWA47 WWW
REID, Isobelle Chestnut (Mrs), b Fredericton 1903– , paint AGO Hu M MM RCA
REID, Jack, b Toronto c 1928– , paint IO M
REID, Laura Evans (m Robert M. Reid), b Guelph, Ont 1883, d Vegreville, Alta 1951, paint M MM RCA
REID, Leslie Mary Margaret, b Ottawa 1947– , paint prt DCA IO M RCA WWA93
REID, Lillian Irene Hoffar (m Neville Reid), b Victoria, BC 1908– , paint M WWNA
REID, Lorna Fyfe, b London, Ont 1887, paint DWA Hu M MM NGC1 RCA TB2
REID, Mary Augusta Hiester (m George Agnew Reid, q.v.), b Reading, Pa 1854, d Toronto 1921, paint AE AGO B CC2 DBA DWA EC H Hu LeJ M MM Mo12 NGC1 RCA TB3 W1–3

REID, Mary Evelyn Wrinch. *See* WRINCH, Mary Evelyn

REID, Richard. *See* REID, William Richard

REID, Robert Dow, b Glasgow 1933– , sculp M

REID, Russell James, b Leeds Village, Que 1920– , paint M RCA

REID, Stuart, b London, Ont 1953– , stgl M

REID, Suzanne (Reid-Gerard), b Montreal, fl 1969– , engr etch pas M

REID, Terence Edward, b Vancouver 1942– , sculp M

REID, Walter. *See* READ/REED/REID, Walter

REID, William, b Smith's Sound, Nfld 1892, paint M

REID, William Richard, b Regina 1930– , paint prt CAE2 M S WWA82

REID, William Ronald (Bill), b Victoria, BC 1920, d Vancouver 1998, sculp CE1,2 Co IBYP M RCA

REID, William Stanford, Rev, b Montreal 1913– , paint CWW93

REIDFORD, James Greig, b Glasgow 1911– , cart paint Des Hu

REIGO, Ants, b England 1948– , paint prt M

REILANDER, Bernard N.J., b Shilo, Man 1948– , des M

REINBLATT, Moses Martin (Moe), b Montreal 1917 – d 1979, paint prt AGO CC1 M MM NGC68 RCA TB2 WWA53

REINDORF, Samuel, b Warsaw, Pol 1914– , Amer, paint M WWA89

REINERT, Bert, b Copenhagen 1924– , paint M

REINHART, Michael, b Kitchener, Ont c 1955– , paint M

REINHOLD, Rudolph H., fl 1869–96, engr litho H

REINHOLDS, Visvaldis, b Latvia 1924– , paint sculp M

REINKE, Reimer, b W Germany c 1929– , carv paint M

REISER, Alice Albertina, b Hamilton, Ont 1917– , paint M

REITAV, Jaan, b Toronto 1951– , prt M

REITZENSTEIN, Reinhard, b Uelzen, Ge 1949– , gra sculp CAE1,2 IO M WWA93

REMEIKA, Vytas, b Lithuania, fl 1968– , paint M

REMILLARD, Abraham B.E., b c 1854, d 1881, paint H K

REMILLARD, Louis, b Quebec 1955– , cart gra illus M

REMINGTON, Frederic Sackrider, b Canton, NY 1861, d Ridgefield, Conn 1909, Amer, paint sculp AAAd28 AAW1 AW B BE DAA DAB DeV1 F H IA2 ICB McC NCAB Sam TB1 WI WWWA Y

REMINGTON, Maureen (m Edward Remington), b Scotland 1938– , paint M

REMPEL, J.G., b Ukraine 1903– , paint CWW73

REMPEL, Myrtle Anne (m Edward I. Rempel), b Swift Current, Sask 1937– , paint prt ABC

REMY, Damase, b Quebec 1833/4, fl 1871–3, sculp K

REMY, Philippe, b Quebec 1801/2, fl 1871, sculp K

RENALS, Dorothy Ann (m Norman Renals), b Toronto 1932– , paint IO M

RENAUD, Danielle, b Quebec c 1957– , drw paint M

RENAUD, M.A., fl 1886–8, paint K

RENAUD, Pierre, b Montreal 1928– , paint M MM

RENAUD, Toussaint-Xenophon, b 1860, d 1946, paint H K MM

RENNICK, Denise Frances Pickering (m Robert Rennick), b Autun, Fr 1883, fl 1966+, paint M

RENNICK, Susan Margaret (Mrs Jolliffe), b Kitchener, Ont 1951– , paint sculp IO

RENNIE, Bill, b c 1953– , fl 1978– , sculp M

RENNIE, John Barrie, b Toronto, fl 1935+, paint M
RENNIE, Robert R., fl 1982– , paint ABC
RENNIE, William Frederick, fl 1862–71, illus DeV4 H
RENNY, Gordon, b England c 1944– , cart des illus M
RENOIR, Pierre, b France c 1958– , prt M
RENTZ, Ewald, b N Dakota c 1908– , fl 1980s, carv M
RENZIUS, Rudy, b Malmoe, Swe 1899, d Newmarket, Ont 1968, carv paint M
REPA, Steve, b Winnipeg 1937– , gra paint M
REPENTIGNY, Rodolphe de (aka Jauran), b Montreal 1926, d nr Lake Louise, Alta 1959, paint M
REPPEN, John Richard (Jack), b Toronto 1933 – d 1964, cart paint AE AGO CC2 CE1,2 Co M MM RCA UG W3
REPPETEAUX, John D., b USA, fl 1951– , paint M
RESTOULE, Tim, b Dokis Res, nr N Bay, Ont 1960– , paint sculp M
RESTOULE, Tracey Leah, b N Bay, Ont 1962– , paint M
RETALLACK, Evelyn Barton (m John L. Retallack), b Dorval, Que 1921– , paint M
RETTIG, Edward P. (Ted), b Germany 1949– , sculp IO M
REUBEN, John, b Moosonee, Ont 1959– , paint prt sculp M
REVEL, Laurent, fl 1909+, paint K MM
REVELL, Ernest John, b Bangalore, India 1934– , paint CWW93 M
REVELL, William, b 1830, d 1902, drgt paint H MM RCA
REYN, Cornelius, b Amsterdam 1917– , paint M
REYNOLDS, Brian Eugene, b Pasco, Wash 1945– , drw sculp CE1,2 DCA M
REYNOLDS, C. Warren, b Toronto 1914– , paint CWW88
REYNOLDS, Catherine, b Detroit, Upper Canada c 1782, d Amherstburgh, Ont 1863/4, paint DWA GW H H74 KB M
REYNOLDS, Edward, b Iowa 1877, d 1931, cart Des
REYNOLDS, Edwin Barrie, b Ottawa 1880 – d 1960, paint M MM
REYNOLDS, Franklin George Armiger, b Newmarket, Ont 1939– , paint sculp IO M
REYNOLDS, John McCombe, b Toronto 1916– , paint sculp M MM
REYNOLDS, Jos (Miss), fl 1891–6, paint H RCA
REYNOLDS, Leslie Alan, b Edmonton 1947– , sculp CE1,2 DCA M
REYNOLDS, Phyllis M. *See* PERCIVAL, Phyllis M. Reynolds
REYNOLDS, William Derek, b Toronto 1947– , paint CWW93 IO M UG
RHEAUME, Jeanne Leblanc. *See* LEBLANC, Jeanne
RHEAUME, Marie-Elmina (Soeur Marie-de-Saint-Virginie), b 1864, d 1956, paint K
RHEAUME, Philippe, b St-Patrice-de-Beaurivage, Que 1932– , paint M
RHO/RAUX/RHEAULT/RHEU, Adolphe (Joseph Adolphe[2]), b Gentilly, Que 1839, d Bécancour, Que 1905, carv paint DCB13 H[2] H77[2] K M[2] MM W1–3
RHO, Auguste, b Bécancour, Que 1867, d 1947, paint K
RHO, Vigor, b Bécancour, Que 1874, d 1954, paint K
RHO, Zotique, b Bécancour, Que 1876, d 1962, paint K
RICARD, Gaston, b Quebec Prov c 1940– , paint M
RICARD, Yves, b St-Sylvère, Que 1931– , paint M
RICCI, Regolo, b Boiano, It 1955– , illus paint M

RICE, Gordon, b Los Angeles 1933– , paint M

RICE, Margaret A., b Canada 1901– , paint WWNA

RICE, Mary. *See* SCHOOLEY, Mary Rice

RICE, Nan (m Hugh Rice), b Winnipeg 1890, d Stockton, Calif 1955, paint AAA33 DWA WWA53d56

RICE, W., fl 1845–6, paint H

RICE-JONES, Dorothy (Mrs), b Dutton, Eng, fl 1963– , paint M

RICE-JONES, Peter, b Little Longlac, Ont 1939– , illus paint M

RICH, Norman, b USA c 1943– , gra tap M

RICHARD, Danielle, b Quebec 1954– , paint M

RICHARD, Hélène, b Quebec 1937– , engr etch paint M

RICHARD, Henri, b Montreal 1879, d 1938, paint K M

RICHARD, Julie Anne. *See* SZABLOWSKI, Julie Anne Richard

RICHARD, Lili Bilodeau (m Claude Archibald), b St-Lazare, Bellechasse Co, Que 1938– , paint CWW93

RICHARD, Louis, b Tours, Fr 1868/9, d W Nyack, NY 1940, Amer, sculp K

RICHARD, Philippe, b L'Assomption, Que 1947– , paint M

RICHARD, René Jean, b La-Chaux-de-Fonds, Swi 1895, d Baie-St-Paul, Que 1982, paint CE2 K M MM WWA53

RICHARD, Rhéal, b Richibucto, NB c 1930– , paint M

RICHARD, Roger, b Ste-Marie-Salomé, Que 1950– , paint M

RICHARDS, Cecil Clarence, b Little Rinsey, nr Penzance, Corn 1907, d Lakefield, Ont 1981, sculp AGO M MM RCA

RICHARDS, Ella Ashbridge, b Howarden, Ches 1892, prt M

RICHARDS, Frances Elswood. *See* ROWLEY, Frances Elswood Richards

RICHARDS, Gerry, b London, Ont 1936– , etch paint M

RICHARDS, Ida, fl 1882–3, paint H RCA

RICHARDS, Jean, b Edmonton 1924– , paint M

RICHARDS, Phil, b Toronto 1951– , paint M

RICHARDS, Phyllis Nelson Harvey. *See* HARVEY, Phyllis Nelson

RICHARDS, William, b Ft Albany, Ont c 1785, d Moose Factory, Ont 1811, paint DCB5 H KB

RICHARDSON, Doris K. (m Ross R. Richardson), b Napanee, Ont 1922– , paint M RCA

RICHARDSON, Edward Mallcott, b London 1839, fl 1865–71, Eng, paint sculp AAW3 AC DCB9 H H77

RICHARDSON, Frederick, b Belleville, Ont, fl 1863–1904, paint H

RICHARDSON, John, Sir, b Nith Place, Scot 1787, d Grasmere, Eng 1865, Scot, drwg DCB9 DNB H W1–3

RICHARDSON, Merv, b Collingwood, Ont c 1943– , paint M

RICHARDSON, Thomas Miles, Jr, b 1813, d 1890, Eng, paint APH DBA G

RICHARDT/REICHARDT, Joachim Ferdinand, b Brede, Dn 1819, d Oakland 1895, paint AAW1 AC B DeV5 GW Sam Y

RICHER, Ovide-Antoine, b Montreal 1830, d 1910, paint H K

RICHER[1], Sinaï (aka Joseph E.[2]), b St-Hyacinthe, Que 1865/7, d 1946, paint H[1,2] K

RICHMAN, Francine Chanceberg (m Hy Richman), b Paris 1928– , sculp CAE1p178 M

RICHMOND, John Russell, b Toronto 1926– , illus paint CWW93 DFA IO M MM O.Ag50 RCA

RICHMOND, Leonard, b Somerset, Eng 1874, d 1965, Eng, paint AAW3 B DBA MM NGC68 RA Sam TB1,2 WBA1 WWB34 WWW

RICHMOND, Lorraine Joy Surcouf. *See* SURCOUF, Lorraine Joy

RICKARD, George P., b Niagara Falls, Ont, fl 1950s, ske M
RICKERSON, Genia Tseretelli (Mrs), b St Petersbourg 1901– , paint M RCA
RICKETTS, Harry E.G., b 1901– , fl 1932–52, paint M MM RCA
RIDDELL/RIDDEL, James, b Glasgow c 1857, d Balerno, Scot 1928, Scot, paint B DBA DScP DVLP DVP G MM RA SW TB1 WBA1 WWBd29
RIDEOUT, Ruth Morton (m V.K. Rideout), b Sydney, NS 1928– , paint M MA
RIDGEWAY, Thomas Henry, b Hillsboro, Eng 1893, fl 1969+, paint M
RIEGLE-BROWN, Shirl (m Samuel Brown), b Ft Erie, Ont 1933– , paint IO M
RIEL, Marie-Sara (Soeur Marguerite-Marie), b St Boniface, Man 1848, d L'Isle-à-la-Crosse, Sask 1883, des K
RIFAAT, Fatma (m Ahmed Rifaat), b Cairo 1915– , paint M
RIFAT, David, b Edinburgh 1934– , drw CAE1 M
RIGALI, Jean, fl 1885–90, sculp K
RIGALI, Michele (Michaeli), b Turin, It 1841, d Quebec 1910, sculp DCB13
RIGAUDIERE, Chevalier de la, b France, fl 1758, Fr, drw K
RIGAUX, Jack, b Pincher Creek, Alta 1951– , paint M
RIGG, William, b Barrhead, nr Glasgow 1877, d Glasgow 1942, Scot, paint DBA M MM
RIGGS, Al, b Newfoundland 1933– , paint M
RIGGS, Alfred, b Fairfield, nr St Martins, NB c 1868, d 1940s, carv DFA KB
RIGHTON, Colin, b Bournemouth, Eng c 1936– , paint M
RIGOLO, Stanislav Dino, b Porcia, It 1924– , paint M RCA
RIGOR, Paul, b Czechoslovakia c 1907– , paint M
RIHA, Stanley, b Prague, Cz 1952– , paint ABC
RILETT, Robert Omar, b Aberfeldy, Ont 1910– , paint CWW70
RILLER, Audrey (m Windston Lyle Leathers, q.v.), b Victoria, BC 1934– , gra paint sculp M
RIMMER, Alfred, b Liverpool 1829, d Chester, Eng 1893, Eng, paint DBA DNB H TB1
RIMMER, David McLellan, b Vancouver 1942– , sculp M RCA WWA82
RIMMER, William, b Liverpool, Eng 1816, d S Milford, Mass 1899, Amer, paint sculp App B DAA DAB F GW NCAB WWWA Y
RINDISBACHER, Peter, b Eggiwil, nr Berne, Swi 1806, d St Louis, Mo 1834, Swi, paint AAW2 APH B CE1,2 Co DCB6 GW H H77 M McC Mo NGC67 PNL ROM Sam St TB1 WWWA Y
RINFRET, Claudette, b Montreal 1932– , paint M
RINFRET, Jean-Claude, b Shawinigan, Que 1929– , paint CC2 M RCA
RINGIUS, Carl Clemens Moritz. *See* RUNGIUS/RINGIUS, Carl Clemens Moritz
RINGNESS, Charles Obert, b Willmar, Minn 1946– , Amer, prt M US WWA93
RIOPELLE, Jean-Paul, b Montreal 1923– , paint ACA AE AGO B CA1–3 CC1 CE1,2 Co CWW93 DCA F H77 L M MM MQ NGC1 NGC67 OC OCD P RCA SC TB2 UG WA WWB80
RIORDON, John Eric Benson, b St Catharines, Ont 1906, d Montreal 1948, paint CWW48A M MM RCA
RIOUX, Jules-Bernadin-Raoul, Père, b Trois-Pistoles, Que 1835, d 1921, paint II K
RIOUX, Pierre-Paul, b Ste-Anne-des-Monts, Gaspé, Que 1932– , paint M
RIOUX, Yolande Rousseau[2] (m Charles Rioux), b Trois-Pistoles, Que 1910– , mur M MM[2]
RIPLEY, David, b London, Ont 1939– , paint M

RIPPLINGER, Henry, b Kendal, Sask 1939– , paint M
RISEBOROUGH, Douglas, b Toronto c 1924– , paint M
RISHEL, Tom, fl 1970s, con CAE1
RISHWORTH, Peter, b Ottawa c 1951– , stgl M
RISSETIERE, Michel de. *See* DESSAILLIANT de RICHETERRE, Michel, dit de RISSETIERE
RISTAU, Eugene, b Toporische, USSR 1932– , paint M
RISTVEDT, Mary (Milly) (Mrs Handerek), b Kimberly, BC 1942– , paint B CAE1,2 DCA IO M RCA
RITCHEL, John E., b Prince Rupert, BC 1913– , paint sculp M
RITCHIE, Alexander Hay, b Glasgow 1822, d New Haven, Conn 1895, engr paint App B DAB GW H TB1 WWWA Y
RITCHIE, James Edward, b Montreal 1929– , sculp M MM
RITCHIE, John, b Bedford, Que 1910– , des paint sculp M
RITCHIE[1], Percival Molson Mackenzie[2] (m Fred Ritchie), b Pointe-au-Pic, Que 1917– , paint AO M MM[1,2]
RITCHIE, Ralph, fl 1794, paint H
RITCHIE, William B., b Windsor, Ont 1954– , prt M
RITCHIE, William Norman (s Norman), b Saint John, NB 1865, fl 1912, cart H Mo12
RITHET, Elizabeth Jane Munro (m Robert Peterson Rithet), b London 1853, d Victoria, BC 1952, paint DWA H
RITTER, Henry, b Montreal 1816, d Dusseldorf, Ge 1853, paint App B H TB1 W1–3
RIVAIT, Susan Elizabeth Collacut, b Windsor, Ont 1948– , paint CAE1 IO M
RIVARD, Jerry, b Willowbunch, Sask c 1944– , paint M
RIVARD, Lyne, b Montreal 1944– , engr paint M
RIVARD, Marlys Vango, b Edmonton 1928– , paint CAE1
RIVARD, Pierre Léon, b Montreal 1947– , paint M
RIVARD, Raymond, b Montreal 1934– , paint M
RIVARD, Suzanne (m Hon Jean Le Moyne), b Quebec 1928– , paint M TB2
RIVARD, Yves, b Sherbrooke, Que 1926– , paint sculp M
RIVIERE (Mme), fl 1785–6, paint H K
RIVIERE, Edward/Edmond/M[2], b France 1803/4, fl 1830–60, paint GW H[2] K TB1
RIVOCHE, Paul, b Ottawa 1959– , cart illus paint M
ROACH, George, b Wales 1897, fl 1986, paint M
ROACH, Gerald, b Windsor, NS 1933– , paint M MM
ROACH, Thomas, b Cheticamp, NS 1891, d Walkerville, NS 1928, paint M
ROACHE, Gordon, b Halifax, NS 1937– , paint CWW93 DCA M T
ROBB, Charles. *See* BUSH, Charles Robert
ROBB, Jim, b Quebec 1933– , paint M
ROBBIE, Enid (m Roderick G. Robbie), b London 1931– , paint prt M
ROBERGE, Daniel, b Victoriaville, Que 1952– , paint CAE1
ROBERT, André, b St-Hyacinthe, Que 1940– , paint M
ROBERT, Gilles, b Montreal 1929– , des gra CWW91 RCA
ROBERT, Guy, b Ste-Agathe-des-Monts, Que 1933– , paint sculp M
ROBERT, Louise, b Montreal 1941– , paint CAE1 DCA M
ROBERT, Luc, b Sudbury, Ont c 1955– , paint M
ROBERTS, Ann. *See* ROBERTS, Theresa Ann
ROBERTS, Arthur George, b Glasgow 1918– , paint IO

ROBERTS, David, b Vancouver 1948– , prt CAE2 SC

ROBERTS, Dorothy Jean, b Port Talbot, Wales 1941– , des fab M

ROBERTS, Goodridge. *See* ROBERTS, William Goodridge

ROBERTS, Grace MacLeod. *See* MacLEOD, Grace

ROBERTS, Guy, b Toronto 1896, d 1969, paint M

ROBERTS, H. Tomtu. *See* ROBERTS, Tomtu Huron

ROBERTS, Henry, Cdr, b Shoreham, Eng c 1747, d W Indies 1796, Eng, paint EMA

ROBERTS, John Gregg Moran, b Toronto 1935– , paint prt AA IO M

ROBERTS, John Herbert, b Saskatoon 1924– , des gra CWW93

ROBERTS, Peter, fl 1983– , paint M

ROBERTS, Ralph, b Vancouver c 1906– , sculp M RA

ROBERTS, Theresa Ann (m Gwilyn Roberts), b Durban, SA 1936– , prt sculp IO M

ROBERTS, Thomas Keith (Tom), b Toronto 1909– , paint CNS40 CWW93 H77 IO M MM O.My48 RCA UG WWA93

ROBERTS, Tomtu Huron, b Collingwood, Ont c 1858, d Caulfield, nr Vancouver 1938, paint H H77 M

ROBERTS, William, fl 1864–75, engr litho H

ROBERTS, William Goodridge, b Barbados, BWI 1904, d Montreal 1974, paint ACA AE AGO B CC2 CE1,2 Co CWW70 H77 M MM MQ NGC1 NGC67 NGC68 RCA S SC TB2 TN UG W3 WWA76 WWB66 WWWA

ROBERTS, William Griffith, b Nelson, BC 1921– , paint AGO M MM NGC1 RCA SC TB2 UG WWA82

ROBERTSON, Archibald, Lt Gen, b Scotland c 1745, d Lawers, nr Cromie, Perthshere, Scot 1813, Scot, drw topog DBWA DScP G GW H SW

ROBERTSON, Beatrice Hagarty. *See* HAGARTY, Beatrice

ROBERTSON, Christine, b London 1957– , paint M

ROBERTSON, David D., fl 1854–70, engr paint DeV5,8 H

ROBERTSON, Donald, b Montreal 1952– , illus paint sculp M

ROBERTSON, Douglas Allan, b Whitehorse, Yukon 1951– , drw paint M

ROBERTSON, Helen Waimel (m A.B. Robertson), b Tartu, Est 1917– , sculp M

ROBERTSON, Hugh Douglas, b Hamilton, Ont 1900– , paint CAE1 Hu IO M MM RCA

ROBERTSON, Kathleen Pratt (Kae) (m J.L. Robertson), b London 1920– , paint BDSA M

ROBERTSON, Madeleine Nixon, b Vancouver 1912– , sculp DAS WWA53

ROBERTSON, Maisie, b Harrison Hot Springs, BC 1910– , paint sculp M WWNA

ROBERTSON, Margaret Mary. *See* WICKENDEN, Margaret Mary Robertson

ROBERTSON, Marjorie, b Vancouver 1912– , sculp M

ROBERTSON, Richard, b 1948– , drw paint M

ROBERTSON, Samuel, b Montreal 1868, d nr Montreal 1943, paint H MM RCA

ROBERTSON, Sarah Margaret Armour, b Montreal 1891 – d 1948, paint AGO CC1 CE2 DWA Hu M MM NGC1 RCA TB2 WWA47d53

ROBERTSON, Sybil Octavia (m Francis Gurzon Dobell[2]), b Montreal, fl 1920s, paint CWW36[2] MM RCA

ROBEZ, Gundai, b Hamilton, Ont 1953– , stgl M

ROBIN. *See* WATT, Henry Robertson

ROBINS, William, b Toronto, fl 1895–1905, paint H RCA

ROBINSON, Agnes Agatha Hammel. *See* HAMMEL, Agnes Agatha

ROBINSON, Al, b Ottawa 1918– , paint prt M

ROBINSON, Alan Marshall, b Toronto 1915– , paint DBA RA WBA1 WWB72

ROBINSON, Albert Henry, b Hamilton, Ont 1881, d Montreal 1956, paint ACA AGO CC1 CWW52 EC FCA H77 Hu M MM Mo12 NGC1 NGC67 NGC68 RCA TB2 TN W2,3 WWA59

ROBINSON, Boardman Michael, b Somerset, NS 1876, d Norotin Heights, Conn 1952, Amer, cart illus paint AAA33 AAW1,3 AC B BE DAA DCAA2,3 F ICB1 Sam TB2 WWA47d53 WWWA

ROBINSON, Clifford Foard, b Bassano, Alta c 1916– , paint CLA GM SC

ROBINSON, Jonas, b 1901– , paint DFA KB

ROBINSON, Katherine Mary Day Ross (m C.W. Robinson), b Trenton, Ont 1928– , paint M RCA

ROBINSON, Kathleen Beverley. *See* INGELS, Kathleen Beverley Robinson

ROBINSON, Maria S. (Mrs Hamilton), fl 1820, d Brighton, Eng 1884, paint DFA ROM

ROBINSON, Michael Robert, b Timmins, Ont 1948– , etch paint CE2 IO M

ROBINSON, Raymond Eric, b London 1931– , drw sculp IO M

ROBINSON, Rob, b 1950– , fl 1970s– , prt sculp CAE1 M

ROBINSON, Ross, b Campbellville, Ont c 1927– , paint M

ROBINSON, Sammy, b Kitimat, BC 1934– , carv M

ROBINSON, Thomas Harris, b Nova Scotia 1834/5, d Providence, RI 1888, Amer, paint ANC B F GW H TB1 Y

ROBINSONG, Lee, b Germany 1955– , paint M

ROBITAILLE, Gérald, b Outremont, Que 1925– , paint M

ROBITAILLE, Ginette, b Montreal 1949– , engr sculp M

ROBLIN, Richard, b Govan, Sask 1940– , paint M

ROBSON, Albert Henry, b Lindsay, Ont 1882, d Toronto 1939, paint CWW36 EC Hu M W1–3

ROBSON, Ebenezer, b Perth, Ont 1835, d British Columbia 1911, paint H Mo12

ROBSON, Peter, b London 1940– , paint M

ROBY, J. Alphonse, fl 1869–97, paint K

ROCH, Edouard, b 1842/3, d 1906, sculp K

ROCH, Ernst, b Osijek, Yu 1928– , gra CGA3 CWW93 M RCA TB3 WWA93 WWGA1,2

ROCHE, Ed, b Middlecove, Nfld c 1945– , paint M

ROCHEFORT, Justin, b Champlain, Que 1917– , paint sculp M

ROCHET, Louis, b Paris 1813 – d 1878, Fr, sculp B K TB1

ROCHON, Daniele, b Ottawa 1946– , engr paint pas M

ROCHON, Flavien, b Ste-Thérèse, Que c 1829, d 1902, carv sculp K M

ROCHON, Naphtali O., b St-Eustache, Que, fl 1881–90, paint H K

ROCHON, Trefflé, fl 1875–95, sculp K

ROCK, Geoffrey A., b Birmingham, Eng 1923– , paint CAE1 M

ROCKBURNE, Dorothea, b Verdun, Que 1934– , paint CA1–3 DCA DCAA2–3 M

ROCKETT, Adeline Strelive (m Harry Rockett), b Blaine Lake, Sask 1929– , paint prt BDSA M SC

ROCKMAN, Arnold Zacharich, b London 1930– , gra paint CWW92 M

ROCKWELL, Anna. *See* COMPTON, Anna Rockwell

ROCKWELL, Augustus, b Manilius, NY 1822, d Buffalo, NY 1882, Amer, paint APH GW

RODERICK, Lulu Rita/Zita. *See* JEFFRIES, Lulu Rita/Zita Roderick
RODEWALT, Vance, b Edmonton 1946– , cart Des M Po86–87
RODGERS, Arthur Wyckoff, Hon, b Amherst, NS 1893, paint CWW64
RODGERS, Bill, b Calgary c 1952– , paint M
RODGERS, Derek, b England 1939– , coll drw gra AA M
RODIER, Olivier, fl 1832–48, paint H K
RODOMAR, Andrew, b Toronto 1957– , paint M
RODRIGUE, Clement, b Thetford Mines, Que, fl 1951+, paint sculp CAE1 M
RODRIGUE, Michel, b St-Césaire, Que 1952– , gra sculp M
RODRIGUE, Rita, b Normétal, Que c 1946– , paint M
RODRIGUEZ, Lupe, b La Linea, Sp 1953– , paint M
RODRIK, Paul (b Paul Johnston), b Toronto 1915, d nr Bancroft, Ont 1983, paint sculp M RCA
ROE, Brent, b Oshawa, Ont 1956– , paint M
ROE, Nigel, b Halifax 1952– , paint M
ROEBUCK, John Arthur, b Madras, India 1802, d London 1879, Eng, paint APH DCB10 DNB H WHC
ROEBUCK, William, b England c 1797, d Côteau-du-Lac, Que 1847, topog H PNL ROM WHC
ROGERS, A. Lee, fl 1871–94, paint H
ROGERS, Donald Otto. *See* ROGERS, Otto Donald
ROGERS, Douglas, b London, Ont 1951– , illus paint M
ROGERS, Florence M. (Mrs), fl 1877–97, paint H RCA
ROGERS, Honor Kever. *See* KEVER, Honor Elizabeth
ROGERS, Hubert. *See* ROGERS, Reginald Hubert
ROGERS, Laura (Rogers-Reid), b 1950– , sculp IO
ROGERS, Marjory. *See* DONALDSON, Marjory Rogers
ROGERS, Otto Donald[2], b Kerroberts, Sask 1935– , paint sculp CC2 CE1,2 H77[2] M MM RCA SC UG US WWA93
ROGERS, Reginald Hubert, b Alberton, PEI 1898, d Ottawa 1982, illus paint APH M NGC1 NGC68 TB3
ROGERS, Robert, b Ft Devens, Mass 1944– , litho M
ROGERS, William Allen, b Springfield, Ohio 1854, d Washington, DC 1931, Amer, cart paint AAAd31 AAW1 B DAB F H McC NCAB Sam TB1 WECa WWWA Y
ROGERSON, John, b 1837, d 1925, carv DFA KB M
ROHNE, Bernd, b Germany 1945– , etch M
ROHRHIRSCH, Eric, b Germany c 1906– , paint M
ROITNER, Joseph, b Austria 1929– , paint MF M
ROLLAND, Dominique, b France 1954– , sculp M
ROLLE, Joan, b Dominica c 1933– , paint M
ROLLIN, Paul, b Longueuil, Que 1789, d Ste-Thérèse, Que 1855, carv DCB8 K
ROLPH, Joseph Thomas, b London 1831, d Toronto 1916, paint H Hu M MM RCA ROM
ROLSTON, Ronald Charles, b Toronto 1947– , paint pas IO M UG
ROMAGNOLI, Brian, b St Catharines, Ont 1957– , paint M
ROMANCE, Patricia (Trisha) (m Gary Peterson), b Hamburg, NY 1951– , paint IO M
ROMANOW, Willis, b Canora, Sask 1940– , paint IO M RCA
RONALD, Gordon Hugh, b Victoria, BC 1929– , paint M
RONALD, William (b William Ronald Smith), b Stratford, Ont 1926– , paint ACA AE AGO CA1 CC1 CE1,2 Co

CWW93 DCAA2 IO M NGC1 NGC67 OC OCD P RCA TB2 WWA93
RONDEAU, Denis, b Chelmsford, Ont 1957– , paint prt M
RONDEAU, Frances Helen Marie Roy (m Victor Rondeau), b Tisdale, Sask 1941– , paint BDSA
RONDO, Lise (m Ronald Rondo, q.v.), fl 1980s, sculp M
RONDO, Ronald (m Lise Rondo, q.v.), b Quebec 1945– , sculp M
RONNING, Chester A., b Fancheng, Chi 1894, sculp CWW73
ROODISH, Betty. *See* GOODWIN, Betty Roodish
ROOKE, Alice Constance (Mrs), b nr Brandon, Man 1886, paint Hu MM
ROOKE, Fay Lorraine, b Chatham, Ont 1934– , enam M WWA93
ROOS, Valerie, b Ottawa 1952– , paint M
ROOSEN, Otto, b Germany c 1895, fl 1984, paint M
ROOT, Derek, b Vancouver 1960– , paint M
ROOT, Frank, b England c 1900– , paint M
ROOTMAN, Jack, fl 1947+, paint M
ROPER, Edward, b Camberwell, London 1833 (x 1854), d Hastings, E Sus 1909 (x 1891), Eng, paint CE2 H H77 Ke NAC PNL ROM Sam
ROQUET, Robert, b Paris 1944– , gra paint M
ROS/ROOS, John Frederick Fitzgerald. *See* DE ROS/DE ROOS, John Frederick Fitzgerald
ROSAIRE, Arthur Dominique. See ROZAIRE, Arthur Dominique
ROSANO, Maria Altilia, b c 1905– , fl 1975, sculp M
ROSCHKOV, Victor, b Kiev, Ukr 1941– , cart Des Po87
ROSE, Augustus Foster, b Hebron Harbour, nr Yarmouth, NS 1873, d Providence, RI 1946, med AAA30 WWA40d47
ROSE, Henry, Capt, fl 1886–8, paint H
ROSE, Joyce Esther Dangoor (m Alan Henry Rose), b Shanghai 1927– , paint M MM
ROSEN, Beulah Irene Jaenicke. *See* JAENICKE, Beulah Irene
ROSEN, David, b Montreal 1955– , car M Po86
ROSENBERG, Henry Mortikar, b New Brunswick, NJ 1858, d Citronelle, Ala 1947, Amer, paint B DBA F H H77 M MM RCA WWA40
ROSENBLATT, Joseph (Joe), b Toronto 1933– , drw prt CE1,2 IO M
ROSENFIELD, Ethel Bernstein (m Ben Rosenfield), b Poland 1910– , sculp CAE1 M
ROSENGARTEN, Morton, b Montreal 1933– , sculp M MM
ROSENTHAL, Joseph (Joe), b Kishinev, Rom 1921– , paint prt sculp CAE1 CWW93 IO M RCA
ROSENZWEIG, Vladimir, b Prague, Cz 1934– , sculp CAE1 M
ROSEWARNE, Frances Martha Jones. *See* JONES, Frances Martha
ROSEWARNE, Robert Victor (m Frances Martha Jones, q.v.), b Ottawa 1925 – d 1974, paint M MM TB3
ROSKRUGE, George W., 1st Lt, fl 1797, topog H
ROSNER/ROSSNER, Charles, b Langendorf, Ge 1894, d Bellport, Long Isld, NY 1975, Amer, paint DMA DSP
ROSNER, Thelma, b Toronto 1941– , paint M
ROSNUK, Larry, b Welland, Ont c 1946– , paint M
ROSS, André, b Rimouski, Que, fl 1982– , sculp M
ROSS, Cathy, b Saint John, NB 1958– , paint prt M
ROSS, David, b Winnipeg 1925– , sculp M
ROSS, Eleanor M., fl 1880–1919, Eng, min DBA H MM RA
ROSS, Eliza, fl 1837–42, min H

ROSS, Frederick Joseph, b Saint John, NB 1927– , drgt paint DCA M MA MM RCA TB2 WWA84

ROSS, Graeme H., b La Tuque, nr Montreal 1929– , paint sculp M MM

ROSS, J. McPherson, b Inverness, Scot 1850, d Toronto 1924, paint H

ROSS, James Clark, R Adm, Sir, b Wigtown, Scot 1800, d Aylesbury, Eng 1862, Scot, topog CE1,2 DCB9 DNB EC H W1–3

ROSS, John, R Adm, Sir, b Balsarroch, Scot 1777, d London 1856, Scot, topog CE1,2 DBWA DCB8 DNB EC H W1–3

ROSS, John Hugh, fl 1860–1903, paint ROM

ROSS, Margaret, fl 1891, paint H RCA

ROSS, Marie E. Banks (m Wilfred A.C. Ross), b Moncton, NB, fl 1952+, paint MA

ROSS, Mildred Peel, Lady. *See* PEEL, Mildred, Lady

ROSS, Oscar, b Toronto 1930– (x 1950), sculp IO M

ROSS, Rick, b Vancouver 1940– , drw sculp M

ROSS, Robert, b Toronto 1902– , drw gra paint AGO Hu M MM RCA TB2

ROSS, Susan Andrina Rutton (m James Ross), b Port Arthur, re Thunder Bay, Ont 1915– , illus paint M

ROSS, William Ernest, b Ponoka, Alta 1947– , illus paint prt IO M

ROSS-HOPPER, Christine, b Helston, Corn 1939– , paint M

ROSSE, Léon, fl 1835–42, Fr, paint GW H K

ROSSEL, Shona, b Calgary c 1961– , paint sculp M

ROSSEL de CERCY, Auguste-Louis de, Marquis, Capt, b Dompierre-sur-Mer, Fr 1736, d Paris 1804, Fr, paint B DeV9 K

ROSSELL, Leonard, b Leicester, Eng 1880, d Ottawa 1953, illus paint M

ROSSI, Armand, b Nova Scotia c 1918– , paint M

ROSSITER, Margaret, b London, Ont 1949– , paint M

ROSSO, Lawrence Joseph (Larry) (Sisakolas), b Burns Lake, BC 1944– , carv prt M

ROSTAND, Michel, b Sadagore-Nice, Au 1895, d 1976, paint B CAE1 M RCA WWA82

ROSTAP. *See* STAPLES, Owen

ROTH, Evelyn Margaret Yakubow (m Klaus Roth), b Mundare, Alta 1936– , des mmed CAE2 DCA M

ROTH, Michael, b Romania 1942– , paint M

ROTHAMMER, Karl, b Bavaria, Ge 1922– , sculp M

ROTHCHILD, Johanna Eleanor (Hanni) (m Frederick Rothschild), b Berlin 1921– , sculp IO M

ROTHROCK, Joseph Trimble, b McVerytown, Pa 1839, d W Chester, Pa 1922, Amer, paint DAB H NCAB WWWA

ROTT, Margaret (Margrit), b Budapest, Hu 1898, paint sculp M MM

ROTTON, R.G., Capt, fl 1840+, paint H

ROUGERON, Marcel-Jules, b Paris 1875, fl 1958, Amer, paint AAA33 B F K MM TB2 WWA40

ROUKES, Nicholas M., b San José, Calif 1925– , paint sculp WWA93

ROULLET, Marie-Anatole-Gaston, b Ars-en-Ré, Fr 1847, d Paris 1925, Fr, paint B H K TB1

ROUS, Herbert Laurence, b Belleville, Ont, des prt CWW61

ROUSSAN, Jacques de. *See* DE ROUSSAN, Jacques

ROUSSEAU, Albert, b Charny, Que 1908, d Quebec 1982, paint M MM

ROUSSEAU, Denis, b Ottawa 1951– , engr paint sculp M

ROUSSEAU, Joseph Thomas, b St-Elzéar, Que 1852, d 1896, paint H K

ROUSSEAU, Mariette (m Claude Vermette), b Trois-Pistoles, Que 1926– , tap DCA M MQ NGC67 US WWA93

ROUSSEAU, Yolande. *See* RIOUX, Yolande Rousseau

ROUSSEL, Claude-Patrice, b Edmundston, NB 1930– , paint sculp CAE1 CWW93 M MA MM WWA93

ROUSSEL, Sylvie, b Montreal 1960– , sculp M

ROUSSIL, Robert, b Montreal 1925– , sculp B CE1,2 DMS M MM MQ NGC67 TB3

ROUSSIN, Jean-Jacques, b Mouscron, Bel 1946– , engr gra paint M

ROUTHIER, Claude, b Quebec Prov c 1947– , carv M

ROWAN, Frederick James, fl 1850s, paint H ROM

ROWAN, William, b Basel, Swi 1891, d Edmonton 1957, drw sculp M RCA W1–3

ROWE, Valentine Francis, fl 1873–4, paint topog H

ROWELL-FREER, Carol Anne, b Sarnia, Ont 1953– , enam IO

ROWLAND, Carolyn (m George Ulman), b Ottawa 1945– , etch IO M

ROWLEY, Frances Elswood Richards[2] (m William Edwin Rowley), b Brockville, Ont 1852, d Glassonby, Cumb 1934, paint B DBA DVP H MM RCA[2]

ROWLEY, Frank, b England 1908– , drw CAE1

ROY, Christiane, b Montreal 1956– , engr prt M

ROY, Diana (Mrs), b Manitoba c 1945– , paint CAE2 M

ROY, Elayne (Mme Mailhot), b Nicolet, Que 1931– , paint M MM NGC1 TB2

ROY, Frances Helen Marie. *See* RONDEAU, France Helen Marie Roy

ROY, Hélène (Roy-Richard), b Cap-de-la-Madeleine, Que 1941– , paint M

ROY, Jean-Claude, b Rochefort-sur-Mer, Fr 1948– , paint M

ROY, Louis-Antoine, b Montreal 1910– , paint sculp M MM

ROY, Louise, b Sullivan Mines, Que 1945– , paint M

ROY, Mario, b Baie-Comeau, Que 1953– , paint CAE1 M

ROY, Maud, b Rimouski, Que 1950– , engr paint tap M

ROY, Philippe, b 1899, d 1982, paint DFA KB

ROY, Raymond, b Ste-Monique-des-Saules, Que 1919– , paint M

ROY, Ruth, b Sherborne, Dor 1915– , paint ABC

ROY-AUDY, Jean-Baptiste, b Charlesbourg, nr Quebec 1778, d nr Trois-Rivières, Que 1848, paint APH CE2 DCB7 GW H H77 K KB M MQ NGC1 NGC67

ROYDS, Mabel Alington (m Ernest Stephen Lumsden, q.v.), fl 1899–1940, Eng, paint DBA MM RCA

ROYER, Henri-Paul, b Nancy, Fr 1869, d Paris 1938, Fr, paint B K TB1

ROYLE, Stanley, b Stalybridge, Lancs 1888, d nr Sheffield, Eng 1961, paint CC1 CWW38 DBA Hu M MM NGC1 RA RCA TB2 WBA1 WWB60d62

ROZAIRE, Arthur Dominique, b Montreal 1879, d Los Angeles 1922, paint AAW2 AC B F Hu MM NGC1 RCA TB1 W1–3

ROZYNSKA, Wanda (m Stanley Rozynski, q.v.), b Montreal 1929– , paint M

ROZYNSKI, Stanley (m Wanda Rozynska, q.v.), b Montreal 1931– , paint sculp M MM

RUBEN, Z. *See* ZELLERMAYER, Ruben

RUBERG, Endel, b Virumaa, Est c 1918– , paint M

RUBIDGE, Frederick Preston, b London 1806, d Montreal 1897, drgt paint DCB12 DeV6 H

RUBIN, Andrew, b Cardiff, Wales c 1951– , paint M

RUBINOFF, Jeffrey, b London, Ont 1946– , sculp M

RUCKLE, Gwen, b Saltspring Isld, BC 1932– , paint ABC M

RUDDICK, Dorothy Cole (m Bruce

Ruddick), b Chicago 1925– , paint M MM
RUDDOCK, Cheryl K., b Detroit, Mich 1949– , paint M
RUDKIN, Robert, b Windsor, Ont 1941– , drw M
RUDMAN, Sean, b Cork, Ire 1951– , engr paint M
RUDNICKI, Richard, b Yorkton, Sask 1951– , prt NGC2p158
RUDYERD, Henry, Lt Gen, b c 1739, d Hammersmith, London 1828, Eng, paint topog H WHC
RUEL, Lise, b Chambord, Que 1943– , paint M
RUEL, William H., fl 1880–94, paint H MM RCA
RUELLAND, Georges, b 1868/9, d Lévis, Que 1915, paint K
RUELLAND, Ludger, b St-Michel, Que 1827, d Lévis, Que 1896, paint H H77 K
RUELLAND, Wilhelmina, b Lévis, Que c 1863/5 – d 1932, paint H K
RUETER, William, b Kitchener, Ont 1940– , des drw gra CWW93 RCA
RUGGLES, John, fl 1983– , paint M
RUHMAN, Walt, b Germany 1899, fl 1967, paint M MM
RUIBER, Hetty Donne, b Grey Yew, Oxon, fl 1884–1906, paint H
RUITER, Linda, fl 1982– , paint M
RUIZ-WILSON, Marcia, b New York, fl 1967– , paint M
RUL-ANGENOT, Angèle (m Pierre Rul-Angenot), b Granville, Normandy, Fr 1946– , paint tap M
RUMPELMAYER, Denise (s Derum), b Chicoutimi, Que 1941– , paint M
RUNGIUS/RINGIUS, Carl Clemens Moritz, b Berlin 1869, d New York 1959, Amer, paint AAA33 AAW1 AC F M McC Sam SC TB1,2 WWA59d62 WWWA Y
RUNIONS, Hazel Fowler (m Arthur Runions), b Belmont, Ont 1904– , fl 1975, paint M UG
RUNTZ, Victor Alexander (s Vic), b Arnprior, Ont 1922– , cart illus CGA2 M
RUSINS. *See* KAUFMANIS, Rusins
RUSK, Hannah. *See* KELLY, Hannah Rusk
RUSK, Sue Rubin (m Marvin Bernard Rusk), b Montreal 1937– , engr paint CWW93 M
RUSSEL, Archibald D., b Dorval, Que 1918– , sculp CWW82
RUSSELL, Alexander Jamieson, b Glasgow 1807, d 1887, paint DeV7 H WHCp53
RUSSELL, Anna MacVicar (m John Russell, q.v.), b Detroit, Mich 1913– , fl 1989, paint M
RUSSELL, Arnold M., b 1900, d 1976, paint DFA KB M
RUSSELL, Charles Marion, b Oak Hill, nr St Louis, Mo 1864, d Great Falls, Mont 1926, Amer, paint sculp AAA26d28 AAW1 AC AW B BE DAA DAS F H IA1,2 McC Sam TB1 WWWA
RUSSELL, Edward John, b I of W, Eng 1832, d Boston, Mass 1906, illus paint DCB13 DeV9 DMA DSA H H77 M PP
RUSSELL, George Ellis, b nr Viscount, Sask 1933– , paint prt CAE1 M US
RUSSELL, George Horne, b Banff, Scot 1861, d St Stephens, NB 1933, paint AGO B CC2 EC H H77 Hu M MM NGC1 NGC68 PMC R2 RCA TB1,3 W1–3
RUSSELL, Gyrth, b Dartmouth, NS 1892, d Penarth, Wales 1970, etch paint AGO B CWW67 DBA Hu M MM NGC1 NGC68 RCA TB1,2 WBA1 WHC WWB70 WWW
RUSSELL, Harold A., b Dartmouth, NS 1874, paint CLA
RUSSELL, John Alonzo (m Shirley B.M. Russell, q.v.), b Hinsdale, NH 1907, d Winnipeg 1966, paint CLA CWW64 RCA
RUSSELL, John Wentworth (m Anna M. Russell, q.v.), b Binbrook, nr

Hamilton, Ont 1879, d Toronto 1959, paint AGO B CC1 CWW52 FCA H77 Hu M Mo12 NGC1 PMC RCA TB1–3

RUSSELL, Loris Shano, b Brooklyn, NY 1904– , paint CWW93

RUSSELL, Lorna Muriel (Mrs Cutting), b Saskatoon 1933– , paint BDSA M

RUSSELL, Mary, b Shepody, NB c 1901– , prt M

RUSSELL, Paul Gary, b Toronto 1942– , drw M

RUSSELL, S., fl 1849–60, Eng, litho DFA ROM

RUSSELL, Shirley B. McKinnon (1940 m John Alonzo Russell, q.v.), b Winnipeg, paint CLA

RUSSOW, Joan Stevenson (m John Russow), b Ottawa 1938– , prt M

RUST, Charles Hammond, b Toronto 1934– , paint CWW93

RUSTON, Hilda Sophia Marquette[2] (m Alfred Ruston), b Kitchener, Ont 1904, d 1984, paint M MM[2] O.Ag50 RCA

RUTHERFORD, Erica, b Edinburgh 1923– , paint prt IO M WWA86

RUTHERFORD, Gail, b Paramatta, Aus 1934– , paint M

RUTHERFORD, Robert William, Maj Gen, b Northumberland 1857, fl 1930, paint DeV9 H M Mo12 RCA

RUYTERS, Stache A.W., b Someren, Neth 1934– , paint sculp M

RYAN, Alonzo, b Montreal 1868, cart Des

RYAN, Noel, b Saint John, NB 1925– , paint CWW93

RYAN, Patric, b Chatham, Ont c 1942– , des prt M

RYAN, Valerie, b Montreal 1958– , paint M

RYBKA, Karel Rudolph, b Vienna, Au 1900– , paint CWW67

RYCE, Doug, b 1952, d nr Sarnia, Ont 1983, prt M

RYCKMAN, Maxwell Redford, b St Thomas, Ont 1910– , carv M

SAARNIIT, Joann Woldemar, b Estonia 1909– , fl 1978, paint M

SABELIS, Huibert, b Wageningen, Neth 1942– , paint prt CAE1,2 IO M WWA93

SABISTON, Carole (m James A. Munro), b London 1939– , paint M

SABOURIN, Claude (m Denise Sabourin, q.v.), b Ontario 1936– , illus M

SABOURIN, Denise (m Claude Sabourin, q.v.), b Val-Barrette, Que 1939– , engr paint M

SACILOTTO, Deli Daniel, b Kimberly, BC 1936– , etch paint prt M UG

SACKHEIM, Frances Krainya (m David Sackheim), b Sudbury, Ont 1902– , des AAA30

SACKVILLE, Peter, b Toronto 1945– , paint sculp ABC

SADAN, Suraj Parkash, b India 1939– , paint M

SADANAND, V.M., b Kerala, India 1940– , etch paint M

SADD, William Harvey, b Toronto c 1864, d Manotick, Ont 1934, paint H M

SADIGH, Mike K., b Iran 1931– , paint M

SADOWSKA, Krystyra Kopczynska (m Konrad Jagmin Sadowski; m Stefan Siwinski), b Lublin, Pol 1918– , paint sculp CWW84 IO M TB2 US

SAFRUK, Alexandria Goota (m Michael Safruk), b Fir Ridge, Sask 1931– , paint sculp BDSA

SAGER, Peter Winchell, b Vancouver 1920– , prt sculp MM S TB2 WWNA WWA53

SAIA, Jorge. *See* ZONTAL, Jorge

SAILA, Pauta. *See* PAUTA, E7-990

SAILA, Pitaloosie. *See* PITALOOSIE, E7-1006

SAINT-AMEDEE (Soeur), fl 1918–39, paint K

SAINTE-ANGELE (Soeur), fl 1865–8, paint K
SAINTE-ANNE (Soeur). *See* GUILLET dit TOURANGEAU, Marie-Mathilde
SAINT-ARNAUD, Damase, fl 1832–62, sculp K
SAINT-ARNAUD, Raymond, b 1942– , paint AA
SAINT-CHARLES, Joseph, b Montreal 1868 – d 1956, paint CC2 CE1,2 CNS36 H77 Hu K MM Mo12 MQ PMC RCA TB2
SAINT-CHARLES, Napoléon, fl 1880–94, paint H K
SAINT CLAIR, Herbert Bruce, b Galt, re Cambridge, Ont 1945– , paint CAE1,2 IO UG
SAINT-FRANCOIS d'ASSISI (Soeur). *See* HALLE, Marie-Joseph
SAINT-FRANCOIS de BORGIA (Soeur). *See* PAINCHAUD, Julie
SAINT GEORGE, Marie Elyse Yates (m Leonard Bruce Saint George), b Merritton, nr St Catharines, Ont 1929– , paint BDSA CAE2 CWW93
SAINT-HILAIRE, Alphonse, b 1895, fl 1920–7, sculp K
SAINT-HILAIRE, Joseph, b USA 1858 – d 1943, Amer, sculp H K
SAINT-HILAIRE, Louis, b 1834, d 1877, sculp K
SAINT-HILAIRE, Louis, b La-Prairie, Que 1860, d Montreal 1922, paint H K
SAINT-JAMES, René. *See* BEAUVAIS dit SAINT-JAMES, René
SAINTE-JEANNE (Soeur), fl 1922, paint K
SAINT-JOSEPH (Soeur). *See* GUILLET dit TOURANGEAU, Flore
SAINT-JUST, Viateur de[2], fl 1918, paint K MM[2]
SAINT-LAURENT-TURCOTTE, Georgine, b 1940– , paint prt CAE1
SAINTE-MARGUERITE (Soeur). *See* GUILLET dit TOURANGEAU, Josephine
SAINTE-MARIE, Judith, fl 1911–39, paint K
SAINT-MEMIN, Charles-Balthazar-Julien Févret de, b Dijon, Fr 1852, Fr, etch paint App B DAA DAB GW H K NCAB TB1 WHC WWWA
SAINT-MICHEL, Jean-Baptiste, fl 1848–68, sculp K
SAINT-PIERRE, Marie-Blanche (Soeur Marie-Irma), b Ile-de-Chênes, Man 1897, d St Boniface, Man 1982, paint K
SAINT-SAUVEUR, Jacques. *See* GRASSET de SAINT-SAUVEUR, Jacques
SAINTE-URSULE (Soeur), fl 1890s, paint K
SAINTE-VIRGINIE (Soeur), fl 1918, paint K
SAITO, Y.T., fl 1892–4, paint H
SAKOWSKI, Robert C., b 1943– , prt SC
SALETTE, Louis, b Montreal 1932– , paint AE
SALOMONIE, Joanassie, b Cape Dorset, NWT 1936– , sculp Co
SALTER, Robert Bruce, b Stratford, Ont 1924– , paint CWW93
SALTER, Ruth. *See* WAINWRIGHT, Ruth Salter
SALTMARCHE, Kenneth Charles, b Cardiff, Wales 1920– , drw paint MM WWA93
SAMCHUK, Alexis, b Toronto 1947– , paint tap IO
SAMETZ, Zenon William, b Winnipeg, paint CWW80
SAMILA, David John, b Winnipeg 1941– , paint IO MM SC
SAMPSON, Joseph Ernest, b Liverpool 1887, d York Mills, Ont 1946, paint AGO CNS40 CWW36 Hu MM NGC1 NGC68 RCA
SAMSON, Olivier, fl 1835–91, sculp K
SAMUEL, Matilda S., b Toronto 1860, fl 1920s, paint DWA H Hu
SAMUELLIE, E7-1004 (m Mary Samuellie, E7-1005, q.v.), b Cape Dorset, NWT 1920– , sculp DEA MM
SAMUELLIE, Mary[2], E7-1005 (m Samuellie, E7-1004, q.v.), b Cape Dorset, NWT 1923– , prt DEAp147[2] UG

SAMUELS, Clara Heirsh (m Victor Samuels), b Winnipeg 1914, d Regina 1988, paint BDSA

SAMUELS, H.S. (Miss), fl 1891, paint DWA H RCA

SAMUELSON, Kenneth, b Calgary 1936– , paint prt CAE2 SC

SANBORN, Margaret Jane, b 1861, d Montreal 1949, paint H MM RCA

SANDBERG, Hannah, b Safed, Is 1904– , Amer, mur paint IO WWA84

SANDERS, Benita Elizabeth, b England 1935– , drw gra prt AGO CAE2 SC

SANDERS, George Minard, b E Orange, NJ 1934/5– , paint IO

SANDHAM, Alfred, b Montreal 1838, d Toronto 1910, cal H Mo98 R1 W1–3

SANDHAM, J. Henry, b Montreal 1842, d London 1910, paint AAA13d28 AAW1 AC AE AGO B CWW10 DAB DBA DCB13 DeV2,3,9 DNB EC F H H77 LeJ McC MM Mo98 NCAB6 NGC1 RA RCA Sam TB1 W1–3 WHC WWW Y

SANFORD, Marion, b Guelph, Ont 1904– , sculp DAS WWA62

SANTBERGEN, Jerry, b Klundert, Neth 1942– , gra paint AGO US

SAPP, Allen (Sapoestaken), b Red Pheasant Res, nr N Battleford, Sask 1929– , paint CE1,2 Co CWW91 RCA SC

SARAFINCHAN, Lillian, b Vegreville, Alta 1935– , paint IO S

SARDELIC, Ante (Antun), b Blato Korcula, Yu 1947 , sculp IO WWA86

SARNER, Susan E., b Montreal 1947– , paint prt CAE1,2 IO

SARONY, Hector, b Quebec 1828, d Burlington, Vt 1856, drw litho GW H K

SARONY, Napoléon, b Quebec 1821, d New York 1896, des litho pas DeV7 DMA F GW H K WWWA

SARTAIN, Emily, b Goring Heath, Oxon 1903– , Eng, paint DBF

SAUCIER, Robert, b Baker Brook, NB 1951– , sculp CAE1

SAUNDERS, Leslie Gale, b London 1895, d Victoria, BC 1968, paint CLA US

SAUNDERS, Lois, fl 1894–6, paint H MM

SAUNDERS, Marlis, b Bonn, Ge, fl 1959– , paint CAE2 S

SAUNDERS, Richard Lorraine de Chasteney Holbourne, b Grahamstown, SA 1908– , ske CWW93

SAVAGE, Anne Douglas, b Montreal 1896 – d 1971, paint AGO CC1 CE1,2 CNS40 DWA Hu NGC1 Sam TB2 WWA62

SAVAGE, Harry, b Camrose, Alta 1938– , paint prt AA CAE1 DCA MM SC

SAVAGE, Isolde, b 1939– , tap CAE1

SAVAGE, Michel M., b Limoges, Ont 1953– , paint IO

SAVAGE, Roger, b Windsor, Ont 1941– , gra paint CAE1,2 WWA93

SAVARD, Napoléon, b Cap-à-l'Aigle, Que 1870, d 1962, illus K

SAVERY, Robert Hubert, b England 1902– , carv paint WWNA

SAVOIE, Robert, b Quebec 1939– , gra paint sculp CAE1 MQ NGC67

SAW, Lew, b W Australia 1922– , cart Des

SAWADA, Miho, b Osaka, Japan 1944– , paint IO UG WWA86

SAWAI, Noboru, b Honmach, Takamatsu, Kagawa-Ken, Japan 1931– , etch prt AA CAE2 RCA UG US WWA91

SAWARD, Gillian (Mrs Phillipson^2), b Maidstone, Eng 1934– , paint IO M^2

SAWATZKY, Peter, b 1922– , paint ABC

SAWCHUK, Oryst H., b Winnipeg 1928– , paint sculp IO

SAWRON, Walter Michal, b Liebersdorf, Ge 1943– , paint IO UG

SAWTELLE, Alice Beirne. *See* MacKENZIE, Alice Beirne Sawtelle

SAWYER, William, b Montreal 1820, d Kingston, Ont 1889, paint AE DCB11 EC H H77 MM NGC1 RCA W1–3

SAXE, Charles Jewett, b St Albans, Vt 1870, d Montreal 1943, paint MM PMC RCA

SAXE, Henry, b Montreal 1937– , engr paint sculp B CA1–3 CWW93 MM MQ NGC67 RCA WWA93

SCADDING, Charles A., fl 1865–85, engr H

SCADDING, Henry, b Dunkeswell, Dev 1813, d 1901, ske H Mo98

SCADDING, S.C., b Columbia, SC 1901– , ske CWW61

SCALABRINI, Rita, b 1919– , paint CAE1

SCARLETT, Rolph, b Guelph, Ont 1889, d Woodstock, NY 1984, fl 1977, paint TB2 UG WWA40

SCHAEFER, Carl Fellman, b Hanover, Ont 1903– , paint ACA AE AGO CC2 CE1,2 Co CWW93 DCA GM H77 IO MM NGC1 NGC67 NGC68 O.Ag49 RCA S SC TB2 TN UG WWA93 WWB90

SCHAFER/SCHAEFFER, Frederick Ferdinand, b Germany 1839, d Oakland, Calif 1927, Amer, paint AAW1,3 AC Sam

SCHAFLEIN, John Edward, b San Diego, Calif 1894, Amer, illus paint GM Hu RCA

SCHALK, Leslie (Laszlo), b Hungary 1900– , paint PHA

SCHAPIRO, Miriam (m Paul Brach), b Toronto 1923– , Amer, paint CA1–3 DCAA2–3 WWA89

SCHEINFELD, Roslyn. *See* SWARTZMAN, Roslyn Scheinfeld

SCHELL, Francis H., b Germantown, Pa 1834 – d 1909, Amer, illus paint AAAd28 B GW RCA TB1 WHC

SCHELL, Frederick B., b Philadelphia, Pa 1838 – d 1902, Amer, illus paint B DeV3,4,6 DMA GW H WHC

SCHELL, James Edgar, b Owen Sound, Ont 1877, paint Hu MM

SCHELLENBERGER, Otto. *See* RAND, Paul

SCHERRER, Jules Joseph, b St-Joseph-de-la-Pointe-de-Lévy, Que 1867, d Montreal 1936, paint H K

SCHEUER, W., fl 1873–83, illus DeV2–7,9 H

SCHIEPERS, Malvina. *See* COBURN, Malvina Schiepers

SCHIFFLEGER, Carole Louise, b USA 1937– , prt IO

SCHIPPER, Gerritt, b Amsterdam c 1775, d England c 1832, min GW H

SCHLEEH, Hans Martin, b Koenigsfeld, Ge 1928– , sculp AE CWW93 MM RCA S TB3 WWA93

SCHLEIMER, Edward A., b Kitchener, Ont 1949– , paint prt sculp IO

SCHLEIN, Lilyan, b Toronto 1914– , prt sculp CAE1 IO

SCHLITTER, Helga, b Mexico City c 1932– , paint sculp WWA93

SCHMID, Annemarie (m John Kenneth Esler, q.v.), b Winnipeg 1937– , sculp AA CAE2 DCA

SCHMERHOLZ, George, b Transylvania, Rom 1949– , sculp ABC

SCHNEID, Otto, b Czechoslovakia 1900 – d 1974, paint sculp WWC73

SCHNEIDER, Mary, b Wilno, Pol 1900– , paint IO

SCHOENMAKERS, Willem, b Rotterdam 1922– , etch paint IO RCA

SCHONBERGER, Fred M.A., b Arnhem, Neth 1930– , paint prt IO WWA93

SCHOOLEY, Mary Rice[2] (m Frederick Theodore Schooley), b London, fl 1920–53, paint CWW49 DBA[2] RA[2]

SCHREIBER, Charlotte Mount Brock Morrell[2] (m Weymouth George Schreiber), b Woodham, Essex 1834, d Paignton, Dev 1922, paint CE1,2 DVP[2] DWA EC G[2] H Mo98 NGC1 TB1[2] W1–3

SCHEIBER-MILICEVIO, Tania[2], b Lodz, Pol 1924– , paint sculp WWA78[2]

SCHREIER, Hilde, b Austria 1926– , wlhg IO RCA

SCHREYER, Edward Richard, Gov-

Gen of Canada (m Lily Schulz Schreyer, q.v.), b Beausejour, Man 1935– , sculp CE1,2 CWW93 WWC82

SCHREYER, Lily Schulz (m Edward Richard Schreyer[2], q.v.), b Grandview, Man, paint sculp CWW93[2] WWC82

SCHRODER/SCHROEDER, C., b Hanau, Ge, fl 1811–31, min G W H

SCHROER, Helmut, b Germany 1928– , paint SC

SCHRYVERS, Wilhelmina Frederica Hendrika de Kan (m W.J. Copper; m Arnold Schryvers) (s W. de Kan, W. Copper, Willy Schryvers), b Bussum, Neth 1916– , paint BDSA

SCHWARZ, Judith, b Vancouver 1944– , drw sculp WWA93

SCIORTINO, Francesco Saverio, b Gitta Rohan, Malta 1875, d Oka, Que 1958, sculp MM PMC RCA

SCOTT, Adam Sherriff, b Galashields, Scot 1887, d Ste-Anne-de-Bellevue, Que 1980, paint AE CNS40 Hu MM NGC1 NGC68 RCA TB2

SCOTT, Campbell, b Milngavie, Scot 1930– , engr etch paint sculp CWW93 IO MM S UG WWA93

SCOTT, Charles Hepburn, b Newmilns, Scot 1886, d Vancouver 1964, paint prt CC1 CLA CWW61 DScP EC H77 Hu MM RCA Sam TB2 WBA2 WWA62

SCOTT, Colin Alexander, b Pakenham, Ont 1861, paint H MM Mo98,12 RCA Y

SCOTT, Gerald William, b Carleton, nr Saint John, NB 1926– , paint AGO RCA

SCOTT, Gerald William, b London 1931– , paint CWW93

SCOTT, Harry Brent, b Calgary 1925– , paint CWW82

SCOTT, James Douglas, fl 1871–80, des engr H

SCOTT, Jeannette, b Kincardine, Ont 1864, d Skaneateles Falls, NY 1937, paint AAA33 DWA F TB2 Y

SCOTT, Jo. *See* SCOTT B, Jo

SCOTT, John, b Windsor, Ont 1950– , paint DCA WWA93

SCOTT, John Wilson, b Toronto 1915– , paint CWW93

SCOTT, Lloyd Edward William, b Foam Lake, Sask 1911– , drw illus WWA70

SCOTT, Marian Mildred Dale (m Francis Reginald Scott), b Montreal 1906 – d 1993, paint AGO B CAE1 CE1,2 CLA Co CWW93 H77 Hu MM MQ NGC1 RCA TB2 WWA93 WWB90

SCOTT, Marie, b Kamloops, BC 1950– , paint ABC

SCOTT, Mary S., fl 1889, paint DWA H MM

SCOTT, R. Stuart, b Nanaimo, BC 1904– , paint RCA WWNA

SCOTT, Ralph C., b Elliston, Nfld 1896, paint AAA33 TB2 WWA40

SCOTT, Robert Austin, b Melfort, Sask 1941– , paint CE2

SCOTT, Samuel, b London 1703, d Bath, Eng 1772, Eng, paint B DMA G H H77 MPE TB1

SCOTT, Stanley, b Ottawa 1889, illus prt AAA30

SCOTT, Sylvia. *See* PALCHINSKI, Sylvia Scott

SCOTT, Thomas Seaton, b Birkenhead, Eng 1826, d Ottawa 1895, paint DCB12 H NGC1 RCA W1–3

SCOTT, W.P., fl 1883–9, paint H MM RCA

SCOTT B, Jo, b Argentina 1941– , paint ABC

SCRANTON, H.H., fl 1872–4, illus DeV9 H

SCRIVEN, Palemon L., fl 1870–98, engr H

SEAGER, b c 1809, fl 1831–50, d 1886, Eng, min paint BM Fo G W H J Y

SEATH, Ethel, b Montreal 1879 – d 1963, paint AGO DWA Hu MM NGC1 RCA TB2 WWA53

SEAVEY, Julian Ruggles, b Boston 1857,

d Hamilton, Ont 1940, illus paint H H77 ROM Sam

SEAWEED, Willie (aka Hiamas; Kwaxitola), b Nugent Sound, BC c 1873, d Blunden Harbour, BC 1967, carv CE1,2

SEBASTIEN, Fred, b Ottawa 1964– , cart Po86–88

SEBELIUS, Helen, b Assiniboia, Sask 1953– , paint CWW93 WWA93

SEBRON, Hippolyte-Victor-Valentine, b Caudebec-en-Caux, Fr 1801, d Paris 1879, Fr, paint B Bry DeV5 GW H K TB1 WHC

SECKA, Passionaria, b Bulgaria 1947– , sculp MFMS

SEDGE, Raymond Joseph, b Windsor, Ont 1952– , paint sculp IO

SEDMINA, Karl, b Czechoslovakia 1950– , sculp CAE1

SEE, J.T., fl 1873–5, paint H

SEELEY[1] /SERLEY[2], Florence, fl 1886–1900, paint AAA01 DWA H[1,2] RCA

SEELY, Walter Frederick, b Monkton, Perth Co, Ont 1886, paint AAA33 AAW2 AC WWA59

SEGAL, Seymour, b Montreal 1939– , paint CAE1 CWW93

SEGUIN, Denys, b Quebec 1937– , paint CC1

SEGUIN, Fernand, b Pittsfield, NY 1927– , paint sculp CAE1

SEGUIN, Jean-Pierre, b Montreal 1951– , paint sculp CAE1 WWA93

SEGUIN, Pierre, b Quebec 1792, fl 1815–23, sculp K

SEGUIN, Tutzi (Bertha). *See* HASPEL-SEGUIN, Tutzi (Bertha)

SEGURO, Nelson, b Columbia 1954– , paint MF

SEH, Elmer (Elemer), b Puspokladany, Hu 1922– , paint sculp PHA

SEIDEN, Regina. *See* GOLDBERG, Regina Seiden

SELCHOW, Roger Hoffman, b Greenwich, Conn 1911– , Amer, paint sculp WWA93

SELKIRK, Thomas Douglas[2], 5th Earl of Selkirk, Baron Daer and Shortcleuch, b St Mary's Isle, Kirc 1771, d Pau, Fr 1820, Scot, paint BPp1215 CE1,2 Co DCB5[2] DNB[2] EC H W1–3

SELWYN, Winifrede, b Brandon, Man 1888, paint Hu

SEMPLE, Margaret Hunter Doty (m Howard Mitchell Semple), b Yarmouth, NS 1900– , paint MA MM RCA

SEN, Ranjan, b W Bengal 1941– , paint DCA

SENECAL, Annette. *See* BELLEFEUILLE, Annette Sénécal de

SENEGAL, Ralph L., b Bolton, Ont 1883, Amer, paint AAA33 Y

SENFT, Douglas, b Vancouver 1950– , gra sculp BCS

SENGGIH (Henk Kreger), b Indonesia 1914– , paint sculp CAE1

SENITT-HARBISON[2], Cathy (m Glen Harbison), b Rochester, NY 1945– , paint CAE2 M[2] MM US

SENIW, Tom, b Montreal 1942– , paint sculp AGO

SENKUS, Slawka Hrystak (m William Senkus), b Alvena, Sask 1919– , paint BDSA

SEPP, Peeter, b Kuressaare, Est 1935– , paint sculp IO

SERAFIN, Sigmund Augustus, b 1920– , paint CAE1 IO

SERGEANT, Edgar, b New York 1877, paint AAA33 WWA62

SERVICE, Patricia Olive (m David Grant), b Alberni, BC 1941– , paint prt CWW93

SETON, George, Maj, b London 1819, d England 1905, Eng, topog APH H PNL ROM

SETON-KARR, Heywood Walter, b 1859, d 1938, illus paint H WWW

SETON-THOMPSON, Ernest Evan. *See* THOMPSON, Ernest Evan Seton

SEVEHON, Paul, b Paris 1931– , paint sculp CAE2

SEVIER, Gerald Leslie (Gerry),

b Hamilton, Ont 1934– , illus paint CWW93 IO RCA
SEWELL, Edward (Rev), b Quebec 1800, paint H
SEWELL, Helen Moore, b Toronto 1906– , paint CAE1
SEWELL, Richard George, b St Louis, Mo 1942– , gra WWA93
SEWELL, Val, b London, fl 1978– , paint ABC
SEWELL, William S., b Quebec 1798 – d 1866, illus paint DeV7 H
SEXTON, Ezekiel, Jr, fl 1842–50, paint H
SEYMOUR, Munsey, b Calcutta 1837, d Barton, Vt 1912, paint H MM NGC1 RCA WHC
SEYSSEL, Alphonse de, Vicomte, fl 1893, Fr, paint K
SGABELLONE, Angelo, b Ferruzzano, It 1948– , sculp IO
SHAA, Aqjangajuk. *See* AQJANGA-JUK/AXANGAYUK, Shaa, E7-289
SH-ADO, Ted W. *See* SHEWCHUK, Theodore William
SHABAEFF, Valentin, b Russia c 1891, gra sculp AGO MM NGC1 RCA TB2
SHACKLETON, Kathleen, b Dublin 1884, d London 1961, Irish, paint AE BP DBA MM RCA
SHADBOLT, Jack Leonard, b Shoeburyness, Eng 1909– , paint ACA AE AGO CA1 CAE2 CC2 CE1,2 Co CWW93 DCA GM H77 MM NGC1 NGC67 NGC68 P RCA S Sam SC TB2 UG US WWA93 WWNA
SHALE, Jeff, b Coventry, Eng 1936– , sculp ABC
SHANE, George, b Winnipeg 1921– , cart Des
SHANKS, Jennifer. *See* LAWSON-SHANKS, Jennifer
SHANLY, Charles Dawson (x Shanley), b Dublin 1811, d Arlington, Fla 1875, paint App DCB10 DeV7 H NCAB ROM W1–3
SHANLY, Charles Dawson, b Yorkville, re Toronto, 1871, d Toronto, paint ROM
SHANLY, Cuthbert William, b 1859, d 1882, paint ROM
SHANLY, Francis James, b St Catharines, Ont 1857, d Yorkville, re Toronto 1877, paint ROM
SHANLY, R.C. (x Shanley), fl 1866, paint H
SHANNON, Eileen. *See* RAYBOULD, Eileen Shannon
SHANNON, James Jebusa, Sir, b Auburn, NY 1862, d London 1923, Irish, paint AAA23d28 B DBA DNB DVP F G H RA TB1 WBA1 WWW Y
SHAPIRO, Helen. *See* TARSHIS-SHAPIRO, Helen
SHARE, Henry Pruett (Harry), b Los Angeles 1853, d Flatbush, NY 1905, Amer, paint AAAd28 B H TB1
SHARP, George Lister Thornton, b England 1880, d Chemainus, BC 1924, paint MM TB2
SHARPE, Norman Blair, b Montreal 1954– , paint IO WWA93
SHARPE, Vera M. (m John McCulloch), b Vernon, BC 1905– , gra WWNA
SHARPLES, Peter, b St-Leonard-de-Portneuf, Que, fl 1860–96, paint H
SHARRER, Honore (m Perez Zagorin), b USA c 1920– , paint MM WWA70
SHAVER, Irene (m H.S. Shaver), b E Williamsburg, Ont 1897, paint CAE1 MM
SHAVER, Mary Julia (s Shaver), b Hamilton, Ont 1941– , paint IO
SHAW, Avery Maynard, b Saint Martin, BWI 1907, d Saint John, NB 1957, drw paint CLA MA MM RCA
SHAW, D.A., fl 1884–96, paint H
SHAW, H. Robertson, fl 1889+, paint H
SHAW, John Palmer, b San Mateo, Calif, paint prt WWA93
SHAW, Shelley Graves, b Toronto, fl 1973– , paint CAE1
SHAW-RIMMINGTON, Barrie, b England 1923– , sculp IO
SHEARD, Matthew, b 1840, d 1910, drw H

SHEARER, James Brodie, b Montreal 1911– , paint IO MM
SHECKTER, Bonnie, b Edmonton 1951– , prt AA
SHEGOAPIK, Charlie. *See* CHARLIE, Shegoapik, E9-1460
SHELDON-WILLIAMS, Inglis, b Elvetham, Sur 1870, d Tunbridge Wells, Eng 1940, Eng, illus paint AH DBA H77 NGC68 RA RCA Sam US WBA2 W1
SHELTON, Margaret Dorothy, b Bruce, nr Drumheller, Alta 1915– , paint GM SC
SHEPHERD, Helen Somerton Parsons[2] (m Reginald S.M. Shepherd, q.v.), b St John's, Nfld 1923– , paint CWW93 M[2] MA MM RCA WWA93
SHEPHERD, Reginald Shirley Moore (m Helen S.P. Shepherd, q.v.), b Portugal Cove, Nfld 1924– , paint CWW93 MM O.Ag49 RCA TB3 WWA93
SHEPPARD, Peter Clapham, b Toronto 1881, d Newmarket, Ont 1965, paint AGO CWW61 MM NGC1 O.My48 RCA TB2 W3 WWA62
SHERRIFF-SCOTT, Adam. *See* SCOTT, Adam Sherriff
SHERWOOD, William Albert, b Omemee, Ont 1855, d Toronto 1919, paint AGO CWW10 H Hu LeJ MM Mo98,12 RCA W1–3
SHEWCHUK, Theodore William (s Ted W. Sh-Ado), b Windsor, Ont 1951– , paint sculp IO
SHIELDS, George S., b Toronto 1872 – d 1952, cart Des
SHIGENO, Kinichi, b Ina, Japan 1953– , sculp ABC
SHILLING, Arthur, b Rama Indian Res, nr Orillia, Ont 1941 – d 1986, paint CE1,2 IO T
SHIMODA, Mel, b Hamilton, Ont 1950– , prt IO
SHINER, Jerry, b Toronto 1949– , prt IO
SHINRAN. *See* KIKUCHI, Mitsugi
SHIRLEY, James R. (Jim), b Bronx, NY 1944– , illus T
SHIVES, Arnold Edward, b Vancouver 1943– , paint prt ABC SC WWA93
SHONE, David John, b Kingston-upon-Thames, Eng 1941– , paint CAE1
SHONIKER, Claire Marie (m Viktoras Brickus), b Toronto 1931– , paint CAE1 IO MM RCA S
SHORE, Henrietta Mary, b Toronto 1875/80, d Carmel, Calif 1963, Amer, paint AAA33 AAW2 AC B DWA F Hu MM NGC1 RCA TB2 WWA53
SHORE, Louis Allen, b Toronto 1912– , paint O.N49
SHORT, Francis Job (Frank), Sir, b Stourbridge, Worc 1857, d Ditchling, Sus 1945, Eng, engr etch paint B DBA DBE DNB DVP DWP G H RA TB1,2 WBA1 WWB34 WWW
SHORT, Hedley Vicars Roycraft, b Toronto 1914– , ske CWW93
SHORT, Richard, fl c 1750–66, paint Co DBLP DBMaP DCB3 DeV7,9 DMA H H77 TB1 W1–3
SHORT, Robert Bond, b Toronto 1917– , paint O.F50
SHORTLIFFE, J. Newton, b Linden, NS 1912– , paint CWW70
SHORTT, Terence Michael, b Winnipeg 1911, d Toronto 1986, paint CE2
SHORTT, Willa Torrance, b Toronto 1913– , paint IO
SHRAPNEL, Edward Scrope, b Gosport, Hants c 1847, d Oak Bay, nr Victoria, BC 1920, paint H Hu MM RCA ROM
SHRAPNEL, Henry Needham, Maj, b England 1812, d Orillia, Ont 1896, paint DNB H
SHUEBROOK, Ronald Lee, b Ft Munro, Va 1943– , paint sculp CAE1,2 CWW93 US WWA93
SHULAMIT (b Shula Steinberg), b Rovno, Pol 1941– , paint MF
SHUSTER, Joe, b Toronto 1914, d Los Angeles 1992, Amer, cart CE2 WECo
SHUTTLEWORTH, Edward Bucking-

ham, b Sheffield, Eng 1842, d 1934, paint H Mo98,12 RCA

SHYKORA, Paul, b Enderby, BC 1945– , paint SC

SIEBNER, Herbert Johannes Josef (von Siebenstein), b Stettin, Ge 1925– , paint CC1 CWW93 MM RCA TB2,3 WWA93

SIEMENS, Gladys Helen Marion Wozny[2] (m Robert George Siemens), b Rabbit Lake, Sask 1943– , paint sculp BDSA US[2]

SIENKIEWICZ, Tatiana, b Bolgrad, Rus 1906– , paint CAE1

SIKKUARK, Nick, b Garry Lake, NWT 1943– , drw prt sculp CWW93

SILVER, Francis (b da Silva), b Portugal 1841, d c 1920, car paint DFA KB

SILVER, Sarah, b Swansea, Wales 1928– , paint IO

SILVERBERG, David, b Montreal 1936– , engr gra AGO MM

SILVERCRUYS, Suzanne (m Henry W. Farnum[2]; m Edward Ford Stevenson), b Maeseyck, Bel 1898, d 1973, Amer, sculp AAA33[2] B DAS DWA[2] K TB2[2] WWA73 WWWA

SILVERSTEIN, Natalie, b Buffalo, NY 1949– , enam IO

SIMA, Caris. *See* MOUNTCASTLE, Clara H.

SIMARD, Claude A., b Quebec 1943– , des paint CWW93

SIMARD, Jean (Sim), b Quebec 1916– , illus paint CC1 MM WWA62

SIMARD, Leonard, b Lac-St-Jean, Que 1933– , paint sculp CAE1

SIMARD, Sylvia, b Arvida, Que 1946– , paint CAE1

SIMARD-LAFLAMME, Carole (m Denis K. Laflamme), b Baie-St-Paul, Que 1945, sculp tap CAE1 CWW93

SIMCOE, Elizabeth Posthuma Gwillim (m John Graves Simcoe[2]), b Aldwincle, Hants 1762, d Wolford Lodge, nr Honiton, Eng 1850, Eng, paint CE1,2[2] Co[2] DCB7[2] DNB[2] H W1–3[2] WHCp236

SIMCOE, Sophia Jemima, b England 1789, fl 1850, Eng, paint ROM

SIMINOVITCH, David, b Montreal 1916– , paint CWW93

SIMON, Ellen Rosalie, b Toronto 1916– , gra illus stgl AGO TB2 WWA78

SIMON, James, b Manitoulin Isld, Ont c 1956– , paint Co IO

SIMON, Madge Bellamy (Mrs), b Chicago 1923– , paint ABC

SIMON, Wendy, b England 1946– , engr BB

SIMON, Wilma J., b Sarnia Res, Ont 1950– , gra paint IO

SIMOND, Raymond Marcel, b N Bay, Ont 1951– , etch paint IO

SIMONIN, Louis-Laurent, b Marseille, Fr 1830, fl 1875, illus K

SIMPKINS, Henry John, b Winnipeg 1906– , illus paint CAE1 CNS40 MM RCA WWA80

SIMPKINS, James N., b Winnipeg 1910– , cart CE2 WECa

SIMPKINSON, Francis Guillemard (c 1858 took the name de Wesselow), b England c 1819, d London 1906, Eng, paint EMA

SIMPSON, Charles Walter, b Montreal 1878 – d 1942, paint CC2 CNS40 EC H77 Hu MM NGC1 NGC68 PMC RCA TB2 W1–3

SIMPSON, Gregg Cairns, b 1947– , paint CAE2

SIMPSON, Isobel Graham. *See* FINLAYSON, Isobel Graham Simpson

SIMPSON, Jeanette Russell (Mrs), fl 1864–88, paint H

SIMPSON, Mary Haldenby, b Toronto 1927– , etch IO

SIMPSON, Minnie A./R., b 1888, paint H MM RCA

SIMPSON, Muriel Jessie Harper (m George William Simpson), b England 1889, d Saskatoon 1963, paint sculp BDSA

SIMPSON, Nancy Griswold (m J.H. Simpson), b Toronto 1902– , paint WWNA

SINCLAIR, Claire, b Glasgow 1931– , paint CAE1
SINCLAIR, Robert A./R.R., fl 1883–9, paint H RCA
SINCLAIR, Robert William, b Saltcoats, Sask 1939– , paint AA CAE1,2 CE1,2 CWW93 RCA SC St UG WWA93
SINDON, Gerard. *See* GECIN, Sindon
SING HOO. *See* HOO SING
SINGER, Sylvia Roberta Weininger[2], b Montreal 1930– , paint IO[2] MM RCA
SINTZENICH, Eugene, fl 1831–57, paint GW H Y
SINTZENICH, Horace H., fl 1862–1919, ske H ROM
SISLER, Rebecca Jean, b Mount Forest, Ont 1932– , sculp AGO CWW93 IO RCA UG WWA91
SISLEY, Edgar Briggs, b Toronto 1900– , gra paint O.Ag49 UG
SISSONS, Lynn E. (Lillian), b Portage La Prairie, Man 1898, d 1985, paint MM WWA76
SITWELL, H.S., Lt, fl 1870s, ske topog H
SIVUARAPIK, Charlie. *See* CHARLIE, Shegoapik, E9-1460
SJOLSETH, Minn Solveig (Mrs Carter), b Todahlen, Nor 1919– , paint WWA80
SKALNIK, Pavel, b Prague, Cz 1941– , paint prt CAE1,2
SKELTON, Leslie James, b Montreal 1848, d Colorado Springs, Colo 1929, paint AAAd29 AAW1 B F H Hu MM NGC1 RCA Sam TB1 WWAd38 WWWA
SKELTON, Liana, b Etobicoke, Ont 1956– , paint MF
SKELTON, Robin, b Easington, Yorks 1925– , paint CWW93 WWA82
SKINNER, Thomas, Col, b England 1759, d Le Havre, Fr 1818, paint DCB5 ROM
SKOBERG, Margaret Ann Overman (m John L. Skoberg), b Hardisty, Alta 1929– , paint BDSA
SKOF, Anna Maria (s Annaskof), b Poland 1937 , paint IO
SKUCE, Thomas Louis (Lou), b Ottawa 1886, d Toronto 1951, cart paint CWW48 Des Mo12 WECa
SLACK, Helen. *See* WICKENDEN, Helen Slack
SLATER, Ruth. *See* WAINWRIGHT, Ruth Slater
SLEEP, Joseph, b 1914, d 1978, paint DFA KB WENA
SLIPPER, Gary Peter, b Calgary 1934– , drw paint AE MM RCA WWA89
SLOAN, John, b Aberdeen, Scot 1891, d Hamilton, Ont 1970, paint sculp MM O.Ag48 RCA
SLOAN, Mack, b Drumheller, Alta 1920– , paint IO
SLOANE, George, b Montreal 1864, paint AAA25
SLOGGETT, Paul, b Campbellford, Ont 1950– , paint IO UG
SLOOT, Rosemary, b Simcoe, Ont 1952– , paint CWW93
SMARDON, Kate I., fl 1888–96, paint H MM RCA
SMART, Edmund Hodgson, b Alnwick, Eng 1873, d Los Angeles 1942, Eng, paint AAW2 AC DBA MM RA RCA TB2,3 WBA1 WWB34 WWW WWWA
SMEATON, Charles, d Rome 1868, paint H
SMEDLEY, Geoffrey, b London 1927– , sculp WWA93
SMEDLEY, William Thomas, b W Bradford, Pa 1858, d Bronxville, NY 1920, Amer, engr paint AAAd28 AAW1 B DAB F H IA1,2 McC NCAB Sam TB1 WWWA Y
SMET, Pierre-Jean de[2], b Termonde, Bel 1801, d St Louis, Mo 1873, paint AAW1 K Sam[2]
SMILLIE, George Frederick Cumming, b New York 1854, d Washington, DC 1924, Amer, paint AAA23 AC F Sam TB1 WWWA Y
SMILLIE, George Henry, b New York

1840, d Bronxville, NY 1921, Amer, paint AAAd28 AAW1 AC ANC App B F GW H Sam TB1 WWWA Y

SMILLIE, James, b Edinburgh, 1807, d Poughkeepsie, NY 1885, Amer, paint ANC App B DeV3,7 F GW H MQ TB1 W1-3 WWWA Y

SMILLIE, James David, b New York 1833 - d 1909, Amer, paint AAA28 AAW1 AC ANC App B DMA F GW H Sam TB1 WWWA Y

SMILLIE, William Cumming, b Edinburgh 1813, fl 1899, Amer, paint App F H TB1 Y

SMITH, Andrew James, b Freedom, Calif 1945– , paint IO

SMITH, Arthur Gordon, b Toronto 1901– , mur paint AGO Hu

SMITH, B. (Rev Benjamin Smith?), fl 1846–60s, drw DeV4 H

SMITH, Barbara Leigh. *See* BODICHON, Barbara Leigh Smith

SMITH, Bryce, fl 1843–61, Eng, min paint B BM DeV4 Fo G H TB1

SMITH, Charles Alexander. *See* ALEXANDER, Charles

SMITH, Charles Gustave, b London 1826, d Ottawa 1896, paint DCB12

SMITH, Charles Hamilton, Lt Col, b Vrommen-Hofen, Flanders 1776, d Plymouth, Eng 1859, Eng, paint B DBMP DBWA DNB H TB1

SMITH, Charles L., b NY State c 1812, fl 1880s, Amer, panor DeV1 GW H Sam

SMITH, Coke. *See* SMYTH/SMITH, John Richard Coke

SMITH, Donald Appelbe, b London 1917– , paint prt IO MM SC

SMITH, E. Gilmour, b Toronto 1892, paint CWW70

SMITH, E. May, fl 1886, paint H MM

SMITH, Edith Agnes, b Halifax 1867, d Petite-Rivière, NS 1954, paint DWA H Hu MM RCA

SMITH, Edith May, b Shaunaton, Sask 1918– , paint prt IO

SMITH, Effie, b Cumberland, Ont 1867, d Guelph, Ont 1960, paint UG

SMITH, Elmer Boyd, b Saint John, NB 1860, d Wilton, Conn 1943, Amer, illus AAA33 AAW2 CWW36 F WWWA

SMITH, Francis Hopkinson, b Baltimore, Md 1838, d New York 1915, Amer, paint AAAd28 AAW1 ANC App B DAB DeV6 GW H MM NCAB5 RCA TB1 Y

SMITH, Frank Vining, b S Abington, re Whitman, Mass 1879, d Hengham, nr Boston 1967, Amer, cart paint DMA DSP WWA62

SMITH, Freda Pemberton, b Montreal 1902, d Vankleek Hill, Ont 1991, paint CLA Hu MM RCA

SMITH, Frederick Marlett Bell. *See* BELL-SMITH, Frederick Marlett

SMITH, George F./P.[2], b England, fl 1880-2, engr H[2] RCA

SMITH, George Neilson, b Edinburgh 1789, d Saint John, NB 1854, paint DMA H H77 ROM WHC

SMITH, Gerald, b W Head, NS 1929– , paint US

SMITH, Gordon Appelbe, b Hove, Brighton, Sus 1919– , paint AE AGO CC1 CE1,2 CWW93 DCA MM NGC1 NGC67 RCA S SC TB2 UG US WWA93

SMITH, Gordon Hammond, b Montreal 1937– , sculp CC2 CWW91 IO MM NGC67 RCA WWA82

SMITH, Harold Thomas Faulkner, b Staffordshire, Eng 1893, d Vancouver 1972, paint WWNA

SMITH, Henry Walter, b Hamilton, Ont 1917– , paint MM NGC1 O.Ag49 RCA TB2

SMITH, Horace S., fl 1865–76, paint H

SMITH, James Agrell, b Stettler, Alta 1913, d Red Deer, Alta 1980, engr BB

SMITH, James Avon, b Macduff, Banf 1832, d Toronto 1918, paint H MM NGC1 RCA W1-3

SMITH, Jean K., b Hythe, Kent 1918– , paint wlhg IO

SMITH, Jeremy Lawrence, b Louth, Eng 1946– , paint CAE2 IO

SMITH, Jerome Howard (J.H.[2]), b Pleasant Valley, Ill c 1861, d Vancouver 1941, cart paint AAW1 H[2] Sam WECa

SMITH, Jill, b Upper Port Latour, NS 1948– , drw CAE2

SMITH, John Ivor, b London 1927– , sculp AE AGO CAE1,2 CC2 Co IO MM RCA UG WWA93

SMITH, John Meredith. *See* MEREDITH, John

SMITH, John Roxburgh, b Greenock, Scot 1883, d Montreal 1975, paint CNS51 CWW73 MM NGC1 RCA

SMITH, Jori. *See* SMITH, Marjorie Thurston (Jori)

SMITH, Joshua, b London c 1880, d Toronto 1938, min paint CWW36 DBA Fo RA RCA W1–3

SMITH, Kate Adeline (m Frank Hoole[2]), b Parkgate, nr Rotherham, Yorks 1878/9, paint MM RCA WWNA[2]

SMITH, Leslie Victor, b Simcoe, Ont 1880, d Toronto 1952, gra paint Hu MM RCA

SMITH, Levi (Levi Smith Alasuak Pirti[2]), E9-1326, b Povungnituk, Que 1927– , sculp Co DEAp131[2] SC

SMITH, Lorna Kidd, b Niagara Falls, Ont 1880, paint Hu

SMITH, Marianne Lee. *See* LEE-SMITH, Marianne

SMITH, Marjorie Thurston (Jori[2]) (m Jean Palardy, q.v.), b Montreal 1907– , paint Hu[2] MM NGC1[2] RCA TB2[2] WWA53[2]

SMITH, Peggy, b O'Leary, PEI 1935– , paint CAE1

SMITH, Robert, b England, fl 1821, Eng, paint DMA

SMITH, Roxann Vivian, b Centre Isld, Toronto 1924– , paint IO

SMITH, Thomas Murray, b Vancouver 1951– , drw paint CAE2 CWW93 SC

SMITH, William Ronald. *See* RONALD, William

SMITH, William Saint Thomas, b Belfast, Ire 1862, d St Thomas, Ont 1947, paint AE CWW36 H Hu MM Mo12 NGC1 PMC RCA S TB2 US

SMITH, Wycliffe Dalton, b Mandeville, Jam 1947– , gra CWW93

SMITHERS, George, b Crewkerne, Som 1810, d Halifax 1868, paint H

SMOLAREK, Waldemar, b Warsaw 1937– , paint ABC WWA93

SMUTYLO, Allen Harry, b Toronto 1946– , paint prt IO

SMYTH, Frederick. *See* SMYTH/SMITH, John Richard Coke

SMYTH/SMYTHE[2], Hervey, Capt, Sir, b Ampton, Eng 1734, d Elmswell, Suf 1811, Eng, paint topog B Co DCB5[2] DeV7 H H77 NGC1 TB1

SMYTH/SMITH[2], John Richard Coke (x Frederick[3]), b England 1808 – d 1882, Eng, paint B Bry[2,3] Co DBLP[3] DeV3,7 DVP G H Red[2] ROM TB1[3] WHC

SMYTH, Samuel Gordon, b Holmesbury, nr Philadelphia, Pa 1891, bu Cape May, NJ 1930, Amer, illus paint AAA32 F WWA47

SMYTH, William, Adm, b England c 1800, d Tunbridge Wells, Eng 1877, Eng, paint topog AAW1 AC DBWA DCB10 DMA DSP EMA G H H77

SNELL, Dawn, b Peterborough, Ont 1928– , paint CAE1

SNELLING, Garry, fl 1970s, paint sculp CAE1

SNEYD, Douglas, b Guelph, Ont 1933– , cart Des

SNOW, John Harold Thomas, b Vancouver 1911– , gra paint sculp AA AE AGO CAE2 CC2 CWW93 MM RCA S SC TB3 UG WWA93

SNOW, Michael James Aleck (m Joyce Wieland, q.v.), b Toronto 1929– , paint sculp AE AGO B CA1–3 CAE1,2 CC1 CE1,2 Co CWW93 DMS

IO MM NGC67 OC RCA St TB3 UG WWA93
SNOW, William Parker, b Poole, Eng 1817, d 1895, Eng, topog DNB H
SNOW, W.R., fl 1863–7, litho paint H
SNOWDON, Michael, b Yorkton, Sask 1948– , paint sculp UG
SOBOLOFF, Simon A., b nr Odessa, Rus 1887, paint PMC
SOHIER, G.H., fl 1856–7, sculp K
SOHON/SOHNS[2], Gustave Frederick, b Tilset, Pru 1825, d Washington, DC 1900, Amer, paint topog AAW1 AC DBA[2] DeV1 GW H McC MM[2] RCA[2] Sam TB1
SOLDATKIN, Paul, b Krasnojarck, Rus 1910– , paint WWNA
SOLE, Stelio, b Caracas, Ven 1932– , paint CAE1
SOLOMON, Daniel, b Topeka, Kans 1945– , paint CAE1 IO MM WWA86
SOMERSALL/SUMMERSKILL, R.H., fl 1868–74, paint Hpp294,301
SOMERSCALES, Thomas Jacques, b Hull, Eng 1842, d c 1927, paint DBA G H RA
SOMERVILLE/SOMMERVILLE, Martin, b England 1796/7, d Quebec 1856, paint DCB8 DeV3 H H77 ROM
SONENBERG, Jack, b Toronto 1925– , Amer, paint sculp CA1 DCAA2,3 WWA93
SONNTAG, August, fl 1853–7, topog H
SOOP, Everette, b Blood Indian Res, nr Cardston, Alta 1943– , cart paint Des
SORENSON, David, b Vancouver 1937– , paint sculp CAE2 RCA
SORGE, Walter Felix, b Forestburg, Alta 1931– , gra paint MM TB3
SORLEY, Queenie Viola Gilverson. *See* GILVERSON, Queenie Viola
SOROKA, Joanne Mary, b Montreal 1949– , tap IO
SOROKOLIT, Michael Marcus, b Toronto 1932– , paint CWW70
SOROSILUTOO/SHOROSHILUTU, E7-1172 (m Kiawak, E7-1103, q.v.), b Cape Dorset, NWT 1941– , prt DEA
SOUCY, Cléophas, b c 1880, d Ottawa 1950, sculp K MM
SOUCY, François, b Montreal 1929– , sculp DMS WWA62
SOUCY, Jean-Baptiste, b St-Antonin, Que 1899, d Quebec 1966, paint K MM RCA WWA62
SOUCY, Jean-Baptiste, b Isle-Verte, Que 1915– , paint CC2
SOUCY, Joseph Alfred Elzear, b Onésime, Que 1876, d 1970, sculp Co K MM PMC RCA
SOULIKIAS, Paul, b Volos, Gr 1926– , paint CAE1
SOUQUERRE/SOQUERE[2], J., b France 1827/8, fl 1862, Amer, drw H[2] K
SOUTHWELL, George H., b England 1865, d 1958, paint H
SOUTHWORTH, Frederick W., b Ontario 1860, d Tacoma, Wash 1946, paint AAA33 AAW3 B F TB1 WWA38d47 WWNA Y
SOWDON, Michael M., b 1948– , fl 1970s, gra illus DCA
SPALDING, Jeffrey John, b Edinburgh 1951– , paint CWW93
SPARLING, John Edmond (Jack), b Winnipeg 1916– , paint sculp DAS
SPATARU, Margareta, b Romania, fl 1970s, drw paint MFMS
SPECTOR, Norma Haller, b Montreal 1937– , drw paint IO
SPECTOR, Sally, b Michigan City, Ind 1946– , drw gra paint CAE1
SPEIRS, Doris Louise Huestis (m W. Gordon Mills; m J. Murray Speirs), b Toronto 1894, paint CWW89
SPENCE, Alexander, b Montreal 1832 – d 1890, stgl H
SPENCE, John C. (and sons), fl 1855, d 1891, stgl H MM
SPENCE, Ruth Elizabeth Bear (Bette), b Little Red Lake Res, Sask 1918– , paint BDSA
SPENCE, W.R., fl 1893, stgl H
SPENCE, Mrs W.R., fl 1884, stgl H
SPENCER, Edna Isbester, b Saint John,

NB 1883, Amer, sculp AAA33 DAS DWA WWA62
SPENCER, James Burton (Sandy), b Toronto 1940– , paint prt CAE1 IO
SPENCER, Joan McCann (s Joan McCann), b London, Ont 1954– , drw paint IO
SPENCER, Samuel A., b England c 1898, carv paint DFA KB WENA
SPICKETT, Ronald John (Gyo-Zo), b Regina 1926– , paint sculp AE AGO CC1 CWW93 MM NGC67 RCA SC TB3 WWA84
SPIERS, Henry (Harry), b Selsea, Sus 1869, Amer, paint AAA33 B F H RCA TB1 WWA40 Y
SPIERS, Raymond (m Patricia Naomi Fulford, q.v.), b Borehamwood, Eng 1934– , sculp CAE2
SPILSBURY, Ashton James (Jim), b Findern, Derb 1905– , paint CWW93
SPINNING, Hester Johnson, b Niagara Falls, Ont 1848, d Detroit 1915, paint DWA
SPITAL, Karl Groenig, b Herne, Ge c 1945– , paint CAE1 DCA
SPOONER, Ruby Young (Mrs), fl 1891–7, paint H MM
SPRAGGE, Ellen Elizabeth Cameron (m Arthur G.M. Spragge), b Toronto 1854, paint DWA H Mo12
SPRAGUE, Stewart, b Belleville, Ont 1943– , engr BB
SPENCER, Myfanwy. *See* PAVELIC, Myfanwy Spencer
SPRINGETT, Martin, b England 1947– , gra illus C
SPROULE, Robert Auchmuty, b Athlone, Ire 1799, d March, nr Ottawa 1845, paint DCB7 DeV3,7 H NGC67 W1–3
SPURR, Gertrude E. *See* CUTTS, Gertrude E. Spurr
SQUIRES, Gerald Leopold, b Change Isld, Nfld 1937– , paint sculp MM WWA93
STAFFER, Charles (Karoly), b Budapest, Hu 1928– , des sculp PHA
STAGG, Pamela Margaret Southwell, b Nottingham, Eng 1949– , illus CWW93
STALKER, George Frederick, b Edinburgh 1845, d Ottawa 1895, paint G H RCA
STANBRIDGE, Harry Andrew, b Quesnel, BC 1943– , paint prt CWW93 WWA93
STANISZKIS, Joanne Katarzyna Kiljanski (m Olgierd Thomas Staniszkis), b Czestochowa, Pol 1944– , tap CWW93 RCA
STANLEY, John Mix, b Canadaigua, NY 1814, d Detroit 1872, Amer, paint AAW1 AC AW B BE DAA DAB DeV1 GW Sam TB1 WWWA Y
STANLEY, Owen, Capt, b Alderley, Ches 1811, d Sydney, Aus 1850, Eng, topog DBWA DMA H PNL
STANNETT, Ralph. *See* STENNETT / STANNETT, Ralph
STANTON, John T., fl 1842, paint H
STAPELLS, Anthony Edward (Tony), b Toronto 1932– , sculp IO
STAPLES, Owen (Rostap[2]) (x Owen Poe), b Stoke-sub-Hamdon, Eng 1866, d Toronto 1949, cart paint AE AGO CNS36 CWW48 Des[2] H Hu MM Mo12 NGC1 O.Ag48 PMC RCA TB2 WWA53
STAPLETON, Archibald Bruce, b Stratford, Ont 1910– , paint O.F50 RCA
STAPPELLS, Tony E., b Toronto 1932– , sculp CAE1
STARK, William Redver, b Toronto 1885, paint Hu RCA
STARKMAN, Bernice, b Canada 1940– , sculp IO
STATHAM, Elizabeth Ursula Zielke. *See* ZIELKE, Elizabeth Ursula
STAUFFER, Sharlene Dee Savage (m Melvyn Roy Stauffer), b Sterling, Kans 1935– , paint BDSA
STEEGMAN, John, b London 1899, d Coffinswell, Dev 1966, Eng, paint CWW55 MM RCA TB2 WWB64 WWW

STEELE, Edwin Albert (Ed), b Toronto 1956– , paint prt IO

STEELE, Robert Cameron (Bob[2]), b Mervin, Sask 1925– , etch CAE2[2] TB3

STEELE, Timothy Walter, b Orillia, Ont 1949– , paint IO

STEEN, Lois E., b London, Ont 1934– , paint CAE1,2 IO

STEEPLE, Georgina M. *See* L'AUBINIERE, Georgina M. Steeple de

STEGEMAN, Charles (m Françoise M. André, q.v.), b Ede, Neth 1924– , paint AGO RCA

STEGEMAN, Françoise André. *See* ANDRE, Françoise Marise Sylviane

STEIGER, Frederic, b Trapau, nr Opava, Au 1899, d Toronto 1990, paint CWW90 MF MM O.F51 RCA TB2 US WWA91d93 WWB90

STEIGER, Rodolphe von, Lt, b Switzerland 1791, d Sorel, Que 1847, paint APH

STEINBERG, Shula. *See* SHULAMIT

STEINER, Jan W., b Znojmo, Cz 1916– , paint CWW90

STEINHOUSE, Tobie Thelma Davis (m Herbert Steinhouse), b Montreal 1925– , paint prt B CAE1,2 CE1,2 DCA MM RCA WWA93

STENNETT /STANNETT, Ralph, fl 1803–15, paint G H

STEPAN, Ursulina Rose McPhee, b New Glasgow, NS 1934– , paint BDSA

STEPHANSON, Loraine Ann, b Edmonton 1950– , paint WWA93

STEPHEN, Lib, b London 1958– , illus C

STEPHENS, Arlene, b Peterborough, Ont 1937– , paint IO

STEPHENS, Herman Archibald, b Canada 1890, paint CWW55

STEPHENSON, Baillie Thomson, b Markham, Ont 1899, paint IO

STEPHENSON, Lionel Macdonald (s LMS), b France 1854, d 1907, paint H H77 WHC

STERLING, Anthony Coningham, Col, Sir, b Dundalk, Ire 1805, d Knightsbridge, London 1871, Eng, topog DFA DNB H ROM

STEVEN, Arthur Gard, b London, Ont 1920– , paint IO

STEVENS, Dorothy (m Reginald de Bruno Austin[2]), b Toronto 1888 – d 1966, etch paint AAA24[2] AGO APH CE1,2 CWW64[2] DWA F MM NGC1 NGC67 O.F48 RCA TB1 W3 WWA62 Y

STEVENS, Dorothy Walpole. *See* COPE, Dorothy Walpole Stevens

STEVENS, J., fl 1745, topog H

STEVENS, Levi, fl 1815, d Toronto 1832, engr min H

STEVENS, Paul, fl 1857–60, des drw H K

STEVENSON, Amy Leanor, b St-Sylvestre, Que, des AAA30 WWA62

STEVENSON, Edith P. (Mrs Wright), b Youngstown, Ohio 1885, paint Mo12

STEVENSON, Suzanne. *See* SILVERCRUYS, Suzanne

STEVENSON, Thomas H., fl 1841–58, min paint GW H TB1 Y

STEVENSON, William Lewy Leroy, b Guelph, Ont 1905, d Calgary 1966, paint GM MM SC TB2 UG

STEWART, Alexander Bishop, fl 1878–90, carv engr H

STEWART, Clair C., b Kenton, Man 1910– , des CWW93 RCA TB2

STEWART, David Murray McCheyne, b Toronto 1919– , paint RCA UG

STEWART, Donald Campbell, b Hamilton, Ont 1912– , sculp CNS44 CWW93 O.My48 RCA TB2 WWA56 WWB72

STEWART, F.A., fl 1827–32, Eng, paint B G H TB1

STEWART, Hilary M., b St Lucia, BWI 1924– , illus paint CWW93

STEWART, Hilda Joyce Pocock[2] (m John Hutcheson Stewart; m Cecil Bell), b London 1892, d Vancouver

1978, paint BDSA CLA CWW70 DBA[2] Hu MM RA TB2 US WWB34

STEWART, Jim, b Toronto 1949– , paint IO

STEWART, Merle, b Flin Flon, Man, fl 1977– , paint SC

STEWART, Murray. *See* STEWART, David Murray McCheyne

STEWART, Rosanna MacLeay. *See* MacLEAY, Rosanna McLeay Stewart

STEWART, William Archibald, b Rivière-du-Loup, Que 1914– , cart paint CWW93

STEWART/STUART, William M./H., b New Brunswick 1829, fl 1850–60, paint GW H

STIKEMAN, Annie, fl 1880–1911, Eng, paint AAA01 DBA DVP DWA H MM RCA

STIKEMAN, Harry Howard, b Montreal 1913– , cart paint CWW93

STOCKWELL, Louise Muir Allison. *See* ALLISON, Louise Muir

STODDARD, Frederick Lincoln, b Coaticook, Que 1861, d Gloucester, Mass 1940, Amer, illus paint AAA33 B F H TB1 WWA40d47 Y

STODDARD, Mary Catherine, b Mador, Ont 1844, paint AAW3 DWA

STODDARD, S.P., fl 1843, paint H ROM

STOGRE, Peter Alexander Zachary, b Ottawa 1949– , paint prt sculp IO

STOHN, John Dale, b Boston, Mass 1922– , paint IO

STOKES, Douglas Dodd, b Newmarket, Eng 1907– , paint CWW67

STOKES, Frank Wilbert, b Nashville, Tenn 1858, Amer, paint sculp AAA33 B DAS F H TB1 WWA40 WWWA Y

STOKES, Louis Walter, b New York 1941– , sculp IO WWA93

STONE, Amy Blanche, b Bristol, Eng 1887, paint CNS40p672 MM RCA

STONE, Caroline Amy, b London 1952– , etch paint IO

STONE, Frank Frederick, b London 1860, d Los Angeles 1939, paint sculp AAA33 AC DAS DBA F MM RA TB1 WWA38d40

STONE, Sylvia, b Toronto 1928– , paint sculp DAS DCAA2,3 WWA93

STONE, Thomas Albert, b Fownhope, Herts c 1894, d 1978, paint AGO Hu IO RCA UG

STOOSHINOFF, Harry, b nr Kamsack, Sask 1956– , paint US

STORM, W.G., Jr, fl 1907–11, d WWI, paint AGO RCA

STORM, William George, b Burton-upon-Strather, Eng 1826, d Toronto 1892, paint Co DCB12 DeV8 H NGC1 W1–3

STOUGHTON, Arthur Alexander, b New York 1867, d Mount Vernon, NY 1955, Amer, etch sculp CWW52

STRAITON, John S., b Kapuskasing, Ont c 1923– , paint sculp CWW93

STRAKHOVSKY, Leonid Ivanovich, b Orenburg, Rus 1898, paint CWW61

STRAKOWSKI, Patricia Elizabeth Dmytrychyn (m John Strakowski), b Calgary 1937– , sculp CWW93

STRANGE, Thomas Bland, Maj Gen (x Stranger), b Meerut, E Indies 1831, d 1925, Eng, paint H Mo98,12 RCA WWW

STREATFIELD, Josephine, b London 1882, paint pas AAA33 DBA DWA F RA Y

STREET, John Michael, b Toronto 1942– , gra CAE1 WWA82

STREETON, Esther Leonora Clinch[2] (Nora) (m Arthur Streeton), b St Mary's, Ont, fl 1890s, paint DBA CWW10 Mo98[2],12

STREN, Patti, b Brantford, Ont 1949– , illus CBC SAA41

STRETTON, Sempronius, Col, b England 1781, d Croydon, Eng 1842, Eng, paint topog H PNL ROM WHC

STRETTON, Severus William Lynam, Lt Col, b 1793, d 1884, Eng, paint topog H MQ PNL ROM WHC

STRICKLAND, Catharine Parr. *See* TRAILL, Catharine Parr Strickland

STRICKLAND, Mary, fl 1870–84, paint DWA H

STRICKLAND, Susanna. *See* MOODIE, Susanna Strickland

STRINGER, Marc T., b Hemmingford, Que 1929– , paint CWW93

STRYJEK, Dmytro, b Lanivtski, Ukr 1899, d 1991, paint DFA KB

STUART, Donald Alexander, b Toronto 1944– , tap IO WWA93

STUBBS, Maurice Claude, b Geraldtown, Aus 1924– , paint IO

STUDHAM, Richard Lynn, b Stanley, Dur 1936– , paint prt CAE1 RCA

STULL, Henry, b Canada 1851, d New Rochelle, NY 1913, Amer, paint AAA14d28 B TB1 Y

STUMP, Sarain (Sock-A-Jaw-Wu), b Fremont, Wyo 1945– , paint CE1,2

STUPNIKOFF, Agatha (m Sam Stupnikoff), b Blaine Lake, Sask 1921– , paint BDSA

STURDY, Kenneth Gordon, b Pen-y-Lan, Wales 1920– , paint CWW85 MM

SUHACEV, Igor P., b Zagreb, Yu 1925– , stgl MF

SULLIVAN, Françoise (m William Patterson Ewen, q.v.), b Montreal 1925– , paint sculp CAE1,2 MM MQ WWA93

SULYOK-PAPP, Joseph de. *See* PAPP, Joseph Sulyok de

SUMMERS, Reta Madeline. *See* COWLEY, Reta Madeline Summers

SUMMERSKILL, R.H. *See* SOMERSALL/SUMMERSKILL, R.H.

SUNAHARA, Walter Toshiyuki, b Vancouver 1935– , paint prt IO

SUNAHARA, Yoshiko/Yoshika, b Tokyo 1939– , sculp IO

SURCOUF, Lorraine Joy (m John Russell Richmond), b Winnipeg 1933– , paint IO RCA

SURES, Jack, b Winnipeg 1934– , cer sculp MM US WWA93

SURIA, Tomàs de, b Madrid 1761, d Mexico City 1835, paint AC B DCB6 EMA GW TB1

SURREY, Philip Henry Howard, b Calgary 1910, d Montreal 1990, paint AGO B CC2 CE1,2 Co CWW90 DCA H77 Hu MM MQ NGC1 RCA WWA89

SURREY, Richard. *See* BROOKER, Bertram Richard

SURVILLA, Ivonka Symaniec, b Beylorussia, USSR 1936– , paint CAE1

SUTCLIFFE, Sarah Erma Lennox (m J. Ingham Sutcliffe), b Toronto 1912/15– , paint IO O.F50

SUTHERLAND, Edward, Maj, fl 1851, topog H

SUTHERLAND, Edward, Capt, fl 1872–5, paint H

SUTHERLAND, Fanny, fl 1858–89, Eng, paint B DBA DVP DWA G H RCA TB1

SUTHERLAND, Florence M., fl 1888, paint H RCA

SUTHERLAND, Frederick William, b 1860, fl c 1920s, engr H RCA

SUTHERLAND, Joan Charlotte, b Ottawa 1942– , paint IO

SUTTON, Carol Lorraine, b Norfolk, Va 1945– , paint IO WWA93

SUZANA, Ken, b Windsor, Ont 1948– , paint IO

SUZOR-COTE[2], Marc-Aurèle de Foy, b Arthabaska, Que 1869, d Daytona Beach, Fla 1937, paint sculp ACA AGO B CC1 CE1,2 CWW36 EC H77 K MM Mo12[2] MQ NGC1 NGC67 PMC RCA TB2 TN UG US

SUZUKI, Aiko, b Vancouver 1937– , des fab CE1,2 DCA IO

SVENDSEN, Svend V., b Christiana, Nor 1864, fl 1886, Nor, paint B H RCA TB1

SWAFFIELD, Myrtle Lewis (m W.A. Swaffield), b USA, fl 1945+, paint CLA

SWAN, Peter, b Greenock, Scot 1941– , paint WWGA2

SWARTZ, Burrell, b Vancouver 1925– , paint MM UG
SWARTZMAN, Roslyn Scheinfeld (m Monte Swartzman), b Montreal 1931– , paint sculp CAE1 DCA MM RCA SC WWA93
SWEENY, Frances Beatrice, b Montreal, fl 1934+, paint CNS40 MM
SWEENY, Kathleen Chipman. *See* LIEBICH, Kathleen Chipman Sweeny
SWIATECKI, Antoni, b Poland 1949– , paint CAE1
SWIFT, Jonathan W., fl 1836–66, paint H
SWIFT, Joseph/James, fl 1872, d c 1889, paint DFA KB ROM
SWIM, Laurie Elizabeth, b Sandy Point, NS 1949– , gra IO
SWINTON, George, b Vienna 1917– , drw paint AE CC1 CWW93 IO MM TB2 WWA84
SYBAL, Philip, b Toronto 1949– , paint IO
SYDIAHA, Joanne Oldring, b Lacombe, Alta 1945– , paint BDSA
SYKES, John, Adm, b London 1724, d Englefield, Eng 1858, Eng, topog AC DeV1 DMA EMA GW H
SYLVESTRE, Micheline. *See* PASSILLE-SYLVESTRE, Micheline de
SYLVESTRE, Yves de. *See* PASSILLE-SYLVESTRE, Yves de
SYME, James, b Edinburgh 1832, d Victoria, BC 1881, carv DCB11
SYMINGTON, Barbara Joan. *See* BOBIER, Barbara Joan Symington
SYMONS, Beatrice Adelaide (Bessie) Fry. *See* FRY, Beatrice Adelaide (Bessie)
SYMONS, Jelinger H. (s JHS), fl 1861, Eng, topog H
SYMONS, Robert David, b Mayfield, Eng 1898, d Regina 1973, paint CWW70
SZABLOWSKI, Julie Anne Richard (m George J. Szablowski), b Sackville, NS 1932– , paint sculp IO MM
SZABO, Zoltan, b Hungary 1928– , paint PHA
SZASZ, Endre, b Hungary 1926– , gra paint PHA
SZEP, Paul, b Hamilton, Ont 1941– , cart illus CGA3 Co WECa
SZILVA, Joseph (Joe), b Budapest, Hu 1950– , gra UG
SZPL. *See* THADDAEUS

T

TABOUILLET, Pierre-Georges, b 1936– , paint CAE1,2
TABUCHI, Sue Sumi, b Cumberland, BC 1928– , paint IO
TABUTEAU, Doris Roosmale Le Cocq. *See* LE COCQ, Doris Roosmale
TACHE, Eugène Etienne, b Montmagny, Que 1836, d Quebec 1912, des paint ACA H K LeJ Mo12 RCA
TACHE, Jules, b Montmagny, Que 1844, d Quebec 1897, drgt paint H K
TACK, Augustus Vincent, b Pittsburgh, Pa 1870, d New York 1949, Amer, mur paint AAA33 B DAA F TB1,2 WWA40 Y
TACON, Edna Jeanette (m Percy Henry Tacon, q.v.), b Milwaukee, Wis 1913, d 1980, paint AGO WWA53
TACON, Percy Henry (m Edna Jeanette Tacon, q.v.), b England 1902– , paint MM O.My49 RCA
TAGGART, William Stuart (s Lance Bilton), b Stouffville, Ont 1859, d Ottawa 1925, paint H W1–3
TAGOONA, Armand, b Baker Lake, NWT 1926– , paint CAE1
TAHEDL, Ernestine (m Richard Ian Ogilvie), b Vienna 1940– , paint stgl CAE1 CWW93 RCA WWA93
TAIARAK, Ituvik, E9-1165, b Sugluk, Que 1898, sculp DEA
TAILFEATHERS, Gerald, b Stand Off, Alta 1925, d Blood Indian Res, Alta 1975, paint sculp CE1,2 DFA SC
TAIT, Douglas, b Medicine Hat, Alta 1944– , illus CBC

TAIT, George Edward, b Sarnia, Ont 1910– , paint CWW93

TAIT, Leslie, b Glasgow 1949– , paint S

TAIT, Sylvia (m Eldon B. Grier), b Montreal 1932– , paint prt CAE2 MM RCA

TAKASHIMA, Shizuye Violet, b Vancouver 1928– , illus paint CBC CGA3 IO SAA13 T WWA93

TALESKI, James, b 1946– , paint CAE1

TALFOURD, Field, b Reading, Eng 1815, d London 1874, Eng, paint B Bry DVP G H Red TB1

TALIRUNILI[2], Joe, E9-818, b Povungnituk, Que 1906, d 1976 prt sculp Co[2] DEAp86

TAMASAUSKAS, Otis Kazys, b Tirschenreuth, Ge 1947– , paint prt IO UG WWA86

TAMOSAITIS, Anastasia, b Vainutas, Lith 1910– , paint prt IO

TAMOSAITIS, Antanas, b Lithuania 1906– , paint prt IO

TAN, Agnes Ivan (s Agnes Ivan), b Budapest, Hu 1950– , paint IO

TAN, Chinkok, b Malaysia 1941– , paint prt IO

TANABE, Takao, b Prince Rupert, BC 1926– , paint AA AE AGO CC2 CE1,2 Co CWW93 MM NGC1 NGC67 RCA SC TB2 UG

TANGREDI, Vincent, b Compobasso, It 1950– , gra paint sculp CAE1,2 IO WWA93

TANGUY, Yves (Raymond-Georges-Yves), b Paris 1900, d Woodbury, Conn 1955, Amer, paint B K L TB1,2 WA

TANIA. *See* SCHREIBER-MILICEVIO, Tania

TANNER, Charlie, b 1904, d 1982, carv DFA KB

TANNER, Harry, b Cuba, fl 1970s, paint MFMS

TANOBE, Miyuki (m Maurice Savignac), b Kamakuro, Japan 1939– , paint CAE1 SAA23 T

TAPPIN, John Robert, b USA 1946– , sculp IO

TAPSON, Kay, b Scotland 1922– , paint CAE1 IO

TARDIVEL, Emile, fl 1861–88, paint H K

TARDIVEL, Jean-Marie, fl 1874–1904, paint H K

TARSHIS-SHAPIRO, Helen, b Montreal 1922– , paint prt IO

TASCONA, Antonio (Tony), b St Boniface, Man 1926– , paint sculp AGO CAE2 CWW93 MM RCA S SC St WWA93

TASSELL, W.H., b England 1880, paint WWNA

TASSEOR TUKSWEETTOK / TUTSWEETOK, Lucy, E1-135 (m Richard Tuksweettok, E1-272), b Eskimo Point, NWT 1934– , sculp CWW93 DEAp229

TATE, James Richard, b Buxton, Eng 1882, d Toronto 1960, paint Hu MM RCA

TATOSSIAN, Armand, b Alexandria, Egy 1948– , paint CWW93 RCA WWA93

TATTNER, George, E2-179, b Baker Lake, NWT 1910– , sculp DEA

TAUFFENBACH, Constantin-Nicolas, b Metz, Fr 1829, d St-Anne-des-Chênes, Man 1890, paint sculp K

TAVARES, Alex, b Zanzibar 1934– , paint sculp MFMS

TAVERNIER, Jules, b Paris 1844, d Honolulu 1899, Fr, paint AAW1 AC B H K Sam TB1

TAYLOR, Alba, b 1931– , sculp CAE2

TAYLOR, Alfred Perring, b Madras, India 1872, paint CWW38 US

TAYLOR, Alice, fl 1895, paint H MM

TAYLOR, Andrew Thomas, Sir, b Edinburgh 1850, d London 1937, Eng, paint CWW36 H MM Mo98,12 NGC1 RCA TB1,3 WBA2 WWB34 WWW

TAYLOR, Anne, fl 1886, paint DWA H MM

TAYLOR, Francis, b Northampton, Eng 1899, Eng, paint DBA Hu RA WBA1 WWB34
TAYLOR Frank Hamilton, b 1846, fl 1874–81, Amer, illus AAA13 H ROM
TAYLOR, Frederick Bourchier, b Ottawa 1906, d 1987, paint AGO B CLA MM NGC1 RCA TB2 WWA86
TAYLOR, G.L., b England 1874, d 1962, paint DFA
TAYLOR, George T., b Fredericton 1838 – d 1913, paint H
TAYLOR, Harriet Jane. *See* PINKERTON, Harriet Jane Taylor
TAYLOR, Jocelyn (m Roy Mitchell), b Toronto 1899, paint DWA IO O.Ag51 RCA WWA70
TAYLOR, John Benjamin, b Charlottetown 1917, d Edmonton 1970, paint CLA MM RCA US
TAYLOR, Lila Caroline. *See* KNOWLES, Lila Caroline Taylor
TAYLOR, Marguerite Judd, b Paris 1884, d Winnipeg 1964, sculp CLA DWA K RCA
TAYLOR, Richard Gordon, b Fergus, Ont 1950– , paint MF
TAYLOR, Richard Lippincott Denison, b Ft William, re Thunder Bay, Ont c 1902, d 1970, cart illus Des RCA TB2 WECa WWA62
TAYLOR, Roberta Jane, b Amherst, NS 1905– , paint MA
TAYLOR, Ron, b Red Lake, Ont 1948– , paint sculp SC
TAYLOR, Stephen, b Merton, Sur 1940– , stgl IO
TAYLOR, Stephen James Lake, 1st Baron Taylor of Harlow, b Marlow-on-Thames 1910– , Eng, paint BPp2614 CWW70
TAYLOR, Thomas, fl 1854–6, paint H
TAYLOR, William Francis, b Hamilton, Ont 1883, paint AAA33 WWA40 Y
TAYLOR, William Hughes, b Port Stanley, Falkland Isld 1891, paint Hu MM NGC1 RCA TB2
TAZEWELL, Samuel Oliver, b England, fl 1820–38, Eng, litho DCB7 H
TEASDALE. *See* GIBSON, Dick
TEITELBAUM, Mashel Alexander, b Saskatoon 1921, d 1985, paint AGO CC1 IO MM RCA
TELARI-O-LIN. *See* VINCENT, Zacharie (Telari-o-lin)
TELLEZ, Eugenio, b 1939– , etch CAE2
TELLIER, Antoinette (Soeur Louise de Savoie), b Montreal 1865, d Outremont, Que 1943, paint K
TEMPEST, John Sugden, b Keighley, Yorks 1864, fl 1933, paint H RCA
TEMPLAR, Albert Edward, b London, Ont 1897, d 1992, paint O.F51 RCA
TEMPLE, Chris, b Ajax, Ont 1957– , paint CWW93
TEMPORALE, Louis Luigi, b Maiana, It 1909, d Port Credit, Ont 1994, sculp IO RCA WWA62
TENGGREN, Gustaf, b Magra, Swe c 1896, d Westport, Me 1970, Amer, illus paint IBYP SAA62
TESSIER, Josephine Hambleton. *See* HAMBLETON, Josephine
TESSIER, Yves, b Quebec 1800, d Montreal 1847, paint H K W1–3
TETREAULT, Pierre-Léon, b Granby, Que 1947– , paint prt CAE2
TETU, Pierre-Narcisse, b Trois-Pistoles, Que c 1836, d Key W, Fla 1878, paint DeV4 H K
TEULON, Edward A., b c 1820, fl 1860, engr GW H Y
THADDAEUS (b Szepielewicz; s SZPL), b Toronto 1955– , sculp CWW93
THATCHER, Charles Gregory, b La Jolla, Calif 1949– , prt CAE1
THAUBERGER, David Allan, b Holdfast, Sask 1948– , paint sculp CAE2 DCA DFA
THEBERGE, Carol Eva Wainio. *See* WAINIO, Carol Eva
THEBERGE-COTE, Odette, b 1947 , paint prt CAE1,2
THEPOT, Roger-François, b Landeleau,

Fr 1925– , paint B CWW84 IO MM RCA TB3 US WWA82

THERRIAULT, André, b Edmundston, NB 1943– , con DCA

THERRIEN, Denise Elena (m Richard John McNeill), b Toronto 1945– , sculp IO

THIBAULT, Gilles (Tibo[2]), b Nicolet, Que 1951– , illus CWW93[2]

THIBAULT, René, b Quebec 1909– , sculp TB2

THIBERT, Patrick Alvin, b Windsor, Ont 1943– , sculp IO WWA93

THICKE, William H., Jr, b England, fl 1873–1910, des engr H

THIELCKE/THIELKE, Henry D., b England c 1789, fl 1805–60, Eng, min paint B Fo G GW H TB1

THOM, Eric, b St Kitts, BWI 1892, d Montreal 1977, cart Des

THOMARAT, Jeanne Aline (m Armand Thomarat), b Lyon, Fr 1893, d Rosthern, Sask 1985, paint BDSA DFA KB

THOMAS, Alice Blair Pollard (m Adolphus Richard Thomas), b Collingwood, Ont c 1865, d Los Angeles c 1945, paint AAA23 AAW2 AC DWA H MM RCA

THOMAS, Edward Harold, b Margate, Kent 1879, paint Hu

THOMAS, Ian, b Nottingham, Eng 1935– , sculp BCS

THOMAS, Jacob Ezra, b Six Nations Res, Tuscarora, nr Brantford, Ont 1922– , carv Co CWW93

THOMAS, Lionel Arthur John, b Toronto 1915– , paint sculp AGO CC2 CWW93 MM NGC1 RCA TB2 WWA86

THOMAS, Roy Harvey, b Longlac, Ont 1949– , paint prt IO

THOMAS, Vincent, b Wales 1915– , paint IO

THOMAS, William, b Suffolk, Eng c 1799, d Toronto 1860, paint ACA CE1,2 Co DCB8 DeV8 H W1–3

THOMAS, William Tutin, b Toronto 1828, d Montreal 1892, paint CE1,2 RCA

THOMPSON, A., Capt, fl 1842, topog DeV4 H

THOMPSON, Carole, b Barrie, Ont 1945– , paint SC

THOMPSON, Dorothy Burr (m Homer Armstrong Thompson), b Delhi, NY 1900– , paint WWA62

THOMPSON, Eleanor Shepherd, b Tillsonburg, Ont 1890, d 1965, paint Hu

THOMPSON, Ernest Evan Seton (aka Seton-Thompson), b S Shields, Eng 1860, d Seton Village, Santa Fe, NM 1946, Amer, paint sculp AAA33 AAW1 AGO B CBC CC2 CE1,2 Co CWW36 DAB DAS DVP EC F H ICB1 McC MM Mo98,12 NCAB RCA SAA18,26 Sam TB1 W2,3 WBA1 WWA40d47 WWW WWWA

THOMPSON, Ernest Thorne, b Saint John, NB 1897, Amer, paint AAA32 B F TB2 WWA89

THOMPSON, Keith, b Craven, Sask 1934– , paint SC

THOMPSON, Margaret Collins Duncan (m Robert Randolph Thompson[2]), b Brooklyn, NY 1884, paint CWW38[2] MM RCA

THOMPSON, Michael, b Montreal 1954– , paint CWW93

THOMSON, David F., b 1872, gra paint Hu

THOMSON, George, b Claremont, Ont 1868, d Owen Sound, Ont 1965, paint AAA33 AGO CWW61 MM NGC1 O.My48 PMC RCA UG WWA62

THOMSON/THOMPSON, John, b Scotland, fl 1803–10, Eng, min paint GW H J

THOMSON, Keith, b Qu'Appelle Valley, Sask 1934– , paint S

THOMSON, Thomas John (Tom), b nr Claremont, Ont 1877, d Canoe Lake, Ont 1917, paint AAW3 ACA AE AGO B CC1 CE1,2 Co EC H77 NGC1

NGC67 OC OCD P R1 RCA S Sam TB1 TN UG W1–3

THOMSON, William James, b Guelph, Ont 1858, d Toronto 1927, etch paint AGO EC H MM RCA W1–3

THOMSON, William Robinson, b Hamilton, Ont 1926– , paint UG WBA2 WWB88

THORN, Anthony (b Arthur Goldman), b Regina 1927– , paint CAE1 TB2

THORN, John, b England, fl 1872–87, paint H

THORNE, Diana (m Arthur North[2]), b Winnipeg 1895, gra illus AAA32 DWA ICB1,2[2] IBYP TB2 WWA40

THORNE, Gordon Kit, b Stanway, Eng 1896, d Vancouver 1982, paint DFA WWA80 WWNA

THORNE, M. Art, b Devon, NB 1909– , mur paint WWA76

THORNTON, James Howard (Jim), b St Stephen, NB 1937– , paint WWA91

THORNTON, Mildred Valley Stinson (m John Henry Thornton), b Dresden, Ont 1890, d Vancouver 1967, paint BDSA CLA DWA Hu MM RCA Sam WWNA

THORPE, Ethel, b Midland, Ont 1881, d Saskatoon 1953, paint BDSA

THORSON, Charles, b Winnipeg 1890, paint CWW58

THORSON, Donald Scarth, b Winnipeg 1925– , sculp CWW89

THRASHER, Mona, b c 1942– , paint SC

THRESHER, Eliza Wilson Brooks (m George Godsell Thresher[2], q.v.), fl 1821–30, paint DCB8[2] H

THRESHER, George Godsell (m Eliza W.B. Thresher, q.v.), b Salisburg, Eng 1780, d Charlottetown 1857, paint DCB8 DMA G W H H77

THUDICHUM/THUDICUM, Roberta. *See* BALFOUR, Roberta

THURMAN, Mark Gordon Ian, b Toronto 1948– , illus paint C CBC SAA63

THURSTON, Edwin, fl 1898–1909, paint H RCA

THURSTON, Jack L., b St Catharines, Ont 1919– , fl 1975, illus sculp Sam

TIBBITS/TIBBETS, Benjamin F., b Banning, Queens Co, NB 1813, fl 1840s, d Grand Lake, NB, paint H

TIBO. *See* THIBAULT, Gilles

TIEDEMANN, Hermann Otto, b Berlin, Ge 1821, d Victoria, BC 1891, topog DeV1 DFA H KB

TIESSEN, George, b 1935– , prt sculp CAE1,2

TIKITOK, E7-1067 (m Lucy Qinnuayuak, E7-1068, q.v.), b Cape Dorset, NWT 1908– , prt sculp DEAp233

TIKTAK, John, b Kareak, nr Whale Cove, NWT 1916, d Ranklin Inlet, NWT 1981, sculp CE1,2 Co DEAp235 RCA

TILEY, James Henry, b London 1933– , paint CAE1,2 CWW93 IO MM

TILLENIUS, Clarence Ingwall, b Sandridge, Man 1913– , paint WWA93

TIMMAS, Osvald, b Tartu, Est 1919– , paint CAE1 WWA93

TIMS, Michael Wayne. *See* BRONSON, A.A.

TINGLEY, Merle R. (s Ting), b Montreal 1921– , cart illus CGA2 Des Po86–88

TINNING, George Campbell, b Saskatoon 1910– , paint CWW93 MM NGC1 NGC68 RCA TB2 WWA93

TINYAN, Chan, b Kwantung, Chi 1942– , paint ABC SC

TIURA, Oliver, b Tampere, Fin c 1943– , paint sculp IO

TOBIN, George, R Adm, b Salisbury, Eng 1768, d Teignmouth, Eng 1838, Eng, drw paint DBWA DMA DNB Ke WHC

TOBIN, Kevin Joseph Michael (s K.T.), b 1958– , cart Po88–90

TOBODANDUNG, Donald, b Parry Sound, Ont 1946– , paint IO

TOD, Joanne, b Montreal 1953– , paint CWW93

TOD, John, b Water Leven, nr Loch

Lomond, Scot 1791, d Victoria, BC 1882, paint DCB11 H W1 3

TODD, Henry Alpheus Randall Cook, b England 1782, d c 1862, paint Co H W1–3

TODD, Jim, b Perotte, NS, cart Po86–91

TODD, Robert Clow, b Berwick-on-Tweed, Eng 1809, d Toronto 1866, carv paint ACA CE1,2 DCB9 H H77 MQ NGC1 NGC67

TOFT/TOFFE/TOOFT/TUFTS, Peter Petersen, b Kolding, Dn 1825, d London 1901, Dn, paint AAW1 AC AW B DBA DVP DWP G H Sam TB1 WBA1

TOKARCHUK, Anne Markowski (m Andrew Tokarchuk), b Sokal, Sask 1912, d Saskatoon 1965, paint BDSA

TOKARCHUK, Sharon Radloff, b Star City, Sask 1940– , paint wlhg CAE1

TOKARYK, John J., b Moose Jaw, Sask 1913– , paint O.N49

TOLER, John George, fl 1808–29, paint H PNL WHC

TOLER, Joseph, b Halifax c 1810, fl 1831–42, paint DCB7 H H77

TOLFREY, Frederick, fl 1845, illus H

TOLGESY, Victor, b Miskolc, Hu 1928, d Ottawa 1980, sculp CAE1 CC1 DCA MM NGC1 RCA TB3 WWA78d82

TOLLES, Walter George, b Zullichau, Ge 1876, d 1946, paint S

TOLMIE, Kenneth Donald, b Halifax 1941– , drw paint CWW93 SAA15 WWA93

TOMAN, Paul Bernard, b Nairobi, Kenya 1947– , paint sculp IO UG

TOMCIK, Andrew Michael, b Cleveland 1938– , des WWA93

TOMLINSON, Noreen Joan, b Toronto 1947– , prt IO

TOMLINSON, Olga Kornavitch (m Roy Tomlinson, q.v.), b Welland, Ont 1929– , litho paint ABC

TOMLINSON, Roy (m Olga K. Tomlinson, q.v.), b Toronto 1928– , gra litho paint ABC

TOMMEO/TOMMEV, Foto Spiro, b Zhelevo, Gr c 1899– , paint Hu MM RCA

TOMMI, Suzanne. *See* GUITE, Suzanne

TONDINO, Gentile, b Montreal 1923– , drw paint CC2 CWW93 MM NGC1 RCA TB2

TONG, John, b Hong Kong 1933– , paint ABC

TONNANCOUR, Jacques Godefroy de[2], b Montreal 1917 , paint ACA AGO B CC2 CE1,2 Co H77 M[2] MM MQ NGC1 NGC67 P RCA S TB2 WWA76

TOOGOOD, Wendy, b Bristol, Eng 1947 , gra paint tap AA CAE1,2

TOOKOOME, Simon, E2-426, b Chantrey Inlet, NWT 1934– , paint prt sculp Co CWW93 DEA

TOOLE, Brigid. *See* GRANT, Brigid Toole

TOOLOOKTOOK, Paul, E2-377, b Baker Lake, NWT 1947– , sculp DEA

TOPHAM, William Thurston, b Spondon, Derb 1888, d Montreal 1966, paint MM NGC68 PMC RCA

TORBETT, Charles W., fl 1810–42, engr DeV9 GW H WHCp195

TORRANCE, Ada Mildred Bruce. *See* BRUCE, Ada Mildred

TORRANCE, Elizabeth M., fl 1895, paint H MM

TORRANCE, Lilias. *See* NEWTON, Lilias Torrance

TOTH, Steven, b Hamilton, Ont 1950– , paint prt IO

TOULMIN, Margaret Clarissa Hayes (m William Toulmin), b Filton, Eng 1916– , sculp CWW89 RCA

TOUPIN, Fernand, b Montreal 1930– , paint B CWW93 H77 MM RCA

TOURBIN, Dennis, b St Catharines, Ont 1946– , paint DCA IO

TOURVILLE, Charles, fl 1880–92, paint H K

TOUSIGNANT, Claude, b Montreal 1932– , paint B CA3 CAE1 CC1 CE1,2 Co CWW93 H77 MM MQ NGC67 OC RCA SC WWA91

TOUSIGNANT, Serge, b Montreal 1942– , paint B CC2 CE1,2 DCA MM SC

TOWN, Harold Barling, b Toronto 1924, d nr Peterborough, Ont 1990, paint sculp ACA AE AGO B CAE1 CC2 CE1,2 Co CWW90 DCA F MM NGC1 NGC67 O.F51 P RCA S SC TB2 UG WWA91d93 WWB90 WWC71

TOWNSEND, Dorothy Jean (m Saul Field[2], q.v.), b Toronto 1921– , etch paint IO[2] WWA93

TOWNSEND, Horace, fl 1880, drw des H RCA

TOWNSEND, Pauline E., fl 1896, paint H RCA

TOWNSEND, William, b London 1909, d Banff, Alta 1973, paint CE1,2 DBA WWB72d74

TOWNSHEND, George, FM, 4th Viscount, 1st Marquess, b England 1724, d Raynham Hall, Norf 1807, Eng, paint B BPp2662 Bry CE1,2 DBE DBWA DCB5 Des DNB EC H H77 LeJ Red TB1 W1–3

TOWNSLEY, Frank, b Vancouver 1948– , paint ABC

TOZER, Marjorie Hughson, b Halifax 1900– , paint Hu MM RCA

TRACY, Arthur John, b S Mymms, Eng 1910– , sculp CWW38 O.F49 RCA

TRAILL, Catharine Parr Strickland[2] (m Thomas Traill), b Rotherhithe, London 1802, d Lakefield, Ont 1899, paint App CBC88 CE1,2 Co DCB12[2] EC R2 W1–3

TRAKAS, George, b Quebec 1944– , sculp CA2 CE1,2 DAS WWA93

TRAQUAIR, Ramsay, b Edinburgh 1874, d Guysborough, NS 1952, paint CWW49 GM MM PMC RCA TB1

TRASK, Fred, b Digby, NS 1946– , paint DFA KB

TRAVERS, Cyril John, b Manchester, Eng 1887, stgl O.N48 RCA

TRAVERS, Frances Emily. *See* PAYNE, Frances Emily Travers

TRAVERS, Gwyneth Mabel Gwillim (m C.H. Travers), b Kingston, Ont 1911 – d 1982, etch paint IO MM TB3 WWA82d84

TRAVERS-SMITH, Brian John, b Tangsham, Chi 1931– , paint WWA93

TREHERNE, Harold J., b 1899, d 1975, drw paint DFA

TREMBLAY, Georges E., b Cap-à-l'Aigle, Que 1878, d Iberville, Que 1939, sculp K MM

TREMBLAY, Gerard, b Les Eboulements, Que 1928– , gra paint MM S TB2

TREMBLAY, Leon, b 1933– , paint CAE1

TREMBLAY, Nicole, b Jonquière, Que 1942– , paint CAE1

TREMBLAY-GILLON, Michele, b 1944– , paint CAE1

TREMEWEN, Vern, b Australia 1913, d 1980, paint S

TRENHOLME, Florence Thompson (x Trentholme; m Frederick Minden Cole[2]), fl 1897–1905, paint H MM Mo12[2]

TRENKA, Stephen, b Budapest, Hu 1909– , med sculp O.My57 WWA62

TREVOR, Leslie J., b Scunthorpe, Lincs 1907– , des gra Hu RCA

TREZE, Anne, b Riga, Lat 1936– , prt CAE1

TRIAUD, Louis-Hubert (aka Briand, Friand, Friend, Triand), b London 1789/90, d Quebec 1836, paint DCB7 H H77 K MQ NGC67 TB1

TRIM, Albertus Hendrikus Franciscus (Bert), b Amsterdam 1946– , paint sculp IO

TROBRIAND, Philippe-Régis-Denis de[2] Keredern, Comte de, b Tours, Fr 1816, d Bayport, NY 1897, des illus paint AAW1 DAB[2] K Sam[2]

TROTTER, Doris Minette. *See* JUDAH, Doris Minette Trotter

TROTTIER, Gerald Mathew, b Ottawa 1925– , paint AGO CC1 H77 IO MM NGC1 RCA TB2

TROWELL, Ian Douglas Lucas, b England 1930– , sculp IO
TROY, Cecil Joseph, b Renfrew, Ont 1935, d 1975, paint S
TRUDEAU, Angus, Manitoulin Isld, Ont c 1910 – d 1984, carv paint DFA KB
TRUDEAU, Randy, b Wikwemikong Res, Ont 1954– , paint IO
TRUDEAU, Yves, b Montreal 1930– , sculp CC2 CE1,2 DMS MM MQ NGC67 RCA WWA93
TRUDELLE, J.-Georges, b Lévis, Que 1877, d 1950, sculp K
TRUE, Werner, b Germany 1934– , sculp BCS
TRUEMAN, Laura, fl 1886, paint H
TRUEMAN, William Peter Main, b Sackville, NB 1934– , paint CWW93
TRUMBULL, John, b Lebanon, Conn 1756, d New York 1843, Amer, min paint AM BM DAA DBHP DBLP DBMP DeV7 Fo G GW Y
TRUTH SEEKER CO. *See* GEUER, Juan W.
TRYON, Dwight William, b Hartford, Conn 1849, d S Dartmouth, Mass 1925, Amer, paint AAA25d28 B DAA F H RCA TB1 Y
TSCHAIKOVSKY, Alexander Nicolaief, b Odessa, Rus 1893, paint WWNA
TUCKER, Gary, b Calgary 1951– , paint AA
TUCKER, Lillian, fl 1894–1901, paint AAA01 DWA H MM RCA
TUCKER, William G., b Cairo, Egy 1935– , Amer, sculp WWA93
TUDIN, Tony, b S Africa 1930– , des IO RCA
TUDLIK, E7-1050, b Cape Dorset, NWT c 1888, d 1960, prt sculp AGO Co DEA
TUDOR-HART, Ernest Percival, b Montreal 1873, d Quebec 1954, paint sculp B DBA Hu NGC1 RA RCA TB1,2 WBA1 WWB34
TUGHAN, Robert James (Jim), b Montreal 1949– , drw paint IO
TULLEY, Charles, b London 1885, d Montreal 1950, paint CNS36 MM
TULLY, Kivas, b Garrarucum, Ire 1820, d Toronto 1905, drw Co H Mo98 RCA W1–3
TULLY, Louise Beresford, fl 1896, d Vancouver 1917, carv H RCA
TULLY, Sydney Strickland, b Toronto 1860 – d 1911 (x d Calgary), paint AAA03 AGO CC1 CWW10 DBA DWA G H Hu MM Mo12 NGC1 RCA W1–3
TULUMELLO, Peter M., b Welland, Ont 1954 , des paint sculp WWA93
TULVING, Ruth Mikkelsaar (m Endel Tulving), b Estonia 1932– , paint prt CWW93 IO RCA WWA93
TUNGILIK/TONGIKIK, Mark, E3-320, b Repulse Bay, NWT 1913, d 1986, sculp DEA
TUNNILLIE, Ovilu, b Cape Dorset, NWT, fl 1981– , sculp CWW93
TUNNILLIE, Qavaroak, b Northwest Territories 1928– , prt sculp CWW93
TUOMI, Brent, b Edmonton 1952– , paint SC
TURCOT/TURCAUT, Joseph, fl 1803–19, sculp H K
TURGEON, Jean (aka Gite), b Quebec 1952– , cart WECa
TURINI, Walter Giovanni, b New York 1883, illus PMC
TURNBULL, Jane Mildred (m Dennis R. Evans; m Richard Spafford), b Milden, Sask 1947– , mmed BDSA
TURNER, Calvin, b Oakland, Calif 1947– , sculp ABC
TURNER, Edwin A., fl 1866–71, litho DeV2 H
TURNER, John Davenall, b Woking, Sur 1900– , paint SC
TURNER, Richard Julian, b Edmonton 1936– , paint sculp AGO CC1 NGC67 RCA
TURNER, Stanley Francis, b Aylesbury, Bucks 1883, d Toronto 1953, paint prt

AGO CNS36 CWW49 GM MM NGC1p431 NGC68 O.My48 RCA TB3 US WWA47

TURNOR, Alicia/Alice Margaret. *See* KILLALY, Alicia/Alice Margaret

TURPIN, James, fl 1833–41, engr paint H

TURQUAND, Helen Elizabeth, b Hamilton, Ont 1885, paint pas AAA32 Hu MM RCA

TWAMMIE/TWAMEE, E9-1452, b Povungnituk, Que 1900 – d 1963, sculp DEA S

TWEEDIE, Jean Frances, b Moncton, NB, fl 1960s, paint MA

TWO GUN. *See* PLAINWOMAN, Percy

TYLER, Gerald Hall, b Birmingham, Eng 1897, paint MM WWNA

TYMOSHENKO, Frederick Joseph, b Windsor, Ont 1937–, paint prt IO UG

TYRRELL, Frances Claire (m Colin J. Philip), b Kirkland Lake, Ont 1959–, illus CWW93

TYSON, Larry, b Pennsylvania 1957–, cart Po88

U

UBERTI, Joseph, b France, fl 1909–17, Fr, paint K

UCHIDA, Bart Shigeru/Shigeri, b Vancouver 1941–, sculp IO

UFFEN, Robert James, b Toronto 1923–, paint CWW93

UHTHOFF, Ina D.D. Campbell, b Scotland 1889, d 1971, paint WWNA

ULLULAQ, Judas, b Thorn Bay, NWT 1937–, sculp CWW93

ULUSCHAK, Edward, b nr Prosperity, Alta 1943–, cart Des Po86–88

UMHOLTZ, David, b Harrisburg, Pa 1943–, paint CWW93 RCA SC US

UNDERHILL, Eldon, fl 1970s, prt CAE2

UNETT, Thomas, Lt Col, fl 1821+, d nr Sebastopol, Crimea 1855, Eng, topog DBMP H WHC

UNGER, James, b London 1937–, cart CE2

URQUHART, Anthony Morse (Tony), b Niagara Falls, Ont 1934–, paint sculp AE AGO B CA1 CC1 CE1,2 Co CWW93 H77 IO MM NGC1 NGC67 RCA TB2 UG US WWA93

USTINOV, Plato Cornelius von, b Jerusalem 1903, d Laguna Hills, Calif 1990, paint RCA WWNA

VACA, Vaclav, b Czechoslovakia 1948–, paint IO

VADEBONCOEUR, Louis-Lévi-Marie, Frère, b Mont-St-Hilaire, Que 1831, d Joliette, Que 1896, des paint K

VALDIS. *See* ILGACS, Valdis Leo

VALE, Florence Gertrude (m Albert Jacques Franck, q.v.), b England 1909–, etch paint CAE2 IO RCA

VALENTINE, William, b Whitehaven, Cumb 1798, d Halifax 1849, min paint BM DCB7 Fo H H77 Hu NGC67

VALIN, Jean-Innocent, b Quebec 1691 – d 1759, sculp K

VALIN, Thomas Henry, b St-Eustache, Que c 1810, d 1850, paint GW H K

VALIUS, Telesforas, b Riga, Lat 1914, d Toronto 1977, prt IO MM WWA80

VAILLANCOURT, Armand Joseph Robert, b Black Lake, Que c 1932–, sculp AE B CC2 CE1,2 Co DMS MM MQ NGC67 TB2 WWA93

VALKO, Andrew, b Prague, Cz 1957–, drw paint CWW93

VALLEE, Claude, b Valleyfield, Que 1944–, paint CAE1

VALLIERE, Lauréat, b New Liverpool, re St-Romuald, Que 1888 – d 1973, carv sculp K

VAN ALSTYNE[2], Thelma Selina

Scribbans (m E. Lloyd Van Alstyne), b Victoria, BC 1913– , paint AKL[2] CWW93 M[2] RCA

VAN BELKUM, Joan, fl 1964, paint CAE1

VAN BENTUM, Henri, b Deurne, Neth 1929– , paint IO S

VAN DAM, Madja, b Amsterdam 1932– , tap CAE1

VAN DAMME, Joan, b Detroit 1936– , prt IO

VAN DE PEER, Robert A., b England 1945– , prt IO

VANDERHAEGHE, Margaret Elizabeth Nagel, b Leader, Sask 1950– , paint BDSA

VANDER HEYDEN, Louise (Soeur Marie de Sainte Croix), b 1827, d 1911, paint K

VAN DER LINDE[2], Louise (Mrs), fl 1882, min DWA H[2] MM

VANDERLIP, F.G., b Milwaukee, Wis, fl 1876–86, paint H

VAN DER MEULEN, Emil George, b Rheden, Neth 1928– , sculp CWW93 RCA

VANDERPOLL, Gerald, b Amsterdam 1882, etch paint CNS36 MM

VANEY, Marie de, b Boston 1938– , paint CAE1

VAN HALM, Renée, b Amsterdam 1949– , gra paint WWA93

VAN HORNE, William Cornelius, Sir, b Chelsea, nr Joliette, Ill 1843, d Montreal 1915, paint CE1,2 Co CWW10 DNB EC H LeJ W1–3 WWW

VAN IEPEREN, Cornelius, b 1899, paint DFA KB

VANIER, Georges, b Montreal 1887, paint K

VANIERE, Henry, b c 1770, d 1848, min H H77 K

VAN KAMPEN, Vlasta (m Jan van Kampen), b Belleville, Ont 1943– , illus C

VAN LAMBALGEN, Gerald, b 1910– , paint DFA KB

VAN LUNE, Ray, b Lacombe, Alta 1951– , paint SC

VAN STOCKUM, Hilda G. (m Erwin Marlin[2]), b Rotterdam 1908– , paint DBA[2] MM WWA53 WWB72

VANTERPOOL, Joanna. *See* KRASNER, Joanna Vanterpool

VAN WIJK, Dirk, b The Hague, Neth 1944– , paint AA

VARLEY, Frederick Horsman, b Sheffield, Eng 1881, d Toronto 1969, paint ACA AGO B CC1 CE1,2 Co CWW67 DBA EC H77 MM NGC1 NGC67 NGC68 O.Ag62 RA RCA S Sam TB1,2 TN UG WBA2

VARNEY, Edwin, b New Rochelle, NY 1944– , prt WWA93

VARVARANDE, Robert Emile, b Lyon, Fr 1922– , paint AE AGO CC1 MM RCA TB2

VASSEUR. *See* LEVASSEUR, François-Noël; LEVASSEUR dit DELORS, Jean-Antoine

VAUGHAN, James Martin, b Bristol, Eng 1943– , cart Des

VAUX, Emma Plimsall, b Brockville, Ont, paint Hu MM RCA

VAZAN, William Joseph, b Toronto 1933– , paint CAE1 DCA MM WWA82

VEKRIS, Terry, b Athens, Gr 1930– , paint IO

VENNE, Emile, b Montreal 1896, paint CNS51 K MM

VENNE, Joseph, b Montreal 1859 – d 1925, paint K MM

VENNE, Lionel, b Verner, Ont 1936– , paint CWW93

VENNE, Ludger, b Quebec 1891, d Montreal 1973, paint K MM

VENOR, Robert George (aka Canada Banner Company), b Montreal 1931– , paint sculp CAE1,2 MM WWA78

VERBOOM, Klaas Willem, b London, Ont 1948– , paint CAE1 IO

VEREKER, Foley Charles Prendergast, Capt, Hon (Gort[2]), b 1850, d 1900, Eng, paint BPp1136[2] DBWA

VERMARE, André-César, b Lyon, Fr 1869, fl 1926, sculp B K
VERMETTE, Mariette Rousseau. *See* ROUSSEAU, Mariette
VERMEULEN, Dirk Martinus, b Zwanenburg, Neth 1940– , prt IO
VERNER, Frederick Arthur, b Hammondville, re Sheridan, nr Oakville, Ont 1836, d London 1928, paint AE AGO CE1,2 DBA DVP EC H H77 G MM Mo12 NGC1 NGC67 RCA Sam TB3 W1–3 WBA2
VERNON, Mary. *See* MORGAN, Mary Vernon
VERNON, Roger, fl 1970s, paint sculp CAE2
VERNON, William H., b 1820, d 1909, Eng, paint DBA DVP G H RCA
VERRAL, Minnie Olive Belcher (m O. Verrall), b Loomis, Mich 1873, paint WWNA
VERRIER, Claude-Etienne, b France 1713 – d 1775, Fr, des K
VERRIER, Etienne, b Aix-en-Provence, Fr 1683, d La-Rochelle, Fr 1747, Fr, topog DCB3 H H77
VERWORN, Charles, b Larrah, Ge 1950– , paint CAE2
VEZINA, Charles, b L'Ange-Gardien, Que 1685, d Les Ecureuils, Que 1755, carv DCB3 K MQ
VEZINA, Emile, b Cap-St-Ignace, Que 1876, d Montreal 1942, car illus paint pas sculp Des K MM RCA
VEZINA, Victor, b Quebec 1859/60, fl 1881–91, sculp K
VIAU, Pierre, fl 1837–48, sculp K
VIAU, Roger, b Montreal 1906– , paint CNS44 MM
VIC. *See* RUNTZ, Victor Alexander
VICAJI, Dorothy E. (Miss), fl 1915, d 1945, Eng, paint DBA DWA MM RA RCA WBA1
VICKERS, Henrietta Moodie, fl 1900–11, paint sculp AAA1900 DWA MM RCA
VICKERS, Henry Harold, b Dudley, Eng 1851, d Ottawa 1918, paint H
VIDAL, Emeric Essex, b Bredford, Eng 1791, d Brighton, Eng 1861, Eng, paint topog DBWA H WHC
VIGER, Denis, b Montreal 1741 – d 1805, carv DCB5 K
VIGER, Jacques, b Montreal 1787 – d 1858, paint CE2 DCB8 DNB EC H K LeJ W1–3
VIGNE, Godfrey Thomas, b England c 1801, d Woodford, Essex 1863, Eng, engr topog DNB DVP G H
VILALLONGA, Jesus Carlos de[2], b Santa Colona, Sp 1927– , paint CWW93[2]
VILDER, Roger, b Beirut, Leb 1938– , mur paint CAE1 WWA82
VILLENEUVE, Ferdinand, b Charlesbourg, Que 1831, d St-Romuald, Que 1909, sculp DCB13 K
VILLENEUVE, Joseph, b 1865, d 1923, sculp K
VILLENEUVE, Joseph Arthur, b Chicoutimi, Que 1910– , paint DFA KB WWA86
VILLENEUVE, Robert de, b France c 1645, fl 1685–92, d France, Fr, des topog DCB1 H K
VILLIERS, Frederick, b London 1852, d Bedhampton, Hants 1922, Eng, illus paint AD BI DBA DBBI DBMP DVP G Sam WBA1 WI WWW
VILSONS, Velta, b Latvia 1919– , wlhg IO
VINCENNES. *See* CHARTRAND dit VINCENNES, Vincent
VINCENT, Antoine, fl 1881–97, sculp K
VINCENT, Arthur, b 1852, d 1903, sculp K
VINCENT, François, b 1737/8, d Loretteville, Que 1804, sculp K
VINCENT, Robert, b Newcastle-on-Tyne, Eng 1908– , paint KB
VINCENT, Zacharie (Telari-o-lin), b Village-des-Hurons, Que 1815, d Quebec 1886, paint DCB11 H H77 K MQ
VINEBERG, Louise (s Louvin[2])

(m Henry Charles Vineberg), b Montreal 1924– , paint M² MM RCA

VINING, Pamela Sarah. See YULE, Pamela Sarah Vining

VIVANT/VENANT/VIRANT, Louis (aka Laurent), b St-Aignan, Fr c 1806, d Montreal 1860, paint DCB8 H K

VIVENZA, Francesca, b Rome 1941– , paint prt sculp CAE2 IO WWA86

VIVOT, Lea Drahomira (Vivot-Fishman), b Prague, Cz 1950– , sculp UG WWA93

VLISMAS, George, b Swansea, Wales 1921– , sculp ABC

VOGT, Adolpha (Adolf), b Bad Liebenstein, Thuringen, Ge 1843, d New York (x Montreal) 1871, paint B DeV2 H H77 Hu MM NGC1 NGC67 RCA TB1

VOISEY, Gordon, b Toronto 1954– , drw SC

VON BOETTICHER, Inga, fl 1980s, paint MFMS

VON BRENTANI, Mario, b St Quirico, It, paint CWW82

VON DER OHE, Dorothy Katie Minna. *See* OHE, Dorothy Katie Minna Von der

VORMITTAG, Irena, b Krakow, Pol 1941– , paint IO

VOSSNACK, Emil (Emile), b Renscheid, Ge 1839, d Halifax 1885, paint DCB11 H

VOYER, Monique, b Magog, Que 1928– , paint CAE1 MM TB2

VOYER, Sylvain Jacques, b Edmonton 1939– , gra paint SC WWA78

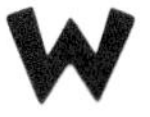

WADE, Nicholas William, b Leigh-on-Sea, Eng 1949– , prt sculp IO

WADMORE, Robinson Lyndhurst, Col, b London 1855, paint CWW10 Mo12

WADOW, Isadore, b Beardmore, Ont 1950– , paint IO

WADSWORTH, Daniel, fl 1771, d 1848, Amer, paint GW H WWWA

WAGHORN, Kerry, b Vancouver 1947– , cart Des

WAGSCHAL, Marion, b Trinidad 1943– , paint prt CAE2

WAINIO, Carol Eva (Mrs Theberge), b Sarnia, Ont 1955– , paint IO

WAINWRIGHT, Robert Barry, b Chilliwack, BC 1935– , gra paint B CWW93 RCA WWA93

WAINWRIGHT, Ruth Salter (m Inglis Lough Wainwright), b Sydney, NS 1902– , drw paint CC2 CLA MA MM TB2

WAKE, Margaret Eveline, b London 1867, d Vancouver 1930, paint DWA H RCA

WAKEMAN, Thomas, b England 1812, d Rome 1850, Eng, paint GW H

WALD, Carol, b Detroit 1935– , illus paint WWA93

WALD, Susana, b Budapest, Hu 1937 , paint sculp CAE2 IO

WALE, George E., b Hamilton, Ont 1948– , sculp IO

WALES, Philip, b Port Louis, Mauritius 1866, fl 1900, paint H MM RCA

WALES, Shirley (m S.J. De Jong), b Montreal 1931– , gra sculp AGO MM NGC67

WALKEM, George Anthony, Hon, b Newry, Ire 1834, d Victoria, BC 1908, drw CE1,2 Des EC H Mo98 W1-3

WALKER, Caroline (Mrs), fl 1859–80, paint DWA H

WALKER, Edmund Murton, b Windsor, Ont 1877, paint CWW67

WALKER, Ella May Jacoby (m Osman James Walker), b Windom, Minn 1892, d 1960, paint CWW58

WALKER, George A., b Brantford, Ont 1960– , engr BB

WALKER, Horatio, b Listowel, Ont 1858, d Ste-Pétronille, Que 1938, paint AAA33 ACA AGO B BE CC2 CE1,2 Co CWW36 DBA EC F FCA G H H77 MM Mo98,12 MQ NGC1

NGC67 P PMC RCA TB1 WBA1 WWA40 WWWA Y

WALKER, John Henry, b Antrim Co, Ire 1831, d Montreal 1899, des engr illus Des DeV2,3 H W1–3

WALKER, Joy, b Tacoma, Wash 1942– , paint prt DCA IO UG

WALKER, Robert, b Montreal 1945– , con prt CAE2 IO

WALKER, Shirley Pearl, b Hamilton, Ont 1933– , paint IO

WALKLEY, David Birdsey, b Rome, Ohio 1849, d 1934, Amer, paint AAA25 AE F Y

WALLACE, George Burton, b Sandy Cove, nr Dublin 1920– , sculp AGO IO MM RCA

WALLACE, Ian, b Shoreham, Eng 1943– , paint DCA MM

WALLACE, Kenneth William, b Penticton, BC 1945– , paint CWW93 DCA SC WWA93

WALLACE, Maj-Len Birgitta, b Helsinki, Fin 1944– , enam paint prt IO

WALLACE, Robert Ian, b Niagara Falls, Ont 1950– , illus CBC CWW93 JAI MF SAA56

WALLACE, William, Capt, b Canterbury, Eng 1804, ret 1842, Eng, topog DeV7 H WHCp32

WALLIS, Katherine Elizabeth, b Peterborough, Ont 1861, d Santa Cruz, Calif 1957, sculp B DBA DWA G H MM Mo12 NGC1 RA RCA TB1,2 W2–3

WALLIS, Provo William Parry, Adm, Sir, b Halifax, NS 1791, d Funtington, Eng 1892, Eng, paint DCB12 DMA DNB

WALLIS, William Henry, b Isle of Wight 1868, d 1946, paint WWNA

WALMSLEY, Lewis Calvin, b Milford, Ont 1897, paint CWW86

WALPER, Ora C., b 1881, d 1961, paint DFA KB

WALSH, Edward, b Waterford, Ire c 1766 (x 1756), d Summerhill, Ire 1832, Irish, paint topog DeV3,5 DNB GW H ROM WHC

WALSH, Francis, b Canada c 1825, fl 1850, engr GW H

WALSH, John Stanley, b Brighton, Eng 1907– , paint AGO CWW93 MM RCA WWA91

WALSH, Vincent Owen, b Toledo, Ohio 1912– , paint CWW70

WALTERS, Emile, b Winnipeg 1893, paint AAA33 AAW1,3 B F RCA Sam TB1,2 US WWA66

WALTERS, Louise (m Mel Malkin), b Big River, Sask 1938– , paint BDSA

WALTON, James Geldard, b Sheffield, Eng 1860, paint PMC

WANDESFORD, James Buckingham (Juan Ivan Wandersforde), b England 1817, d Hayward, nr San Francisco 1902, Eng, paint AAW1 AC GW H H77 McC Sam Y

WARD, Charles Caleb, b Saint John, NB c 1831, d Rothesay, NB 1896, paint GW H H77 ROM Sam

WARD, Donella Joy Macaulay, b London 1920– , etch paint IO

WARD, John, b Hull, Eng 1798 – d 1849, Eng, paint DBLP DBMaP DBWA DMA DSP DVP DWP H MP MPE OELP PP PS SP

WARD, Kathleen Louise Campbell. *See* PINKERTON, Kathleen Louise Campbell Ward

WARD, William Dudley Burnett, b Graveley Bank, Staf 1879, d Toronto 1935, gra paint AGO Hu MM RCA

WARE, L. Graeme, fl 1891–2, paint H MM RCA

WARE, Titus Hibbert, Capt, b Cheshire, Eng 1810, d 1890, paint topog H

WARGIN, Nancy Petry. *See* PETRY, Nancy

WARKOV, Esther (m Franz Visscher), b Winnipeg 1941– , paint sculp CAE2 DFA MM NGC67 SC WWA93

WARNOCK, Betty Meyers. *See* MEYERS, Betty

WARRE, Henry James, Gen, Sir, b Cape

of Good Hope 1819, d London 1898, Eng, topog AAW1 APH DeV3 G W H H77 McC PNL ROM Sam W1–3 WHC WWW

WARREN, Asa Coolidge, b Boston 1815/19, d New York 1904, Amer, engr paint AAAd28 B DeV4 F GW TB1

WARREN, Emily Mary Bibbens, b 1869, d Dunrobin, nr Ottawa 1956, paint B DBA DWA MM RA TB1,2 WBA WWB34

WARREN, Raymond, b Vancouver, fl 1967, paint ABC

WARRENER, Lowrie Lyle, b Sarnia, Ont 1900, d Toronto 1983, gra paint GM Hu RCA S

WARTERS, Winnifred M., b Birmingham, Eng 1898, d 1963, paint DFA

WASHBURN, Lawrence (Larry), b Fernie, BC 1942– , paint SC

WASHCHUK, Friedel (s Friedel), b Regensburg, Ge 1917– , sculp IO

WATERBURY, Catherine, fl 1895–8, paint H

WATKINS, Alexandra Nugent Johnson (1892 m Benjamin Watkins[2], q.v.), paint MM Mo98[2],12

WATKINS, Benjamin (m Alexandra N.J. Watkins, q.v.), b Mon, Wales 1853, d Warwicks, Eng 1913, paint MM Mo98,12 UG

WATKINS, Cathrine W. (Mrs), b Hamilton, Ont, fl 1904+, paint AAA33 AAW2 AC DWA WWA40

WATSON, Alexander, b Saint John, NB 1858 – d 1923, paint H MM RCA

WATSON, Bruce, b Br Guiana 1925– , sculp IOp288

WATSON, Dawson. *See* DAWSON-WATSON, Dawson

WATSON, Homer Ransford, b Doon, Ont 1855 – d 1936, paint ACA AE AGO B CC1 CE1,2 Co DBA DVLP EC FCA G H H77 MM Mo98,12 NGC1 NGC67 NGC68 PMC R2 RA RCA St TB1,2 UG W1–3 WBA1

WATSON, Mary Anne Louise, b Canada 1923– , paint prt WWA93

WATSON, Phoebe Amelia, b Doon, Ont 1858 – d 1947, paint DWA H

WATSON, Susan (m Harvey Cowan), b Toronto 1949– , sculp IO RCA

WATSON, Sydney Hollinger, b Toronto 1911, d 1981, paint AE CWW81 IO NGC1 NGC68 O.My48 RCA TB2 WWA82

WATT, Henry Robertson (s Robin[2]), b Victoria, BC 1896, d Cowansville, Que 1964, paint DBA[2] MM RA[2] RCA TB2[2]

WATTS, Etta (m W.H. Watts), fl 1895–1900, paint AAA1900 DWA H MM RCA

WATTS, John William Hurrell, b Teigmouth, Eng 1850, d Ottawa 1917, etch paint DeV6 H MM Mo98 NGC1 RCA

WAUGH, De Witt C., fl 1872–4, paint H

WAUGH, Samuel Bell, b Mercer, Pa 1814, d Janesville, Wis 1885, Amer, paint B F GW H H77 TB1 Y

WAWRA, Margaret Lucie Walter (Mara, Margot) (m Helmut Frank Wawra), b Landsberg, Ge 1923– , paint sculp BDSA CAE1

WAY, Annie M., fl 1899–1915, paint H MM RCA

WAY, Charles Jones, b Dartmouth, Eng 1834, d Lausanne, Swi 1919, Eng, paint B DBA DBWA DVLP DVP EC G H Hu MM Mo98,12 NGC1 RA RCA ROM TB1 UG W1–3

WAYNE-VON KONIGSLOW, Andrea (m Rainer von Konigslow), b Toronto 1958– , illus C

WAYWELL, Alice Doreen, b Manchester, Eng 1920– , paint CAE1 IO

WEATHERBIE, Vera Olivia (m Harold Mortimer Lamb, q.v.), b Vancouver 1909, d Burnaby, BC 1977, paint DFA WWNA

WEATHERILL, Timothy Douglas Stinson, b Toronto 1960– , paint sculp CWW93

WEATHERSTON, Mary Helen Moss. *See* MOSS, Mary Helen
WEAVER, John, fl 1798, paint H
WEAVER, John Barney, b Anaconda, Mont 1920– , sculp WWA93
WEAVER, Larry E., b 1937– , prt sculp CAE2
WEBBER, Gordon McKinley, b Sault Ste Marie, Ont 1909, d Montreal 1965, paint AGO CC2 CLA Hu MM RCA TB2 WWA62
WEBBER, John (b Johann Weber), b London c 1751 – d 1793, Eng, paint AAW1 B Bry DBLP DBMaP DBWA DCB4 DeV1 DMA DNB DWP EMA Fo G GW H OELP PNL Red ROM Sam TB1
WEBER, Anne (aka Nancy), b Earl Tp, Lancaster Co, Pa 1814, d Woolwich, Waterloo Co, Ont 1888, drw DCB11
WEBER, George, b Munich, Ge 1907– , gra paint WWA62
WEBER, Kathleen Nichol Murray[2] (m L. George Weber), b Ayr, Ont 1919– , paint prt CAE2 CWW93[2] IO RCA UG
WEBSTER, Clarence, b Hawaii c 1900, fl 1978, paint DFA KB
WEBSTER, George, b 1775, fl 1832, Eng, paint B Bry DBLP DBMaP DBWA DMA DSP DWP G H OELP ROM TB1
WEBSTER, Herbert Henry, b Windsor, Ont 1909– , paint MM O.My50
WEBSTER, John Bruce, b Ottawa 1947– , paint CWW93
WECHSLER, Dora Harris (m John Wechsler), b Ottawa, Ont 1897, d Toronto 1952, paint sculp O.Ag48 RCA
WEININGER, Sylvia Roberta. *See* SINGER, Sylvia Roberta Weininger
WEINSTEIN, Alan Herbert, b Toronto 1939– , paint tap CAE1 IO UG
WEIR, Albert George (Bert), b Sandwich, Ont 1925– , paint IO
WEISBRICH, Les, b New Jersey 1927– , paint ABC
WEISMAN, Gustav Oswald, b Lithuania 1926– , paint sculp AGO RCA S TB2
WEISS, Ephrum Philip, b Montreal 1924– , paint sculp AGO CWW93
WEISS, Jeannette, b 1934– , paint CAE1
WELD, Isaac, b Dublin 1774, d Ravenswell, nr Bray, Ire 1856, Irish, illus paint DeV5 DNB GW H
WELLES/WELLS[2], J., fl 1783–4, Eng, paint DBLP DBMaP[2] G
WELLGE, H., fl 1884, paint DeV2
WELLS, Albert Eugene, b W Saint John, NB 1859, d Lakeview, Wash 1931, paint H
WELLS, Ethel Lucille Oille. *See* OILLE, Ethel Lucille
WELLS, Frederick, b Toronto, fl 1840–55, paint H
WELLS, John, b 1789, d 1864, drw DeV3 H
WELSFORD, Augustus, Maj, b Windsor, NS 1811, d nr Sevastopol, Crimea 1855, paint DCB8 H
WELSH, Ruth P., b Prince Albert, Sask 1949– , paint sculp BDSA CAE2
WENTWORTH, Thomas Hanford, b Norwalk, Conn 1781, d Oswego, NY 1849, Amer, paint DCB7 F GW H H77 ROM Y
WENTWORTH, William Henry, b Oswego, NY 1813, fl 1859, Amer, paint GW H
WERTHEIMER, Esther, b 1926– , paint sculp SC
WERTHMAN, William C., b Germany, fl 1950+, cart Des
WESBROOM, William N., fl 1889, paint H MM
WESSELOW, Francis Guillemard de. *See* SIMPKINSON, Francis Guillemard
WEST, Barbara, b London 1900– , paint WWNA
WEST, Ingrid, b Norfolk, Eng 1939– , paint BDSA
WEST, John, b Farnham, Eng 1778,

d Chettle, Eng 1845, Eng, topog DCB7 H W1–3
WEST, R. Rolleston, b London 1894, paint WWNA
WESTERGARD, Jim, b Ogden, Utah 1939– , drw AA BB
WESTERLUND, Mia, b New York 1942– , drw sculp CAE2
WESTMACOTT, E.K./K.E., Miss, fl 1874, d 1890, Eng, paint DWA H RCA
WESTMACOTT, John, Capt, b England, d Halifax 1815, paint H
WESTMACOTT, Stewart, b England c 1818, fl 1841–69, Eng, paint DVP G H
WESTMORLAND, Priscilla Anne Pole, Countess (aka Lady Burghersh) (m John Fane[2], Lord Burghersh, 11th Earl of Westmorland), b England 1793, d London 1879, Eng, paint B BPp2802 DNB[2] DWA H TB1
WESTON, Eloise, fl 1880–1, paint H MM
WESTON, James L., b England c 1815, d 1896, cart paint DeV2,3,5,6,8 Des H MM RCA
WESTON, Julia, fl 1880–6, paint H MM
WESTON, William Percy (Bill), b London 1879, d New Westminster, BC 1967, drw paint CC2 CWW67 GM H77 Hu MM NGC1 RCA Sam TB2 WWA62 WWNA
WETENHALL, John, b Nelson, Ont 1807 – d 1850, paint H
WEYMAN, Ronald Charles Toshach, Lt Cdr, b Erith, Kent 1915– , paint MM NGC68
WHALE, John Claude, b at sea (England to Canada) 1852, d Brantford, Ont 1905, paint H
WHALE, John Hicks, b Liskeard, Corn 1829, d Brantford, Ont 1905, paint H
WHALE, Robert Heard, b Burford, nr Brantford, Ont 1857, d S Africa 1906, paint H
WHALE, Robert Reginald, b Altamun, Corn 1805, d Brantford, Ont 1887, paint ACA DCB11 DeV3 H H77 Hu NGC1 NGC67 RCA UG W1–3
WHALLEY, Peter Graham, b Brockville, Ont 1921– , cart gra illus paint AE Co Des MM TB2
WHATMOUGH, Grant Allan, b Toronto 1921– , sculp IO RCA
WHEALE, Ivan Trevor, b Sunderland, Eng 1934– , des sculp CWW93 IO
WHEELER, Louis Ward, Lt Col, b St Joseph, Mich 1893, paint CWW58
WHEELER, Orson Shorey, b Barnston, Que 1902, d Montreal 1990, sculp CWW89 MM NGC1 RCA TB2 WWA91
WHEELER, Thomas, b England c 1809, fl 1847–71, des engr H
WHERRY, Sheila, fl 1939+, sculp CWW80
WHILLANS, Morley Gray, b Manitoba 1911– , ske CWW93
WHITE, George Harlow, b London c 1817, d Charter House, London 1887, Eng, paint AE AGO B DBA DBLP DCB11 DVLP DVP G H H77 Hu MM NGC1 RCA Sam TB1 W1–3
WHITE, John, Col, b England c 1540/50, fl 1570–93, Eng, drw paint DAA DAB DBLP DBWA DCB1 GW H Sam TB1 WWWA
WHITE, John Clayton, b England 1835, d Berkeley, Calif 1907, paint H
WHITE, Linda. *See* MELNICK, Linda White
WHITE, Michael. *See* GRADOWSKI, Michael Willard
WHITE, Norman Triplett, b San Antonio, Tex 1938– , sculp WWA93
WHITE, Richard Leonard, b Hamilton, Ont 1954– , paint CWW93
WHITEFIELD, Edwin, b E Lulworth, Eng 1816, d Dedham, Me 1892, Amer, paint DeV3,5–8 DFA GW H PNL ROM Sam WWWA Y
WHITEHEAD, Alfred Ernest, b Peterborough, Eng 1887, d Amherst, NS 1974, paint CWW70 MA MM PMC WWA73

WHITEHOUSE, Diane, b Birmingham, Eng 1940– , paint AA

WHITEN, Colette M., b Birmingham, Eng 1945– , sculp CAE1,2 CE1,2 IO WWA93

WHITEN, Grover Timothy, b Inkster, Mich 1941– , sculp CAE1 IO WWA93

WHITLOCK, An, b Guelph, Ont 1944– , tap CAE1

WHITMAN, Linley Vail (s Lin), b Emerson, Man 1929– , sculp CWW93

WHITMORE, George St Vincent, Maj, b Charlton, Kent 1798 – d 1851, Eng, paint APH

WHITNEY, Elizabeth, fl 1876–98, paint DWA H MM RCA

WHITTLESEY, Mary Ann Bacon[2] (m M. Chauncy Whittlesey), b Canada, paint DWA[2] GW[2] H

WHITTOME, Irene F., b Vancouver 1942– , prt sculp CAE2 DCA RCA WWA93

WHITWELL, Henry William, b Wales 1911– , paint prt CAE1 IO

WHITZMAN, David, b Halifax 1915– , paint CLA MA MM

WHYMPER, Frederick, b Lambeth, London 1838, d London 1901, Eng, engr illus topog AAW1,3 AC DCB13 DeV1 DVP G H H77 P PNL

WHYTE, Peter, b Banff, Alta 1905, d 1966, paint DFA NGC68

WICHERTS, Audie, b Netherlands 1930– , prt SC

WICKENDEN, Helen Slack (m Alfred Athier Wickenden), b Bethel, Conn 1887, paint CNS40 MM

WICKENDEN, Horace Watson (m Margaret Robertson Wickenden, q.v.), b England 1901– , gra sculp US

WICKENDEN, Margaret Mary Robertson (m Horace Wickenden, q.v.), b Winnipeg 1915– , paint BDSA

WICKENDEN, Robert John, b Rochester, Eng 1861, d Brooklyn, NY 1931, Amer, paint AAAd31 B H MM Mo12 RCA TB2

WICKENS, Wilfred Stanley, b Toronto 1889, paint Hu

WICKHAM, Caroline, b Montreal 1945– , paint wlhg CAE1

WICKS, Ben (Alfred[2]), b London 1926, d 2000, cart CE2[2] CWW93 Des Po86–88 WECa

WICKS, Victor, b Calgary 1950– , cart Po88

WICKSON, Alfred Morton, b Toronto 1882/4, d 1947, paint Hu

WICKSON, Paul Giovanni, b Toronto 1860, d Paris, Ont 1922, paint CWW10 DBA G H LeJ MM Mo12 R1 RA RCA UG W1–3

WIELAND, Joyce (m Michael Snow, q.v.), b Toronto 1931– , fab paint AGO B CA1–3 CC1 CE1,2 Co CWW93 Des IO MM OC RCA St UG WWA93

WIGGIN, C.E., fl 1841, paint H

WIGGINS, Samuel A., b New Brunswick 1834, fl 1860, Amer, engr GW H

WIGGS, Henry Ross, b Quebec 1895, d Hamilton, Ont 1986, paint CNS47 CWW88 MM PMC

WIGHTMAN, Donald Albert, b London 1935– , paint prt IO

WIITASALO, Shirley, b Toronto 1949– , paint DCA IO WWA93

WILCOX, Georgie M. Crawford (m Howard Buell Wilcox), b Winnipeg 1889, paint CLA MM RCA

WILDMAN, Sally Anne, b Tynemouth, Eng 1939– , paint CAE1 CWW93 IO RCA S US

WILEK. *See* MARKIEWICZ, William

WILKIE, Robert D., b Halifax 1828, d Swampscott, Me 1903, paint DMA GW H Y

WILKINS, Louisa A., fl 1879–86, drw drgt paint DWA H RCA

WILKINSON, Caroline Helena. *See* ARMINGTON, Caroline Helena Wilkinson

WILKINSON, John B., b England, fl 1863–1915, paint DeV7 H ROM WHC

WILKINSON, Jon Frederick, b 1940– , paint CAE1

WILKINSON, Thomas Harrison, b Bradford, Yorks 1847, d Hamilton, Ont 1929, paint H Hu RCA

WILL, John A., b Waterloo, Iowa 1939– , drw gra CAE1,2 WWA93

WILL, Mary Shannon, b Ithaca, NY 1944– , cer sculp DCA WWA82

WILLER, James Sidney Harold, b Fulham, Eng 1921– , paint sculp CWW93 MM NGC1 TB2 WWA82

WILLEY, Philip, b Hampshire, Eng 1941– , paint ABC

WILLIAM IV, King of England (Duke of Clarence), b Buckingham Palace 1765, d Windsor Castle 1837, Eng, paint DNB DPp117 H

WILLIAMS, Arch, b Ferryland, Nfld 1909, d 1982, paint DFA KB

WILLIAMS, C.L., Capt, fl 1860–1, Eng, paint DeV7 H PNL

WILLIAMS, Christopher, b Windsor, Ont 1947– , paint UG

WILLIAMS, Colin, b Byhope, Dur 1935– , paint SC

WILLIAMS, Dorothy May Bentley (1934 m George R. Williams), b Brooklyn Corner, King's Co, NS, fl 1940s, paint CLA MM

WILLIAMS, Eva Marie Brook Donly. *See* DONLY, Eva Marie Brook

WILLIAMS, Henry (Harry), b Allan, Sask, fl 1930s, paint CLA

WILLIAMS, Inglis Sheldon. *See* SHELDON-WILLIAMS, Inglis

WILLIAMS, Leonore Ethel. *See* BENOLKEN, Leonore Ethel Williams

WILLIAMS, Mary Bertha. *See* CLEMES, Mary Bertha Williams

WILLIAMS, Maxine. *See* HUGHSON, Maxine Williams

WILLIAMS, Paul Stanley, b Toronto 1949– , sculp IO

WILLIAMS, Richard Edmund, b Toronto 1933– , anim cart WECa

WILLIAMS, Richard Emerson, b Pittsburgh, Pa 1921– , paint sculp MM RCA TB2

WILLIAMS, Saul John, b N Caribou Lake, Ont 1954– , paint prt Co IO

WILLIAMS, W.J., b England, fl 1833–72, paint H

WILLIAMS, Yvonne, b Port of Spain, Tri 1901– , fl 1985, stgl MM RCA TB2

WILLIAMSON, Albert Curtis, b Brampton, Ont 1867, d Toronto 1944, paint AGO B CC1 CE1,2 CWW36 FCA H Hu Mo12 NGC1 PMC RCA TB1,2 W1–3

WILLIAMSON, Elizabeth Fraser, b Vancouver 1914– , sculp IO

WILLING, John Thomson, b Toronto 1860, des illus AAA31 B CWW36 F H Mo98 RCA TB1 Y

WILLIS, Dorothy Gwendolyn Henzell (m Charles B. Willis), b Newcastle, Eng 1899, paint CLA MM

WILLIS, George Brander, Lt, fl 1809–66, Eng, topog H ROM

WILLIS, Rose MacDonald (Rosa) (m William Arthur Willis), b Newport, Scot 1866, d Victoria, BC 1960, paint DWA H MM WWNA

WILLSHER-MARTEL, Joan Frances. *See* MARTEL, Joan Frances

WILLSON, Frederick J.[1] / John[2], fl 1881–1900, cart H[1,2]

WILSON, Al, fl 1970s, paint sculp CAE1

WILSON, Budge (b Marjorie MacGregor Archibald) (m Alan Wilson), b Halifax 1927– , illus C SAA53

WILSON, Bunny, b Kingston, Jam 1934– , paint sculp CAE1

WILSON, Daniel, Sir, b Edinburgh 1816, d Toronto 1892, paint AGO CE1,2 DCB12 DNB EC H Hu LeJ TB1 W1–3 WHC

WILSON, Dorothy R., b Jamaica 1934– , sculp IO

WILSON, Edward Francis, Rev, b 1841, fl 1876, d 1915, illus H

WILSON, Frank Howard, b Montreal 1908– , paint CWW58 MM

WILSON, Harry, b Nelson, Eng 1905– , paint CWW67

WILSON, James, b Montreal 1852, d Pickanock, Que 1932, paint H MM RCA

WILSON, Joanna Simpson (Mrs), b Scotland 1896, paint WWNA

WILSON, John Albert, b New Glasgow, NS 1878, sculp AAA13 DAS

WILSON, John Francis, b Whitby, Eng 1865, fl 1940, drw H

WILSON, Katharine E. McDougall (m J.E. Wilson), b Antigonish, NS 1833, d 1893, paint DWA H

WILSON, Marcia Ruiz. *See* RUIZ-WILSON, Marcia

WILSON, Marjorie. *See* WILSON, Budge

WILSON, Percy Roy, b Birmingham, Eng 1900, fl 1987, paint CLA MM RCA

WILSON, Robert (Scottie) (b Louis/Lewis Freeman), b Glasgow c 1890, d London 1972, Scot, paint ABH DFA H74 KB NGC1 OC OCD P S TB2 WBA1,2 WENA

WILSON, Ronald York, b Toronto 1907 – d 1984, paint AE AGO CC1 CE1,2 CWW84 IO MM NGC1 O.My48 RCA S SC TB2 WWA84

WILSON, Scottie. *See* WILSON, Robert (Scottie)

WILSON, Stanley B., b 1881, d 1960, paint H MM

WILSON, William F., fl 1842–54, engr paint GW H Y

WILSON, York. *See* WILSON, Ronald York

WILSON-HAMMOND, Charlotte Emily, b Montreal 1941– , paint prt WWA93

WINDEAT, Emma S., b Brockville, Ont, fl 1884, d 1922, paint AAA01 DWA H Hu MM RCA

WINDEAT, William, b England 1826, fl 1871, paint GW H Y

WINDEYER, Richard Cunningham, b Ft Amherst, Chatham, Kent c 1831, d Toronto 1900, paint H MM

WINDLE, Edith Mary Nazer, Lady (1901 m Bertram Coghill Alan Windle[2], Sir), b England, paint CWW36 WWW[2]

WINEMAN, Marsha, b 1947– , drw CAE2

WING, Theresa, fl 1895, min H MM

WINKLER, Friedrich (Fred, Fritz), b Dresden 1894, d Toronto 1974, sculp B MM RCA TB2

WINKLER, Robert M., b London, Ont 1952– , paint IO

WINSOR, V. Jacqueline, b Newfoundland 1941– , Amer, sculp DAS WWA93

WINTER, William Arthur, b Winnipeg 1909– , illus paint AGO B CC2 CWW89 IO NGC1 O.My48 RCA S TB2 UG WWA53 WWB72

WIRTH, H., b Labrador, fl 1877, sil H J

WISE, Jack Marlowe, b Centerville, Iowa 1928– , paint CAE2 CWW91 CE1,2 RCA SC US WWA76

WISEMAN, James Lovell, b Montreal 1847 – d 1912, engr DeV2,3 H RCA

WISHART, Jean Wylie, b Toronto 1902– , paint CAE1 IO

WISSMEYER, Gunter Gustav, b Hamburg, Ge 1940– , paint WWA93

WITT, Gerard de, b Cape Town, SA 1884, paint NGC68

WITTE, Gontran de, b Dauphiné, Fr, d nr Verdun, Fr c 1914/18, car paint K

WOERKOM, Fons van (s Fons[2]), b Netherlands 1943– , cart Des[2]

WOHLFARTH, Harry Karl Heinz, b Oberstdorf, Ge 1921– , paint sculp CAE1 CWW93 WWA76

WOJTOWICZ, Evelyn, b Dry River, Man 1926– , paint CAE1

WOLFE, James, Lt, b England c 1800 – d 1849, Eng, paint EMA

WOLFE, Wallace Leroy de, b Chicago 1854, d Pasadena, Calif 1930, Amer, engr paint AAA29d31 AAW1 AC B F Sam TB1,2 WWWA

WOLFF, Louis Augustin, b Germany, fl 1760–1818, paint H H77
WOLOSHYN, Caroline E. (Mrs), b Michel, BC, fl 1966– , paint ABC
WONG, Anna Chou Ying, b 1930– , prt CAE2
WONG, Viviane, fl 1970s, paint CAE2
WOOD, Abraham (Abram), Rev, b c 1791, d 1879, paint topog H
WOOD, Alan, b Widnes, Lincs 1935– , paint sculp CAE2 RCA WWA93
WOOD, Alexander M., fl 1887–95, paint AAW1,3 AC H
WOOD, Candace, fl 1883, paint DWA H MM RCA
WOOD, Elizabeth Wyn[2] (m Emanuel Hahn, q.v.), b Orillia, Ont 1903, d Toronto 1966, sculp ACA AGO CC1 CE1[2],2 Co CWW61 DWA EC NGC1 NGC67 O.F49 RCA TB2 WWA66 WWB68
WOOD, Faith (m Mel Breen), b Devon 1917– , paint pas IO MM RCA
WOOD, George Melville, b Regina 1932– , paint AA MM S US
WOOD, Thomas Charles, Lt, b Westborough, nr Ottawa 1913– , paint AGO MM NGC68 TB2 WWA53
WOOD, Thomas Waterman (s T.W. Wood), b Montpelier, Vt 1823, d New York 1903, Amer, paint AAAd28 App B DAA F GW H NCAB TB1 WWWA Y
WOOD, William, b Cheshire, Eng 1836, d Rockwood, Ont 1919, drw H
WOOD, William John, b Ottawa 1877, d Midland, Ont 1954, paint AGO CC2 CE1,2 H77 Hu MM NGC1 PMC RCA TB1
WOODCOCK, Joseph, b Allhallowes, London 1767, fl 1785–9, Eng, paint DeV1 EMA
WOODCOCK, Percy Franklin, b Farmersville, re Athens, Ont 1855, d Montreal 1936, paint B CC1 H H77 Hu MM Mo98,12 NGC1 PMC RCA TB1,2
WOODHOUSE, Edith, fl 1898–9, paint AAA01 DWA H MM RCA
WOODHOUSE, Margaret E., b Torrance, Calif 1933– , paint CAE1
WOODLEY (Mr), fl 1830–4, min H
WOODLEY, Clifford Beverley, b St Catharines, Ont 1920– , paint CWW67
WOODROW, Paul, b 1941– , con CAE2
WOODS, Chris W. *See* WOODS, William Christopher
WOODS, Elizabeth Ann (Lillie), b 1849, d Victoria, BC 1930, paint DWA H
WOODS, Emily Henrietta (x Wood[2]), b Ireland 1852, d 1916, paint Hpp339,338[2]
WOODS, Rex Norman, b Gainsborough, Lincs 1903– , illus paint CNS40 WWA70
WOODS, William Christopher, b Edmonton 1949– , litho prt IO UG
WOODVILLE, Richard Caton, b London 1856 – d 1927, Eng, paint AAW1 AH B1 DAA DBA DBHP DBMP DVP G H RA Sam TB1 WBA1 W1 WWW
WOODWARD, Gwladys Clovelly, b England 1885, paint WWNA
WOODWARD, John Douglas, b Monte Bello, Va 1846, d New Rochelle, NY 1924, Amer, paint AAA24d28 B DeV7 H NCAB TB1 Y
WOODWARD, Thomas, fl 1811–51, topog H
WOOLFIT, Benjamin Clayton, b Oxbow, Sask 1946– , paint IO
WOOLFORD, John Elliott, b London 1778, d Fredericton 1866, paint APH DCB9 DeV9 H H77 Hu ROM WHC
WOOLNOUGH, Hilda Mary (m Reshard W. Gool), b Northampton, Eng 1934– , drgt sculp tap CWW89 DCA RCA
WORKMAN, Lennie Elizabeth, b Belleville, Ont 1949– , paint IO
WORKMAN, Thomas/J.T., fl 1877–95, paint H

WORLING, Vera Kochanski. *See* KOCHANSKI, Vera

WORSLEY, Harriette Keating. *See* KEATING, Harriette

WORSLEY, John, b Kenya 1919– , Eng, paint DBMaP DSP RA WBA1 WWB72

WOZNY, Gladys Helen Marion. *See* SIEMENS, Gladys Helen Marion Wozny

WRANGEL, Geraldine Major. *See* MAJOR, Geraldine

WREFORD, Bertram Stanley (m Lorna B. Wreford, q.v.), b Bristol, Eng 1926– , carv paint prt IO

WREFORD, Lorna Bentley (m Bertram Stanley Wreford, q.v.), b Peterborough, Ont 1938– , etch paint prt IO

WREN, Bernie, b 1917– , carv DFA KB

WRIGHT, Charles, Col, b Bengal, India 1793, d London 1866, Eng, paint H ROM WHCp8

WRIGHT, David Thomas, b Coventry, Eng 1947– , paint IO WWA93

WRIGHT, Donald, b Timmins, Ont 1931– , gra paint S

WRIGHT, Douglas, b Dover, Eng 1917– , cart Des WECa

WRIGHT, Edith P. Stevenson. *See* STEVENSON, Edith P.

WRIGHT, Evelyn R. Foster (1919 m H.S. Wright), b London, fl 1920–67, paint MA

WRIGHT, Fanny Amelia. *See* BAYFIELD, Fanny Amelia Wright

WRIGHT, George Hand Charles, b Fox Chase, Pa 1872, d Westport, Conn 1951, Amer, prt AAA33 B F TB1,2 WHC WWA47d53 WWWA Y

WRIGHT, Graham, b Rochford, Eng 1950– , sculp IO

WRIGHT, Henry Charles Sepping, b England 1850, d Bosham, Sus 1937, Eng, paint AH DBA G RA Sam WBA2

WRIGHT, Monte M. (s Monte), b Moose Jaw, Sask 1934– , paint IO

WRIGHT, Sam L., fl 1888–95, paint H RCA

WRIGHT, W.E., fl 1864–6, paint H

WRINCH, Mary Evelyn (m George Agnew Reid[2], q.v.), b Kirby-le-Soken, Essex 1877, d Toronto 1969, paint AAA01 AGO DWA[2] FCA GM MM NGC1 O.My48 RCA S TB2 UG

WYANT, Alexander Helwig, b Evans Creek/Port Washington, Ohio 1836, d New York 1892, Amer, paint AAW1,3 ANC App B DAA F GW H MM NCAB RCA TB1 WWWA Y

WYATT, Charles Oliver, fl 1876–8, illus DeV6 H

WYERS, Jan Gerrit, b Steenderen, Neth 1888, d 1973, paint CC2 Co DFA H77 KB MM WENA

WYLE, Florence, b Trenton, Ill 1881, d Newmarket, Ont 1968, sculp AGO CC2 CE1,2 Co CWW64 DAS DWA EC MM NGC1 NGC67 NGC68 O.N48 RCA S Sam St TB2 W3 WWA62 WWB62

WYLIE, Alan, b Glasgow 1938– , paint SC

WYLIE, Robert J., Jr, fl 1886–1908, paint ROM

WYNDHAM, Alfred, Lt Col, b England 1837, d Alberta 1914, paint APH

WYNDHAM-LEWIS, Percy. *See* LEWIS, Percy Wyndham

WYSE, Alexander John, b Tewkesbery, Glos 1938– , paint sculp CAE1 DCA IO WWA82

WYSE, Frederick Horatio, b Quebec c 1826 – d 1884, engr H

XAVIER, Llewellyn Charles, b St Lucia, BWI 1945– , paint IO

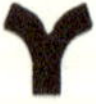

YAMADA, Ruth Chizuko Hagino (m Sam Isamu), b Vancouver 1923– , paint CWW93 IO

YANEFF, Christopher, b Toronto

1928– , drw gra paint Co CWW93 RCA WWA93 WWC89
YANOVSKY, Avrom (s Avrom[2]), b Krivoirog, Ukr 1911– , cart prt Des[2] O.Ag48
YARDLEY-JONES, John, b Liverpool 1930– , cart paint Des
YAROSLAWSKY, Semen, b 1899, d 1966, paint DFA
YARWOOD, Walter Hawley, b Toronto 1917– , paint sculp AE AGO CC2 Co H77 MM O.F51 RCA TB2
YATES, Norman, b Calgary 1923– , paint AA CAE1,2 SC
YATES, Whynona, b Leicester, Eng 1926– , wlhg AA
YEE BON. *See* BON, Yee
YEIGH, Frank, b Burford, Ont 1860, illus CWW10 Mo98,12
YEOMANS, Naneen, b Kingston, Ont 1923– , etch IO
YEREX, Elton James, b Neepawa, Man 1934– , paint CAE1 IO UG WWA82
YERXA, Leo, b Couchiching Res, nr Ft Frances, Ont 1947– , drw paint prt Co IO
YERXA, Wayne, b Couchiching Res, nr Ft Frances, Ont 1945– , drw paint prt Co IO
YGARTUA, Paul, b nr Liverpool 1945– , paint ABC
YIP, Chuck Wing, b Vancouver 1923– , paint sculp MM TB2
YORKE, Joseph Sydney, Adm, Sir, b 1768, d Stokes Bay, Eng 1831, Eng, topog DBWA DNB H KB
YORKE, William Guy, b Saint John, NB 1817 – d 1882, paint DMA DSP
YORKE, William Howard (x Hoard), b Saint John, NB 1847, d Liverpool 1921, paint DBA DBMaP DBMA H
YOSHIKAWA, Akira, b Hiroshima, Japan 1949– , sculp IO
YOUDS, Robert F., b Burnaby, BC 1954– , paint DCA
YOUNG, Clarence Richard, b nr Picton, Ont 1879, paint CWW58
YOUNG, George, Adm, Sir, b Dorset 1732, d England 1810, Eng, drgt DNB H
YOUNG, George MacDonald, b 1908– , paint CWW73
YOUNG, John (Jack), b Salisbury, Eng 1894, d Montreal 1963, paint MM S
YOUNG, John Crawford, Col, b Dalkeith, Scot 1788, d c 1859, Scot, paint H ROM WHC
YOUNG, L. Juliet (Mrs), b Vineland, NJ 1878, paint WWNA
YOUNG, Myrtle (Mattie) (Mrs), b Hillier, Ont 1876, paint AAA23 AAW2 DWA WWA59
YOUNG, Paul, b Toronto 1937– , paint IO RCA
YOUNG, Robert John, b Vancouver 1938– , gra paint CAE2 UG WWA93
YOUNG, Ross, b 1952– , paint CAE2
YOUNG, Thomas, b England c 1805, fl 1835–47, d Toronto 1860, paint DCB8 DeV5,8 H H77 W1–3
YOUNGER, Piercy Evelyn Frances Porteous. *See* PORTEOUS, Percy Evelyn Frances
YOUVILLE (Soeur). *See* L'ESPERANCE, Marie-Cécile-Christine Talon
YUEN, Sing Hoo. *See* HOO SING
YUHASZ, Kim Elizabeth, b Montreal 1953– , etch paint prt IO
YULE, Pamela Sarah Vining[2] (m James Cotton Yule), b Clarenden, NY 1826, d Ingersoll, Ont 1897, paint DCB12[2] W1–3
YURISTY, Russel Michael, b Goodeve, Sask 1936– , paint sculp CAE1 DFA WWA86
YUZBASIYAN/YUZBASIGAN, Arto, b Istanbul, Tur 1948– , paint CWW93 IO

Z

Z, Ruben. *See* ZELLERMAYER, Ruben
ZACK, Badanna Bernice, b Montreal 1933– , sculp CWW93 DCA IO RCA WWA93

ZACK, David, b New Orleans 1938– , des WWA78

ZACK, Gertrude Fouks (m Sidney Zack), b Edmonton 1918– , paint ABC

ZADAK, Zdenek Anthony, b Prague, Cz 1918– , paint CAE1

ZADDEN, Tanzara, fl 1970s, sculp CAE2

ZADOWSKA, Barbara Bailey, b Toronto 1948– , tap IO

ZAJFMAN, E. Pulver, b Toronto 1948– , wlhg CAE1

ZALAN, Zoltan, b Sopron, Hu 1938– , gra paint sculp PHA

ZAMMI, H. Norman, b Toronto 1931– , Amer, sculp DAS WWA91

ZANDER, Dik, b Berlin, Ge 1943– , sculp CAE1 IO

ZARAND, Julius John, b Nagyvarad, Hu 1913– , paint WWA93

ZATZKOY, Catherine, b Netherlands, fl 1960s, paint ABC

ZEDNIK, Jane, b Toronto 1953– , gra paint US

ZEIDLER, Eberhard Heinrich, b Braunsdorf, Ge 1926– , drw CWW93 RCA TB2 WWA93

ZEIGLER-SUNGUR, Barbara, b London, Ont 1949– , prt AA SC UG

ZELDIN, Annette Françoise. *See* FRANCOISE, Annette

ZELDIN, Gerald, b Toronto 1943– , paint CAE2 RCA

ZELENAK, Edward John, b St Thomas, Ont 1940– , sculp B CAE1 IO MM RCA WWA93

ZELLER, Ludwig, b Riohoa, Chile 1927– , coll Co IO

ZELLERMAYER, Ruben (s Ruben Z.), b Israel 1949– , sculp IO

ZEWENIUK, Garry, b Parksville, BC 1944– , paint CAE2

ZIELKE, Elizabeth Ursula (m Edwin Robert Statham), b New Osgoode, Sask 1936– , paint BDSA

ZIELKE, Peter J., b Berlin, Ge 1937– , paint CAE1

ZIGER, Joanne, b Montreal 1951– , prt CAE1

ZILAHI, Edit. *See* IVAN, Edit Zilahi

ZIMMER, Morand Herman Joseph, b Thamesville, Ont 1925– , paint O.My50

ZONTAL, Jorge (aka Jorge Saia) (General Idea, q.v.), b Parma, It 1944, d Toronto 1994, mmed WWA93

ZOUCHE, George-C. de, fl 1868–96, paint K

ZOUDIS, Panagiotis (Peter), b Kavala, Gr 1952– , met MFMS

ZUNTI, M. Saleria, b Luseland, Sask 1916– , paint CAE1

ZUROSKY, Louise, b Toronto 1942– , paint prt CAE1 IO

ZWICKER, LeRoy Judson (m Mary M.P. Zwicker, q.v.), b Halifax 1906– , paint CLA MA MM RCA TB2 WWA82

ZWICKER, Mary Marguerite Porter (m LeRoy Judson Zwicker, q.v.), b Yarmouth, NS 1904– , paint CLA MA MM RCA

www.ingramcontent.com/pod-product-compliance
Lightning Source LLC
LaVergne TN
LVHW090806070826
844660LV00022B/1096

* 9 7 8 1 4 8 7 5 8 6 8 8 1 *